Global Mental Health and Psychotherapy

Global Mental Health and Psychotherapy

Adapting Psychotherapy for Low- and Middle-Income Countries

Edited By:

Dan J. Stein
Judith K. Bass
Stefan G. Hofmann

ELSEVIER

ACADEMIC PRESS
An imprint of Elsevier

Academic Press is an imprint of Elsevier
125 London Wall, London EC2Y 5AS, United Kingdom
525 B Street, Suite 1650, San Diego, CA 92101, United States
50 Hampshire Street, 5th Floor, Cambridge, MA 02139, United States
The Boulevard, Langford Lane, Kidlington, Oxford OX5 1GB, United Kingdom

Library of Congress Cataloging-in-Publication Data
A catalog record for this book is available from the Library of Congress

British Library Cataloguing-in-Publication Data
A catalogue record for this book is available from the British Library

ISBN 978-0-12-814932-4

For information on all Academic Press publications visit our website at https://www.elsevier.com/books-and-journals

Publisher: Nikki Levy
Acquisition Editor: Emily Ekle
Editorial Project Manager: Carlos Rodriguez
Production Project Manager: Anusha Sambamoorthy
Cover Designer: Vicky Pearson

Typeset by SPi Global, India

Contents

Contributors

Cyrilla Amanya Ace Africa, Bungoma, Kenya

Lena S. Andersen HIV Mental Health Research Unit, Department of Psychiatry and Mental Health, University of Cape Town, Cape Town, South Africa

Ricardo Araya Centre of Global Mental Health, Institute of Psychiatry, Psychology and Neurosciences, King's College London, London, United Kingdom

Judith K. Bass Department of Mental Health, Johns Hopkins University Bloomberg School of Public Health, Baltimore, MD, United States

Anvita Bhardwaj Department of Psychiatry, George Washington University, Washington, DC, United States

Paul Bolton Department of International Health; Department of Mental Health, Johns Hopkins University Bloomberg School of Public Health, Baltimore, MD, United States

Karis Callaway Department of Psychology, Western Michigan University, Kalamazoo, MI, United States

Dixon Chibanda Department of Psychiatry, University of Zimbabwe, Harare, Zimbabwe

Lydia Chwastiak Department of Psychiatry and Behavioral Sciences, School of Medicine, University of Washington, Seattle, WA, United States

Jessica N. Coleman Department of Psychology and Neuroscience, Duke Global Health Institute, Duke University, Durham, NC, United States

Pim Cuijpers Department of Clinical, Neuro and Developmental Psychology, Amsterdam Public Health Research Institute, Vrije Universiteit Amsterdam, Amsterdam, Netherlands

Thandi Davies Alan J Flisher Centre for Public Mental Health, Department of Psychiatry and Mental Health, University of Cape Town, Cape Town, South Africa

Lucy X. Dong School of Public Health, University of Washington, Seattle, WA, United States

Shannon Dorsey Department of Psychology, University of Washington, Seattle, WA, United States

Laura M. Eise Department of Psychology, University of Washington, Seattle, WA, United States

Ozlem Eylem Department of Clinical, Neuro and Developmental Psychology, Amsterdam Public Health Research Institute, Vrije Universiteit Amsterdam, Amsterdam, Netherlands

Engelina Groenewald Department of Psychiatry, University of Stellenbosch and Stikland Hospital, Cape Town, South Africa

Syed Usman Hamdani Human Development Research Foundation, Islambad, Pakistan

Stefan G. Hofmann Dept of Psychological and Brain Sciences, Boston University, Boston, MA, United States

Muhammad Irfan Department of Mental Health, Psychiatry and Behavioural Sciences, Peshawar Medical College, Riphah International University, Islamabad, Pakistan

John Joska Department of Psychiatry and Mental Health, University of Cape Town, Cape Town, South Africa

Eirini Karyotaki Department of Clinical, Neuro and Developmental Psychology, Amsterdam Public Health Research Institute, Vrije Universiteit Amsterdam, Amsterdam, Netherlands

David Kingdon Clinical Trials Facility, Tom Rudd Unit, Southern Health NHS Foundation Trust, Hampshire, United Kingdom

Brandon A. Kohrt Department of Psychiatry, George Washington University, Washington, DC, United States

Caroline Kuo Department of Behavioral and Social Sciences, Brown University School of Public Health, Providence, RI, United States

Jessica Leith Psychiatry and Behavioral Sciences, University of Washington School of Medicine, Seattle, WA, United States

Leah Lucid Department of Psychology, University of Washington, Seattle, WA, United States

Crick Lund Alan J Flisher Centre for Public Mental Health, Department of Psychiatry and Mental Health, University of Cape Town, Cape Town, South Africa; Centre for Global Mental Health, Department of Health Service and Population Research, Institute of Psychiatry, Psychology and Neuroscience, King's College London, London, United Kingdom

Jessica F. Magidson Department of Psychology, University of Maryland, College Park, MD, United States

Kristina Metz Department of Mental Health; Department of International Health, Johns Hopkins Bloomberg School of Public Health, Baltimore, MD, United States

Laura K. Murray Department of Mental Health; Department of International Health, Johns Hopkins Bloomberg School of Public Health, Baltimore, MD, United States

Saadia Muzaffar Southern Health NHS Foundation Trust, Hampshire, United Kingdom

Bronwyn Myers Alcohol, Tobacco and Other Drug Research Unit, South African Medical Research Council and Division of Addiction Psychiatry, Department of Psychiatry and Mental Health, University of Cape Town, Cape Town, South Africa

Farooq Naeem University of Toronto and Centre for Addiction and Mental Health, Toronto, Canada

Mark van Ommeren Dept of Mental Health and Substance Abuse, World Health Organization, Geneva, Switzerland

Inge Petersen Centre for Rural Health, University of KwaZulu-Natal, Durban, South Africa

Atif Rahman Institute for Psychological Health and Society, University of Liverpool, Liverpool, United Kingdom

Deepa Rao Department of Global Health; Department of Psychiatry and Behavioral Sciences, School of Medicine, University of Washington, Seattle, WA, United States

Shanaya Rathod Clinical Trials Facility, Tom Rudd Unit, Southern Health NHS Foundation Trust, Hampshire; Portsmouth-Brawijaya Centre for Global Health, Population, and Policy, University of Portsmouth, Portsmouth, United Kingdom

Susan Rees Psychiatry Research and Teaching Unit, School of Psychiatry, University of New South Wales, Sydney, NSW, Australia

Kristen S. Regenauer Behavioral Medicine Service, Department of Psychiatry, Massachusetts General Hospital, Boston, MA, United States

Steven A. Safren Department of Psychology, University of Miami, Coral Gables, FL, United States

Marit Sijbrandij Department of Clinical, Neuro and Developmental Psychology, Amsterdam Public Health Research Institute, Vrije Universiteit Amsterdam, Amsterdam, Netherlands

Kathleen J. Sikkema Department of Psychology and Neuroscience, Duke Global Health Institute, Duke University, Durham, NC, United States

Derrick Silove Psychiatry Research and Teaching Unit, School of Psychiatry, University of New South Wales, Sydney, NSW, Australia

Maxine F. Spedding Department of Psychiatry & Mental Health, Alan J. Flisher School for Public Mental Health, University of Cape Town, Cape Town, South Africa

Dan J. Stein SA Medical Research Council Unit on Risk & Resilience in Mental Disorders, Dept of Psychiatry and Mental Health, University of Cape Town, Cape Town, South Africa

Alvin Tay Perdana University-Royal College of Surgeons in Ireland School of Medicine, Early Career Research Fellow, National Health & Medical Research Council (NHMRC), School of Psychiatry, University of New South Wales, Sydney, NSW, Australia

Bradley H. Wagenaar Department of Global Health, University of Washington, Seattle, WA, United States

Xinyu Zhou Department of Psychiatry, First Affiliated Hospital of Chongqing Medical University, Chongqing Medical University, Chongqing, China

Foreword

Psychological therapies have, for a long time, been relegated to an adjunctive or secondary role in the treatment of mental health problems, in comparison with pharmacological therapies, not least because most mental health professionals, particularly in low- and middle-income countries, are psychiatrists who had neither the training nor the inclination to deliver these therapies. Additionally, they were also seen as poorly defined interventions, prone to huge levels of variability and inconsistency in content and delivery. As a result, they were perceived to be neither replicable nor active in a specific theoretical context. Unsurprisingly, what often passed for psychological therapies was little more than a supportive chat with a well-meaning provider. The advent of the WHO's Mental Health Gap Action Program (mhGAP) guidelines reminded the global mental health community that the evidence base for psychological therapies was so strong that not only were they recommended as first-line treatments for the majority of mental and substance use disorders but also, for some of them, they were the *only* such treatment.

This volume lays out the impressive evidence of the acceptability and effectiveness for a range of mental health problems across the life course and in diverse contexts and for a range of goals from promotion and prevention, to the treatment of acute phases of illness, to rehabilitation and recovery. The effect sizes from a range of meta-analyses for these interventions often range from moderate to large, and the occurrence of side effects is rare. Further, the current generation of therapies is grounded in a robust orientation of cognitive, behavioral, and interpersonal theories, and there is a growing mediation evidence base testifying to their mechanisms of action. The evolving understanding of brain plasticity offers a coherent biological explanatory framework for the effectiveness of these therapies. Because the focus of these therapies is to teach a person the skills to target the factors that lead to and sustain psychological distress, they are also associated with longer-term enduring effects. Quite simply, psychological therapies not only are among the most effective interventions for mental health care but also are of equivalent effectiveness when compared with interventions for a range of other chronic conditions. In practice, however, in most countries, there is very limited access to these therapies, and their effective coverage is less than 10% in most of the global population.

Global mental health has been a fertile discipline for the generation of a substantial body of evidence to reduce this enormous treatment gap by designing and evaluating innovations to address the demand and supply side barriers to the effective delivery of these therapies. Indeed, much of the intervention and implementation research in the field has been heavily dominated by psychological therapies. This volume is not only the first comprehensive account of this rich body of evidence but also a very timely one, with the goal of taking stock of the progress to date, addressing some key questions that have hindered the global application of these therapies, and allowing reflection on the implications of this evidence for transforming mental health globally. Two key questions have, in my mind, been comprehensively addressed by the existing evidence.

The first is with regard to the transportability of the theories that underlie the design of psychological therapies, the vast majority of which were originally developed and tested in relatively homogenous European populations in a few high-income countries, to diverse cultures and contexts. It is clear that these theories are, indeed, universally applicable, opening the doors to the possibility of exchanging experiences on therapy design globally, and this is already happening in a dynamic and multipolar way. The effectiveness and acceptability of these therapies in diverse contexts is further proof that that nature of psychological suffering is a fundamental, universal human experience. The second question is the delivery of these interventions. There are very few skilled practitioners of psychological therapies in most countries, and the large number of "empirically supported treatments" that now exist for a range of targets and conditions makes it impossible for the available providers to meet the needs of populations, even in high-resourced settings. Global mental health innovators (in both high-income countries and low- and middle-income countries) have been addressing these barriers through task sharing (often described as task shifting) to less specialized providers. The sum of this substantial evidence base points to a fundamental rethinking of psychological therapies in several respects.

The *content* of psychological therapies needs significant modification to incorporate local metaphors and beliefs about the target (e.g., avoiding the use of psychiatric labels that are incomprehensible and even stigmatizing), include social work components in settings where there is no parallel social welfare system (e.g., practical problem-solving support for social difficulties that are very commonly associated with the distress), and adapt the tasks to ensure acceptability for people with limited literacy (e.g., completing homework in sessions). The *delivery agent* is most often a community health worker or lay counselor who belongs to the same community as the beneficiary population. The selection of this cadre reflects the need for scalability and acceptability. The provider is trained for an average of a period of a few weeks to achieve competency to deliver the treatment, followed by a structured supervision protocol to ensure continuing quality. The *setting* for the delivery is typically in the community (including the person's home) or in primary health care or other routine care delivery platforms, rather than a specialist setting. The treatment *format* comprises a relatively small number of sessions, on average between 6 and 10 for adult common mental disorders, in order to enhance acceptability and engagement and to maximize the number of people who can be served. Typically, the provider works within a collaborative care framework with access to a specialist provider, who may be remotely located, who participates in training, oversees quality, and provides guidance or referral options for complex clinical presentations.

This rich evidence base provides a robust foundation for the wider dissemination and scaling up of psychological therapies. A number of newer innovations are pointing to strategies that can enable this goal. *First*, a major bottleneck to task sharing is the reliance on traditional face-to-face methods for training and on experts for supervision. Both these barriers are now being addressed through online training for learning psychological therapies and the use of peers to supervise therapy quality using structured scales with feedback. Utilizing a digital platform for learning and supervision may eventually lead to these therapies being made available to any provider anywhere in the world. *Second*, the plethora of trials potentially leads to the same problem where the multiplicity of treatment packages for specific disorders or groups of persons (e.g., for maternal depression), perhaps paradoxically, makes it more difficult for potential practitioners to decide which package to learn. Yet, most therapies share a common theoretical foundation and comprise a relatively limited number of similar "elements" (as described by Murray) spanning behavioral, interpersonal, cognitive, and emotional domains (i.e., with specific therapeutic targets such as activation or relaxation). This has led to the development of "transdiagnostic" psychological therapies that target multiple disorders either through a common ("unified") approach for all or through matching of specific treatment elements for specific syndromes (e.g., activation for depression). The *third* approach to scale up psychological therapies is their dissemination directly to the beneficiaries, that is, persons with mental health problems. This is potentially the most disruptive innovation of all as it removes the health professional entirely. There is a burgeoning industry of apps and websites offering self-delivered psychological therapies and an emerging body of evidence demonstrating the effectiveness of self-delivered psychological therapies, especially when supported remotely by a counselor, when compared with traditional face-to-face delivery of psychological therapies. There is also evidence in support of traditional manual guidance that is relevant for populations with limited Internet coverage.

A key goal is to figure out the steps through which this body of evidence, largely comprising trials and discrete projects, can be scaled up at national or subnational levels. Ideally, this might be done through a stepped care architecture in which low-intensity interventions are delivered at the level of populations (e.g., in schools) from the first step or the "base of the pyramid." The strategies to achieve these will include a mix of digital platforms, task sharing and transdiagnostic approaches. The second step will require therapy for individuals with more enduring or severe mental health problems and may take the form of guided self-care or traditional face-to-face therapy delivered in routine care settings or homes by lay counselors. The final step may take the form of a specialist or physician consultation, and intervention options may expand to include drugs or other physical therapies. There are very few examples of such scale-up for now, perhaps the most well-described one being England's Improving Access to Psychological Therapies program, but these indicate that additional resources invested in this architecture of care can greatly improve the effective coverage of psychological therapies and reduce the suffering due to mental and substance use disorders. This book serves as a call to action to realize this goal to transform mental health globally.

Vikram Patel

Rethinking psychotherapy

Dan J. Stein, Judith K. Bass†, Stefan G. Hofmann‡, Mark van Ommeren§*
*SA Medical Research Council Unit on Risk & Resilience in Mental Disorders, Dept of Psychiatry and Mental Health, University of Cape Town, Cape Town, South Africa, †Department of Mental Health, Johns Hopkins University Bloomberg School of Public Health, Baltimore, MD, United States, ‡Dept of Psychological and Brain Sciences, Boston University, Boston, MA, United States, §Dept of Mental Health and Substance Abuse, World Health Organization, Geneva, Switzerland

It is perhaps the best and worst of times for mental health practitioners and scientists. Advances in psychiatric epidemiology not only have quantified the prevalence and burden of mental disorders but also have emphasized the significant treatment gap, particularly in low- and middle-income countries (LMIC) (Demyttenaere et al., 2004; Stein et al., 2015). Advances in neuroscience not only have led to a better understanding of the psychobiology of mental disorders but also have underscored how far we are away from a personalized psychiatry that targets specific brain circuitry in order to achieve symptom remission in the clinic (Stein et al., 2015).

In this context, psychotherapy remains a key intervention in the clinic and a key focus of research. Several decades of research have established the efficacy of specific psychotherapies for particular conditions, and they are therefore recommended as first-line interventions in a broad range of evidence-based clinical guidelines. Furthermore, there have been gradual advances in our understanding of how psychotherapies effect psychological change, raising the possibility that in the future, clinician-scientists will be able to forge personalized psychotherapy plans that improve treatment outcomes.

At the same time, further progress in psychotherapy requires important conceptual and empirical questions to be addressed. The diverse historical roots of psychotherapy, ranging from psychoanalytic to cognitive behavioral theories, raise the conceptual questions of how best to explain the nature of psychopathology and how best to account for changes that may be seen during psychotherapy. The broad range of scholarship on psychotherapy, ranging from qualitative accounts to randomized controlled trials, raises the empirical questions of what works best, for whom, and why.

Within this context, the emerging discipline of global mental health has a key role to play in reinvigorating the search for answers to these questions and so in advancing the science and art of psychotherapy. First, global mental health has emphasized the enormity of the mental health treatment gap, particularly in LMIC, and has put forward the hypothesis that a range of nonspecialized mental health workers may be able to undertake efficacious psychotherapy (Patel, 2012). Second, global mental health has emphasized the heterogeneous contexts in which psychotherapy must be delivered, particularly in LMIC, and has put forward a range of ideas about how best to

Global Mental Health and Psychotherapy. https://doi.org/10.1016/B978-0-12-814932-4.09998-5

adapt existing or forge new psychotherapeutic techniques and tools (Singla et al., 2017).

In this introductory chapter, we summarize ongoing contributions to psychotherapy from the emerging discipline of global mental health and outline the subsequent chapters of this volume, which provide more detailed accounts. We also emphasize the importance of an integrative theoretical and research framework. While the novelty of the intersection between global mental health and psychotherapy may well require that a broad range of ideas and activities are robustly explored, this intersection also arguably provides an opportunity for the field to move beyond past schisms and to tackle future challenges in the field in a way that ensures that focused progress is in fact made.

1 Nature of psychotherapy

The complexity of current debates on the nature of psychopathology is exemplified in recent controversies regarding the revision of the *Diagnostic and Statistical Manual of Mental Disorders* (DSM) and the International Classification of Diseases (ICD) and the formulation of the Research Domain Criteria (RDoC) framework (Clark, Cuthbert, Lewis-Fernandez, Narrow, & Reed, 2017). Key questions that have been raised include whether psychopathology is best described using categories or dimensions, the extent of the link between clinical symptoms and brain changes, and the extent to which syndromes and symptoms are context-bound.

Psychotherapy has its own diverse historical roots and is influenced in an ongoing way by these debates on psychopathology. Psychoanalytic authors, for example, have emphasized links between psychodynamic formulations and neuroscience discoveries and have argued that empirical literature supports psychoanalytic interventions (Stein, Solms, & van Honk, 2006). Cognitive behavioral authors have similarly addressed the biological basis of their theoretical formulations and have focused a great deal of effort on accumulating data in support of their psychotherapeutic interventions (Clark & Beck, 2010).

Global mental health raises a range of additional conceptual questions for psychotherapy. First, there are questions about who is best able to deliver psychotherapy; in Chapter 1 of this volume, Paul Bolton, who has undertaken seminal work on psychotherapy in LMIC, makes the argument that task-shifting interventions are crucial in this context. Second, there are questions about how best to formulate psychotherapies in a resource-constrained environment; in Chapter 2 of the volume, Laura Murray argues that transdiagnostic approaches are particularly relevant. Third, there are questions about how best to implement and scale up psychotherapy; in Chapter 3, Brandon Kohrt and colleagues discuss the importance of supervision, and in Chapter 4, Judith Bass and Usman Hamdani emphasize the role of implementation science in addressing this issue.

There are, however, surely deeper theoretical questions, which practical efforts to improve psychotherapies in a global context must address. In particular, what psychobiological structures and processes do psychotherapies target in which individuals, and how do they optimally do so? We might imagine that target structures and processes differ across mental disorders and across individual patients; how are these differences best articulated and assessed? While the RDoC effort has provided one recent conceptual framework for understanding psychopathology, is this the most suitable one for progressing efforts in psychotherapy?

2 Evidence of efficacy

Some might respond that no matter the conceptual foundations of psychotherapy, it has shown good evidence of efficacy. However, despite a growing body of randomized controlled trials demonstrating efficacy, the question of psychotherapy efficacy is far from fully resolved. First, the quality of much of the evidence has been questioned, with critics emphasizing factors such as the weakness of methods that too often rely on waiting-list controls and the avoidance of rigorous assessment of adverse events of psychotherapy. Second, the generalizability of the evidence has been questioned; the vast majority of psychotherapy research has focused on explanatory trials in academic settings, with much less work undertaken in pragmatic or real-world contexts, including LMIC settings (van't Hof, Cuijpers, Waheed, & Stein, 2011). Third, many of the trials in global mental health are by authors who have an allegiance to the intervention, raising conflict of interest issues.

The diverse historical roots of psychotherapy have arguably contributed to the heterogeneity and weakness of the literature. Many schools of psychotherapy have taken a predominantly qualitative approach to describing their concepts and outcomes. Even within paradigms that emphasize the importance of quantitative research, there is a substantial clinical research gap, with practitioners emphasizing, for example, that they are not able to rely on standardized research manuals that address narrow populations in a real-world setting (Pilecki & McKay, 2013; Teachman et al., 2012).

Global mental health has, however, made an important qualitative and quantitative contribution to the literature. In Chapter 5, Caroline Kuo not only emphasizes how cognitive behavioral therapy provides a useful framework for psychotherapy intervention around the world but also discussed how adaptations need to be made to ensure success in diverse contexts. In Chapter 6, Maxine Spedding and Dixon Chibanda describe a range of other psychotherapeutic interventions that may be useful in global settings; these include the World Health Organization's Problem Management Plus (PM+), a transdiagnostic treatment for delivery by nonspecialist providers. In Chapter 7, Bradley Wagenaar and colleagues emphasize the data demonstrating the value of primary care collaborative interventions, as comprising a key platform for delivery of psychotherapy.

Global mental health research has also addressed a broad range of mental disorders. In Chapter 8, Pim Cuijpers and colleagues summarize the growing literature on interventions for mood and anxiety disorders in LMIC. In Chapter 9, Kathleen Sikkema and colleagues address the valuable interventions that have been developed to address trauma- and stressor-related disorders, such as post-traumatic stress disorder, across the globe. In Chapter 10, Muhammad Irfan and colleagues cover psychotherapeutic interventions for schizophrenia and bipolar disorder in diverse settings. In Chapter 11, Bronwyn Myers summarizes work on substance use disorders around the world. Taken together, this is a large and important contribution to psychotherapy research.

Furthermore, global mental health research has also addressed a range of important populations. In Chapter 12, Jessica Magidson and colleagues tackle chronic physical disorders, including HIV/AIDS, complementing the earlier chapter on the importance of collaborative care. In Chapter 13, Shannon Dorsey and colleagues summarize work that has been undertaken in child and adolescent populations in global settings. In Chapter 14, Thandi Davies reviews research that has been undertaken on perinatal common mental disorders across the world. In Chapter 15, Engelina Groenewald focuses on global mental health research that has been undertaken in the elderly. Finally, in Chapter 16, Derrick Silove focuses on research that has been undertaken on refugee and similar populations in the context of humanitarian crises.

3 Towards an integrative theoretical framework

In this brief section, we wish to argue that contemporary cognitive-affective neuroscience provides a useful and integrative framework for psychotherapy. Although psychoanalytic theory provided some of the historical foundation for the development of psychotherapy, its conceptual basis is now outdated. This gap means that even thoughtful efforts to integrate psychoanalysis with neuroscience typically do not find their way into contemporary neuroscientific journals (Ramus, 2013). Cognitive behavioral therapy, on the other hand, has long attempted to integrate its underlying theory with neuroscientific findings. Advances in the psychobiology of emotion can therefore be incorporated into its theories and approaches (Beck, 2008).

Consider, for example, contemporary work on fear conditioning and extinction. A range of neuroscientific methods have been useful in delineating the relevant psychobiological structures and processes involved in these phenomena in the laboratory; we therefore have a growing understanding of the underlying neurocircuitry and of the role of different molecules that play a role (Stein, 2006). In the clinic, we are therefore well placed to study how psychotherapy leads to alterations in this circuitry, as assessed by modern brain imaging techniques (Brooks & Stein, 2015). Furthermore, we can use this knowledge to target specific mechanisms; for example, it was hypothesized that the glutamatergic drug, D-cycloserine, would augment CBT in anxiety disorders by improving fear extinction (Mataix-Cols et al., 2017).

Clearly, much further work is needed in order to consolidate this sort of conceptual framework. The psychobiological basis of anxiety and threat responses, where there are good animal models, is perhaps easier to understand than that of the psychoses, where animal models are only partially useful. Clinical research tools are often relatively blunt compared with laboratory techniques; the fear circuitry of a rodent can literally be dissected out, while current brain imaging methods have limited temporal and spatial resolution. The complexity of mental disorders and of the experiences of individuals who suffer from these conditions cannot be overestimated; simple models of dysfunction and of intervention will invariably fail to fully address this complexity.

Nevertheless, considerable progress has been made in recent years toward an integrative cognitive-affective neuroscience approach to the brain-mind and its pathologies. Although much further work needs to be done to fully delineate the relevant structures and processes that underlie mental disorders and symptoms, important advances have been made in delineating key relevant phenomena, such as fear conditioning and extinction, emotional dysregulation and control, and reward processing and regulation. Such advances provide the framework for an integrative psychobiology of psychotherapy and for research on the neurocircuitry underlying particular therapeutic interventions. Ultimately, therefore, there is scope for integrating global mental health, neuroscience, and psychotherapy (Stein et al., 2015).

4 Towards a translational research framework

In this brief section, we wish to argue that global mental health has provided a unique opportunity for advancing psychotherapy. Psychotherapy practice and research have been constrained by being confined to a narrow set of contexts. While early efforts to expand psychotherapy by inclusion of nurse practitioners and computerization should certainly be acknowledged (Ginsberg, Marks, & Waters, 1984; Greist et al., 1998), the emergence of global mental health as a distinct discipline has ensured a focus on the extension of psychotherapy to a range of practitioners, to novel contexts, and to new delivery platforms (Patel, 2012; Singla et al., 2017).

Furthermore, a focus in global mental health research on moving from initial feasibility and acceptability studies, to efficacy research, and to larger implementation and scale-up has ensured that psychotherapy research is not merely an academic activity, but rather is embedded within a real-world context. This framework allows translation between initial hypotheses about what might be useful and the lived experience of practitioners and patients as they try out psychotherapy techniques and tools. There is acknowledgment of key societal variables including the role of psychotherapy supervisors, the role of family members and peers, and other aspects of the context in which psychotherapy occurs.

Again, much further work is needed in order to consolidate this sort of research framework. A range of approaches toward psychotherapy adaptation and implementation are outlined in this volume; further elaboration and refinement of these models are likely to occur in future years. One key challenge is ensuring that mental disorders and psychotherapy are not stigmatized, and rather and that psychotherapies are viewed as potentially efficacious and cost-effective health interventions. A second key challenge is establishing mechanisms that support psychotherapy research on efficacy and implementation and that use lessons learned to further improve interventions.

Considerable progress has been made toward establishing such a framework. The development of an integrative conceptual foundation for psychotherapy is important in overcoming past schisms and persuading funders and communities that this is an important field. Developments such as rigorous syntheses of the literature (e.g., the Cochrane Collaboration), the promotion of evidence-based guidelines, and other efforts to address the practitioner-researcher gap have all been key in promoting the field of psychotherapy. WHO policies and products including the *Mental Health Action Gap Action Programme* (mhGAP) have been key in advancing support for psychotherapy (Keynejad, Dua, Barbui, & Thornicroft, 2018). The Sustainable Development Goals emphasize that mental health and sustainable development are intertwined in important ways, and this will hopefully encourage further investment in this area (Votruba, Eaton, Prince, & Thornicroft, 2014).

5 Conclusion

Recent attempts to address the mental health treatment gap in LMIC by adapting psychotherapies for these contexts have drawn attention to key conceptual and empirical questions in the field. By so doing, we would suggest that they have reinvigorated the field. This introductory chapter has summarized ongoing contributions to psychotherapy from the emerging discipline of global mental health; in succeeding chapters, these will be further expanded on. In the interim, we wish to emphasize the value of integrative theoretical and research frameworks for psychotherapy. Important progress has been made in establishing such frameworks, but much further work is required to consolidate them. Our hope is that this volume contributes to such efforts.

References

Beck, A. T. (2008). The evolution of the cognitive model of depression and its neurobiological correlates. *American Journal of Psychiatry*, *165*(8), 969–977.

Brooks, S. J., & Stein, D. J. (2015). A systematic review of the neural bases of psychotherapy for anxiety and related disorders. *Dialogues in Clinical Neuroscience*, *17*(3), 261–279.

Clark, D. A., & Beck, A. T. (2010). Cognitive theory and therapy of anxiety and depression: Convergence with neurobiological findings. *Trends in Cognitive Sciences*, *14*(9), 418–424.

Clark, L. A., Cuthbert, B., Lewis-Fernandez, R., Narrow, W. E., & Reed, G. M. (2017). Three approaches to understanding and classifying mental disorder: ICD-11, DSM-5, and the national institute of mental health's research domain criteria (RDoC). *Psychological Science in the Public Interest*, *18*(2), 72–145.

Demyttenaere, K., Bruffaerts, R., Posada-Villa, J., Gasquet, I., Kovess, V., Lepine, J. P., et al. (2004). Prevalence, severity, and unmet need for treatment of mental disorders in the World Health Organization World Mental Health Surveys. *JAMA: The Journal of the American Medical Association*, *291*(21), 2581–2590.

Ginsberg, G., Marks, I., & Waters, H. (1984). Cost-benefit analysis of a controlled trial of nurse therapy for neuroses in primary care. *Psychological Medicine*, *14*(3), 683–690.

Greist, J. H., Marks, I. M., Baer, L., Parkin, J. R., Manzo, P. A., Mantle, J. M., et al. (1998). Self-treatment for obsessive compulsive disorder using a manual and a computerized telephone interview: a U.S.-U.K. study. *M.D. Computing*, *15*(3), 149–157.

Keynejad, R. C., Dua, T., Barbui, C., & Thornicroft, G. (2018). WHO mental health gap action programme (mhGAP) intervention guide: A systematic review of evidence from low and middle-income countries. *Evidence-Based Mental Health*, *21*(1), 30–34.

Mataix-Cols, D., Fernández de la Cruz, L., Monzani, B., Rosenfield, D., Andersson, E., Pérez-Vigil, A., … Rück, C. (2017). D-Cycloserine augmentation of exposure-based cognitive-behavior therapy for anxiety, obsessive-compulsive, and posttraumatic stress disorders: Systematic review and meta-analysis of individual participant data. *JAMA Psychiatry*, *74*, 501–510. https://doi.org/10.1001/jamapsychiatry.2016.3955.

Patel, V. (2012). Global mental health: from science to action. *Harvard Review of Psychiatry*, *20*(1), 6–12.

Pilecki, B., & McKay, D. (2013). The theory-practice gap in cognitive-behavior therapy. *Behavior Therapy*, *44*(4), 541–547.

Ramus, F. (2013). What's the point of neuropsychoanalysis? *British Journal of Psychiatry: The Journal of Mental Science*, *203*(3), 170–171.

Singla, D. R., Kohrt, B. A., Murray, L. K., Anand, A., Chorpita, B. F., & Patel, V. (2017). Psychological treatments for the world: Lessons from low- and middle-income countries. *Annual Review of Clinical Psychology*, *13*, 149–181.

Stein, D. J. (2006). Advances in understanding the anxiety disorders: The cognitive-affective neuroscience of 'false alarms. *Annals of Clinical Psychiatry: Official Journal of the American Academy of Clinical Psychiatrists*, *18*(3), 173–182.

Stein, D. J., He, Y., Phillips, A., Sahakian, B. J., Williams, J., & Patel, V. (2015). Global mental health and neuroscience: Potential synergies. *Lancet Psychiatry*, *2*, 178–185.

Stein, D. J., Solms, M., & van Honk, J. (2006). The cognitive-affective neuroscience of the unconscious. *CNS Spectrums*, *11*(8), 580–583.

Teachman, B. A., Drabick, D. A., Hershenberg, R., Vivian, D., Wolfe, B. E., & Goldfried, M. R. (2012). Bridging the gap between clinical research and clinical practice: introduction to the special section. *Psychotherapy (Chicago, Ill.)*, *49*(2), 97–100.

van't Hof, E., Cuijpers, P., Waheed, W., & Stein, D. J. (2011). Psychological treatments for depression and anxiety disorders in low- and middle-income countries: A meta-analysis. *African Journal of Psychiatry*, *14*(3), 200–207.

Votruba, N., Eaton, J., Prince, M., & Thornicroft, G. (2014). The importance of global mental health for the sustainable development goals. *Journal of Mental Health*, *23*(6), 283–286.

Section A

Conceptual issues

Global mental health and psychotherapy: Importance of task-shifting and a systematic approach to adaptation

1

Paul Bolton[*,†]
*Department of International Health, Johns Hopkins University Bloomberg School of Public Health, Baltimore, MD, United States, †Department of Mental Health, Johns Hopkins University Bloomberg School of Public Health, Baltimore, MD, United States

1.1 The importance of task shifting

1.1.1 Background and rationale

The key public health challenge in providing health care is how to provide good access to appropriate services with the resources available. Task shifting exists as one means to meet this challenge. It has been described as "a process whereby specific tasks are moved, where appropriate, to health workers with shorter training and fewer qualifications… [to] make more efficient use of existing human resources and ease bottlenecks in service delivery" (WHO, 2008). The assumption is that shorter training and fewer qualifications equates with the ability to train and support more health workers with the same resources. Task shifting is used in high-, middle-, and low-income countries as a response to broad access in the face of limited resources for a range of health services, notably primary care, maternal and child care, and HIV.

To appreciate the rationale of the task shifting approach in mental health, it is useful to review its origins that lay in physical health care prior to the global mental health movement. Health-care systems in high-income countries have a flat structure with only three basic levels. Clients can directly consult highly trained primary care physicians and nurses who treat most cases that present to them. This level is called primary care. These providers also act as gatekeepers to secondary care that consists of health-care specialists who, in turn, act as gatekeepers for tertiary care in the form of hospitals or inpatient clinics. Almost all medical care in high-income countries takes place at one of these three levels. Only three care levels are needed because high-income health systems can afford to support large numbers of highly trained physicians and nurses at the primary level to deal with the many clients with minor problems requiring little attention. In other words, while most patients present with problems that do require full medical or nursing training, the system can afford to have these workers spend much of their time doing just that.

Global Mental Health and Psychotherapy. https://doi.org/10.1016/B978-0-12-814932-4.00001-X

Low- and middle-income countries (LMIC) require systems that make more efficient use of the few fully trained medical workers that they can afford. This requires a system with additional treatment and gatekeeping levels before doctors and nurses. These levels need to be populated by workers who have less training and work at lower cost yet can treat the most common problems. They also refer more serious problems or problems that do not improve with their treatment. The result is smaller numbers of doctors and nurses treating those patients who really require their expertise.

This tiered approach to health care is not new. It can be traced back to Lord Dawson of Penn who in 1920 proposed a system of primary, secondary, and supplementary services to the UK government that included a "health visitor" at the primary level who had limited training, did not treat, and focused on preventive services (Dawson, 1920). The first tiered system in which the first level of treatment was provided by workers with limited medical education was designed by James Yen and first implemented as part of the Ding Xian experiment in rural China (1926–37) (Taylor & Taylor, 2002). For the first time, village health workers were trained to provide basic treatment and refer cases outside their expertise. In 1965, this approach was revived and widely implemented by the Chinese government as a major part of health services in rural areas; its practitioners famously referred to "barefoot doctors" to emphasize their rural community roots and their work in rural villages.

In 1978, the barefoot doctor program was the major inspiration for the Alma-Ata Conference on Primary Health Care convened by WHO and the United Nations Children's Fund (UNICEF) with representatives from 134 countries, 67 international organizations, and many nongovernmental organizations. "Primary Health Care" was the name given to task shifting based on the barefoot doctor experience. The Alma-Ata declaration called on all countries to implement primary health care "based on practical, scientifically sound and socially acceptable methods and technology made universally accessible through people's full participation and at a cost that the community and country can afford...[and] addresses the main health problems in the community" (WHO Publications, 1978). This global policy change began the mass movement to implementing primary health care as the basis for health services in many countries, particularly LMIC. The barefoot doctor approach was necessarily the most feasible approach in these countries—people who live locally trained in sufficient numbers to make health care locally available. As per the declaration, WHO and other organizations have expended much effort in developing training models and materials to quickly train community health workers in the treatment and prevention of physical illness.

The history and rationale of the Primary (physical) Health Care movement has parallel with the incipient field of global mental health. In the 1950s, the health field was newly ripe with a variety of evidence-based treatments for the major problems affecting people in high-, middle-, and low-income countries. This was concurrent with a broadly supported humanitarian mission based on an emerging view that all people have the right to health care if we could only figure out how to do it. After years of trying to figure out how to provide enough doctors, nurses, and hospitals to the entire world, the world health community abandoned this approach as unfeasible in LMIC and settled on the primary health-care model as the only reasonable alternative.

In 2018, the global mental health community finds itself in a similar situation to the physical health field in the 1950s because of two critical advances over the last two decades: demonstration that the most common mental disorders occur across cultures (albeit with some variation) and scientific evidence-based services for the treatment of these common disorders that (with adaptation) transcends cultural boundaries. These advances have formed a scientific basis for global mental health, while recognition of the cross-cultural importance of these disorders has together fueled the global mental health movement and its humanitarian mission to provide global access to effective services. Like the health proponents of the 1950s, global mental health workers are considering how best to provide evidence-based services to as many people as possible with limited resources.

In some ways, the situation is more compelling than for our predecessors in physical health. Psychotherapeutic treatments are labor-intensive compared with physical health care. While most of the common physical disorders can be treated by 1–3 brief outpatient visits and readily available and cheap drugs, psychotherapy for the common mental disorders (in LMIC: depression, anxiety, and post-traumatic stress disorder (PTSD)) currently consists of 5–12 weekly visits of an hour or more. Universal access to these treatments is therefore even further beyond the workforce resources of most countries than for physical health. Some attempts at task shifting have trained doctors, (and particularly) nurses, and other physical health providers to provide these services as part of their current duties. However, in most low- and middle-income countries, these workers do not have the available time. Moreover, in the author's experience, even when physical health workers do provide these services, they are dropped when other temporary or permanent tasks are added to their workload or client numbers increase. The only feasible option is a separate cadre of providers dedicated to these services.

While labor requirements are increased, resources are more limited. Around the world, mental health has never enjoyed the level of public, political, and therefore funding support as physical health. WHO has reported that only 1% of the global health workforce works in mental health and in low-income countries there is less than one mental health worker per 100,000 people. Low- and middle-income countries collectively spend less than $2/capita on mental health, most of it on hospitals that serve few (WHO, 2015).

Why is this so? Stigma likely plays a major role since it reduces the value placed on its targets and is as pervasive across societies as the lack of resources to deal with mental illness. Why stigma is attached to mental illness (or other conditions) is not clear but may be a result of a perceived threat (Stangor & Crandall, 2000). The common attribution of mental illness to "weakness," laziness, or other "flaws" under the control of the sufferer makes them a threat to societal expectations. Perceptions of unpredictable behavior by the mentally ill add another and more direct threat of violence (Arboleda-Florez, 2002). The result is that the mentally ill is not seen as a sympathetic group worthy of precious resources, particularly health resources. The perceived inability to treat the purported causes of mental illness additionally reduces the impetus to expend resources. Reluctance to be identified as mentally ill hides the extent of the problem and reduces demand for services and visible advocacy for change. Such diverse, universal, and deeply embedded stigma against the mentally ill is not going to dramatically change anytime soon. The field of global mental health will likely have to accept a paltry share of health resources for the foreseeable future to support labor-intensive treatments, creating a large need for task shifting for the foreseeable future.

Implementing task shifting may also help to reduce stigma against those with common mental disorders. Mental health problems and disorders are typically referred to collectively, lumping the few who have severe and potentially threatening disorders of thinking and behavior with those whose disorders are more acceptable as extensions of common experience. Few persons will ever experience psychosis, but most will at some time experience sadness, anxiety, and physical threat, making depression, anxiety, and posttraumatic stress more relatable. Taking primary care for the bulk of these more relatable disorders out of the hands of mental health professionals emphasizes their distinctness from the more severe disorders. In some countries, the author and colleagues have made this part of an argument that these disorders are not "medical" in the sense of necessarily requiring drugs, which has helped to explain why the "talking" approach is appropriate. For many populations, seeing a mental health professional is itself part of the stigma of mental illness, and so access to treatment from a nonprofessional for problems that are seen as extensions of normal life can help to increase access while reducing stigma for the common disorders.

1.1.2 What interventions should be task shifted?

1.1.2.1 Effectiveness and acceptability

Treatments appropriate for task shifting are those known to be effective for common mental health problems when provided using local available resources. Demonstrating which treatments are effective across cultures and situations has therefore been an early primary focus of global mental health research in the form of randomized controlled trials. The first decade of the twenty-first century saw the advent of trials in LMIC exploring the local impact of treatments previously found to be effective in Western countries. Versions of cognitive behavioral therapy were the primary target of these trials because of their success in Western countries, and this has largely been repeated in LMIC (Singla et al., 2017). Other therapies, such as eye movement desensitization and reprocessing, also have supportive evidence although none has been the subject of as many trials with such consistent results. At the timing of writing, variants of cognitive behavioral therapy continue to be the source for most task shifting efforts.

While some interventions like cognitive behavioral therapy have been found to be effective and culturally acceptable where they have been tested, some important problems have emerged. One issue is that many of the populations for whom mental health is a priority are affected by multiple problems including conflict, poverty, and instability. Existing psychotherapies typically focus on a single disorder, requiring therapists to learn multiple interventions. This is feasible for mental health professionals but daunting for paraprofessionals and costly to train and supervise. Even if this were feasible, it would not be appropriate. Among populations affected by conflict, poverty, and instability, comorbidity is much more common among other populations. The author's own experience is that among clients in these populations who have significant mental health problems, the presence of a single disorder is uncommon. Most people who have post-traumatic stress disorder also have both depression and anxiety. Since these problems interact with each other, using a series of single focused psychotherapies would be difficult for both the provider and the client.

While this has been less of a problem in Western countries, it has been recognized and resulted in the development of "transdiagnostic therapies." This is based on recognition that many versions of cognitive behavioral therapy and exposure therapy that have been adapted to treat different disorders share common elements or activities. Therapists could therefore receive a single training that consists of learning these elements, procedures for determining what problem(s) the client has, and planning a treatment approach that consists of an appropriate combination of elements to address these problems (McHugh, Murray, & Barlow, 2009).

This approach has since been adapted and tested among persons with high degrees of comorbidity in LMIC (Murray, Dorsey, et al., 2014) (Chapter 2). Results so far suggest that the approach can be learned by paraprofessionals and used by them to successfully treat common mental disorders and associated psychosocial problems (Bolton et al., 2014; Weiss et al., 2015).

1.1.2.2 Feasibility

While most trials have studied effectiveness under program-like or "real life" settings, they cannot demonstrate the maintenance of effect during scale-up or over time. There has been a recent change in research emphasis to focus on these issues in implementation studies, informing a discussion on what interventions can really be provided sustainably and effectively (Chapter 3). One view is leaning toward simpler interventions based on concerns that Western-style interventions and cognitive behavioral therapy in particular are too complex and/or costly for the training and maintenance of quality among sufficient numbers of paraprofessional workers. This view has required revisiting effectiveness; new trials are being conducted of new simplified or partial versions of interventions already found to be effective. Examples include Problem Management Plus developed under WHO auspices that focuses on problem management aspects of cognitive behavioral therapy and less on cognitive restructuring, regarded as too complex or difficult (Sijbrandij et al., 2015) (Chapter 7). The main alternative view pursues exploration of how to implement the full interventions in their original form. The rationale is that they are demonstrably effective and likely to be more so than simplified or partial versions. High effectiveness at the primary level equates with greater access to truly effective services and a greater shift of the treatment burden from professionals to local providers. This view holds that the poorer the country and the fewer professional resources available, the higher the level of services that should be task shifted.

If simplified versions of interventions prove similarly effective to the full versions, this will resolve this discussion. But at the time of writing, there are too few studies to suggest what the future will be. Meanwhile, discussion and research continue on the capabilities of the available human resources in LMIC who will form the pool for paraprofessional mental health providers. At minimum, they are persons who can read and write and are familiar with didactic instruction and supervision, usually the equivalent of an American middle school (or British primary school) education. How well can they learn and provide services with the available financial and system support in these countries? While the author and colleagues have demonstrated in multiple LMIC that these workers can correctly provide the highest level of effective nondrug treatments for common mental disorders—psychotherapy based on cognitive behavioral therapy—this requires didactic instruction followed by a training apprenticeship of up to a year (Murray et al., 2011). Some global mental health workers believe that this is too great effort and expense, which has been the impetus for the development of new simpler interventions mentioned earlier, including WHO support of "low intensity" interventions focused on reduced training and supervision needs of local paraprofessional workers. If future research suggests that the fuller versions of cognitive behavioral therapy are more effective generally or more effective for some groups, then decisions about which approaches are appropriate will vary according to a country's available resources, and both may ultimately be used together or separately in different parts of the world.

1.1.3 Problems with task shifting

Whether provided individually or even in a group format, psychotherapy takes much more of the provider's time per client than most physical treatments. This makes it unsuitable for uptake by existing health workers (nurses, doctors, and community health workers) who are usually already busy. These workers tend to see few psychotherapy clients, and when numbers of physical health clients increase, mental health services are often the first thing to be dropped. This is not only a function of the time demands of psychotherapy but also due to the priority given to physical health services and a common lack of interest among physical health workers in dealing with mental health problems. Rather than learning and providing psychotherapy, physical health workers tend to be more interested in adopting new physical health services, while their main concern with mental health clients is in referring them elsewhere.

For all these reasons, psychotherapy should be task shifted to paraprofessionals who focus primarily or solely on providing mental health services. This requires the creation of a new type of position to local health services, something that is usually difficult to implement. Departments of Health are leery of creating new positions because of budget issues, and the approvals and procedures for making this happen are usually complex and slow. Where task shifting has been done to dedicated positions, primarily by NGOs, these positions lack formal recognition, job security, and adequate pay. This produces mental health paraprofessionals who tend to be less committed to this work than professionals, causing high turnover that increases training costs and decreases morale and service quality. In some countries, the stigma attached to persons with mental health problems results in lower regard for those who treat them, which exacerbates the turnover problem. This may change as mental health is receiving increasing attention. If changes in attitude by populations and governments improve, particularly regarding the need for mental health programs and their effectiveness, funding and recognition of community mental health workers should also improve. Progress should be directed to an ultimate goal of formal integration of these positions into health services as career positions with ongoing supervision, appropriate pay, and similar conditions to other health workers.

Recently, a more extreme version of task shifting is being investigated (Ruzek, Kuhn, Jaworski, Owen, & Ramsey, 2016). Smartphone- and internet-based mobile mental health interventions are continually being developed, some of which consist of software to be used by clients with little or no mental health worker intervention (Epping-Jordan et al., 2016). This represents task shifting to the client. While these interventions are largely based on various elements of cognitive behavioral therapy known to be effective, their effectiveness in a mobile format across cultures is still being investigated. Should they prove effective, they could provide a major alternative form of access to mental health services for those persons with smartphone or internet access. For them, mobile health platforms are not only cheaper and less time-consuming than traveling to a provider but also more confidential, particularly in small communities where provider visits are noticed. Mobile mental health platforms may therefore prove to be a powerful means of expanding access to some communities. At the present time, there are many limitations. These include the need for pre-existing phone access; difficulties in programming some of the more complex elements of psychotherapy; reduced ability to tailor treatment to the client's current situation, both at the beginning and during treatment; and accessibility to people who are unused to confiding in technology instead of another person. As these issues are resolved, it is probable that software-based interventions will find a useful place supplementing the other approaches described in this chapter.

1.2 Systematic adaptation of psychotherapies

1.2.1 The need for systematic adaptation

When mental health first emerged in the 1990s as a potential area of concern within the field of International Health, attention focused on the identification and treatment of mental disorders. A debate immediately began as to whether people in non-Western countries developed the same disorders as those described in the West and codified in the standard Diagnostic and Statistical Manual that originated in the United States. Some authors took the view that disorders described in the West must be culturally bound, and it was therefore unreasonable to expect to find them elsewhere (Bracken, Giller, & Summerfield, 1995). Proponents seemed to ignore the possibility that what had been described in the West might refer to human rather than culturally-defined states and offered little evidence to support their objections. This view has persisted in some quarters, but where mental disorders have been investigated cross-culturally, they have been found to be similar to those originally described in the West in terms of symptomatology and causation (e.g., Haroz et al., 2017; Michalopoulos, Haroz, Bass, Murray, & Bolton, 2015).

This has been an important finding as it suggests that interventions found to be effective for these disorders in Western countries might be similarly effective for the same disorders elsewhere. A series of studies have supported this hypothesis for some interventions. Of these, the most widely tested and supported are the cognitive behavioral therapies (van Ginneken et al., 2013).

But while the disorders themselves are similar across cultures and populations, they are not identical. A global review of depression symptoms found that while many core symptoms occur across populations, other symptoms appear to be important in some populations but not others (Haroz et al., 2017). The differences are important when it comes to adaptation of treatment approaches for task shifting. Ability to assess the presence of the problems to be addressed by the intervention forms an important part of the task shifting process and so needs to be included in training. Training of paraprofessionals requires that these descriptions are not based on Western descriptions but on how these problems are described locally. This is not so necessary when training professional mental health workers such as psychiatrists and social workers. They are trained with a thorough conceptual understanding of mental health and illness that they can adapt to their own culture. But when adapting psychotherapies for task shifting, where the providers are paraprofessionals who do not receive in-depth conceptual training, the description of problems must be adapted a priori to the local culture in order to make sense to clients and to the providers.

Just as Western descriptions of illness are relevant but still need to be adapted to other contexts, the same is true of Western methods of treatment. Demonstrated effectiveness in other cultures confirms the appropriateness of the basic concepts, but in each case, success has also depended on successful local adaptation.

Adaptation is therefore a critical aspect of task shifting success. Developing an adapted treatment suitable for task shifting can be a difficult task. The final version must explain the material in ways that are understandable and acceptable to both providers and clients. Ensuring this requires a systematic iterative process. The remainder of this chapter is a summary of a recommended stepwise process successfully used by the authors and colleagues in diverse regions of the world. The steps are presented here in order to explain their rationale. A detailed description of these steps is available elsewhere (AMHR, 2013a; Murray et al., 2011; Murray, Tol, et al., 2014) (see also Chapter 5).

1.2.2 Steps in the adaptation process

1.2.2.1 Preliminary understanding of local priority mental problems

This step should precede selection of the intervention or at least before selection has been finalized. Key pieces of information to collect at this step include the priority mental health problems of the population in terms of frequency and their impact and severity. This is because interventions should be selected that address at least some of these problems as failure to do so is likely to result in programs that are poorly utilized by the population. Providers will also feel less committed. Other important information includes how the problems are understood in terms of perceived causes and appropriate treatments. An intervention that does not appear to address the perceived cause will require more explanation and convincing to motivate clients to try it. These efforts may fail. For example, if a mental health problem is thought to be due to witchcraft, then interventions that consist of weekly meetings to talk about the problem may appear irrelevant. Similarly, it is important to explore what are acceptable treatments. If talking about mental health problems is not acceptable, then group-based interventions or even individual talking sessions may not be well received. Where mental health problems are acknowledged as health issues, there may be an expectation of drug treatment. Anything less may be regarded as not taking the problem seriously. Finally, knowledge of the language used to name and describe the priority problems is important. The manual and training materials should rely on local terminology as much as possible in order to be well understood by both providers and clients.

Where this information does not already exist, preliminary research is warranted. Qualitative methods are recommended because of their emphasis on nonleading and on open-ended detailed descriptions. A detailed description of one qualitative approach for this purpose is available online (AMHR, 2013b).

1.2.2.2 Selection of treatment approach

Selection begins with the identification of the community's perception of the priority mental health problems as described above. The primary consideration in selecting candidate interventions (or versions of interventions) is that they are known to be effective in addressing at least one of these priorities. Effectiveness criteria are relative; the most preferred is demonstrated effectiveness among the target population, followed by effectiveness among populations similar in terms of culture, situation (war, displacement, etc.), or geography. The minimum criterion is that the intervention has been found to be effective for the priority problems among unrelated populations somewhere in the world.

The acceptability and feasibility of the candidate effective interventions are then considered. Choosing an intervention that is likely to be acceptable will make training and uptake by clients easier to achieve. The lack of face acceptability is not a contraindication; if no interventions appear suitable, then a choice is still made. Choosing an intervention that does not appear to be acceptable may simply indicate that more groundwork will likely be required with the trainees and clients to convince them to try the intervention, and progress will be slower. In the author's experience, psychotherapeutic interventions are looked on with distrust in many cultures, but few reject them totally. Some work-around is usually possible to deal with cultural or practical objections.

Feasibility among the candidate options is also important. Ideally, conversations with governments or other organizations who would be expected to support the program have occurred prior to step 1, but no later than this step. Negotiation should establish what resources a program can expect in order to match the intervention choice and logistics to what is available. Depending on the circumstances, feasibility may be less important than acceptability (in situations like post disaster where programs will likely wind down) but more important for programs that are planned to be permanent or at least over many years. In some cases, programs may begin where long-term resources are not available to sustain them, in the expectation that if the programs show significant impact, funding may be made available. This depends on conversations with the government or supporting organizations to establish that this will occur.

1.2.2.3 Conversion of manual and training materials into simple language

This applies to materials originally written for professional mental health workers and students. Most include technical or complex language that is difficult to translate by persons who lack technical knowledge and are not MH professionals. Before they can begin, the materials need to be rewritten in a form that uses simple language. Examples include substituting "verbalize" or "focus on" with "talk about," "motivated" with "want to," and "facilitate the process" with "make it work." While it is true that the more complex terms are subtly different from the simple terms suggested here, most subtleties are lost in translation anyway (or worse when the terms are mistranslated).

Below is an example of mistranslated term from a manual on cognitive processing therapy (CPT):

> *"It is helpful to provide an expectation that the patient provide a brief, less affect-charged event by providing a timeframe in the request." (Resick, Monson, & Chard, 2006)*

This is immediately followed by advice on how to state this to the client:

> *"In order for me to have a clearer picture of what we will be working on first, could you please give me a brief description, about five minutes, of the most traumatic event…".*

The first explanation is complex and difficult to translate. The second version is much clearer, as it is designed for the client. Since the translators are usually nonprofessionals and so are closer to the clients in terms of education than they are to professional mental health workers, it would be better for them if the entire manual was written using this type of simple and direct language.

There is also a preference for using multiple words that mean the same thing, to give some variety to the writing (e.g., sometimes referring to one's "house" and later to one's "home"). As much as possible, the manual should use the same word to express the same meaning.

Simplifying existing materials in this way is an important step to producing accurately translated and understandable materials.

1.2.2.4 Translation of the manual and training materials into local language

The simplified language version of the materials is then translated into the local language. This should be done by a group of translators if available. Available translators are unlikely to be familiar with mental health concepts. In fact, it is better if their familiarity with concepts is no better than that of the trainees, so that any questions or problems they have with the material will be similar to those of the trainees.

During the translation process, they need frequent access to the trainers in order to ask questions and raise concerns that are then negotiated with the trainers. Here, "negotiation" means collaboratively coming up with solutions that are understandable to translators (and other local people) yet remain true to the material. Translators who belong to the local population may also raise concerns about the appropriateness of the content of the material. Most often concerns refer to situations or activities considered too specific to the Western culture (such as referring to shopping in a supermarket if none exist locally) but may also refer to people thinking or acting in ways that would be alien to local people. Where translators agree on a problem as being significant, this is noted along with any changes they can agree on. If the changes are clearly warranted and do not affect content, they are made.

1.2.2.5 On-site provider training

Adaptation continues during on-site training. Trainers explain the material, but trainees also provide feedback as to how understandable and relevant the materials and explanations are. Where trainees cannot understand the trainer or have concerns that the clients will not understand the material, the trainer must negotiate an alternate explanation. In some cases, trainees will understand the trainer and the material but still suggest better ways to explain concepts. These changes are then made to the manual during (or very soon after) the on-site training.

1.2.2.6 Piloting

By the end of the class-based training trainers and trainees will have produced an adapted version of the materials and approach that is understandable to the trainees and hopefully to the clients. A piloting stage then follows the on-site training. Trainees take on no more than 1–2 clients each and report in detail how well treatment is proceeding, in particular problems with the content or its presentation, compliance and acceptance, or the practicality of treatment for both providers and clients (such as length of sessions, timing, frequency, and accessibility). Problems are discussed, and alternative language or approaches are negotiated and tried. Those that are successful are incorporated into the approach as permanent changes or options.

1.2.2.7 On-going adaptation

After the pilot phase and during normal implementation, training and supervision of providers continue. The author works with trainer clinicians who implement an "apprenticeship" approach to training; after on-site training of both providers and local supervisors, the providers report weekly to their supervisors who in turn report remotely to trainers. This facilitates "on the job" training that lasts months and continues until the trainees are considered skilled and knowledgeable enough to graduate to less frequent ongoing supervision. The process is also important because it continues the trainee-trainer connection that allows for further identification of problems and further adaptation as indicated.

The author's experience is that all seven steps are necessary for successful adaptation. Information on local perceptions of mental health (step 1) helps intervention selection and can also suggest some changes but not comprehensively. Review by local translator and providers forms a major part of adaptation but is also rarely comprehensive. Even the clients themselves, as they begin treatment, cannot predict all the problems that they and later clients will encounter. Therefore, even during step 7, new and important issues continue to be identified and addressed.

1.3 Conclusion

The lack of mental health professionals in most LMIC and the high cost of increasing their numbers make task shifting currently the most viable approach to improving global access to psychotherapy. The labor intensiveness of these interventions prevents the transfer of tasks to other health professionals, necessitating the training of paraprofessionals who focus on these treatments. However, ongoing concerns about the ability of paraprofessionals to learn and provide these treatments at scale have led to the development of expurgated versions of the standard psychotherapies that are still undergoing testing. There are also efforts to reduce or remove reliance on paraprofessionals through technology-based self-administered treatments. At this time, it is not clear what the balance will be in the future. However, a single approach is unlikely. Variations in resources and level of need in countries around the world will likely result in varying combinations of full or partial interventions provided by combinations of mental health and paraprofessionals and supplemented by technology. Even if technology provides to be highly effective, the lack of access to technology and the high cost of mental health professionals will maintain task shifting as an important element in mental health practice globally for the foreseeable future.

References

Applied Mental Health Research Group (AMHR). (2013a). *Design, implementation, monitoring and evaluation of cross-cultural trauma related mental health and psychosocial assistance programs: A user's manual for researchers and program implementers. Modules 1, 2, 4, and 5. Available from* https://www.jhsph.edu/research/centers-and-institutes/global-mental-health/resource-materials/design-implementation-monitoring-and-evaluation-dime/ (accessed 15.03.18).

Applied Mental Health Research Group (AMHR). (2013b). *Design, implementation, monitoring and evaluation of cross-cultural trauma related mental health and psychosocial assistance programs: A user's manual for researchers and program implementers. Module 1.* Available from http://hopkinshumanitarianhealth.org/assets/documents/VOT_DIME_MODULE1_FINAL.PDF (accessed 15.03.18).

Arboleda-Florez, J. (2002). What causes stigma? *World Psychiatry, 1*(1), 25–26. PMCID: PMC1489829.

Bolton, P., Bass, J., Zangana, G., Kamal, T., Murray, S., Kaysen, D., ... Rosenblum, M. (2014). A randomized controlled trial of mental health interventions for survivors of systematic violence in Kurdistan, Northern Iraq. *BMC Psychiatry, 14*, 1693. https://doi.org/10.1186/s12888-014-0360-2.

Bracken, P. J., Giller, J. E., & Summerfield, D. (1995). Psychological responses to war and atrocity: The limitations of current concepts. *Social Science & Medicine, 40*(8), 1073–1082. https://doi.org/10.1016/0277-9536(94)00181-r.

Epping-Jordan, J. E., Harris, R., Brown, F. L., Carswell, K., Foley, C., García-Moreno, C., ... van Ommeren, M. (2016). Self-help plus (SH+): A new WHO stress management package. *World Psychiatry, 15*(3), 295–296. https://doi.org/10.1002/wps.20355. PMCID: PMC5032500.

Haroz, E., Bolton, P., Gross, A., Chan, K. S., Michalopolous, L., & Bass, J. (2017). Depression symptoms across cultures: An IRT analysis of standard depression symptoms using data from eight countries. *Social Science and Medicine, 183*, 151–162.

Lord Dawson of Penn. (1920). Interim report on the future provision of medical and allied services 1920. Ministry of Health Consultative Council on Medical and Allied Services. In *Presented to parliament by command of his majesty. London Published by his Majesty's Stationery Office.* Available from https://www.sochealth.co.uk/national-health-service/healthcare-generally/history-of-healthcare/interim-report-on-the-future-provision-of-medical-and-allied-services-1920-lord-dawson-of-penn/ (accessed 12.02.18).

McHugh, R. K., Murray, H. W., & Barlow, D. H. (2009). Balancing fidelity and adaptation in the dissemination of empirically-supported treatments: The promise of transdiagnostic interventions. *Behaviour Research and Therapy, 47*, 946–953.

Michalopoulos, L., Haroz, E., Bass, J., Murray, L., & Bolton, P. (2015). Exploring the fit of Western PTSD models across three non-Western low and middle income countries. *Traumatology, 21*(2), 55–63. https://doi.org/10.1037/trm0000020.

Murray, L. K., Dorsey, S., Bolton, P., Jordans, M., Rahman, A., Bass, J., & Verdeli, H. (2011). Building capacity in mental health interventions in low resource countries: An apprenticeship model for training local providers. *International Journal of Mental Health Systems, 5*, 30. https://doi.org/10.1186/1752-4458-5-30. http://www.ijmhs.com/content/5/1/30.

Murray, L. K., Dorsey, S., Haroz, E., Lee, C., Alyasiry, M. M., Haydary, A., ... Bolton, P. (2014). A common elements treatment approach for adult mental health problems in low- and middle income countries. *Cognitive and Behavioral Practice, 21*(2), 111–123. https://doi.org/10.1016/j.cbpra.2013.06.005.

Murray, L. K., Tol, W., Jordans, M., Zangana, G. S., Amin, A. M., Bolton, P., ... Thornicroft, G. (2014). Dissemination and implementation of evidence-based mental health interventions in post-conflict, low-resource settings. *Intervention, 12*(1), 94–112.

Resick, P. A., Monson, C. M., & Chard, K. M. (2006). *Cognitive processing therapy veteran/military version. Copyright, © Patricia A. Resick, Ph.D. and Candice M. Monson, Ph.D.* http://www.alrest.org/pdf/CPT_Manual_-_Modified_for_PRRP(2).pdf (accessed 10.02.18).

Ruzek, J. I., Kuhn, E., Jaworski, B. K., Owen, J. E., & Ramsey, K. M. (2016). Mobile mental health interventions following war and disaster. *Mhealth*, *2*, 37. https://doi.org/10.21037/mhealth.2016.08.06 PMCID: PMC5344166.

Sijbrandij, M., Farooq, S., Bryant, R. A., Dawson, K., Hamdani, S. U., Chiumento, A., … Rahman, A. (2015). Problem Management Plus (PM+) for common mental disorders in a humanitarian setting in Pakistan; study protocol for a randomised controlled trial (RCT). *BMC Psychiatry*, *15*, 232. https://doi.org/10.1186/s12888-015-0602-y©.

Singla, D. R., Kohrt, B. A., Murray, L. K., Anand, A., Chorpita, B. F., & Patel, V. (2017). Psychological treatments for the world: Lessons from low- and middle-income countries. *Annual Review of Clinical Psychology*, *8*(13), 149–181. https://doi.org/10.1146/annurev-clinpsy-032816-045217.

Stangor, G., & Crandall, C. S. (2000). Threat and the social construction of stigma. In T. F. Heatherton, R. E. Kleck, M. R. Heblet al. *(Eds.), The social psychology of stigma* (pp. 62–87). New York: Guilford Press.

Taylor, D. C., & Taylor, C. E. (2002). Just and lasting change. When communities own their futures. In *Chapter 7: The World's first example of intentional, community-based development* (2nd ed.). Ding Xian, China: Johns Hopkins University Press.

van Ginneken, N., Tharyan, P., Lewin, S., Rao, G. N., Meera, S. M., Pian, J., … Patel, V. (2013). Non-specialist health worker interventions for the care of mental, neurological and substance-abuse disorders in low- and middle-income countries. *Cochrane Database of Systematic Reviews. 11*, CD009149. https://doi.org/10.1002/14651858.CD009149.pub2.

Weiss, W. M., Murray, L. K., Zangana, G. A., Mahmooth, Z., Kaysen, D., Dorsey, S., … Bolton, P. (2015). Community-based mental health treatments for survivors of torture and militant attacks in Southern Iraq: A randomized control trial. *BMC Psychiatry*, *15*, 249. https://doi.org/10.1186/s12888-015-0622-7.

WHO. (2015). *Mental health atlas 2014*. ISBN 978.92.4.156501.1 (NLM classification: WM 17) © World Health Organization http://www.who.int/mediacentre/news/notes/2015/finances-mental-health/en/ (accessed 10.03.18).

WHO Publications. (2008). *Task shifting: rational redistribution of tasks among health workforce teams: global recommendations and guidelines. 1. HIV infections – prevention and control. 2. Health services administration. 3. Health personnel – organization and administration. 4. Health services accessibility*. I. World Health Organization. II. PEPFAR. III. UNAIDS. ISBN 978-92-4-159631-2 (NLM classification: WC 503.6) © World Health Organization http://www.who.int/healthsystems/TTR-TaskShifting.pdf (accessed 04.03.18).

WHO Publications. (1978). http://www.who.int/publications/almaata_declaration_en.pdf (accessed 05.03.18).

Transdiagnostic therapeutic approaches: A global perspective

2

Laura K. Murray[*,†], *Kristina Metz*[*,†], *Karis Callaway*[‡]
*Department of Mental Health, Johns Hopkins Bloomberg School of Public Health, Baltimore, MD, United States, †Department of International Health, Johns Hopkins Bloomberg School of Public Health, Baltimore, MD, United States, ‡Department of Psychology, Western Michigan University, Kalamazoo, MI, United States

2.1 Introduction/background

As laid out elsewhere in this book, there is a significant mental health treatment gap in low- and middle-income countries (LMIC). Funders, policymakers, and researchers have encouraged a focus on the reduction of the mental health treatment gap (Collins, Insel, Chockalingam, Daar, & Maddox, 2013; Patel et al., 2008, 2013), which has led to worthy advances in global mental health, including multiple clinical trials on mental health treatments in LMIC (see also later chapters). Most of these clinical trials included "focal disorder treatments"—or treatments that focus primarily on one disorder. For example, interpersonal psychotherapy (IPT), which was developed to target major depressive disorder, was one of the first treatments tested in LMIC with both adults and youth (Bolton et al., 2003; Bolton et al., 2007). Other focal treatments tested in LMIC include, but are not limited to, behavioral activation (BA), narrative exposure therapy (NET, kidNET), cognitive processing therapy (CPT), and trauma-focused cognitive behavioral therapy (TF-CBT) (Bass et al., 2013; Bolton et al., 2014; Hensel-Dittmann et al., 2011; Magidson et al., 2016; Murray et al., 2015; O'Callaghan, McMullen, Shannon, Rafferty, & Black, 2013; Robjant & Fazel, 2010; Ruf et al., 2010; Weiss et al., 2015). These trials document the acceptability of mental health treatments cross-culturally, with modifications (e.g., simplified terminology and culturally appropriate application methods) that did not include changes to core treatment elements (Kaysen et al., 2013; Murray et al., 2013; Patel, Chowdhary, Rahman, & Verdeli, 2011; Verdeli et al., 2008). Furthermore, many of the studies cited above have demonstrated the effectiveness of evidence-based treatments (EBTs) using lay community workers known as task sharing (see Chapter 1). This research is noteworthy in that collectively, it has shown that EBTs from high-income countries (HIC) are effective for reducing common mental health symptomology in real-world and frequently unstable settings. Furthermore, it demonstrates that EBTs can be implemented with fidelity and effectiveness by non-professional providers.

Although there have been significant gains in understanding the effectiveness of mental health treatments and potential delivery methods to increase sustainability

Global Mental Health and Psychotherapy. https://doi.org/10.1016/B978-0-12-814932-4.00002-1

and build capacity (e.g., task sharing), there continue to be barriers in providing and scaling up mental health services in LMIC. This chapter will focus on the relatively new transdiagnostic approach in LMIC that may help to further bridge the mental health treatment gap. We will begin by defining transdiagnostic approaches, walk through the historical theory and rationale, and discuss its potential utilization and benefits in LMIC. We will then review the current evidence for transdiagnostic treatments, pulling from both HIC and LMIC. Finally, we will deliberate possible future directions of transdiagnostic approaches in LMIC.

2.2 What is a transdiagnostic intervention?

Given the range of terms and qualifiers used to describe transdiagnostic treatments for mental health problems, it is important to carefully define terminology. Three recently published papers help clarify language used to describe various types of transdiagnostic treatments (see Table 2.1). Sauer-Zavala et al. (2017) categorize transdiagnostic treatments into three approaches: (1) a *universally applied principles approach*, which is a "top-down" (p. 131) approach leading to interventions based on a school of thought (e.g., psychodynamic, cognitive behavioral, humanistic, and mindfulness-based approaches) that is then applied to multiple disorders regardless

Table 2.1 Terms and definitions of transdiagnostic

Names	Definitions
Approaches	
Common elements approach	Involves assembling commonly used components or strategies of EBTs that can be delivered in varying combinations to address a range of problems. Decision rules based on research evidence guide selection, sequencing, and dosing of elements but allow for flexibility in individual symptom presentation (Chorpita & Daleiden, 2009; Sauer-Zavala et al., 2017)
Principle-guided approach	"Principles" do not refer to a school of thought (e.g., cognitive behavioral or humanistic) to guide therapeutic strategies (as in Sauer-Zavala et al., 2017), but rather a limited number of broad evidence-based assumptions underlying effective psychological treatments for multiple disorders, each of which is associated with improvement even when used alone (Weisz et al., 2017)
Shared mechanisms approach	Targets underlying processes implicated in the development and maintenance of multiple disorders (Ehrenreich-May & Chu, 2014). Interventions based on this approach are informed by theoretical models of psychopathology rather than treatment, and target core features that appear across disorders (Sauer-Zavala et al., 2017)
Universally applied principles approach	A "top-down" approach leading to interventions based on a school of thought (e.g., psychodynamic, cognitive behavioral, humanistic, and mindfulness-based approaches, including acceptance and commitment therapy) that this is then applied to multiple disorders regardless of symptom presentation (Sauer-Zavala et al., 2017)

Table 2.1 Continued

Names	**Definitions**
Terms	
Dosage	The amount of an element or component used in treatment, measured by session number, minutes focused on any one element or component
Flexible	A flexible program can be adapted and individualized during its delivery. They can have manuals providing guidance, but they need not dictate strict session-by-session content, scripts, or prescribed number of sessions (Boustani et al., 2017)
Linear	A linear program is designed so that elements are provided in a specific sequence from beginning to end with each client getting the same elements and order of elements. There is no deviation in this sequence, but there can be variations in dosing of an element
Modular	Four principles define this: (a) they are partially decomposable (i.e., a modular treatment can be divided into independent units or subunits); (b) each module should have its own goal and purpose, independent of other modules; (c) modules have an interface that allows them to connect to other modules in a standardized way (i.e., they are immediately compatible when linked); and (d) a module should be self-contained, such that all the information needed to deliver that module should be contained internally and not dependent on another module (Boustani et al., 2017)
Multiproblem	A treatment with multiple foci, that is, a treatment that addresses a range of problems like depression, anxiety, trauma, and substance use. This does not refer to treatments that address multiple *disorders* within one problem area (e.g., different anxiety disorders) (Boustani et al., 2017)
Transdiagnostic	A treatment that addresses multiple diagnoses. These can be multiple disorders within one problem area (e.g., different anxiety disorders) or multiple problem areas (e.g., depression, anxiety, and trauma) (Boustani et al., 2017; Marchette & Weisz, 2017)

of symptom presentation; (2) a *modular or common elements approach*, which involves assembling commonly used components, elements, or strategies of EBTs that can be delivered in varying combinations to address a range of problems, with flexibility in component selection, sequencing, and dosing of elements; and (3) a *shared mechanisms approach*, which are informed by theoretical models and target underlying processes implicated in the development and maintenance of certain disorders (Chorpita & Daleiden, 2009; Ehrenreich-May & Chu, 2014). More recently, Marchette and Weisz (2017) proposed a fourth category, a *principle-guided approach*, in which a "principle" refers to an evidence-based assumption underlying effective psychological treatments for multiple disorders and is associated with improvement even when used alone (Weisz, Bearman, Santucci, & Jensen-Doss, 2017).

Boustani, Gellatly, Westman, and Chorpita (2017) added to this work by providing an extensive glossary of terms used in the transdiagnostic literature, including distinguishing between *transdiagnostic* and *common elements*. Other descriptors depict how the transdiagnostic treatment is utilized including terms such as dosage, linear, multiproblem, modular, and flexible (see Table 2.1 for definitions). Treatments often meet the criteria for some but not all of these terms—all of which may have advantages and disadvantages for use and sustainability in LMIC. In summary, "transdiagnostic" is an umbrella term. Therefore, it is increasingly important to delineate treatment characteristics to fully understand their potential benefits and challenges, utilization, and implementation within LMIC.

2.3 Why transdiagnostic? A historical look and lessons learned from high-income countries

Historically in HIC, mental health treatment was based in psychological theory and highly variable across clinicians. However, in the 1980s, there was movement to provide evidence that these theoretically driven treatments were effective, and thus, treatment manuals were developed and rigorously evaluated for effectiveness (Luborsky & DeRubeis, 1984). Treatment manuals have advantages as they allow for clinical trials and track fidelity closely and provide specific guidance on how to effectively treat mental health disorders. Many of the treatment manuals tested were focal cognitive behavioral therapy (CBT) interventions (i.e., CBT for depression), which typically provide treatment in a linear, proscribed fashion (McEvoy, Nathan, & Norton, 2009; McManus, Shafran, & Cooper, 2010). From this line of research, multiple now-manualized focal treatments for mental health disorders were found to be efficacious in HIC (e.g., https://www.effectivechildtherapy.org; https://www.div12.org/psychological-treatments/treatments; and National Collaborating Centre for Mental Health, 2011).

While this proliferation of treatment manuals beneficially moved mental health into the evidence-based care movement, there were criticisms such as overemphasizing technique, ignoring the role of the therapist, and overfocusing on diagnostic categories (Addis & Krasnow, 2000). In addition, a number of meta-analyses began demonstrating that the manualized treatment effect sizes significantly decreased when applied within real-world settings (e.g., community clinics) in comparison with hospitals or universities where the trials were conducted (Weisz & Donenberg, 1992; Weisz, Donenberg, Han, & Kauneckis, 1995). These metaanalyses suggested that although evidence-based psychotherapeutic manuals were available, professionals in applied settings either were not trained to utilize them or were not implementing them at all or with fidelity. It was also suggested that these treatments may be no longer effective within applied contexts. Weisz et al. (1995) hypothesized that the beneficial therapy effects in contrived settings were associated with three factors: (a) the use of behavioral or cognitive behavioral methods, (b) reliance on specific therapy methods rather than eclectic approaches, and (c) provision of structure through treatment manuals and monitoring to promote fidelity.

This difficulty with transferring effective manualized treatments to the greater population was identified as a public health issue in the United States, and significant efforts moved toward identifying ways to disseminate and maintain the effectiveness of EBTs (Insel, 2009; President's New Freedom Commission on Mental Health, 2004). Although multiple funding opportunities emerged to disseminate EBTs, states and organizations began struggling with the cost and resources necessary to train a workforce (with high turnover) in *multiple* EBTs (Marsenich, 2007; McHugh, Murray, & Barlow, 2009). Another challenge was that providers were having difficulty deciding which EBTs to use given significant overlap in elements and targeted problems (Harvey & Gumport, 2015). Chu et al. (2015) interviewed clinical practitioners to determine the uptake and implementation difficulties with manualized treatments. Qualitative interviews found that practitioners tended to randomly select from different manuals instead of adhering to one completely. The findings suggested that the CBT protocols did contain elements the practitioners found useful for everyday practice, but due to heterogeneity in caseloads, comorbidity, and fluctuations in symptoms, they preferred to build personalized treatments by selecting subsets of the components provided by the EBT manuals. At this time, there was a convergence of multiple mental health leaders calling for a move to transdiagnostic approaches to address the public health- and implementation-related challenges with focal treatments. The rationale for moving to transdiagnostic approaches included the following: (a) to achieve a better balance of fidelity and flexibility to address dissemination and transportability issues, (b) to reduce the number of model clinicians need to be trained in, (c) to minimize the cost of retraining due to high clinician turnover rates, (d) to reduce the confusion around what EBT to choose, (e) to capitalize on similarities across diagnoses and elements within existing EBTs, (f) a possible method to deal with comorbidity more effectively and efficiently, (g) to systematize the selection process in the case of modular approaches, (h) to reduce the strict order and timeline disliked by clinicians to create more personalized mental health care, and (i) to (hopefully) produce substantial cost reductions (Chorpita, Daleiden, & Weisz, 2005a, 2005b; Chu, Temkin, & Toffey, 2016; Insel, 2009; Mansell, Harvey, Watkins, & Shafran, 2008; McHugh et al., 2009; Weisz, Krumholz, Santucci, Thomassin, & Ng, 2015; Weisz, Ugueto, Herren, Afienko, & Rutt, 2011). The cost issue was critical in that even at specialty outpatient clinics in the United States, clinicians would need to receive training and maintain high fidelity in multiple individual EBTs (e.g., 5–8) to be able to treat the target population. Often, community mental health centers would require even more protocol trainings. The task to then maintain fidelity to each of these treatments was an enormous weight on the entire mental health system (McHugh et al., 2009). Thus, multiple HIC began developing and evaluating transdiagnostic approaches in the early 2000s, with 400 publications from 2013 to 2014 (Chu et al., 2016).

2.4 Evidence review of existing transdiagnostic literature in high-income countries

We begin by reviewing some transdiagnostic models developed and tested within HIC, focusing on those that have multiple completed trials.

2.4.1 Unified protocol for the treatment of emotional disorders (UP)

The UP is a transdiagnostic treatment designed for mental health professionals to target a range of anxiety and unipolar mood disorders (Barlow et al., 2011; Boisseau, Farchione, Fairholme, Ellard, & Barlow, 2010). Based on the theory that psychological disorders share the underlying mechanism of neuroticism, the UP underscores the functional nature of emotions, promotes the tolerance of intense emotions, and corrects maladaptive attempts to regulate these experiences (Barlow, Ellard, Sauer-Zavala, Bullis, & Carl, 2014). It utilizes fundamental principles such as the interoceptive exposure, extinction learning, and identification and modification of maladaptive thoughts. It also uniquely emphasizes the importance of how one experiences and responds to emotions. Through this, the UP seeks to promote appropriate emotional processing and eliminate excessive emotionally driven responses to internal and external cues (Wilamowska et al., 2010).

The UP consists of eight modules, five of which form the core treatment components. The beginning modules start with a functional assessment to increase the client's readiness for behavioral change, foster self-efficacy, and psychoeducation on emotions. Modules three through seven make up the UP's "core modules" that are tailored to support the development of emotion objectivity, reappraisal and processing of emotionally charged situations, and effective coping. The final module reviews success and reemphasizes the typical fluctuating nature of emotions (Boisseau et al., 2010; Wilamowska et al., 2010). The developers describe the UP as a shared mechanism approach (Sauer-Zavala et al., 2017). Based on the definitions of other terms, it would also be linear in that the modules are given in the same order for clients.

The UP has been investigated through a case study, various open clinical trials, and randomized controlled trials (RCTs). It has been found to be effective in significantly reducing adults' symptoms of anxiety and unipolar depression, and preliminary research shows favorable results for somatoform and dissociative disorders (Barlow et al., 2017; Bullis, Fortune, Farchione, & Barlow, 2014; Ellard, Fairholme, Boisseau, Farchione, & Barlow, 2010; Farchione et al., 2012; Mazaheri, Daghaghzadeh, Afshar, & Mohammadi, 2014). There is also some early evidence for its applicability with youth and more nationally diverse samples including Japanese, Spanish, and Iranian participants (Barlow et al., 2017; Bilek & Ehrenreich-May, 2012; Ehrenreich-May et al., 2017; Ito et al., 2016; Mazaheri et al., 2014; Osma, Castellano, Crespo, & García-Palacios, 2015). Predominately researched as an individual treatment, the UP has recently been pilot tested within a group format (Osma et al., 2015). All studies have utilized mental health professionals.

2.4.2 Cognitive-behavioral therapy-enhanced (CBT-E)

CBT-E is a transdiagnostic treatment for eating disorders. It is a shared mechanism approach specifying overevaluation of weight and shape as a core maintaining mechanism across anorexia nervosa, bulimia nervosa, and eating disorders not otherwise specified (Fairburn, Cooper, & Shafran, 2003). Originally developed to address bulimia nervosa, CBT-E has been successfully expanded to treat multiple other categories of eating disorders by targeting their similar maintenance mechanisms. Therefore, it addresses multiple disorders within one category but is not considered multiproblem as it does not address other categories (e.g., depression and substance use).

CBT-E begins with stage one in which sessions are held twice a week and concentrate on collaboration to mutually understand the problem and to stabilize the client's preexisting eating patterns. Stage two reviews and reinforces initial successes and addresses any potential barriers to change. Stage three is the bulk of the treatment and incorporates several modules on body image, dietary restraint, and triggers for maladaptive eating behaviors. Stage four promotes the maintenance of treatment gains and emphasizes how to cope appropriately with possible future setbacks. For underweight clients, an additional module can be added to further individualize the treatment to assist in weight gain (Fairburn et al., 2003).

CBT-E has been found to be effective in increasing body mass index scores in clients with anorexia nervosa, a change that remained stable for more than several months of posttreatment (Fairburn et al., 2013). A recent RCT found that CBT-E showed significant remission rates (66% at posttreatment) for both participants with anorexia and bulimia nervosa and that these remission rates increased (69%) throughout a 60-week follow-up. These remission rates were found to be superior to the IPT participants' rates (33% posttreatment and 49% follow-up; Fairburn et al., 2015). CBT-E is provided in a variety of settings (e.g., intensive day programs, inpatient) and is used to treat youth and adult populations (Grave, 2012; Grave, Calugi, Conti, Doll, & Fairburn, 2013; Grave, Calugi, Doll, & Fairburn, 2013). It adheres to a 20- or 40-week session schedule, treatment length being dependent on the client's initial ability and willingness to maintain a healthy weight as treatment progress. Both schedule lengths consist of 40–50 min sessions. Like the UP, CBT-E utilizes mental health professionals to deliver the treatment.

2.4.3 The modular approach to therapy for children with anxiety, depression, trauma, or conduct problems (MATCH-ADTC)

MATCH-ADTC (referred to as MATCH) is a transdiagnostic manual designed to treat four clinical problem areas including anxiety, depression, traumatic stress, and conduct problems in youth aged 6–15 (Chorpita & Weisz, 2009). The manual incorporates a menu of 33 modules, each addressing one of the separate treatment components frequently included in EBT for common youth mental health problems (see Chorpita et al., 2005a, 2005b), including CBT for anxiety (e.g., graduated exposure), CBT for depression (e.g., behavioral activation), and behavioral parent training (BPT) for conduct problems (e.g., labeled praise). The modules are clustered together under various problem areas with some being included in multiple areas (e.g., exposure is used for both anxiety and trauma). MATCH begins with an initial assessment of mental health symptoms that is used to determine which of the four problem areas to initially focus on. It also includes flowcharts for each primary problem area to guide practitioners in clinical decision-making, including module choice, order, and whether and when to shift to another problem area (Hersh, Metz, & Weisz, 2016).

MATCH was specifically developed to address the three common challenges faced by mental health professionals using focal EBT: heterogeneity of clinical populations, comorbidity, and fluctuations in symptoms (Chorpita & Weisz, 2009; Hersh et al., 2016). It was designed to address the heterogeneity and comorbidity of youth by encompassing components to treat three high-prevalence clusters of disorders and problems—anxiety (including posttraumatic stress), depression, and misconduct. Furthermore, MATCH addresses fluctuations in problem area severity by incorporating strategies for changing treatment focus when a youth's needs shift markedly or when new problems that were not the original focus of therapy interfere with the treatment plan and goals. Overall, its modular, flexible, multiproblem approach allows for the treating of singular or multiple disorders and/or problems and provides the flexibility to individualize treatment to address fluctuation in symptoms or treatment interference.

Two RCTs have found that MATCH outperforms focal manual (standard) treatment, including Coping Cat, primary and secondary control enhancement training, defiant child (effect size = 0.71), usual care without specific EBT training (effect size = 0.59), and usual care with county mandated use of EBT (effect size = 0.51) on total symptoms (Weisz et al., 2012; Chorpita et al., 2017). These effects were sustained at a 2-year follow-up compared with those of usual care (Chorpita et al., 2013). Additionally, compared with usual care treatment, MATCH was associated with shorter treatment duration (averages: MATCH, 16.17–21.65; focal EBT, 16.17; and usual care, 30.22 sessions), fewer diagnoses at posttreatment, lower use of other mental health services, and lower rates of starting or increasing psychotropic medication (Weisz et al., 2012; Chorpita et al., 2017). Overall, findings suggest that a modular, flexible, transdiagnostic intervention may be helpful for both internalizing and externalizing problems and that the benefits may extend over a 2-year period. Providers of MATCH to date have included mental health professionals in the United States (e.g., licensed social workers and psychologists).

2.4.4 Feeling calm, increasing motivation, repairing thoughts, solving problems, trying the opposite (FIRST)

Although this transdiagnostic treatment does not have multiple trials, we choose to include FIRST as it was developed in an effort to provide more efficient access to evidence-based practices for service providers of youth mental health—and thus potentially more relevant to LMIC. FIRST was developed in the United States as an alternative to the more complex, multimodule approach illustrated by MATCH (Weisz et al., 2017). FIRST involves teaching service providers to use five intervention principles that (a) are often included in youth evidence-based practices (EBPs) for common internalizing and externalizing disorders, (b) have been shown to be efficacious as stand-alone interventions, (c) can be applied to multiple youth problems that often cooccur, and (d) can be learned efficiently by mental health professionals. The principles include *feeling calm* (relaxation), *increasing motivation* (using environmental contingencies to make adaptive behavior more rewarding than maladaptive behavior), *repairing thoughts* (identifying and changing biased or distorted cognitions), *solving problems* (identifying the problem, thinking of solutions, examining the solutions, selecting a solution, and testing the solution), and *trying the opposite* (e.g., engaging in activities that are incompatible with the targeted problem, such as behavioral activation). The protocol includes an initial overview of the principles and their potential role in the treatment of anxiety, depression, and conduct problems, followed by guidelines that assist the clinician in treatment (e.g., how to begin treatment and determining primary problem area). Mental health clinicians learn over time to apply these principles to different problem areas. There is additionally an appendix focused on special cases (e.g., how to address panic disorder), frequently asked questions, additional treatment resources for the clinician (e.g., sample fear hierarchies and sample reward system plans), and a research bibliography. Furthermore, the manual includes a decision tree to use with weekly symptom reports to guide practitioners' clinical decision-making. It is believed that by offering a simpler design (only five principles and additional information as needed versus 33 modules in MATCH) and fewer detailed instructions, paired with a conceptual approach to learning, it might enhance training efficiency (2-day training versus 6-day training of MATCH for mental health professionals) and thus increase uptake in applied settings.

An open trial of FIRST utilized by mental health professionals showed promising effects in feasibility for use in everyday clinical practice and acceptability of use by practitioners and clinical outcomes. Observational coding of sessions showed high levels of fidelity (86.6%), which is somewhat higher than the MATCH protocol in two previous studies (82.95% and 80.1%; Weisz et al., 2012, 2016). Additionally, therapist satisfaction with the treatment was high and, in comparison, similar to the MATCH manual and significantly higher than for EBPs and usual care in similar studies (Chorpita et al., 2015). Both youth and caregivers reported significant improvements in total problems (youth effect size = 1.15; caregiver effect size = 0.85), internalizing problems (youth effect size = 0.94; caregiver effect size = 0.51), and externalizing problems (youth effect size = 0.94; caregiver effect size = 0.93). Furthermore, there were significant reductions (58.6%) in total number of diagnoses pre- to posttreatment. This reduction achieved by FIRST can be compared with the 59.9% reduction achieved by MATCH, 52.6% by standard EBPs, and 24.7% by usual care (Weisz et al., 2012). These findings suggest that FIRST may be a promising scaled-down modular transdiagnostic approach but requires further evidence to show its effectiveness.

2.5 Evidence review of existing transdiagnostic literature in low- and middle-income countries

It is important to mention that many of the focal treatments that have been tested in LMIC are now described as transdiagnostic as they affect different problem areas (e.g., models like TF-CBT or CPT impact trauma and depressive symptoms).

These treatments would not be considered modular or flexible as they are linear and thus proscribed the same for every individual (i.e., every individual would receive the sessions as laid out in the manual order). These approaches are not individualized to client symptom course and fluctuations nor were they technically or theoretically built as transdiagnostic models with shared mechanisms across disorders. They provide an impact on the primary target (e.g., trauma symptoms) and by treating that, they subsequently reduce other secondary symptoms (e.g., depression).

2.5.1 Problem management plus (PM+)

Problem management plus (PM+) was developed as a transdiagnostic model by the World Health Organization in an attempt to address the treatment gap specifically in LMIC (Dawson et al., 2015) (see also Chapter 7). The developers state that PM+ is designed for use by lay providers to treat adult depression, anxiety, stress, or grief and address client self-identified practical problems, such as interpersonal conflict and financial problems. Utilizing the definitions from Boustani et al. (2017), this would be a transdiagnostic, multiproblem approach but would not be defined as modular or flexible as the same order and dose are given to all recipients. PM+ consists of five 90 min sessions. Dawson and colleagues describe PM+ as consisting of only behavioral elements, which are perceived by the developers to be lower in complexity and to require less theoretical background than cognitive elements. Specifically, PM+ integrates evidence-based problem-solving and behavioral treatment techniques into four core strategies: (a) managing stress (simple stress management strategies such as deep breathing); (b) managing problems (teaching basic problem-solving skills to address practical problems); (c) get going, keep doing (behavioral activation strategies to increase positive reinforcement from the environment to improve mood and functioning); and (d) strengthening social support (increasing one's capacity to reengage in their community and elicit support from other individuals and agencies; Dawson et al., 2015). In addition to these, PM+ includes psychoeducation and engagement components and a relapse prevention component.

To date, there have been two pilot studies and one large trial in Kenya (Bryant et al., 2017; Dawson et al., 2016; Rahman et al., 2016). Results from the pilot trials comparing PM+ to an enhanced treatment as usual (ETAU) condition included small or no effects for general psychological distress and varying effects for functioning and posttraumatic stress (Dawson et al., 2016; Rahman et al., 2016). In the large RCT, PM+ was compared with ETAU for a gender-based violence-affected sample. Results showed moderate effects for psychological distress ($d=0.57$) and for idiographic outcomes (i.e., participants' top two identified problems; $d=0.67$) and small effects for functioning ($d=0.26$) and PTSD ($d=0.21$; Bryant et al., 2017). Multiple PM+ effectiveness trials are underway examining cost-effectiveness, utilization of PM+ by primary care attendees in Kenya, management of common mental disorders in a specialized mental health-care facility in Pakistan, and group PM+ for women in conflict-affected rural Pakistan (Chiumento et al., 2017; Hamdani et al., 2017; Sijbrandij et al., 2015).

2.5.2 The common elements treatment approach (CETA)

CETA is a transdiagnostic approach that is specifically designed for task sharing (i.e., the use of lay providers) in LMIC (Murray et al., 2014). With significant input from the MATCH developers, CETA was created to mimic MATCH's model, design, and goals. However, given its focus on use by lay providers in LMIC, there are some significant differences from MATCH. These include (a) fewer elements and a lower complexity level to meet the needs of the target provider; (b) descriptions and "step sheets" of each element that are brief and concrete, utilize simple language, and act as a guide to non-professionals; and (c) simplified clinical decision-making. Similar to MATCH, CETA is modular, flexible and built to address heterogeneity, comorbidity, and symptom fluctuations. CETA initially focused on anxiety, traumatic stress, depression, and behavioral problems (for youth) as its primary problem areas. Given its design, when qualitative research indicated substance misuse as another primary concern in LMIC, an element of CBT for substance misuse was included. CETA materials are simplified for both lay provider use and low-resourced settings (e.g., shorter documents to help with translation and printing). Training materials include a short manual section (1–5 pages) and a "step" sheet (1–2 pages) for each element.

CETA has a small set of common elements found to be efficacious and prevalent in other EBTs to treat common mental health problems. Elements include (1) introduction, (2) encouraging participation (engagement), (3) thinking in a different way parts I and II, (4) talking about difficult memories (imaginal exposure), (5) live exposure, (6) getting active (behavioral activation), (7) relaxation, (8) problem-solving, (9) safety, (10) CBT for substance use, and (11) parenting skills (youth). Core, crosscutting cognitive behavioral strategies were included in the "step" sheet for each element (e.g., Sburlati, Schniering, Lyneham, & Rapee, 2011). These include (a) a weekly symptom monitoring (i.e., measurement-based care); (b) the "what" (e.g., describing the element) and "why" (e.g., rationale); (c) in-session, guided practice of elements (modeling and role-plays); and (d) weekly homework assignment, review, and problem-solving completion barriers. Each element has "step" sheets that can be used to practice and prepare prior to sessions and as in-session provider guides. This level of guidance was particularly geared toward task shifting, where providers likely had no experience conducting a talk therapy session, and also for maintaining fidelity over time.

CETA has demonstrated effectiveness in low-resourced settings. An RCT in southern Iraq using nonspecialized community health workers to provide CETA to adult survivors of systematic violence (i.e., experienced or witnessed physical torture or militant attacks) demonstrated large effect sizes for trauma ($d=2.4$), anxiety ($d=1.6$), depression ($d=1.82$), and dysfunction ($d=0.88$) and outperformed both waiting-list control and CPT in symptom reduction (Weiss et al., 2015). A second trial conducted in Thailand with displaced Burmese adults demonstrated large effect sizes for posttraumatic stress ($d=1.19$), depression ($d=1.16$), and anxiety ($d=0.79$) with more moderate effect sizes observed for impaired function ($d=0.63$; Bolton et al., 2014). Furthermore, an open trial of CETA-Youth with displaced Somali youth in Ethiopian refugee camps showed promising results with significant decreases in internalizing ($d = 1.37$) and externalizing symptoms ($d = 0.85$), posttraumatic stress ($d = 1.71$), and improvements in well-being ($d = 0.75$; Murray et al., 2018). Overall, CETA provided by lay counselors was highly effective across multiple problem areas among adults, and CETA-Youth shows preliminary effectiveness as well. Ongoing CETA trials include (a) group versus individual delivery, (b) use with couples and families experiencing both violence and substance misuse, and (c) evaluation of a shortened version of CETA (Kane et al., 2017; Murray et al., 2018).

2.6 Clinical decision making

Inherent to many transdiagnostic models, particularly modular, flexible, and multiproblem ones, is the need for clinical decision-making. In HIC, there is an assumption that mental health professionals are already trained to make clinical decisions and do so on a daily basis. Some models have attempted to systematize or help enhance clinicians' clinical decision-making (e.g., flowcharts in MATCH; Dorsey, Berliner, Lyon, Pullmann, & Murray, 2016; Hersh et al., 2016; Lyon, Dorsey, Pullmann, Silbaugh-Cowdin, & Berliner, 2015). As transdiagnostic approaches are now being developed and tested in LMIC, a valid concern is training lay providers in clinical decision-making.

One of the initial challenges in the development of CETA, given its modular, multiproblem, and flexible design, was devising a clinical decision-making process that was simple enough for lay providers to master independently overtime. This was particularly critical given the overall goal of sustainability without expert involvement. The clinical decision-making training process for CETA was simplified to three main steps. First, lay providers are taught the elements and order for each primary common mental health problems (i.e., depression, trauma, anxiety, substance use, and behavioral problems for youth). These simplified "default flows" were created based on existing EBTs for these problem areas and on elements that overlapped between treatment manuals. They also represent the least amount of "key elements" likely needed for symptom reduction. Second, lay providers are taught to assess and understand the primary problem(s). This is based on self-report assessment results (ideally of a locally validated measure), clinical presentation, and discussion with a local supervisor who consults with CETA trainers (Murray et al., 2011). For the self-report assessment, certain items are identified as correlating to certain problem areas such as "sadness or crying" linking to depression. The lay providers learn how to fill out a "clinical decision-making table" where items from the assessment are linked and grouped to problem areas. Third, in the training, lay providers participate in an activity called "card sort" whereby the trainers read a short (3–5 sentences) vignette and providers are asked to choose and arrange the elements in order of the primary problem(s). Lay providers are in small groups during this activity and must provide a rationale for their arrangement to the trainer. Trainers are specifically coaching lay providers to think through the "data points of information" that are included in the vignette (i.e., assessment score, client presentation, and supervisor consultation). As lay providers become more skilled, the vignettes become more challenging to include equally severe comorbidities. Card sorting also includes asking providers to think about "dosage." For instance, adding another session of an element if the client does not seem to understand it yet has not done their homework, or the assessment score for the corresponding item(s) is high. This practical activity allows for lay providers to build clinical decision-making skills and develop the understanding of "flexibility within fidelity" (Kendall & Beidas, 2007, p. 13), which is particularly important given the culturally diverse contexts. In this way, the treatment is based on symptomatology, can account for interference of other symptoms, and can stop or continue based on need and not a set number of sessions or elements.

2.7 Conclusion

The field of mental health has advanced greatly in further understanding the efficacy of treatments, implementation barriers, and how to adapt existing EBTs to increase effectiveness in real-world contexts. However, there remain barriers of treatment scale-up and sustainability in LMIC. Some of these barriers can be seen in our historical look at HIC, for example, the unfeasible cost of scaling up multiple treatments needed to address a wide range of problems and comorbidities effectively.

Perhaps largely due to a public health approach and recent focus on implementation science, there has been development of transdiagnostic treatments for LMIC and evidence that these approaches may be feasible, teachable, and effective, even when delivered by nonspecialist providers (Martin, Murray, Darnell, & Dorsey, in press). This represents an innovation in mental health care. Diffusion of innovation in health care is usually difficult, nonlinear, and full of barriers (Ferlie, Fitzgerald, Wood, & Hawkins, 2005). Researchers have examined diffusion of innovation and identified certain required attributes including the following: (a) the innovation has relative advantage, (b) the innovation is compatible with the context, (c) the innovation is perceived as uncomplicated with benefits, and (d) the adopter context needs to be ready and open to change. Global mental health would benefit from a litmus test of stakeholders on these attributes. It will be important to understand readiness not only from health-care systems, communities, contexts, and implementers but also leaders, researchers, and treatment developers in the field (Greenhalgh, Robert, MacFarlane, Bate, & Kyriakidou, 2004).

The two models specifically designed as transdiagnostic and for lay providers are PM+ and CETA. Although both transdiagnostic approaches, these treatments have unique attributes that may have varying implications on effectiveness, implementation (e.g., reach, cost, and fidelity), and sustainability. PM+ is linear and is built to address specific problem areas and has no clinical decision-making requirements. This would potentially lead to easier training and implementation. CETA is modular, multiproblem, and flexible, requiring decision-making. Theoretically, this may increase the difficulty in training but would allow for potential increased effectiveness and utility for heterogeneous populations with a variety of presenting problems and thus a wider breadth of population service. So far, the trials of PM+ and CETA have similar training and supervision models and resource requirements (i.e., hours and days). CETA trials have shown that it is possible to teach decision-making but have not yet quantified the effectiveness to which a supervisor and clinician can make these decisions without expert level support. One important future direction is to begin to understand competency. Competence has received increasing attention as critical in dissemination and implementation of psychological therapies and is defined as "the extent to which a therapist has the knowledge and skill required to deliver a treatment to the standard needed for it to achieve its expected effects" (Fairburn & Cooper, 2011, p. 374; Kohrt et al., 2015). Measurement of competency needs to assess (a) knowledge and (b) ability to apply this knowledge in clinical practice. This will answer important questions about the resources (e.g., time to competency and money) required to train lay providers in any one element and the different types of transdiagnostic approaches. Investigations should also factor in supervisory requirements and skill as a mediating variable (Dorsey et al., 2016).

PM+ and CETA also chose two different approaches in selecting elements to include. PM+ developers write that in addition to choosing elements that were effective across different problem areas, they specifically chose elements that they believed would be easier to teach lay providers, and they did not develop PM+ to treat PTSD. PM+ does not have exposure elements or cognitive work. CETA developers focused on elements that research analyses (Chorpita & Daleiden, 2009) and EBT developers thought were key "mechanisms of action" or the cause of symptom decrease and open to addressing all common mental health problems inclusive of PTSD. These are both valid hypotheses, and future research needs to focus on element-level analysis to better understand which ones are the primary indicators of change for various presenting problem(s) within LMIC.

Given the scarcity of mental health providers, even lay providers, in LMIC, an important consideration is how to reach more people in need with effective services (i.e., implementation construct of reach or penetration). Central to reach is the amount of time in treatment, looking for the shortest duration of treatment that can be provided to achieve effective outcomes. With shorter *and* effective treatments, more people in need can receive services with the same number of providers. PM+ is designed to be five 90min sessions (450min total) for every client; CETA not only averages eight 60min sessions and fluctuates based on need (average 480min) but also allows for less or more depending on need. Most focal treatments are set at about 12, 60–90min sessions (average 720+ min). So far, trial results suggest that CETA and PM+ are effective, with CETA showing larger effect sizes across some areas (e.g., trauma). However, none of the trials have evaluated reach or the effectiveness with shorter durations of care. Implementation study designs like a pragmatic rollout implementation trial design would be helpful in understanding how variations in approaches and duration help or hinder implementation and sustainability challenges and how these are linked to client outcomes (Brown & Lilford, 2006; Brown et al., 2017Landsverk et al., 2012).

In HIC settings, some researchers are suggesting that a modular and flexible approach allows for individualized treatment to occur. These approaches can address heterogeneity in clinical cases, comorbidity, and symptom fluctuations, thereby tailoring treatment to give the client exactly what they need and when (Chu, 2012;

Rohde, 2012). This "precision approach" to psychotherapy has the potential to both shorten treatment and increase retention. This has been suggested in psychotherapy research (Carroll, 1997) and shown to influence retention rates in other community-based interventions (Ingoldsby et al., 2013; O'Brien et al., 2012). When clients feel like their specific needs are met, they are more likely to engage in the treatment and receive sufficient dose of a program without more than needed. Spoth and colleagues suggest that tailoring treatment to fit a client's needs is a critical strategy to "translate science to population impact" (Spoth et al., 2013).

Precision psychotherapy overlaps with the need to guide lay providers in how to deal with comorbidity. Focal treatments do not provide guidance on comorbidity nor do linear, nonflexible transdiagnostic treatments. These models rely on theoretical principles that suggest comorbid conditions are addressed through the same delivery of set elements. Modular, flexible, multiproblem transdiagnostic models that require clinical decision-making are specifically built to teach management of comorbidity. As a concrete example, if a linear, nonflexible transdiagnostic treatment addresses depression and anxiety and a client presents with substance use, then in a low-resource setting, the provider is back to learning multiple treatment protocols. Future research would benefit from cost analysis work on the gains of one provider learning to treat the gamete of common mental health problems (i.e., clinical decision-making) versus learning 2–3 protocols to cover the same scope of problems.

Collectively, current literature crossing high- and low-income settings support the further development and investigation of transdiagnostic approaches that utilize lay community workers as viable treatment options that could help address implementation and sustainability barriers. Theoretically, from a clinical and public health prospective, transdiagnostically built approaches are likely more feasible and sustainable to improving mental health care in LMIC than focal treatments. It is important to remember that these treatments are not build as universal prevention and are directed toward populations that are presenting with mental and/or behavioral health problems.

References

Addis, M. E., & Krasnow, A. D. (2000). A national survey of practicing psychologists' attitudes toward psychotherapy treatment manuals. *Journal of Consulting and Clinical Psychology, 68*(2), 331–339. https://doi.org/10.1037/0022-006X.68.2.331.

Barlow, D., Ellard, K., Sauer-Zavala, S., Bullis, J., & Carl, J. (2014). The origins of neuroticism. *Perspectives on Psychological Science: A Journal of the Association for Psychological Science, 9*(5), 481–496. https://doi.org/10.1177/1745691614544528.

Barlow, D. H., Farchione, T. J., Bullis, J. R., Gallagher, M. W., Murray-Latin, H., Sauer-Zavala, S., … Cassiello-Robbins, C. (2017). The unified protocol for transdiagnostic treatment of emotional disorders compared with diagnosis-specific protocols for anxiety disorders. *JAMA Psychiatry. 2215*. https://doi.org/10.1001/jamapsychiatry.2017.2164.

Barlow, D. H., Farchione, T. J., Sauer-Zavala, S., Murray-Latin, H., Ellard, K. K., Bullis, J. R., … Cassiello-Robbins, C. (2011). *Unified protocol for transdiagnostic treatment of emotional disorders, therapist guide*. New York, NY: Oxford University Press.

Bass, J. K., Annan, J., McIvor, J., Murray, S., Kaysen, D., Griffiths, S., … Bolton, P. A. (2013). Controlled trial of psychotherapy for Congolese survivors of sexual violence. *New England Journal of Medicine*, *368*(23), 2182–2191. https://doi.org/10.1056/NEJMoa1211853.

Bilek, E. L., & Ehrenreich-May, J. (2012). An open trial investigation of a transdiagnostic group treatment for children with anxiety and depressive symptoms. *Behavior Therapy*, *43*(4), 887–897. https://doi.org/10.1016/j.beth.2012.04.007.

Boisseau, C. L., Farchione, T. J., Fairholme, C. P., Ellard, K. K., & Barlow, D. H. (2010). The development of the unified protocol for the transdiagnostic treatment of emotional disorders: A case study. *Cognitive and Behavioral Practice*, *17*(1), 102–113. https://doi.org/10.1016/j.cbpra.2009.09.003.

Bolton, P., Bass, J., Betancourt, T., Speelman, L., Onyango, G., Clougherty, K. F., … Verdeli, H. (2007). Interventions for depression symptoms among adolescent survivors of war and displacement in northern Uganda: A randomized controlled trial. *JAMA*, *298*(5), 519–527. https://doi.org/10.1001/jama.298.5.519.

Bolton, P., Bass, J., Neugebauer, R., Verdeli, H., Clougherty, K. F., Wickramaratne, P., … Weissman, M. (2003). Group interpersonal psychotherapy for depression in rural Uganda: A randomized controlled trial. *JAMA*, *289*(23), 3117. https://doi.org/10.1001/jama.289.23.3117.

Bolton, P., Lee, C., Haroz, E. E., Murray, L., Dorsey, S., Robinson, C., … Bass, J. (2014). A transdiagnostic community-based mental health treatment for comorbid disorders: Development and outcomes of a randomized controlled trial among Burmese refugees in Thailand. *PLoS Medicine*. *11*(11), e1001757https://doi.org/10.1371/journal.pmed.1001757.

Boustani, M. M., Gellatly, R., Westman, J. G., & Chorpita, B. F. (2017). Advances in cognitive behavioral treatment design: Time for a glossary. *Behavior Therapist*, *40*(6), 199–208. Retrieved from www.abct.org/docs/PastIssue/40n6.pdf.

Brown, C. H., Curran, G., Palinkas, L. A., Aarons, G. A., Wells, K. B., Jones, L., … Cruden, G. (2017). An overview of research and evaluation designs for dissemination and implementation. *Annual Review of Public Health*, *38*(1), 1–22. https://doi.org/10.1146/annurev-publhealth-031816-044215.

Brown, C. A., & Lilford, R. J. (2006). The stepped wedge trial design: A systematic review. *BMC Medical Research Methodology*, *6*(1), 54. https://doi.org/10.1186/1471-2288-6-54.

Bryant, R. A., Schafer, A., Dawson, K. S., Anjuri, D., Mulili, C., Ndogoni, L., … van Ommeren, M. (2017). Effectiveness of a brief behavioural intervention on psychological distress among women with a history of gender-based violence in urban Kenya: A randomised clinical trial. *PLoS Medicine*. *14*(8), e1002371. https://doi.org/10.1371/journal.pmed.1002371.

Bullis, J. R., Fortune, M. R., Farchione, T. J., & Barlow, D. H. (2014). A preliminary investigation of the long-term outcome of the unified protocol for transdiagnostic treatment of emotional disorders. *Comprehensive Psychiatry*, *55*(8), 1920–1927. https://doi.org/10.1016/j.comppsych.2014.07.016.

Carroll, K. M. (1997). Integrating psychotherapy and pharmacotherapy to improve drug abuse outcomes. *Addictive Behaviors*, *22*(2), 233–245. https://doi.org/10.1016/S0306-4603(96)00038-X.

Chiumento, A., Hamdani, S. U., Khan, M. N., Dawson, K., Bryant, R. A., Sijbrandij , M., … Wang, D. (2017). Evaluating effectiveness and cost-effectiveness of a group psychological intervention using cognitive behavioural strategies for women with common mental disorders in conflict-affected rural Pakistan: Study protocol for a randomised controlled trial. *Trials*, *18*(1), 190. https://doi.org/10.1186/s13063-017-1905-8.

Chorpita, B. F., & Daleiden, E. L. (2009). Mapping evidence-based treatments for children and adolescents: Application of the distillation and matching model to 615 treatments from 322 randomized trials. *Journal of Consulting and Clinical Psychology*, *77*(3), 566–579. https://doi.org/10.1037/a0014565.

Chorpita, B. F., Daleiden, E. L., Park, A. L., Ward, A. M., Levy, M. C., Cromley, T., … Krull, J. L. (2017). Child STEPs in California: A cluster randomized effectiveness trial comparing modular treatment with community implemented treatment for youth with anxiety, depression, conduct problems, or traumatic stress. *Journal of Consulting and Clinical Psychology*, *85*(1), 13–25. https://doi.org/10.1037/ccp0000133.

Chorpita, B. F., Daleiden, E. L., & Weisz, J. R. (2005a). Identifying and selecting the common elements of evidence based interventions: A distillation and matching model. *Mental Health Services Research*, *7*(1), 5–20. https://doi.org/10.1007/s11020-005-1962-6.

Chorpita, B. F., Daleiden, E. L., & Weisz, J. R. (2005b). Modularity in the design and application of therapeutic interventions. *Applied and Preventive Psychology*, *11*(3), 141–156. https://doi.org/10.1016/j.appsy.2005.05.002.

Chorpita, B. F., Park, A., Tsai, K., Korathu-Larson, P., Higa-McMillan, C., Nakamura, B. J., … Krull, J. (2015). Balancing effectiveness with responsiveness: Therapist satisfaction across different treatment designs in the child STEPs randomized effectiveness trial. *Journal of Consulting and Clinical Psychology*, *83*(4), 709–718. https://doi.org/10.1037/a0039301.

Chorpita, B. F., & Weisz, J. R. (2009). *Match-ADTC: Modular approach to therapy for children with anxiety, depression, trauma, or conduct problems*. Satellite Beach, FL: PracticeWise.

Chorpita, B. F., Weisz, J. R., Daleiden, E. L., Schoenwald, S. K., Palinkas, L. A., Miranda, J., … Borntrager, C. F. (2013). Long-term outcomes for the child STEPs randomized effectiveness trial: A comparison of modular and standard treatment designs with usual care. *Journal of Consulting and Clinical Psychology*, *821*(6), 999.

Chu, B. C. (2012). Translating transdiagnostic approaches to children and adolescents. *Cognitive and Behavioral Practice*, *19*(1), 1–4. https://doi.org/10.1016/j.cbpra.2011.06.003.

Chu, B. C., Crocco, S. T., Arnold, C. C., Brown, R., Southam-Gerow, M. A., & Weisz, J. R. (2015). Sustained implementation of cognitive-behavioral therapy for youth anxiety and depression: Long-term effects of structured training and consultation on therapist practice in the field. *Professional Psychology, Research and Practice*, *46*, 70–79. https://doi.org/10.1037/a0038000.

Chu, B. C., Temkin, A. B., & Toffey, K. (2016). Transdiagnostic mechanisms and treatment for children and adolescents: An emerging field. In *Oxford handbooks online (clinical psychology)*. New York, NY: Oxford University Press. https://doi.org/10.1093/oxfordhb/9780199935291.013.10.

Collins, P. Y., Insel, T. R., Chockalingam, A., Daar, A., & Maddox, Y. T. (2013). Grand challenges in global mental health: Integration in research, policy, and practice. *PLoS Medicine* *10*(4), e1001434. https://doi.org/10.1371/journal.pmed.1001434.

Dawson, K. S., Bryant, R. A., Harper, M., Kuowei Tay, A., Rahman, A., Schafer, A., & van Ommeren, M. (2015). Problem management plus (PM+): A WHO transdiagnostic psychological intervention for common mental health problems. *World Psychiatry*, *14*(3), 354–357. https://doi.org/10.1002/wps.20255.

Dawson, K. S., Schafer, A., Anjuri, D., Ndogoni, L., Musyoki, C., Sijbrandij, M., … Bryant, R. A. (2016). Feasibility trial of a scalable psychological intervention for women affected by urban adversity and gender-based violence in Nairobi. *BMC Psychiatry*, *16*(1), 410. https://doi.org/10.1186/s12888-016-1117-x.

Dorsey, S., Berliner, L., Lyon, A. R., Pullmann, M. D., & Murray, L. K. (2016). [MOU1] [k2] A statewide common elements initiative for children's mental health. *The Journal of*

Behavioral Health Services and Research, *43*(2), 246–261. https://doi.org/10.1007/s11414-014-9430-y.

Ehrenreich-May, J., & Chu, B. C. (2014). *Transdiagnostic treatments for children and adolescents: Principles and practice*. New York, NY: Guilford Press.

Ehrenreich-May, J., Rosenfield, D., Queen, A. H., Kennedy, S. M., Remmes, C. S., & Barlow, D. H. (2017). An initial waitlist-controlled trial of the unified protocol for the treatment of emotional disorders in adolescents. *Journal of Anxiety Disorders*, *46*, 46–55. https://doi.org/10.1016/j.janxdis.2016.10.006.

Ellard, K. K., Fairholme, C. P., Boisseau, C. L., Farchione, T. J., & Barlow, D. H. (2010). Unified protocol for the transdiagnostic treatment of emotional disorders: Protocol development and initial outcome data. *Cognitive and Behavioral Practice*, *17*(1), 88–101. https://doi.org/10.1016/j.cbpra.2009.06.002.

Fairburn, C. G., Bailey-Straebler, S., Basden, S., Doll, H. A., Jones, R., Murphy , R., … Cooper, Z. (2015). Behaviour research and therapy a transdiagnostic comparison of enhanced cognitive behaviour therapy (CBT-E) and interpersonal psychotherapy in the treatment of eating disorders. *Behaviour Research and Therapy*, *70*, 64–71. https://doi.org/10.1016/j.brat.2015.04.010.

Fairburn, C. G., & Cooper, Z. (2011). Therapist competence, therapy quality, and therapist training. *Behaviour Research and Therapy*, *49*(6–7), 373–378. https://doi.org/10.1016/j.brat.2011.03.005.

Fairburn, C. G., Cooper, Z., Doll, H. A., O'Connor, M. E., Palmer, R. L., & Dalle Grave, R. (2013). Enhanced cognitive behaviour therapy for adults with anorexia nervosa: A UK-Italy study. *Behaviour Research and Therapy*, *51*(1), R2–R8. https://doi.org/10.1016/j.brat.2012.09.010.

Fairburn, C. G., Cooper, Z., & Shafran, R. (2003). Cognitive behaviour therapy for eating disorders: A "transdiagnostic" theory and treatment. *Behaviour Research and Therapy*, *41*(5), 509–528. https://doi.org/10.1016/S0005-7967(02)00088-8.

Farchione, T. J., Fairholme, C. P., Ellard, K. K., Boisseau, C. L., Thompson-Hollands, J., Carl, J. R., … Barlow, D. H. (2012). Unified protocol for transdiagnostic treatment of emotional disorders: A randomized controlled trial. *Behavior Therapy*, *43*(3), 666–678. https://doi.org/10.1016/j.beth.2012.01.001.

Ferlie, E., Fitzgerald, L., Wood, M., & Hawkins, C. (2005). The (non) spread of innovations: The mediating role of professionals. *Academy of Management Journal*, *48*(1), 117–134.

Grave, R. D. (2012). *Intensive cognitive behaviour therapy for eating disorders*. Haupauge, NY: Nova.

Grave, R. D., Calugi, S., Conti, M., Doll, H., & Fairburn, C. G. (2013). Inpatient cognitive behaviour therapy for anorexia nervosa: A randomized controlled trial. *Psychotherapy and Psychosomatics*, *82*, 390–398. https://doi.org/10.1159/000350058.

Grave, R. D., Calugi, S., Doll, H. A., & Fairburn, C. G. (2013). Enhanced cognitive behaviour therapy for adolescents with anorexia nervosa: An alternative to family therapy? *Behaviour Research and Therapy*, *51*, R9–R12. https://doi.org/10.1016/j.brat.2012.09.008.

Greenhalgh, T., Robert, G., MacFarlane, F., Bate, P., & Kyriakidou, O. (2004). Diffusion of innovations in service organizations: Systematic review and recommendations. *Milbank Quaterly*, *82*(4), 581–629. https://doi.org/10.1111/j.0887-378X.2004.00325.x.

Hamdani, S. U., Ahmed, Z., Sijbrandij, M., Nazir, H., Masood, A., Akhtar, P., … Ommeren, M. (2017). Problem management plus (PM+) in the management of common mental disorders in a specialized mental healthcare facility in Pakistan; study protocol for a randomized controlled trial. *International Journal of Mental Health Systems*, *11*(1), 40. https://doi.org/10.1186/s13033-017-0147-1.

Harvey, A. G., & Gumport, N. B. (2015). Evidence-based psychological treatments for mental disorders: Modifiable barriers to access and possible solutions. *Behaviour Research and Therapy*, *68*, 1–12. https://doi.org/10.1016/j.brat.2015.02.004.

Hensel-Dittmann, D., Schauer, M., Ruf, M., Catani, C., Odenwald, M., Elbert, T., & Neuner, F. (2011). Treatment of traumatized victims of war and torture: a randomized controlled comparison of narrative exposure therapy and stress inoculation training. *Psychotherapy and Psychosomatics*, *80*(6), 345–352. https://doi.org/10.1159/000327253.

Hersh, J., Metz, K. L., & Weisz, J. R. (2016). New frontiers in transdiagnostic treatment: Youth psychotherapy for internalizing and externalizing problems and disorders. *International Journal of Cognitive Therapy*, *9*(2), 140–155. https://doi.org/10.1521/ijct.2016.9.2.140.

Ingoldsby, E. M., Baca, P., McClatchey, M. W., Luckey, D. W., Ramsey, M. O., Loch, J. M., … Olds, D. L. (2013). Quasi-experimental pilot study of intervention to increase participant retention and completed home visits in the nurse-family partnership. *Prevention Science*, *14*(6), 525–534. https://doi.org/10.1007/s11121-013-0410-x.

Insel, T. R. (2009). Translating scientific opportunity into public health impact. *Archives of General Psychiatry*, *66*(2), 128. https://doi.org/10.1001/archgenpsychiatry.2008.540.

Ito, M., Horikoshi, M., Kato, N., Oe, Y., Fujisato, H., Nakajima, S., … Ono, Y. (2016). Transdiagnostic and transcultural: Pilot study of unified protocol for depressive and anxiety disorders in Japan. *Behavior Therapy*, *47*(3), 416–430. https://doi.org/10.1016/j.beth.2016.02.005.

Kane, J. C., Skavenski Van Wyk, S., Murray, S. M., Bolton, P., Melendez, F., Danielson, C. K., … Murray, L. K. (2017). Testing the effectiveness of a transdiagnostic treatment approach in reducing violence and alcohol abuse among families in Zambia: study protocol of the violence and alcohol treatment (VATU) trial. *Global Mental Health (Cambridge)*, *4*, e18. https://doi.org/10.1017/gmh.2017.10.

Kaysen, D., Lindgren, K., Sabir Zangana, G. A., Murray, L., Bass, J., & Bolton, P. (2013). Adaptation of cognitive processing therapy for treatment of torture victims: Experience in Kurdistan, Iraq. *Psychological Trauma: Theory, Research, Practice, and Policy*, *5*(2), 184–192. https://doi.org/10.1037/a0026053.

Kendall, P. C., & Beidas, R. S. (2007). Smoothing the trail for dissemination of evidence-based practices for youth: Flexibility within fidelity. *Professional Psychology: Research and Practice*, *38*(1), 13–20. https://doi.org/10.1037/0735-7028.38.1.13.

Kohrt, B. A., Jordans, M. J. D., Rai, S., Shrestha, P., Luitel, N. P., Ramaiya, M. K., … Patel, V. (2015). Therapist competence in global mental health: Development of the ENhancing Assessment of Common Therapeutic factors (ENACT) rating scale. *Behaviour Research and Therapy*, *69*, 11–21. https://doi.org/10.1016/j.brat.2015.03.009.

Landsverk, J., Brown, C. H., Chamberlain, P., Curran, G. M., Palinkas, L., Ogihara, M., … Horwitz, S. M. (2012). Design and analysis in dissemination and implementation research. In R. C. Brownson, G. A. Colditz, & E. K. Proctor (Eds.), *Dissemination and implementation research in health translating science to practice* (pp. 255–260). Oxford, UK: Oxford University Press.

Luborsky, L., & DeRubeis, R. J. (1984). The use of psychotherapy treatment manuals: A small revolution in psychotherapy research style. *Clinical Psychology Review*, *4*(1), 5–14. https://doi.org/10.1016/0272-7358(84)90034-5.

Lyon, A. R., Dorsey, S., Pullmann, M., Silbaugh-Cowdin, J., & Berliner, L. (2015). Clinician use of standardized assessments following a common elements psychotherapy training and consultation program. *Administration and Policy in Mental Health*, *42*(1), 47–60. https://doi.org/10.1007/s10488-014-0543-7.

Magidson, J., Lejuez, C., Kamal, T., Blevins, E., Murray, L., Bass, J., ... Pagoto, S. (2016). Adaptation of community health worker-delivered behavioral activation for torture survivors in Kurdistan, Iraq. *Global Mental Health*, *2*(1), e24. https://doi.org/10.1017/gmh.2015.22.

Mansell, W., Harvey, A., Watkins, E. R., & Shafran, R. (2008). Cognitive behavioral processes across psychological disorders: A review of the utility and validity of the transdiagnostic approach. *International Journal of Cognitive Therapy*, *1*(3), 181–191. https://doi.org/10.1680/ijct.2008.1.3.181.

Marchette, L. K., & Weisz, J. R. (2017). Practitioner review: Empirical evolution of youth psychotherapy toward transdiagnostic approaches. *Journal of Child Psychology and Psychiatry and Allied Disciplines*, *58*(9), 970–984. https://doi.org/10.1111/jcpp.12747.

Marsenich, L. (2007). *Using evidence-based programs to meet the mental health needs of California children and youth*. Retrieved from. www.cibhs.org/sites/main/files/file-attachments/ebp_children_youth_070811.pdf.

Martin, P., Murray, L. K., Darnell, D., & Dorsey, S. (in press). Implementing transdiagnostic mental health interventions for greater public health impact in low resource settings. Clinical Psychology: Science and Practice

Mazaheri, M., Daghaghzadeh, H., Afshar, H., & Mohammadi, N. (2014). The effectiveness of the unified protocol on emotional dysregulation and cognitive emotion regulation strategies in patients with psychosomatic disorders. *International Journal of Body, Mind & Culture*, *1*(1), 73–82.

McEvoy, P. M., Nathan, P., & Norton, P. J. (2009). Efficacy of transdiagnostic treatments: A review of published outcome studies and future research directions. *Journal of Cognitive Psychotherapy*, *23*(1), 20–33. https://doi.org/10.1891/0889-8391.23.1.20.

McHugh, R. K., Murray, H. W., & Barlow, D. H. (2009). Balancing fidelity and adaptation in the dissemination of empirically-supported treatments: The promise of transdiagnostic interventions. *Behaviour Research and Therapy*, *47*(11), 946–953. https://doi.org/10.1016/j.brat.2009.07.005.

McManus, F., Shafran, R., & Cooper, Z. (2010). What does a transdiagnostic approach have to offer the treatment of anxiety disorders? *British Journal of Clinical Psychology*, *49*(4), 491–505. https://doi.org/10.1348/014466509X476567.

Murray, L. K., Dorsey, S., Bolton, P., Jordans, M. J., Rahman, A., Bass, J., & Verdeli, H. (2011). Building capacity in mental health interventions in low resource countries: An apprenticeship model for training local providers. *International Journal of Mental Health Systems*, *5*(1), 30. https://doi.org/10.1186/1752-4458-5-30.

Murray, L. K., Dorsey, S., Haroz, E., Lee, C., Alsiary, M. M., Haydary, A., ... Bolton, P. (2014). A common elements treatment approach for adult mental health problems in low- and middle-income countries. *Cognitive and Behavioral Practice*, *21*, 111–123. https://doi.org/10.1016/j.cbpra.2013.06.005.

Murray, L. K., Dorsey, S., Skavenski, S., Kasoma, M., Imasiku, M., Bolton, P., ... Cohen, J. A. (2013). Identification, modification, and implementation of an evidence-based psychotherapy for children in a low-income country: The use of TF-CBT in Zambia. *International Journal of Mental Health Systems*, *7*(1), 24. https://doi.org/10.1186/1752-4458-7-24.

Murray, L., Hall, B., Dorsey, S., Ugeuto, A., Puffer, E., Ismael, A., ... Bolton, P. A. (2018). An open trial of a common elements approach to address children's mental health in Somali refugee camps. Global Mental Health.

Murray, L. K., Skavenski, S., Kane, J. C., Mayeya, J., Dorsey, S., Cohen, J. A., ... Bolton, P. A. (2015). Effectiveness of trauma-focused cognitive behavioral therapy among trauma-affected children in Lusaka, Zambia: A randomized clinical trial. *JAMA Pediatrics*. *169* (8). https://doi.org/10.1001/jamapediatrics.2015.0580.

National Collaborating Centre for Mental Health. *Common mental health disorders*. (2011). In *Retrieved from*. www.nice.org.uk/guidance/cg123/evidence/full-guideline-pdf-181771741.

O'Brien, R. A., Moritz, P., Luckey, D. W., McClatchey, M. W., Ingoldsby, E. M., & Olds, D. L. (2012). Mixed methods analysis of participant attrition in the nurse-family partnership. *Prevention Science*, *13*(3), 219–228. https://doi.org/10.1007/s11121-012-0287-0.

O'Callaghan, P., McMullen, J., Shannon, C., Rafferty, H., & Black, A. (2013). A randomized controlled trial of trauma-focused cognitive behavioral therapy for sexually exploited, war-affected Congolese girls. *Journal of the American Academy of Child and Adolescent Psychiatry*, *52*(4), 359–369. https://doi.org/10.1016/j.jaac.2013.01.013.

Osma, J., Castellano, C., Crespo, E., & García-Palacios, A. (2015). The unified protocol for transdiagnostic treatment of emotional disorders in group format in a Spanish public mental health setting. *Behavioral Psychology*, *23*(3), 447–466.

Patel, V., Belkin, G. S., Chockalingam, A., Cooper, J., Saxena, S., & Unützer, J. (2013). Grand challenges: Integrating mental health services into priority health care platforms. *PLoS Medicine*. *10*(5)e1001448https://doi.org/10.1371/journal.pmed.1001448.

Patel, V., Chowdhary, N., Rahman, A., & Verdeli, H. (2011). Improving access to psychological treatments: Lessons from developing countries. *Behaviour Research and Therapy*, *49*(9), 523–528. https://doi.org/10.1016/j.brat.2011.06.012.

Patel, V., Garrison, P., Mari, J. D. J., Minas, H., Prince, M., & Saxena, S. (2008). The lancet's series on global mental health: 1 year on. *The Lancet*, *372*(9646), 1354–1357. https://doi.org/10.1016/S0140-6736(08)61556-1.

President's New Freedom Commission on Mental Health (2004). *Report of the President's new freedom commission on mental health. In Available from*. www.mentalhealthcommission.gov/reports/FinalReport/toc.html.

Rahman, A., Riaz, N., Dawson, K. S., Usman Hamdani, S., Chiumento, A., Sijbrandij, M., … van Ommeren, M. (2016). Problem management plus (PM+): Pilot trial of a WHO transdiagnostic psychological intervention in conflict-affected Pakistan. *World Psychiatry*, *15* (2), 182–183. https://doi.org/10.1002/wps.20312.

Robjant, K., & Fazel, M. (2010). The emerging evidence for narrative exposure therapy: a review. *Clinical Psychology Review*, *30*(8), 1030–1039. https://doi.org/10.1016/j.cpr.2010.07.004.

Rohde, P. (2012). Applying transdiagnostic approaches to treatments with children and adolescents: Innovative models that are ready for more systematic evaluation. *Cognitive and Behavioral Practice*, *19*(1), 83–86. https://doi.org/10.1016/j.cbpra.2011.06.006.

Ruf, M., Schauer, M., Neuner, F., Catani, C., Schauer, E., & Elbert, T. (2010). Narrative exposure therapy for 7- to 16-year-olds: a randomized controlled trial with traumatized refugee children. *Journal of Traumatic Stress*, *4*, 437–445. https://doi.org/10.1002/jts.20548.

Sauer-Zavala, S., Gutner, C. A., Farchione, T. J., Boettcher, H. T., Bullis, J. R., & Barlow, D. H. (2017). Current definitions of "transdiagnostic" in treatment development: A search for consensus. *Behavior Therapy*, *48*(1), 128–138. https://doi.org/10.1016/j.beth.2016.09.004.

Sburlati, E. S., Schniering, C. A., Lyneham, H. J., & Rapee, R. M. (2011). A model of therapist competencies for the empirically supported cognitive behavioral treatment of child and adolescent anxiety and depressive disorders. *Clinical Child and Family Psychology Review*, *14*(1), 89–109. https://doi.org/10.1007/s10567-011-0083-6.

Sijbrandij, M., Farooq, S., Bryant, R. A., Dawson, K., Hamdani, S. U., Chiumento, A., … van Ommeren, M. (2015). Problem management plus (PM+) for common mental disorders in a humanitarian setting in Pakistan: Study protocol for a randomised controlled trial (RCT). *BMC Psychiatry*, *15*(1), 232. https://doi.org/10.1186/s12888-015-0602-y.

Spoth, R., Rohrbach, L. A., Greenberg, M., Leaf, P., Brown, C. H., Fagan, A., & Hawkins, J. D. (2013). Addressing core challenges for the next generation of type 2 translation research and systems: the translation science to population impact (TSci impact) framework. *Prevention Science*, *14*(4), 319–351. https://doi.org/10.1007/s11121-012-0362-6.

Verdeli, H., Clougherty, K., Onyango, G., Lewandowski, E., Speelman, L., Betancourt, T. S., … Bolton, P. (2008). Group interpersonal psychotherapy for depressed youth in IDP camps in northern Uganda: Adaptation and training. *Child and Adolescent Psychiatric Clinics of North America*. https://doi.org/10.1016/j.chc.2008.03.002.

Weiss, W. M., Murray, L. K., Zangana, G. A. S., Mahmooth, Z., Kaysen, D., Dorsey, S., … Bolton, P. (2015). Community-based mental health treatments for survivors of torture and militant attacks in southern Iraq: A randomized control trial. *BMC Psychiatry*, *15* (1), 249. https://doi.org/10.1186/s12888-015-0622-7.

Weisz, J., Bearman, S. K., Santucci, L. C., & Jensen-Doss, A. (2017). Initial test of a principle-guided approach to transdiagnostic psychotherapy with children and adolescents. *Journal of Clinical Child and Adolescent Psychology*, *46*(1), 44–58. https://doi.org/10.1080/15374416.2016.1163708.

Weisz, J. R., Bearman, S. K., Ugueto, A. M., Herren, J., Allene, A., Cheron, D. M., … Tweed, L. (2016). *Pragmatic trial of transdiagnostic intervention for youth mental health problems.* Cambridge, MA: Harvard University.

Weisz, J. R., Chorpita, B. F., Palinkas, L. A., Schoenwald, S. K., Miranda, J., Bearman, S. K., … Martin, J. (2012). Testing standard and modular designs for psychotherapy treating depression, anxiety, and conduct problems in youth: A randomized effectiveness trial. *Archives of General Psychiatry*, *69*(3), 274–282. https://doi.org/10.1001/archgenpsychiatry.2011.147.

Weisz, J. R., & Donenberg, G. R. (1992). The lab versus the clinic: Effects of child and adolescent psychotherapy. *American Psychologist*, *47*(12), 1578–1585. https://doi.org/10.1037/0003-066X.47.12.1578.

Weisz, J. R., Donenberg, G. R., Han, S. S., & Kauneckis, D. (1995). Child and adolescent psychotherapy outcomes in experiments versus clinics: Why the disparity? *Journal of Abnormal Child Psychology*, *23*(1), 83–106. https://doi.org/10.1007/BF01447046.

Weisz, J. R., Krumholz, L. S., Santucci, L., Thomassin, K., & Ng, M. Y. (2015). Shrinking the gap between research and practice: Tailoring and testing youth psychotherapies in clinical care contexts. *Annual Review of Clinical Psychology*, *11*, 139–163. https://doi.org/10.1146/annurev-clinpsy-032814-112820.

Weisz, J. R., Ugueto, A. M., Herren, J., Afienko, S. R., & Rutt, C. (2011). Kernels vs. ears, and other questions for a science of treatment dissemination. *Clinical Psychology: Science and Practice*, *18*(1), 41–46. https://doi.org/10.1111/j.1468-2850.2010.01233.

Wilamowska, Z. A., Thompson-Hollands, J., Fairholme, C. P., Ellard, K. K., Farchione, T. J., & Barlow, D. H. (2010). Conceptual background, development, and preliminary data from the unified protocol for transdiagnostic treatment of emotional disorders. *Depression and Anxiety*, *27*(10), 882–890. https://doi.org/10.1002/da.20735.

Training and supervision

3

Brandon A. Kohrt, Anvita Bhardwaj
Department of Psychiatry, George Washington University, Washington, DC, United States

A pervasive challenge in reducing the treatment gap between the burden of mental illness and the availability of evidence-based services is the lack of a trained workforce able to deliver mental health care (Kakuma et al., 2011), such as psychological interventions. To address this, it is crucial to consider how best to conduct trainings and implement supervision to establish a workforce competent in delivering psychological interventions. In this chapter, we discuss key considerations and best practices for training and supervision for psychological interventions in low-resource settings. First, we discuss what aspects of training and supervision require special consideration in the context of global mental health. Then, we review the hierarchy of skills needed for psychological interventions including skills related to common factors in psychotherapy, treatment-specific skills, and skills for particular contexts. We continue by exploring how training and supervision considerations should go into the formative research phase when devising interventions. The subsequent sections are broken down into who does training, who is trained, and the content and structure of trainings. We then present a section dedicated to the often overlooked issues of attitudes and motivation in trainings. This is followed by a section on training evaluation with particular emphasis on evaluating competency in global mental health. The final sections address supervision models, evaluating quality and fidelity in implementation, and issues of accreditation, certification, and workforce development. By conclusion of this chapter, readers will be aware of key considerations in global mental health training and supervision for psychological interventions, and they will have the building blocks to assemble a training and supervision programs for global mental health initiatives.

3.1 Considerations for training and supervision in global mental health

There are a number of considerations that require special attention in global mental health (GMH) and, when taken into account, can guide how trainings and supervisions should differ from standard models set in high-income countries. Below, we list some of these key considerations:

(1) *Use of nonspecialists to deliver psychological interventions*: Psychological interventions such as cognitive behavioral therapy, interpersonal therapy, and exposure therapies are delivered by persons with a professional mental health-related degree in high-income countries, whereas in low-resource settings, nonspecialists are trained and subsequently tasked

Global Mental Health and Psychotherapy. https://doi.org/10.1016/B978-0-12-814932-4.00003-3

with delivering these treatments (Singla et al., 2017; van Ginneken et al., 2013). This is the hallmark of task-sharing interventions (WHO, 2008). Because nonspecialists, who may range for laypersons with minimal literacy to community health volunteers to teachers, are asked to deliver these psychological interventions, the training and supervision models potentially need to be adapted to limited educational backgrounds and the lack of familiarity with physical health and mental health care.

(2) *Limited availability of mental health specialists with training expertise*: In high-resource settings, trainers are often faculty in academic institutions and other experts who work for companies charging high rates for specialized trainings. In low-resource settings, there is often a gap in expertise for such trainings, and the prices charged by training companies often exceed monthly or even annual wages of the nonspecialists asked to deliver the intervention. To date, many psychological therapy trainings have been conducted in the context of research trials, involving trainers from universities in high-income countries (Singla et al., 2017), thus presenting challenges in cultural and linguistic differences between the trainers and trainees. Also, with trainers often departing the country after the trainings, supervision may not be in place. This has led to the phrase "train and hope" to describe some of these GMH endeavors—that is, train folks and *hope* everything works after the international expert has departed. A gradual shift to trainers from institutions in low- and middle-income countries (LMIC) has been seen.

(3) *Cultural frameworks for the adaptation of training and other materials*: Psychological interventions are often uncommon in low-resource settings that characterize GMH initiatives. Therefore, trainings also need to be adapted to take into account cultural models of healing and cultural frameworks to explain psychological therapies (Kohrt, Maharjan, Timsina, & Griffith, 2012; Ramaiya, Fiorillo, Regmi, Robins, & Kohrt, 2017). Not only do the ways in which trainings are administered need to be adapted, but also often the materials that guide training and supervision need to be adjusted for low literacy rates, translation into local languages, and cultural concepts and frameworks (Patel, Chowdhary, Rahman, & Verdeli, 2011).

(4) *Methods used for training*: Given the often lack of prior expertise and adults with limited formal education, there is often a need for methods more typically associated with adult education, nonformal education, and participatory engagement.

(5) *Location for delivering psychological interventions*: GMH psychological interventions typically will not happen in a consultant's office. Instead, these may happen in settings ranging from a bench outside of a clinic to a home or community center. Moreover, many GMH initiatives are in settings of humanitarian emergencies where there needs to be flexibility in how and where psychological interventions are delivered.

(6) *Need for and methods of supervision*: Because trainees may not have full competency at the end of trainings based on their prior lack of exposure and also the challenges of trainers not being available in person after trainings, this has necessitated creative approaches using peer supervision, a mix of in-person and virtual supervision, and apprentice-based supervision (Patel, Chowdhary, et al., 2011; Singla et al., 2014).

(7) *Evaluation of competency, quality, and fidelity*: Because of the types of psychological interventions and the persons delivering them, traditional approaches to what is measured and how it is measured for competency, quality, and fidelity are not adequate. New tools and approaches are needed for evaluation at different stages ranging from evaluations during and after training to evaluation during supervision and implementation (Kohrt, Jordans, et al., 2015; Singla et al., 2014).

(8) *Workforce development*: Finally, the need for training programs to be not only one-off but also scalable models that can be sustained and expanded to develop nationwide workforces for psychological interventions also changes the development and scope of training and supervision programs.

This chapter takes these issues as priorities when describing how training and supervision needs to be designed and implemented in GMH endeavors. In the next section, we briefly review the basics of clinical skill hierarchies that guide trainings; then, we go on to address the considerations mentioned above.

3.1.1 Fundamentals of training and supervision for psychological interventions

Training and supervision in the domain of psychological therapies has been framed by Miller according to a hierarchy of clinical skills. To conceptualize the acquisition of clinical skills and knowledge, we employ Miller's hierarchy of clinical skills, which have been used to evaluate training and supervision practices for mental health treatments in high-income settings (Miller, 1990; Muse & McManus, 2013). Miller's hierarchy includes four levels: Level 1 "knows" refers to conceptual knowledge of mental health care and typically is assessed through multiple-choice questions. Level 2 "knows how" refers to knowledge of how to apply conceptual information and theory, which can be assessed through decision-making questions following clinical vignettes. Level 3 "shows" refers to competence, which is the degree to which a provider demonstrates "the knowledge and skill required to deliver a treatment to the standard needed for it to achieve its expected effects" (Fairburn & Cooper, 2011, p. 373), and it can be assessed by demonstrating skills through role plays with standardized patients. Level 4 "does" refers to how providers apply skills in practice, which reflects treatment quality and is assessed through rating treatment sessions. Treatment quality refers to the degree to which a mental health "treatment was delivered well enough for it to achieve its expected effects" (Fairburn & Cooper, 2011, p. 373). This hierarchy is designed for the evaluation of those provider attributes expected to be most predictive of patient outcomes. Fig. 3.1 illustrates the components of training and supervision that contribute to clinical knowledge, attitudes, skills, and related factors, which ultimately influence patient outcomes.

Working backward from the goal of a positive patient interaction, the many elements of trainings and supervisions necessary to reach that goal are elucidated. Overarchingly, in order to achieve this goal, evidence-based care needs to be delivered. Prior to that, providers need to achieve competency in the psychological intervention in order to deliver it with quality. Prior to that, persons need to have the knowledge and attitudes to support development and demonstration of competency. To achieve that, they need successful training. This requires appropriate selection of trainees, preparation of trainers, and availability of appropriate materials (see Fig. 3.2). Below, we review those key steps.

One of the key issues to consider is what competencies are needed from trainings; there are three types of competencies needed that are laid out below. What often comes to mind first is competency in the specific manualized intervention. This, in delivery, is referred to as fidelity to the intervention—that a person delivers the intervention

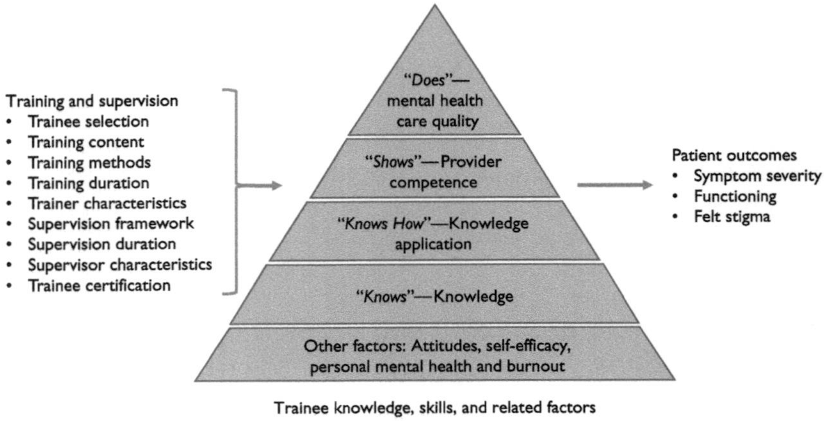

Fig. 3.1 Pathway from training and supervision to patient outcomes as mediated by nonspecialist provider knowledge, attitudes, and clinical skills.
Adapted from Miller's hierarchy of clinical skills (1990).

Fig. 3.2 Sequence of training and supervision to achieve improved patient outcomes. Assessment points: (1) assess trainees communication skills prior to enrollment in training; (2) assess knowledge, attitudes, and competency at the conclusion of training; (3) assess competency after period of initial supervision; (4) assess quality of care delivered.

according to what are viewed as the key components to achieve the mechanisms of action. The second competency is competency in common factors. Common factors include concepts such as therapist qualities including empathy and genuineness, patient and extracontextual factors such as mobilization of social support and bolstering prior positive coping strategies, aspects of the therapist-patient relationship including collaborative goal setting, and overall promotion of hope and expectancy of change among patients (Garfield, 1973; Greenberg, 2004; Karson & Fox, 2010; Sparks, Duncan, & Miller, 2008; Wampold, 2011). These common factors, also referred to as nonspecific factors, are elements thought to cut across all successful forms of intervention. Early research suggested that common factors explain 85% of the differences in therapy outcomes with treatment-specific factors explaining 15% of the difference (Lambert & Bergin, 1994). More recent research suggests that the division between treatment-specific and common factors cannot be so easily apportioned (Wampold, 2011), but the role of common factors continues to be promoted as the dominant contributor to improvement with a lack of significant differences across types of specific therapies when implemented by mental health specialists in high-income countries (Barth et al., 2013; Drisko, 2004; Imel & Wampold, 2008; Karson & Fox, 2010). Studies also point toward common factors being important for nonspecialists; however, this has been limited to research conducted in high-income countries (Armstrong, 2010; Brown & Wissow, 2012; Montgomery, Kunik, Wilson, Stanley, & Weiss, 2010; Zirkelback & Reese, 2010). The central role of common factors for positive patient outcomes is also likely to be true for nonspecialists in LMIC. The third competency is related to contextual factors or the ability to navigate the specific context in which the psychological intervention will be delivered. This relates to the ability to function in the health system or a community setting or navigating a refugee camp. These are important to be able to deliver care. Even if one is competent in the intervention and with common factors, being unable to work in the setting will lead to low-quality services. Some aspects of contextual competency may include needing to work with groups or work with vulnerable populations that have specific needs in a population such as persons living with HIV/AIDS, transgender groups, and members of ethnic minorities. Ultimately, the goal of training and supervision should be to assure competence and quality in common factors of psychotherapy, treatment-specific elements of a manualized intervention, and contextual factors relevant to delivery in particular structural and cultural setting. Next, we describe the key considerations in training and supervision as they relate to GMH context.

3.2 Consideration 1. How should feasibility of training and supervision in specific context influence selection of a psychological intervention?

Before training begins, the first step is the selection of an appropriate psychological intervention. Psychological interventions should be dictated by the local needs and populations. For example, the key concerns may be interpersonal stressors, exposure to trauma, high rates of suicidality, or other sources of distress. These should influence the type of psychological intervention selected. Equally important is the context related to training and supervision. What is the available workforce that can be trained, and what are their prior competencies? What are the available human resources for training and supervision—for example, are their experts available on-site for training and/or supervision? What is the context and duration under which training can be delivered? These training and supervision factors are crucial for effective implementation of the intervention. Although some types of interventions may have a strong fit, if the training and supervision environment is not adequate, other interventions may need to be considered.

A helpful aid for this evaluation is to employ a framework from the field of implementation science. There are a range of appropriate frameworks; one example is replicating effective programs (REP) (Kilbourne, Neumann, Pincus, Bauer, & Stall, 2007). REP is a systematic approach to select and implement interventions within a particular context. It was developed by the United States' Centers for Disease Control and Prevention for scaling up and implementation of HIV/AIDS programs in diverse settings. In the area of psychological interventions in global health, it has been used to select, adapt, and implement a psychological intervention for caregivers of children affected by nodding syndrome in Northern Uganda (Mutamba et al., 2018). The hallmark of REP is balancing fidelity to the core intervention components while promoting flexibility to maximize the diversity of settings for implementation (Kilbourne et al., 2007). REP is divided into four phases: (i) preconditions, (ii) preimplementation, (iii), implementation, and (iv) maintenance and evolution (Kilbourne et al., 2007). In the context of health-care interventions, the precondition phase consists of identifying and packaging of the intervention for training and assessment; preimplementation consists of customization, training, and establishing technical assistance services; implementation consists of delivery and evaluation; and maintenance and evolution requires models for financial sustainability, nationwide dissemination, and iterative recustomization (Kilbourne et al., 2007).

In the first phase, formative research is used to determine what the needs are for the intervention. In addition, this phase includes exercises to determine what would be appropriate in terms of human resources, training, and supervision. For this Uganda study, Mutamba and colleagues identified group interpersonal psychotherapy (IPT) as an intervention that would fit the psychological needs, but they had to adapt prior training and supervision approaches because prior work was within an NGO setting but this IPT program was delivered within the government infrastructure (Mutamba et al., 2018). Similarly, in Nepal, formative research with psychosocial counselors, gender-based violence counselors, religious leaders, and traditional healers was used to determine whom would be ideal to deliver culturally adapted dialectical behavior therapy (DBT) (Ramaiya et al., 2017).

3.3 Consideration 2. Who will deliver the training?

Once formative work has been done on selecting the psychological intervention taking into account both the need and the existing resources, then, there should be a proposed composition for the training team. This will often include a mental health expert and an expert in the specific intervention. NGO members are included as trainers, as seen in Bass et al. where workers of an international nongovernmental organization trained the counselors (Bass et al., 2013). In some instances, peers of the trainees who have previously participated in the training may be promoted to facilitator after sufficient experience as seen in Becker (Becker, 2009). One of the pitfalls is the assumption that simply because someone is a mental health expert means that they are also competent to be an effective trainer. In many instances, trainers need both to be trained on the content of the intervention and also to develop training skills. In instances where a foreign trainer is used because they have expertise in the intervention and/or in other mental health skills, it is important to consider language. When trainers are unable to communicate in the local language, it will be important to have an interpreter who is skilled in mental health and psychological terminology. Ideally, after the first few trainings, persons from the same country as the trainee who have adequate linguistic and cultural knowledge support knowledge transfer. Kabura et al. found that having the main trainer be a native Ugandan helped to the make the training more effective by using local proverbs, a culturally relevant teaching method (Kabura, Fleming, & Tobin, 2005).

3.4 Consideration 3. Who will receive the training?

Trainees are typically laypersons, primary care workers, or community health workers. Primary care workers included doctors, nurses, health auxiliaries, and other providers in generalist settings. In Singla et al.'s review of psychological interventions delivered by nonspecialist workers in LMIC, the authors found that community health workers employed through the health system comprised trainees in a third of all trials, followed by groups such as peers or individuals specifically recruited for the trial from the same community (29.6%), nurses (18.5%), and midwives (14.8%) (Singla et al., 2017). The most common rationale was that the nonspecialists were close to and had frequent contact with the target community (46.2%); also important were acknowledging the value of peer support (30.7%) and seeing the chosen individuals as a sustainable resource (23.1%) (e.g., by being employed at a local health center). Only half of the trials ($n = 14$) reported the gender of the nonspecialists; of these, all included females (100%), and the majority included only females (64.3%). Only three trials reported the age of the nonspecialists, which averaged 35 years (range = 30–50) (Singla et al., 2017).

The majority of programs selected trainees based on demographic educational criteria, such as having a 10th-grade education or being able to speak English. In other training programs, nominations from governmental and nongovernmental organizations have been used. In one psychological therapy training, participants were selected by passing a written and skill-based exam (Neuner et al., 2008). In Singla's review, among the 13 trials that reported education levels for nonspecialists, 30.8% reported that nonspecialists had up to a postgraduate education, but nearly one-quarter (23.1%) reported nonspecialists had only primary education (23.1%) (Singla et al., 2017). One trial included literate nonspecialists as the criteria for selecting delivery agents, although they had had no formal schooling.

3.5 Consideration 4. How will the training be structured?

Trainings in psychological interventions may be as brief as a few days or up to 6 months as with a psychosocial counselor training that has been regularly conducted for more than a decade in Nepal (Jordans, Tol, Sharma, & van Ommeren, 2003). For trainings of nonspecialists to deliver psychological interventions for common mental disorders in LMIC, the duration of their training period varied from 3 h to 2 months (Singla et al., 2017). Overall, training lasted a mean of 78.82 h (95% CI = 21.81–135.84). However, the mean was 53.80 h (95% CI = 31.72–75.84) when the one outlier (Patel et al., 2010) was excluded because the MANAS (MANAshanti Sudhar shodh, which means "project to promote mental health" in Konkani) training lasted 2 months due to inclusion of skills that went beyond psychological intervention (e.g., case management and yoga).

The trainings typically involve a combination of didactic and practical skill sessions. Participants are given information about the intervention and theory, but then, there is often a great deal of practicing skills and use of role plays. In some trainings, there is an opportunity to work with patients, clients, or practice groups to work on developing the appropriate skills. Because in many GMH settings persons may have limited formal education, repetition and participatory methods are often vital. Adult informal educational approaches are used, especially when working with populations that have limited literacy (Verdeli et al., 2003). Many trainings use vignettes or role-playing scenarios that were adapted to include local constructs of distress and culturally relevant details to make them look, sound, and feel more realistic to the trainees. As part of a training of school teachers and principals in Jamaica, Baker-Henningham et al. included vignette videos filmed in Jamaican classrooms and revised handouts to include examples that were relevant to the local context (Baker-Henningham, Scott, Jones, & Walker, 2012). There were a limited number of studies that described training adaptation to meet the cultural and educational learning styles of lay health workers. One study explicitly identified the use of problem-based learning (Chadda, Sood, & Kumar, 2009). In the satisfaction evaluation from one study, the participants reported that they learned better through discussions rather than didactics. Because of the increasing penetration of technology, there are growing opportunities to use recordings, interactive digital programs, and online resources. However, technology feasibility for training sites and technological literacy of trainees need to be taken into account.

3.6 Consideration 5. What will be the content of the training?

Common factors for psychotherapy are included in some trainings, for example, listening, communication, psychoeducation, and basic problem-solving skills (Kohrt, Ramaiya, Rai, Bhardwaj, & Jordans, 2015). One training focuses specifically on microcounseling skills (Kabura et al., 2005). The materials for training often include a manual for trainees. Manuals for counseling skills, CBT, IPT, and other therapies also have been developed for LMIC. In multiple trials, a manual specific to that study has been designed. Formal interventions included "Incredible Years" for Jamaican children; "Helping Challenging Children" used in Lebanon; "Playing to Grow" for children in Mexico; and "Classroom-Based Intervention" for Indonesia, Burundi, Nepal, Sri Lanka, and Sudan (Baker-Henningham et al., 2012; Baker-Henningham, Walker, Powell, & Gardner, 2009; Jordans et al., 2010; Miller & Billings, 1994; Tol et al., 2008, 2014).

The adaptation of training materials to meet the needs of participants or other contextual factors has been reported for some psychological intervention trainings. Most of the adaptations listed focused on adapting interventions, but there are only a few studies that described adapting the training itself. Trainings and implementation often included the adoption of simplified scripts and figures (Patel, Weiss, et al., 2011). In order to address stigma issues in an Indian community-based program for persons with schizophrenia, additional training was included to improve attitudes, the intervention was modified for stigma and confidentiality, and a neighborhood script was prepared when encountering persons not in the direct family (Balaji et al., 2012). Vignettes were developed and adapted as these appeared to communicate effectively about the disorders, and symptom checklists disembodied from personal narratives anecdotally were not effective as the vignettes.

A significant number of the articles reviewed mention some form of adaption to training materials, training content, and/or the training methods (Chowdhary et al., 2014; Singla et al., 2017). Examples of adaptations include translating training materials, adapting the complexity of the language and content for use with nonprofessionals, adding visual materials, and including culturally relevant explanatory causal models and treatment models. Often, local experts in the field were included in the cultural adaptation of training materials and content. However, the amount of detailed information on the adaption of training materials, content, or methods is often limited.

The majority of articles that mention adaptation refer to the adaptation of treatment models, such as cognitive behavioral therapy or interpersonal therapy, with few details on how the adaption of the treatment models affects the training methods, materials, or content. In several studies, the adaptation of treatment modalities has led to the creation or adaption of a treatment manual. For example, Patel et al. adapted a behavioral activation manual and motivational enhancement therapy manual to develop a manual for primary health-care workers to provide psychological interventions in India (Patel et al., 2014). However, there is often limited information on how these manuals were used for training purposes.

Training materials and content were often translated into the local language. Several trainings changed the complexity of the language and information in the training to better suit the trainees (Bass et al., 2013; Bolton et al., 2003, 2007). Several authors found that using local constructs of distress in the training materials and activities enhanced the experience of the trainees (Gelkopf, Ryan, Cotton, & Berger, 2008; Kabura et al., 2005). Bolton et al. found that using simplified jargon-free language that is reflective of local understandings of distress was beneficial for training nonclinicians on group interpersonal therapy in rural Uganda (Bolton et al., 2003).

Additionally, several adaptations included incorporating local cultural norms and religious activities to enhance the training and, ultimately, the intervention. To enhance the cultural relevance of a training course for Sri Lanka disaster workers, Gelkopf avoided using diagnostic labels and instead trained participants to focus on decreasing negative thought patterns and increasing social interactions, such as group prayer (Gelkopf et al., 2008). Similarly, Das incorporated concepts from the biomedical model of mental health while intentionally not challenging local belief and understandings in a training of relatives of people with schizophrenia in India (Das et al., 2006).

There are multiple examples of collaborating with local lay or mental health professionals to adapt training materials, methods, and content to increase cultural relevance. In a training discussed by Murray and colleagues, an iterative process was used where local counselors made cultural adaptations throughout the training and intervention process (Murray et al., 2013). In another setting—Nepal—a psychological intervention was needed to address high suicide rates among women in rural areas. Formative research was used to determine existing practices that could be included in the training (Ramaiya et al., 2017).

3.7 Consideration 6. How will motivation be enhanced and stigma reduced?

One of the major challenges in training in GMH initiatives is the willingness and motivation of trainees to participate in trainings and then to deliver the intervention with adequate quality after training. Stigma against persons with mental illness across cultures around the world may limit the motivation to engage in these endeavors. Stigma including both conscious and unconscious bias against persons with mental illness may especially impede competency and quality in common factors that require empathy, rapport building, and a collaborative approach. It is not uncommon for trainings to not specifically mention if any stigma reduction content was included in the overall training. In some trainings, a short component of the training focused on stigma reduction is added; this ranges from brief educational activities to more active methods of addressing stigma reduction. Kermode et al. used a brainstorming activity to engage participants in a discussion about stigma and discrimination that people with mental illnesses face (Kermode et al., 2008). Unfortunately, simply developing skills for a psychological intervention is often inadequate to reduce stigma and enhance motivation. One alternative strategy is to employ mental health service users as cofacilitators in the training. When persons who have participated in the intervention and benefited from it participate in the training, they are living examples of how delivery of care can make a major difference for individuals, families, and communities. REducing Stigma among HealthcAre ProvidErs (RESHAPE) is a program that trains persons living with mental illness who have received treatment to be cofacilitators in trainings ranging from mental health Gap Action Program (mhGAP) trainings to psychological interventions including the Healthy Activity Program (HAP) and Counseling for Alcohol Problems (CAP) (Kohrt et al., 2018).

3.8 Consideration 7. How will training outcomes be evaluated?

To assure that trainings are well designed and effective, it is important to conduct training evaluations. Unfortunately, many trainings limit such evaluations to satisfaction surveys in which participants are asked to rate how much they liked certain aspects of the training. If we return to Miller's hierarchy of skills, which was presented at the beginning, then we can identify the different domains that need to be assessed. At the bottom of Miller's pyramid, we can consider the need to evaluate changes in attitudes and motivation. Subjective ratings of self-efficacy would also fall under this section. An example of attitudinal scales is the Depression Attitude Questionnaire, which includes questions about treating persons with depression, preferences for medication or psychotherapy, and character attributes of persons with depression (Ola, Crabb, Adewuya, Olugbile, & Abosede, 2013). The social distance scale can be used to assess ones comfort in interacting with persons with mental illness, and this scale may be a good predictor of empathy toward persons with mental illness (Broussard et al., 2011; Kirmayer, Fletcher, & Boothroyd, 1997; Reinke, Corrigan, Leonhard, Lundin, & Kubiak, 2004). The Mental Illness: Clinician's Attitudes (MICA) is a brief self-report of interest in mental illness and attributes toward providing mental health care (Gabbidon et al., 2013; Kassam, Glozier, Leese, Henderson, & Thornicroft, 2010). There is a wide range of other scales related to stigma, discrimination, and intended behaviors (Brohan, Slade, Clement, & Thornicroft, 2010).

At the next level of assessment "*knows*," multiple-choice assessments, true-false, and other similar closed-ended questions are often used to assess knowledge about mental health and familiarity with the intervention and its elements. Often, "*knows*" assessed pretraining and posttraining such that there is a comparison between the two time points. Paper-based assessments can be supplemented with qualitative methods to assess knowledge such as oral exams and case-based discussions and focus groups to evaluate knowledge. Basic knowledge about the intervention is typically necessary but not often sufficient to assure quality of care delivered. The next level is "*knows how*" that refers to the application of knowledge. This is typically done through structured vignettes in which participants are asked questions about diagnosing and delivering the psychological intervention. A layered vignette system can be used to determine if participants have been adequately trained to select the correct intervention or components of the intervention and to know when to deliver them. Often, responses are open-ended in this part of the evaluation in comparison with "*knows*" allowing for more insight to the participants' thought processes. As with the above, correct answering is an important part of the process, but a "knows how" does not directly predict the manner in which the intervention will actually be delivered.

The next level "shows" refers to competence with which a trainee can deliver the intervention under a controlled setting. Some form of observed structured clinical evaluation (OSCE) is useful here and can be standardized across participants to compare the range of outcomes. The competency component can be used to evaluate treatment-specific features, common factors, and contextual factors. Treatment-specific measures of competency are typically developed by the intervention designers. For common factors, a competence evaluation tool has been developed that can be administered for and by nonspecialists in GMH endeavors. This tool, the Enhancing Assessment of Common Therapeutic Factors (ENACT), comprises 18 observations that can be garnered from a 10min standardized role play with someone trained to be a mock client (Kohrt, Jordans, et al., 2015; Kohrt, Ramaiya, et al., 2015). The ENACT be administered right after a training and over time to evaluate changes in competence as trainees begin real-life practice of implementing the therapy. The final level of evaluation "does" refers to quality, which we will discuss separately below.

3.9 Consideration 8. How will supervision be conducted?

Supervision formats can be diverse ranging from clinical observation, individual supervision sessions, group supervision, and online/internet supervision to review of case documentation. Some studies have incorporated phone or Skype calls into the supervision strategies. For psychological interventions for common mental disorders delivered by nonspecialists in LMIC, all trials conducted supervision in person, and almost half of these supplemented this supervision with telephone (46.7%) or Skype (40.0%) support (Singla et al., 2017). Supervision was conducted in groups (86.7%) and/or individually (66.7%)—some trials included both group and individual supervision; only one trial exclusively used peers to conduct supervision (5.9%) (Singla et al., 2017). Supervision methods were reported in 19 trials and typically involved discussing a particular case (63.1%), observing a session (26.3%), or listening to an individual session via audio (10.5%) or some combination of these methods (Singla et al., 2017).

Supervisors in GMH initiatives have included research coordinators, psychiatrists, psychologists, and other mental health experts. Some studies worked with external organizations to supervise the individuals trained. In one study conducted in the Democratic Republic of Congo, Bass et al. partnered with the International Rescue Committee and trained employees to serve as supervisors (Bass et al., 2013). IRC employees were supported throughout the initial training process through weekly phone calls with the research team to troubleshot, to bolster supervision efficacy, and to maintain quality control. Ager et al. partnered with the Child Resilience Project to conduct supervisory meetings with individual trainees in Uganda (Ager et al., 2011). Bolton et al. used existing World Vision staff to assist with supervision of trainees in their 2007 Uganda study (Bolton et al., 2007). In this study, the supervisors had prior experience with the intervention, and supervisors were in turn supervised by a US-based trainer.

The apprenticeship model by Murray et al. has been explicitly cited by studies conducted in Uganda and South Africa (Murray et al., 2011, 2014; Petersen, Fairall, Egbe, & Bhana, 2014; Petersen, Hancock, Bhana, & Govender, 2014). This model aims to build local mental health capacity by selecting locals to serve as trainees and supervisors, with long-term extensive supervision shortening the time required for initial training. Aspects of the apprenticeship model include selection of trainees and supervisors based on demonstrated aptitude and interest, initial on-site training, supervisor-specific training, practice groups with local supervision, supervision groups, additional coaching of supervision techniques, a balance of flexibility and fidelity, use of self-report and observation of sessions, and mutual problem-solving ethic for trainers and apprentices (Murray et al., 2011). Fig. 3.3 outlines the process of conducting the apprenticeship approach.

Frequency in some studies is weekly or biweekly but may be monthly or eventually decrease to monthly after achieving minimal standards of quality. Others may use ad hoc supervision. Jordans et al. report that their paraprofessional training course in Nepal included 150h of clinical supervision. The teachers trained to deliver Wolmer et al.'s intervention in Turkey received 2h of supervision weekly for the 8-week duration of the intervention, for a total of 16h of supervision (Wolmer, Laor, & Yazgan, 2003).

Systematic supervision reporting tools have had limited use. In the Thinking Healthy Program Peer-delivered (THPP), a tool similar to the ENACT was used in which THPP group facilitators listened to session recordings and completed the checklist to give one another structured feedback.

3.10 Consideration 9. How will quality and fidelity be evaluated in actual implementation?

The evaluation of "does" determines the fidelity of the training intervention. This requires scoring the actual practice and clinical quality that the trainees are performing at after taking part in the training. This part of the evaluation is normally over a period of time and can be included into the supervision category as well. The apprenticeship model seemed to be a popular modality to evaluate the trainee's clinical ability as seen in Murray et al. (2014). Most of the articles reported the method by which this was

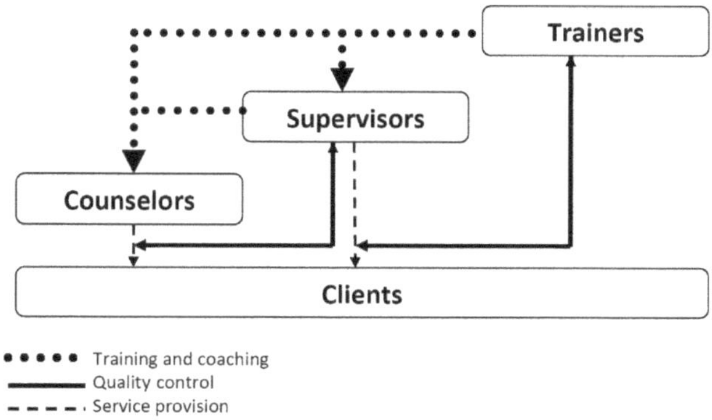

Fig. 3.3 Apprenticeship model for training and supervision.
Figure from Murray et al., 2011 *Intl Jrnl Mental Health Systems*.

evaluated and then broadly just mentioned if the training had seemed to be successful. Murray et al. (2013) is an example of this as the trainees were monitored, and it stated in the article that "clinical monitoring suggestions that TF-CBT was conducted by local lay counselors with fidelity." Some studies such as in Patel et al. (2014) used scales to assess the quality of care that the trainees were providing. The use of scales allows for numeric outputs to evaluate the fidelity of the training intervention, which hence are often chosen to be used. Some interventions use less structured tools such as focus groups and case discussions with the trainees to assess the "does" component of the training, for example, Ertl and colleagues (Ertl, Pfeiffer, Schauer, Elbert, & Neuner, 2011). Due to the longitudinal evaluation of this category, there are some studies, for example, Singla et al. (2014), where the data are yet to be collected as the supervision of the trainees is still going on.

3.11 Consideration 10. How will trainees be certified or accredited?

Trainings may lead to certification, employment, completion of a professional degree, or tokens that help those in the community recognize that participants have taken a training. In a trial IPT-G in Uganda, the trained lay counselors were hired by World Vision after the trial was completed. Some trainings have been incorporated into nursing or medical diploma programs, and the mental health training was part of the diploma completion process, or academic credit has been given for the training. In the case of the Friendship Bench intervention in Zimbabwe, along with a certificate, participants were given an apron and T-shirt to wear when they were sitting on the bench or going for home visits as a way for the community to identify that he or she had gone through the training (Chibanda et al., 2011). In some instances, trainees may go on to be employed as trainers. In response to the Tsunami disaster in India, nongovernmental organizations were quickly trained and subsequently employed and dispersed as trainers for community health workers on basic psychosocial care for disaster survivors (Becker, 2009).

3.12 Conclusion

Training and supervision approaches have been developed, and many of these are effective as suggested by the results of psychological interventions (Singla et al., 2017). However, less is known about what training and supervision approaches are best suited to scaling up and implementation throughout government systems. More research is needed to innovate and evaluate training and supervision approaches that will assure universal access to evidence-based psychological interventions that are delivered with appropriate quality to ultimately reduce the global treatment gap for mental illness.

References

Ager, A., Akesson, B., Stark, L., Flouri, E., Okot, B., McCollister, F., & Boothby, N. (2011). The impact of the school-based psychosocial structured activities (PSSA) program on conflict-affected children in northern Uganda. *Journal of Child Psychology and Psychiatry, 52*(11), 1124–1133.

Armstrong, J. (2010). How effective are minimally trained/experienced volunteer mental health counsellors? Evaluation of CORE outcome data. *Counselling and Psychotherapy Research, 10*(1), 22–31.

Baker-Henningham, H., Scott, S., Jones, K., & Walker, S. (2012). Reducing child conduct problems and promoting social skills in a middle-income country: Cluster randomised controlled trial. *British Journal of Psychiatry, 201*, 101–108. https://doi.org/10.1192/bjp.bp.111.096834.

Baker-Henningham, H., Walker, S. P., Powell, C., & Gardner, J. M. (2009). Preventing behaviour problems through a universal intervention in Jamaican basic schools a pilot study. *West Indian Medical Journal, 58*(5), 460–464.

Balaji, M., Chatterjee, S., Koschorke, M., Rangaswamy, T., Chavan, A., Dabholkar, H., ... Patel, V. (2012). The development of a lay health worker delivered collaborative community based intervention for people with schizophrenia in India. *BMC Health Services Research. 12*, 42. https://doi.org/10.1186/1472-6963-12-42.

Barth, J., Munder, T., Gerger, H., Nüesch, E., Trelle, S., Znoj, H., ... Cuijpers, P. (2013). Comparative efficacy of seven psychotherapeutic interventions for patients with depression: A network meta-analysis. *PLoS Medicine/Public Library of Science. 10*(5)e1001454. https://doi.org/10.1371/journal.pmed.1001454.

Bass, J. K., Annan, J., McIvor Murray, S., Kaysen, D., Griffiths, S., Cetinoglu, T., ... Bolton, P. A. (2013). Controlled trial of psychotherapy for Congolese survivors of sexual violence. *New England Journal of Medicine, 368*(23), 2182–2191.

Becker, S. M. (2009). Psychosocial care for women survivors of the tsunami disaster in India. *American Journal of Public Health, 99*(4), 654.

Bolton, P., Bass, J., Betancourt, T., Speelman, L., Onyango, G., Clougherty, K. F., ... Verdeli, H. (2007). Interventions for depression symptoms among adolescent survivors of war and displacement in northern Uganda: A randomized controlled trial. *JAMA, 298*(5), 519–527.

Bolton, P., Bass, J., Neugebauer, R., Verdeli, H., Clougherty, K., Wickramaratne, P., ... Weissman, M. (2003). Group interpersonal psychotherapy for depression in rural Uganda: A randomized controlled trial. *JAMA, 289*(23), 3117–3124.

Brohan, E., Slade, M., Clement, S., & Thornicroft, G. (2010). Experiences of mental illness stigma, prejudice and discrimination: A review of measures. *BMC Health Services Research, 10*, 80. https://doi.org/10.1186/1472-6963-10-80.

Broussard, B., Krishan, S., Hankerson-Dyson, D., Husbands, L., Stewart-Hutto, T., & Compton, M. T. (2011). Development and initial reliability and validity of four self-report measures used in research on interactions between police officers and individuals with mental illnesses. *Psychiatry Research, 189*(3), 458–462. https://doi.org/10.1016/j.psychres.2011.06.017.

Brown, J. D., & Wissow, L. S. (2012). Rethinking the mental health treatment skills of primary care staff: A framework for training and research. *Administration and Policy in Mental Health and Mental Health Services Research, 39*(6), 489–502.

Chadda, R. K., Sood, M., & Kumar, N. (2009). Experiences of a sensitization program on common mental disorders for primary care physicians using problem-based learning approach. *Indian Journal of Psychiatry, 51*(4), 289–291. https://doi.org/10.4103/0019-5545.58296.

Chibanda, D., Mesu, P., Kajawu, L., Cowan, F., Araya, R., & Abas, M. (2011). Problem-solving therapy for depression and common mental disorders in Zimbabwe: Piloting a task-shifting primary mental health care intervention in a population with a high prevalence of people living with HIV. *BMC Public Health, 11*(1), 828.

Chowdhary, N., Jotheeswaran, A., Nadkarni, A., Hollon, S., King, M., Jordans, M., … Patel, V. (2014). The methods and outcomes of cultural adaptations of psychological treatments for depressive disorders: A systematic review. *Psychological Medicine, 44*(06), 1131–1146.

Das, S., Saravanan, B., Karunakaran, K. P., Manoranjitham, S., Ezhilarasu, P., & Jacob, K. S. (2006). Effect of a structured educational intervention on explanatory models of relatives of patients with schizophrenia randomised controlled trial. *British Journal of Psychiatry, 188*(3), 286–287.

Drisko, J. W. (2004). Common factors in psychotherapy outcome: Meta-analytic findings and their implications for practice and research. *Families in Society, 85*(1), 81–90.

Ertl, V., Pfeiffer, A., Schauer, E., Elbert, T., & Neuner, F. (2011). Community-implemented trauma therapy for former child soldiers in northern Uganda a randomized controlled trial. *Journal of the American Medical Association, 306*(5), 503–512.

Fairburn, C. G., & Cooper, Z. (2011). Therapist competence, therapy quality, and therapist training. *Behaviour Research and Therapy, 49*(6), 373–378.

Gabbidon, J., Clement, S., van Nieuwenhuizen, A., Kassam, A., Brohan, E., Norman, I., & Thornicroft, G. (2013). Mental illness: Clinicians' attitudes (MICA) scale-psychometric properties of a version for healthcare students and professionals. *Psychiatry Research, 206*(1), 81–87. https://doi.org/10.1016/j.psychres.2012.09.028.

Garfield, S. L. (1973). Basic ingredients or common factors in psychotherapy? *Journal of Consulting and Clinical Psychology, 41*(1), 9–12. https://doi.org/10.1037/h0035618.

Gelkopf, M., Ryan, P., Cotton, S. J., & Berger, R. (2008). The impact of "training the trainers" course for helping tsunami-survivor children on Sri Lankan disaster volunteer workers. *International Journal of Stress Management, 15*(2), 117.

Greenberg, R. P. (2004). Essential ingredients for successful psychotherapy: Effect of common factors. In M. J. Dewan, B. N. Steenbarger, & R. P. Greenberg (Eds.), *The art and science of brief psychotherapies: A practitioner's guide* (pp. 231–241). Arlington, VA: American Psychiatric Publishing, Inc.

Imel, Z. E., & Wampold, B. E. (2008). The importance of treatment and the science of common factors in psychotherapy. In S. D. Brown & R. W. Lent (Eds.), *Handbook of counseling psychology* (4th ed., pp. 249–266). Hoboken, NJ: John Wiley & Sons Inc.

Jordans, M. J. D., Komproe, I. H., Tol, W. A., Kohrt, B. A., Luitel, N. P., Macy, R. D., & de Jong, J. T. V. M. (2010). Evaluation of a classroom-based psychosocial intervention in conflict-affected Nepal: A cluster randomized controlled trial. *Journal of Child Psychology & Psychiatry & Allied Disciplines, 51*(7), 818–826.

Jordans, M. J. D., Tol, W. A., Sharma, B., & van Ommeren, M. (2003). Training psychosocial counselling in Nepal: Content review of a specialised training programme. *Intervention: International Journal of Mental Health, Psychosocial Work & Counselling in Areas of Armed Conflict, 1*(2), 18–35.

Kabura, P., Fleming, L. M., & Tobin, D. J. (2005). Microcounseling skills training for informal helpers in Uganda. *International Journal of Social Psychiatry, 51*(1), 63–70. https://doi.org/10.1177/0020764005053282.

Kakuma, R., Minas, H., van Ginneken, N., Dal Poz, M. R., Desiraju, K., Morris, J. E., … Scheffler, R. M. (2011). Human resources for mental health care: Current situation and strategies for action. *The Lancet, 378*(9803), 1654–1663.

Karson, M., & Fox, J. (2010). Common skills that underlie the common factors of successful psychotherapy. *American Journal of Psychotherapy, 64*(3), 269–281.

Kassam, A., Glozier, N., Leese, M., Henderson, C., & Thornicroft, G. (2010). Development and responsiveness of a scale to measure clinicians' attitudes to people with mental illness (medical student version). *Acta Psychiatrica Scandinavica*, *122*(2), 153–161.

Kermode, M., Devine, A., Chandra, P., Dzuvichu, B., Gilbert, T., & Herrman, H. (2008). Some peace of mind: Assessing a pilot intervention to promote mental health among widows of injecting drug users in north-east India. *BMC Public Health*, *8*(1), 294.

Kilbourne, A. M., Neumann, M. S., Pincus, H. A., Bauer, M. S., & Stall, R. (2007). Implementing evidence-based interventions in health care: Application of the replicating effective programs framework. *Implementation Science*, *2*(1), 1–10. https://doi.org/10.1186/1748-5908-2-42.

Kirmayer, L. J., Fletcher, C. M., & Boothroyd, L. J. (1997). Inuit attitudes toward deviant behavior: A vignette study. *Journal of Nervous and Mental Disease*, *185*(2), 78–86.

Kohrt, B. A., Jordans, M. J. D., Rai, S., Shrestha, P., Luitel, N. P., Ramaiya, M., ... Patel, V. (2015). Therapist competence in global mental health: Development of the Enhancing assessment of common therapeutic factors (ENACT) rating scale. *Behaviour Research and Therapy*, *69*, 11–21. https://doi.org/10.1016/j.brat.2015.03.009.

Kohrt, B. A., Jordans, M. J. D., Turner, E. L., Sikkema, K. J., Luitel, N. P., Rai, S., ... Patel, V. (2018). Reducing stigma among healthcare providers to improve mental health services (RESHAPE): Protocol for a pilot cluster randomized controlled trial of a stigma reduction intervention for training primary healthcare workers in Nepal. *Pilot and Feasibility Studies*, *4*(1), 36. https://doi.org/10.1186/s40814-018-0234-3.

Kohrt, B. A., Maharjan, S. M., Timsina, D., & Griffith, J. L. (2012). Applying Nepali ethnopsychology to psychotherapy for the treatment of mental illness and prevention of suicide among Bhutanese refugees. *Annals of Anthropological Practice*, *36*(1), 88–112.

Kohrt, B. A., Ramaiya, M. K., Rai, S., Bhardwaj, A., & Jordans, M. J. D. (2015). Development of a scoring system for non-specialist ratings of clinical competence in global mental health: A qualitative process evaluation of the enhancing assessment of common therapeutic factors (ENACT) scale. *Global Mental Health*. *2*, e23. https://doi.org/10.1017/gmh.2015.21.

Lambert, M. J., & Bergin, A. E. (1994). The effectiveness of psychotherapy. In A. E. Bergin & S. L. Garfield (Eds.), *Handbook of psychotherapy and behavior change*. New York: John Wiley.

Miller, G. E. (1990). The assessment of clinical skills/competence/performance. *Academic Medicine*, *65*(9), S63–S67.

Miller, K. E., & Billings, D. L. (1994). Playing to grow: A primary mental health intervention with Guatemalan refugee children. *American Journal of Orthopsychiatry*, *64*(3), 346–356.

Montgomery, E. C., Kunik, M. E., Wilson, N., Stanley, M. A., & Weiss, B. (2010). Can paraprofessionals deliver cognitive-behavioral therapy to treat anxiety and depressive symptoms? *Bulletin of the Menninger Clinic*, *74*(1), 45–62.

Murray, L. K., Dorsey, S., Bolton, P., Jordans, M. J., Rahman, A., & Bass, J. (2011). Building capacity in mental health interventions in low resource countries: An apprenticeship model for training local providers. *International Journal of Mental Health Systems*. *5*. https://doi.org/10.1186/1752-4458-5-1.

Murray, L. K., Familiar, I., Skavenski, S., Jere, E., Cohen, J., Imasiku, M., ... Bolton, P. (2013). An evaluation of trauma focused cognitive behavioral therapy for children in Zambia. *Child Abuse & Neglect*, *37*(12), 1175–1185.

Murray, L. K. P., Skavenski, S. M. S. W. M. P. H., Bass, J. P., Wilcox, H. P., Bolton, P. M. M. P. H., Imasiku, M. P., & Mayeya, J. M. P. H. (2014). Implementing evidence-based mental health Care in low-Resource Settings: A focus on safety planning procedures. *Journal of Cognitive Psychotherapy*, *28*(3), 168–185.

Muse, K., & McManus, F. (2013). A systematic review of methods for assessing competence in cognitive–behavioural therapy. *Clinical Psychology Review*, *33*(3), 484–499. https://doi.org/10.1016/j.cpr.2013.01.010.

Mutamba, B. B., Kane, J. C., De Jong, J., Okello, J., Musisi, S., & Kohrt, B. A. (2018). Psychological treatments delivered by community health workers in low-resource government health systems: Effectiveness of group interpersonal psychotherapy for caregivers of children affected by nodding syndrome in Uganda. *Psychological Medicine*. https://doi.org/10.1017/S0033291718000193.

Neuner, F., Onyut, P. L., Ertl, V., Odenwald, M., Schauer, E., & Elbert, T. (2008). Treatment of posttraumatic stress disorder by trained lay counselors in an African refugee settlement: A randomized controlled trial. *Journal of Consulting & Clinical Psychology*, *76*(4), 686–694.

Ola, B., Crabb, J., Adewuya, A., Olugbile, F., & Abosede, O. A. (2013). The state of readiness of Lagos state primary health care physicians to embrace the care of depression in Nigeria. *Community Mental Health Journal*. https://doi.org/10.1007/s10597-013-9648-9.

Patel, V., Chowdhary, N., Rahman, A., & Verdeli, H. (2011). Improving access to psychological treatments: Lessons from developing countries. *Behaviour Research and Therapy*, *49*(9), 523–528. https://doi.org/10.1016/j.brat.2011.06.012.

Patel, V., Weiss, H. A., Chowdhary, N., Naik, S., Pednekar, S., Chatterjee, S., … Kirkwood, B. R. (2011). Lay health worker led intervention for depressive and anxiety disorders in India: Impact on clinical and disability outcomes over 12 months. *British Journal of Psychiatry*, *199*(6), 459–466.

Patel, V., Weiss, H. A., Chowdhary, N., Naik, S., Pednekar, S., Chatterjee, S., … Kirkwood, B. R. (2010). Effectiveness of an intervention led by lay health counsellors for depressive and anxiety disorders in primary care in Goa, India (MANAS): A cluster randomised controlled trial. *Lancet*, *376*(9758), 2086–2095.

Patel, V., Weobong, B., Nadkarni, A., Weiss, H., Anand, A., Naik, S., … Kirkwood, B. (2014). The effectiveness and cost-effectiveness of lay counsellor-delivered psychological treatments for harmful and dependent drinking and moderate to severe depression in primary care in India: PREMIUM study protocol for randomized controlled trials. *Trials*, *15*(1), 101.

Petersen, I., Fairall, L., Egbe, C. O., & Bhana, A. (2014). Optimizing lay counsellor services for chronic care in South Africa: A qualitative systematic review. *Patient Education and Counseling*, *95*(2), 201–210.

Petersen, I., Hancock, J. H., Bhana, A., & Govender, K. (2014). A group-based counselling intervention for depression comorbid with HIV/AIDS using a task shifting approach in South Africa: A randomized controlled pilot study. *Journal of Affective Disorders*, *158*, 78–84.

Ramaiya, M. K., Fiorillo, D., Regmi, U., Robins, C. J., & Kohrt, B. A. (2017). A cultural adaptation of dialectical behavior therapy in Nepal. *Cognitive and Behavioral Practice*, *24*(4), 428–444. https://doi.org/10.1016/j.cbpra.2016.12.005.

Reinke, R. R., Corrigan, P. W., Leonhard, C., Lundin, R. K., & Kubiak, M. A. (2004). Examining two aspects of contact on the stigma of mental illness. *Journal of Social and Clinical Psychology*, *23*(3), 377–389. https://doi.org/10.1521/jscp.23.3.377.35457.

Singla, D. R., Kohrt, B. A., Murray, L. K., Anand, A., Chorpita, B. F., & Patel, V. (2017). Psychological treatments for the world: Lessons from low- and middle-income countries. *Annual Review of Clinical Psychology*, *13*(April), 5.1–5.33. https://doi.org/10.1146/annurev-clinpsy-032816-045217.

Singla, D. R., Weobong, B., Nadkarni, A., Chowdhary, N., Shinde, S., & Anand, A. (2014). Improving the scalability of psychological treatments in developing countries: An evaluation of peer-led therapy quality assessment in Goa, India. *Behaviour Research and Therapy*. *60*. https://doi.org/10.1016/j.brat.2014.06.006.

Sparks, J. A., Duncan, B. L., & Miller, S. D. (2008). Common factors in psychotherapy. In J. L. Lebow (Ed.), *Twenty-first century psychotherapies: Contemporary approaches to theory and practice* (pp. 453–497). Hoboken, NJ: John Wiley & Sons Inc.

Tol, W., Komproe, I., Jordans, M., Ndayisaba, A., Ntamutumba, P., Sipsma, H., … de Jong, J. (2014). School-based mental health intervention for children in war-affected Burundi: A cluster randomized trial. *BMC Medicine*, *12*(1), 56.

Tol, W. A., Komproe, I. H., Susanty, D., Jordans, M. J. D., Macy, R. D., & De Jong, J. T. V. M. (2008). School-based mental health intervention for children affected by political violence in Indonesia: A cluster randomized trial. *JAMA*, *300*(6), 655–662.

van Ginneken, N., Tharyan, P., Lewin, S., Rao, G. N., Meera, S., Pian, J., … Patel, V. (2013). Non-specialist health worker interventions for the care of mental, neurological and substance-abuse disorders in low-and middle-income countries. *Cochrane Database of Systematic Reviews*, *11*, CD009149.

Verdeli, H., Clougherty, K., Bolton, P., Speelman, L., Lincoln, N., Bass, J., … Weissman, M. M. (2003). Adapting group interpersonal psychotherapy for a developing country: Experience in rural Uganda. *World Psychiatry: Official Journal of the World Psychiatric Association (WPA)*, *2*(2), 114–120.

Wampold, B. E. (2011). The research evidence for common factors models: A historically situated perspective. In B. L. Duncan, S. D. Miller, B. E. Wampold, & M. A. Hubble (Eds.), *The heart and soul of change: Delivering what works in therapy* (2nd ed., pp. 49–82). Washington, DC: American Psychological Association.

WHO (2008). *Task shifting: Rational redistribution of tasks among health workforce teams: Global recommendations and guidelines*. (Retrieved from Geneva).

Wolmer, L., Laor, N., & Yazgan, Y. (2003). School reactivation programs after disaster: Could teachers serve as clinical mediators? *Child and Adolescent Psychiatric Clinics of North America*, *12*(2), 363–381.

Zirkelback, E. A., & Reese, R. J. (2010). A review of psychotherapy outcome research: Considerations for school-based mental health providers. *Psychology in the Schools*, *47*(10), 1084–1100.

Scaling up and implementing psychotherapies in low-resource settings

4

Judith K. Bass, Syed Usman Hamdani*[†]

*Department of Mental Health, Johns Hopkins University Bloomberg School of Public Health, Baltimore, MD, United States, [†]Human Development Research Foundation, Islambad, Pakistan

4.1 Definitions and goals of dissemination and implementation research for global mental health

Dissemination and *implementation* are two distinct but interrelated terms. Dissemination refers to the spread and scale-up of knowledge and practice, while implementation refers to the strategies and approaches used to support the adoption, integration, and sustainability of knowledge and practice. The growth of the field of dissemination and implementation (D&I) research in the field of psychotherapy in global mental health builds on nearly two decades of research that developed, adapted, and tested talk therapies in low- and middle-resource settings, frequently using rigorous randomized controlled trial designs (Bass et al., 2013; Bolton, Bass, et al., 2014; Rahman et al., 2013; van Ginneken et al., 2013; Weiss et al., 2015). These trials provide good evidence that psychotherapies can be feasibly implemented in contexts with few or no formally trained mental health professionals and can have clinically significant impacts of reducing the burden of mental health problems and improving functioning and tasks of daily living. The role of D&I research now is important for translating those research results into practice. Like much of the health-care field, there still remains a wide gap between what is known to work in research and what is actually being implemented in practice. While this gap exists in high-income countries, it is exacerbated in contexts with few health resources generally and fewer if any mental health resources.

The field of D&I research provides frameworks and approaches for investigating how to transfer knowledge and services, like evidence-based psychotherapies, from efficacy and effectiveness trials to settings that lack the concentrated oversight and rigorous monitoring that trials bring with them. This is often referred to as "real-world" settings where inclusion criteria, research-dedicated staff, and highly regulated systems of care and data collection are not standard practice. The challenge to the field is to develop strategies and models that allow for these interventions to be disseminated in ways that are sustainable and accessible while retaining quality and impact.

Global Mental Health and Psychotherapy. https://doi.org/10.1016/B978-0-12-814932-4.00004-5

D&I researchers in global mental health are approaching this translational challenge through developing innovative approaches to training and supervising psychotherapy providers, through adapting and designing models of mental health services integration into clinical and social service delivery systems and through comparing and contrasting the human and financial costs associated with different delivery models. The rest of this chapter will present some of the conceptual frameworks and theoretical models driving this current research agenda as well as concrete examples of dissemination and implementation research in the field.

4.2 Conceptual frameworks and theoretical models for global mental health psychotherapy research

There are several frameworks and theoretical models that researchers have developed to guide thinking around dissemination and implementation research and strategy. One of the most frequently used conceptual models for mental health implementation research is that designed by Proctor et al. (2009), which promotes thinking about implementation research across multiple levels for multiple outcomes with recognition of the bidirectionality of learning informing practice and practice informing learning. In this model, intervention strategies are distinguished from implementation strategies—the former are the interventions that are being disseminated (i.e., evidence-based psychotherapies), while the latter are interventions or strategies that facilitate the uptake and integration of the evidence-based psychotherapy aimed at different parts of the service system. For example, developing a mobile-health-based supervision system would be an implementation strategy that could facilitate remote supervision of psychotherapy providers in contexts where face-to-face supervision is not logistically feasible. In addition to the distinction between implementation and intervention strategies, this model provides a helpful way to illustrate the complexity of multiple types of outcomes across multiple levels. Specifically, Proctor and colleagues define outcomes at the implementation, service, and client levels recognizing that each level has its own set of distinct outcomes while being interrelated with the outcomes of the other levels (Proctor et al., 2009). This complexity recognizes that implementation research requires a multilevel approach that incorporates the needs and perspectives of multiple stakeholders.

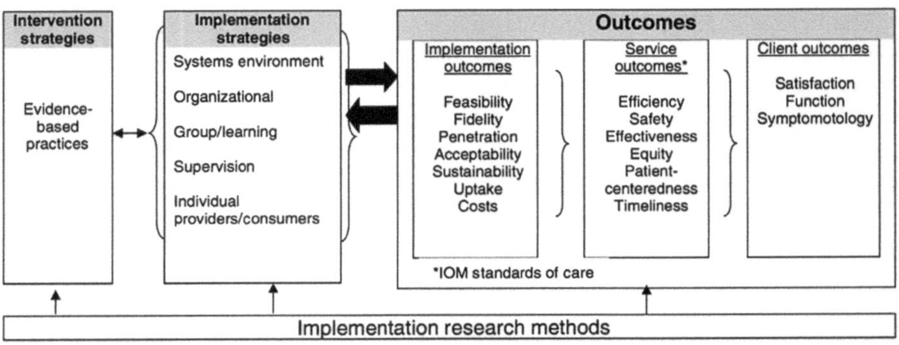

Another frequently used model in services implementation research is the Consolidated Framework for Implementation Research (CFIR) proposed by Damschroder et al. (2009). Following a thorough review of published theories that identified constructs related to health services implementation, they identified five major domains that encompass the areas that need to be considered when approaching the complex, multilevel field of systems research. They characterized the five domains as (1) intervention characteristics, (2) outer setting, (3) inner setting, (4) characteristics of the individuals involved, and (5) process of implementation. For each of these domains, multiple constructs were identified that could be seen as targets for implementation strategies in our outcomes research.

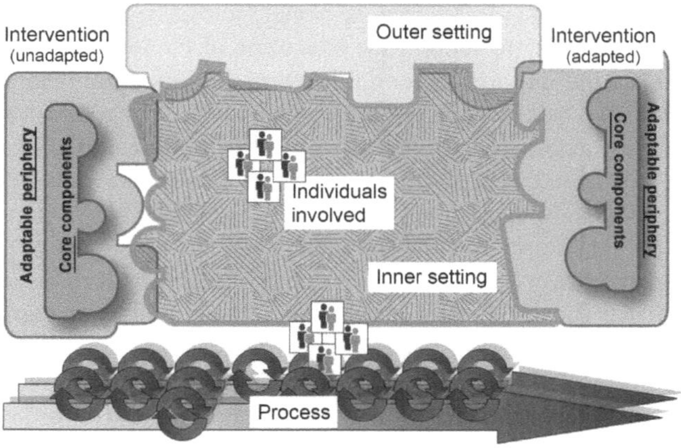

From: http:/cfirwiki.net/wiki/index.php?title=Talk:Main_Page.

This model is particularly amenable to implementation of services in different cultural and contextual settings with domain 2 (outer setting) focusing on the economic, political, and social context in which the service organization providing the psychotherapy is nested within and domain 3 (inner setting) encompassing the structural, political, and cultural contexts of the service organization itself. This intrinsically recognizes that health systems exist within social-political-cultural contexts that may have similarities across countries but more frequently have differences, particularly when comparing contexts in high-income countries with well-developed health infrastructures and policies with low- and middle-income countries (LMIC) where the quality of health infrastructures and the existence and regard of health policies will vary more widely.

One additional model that is helpful to include is proposed by Aarons, Hurlburt, and Horwitz (2011) that was specifically designed for implementing evidence-based programs in the public service sector, as opposed to the standard clinical setting for which most other models were designed. Building on conceptual models that present the different levels and domains that need to be considered when implementing programs, such as the two frameworks presented above, this model proposes an actual implementation process for incorporating a new intervention into an existing service system. Like the Damschroder CFIR framework (Damschroder et al., 2009), this model includes outer and inner contexts during each implementation phase and incorporates them into a multilevel, multistage process across four phases of implementation: exploration, adoption/preparation, implementation, and sustainment. Relating this to mental health services, the exploration phase is the stage during which there is recognition that a new service, or an improvement of existing services, is needed to meet the needs of the client base. This is followed by the phase during which the new intervention is determined to be appropriate and a good "fit" for the service providers, and thus, they decide to *adopt* the intervention and begin preparation for its implementation and integration within their own service system. This is followed by a period of active implementation during which the new intervention is rolled out and provided to the clients, with all the organizational factors—again including inner and outer contexts—interacting to support the execution of the intervention. And finally, this model includes the important recognition that the inner and outer contexts also play important roles in establishing the sustainment of the intervention as an integral, and hopefully now fundamental, program within the organizational system of care.

These conceptual frameworks and theoretical models remind researchers and program implementers just how complex service systems are and how there is never just one or two factors that are in play that will lead to the success or failure of a specific health intervention. However, like much of mental health services research, the conceptual frameworks and theoretical models for dissemination and implementation research have been predominantly developed in high-income country contexts. The lack of frameworks and models that are specific to other resource contexts is in part due to the generally limited amount of implementation research focus in global health (Ridde, 2016). However, despite the lack of frameworks and models specifically developed or adapted to low-resource settings, there has been a sizable growth in innovative programming and research to address specific domains and barriers that global mental health services researchers face as we design, evaluate, and implement psychotherapy services across diverse settings. The rest of this chapter will highlight several of these promising approaches that have been developed with an understanding of the social, cultural, and resource constraints existing in LMIC settings.

4.3 Training and supervising psychotherapy providers

The availability of mental health professionals in most LMIC settings is limited, and the availability of mental health services outside of urban settings and hospital settings is minimal (Kakuma et al., 2011). This has resulted in the use of "task-sharing" models for service provision, that is, services that traditionally are provided by professionals with specialized mental health training are delegated to nonmental health workers who work within a system of care that includes supervision and monitoring by those with more experience and training. A Cochrane review of nonspecialist health worker interventions for the care of mental, neurological, and substance abuse disorders in LMIC has shown that the delivery of mental health services by nonmental health professionals in primary care and community-based settings can be an effective strategy for meeting this treatment need (van Ginneken et al., 2013) (see Chapter 2).

4.3.1 Apprenticeship training

Building the capacity of nonmental health professionals to provide mental health services in LMIC settings is an implementation challenge that requires thinking about the training needs not only from a one-time didactic training point of view but also from an ongoing perspective of professional development.

To do this, Murray et al. (2011) developed an apprenticeship model to support intervention implementation fidelity and quality. The apprenticeship model is a generalized approach to training psychotherapy interventions, rather than a training model for a particular evidence-based therapy. This model, which we have successfully used in multiple RCTs (Bolton, Bass, et al., 2014; Bolton, Lee, et al., 2014; Murray et al., 2015), relies on three main roles: (1) trainers, experts in the mental health intervention who typically are from outside the project area; (2) supervisors, local individuals with prior counseling experience or who demonstrate aptitude for an advanced clinical role; and (3) counselors, local individuals, usually with no prior mental health experience and often limited formal education (e.g., high school), who actually provide the mental health intervention to clients. In contrast to trainings conducted with mental health professionals in high-income contexts, trainings in the apprenticeship model include simplification of materials, more skilled rehearsal (e.g., role-plays), cultural modifications, and modifications to address contextual challenges. Training highlights active learning and quickly transitions from didactic instruction to practice: a relatively brief (e.g., 8–10 days) training delivered in person with additional training for supervisors, followed by practice groups where counselors role-play skills under observation of the supervisor, followed by completion of 1–2 practice cases in which the intervention is delivered to real clients by counselors who do not yet have an active caseload. Only after successful completion of these initial cases is the counselor ready to take on a regular client caseload. This process supports the concept that initial training is necessary but not sufficient in building the skill level of providers and that supervision is one of the most critical factors for effective implementation (Herschell, Kolko, Baumann, & Davis, 2010). While this process has been implemented with lay workers, community health providers, and nonmental health professionals, it has not been rigorously evaluated to identify the time and resources needed for different types of providers to reach a level of skill and fidelity indicative of a sustainable program.

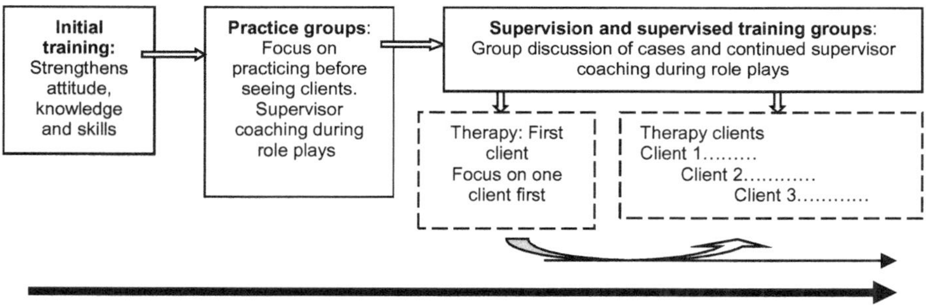

4.4 Integrating interventions into existing systems

In LMIC, the infrastructure for delivery of psychotherapy often does not exist, and therefore, integrating these services into existing priority health-care platforms such as primary health care, maternal care, HIV care, and other noncommunicable disease (NCD) programs is suggested (Patel et al., 2013) (see Chapter 13). Integration of interventions for common mental health problems such as depression, anxiety, and alcohol and substance abuse disorders into priority health-care platforms is logical because (a) these mental disorders are highly prevalent and contribute greatly to the global burden of disease; (b) these mental disorders frequently are accompanied by comorbid acute and chronic medical conditions; and (c) frequently, the outcome of care for medical conditions is linked with mental health outcomes in patients with comorbidity and vice versa. The sections below describe some examples of implementation research leading to integration of interventions for common mental health disorders into priority health-care platforms.

4.4.1 Integrating into primary care

Primary health care (PHC) systems are the mainstay of treatment for priority health conditions in many settings globally (Regier et al., 1993). Evidence suggests that the PHC system may be one of the most appropriate platforms for the integration of psychotherapeutic interventions in LMIC and HIC alike for a number of reasons: (a) the PHC system is often community-based, allowing treatment to reach populations at a grass-root level; (b) the PHC model is frequently "patient-centered," lending itself to providing individualized psychotherapy care; (c) the PHC systems are often staffed by clinicians and community health workers, with the latter available to be trained in psychotherapy interventions; and (d) the PHC approach is not specialty service focused, reducing the potential for stigma related to accessing care for mental health problems that might be experienced if services were at mental health specific centers (Patel et al., 2013).

Integration of care, including psychotherapy, for mental health conditions in the PHC platform is in line with the global goals for development such as universal health coverage (UHC) to increase equitable access to quality health-care services worldwide (World Health Organization, 2010) and is recommended by the WHO mental health gap action program (mhGAP) to bridge the treatment gap for mental health in low-resource settings (World Health Organization, 2017). However, a number of barriers to sustainable integration in low-resource settings exist, including the lack of trained human resource; the lack of case identification mechanisms in community settings; and the lack of training, supervision and monitoring at scale, and sustainability (Saraceno et al., 2007). Other limitations include limited evidence based on the effectiveness and cost-effectiveness of scale-up; integrated psychological intervention programs; weak, fragile, overburdened primary health-care systems; high staff turnover rates; and poor financing and governance issues in PHC systems of low-resource settings globally. Implementation strategies and innovations to integrate psychological interventions in PHC system have the potential to bridge the treatment gap for priority mental health conditions in low-resource settings. While there is a risk to overburden an already weak PHC systems by integration of mental health care, there is a possibility of system strengthening as well (Davies & Lund, 2017).

The last decade has seen concerted efforts by the global mental health community and research funders such as the US National Institute of Mental Health (NIMH), the European Commission (EC), the UK Department for International Development (DFID), Grand Challenges Canada, and the Wellcome Trust to address the "real-world" barriers to the scale-up of evidence-based psychological interventions in low-resource settings (Collins, Insel, Chockalingam, Daar, & Maddox, 2013; Davies & Lund, 2017). Although conclusive evidence for the effectiveness and cost-effectiveness of scaled-up services for mental health remains patchy, key insights obtained from implementation research projects highlight the need to integrate mental health services into primary health-care system by collaboratively engaging local stakeholders using participatory methods such as theory of change (ToC) workshops to inform program development and implementation (Breuer et al., 2015), improving access to target population through collaborative care (CC) models, and using the PHC systems to identify vulnerable individuals in need of mental health service.

Psychotherapy implementation in humanitarian settings, where systems are fragile and fragmented, has its unique dimensions. Providing evidence-based psychological therapies integrated in PHC systems in postconflict or humanitarian contexts

Box 4.1 Providing psychological support to adults impaired by psychological distress in postconflict setting of Pakistan: WHO Problem Management Plus (PM+) program.

Settings: Peri-urban primary health care (PHC) centers in a postconflict setting.
Target population: Adults impaired by psychological distress post humanitarian crisis.
Psychological intervention: WHO Problem Management Plus (PM+) program.
Intervention strategies: Motivational interviewing techniques, basic stress management strategy (slow breathing), problem-solving techniques, behavioral activation, stress management, and strengthening social support networks.
Implementation strategies: Formative research was conducted to adapt the intervention to suit the local context; stakeholder buy in through consultation meetings and integration in primary health-care systems; the psychological intervention was delivered by nonspecialist health workers; cascade model of training, supervision, and monitoring was employed.
Findings: The intervention was feasible, acceptable, and effective and resulted in improvement in depression and anxiety scores. The gains were sustained after 3 months of treatment.

provides additional challenges. Box 4.1 illustrates a case study that used nonspecialist health-care providers, integrated in the PHC system to provide mental health and psychosocial support in a postconflict setting of Pakistan (Rahman et al., 2016).

4.4.2 Integrating into maternal and child health care platforms

Psychotherapies for maternal depression are ideally suited for integration in maternal and child health platforms. The World Health Organization defines maternal mental health as "a state of well-being in which a mother realizes her own abilities, can cope with the normal stresses of life, can work productively and fruitfully and is able to make a contribution to her community" (Herrman et al., 2005). Depressive symptoms in pregnant women and mothers are associated with preterm birth, low birth weight (Grote et al., 2010), undernutrition in the first year of life (Surkan, Kennedy, Hurley, & Black, 2011), higher rates of diarrhea, and early cessation of breastfeeding (Wachs, Black, & Engle, 2009). Maternal depression adversely impacts the long-term cognitive and socioemotional development in children and has a profound intergenerational impact (Wachs et al., 2009). The economic burden of depression in pregnant and postnatal women not only includes the cost of treating depression but also includes the cost of complications, such as preterm birth and low birth weight (Grote et al., 2010). This strong body of evidence has been used to make the case for integration of psychotherapies for maternal depression into maternal and child health platforms (Rahman et al., 2013).

Baker-Henningham, Powell, Walker, and Grantham-McGregor (2005) integrated maternal mental health program in a nutrition and positive parenting program. The program resulted in decline in depressive symptoms in mothers and improved development quotient (DQ) in boys at 1 year following intervention ($n=139$ mother-infant dyads) (Baker-Henningham et al., 2005). Rahman, Malik, Sikander, Roberts, and Creed (2008) integrated maternal mental health program into a community health program in two rural subdistricts of Pakistan. The manualized Thinking Healthy Program (THP) incorporated cognitive behavioral techniques for postnatal depression in women, aged 16–45 years in third trimester of pregnancy ($n=903$). The program resulted in decreased incidence of depression, improved perceived social support, and improved infant health and development outcomes at 6–12 months postpartum (Rahman et al., 2008). Cooper et al. (2009) integrated maternal mental health program into a child development program that resulted in lower prevalence of depression, improved mother-infant interaction, and infant attachment outcomes at 6–12 months ($n=449$) (Cooper et al., 2009). These studies were conducted in different regions of the world and employed different implementation strategies of task shifting, integration, and intervention adaptation to suit inner and outer contexts. Integration of psychotherapies in these platforms needs careful adaptation to suit the local context. Box 4.2 illustrates a case study about the integration of WHO Thinking Health Program into the community health program in rural Pakistan.

The issues in scaling up the coverage of maternal mental health interventions include the costs, equity and quality concerns and service delivery issues including training, and supervision and monitoring of nonspecialist health force at scale

Box 4.2 Case study: WHO Thinking Healthy Program integration in Mother and Child Health (MCH) Program.

Settings: Rural community settings of Pakistan.
Target population: Mothers with postnatal depression.
Psychological intervention: Thinking Healthy Program (THP) delivered by community health workers (CHWs).
Intervention strategies: CBT, improving family support, empathic listening, guided discovery using pictures, behavioral activation, and problem-solving.
Implementation strategies: Integration of THP into existing work pattern of the community health workers (CHWs); simplifying CBT strategies, using pictures and stories to communicate key intervention messages; using "child development" as an agenda to ensure family buy-in and common elements treatment approach including family support, empathic listening, behavioral activation, and problem-solving were added to increase adoption and integration of THP.
Implications: The intervention was designed to be integrated into the routine work of the CHWs. The training was short (2 days followed by a 1-day refresher after 4 months) and therefore feasible on a large scale. Regular and reliable training and half-day group supervision were considered essential for the success of community health worker-based program.

(Mangham & Hanson, 2010). The limited number of specialist services for maternal mental health in LMIC (Van Damme, Kober, & Kegels, 2008) is magnified in humanitarian crisis settings (Mollica et al., 2004). Development and evaluation of technology-assisted training and supervision platforms offer potential opportunities to assist scale-up of integrated, evidence-based interventions for maternal mental health in fragile, low-resource community settings (Zafar et al., 2016).

4.4.3 Integration of mental health care into HIV care program

Grand challenges in global mental health (Collins et al., 2011) emphasized the need to integrate care for mental, neurological, and substance use (MNS) disorders with other chronic disease care models. HIV treatment and care programs offer one such opportunity of integration. This opportunity is based on a number of synergies including common socioeconomic adversities such as poverty and stigma experienced by people with HIV and with mental health problems (Collins, Holman, Freeman, & Patel, 2006), the chronic debilitating nature of mental health problems and HIV (Sherbourne et al., 2000; Patel et al., 2009), the association of HIV prevalence with neurocognitive disorders (HAND), and cooccurring depression and alcohol abuse disorders. Comorbid MNS disorders in people with HIV are associated with poor adherence to antiretroviral therapies (ARTs), poor treatment outcomes, and poor quality of life (Kaaya et al., 2013).

Psychotherapies, including cognitive behavioral therapy (CBT), interpersonal therapy (IPT), and problem-solving therapy (PST), have been evaluated for effectiveness in people with HIV in LMIC and HIC (Himelhoch, Medoff, & Oyeniyi, 2007). Evidence suggests that these psychotherapies can be delivered by nonspecialist health workers to reduce depression symptom severity; increase coping, social support, and self-esteem; and improve health-related behavior change and adherence to ARTs in people with HIV. Similar effective psychotherapeutic interventions exist for hazardous alcohol use in HIV (Chibanda et al., 2011). Group psychotherapy interventions in HIV-positive individuals with depressive symptoms have demonstrated a moderate effect size (Himelhoch et al., 2007). Similar findings on the effectiveness of cognitive behavioral therapies (CBTs) for treatment of common mental disorders (CMDs) in people with HIV have been reported by Crepaz et al. (2008).

Although there is good evidence for cooccurrence of MNS disorders with HIV and existence of effective psychotherapeutic intervention strategies, there is little evidence to demonstrate the effectiveness of integration of care for MNS disorders within HIV care at scale. Box 4.3 describes a case study of integration of care for depression in people with HIV, in the primary health-care settings in Zimbabwe (Chibanda et al., 2011).

Integration of care for CMDs in HIV care programs holds much promise. Historically, HIV care programs have been organized as vertical programs, but recently,

Box 4.3 A task-shifting primary mental health-care intervention in a population with a high prevalence of people living with HIV—The Friendship Bench.

Settings: Primary health-care settings in Zimbabwe.
Target population: 395 HIV-positive adults with common mental disorders (CMDs).
Psychological intervention: Problem-solving therapy (PST) (problem identification, problems exploration, action plan, implementation, and follow-up). Six weekly sessions of 30–45 min delivered through the Friendship Bench.
Implementation strategies: Task shifting and integration into PHC settings, 2-week training of lay health workers before onset of Friendship Bench. Ongoing training every 2 weeks for the first 6 months, thereafter monthly. Weekly 1 h group supervision by a general nurse with training in counseling. Group supervision from a clinical psychologist 1 h every 2 weeks and group supervision by a psychiatrist every 4 weeks, 45 min.
Implications: Clinically meaningful improvement in CMD associated with locally adapted problem-solving therapy delivered by lay health workers through routine primary health care in an African setting.

there has been an increased realization to integrate HIV care with other priority health programs to promote "whole patient approach" to care and increase coverage and cost-effectiveness of such programs. Such an approach to integration of HIV care is in line with the principles of "grand challenges" in global mental health that emphasizes the use of a life course approach, use of evidence-based intervention strategies, understanding the role of context, and use of systems' approach to integration of care for priority mental health conditions (Kaaya et al., 2013).

The availability of evidence-based psychological intervention packages and emergence of implementation research frameworks in global mental health have made it possible to begin to scale-up care for mental health integrated in the HIV care platforms. Such integration provides the opportunity for holistic care for MNS in people with HIV in the form of early identification and implementation of effective intervention strategies along a life-course approach. The evidence for feasibility and acceptability for such integration exists; however, further research on scaled-up model of integration is needed.

4.4.4 Collaborative care models

The last decade has witnessed an increase in global mental health research leading to the development of evidence-based intervention packages that can potentially be integrated into existing health systems (Patel & Thornicroft, 2009) (see Chapter 8). The question now facing the global mental health community is "how can mental health care be made available at scale to populations with systems that have neither the means nor the expertise to deliver it (Eaton et al., 2011)?" The need for implementation research in low-income countries (LICs) has been highlighted (Sanders & Haines, 2006), but conventional health services research has been unable to overcome the challenges limiting mental health service scale-up.

A promising strategy in such low-resource settings is the "collaborative care models." In a collaborative care model, the role of specialist health-care provider is restructured, and a team-based approach to the management of complex mental health problems is introduced. Task sharing—"specialists supporting the nonspecialists"—in the delivery of psychotherapy care for mental health has proved to be an effective implementation strategy in collaborative care models in low-resource settings. Specific tasks are moved from specialists to nonspecialists who are trained over a shorter period of time and deliver services under the supervision of specialists. In task sharing, specialists build capacity of nonspecialists, ensure quality of service delivery, and offer a referral pathway when needed (Community Preventive Services Task Force, 2012; Gilbody, Bower, & Whitty, 2006; Glied, Herzog, & Frank, 2010; Thota et al., 2012).

While evidence on the feasibility, acceptability, and effectiveness of collaborative care model in the treatment of adult CMDs in LMIC exists (van Ginneken et al., 2013), similar evidence for child mental health problems is scarce. However, community-based nonspecialist lay health workers can be a potential source of delivery of psychosocial interventions for child mental health at scale (Reichow, Volkmar, &

Box 4.4 Integrated model of service delivery for children with developmental disorders in low-resource settings.

Settings: Community-based "family networks".
Target population: Caregivers of children with developmental disorders.
Psychological intervention: WHO caregiver skills training (CST) program for children with developmental disorders and delays (psychoeducation, daily life skills training, behavioral management, supporting communication, problem-solving skills, and self-care for caregivers).
Implementation strategies: Technology-assisted task shifting-technology-assisted identification, training, supervision, and monitoring of "champion family volunteers;" community-based "family networks" to support caregivers in the delivery of intervention; embedded within the implementation of WHO mhGAP program (collaborative care) in PHC settings; social franchise model to "box up" the program for scale-up.
Implications: The whole field of global mental health suffers from implementation bottlenecks. Integrated, innovative solutions from social, technological, and business domains will need to be incorporated into the framework of implementation research to make scale-up of psychotherapeutic interventions a real possibility in global mental health.

Bloch, 2013). Hamdani, Minhas, Iqbal, and Rahman (2015) reported an integrated, innovative, group-based, peer-mediated parent training for caregivers of children with developmental disorders in Pakistan. The program led to improvement in children's disability and socioemotional difficulties, reduction in stigmatizing experiences, and enhanced family empowerment to seek services and community resources for the child (Hamdani et al., 2015) (Box 4.4).

Barry, Clarke, Jenkins, and Patel (2013) systematically evaluated the effectiveness of interventions promoting the mental health of young people and concluded that mental health promotion interventions can be implemented effectively in LMIC school and community settings by peers, teachers, and nonspecialist lay health workers. However, the study highlighted the need for evidence on scale-up and sustainability of child and adolescent mental health promotion interventions in LMIC.

Bridging the treatment gap for mental health in low-resource settings is a challenge. Research from LMIC demonstrates that the collaborative care model can be extended by including nonspecialist health force in the delivery of evidence-based psychological interventions. A cascaded model of training, supervision, and monitoring between specialist, nonspecialist primary health-care workers, and lay health workers is feasible, acceptable, and effective (Murray et al., 2011). Although the evidence on the sustainability and scale-up of such models is still emerging, the integration of collaborative care models within existing care systems offers potentially financially feasible, sustainable, and scalable solutions to bridge the treatment gap in low-resource settings.

4.5 Human and financial costs associated with different delivery models

Human, financial, and physical resources are needed to deliver evidence-based mental health interventions at scale. The magnitude of resources needed to scale-up psychotherapy services is determined by the prevalence of the target mental health conditions, the population in need, and the desired coverage level. A frequently missing piece in dissemination and implementation research in global mental health is research on the human and financial costs associated with different delivery models. Although health economic evaluations of mental health services scale-up is a cornerstone of implementation research frameworks in global mental health, literature on estimates of resource needs for scale-up of mental health service in LMIC is limited to a few studies. Chisholm et al. (2016) evaluated the resources needed to scale-up WHO mhGAP IG-based packages of care at district level in five LMIC. The cost of delivering integrated mental health care in primary and maternal and child care platforms at district level ranged from US$0.21 to 0.56 per head of population in four LMIC districts. The per head cost was higher in the higher-income context of South Africa (US$1.86). In all five districts, the incremental cost to reach target coverage goals in 10 years was estimated at less than US$0.10 per head of population. In a similar study, Buttorff et al. (2012) conducted cost utility and cost-effectiveness analyses of a task-shifting intervention for the treatment of depressive and anxiety disorders in 24 public and private primary care facilities in Goa, India. In the intervention arm, lay health workers provided psychoeducation, case management, interpersonal psychotherapy, and/or antidepressants to the participants. In the control arm, routine care was provided to the study participants by physicians. The authors concluded that lay-health-worker-administered care for CMDs was cost-effective and also cost-saving in public primary care facilities.

Innovations to scale-up care for mental health such as use of technology can reduce the costs for service delivery at scale dramatically. In a study by Hamdani et al. (2015), the cost of identifying a child with developmental disorders in community setting using an interactive voice response technology was US$0.07, compared with a cost of US$7.0 of identifying a child through a house-to-house survey.

Developing and feasibility testing of business models to ensure sustainability and scale-up of evidence-based psychological interventions have been reported in the literature (http://www.basicneeds.org/social-franchise/; Hamdani et al., 2015) and should be part of any implementation research in global mental health.

Lastly, the task-sharing strategies in global mental health have their own health economics implications. The current published health economics literature in global mental health is limited to direct health-care costs and health-related outcomes for a particular intervention. It does not typically include the nonhealth or wider economic or social value of investing in mental health, long-term benefits of reducing psychological distress, protection from chronicity of disorder, and relapse prevention that may be quite significant for a condition in a given context. Going forward, health economic evaluations in global mental health will benefit by integrating the opportunity and time cost of peers, caregivers, and nonspecialist lay health workers and the value that accompanies such task-sharing implementation strategies in terms of empowerment, opportunities, and career growth for nonspecialist health work force in low-resource settings globally.

4.6 Conclusion

Research has shown that psychotherapy treatment for common mental health problems can be provided with quality and fidelity in settings that lack formal mental health-care services and formally trained mental health professionals. Trials have been completed showing that these treatments can be efficacious in reducing symptom severity compared with control or other comparison conditions. The field of implementation science is providing a formalized approach to investigating how to translate the results of these trials into programmatic strategies that can be scaled up in order to broadly reach populations in need of mental health services. While implementation strategies such as task-sharing approaches, apprenticeship models of training and supervision, and integrated and collaborative care models provide the basis by which intervention dissemination can be realized, challenges remain in how to sustain these strategies and ensure quality service delivery. These challenges are not unique to low-resource settings, but the resource limitations intrinsic to these contexts make the task of sustainability more difficult to achieve. Technological innovations and community-based strategies that harness local capital will need to be utilized if we are to continue to reduce the mental health treatment gap.

References

Aarons, G. A., Hurlburt, M., & Horwitz, S. M. (2011). Advancing a conceptual model of evidence-based practice implementation in public service sectors. *Administration and Policy in Mental Health*, *38*(1), 4–23.

Baker-Henningham, H., Powell, C., Walker, S., & Grantham-McGregor, S. (2005). The effect of early stimulation on maternal depression: A cluster randomised controlled trial. *Archives of Disease in Childhood*, *90*(12), 1230–1234.

Barry, M. M., Clarke, A. M., Jenkins, R., & Patel, V. (2013). A systematic review of the effectiveness of mental health promotion interventions for young people in low and middle income countries. *BMC Public Health*, *13*(1), 835.

Bass, J. K., Annan, J., McIvor Murray, S., Kaysen, D., Griffiths, S., Cetinoglu, T., et al. (2013). Controlled trial of psychotherapy for Congolese survivors of sexual violence. *New England Journal of Medicine*, *368*(23), 2182–2191.

Bolton, P., Bass, J. K., Zangana, G. A., Kamal, T., Murray, S. M., Kaysen, D., et al. (2014). A randomized controlled trial of mental health interventions for survivors of systematic violence in Kurdistan, Northern Iraq. *BMC Psychiatry*, *14*, 360.

Bolton, P., Lee, C., Haroz, E. E., Murray, L., Dorsey, S., Robinson, C., et al. (2014). A transdiagnostic community-based mental health treatment for comorbid disorders: Development and outcomes of a randomized controlled trial among Burmese refugees in Thailand. *PLoS Medicine*, *11*(11).

Breuer, E., De Silva, M. J., Shidaye, R., Petersen, I., Nakku, J., Jordans, M. J., et al. (2015). Planning and evaluating mental health services in low-and middle-income countries using theory of change. *British Journal of Psychiatry*, https://doi.org/10.1192/bjp.bp.114.153841.

Buttorff, C., Hock, R. S., Weiss, H. A., Naik, S., Araya, R., Kirkwood, B. R., et al. (2012). Economic evaluation of a task-shifting intervention for common mental disorders in India. *Bulletin of the World Health Organization*, *90*(11), 813–821.

Chibanda, D., Mesu, P., Kajawu, L., Cowan, F., Araya, R., & Abas, M. A. (2011). Problem-solving therapy for depression and common mental disorders in Zimbabwe: Piloting a task-shifting primary mental health care intervention in a population with a high prevalence of people living with HIV. *BMC Public Health*, *11*(1), 828.

Chisholm, D., Burman-Roy, S., Fekadu, A., Kathree, T., Kizza, D., Luitel, N. P., et al. (2016). Estimating the cost of implementing district mental healthcare plans in five low- and middle-income countries: The PRIME study. *British Journal of Psychiatry*, *208*(Suppl. 56), s71–s78.

Collins, P. Y., Holman, A. R., Freeman, M. C., & Patel, V. (2006). What is the relevance of mental health to HIV/AIDS care and treatment programs in developing countries? A systematic review. *AIDS (London, England)*, *20*(12), 1571.

Collins, P. Y., Insel, T. R., Chockalingam, A., Daar, A., & Maddox, Y. T. (2013). Grand challenges in global mental health: Integration in research, policy, and practice. *PLoS Medicine*, *10*(4).

Collins, P. Y., Patel, V., Joestl, S. S., March, D., Insel, T. R., Daar, A. S., et al. (2011). Grand challenges in global mental health. *Nature*, *475*(7354), 27.

Community Preventive Services Task Force (2012). Recommendation from the community preventive services task force for use of collaborative care for the management of depressive disorders. *American Journal of Preventive Medicine*, *42*(5), 521–524.

Cooper, P. J., Tomlinson, M., Swartz, L., Landman, M., Molteno, C., Stein, A., et al. (2009). Improving quality of mother-infant relationship and infant attachment in socioeconomically deprived community in South Africa: Randomised controlled trial. *BMJ*, *338*, b974.

Crepaz, N., Passin, W. F., Herbst, J. H., Rama, S. M., Malow, R. M., Purcell, D. W., et al. (2008). Meta-analysis of cognitive-behavioral interventions on HIV-positive persons' mental health and immune functioning. *Health Psychology*, *27*(1), 4.

Damschroder, L. J., Aron, D. C., Keith, R. E., Kirsh, S. R., Alexander, J. A., & Lowery, J. C. (2009). Fostering implementation of health services research findings into practice: A consolidated framework for advancing implementation science. *Implementation Science*, *4*, 50.

Davies, T., & Lund, C. (2017). Integrating mental health care into primary care systems in low-and middle-income countries: Lessons from PRIME and AFFIRM. *Global Mental Health*, *4*.

Eaton, J., McCay, L., Semrau, M., Chatterjee, S., Baingana, F., Araya, R., et al. (2011). Scale up of services for mental health in low-income and middle-income countries. *Lancet*, *378* (9802), 1592–1603.

Gilbody, S., Bower, P., & Whitty, P. (2006). Costs and consequences of enhanced primary care for depression: Systematic review of randomised economic evaluations. *British Journal of Psychiatry*, *189*(4), 297–308.

Glied, S., Herzog, K., & Frank, R. (2010). Review: The net benefits of depression Management in Primary Care. *Medical Care Research and Review*, *67*(3), 251–274.

Grote, N. K., Bridge, J. A., Gavin, A. R., Melville, J. L., Iyengar, S., & Katon, W. J. (2010). A meta-analysis of depression during pregnancy and the risk of preterm birth, low birth weight, and intrauterine growth restriction. *Archives of General Psychiatry*, *67*(10), 1012–1024.

Hamdani, S. U., Minhas, F. A., Iqbal, Z., & Rahman, A. (2015). Model for service delivery for developmental disorders in low-income countries. *Pediatrics*, *136*(6), 1166–1172.

Herrman, H., Saxena, S., Moodie, R., & World Health Organization (2005). *Promoting mental health: Concepts, emerging evidence, practice: A report of the World Health Organization, Department of Mental Health and Substance Abuse in collaboration with the Victorian Health Promotion Foundation and the University of Melbourne.*

Herschell, A. D., Kolko, D. J., Baumann, B. L., & Davis, A. C. (2010). The role of therapist training in the implementation of psychosocial treatments: A review and critique with recommendations. *Clinical Psychology Review*, *30*(4), 448–466.

Himelhoch, S., Medoff, D. R., & Oyeniyi, G. (2007). Efficacy of group psychotherapy to reduce depressive symptoms among HIV-infected individuals: A systematic review and meta-analysis. *AIDS Patient Care and STDs*, *21*(10), 732–739.

Kaaya, S., Eustache, E., Lapidos-Salaiz, I., Musisi, S., Psaros, C., & Wissow, L. (2013). Grand challenges: Improving HIV treatment outcomes by integrating interventions for co-morbid mental illness. *PLoS Medicine*, *10*(5).

Kakuma, R., Minas, H., van Ginneken, N., Dal Poz, M. R., Desiraju, K., Morris, J. E., et al. (2011). Human resources for mental health care: Current situation and strategies for action. *Lancet (London, England)*, *378*(9803), 1654–1663.

Mangham, L. J., & Hanson, K. (2010). Scaling up in international health: What are the key issues? *Health Policy and Planning*, *25*(2), 85–96.

Mollica, R. F., Cardozo, B. L., Osofsky, H. J., Raphael, B., Ager, A., & Salama, P. (2004). Mental health in complex emergencies. *Lancet*, *364*(9450), 2058–2067.

Murray, L. K., Dorsey, S., Bolton, P., Jordans, M. J., Rahman, A., Bass, J., et al. (2011). Building capacity in mental health interventions in low resource countries: An apprenticeship model for training local providers. *International Journal of Mental Health Systems*, *5* (1), 30.

Murray, L. K., Skavenski, S., Kane, J. C., Mayeya, J., Dorsey, S., Cohen, J. A., et al. (2015). Effectiveness of trauma-focused cognitive behavioral therapy among trauma-affected children in Lusaka, Zambia: A randomized clinical trial. *JAMA Pediatrics*, *169*(8), 761–769.

Patel, V., Belkin, G. S., Chockalingam, A., Cooper, J., Saxena, S., & Unützer, J. (2013). Grand challenges: Integrating mental health services into priority health care platforms. *PLoS Medicine*, *10*(5).

Patel, R., Kassaye, S., Gore-Felton, C., Wyshak, G., Kadzirange, G., Woelk, G., et al. (2009). Quality of life, psychosocial health, and antiretroviral therapy among HIV-positive women in Zimbabwe. *AIDS Care*, *21*(12), 1517–1527.

Patel, V., & Thornicroft, G. (2009). Packages of care for mental, neurological, and substance use disorders in low-and middle-income countries: PLoS medicine series. *PLoS Medicine*, *6*(10).

Proctor, E. K., Landsverk, J., Aarons, G., Chambers, D., Glisson, C., & Mittman, B. (2009). Implementation research in mental health services: An emerging science with conceptual, methodological, and training challenges. *Administration and Policy in Mental Health*, *36* (1), 24–34.

Rahman, A., Fisher, J., Bower, P., Luchters, S., Tran, T., Yasamy, M. T., et al. (2013). Interventions for common perinatal mental disorders in women in low- and middle-income countries: A systematic review and meta-analysis. *Bulletin of the World Health Organization, 91*(8), 593–601.

Rahman, A., Hamdani, S. U., Awan, N. R., Bryant, R. A., Dawson, K. S., Khan, M. F., et al. (2016). Effect of a multicomponent behavioral intervention in adults impaired by psychological distress in a conflict-affected area of Pakistan: A randomized clinical trial. *Journal of the American Medical Association, 316*(24), 2609–2617.

Rahman, A., Malik, A., Sikander, S., Roberts, C., & Creed, F. (2008). Cognitive behaviour therapy-based intervention by community health workers for mothers with depression and their infants in rural Pakistan: A cluster-randomised controlled trial. *Lancet, 372* (9642), 902–909.

Regier, D. A., Narrow, W. E., Rae, D. S., Manderscheid, R. W., Locke, B. Z., & Goodwin, F. K. (1993). The de facto US mental and addictive disorders service system: Epidemiologic catchment area prospective 1-year prevalence rates of disorders and services. *Archives of General Psychiatry, 50*(2), 85–94.

Reichow, B., Volkmar, F. R., & Bloch, M. H. (2013). Systematic review and meta-analysis of pharmacological treatment of the symptoms of attention-deficit/hyperactivity disorder in children with pervasive developmental disorders. *Journal of Autism and Developmental Disorders, 43*(10), 2435–2441.

Ridde, V. (2016). Need for more and better implementation science in global health. *BMJ Global Health, 1*(2).

Sanders, D., & Haines, A. (2006). Implementation research is needed to achieve international health goals. *PLoS Medicine, 3*(6).

Saraceno, B., van Ommeren, M., Batniji, R., Cohen, A., Gureje, O., Mahoney, J., et al. (2007). Barriers to improvement of mental health services in low-income and middle-income countries. *Lancet, 370*(9593), 1164–1174.

Sherbourne, C. D., Hays, R. D., Fleishman, J. A., Vitiello, B., Magruder, K. M., Bing, E. G., et al. (2000). Impact of psychiatric conditions on health-related quality of life in persons with HIV infection. *American Journal of Psychiatry, 157*(2), 248–254.

Surkan, P. J., Kennedy, C. E., Hurley, K. M., & Black, M. M. (2011). Maternal depression and early childhood growth in developing countries: Systematic review and meta-analysis. *Bulletin of the World Health Organization, 89*(8), 607–615.

Thota, A. B., Sipe, T. A., Byard, G. J., Zometa, C. S., Hahn, R. A., McKnight-Eily, L. R., et al. (2012). Collaborative care to improve the management of depressive disorders: A community guide systematic review and meta-analysis. *American Journal of Preventive Medicine, 42*(5), 525–538.

Van Damme, W., Kober, K., & Kegels, G. (2008). Scaling-up antiretroviral treatment in southern African countries with human resource shortage: How will health systems adapt? *Social Science & Medicine, 66*(10), 2108–2121.

van Ginneken, N., Tharyan, P., Lewin, S., Rao, G. N., Meera, S. M., Pian, J., et al. (2013). Non-specialist health worker interventions for the care of mental, neurological and substance-abuse disorders in low- and middle-income countries. *Cochrane Database of Systematic Reviews, 11*, Cd009149.

Wachs, T. D., Black, M. M., & Engle, P. L. (2009). Maternal depression: A global threat to children's health, development, and behavior and to human rights. *Child Development Perspectives, 3*(1), 51–59.

Weiss, W. M., Murray, L. K., Zangana, G. A., Mahmooth, Z., Kaysen, D., Dorsey, S., et al. (2015). Community-based mental health treatments for survivors of torture and militant attacks in Southern Iraq: A randomized control trial. *BMC Psychiatry, 15*, 249.

World Health Organization (2010). *World Health Report, 2010: Health systems financing the path to universal coverage. World Health Report, 2010: Health systems financing the path to universal coverage.*

World Health Organization (2017). *mhGAP training manuals for the mhGAP intervention guide for mental, neurological and substance use disorders in non-specialized health settings-version 2.0 (for field testing).*

Zafar, S., Sikander, S., Hamdani, S. U., Atif, N., Akhtar, P., Nazir, H., et al. (2016). The effectiveness of technology-assisted cascade training and supervision of community health workers in delivering the thinking healthy program for perinatal depression in a post-conflict area of Pakistan—Study protocol for a randomized controlled trial. *Trials*, *17*(1), 188.

Section B

Globalizing Psychotherapies

Cognitive behavioral therapy around the globe

5

Caroline Kuo
Department of Behavioral and Social Sciences, Brown University School of Public Health, Providence, RI, United States

5.1 Overview of cognitive behavioral therapy

Cognitive behavioral therapy (CBT) is a widely used psychotherapy approach. The core theoretical premise of CBT is that maladaptive ways of thinking and behaving can generate mental and behavioral problems. CBT originally emerged from a combination of Aaron Beck's therapeutic approach called cognitive therapy (Beck, 1970) and Albert Ellis's early work on behavioral therapy (Ellis, 1957). Since these original iterations, CBT has gone through a rapid evolution built on a large number of clinical trials tested in a variety of populations, outcomes, and settings.

In its current iterations, CBT is utilized to treat a large number of mental disorders. These range from depressive and anxiety disorders (Cuijpers, Cristea, Karyotaki, Reijnders, & Huibers, 2016; Jakobsen, Lindschou Hansen, Storebø, Simonsen, & Gluud, 2011; Kaczkurkin & Foa, 2015; Ougrin, 2011) to schizophrenia (Jones, Hacker, Cormac, Meaden, & Irving, 2012). CBT is also utilized to treat behavioral challenges ranging from insomnia (Seyffert et al., 2016; van Beugen et al., 2014) to anger (Henwood, Chou, & Browne, 2015). There are also wide variations in how CBT is applied. For example, CBT therapies can involve problem-solving therapy, mindfulness-based cognitive therapy, dialectical behavior therapy, and many more approaches in various combinations and delivery modalities (Gaudiano, 2008).

Thus, in its current form, CBT should not be conceived of as one singular approach. Rather, CBT represents a large body of related interventions using a therapeutic approach with common elements. These elements include a focus on developing ways of recognizing maladaptive thinking and behaviors and then building skills for positive coping to alleviate mental distress and problem behaviors. Changing maladaptive cognitive and behavioral patterns using CBT often incorporates goal-oriented therapy and some form of talk-based therapy. This chapter describes evidence on the efficacy of CBT generally and in low- and middle-income country (LMIC) settings. Then, a conceptual model for adapting empirically supported CBT models in LMIC settings is presented.

Global Mental Health and Psychotherapy. https://doi.org/10.1016/B978-0-12-814932-4.00005-7

5.2 Evidence on efficacy of cognitive behavioral therapy

The appeal of CBT is fourfold. First, as a therapeutic approach, CBT can be captured in manual-based protocols to facilitate standardized, high-quality, and consistent delivery. Second, CBT can be delivered by a wide range of practitioners, ranging from clinical specialists to well-trained and supervised lay providers (Kraus-Schuman et al., 2015; Patel, Chowdhary, Rahman, & Verdeli, 2011). The use of well-trained and supervised lay providers holds great promise for meeting the mental health gap in LMIC. Third, CBT can be adapted to a wide range of modalities ranging from the more traditional approaches of in-person delivery via one-to-one therapy and group-based therapy to phone- and internet-based delivery (Fann et al., 2015; Farrer, Christensen, Griffiths, & Mackinnon, 2011; Gratzer & Khalid-Khan, 2016). Fourth and most importantly, there is a large body of evidence supporting the efficacy of CBT. This body of evidence has catalyzed the uptake of CBT as one of the most widely used forms of psychotherapy across the globe.

A pivotal and comprehensive review aggregated evidence from 106 existing meta-analyses to determine the efficacy of CBT for a wide range of populations. The review examined the strength of CBT evidence for outcomes including substance use disorder, schizophrenia and other psychotic disorders, depression and dysthymia, bipolar disorder, anxiety disorders, somatoform disorders, eating disorders, insomnia, personality disorders, anger and aggression, criminal behaviors, general stress, distress due to general medical conditions, chronic pain and fatigue, distress related to pregnancy complications, and female hormonal conditions. The review concluded that "the evidence base of CBT is very strong" (Hofmann, Asnaani, Vonk, Sawyer, & Fang, 2012).

Recent meta-analyses of CBT—all conducted in the past 5 years for various outcomes—provide further indication of CBT as an efficacious approach. These meta-analyses also demonstrate that the existing evidence base on CBT continues to grow rapidly in terms of size and strength. As a whole, the evidence base on CBT provides strong data supporting the efficacy of CBT for a diverse spectrum of treatment targets (e.g., anxiety disorders, bipolar disorder, migraines, and insomnia), populations (e.g., children and adults), and using a range of comparator groups (e.g., active control, waiting list, placebo, and no treatment) (Adelman, Panza, Bartley, Bontempo, & Bloch, 2014; Chiang et al., 2017; Montero-Marin, Garcia-Campayo, López-Montoyo, Zabaleta-Del-Olmo, & Cuijpers, 2017; Ng, Venkatanarayanan, & Kumar, 2017; van Straten et al., 2017; Wang et al., 2017). Despite the wealth of CBT evidence—including evidence that supports the efficacy of CBT for a wide range of outcomes and populations—the existing literature must be evaluated with care when considering its applicability to LMIC settings.

In LMIC, there is a significant treatment gap. The most recent Global Burden of Disease Study from 2010 estimated that LMIC bear three-quarters of the burden of global mental, neurological, and substance disorders (Murray et al., 2012). Yet, the majority (75%) of people with mental disorders in LMIC lack access to care (World Health Organization, 2017). This treatment gap reflects low investment in mental health spending in these settings. For example, the World Health

Organization's Mental Health Atlas report estimated that low-income countries spend just $0.20 per capita on mental health. Middle-income countries spend only marginally more, at $0.59 per capita on mental health (World Health Organization, 2011). This treatment gap also reflects differences in health systems and human resource capacity. For example, in low-income countries, the median rates of mental health professionals per 100,000 population are as follows: 0.1 psychiatrists; 0.0 psychologists, social workers, and occupational therapists; and 0.2 other mental health workers (World Health Organization, 2009).

Task shifting—or the process of training and supervising lay providers for use in certain forms of mental health treatment and prevention—is a key strategy for addressing global mental health resource challenges (Saraceno et al., 2007). Task shifting may be particularly appropriate for CBT, which can be implemented by a range of providers. Thus far, studies indicate that task shifting is an effective strategy for mental health delivery in LMIC (Chibanda et al., 2011; Kakuma et al., 2011; Patel et al., 2010). Strengthening human capacity and health systems will require these types of innovations and others to develop novel new forms of mental health delivery to fill the treatment gap. Finally, this treatment gap reflects a need for resource reallocation, stronger political will, and the creation of a facilitating legislative environment that promotes strategies to close the treatment gap (Rathod et al., 2017). Against the backdrop of high burden of mental disorders and correspondingly high unmet need in LMIC, the use of CBT holds great promise. However, several patterns in the existing evidence base for CBT give pause for concern in the potential application of existing evidence to these settings without first evaluating whether adaptation is needed. First, the existing CBT evidence base is geographically biased. The vast majority of existing CBT evidence has been generated from randomized controlled trials (RCTs) in high-income countries. For example, in a 2016 global meta-analysis of 144 RCTs that examined the efficacy of CBT for four common mental disorders (major depression, generalized anxiety disorder, panic disorder, and social anxiety disorder), only 8 RCTs (0.05 %) occurred outside of North America, European countries, Australia, East Asia, and the United Kingdom (Cuijpers et al., 2016). Second, there is relatively limited knowledge of how CBT may perform in socioeconomic and racially/ethnically diverse subgroups compared with middle-class and white study populations (Hofmann et al., 2012). Combined, these two factors introduce doubt regarding whether evidence can be transported to socioeconomic and racially/ethnically diverse populations in LMIC where contextual factors such as health systems, human resource shortages, and cultural differences may be very different (Hofmann et al., 2012).

5.3 Cognitive behavioral therapy evidence in low- and middle-income countries

In an ideal scenario, original CBT treatment models should be developed and tested for use in LMIC. A search of PubMed was conducted to identify existing CBT research in LMIC. This search focused on RCTs and quasi-randomized study designs.

The search protocol involved the use of Boolean operators combining the following key terms and variations: cognitive therapy (MeSH), randomized controlled trial (MeSH), and existing Cochrane search terms for LMIC based on World Bank Country classifications (The Cochrane Group, 2012). CBT interventions for any outcome were included. Furthermore, intervention studies were included if they met the following criteria: (1) CBT was used as the primary component of the intervention component or as one component of the intervention approach, (2) and the intervention was tested in LMIC, as defined by the World Bank. The search did not set any date restrictions but included English-only full-text articles. The initial search resulted in 249 citations excluding 8 duplicates. Full-text review was conducted on these citations. Based on the previously defined criteria, 110 citations failed to meet search parameters, resulting in a final inclusion of 139 citations. These 139 citations represent 136 unique interventions tested in LMIC.

An analysis of the 139 citations detailing CBT treatment models that have been tested in LMIC revealed several themes. First, this body of evidence is proportionally smaller in number compared with the body of evidence of CBT treatment models developed in high-income country settings (e.g., compared with the meta-analyses detailed previously). The 136 unique interventions were tested in a wide range of LMIC including China ($n=30$), Iraq ($n=15$), Pakistan ($n=11$), South Korea ($n=10$), Thailand ($n=9$), Brazil ($n=6$), Turkey ($n=4$), India ($n=4$), Democratic Republic of the Congo ($n=4$), Mexico ($n=4$), South Africa ($n=4$), Chile ($n=3$), Nigeria ($n=3$), Egypt ($n=3$), Uganda ($n=3$), Greece ($n=2$), Malaysia ($n=2$), Romania ($n=2$), Myanmar ($n=1$), Malta ($n=1$), Nepal ($n=1$), Cuba ($n=1$), Ghana ($n=1$), Jordan ($n=1$), Kenya ($n=1$), Kosovo ($n=1$), Palestine ($n=1$), Russia ($n=1$), Saudi Arabia ($n=1$), Sierra Leone ($n=1$), Sri Lanka ($n=1$), Trinidad and Tobago ($n=1$), Venezuela ($n=1$), and Zambia ($n=1$). The largest proportion of intervention trials occurred in China (22%). However, many LMIC were completely unrepresented in this evidence base. The interventions targeted a wide range of outcomes with the most dominant target outcomes consisting of depression, anxiety, or both (30%). A quarter of the interventions tested (26%) were explicitly adapted from models developed outside of the setting (typically high-income country settings) (see details in Table 5.1).

In general, the body of evidence of CBT interventions in LMIC is growing in size and holds great promise for guiding the use of CBT treatment models in LMIC populations. However, the comparative paucity of evidence on CBT treatment models in LMIC reflects global disparities in the mental health research. A selective review examining the global distribution of RCTs for mental health interventions revealed that just 3% ($n=176$ trials) of RCTs occurred in LMIC (Sheriff, Adams, Tharyan, Jayaram, & Duley, 2008). Indeed, developing parity in investment in mental health research was identified as a grand challenge in a Delphi panel that aggregated views from 422 mental health experts representing 60 countries in a Grand Challenges in Global Mental Health initiative published in *Nature* (Collins et al., 2011). In spite of the uneven geographic distribution of the evidence base on psychological interventions globally, important insights have emerged from work on CBTs in LMIC. Key considerations emerging from this evidence base of CBTs will be discussed in the next section.

Table 5.1 Summary of randomized and quasi-randomized trials testing interventions with CBT elements in LMIC

Author	Adaptation	Study design	Location	Outcome(s)	Findings
Abedi and Vostanis (2010)	Original	Pilot RCT	Iran	Quality of life	Significant
Aboulafia-Brakha, Suchecki, Gouveia-Paulino, Nitrini, and Ptak (2014)	Original	RCT	Brazil	Cortisol	Significant
Alavi, Hirji, Sutton, and Naeem (2016)	Original	Pilot RCT	Iran	Depression	Significant
Araya et al. (2013)	Original	RCT	Chile	Depression	Nonsignificant
Arefnasab et al. (2016)	Original	Pilot RCT	Iran	Psych immunologic condition	Nonsignificant
Azhar (2000)	Original	RCT	Malaysia	Panic	Significant
Bass et al. (2013)	Adaptation	RCT	Demographic Republic of Congo	Trauma	Significant
Bello, Quartey, and Lartey (2015)	Original	Pilot RCT	Ghana	Pain	Nonsignificant
Betancourt et al. (2014)[a]	Adaptation	RCT	Sierra Leone	Emotion regulation, psychological distress, prosocial attitudes/behaviors, social support, functional impairment, and post-traumatic stress disorder (PTSD) symptoms	Significant
Bolton et al. (2014)	Adaptation	RCT	Iraq	Depression, functional impairment	Significant
Bryant et al. (2011)	Adaptation	RCT (stopped early, not fully powered)	Thailand	Trauma	Trial stopped early

Continued

Table 5.1 Continued

Author	Adaptation	Study design	Location	Outcome(s)	Findings
Chan, Ngai, Leung, and Wong (2010)	Original	Pilot RCT	China	Cognitive functioning	Significant
Chen et al. (2014)	Adaptation	RCT	China	Depression and trauma	Significant
Chetty and Hoque (2013)	Adaptation	Pilot RCT	South Africa	Depression	Significant
Chien and Thompson (2014)	Original	RCT	China	Psychiatric symptoms	Significant
de Oliveira et al. (2012)	Original	Pilot RCT	Brazil	Social anxiety	Significant
Deng et al. (2014)	Original	RCT	China	OCD	Significant
D'Souza et al. (2013)	Original	Pilot RCT	India (and the United States)	Schizophrenia	Significant
Duarte, Miyazaki, Blay, and Sesso (2009)	Original	Pilot RCT	Brazil	Depression	Significant
Edries, Jelsma, and Maart (2013)	Original	RCT	South Africa	Quality of life	Significant
Fabrizio et al. (2015)	Original	RCT	China	Emotion management	Significant
Faramarzi et al. (2008)	Original	RCT	Iran	Depression and anxiety	Significant
Faramarzi, Yazdani, and Barat (2015)	Original	RCT	Iran	Nausea/vomiting, psychological symptoms, and pregnancy distress	Significant
Gaete et al. (2016)	Adaptation	RCT	Chile	Depression	Significant
Giasuddin, Nahar, Morshed, Balhara, and Sobhan (2013)	Original	Pilot RCT	Pakistan	OCD	Significant

Gohar, Hamdi, El Ray, Horan, and Green (2013)	Original	Pilot RCT	Egypt	Schizophrenia	Significant
Gomes et al. (2011)	Original	Pilot RCT	Brazil	Bipolar	Nonsignificant
Gorayeb, Borsari, Rosa-e-Silva, and Ferriani (2012)	Original	RCT	Brazil	Pregnancy rates	Significant
Guo et al. (2010)	Original	RCT	China	Schizophrenia	Significant
Guo et al. (2017)	Original	RCT	China	Schizophrenia	Significant
Habib, Dawood, Kingdon, and Naeem (2015)	Adaptation	Pilot RCT	Pakistan	Psychosis	Significant
Hall et al. (2014)	Adaptation	RCT	Demographic Republic of Congo	Social capital	Significant
Hamdan-Mansour, Puskar, and Bandak (2009)	Adaptation	RCT	Jordan	Depression, stress, positive coping	Significant
Henwood, Browne, and Chou (2016)	Original	Pilot RCT	Malta	Anger	Significant
Huang et al. (2017)	Original	RCT	China	ADHD	Significant
(2015)	Original	Pilot RCT	Saudi Arabia	Quality of life	Significant
Husain, Afsar, et al. (2014)	Adaptation	Pilot RCT	Pakistan	Depression	Nonsignificant
Husain, Chaudhry, et al. (2014)	Adaptation	RCT	Pakistan	Self-harm	Significant
Husain et al. (2017)	Adaptation	RCT	Pakistan	Depression	Significant
Hutchinson, Willner, Rose, Burke, and Bastick (2017)	Adaptation	RCT	Trinidad and Tobago	Anger	Significant

Continued

Table 5.1 Continued

Author	Adaptation	Study design	Location	Outcome(s)	Findings
Hyun, Chung, and Lee (2005)	Original	Pilot RCT	South Korea	Depression, self-esteem, self-efficacy	Significant
Hyun, Nam, and Kim (2010)	Original	Pilot RCT	South Korea	Resilience	Significant
Iftene, Predescu, Stefan, and David (2015)	Original	RCT	Romania	Depression	Significant
Ishola and Chipps (2015)	Original	RCT	Nigeria	Acceptance and treatment commitment	Significant
Jiang and He (2012)	Original	Pilot RCT	China	Uncertainty, anxiety, depression, and quality of life	Significant
Jordans et al. (2010)	Adaptation	RCT	Nepal	Depression, anxiety, post-traumatic stress disorder, psychological difficulties, resilience indicators (hope and prosocial behavior), and function impairment	Significant
Jung, Lee, and Park (2015)	Original	RCT	South Korea	Cortisol, blood glucose, plasminogen activator inhibitor-1 (PAI-1), and tissue plasminogen activator (t-PA)	Significant
Kalantari, Yule, Dyregrov, Neshatdoost, and Ahmadi (2012)	Adaptation	Pilot RCT	Iran	Traumatic grief	Significant
Karairmak and Aydin (2008)	Original	RCT or pilot RCT (unable to determine)	Turkey	Fear	Nonsignificant

Khanlary, Maarefvand, Biglarian, and Heravi-Karimooi (2016)	Unable to determine	Pilot RCT	Iran	Abuse	Significant
Khodayarifard, Shokoohi-Yekta, and Hamot (2010)	Adaptation	RCT	Iran	Psychological symptoms	Significant
Kim, Lee, Kim, Noh, and Lee (2016)	Original	RCT	South Korea	Life stress, stress coping, psychological distress, and cortisol	Significant
Lam et al. (2015)	Adaptation	RCT	China	Psychosis	Significant
Lau, Chan, Li, and Au (2010)	Adaptation	RCT	China	Anxiety	Significant
Lee and Kwon (2013)	Adaptation	RCT	South Korea	Phobia	Significant
Lee (2013)	Unable to determine	RCT	South Korea	Schizophrenia	Nonsignificant
Lee and Yeun (2017)	Original	RCT	South Korea	Stress	Significant
Lerma et al. (2017)	Adaptation	RCT	Mexico	Depression and anxiety	Significant
Li et al. (2015)	Original	RCT	China	Schizophrenia	Significant
Lim et al. (2010)	Original	Pilot RCT	South Korea	Career attitude maturity, self-esteem, decision-making style	Significant
Lin et al. (2016)	Original	RCT	China	Sleep	Significant
Lou et al. (2013)	Original	RCT	China	Smoking	Significant
Lundgren, Dahl, and Hayes (2008)	Original	RCT	South Africa	Epilepsy	Significant
Mahdizadeh, Peymam, Taghipour, Esmaily, and Mahdizadeh (2013)	Original	RCT	Iran	Physical activity	Significant

Continued

Table 5.1 Continued

Author	Adaptation	Study design	Location	Outcome(s)	Findings
Maneesakorn, Robson, Gournay, and Gray (2007)	Adaptation	RCT	Thailand	Adherence	Significant
Manjula, Prasadarao, Kumaraiah, and Raguram (2014)	Adaptation	RCT	India	Panic disorder	Significant
Mantell et al. (2015)	Original	RCT	South Africa	Condom use	Nonsignificant
McBain et al. (2015)[a]	Adaptation	RCT	Sierra Leone	Mental health	Significant
McCann, Songprakun, and Stephenson (2015)	Original	RCT	Thailand	Expressed emotion	Significant
McCann, Songprakun, and Stephenson (2016)	Original	RCT	Thailand	Resilience	Nonsignificant
McMullen, O'Callaghan, Shannon, Black, and Eakin (2013)	Adaptation	RCT	Demographic Republic of Congo	Psychological symptoms	Significant
Min et al. (2011)	Adaptation	Pilot RCT	China	Heroin use	Significant
Momeni, Omidi, Raygan, and Akbari (2016)	Original	RCT	Iran	Blood pressure, perceived stress, and anger	Significant
Mon, Liabsuetrakul, and Htut (2016)	Original	RCT	Myanmar	Emotional, conduct, and social behaviors	Significant
Moustafa and Diab (2015)	Original	RCT	Egypt	Fibromyalgia management	Nonsignificant

Murray et al. (2015)	Original	RCT	Zambia	Trauma	Significant
Naeem, Gul, et al. (2015)	Adaptation	RCT	Pakistan	Depression	Significant
Naeem, Saeed, et al. (2015)	Adaptation	RCT	Pakistan	Depression	Significant
Naeem et al. (2014)	Adaptation	RCT	Pakistan	Depression	Significant
Naeem, Waheed, Gobbi, Ayub, and Kingdon (2011)	Adaptation	RCT	Pakistan	Schizophrenia	Significant
Nance (2012)	Unable to determine	RCT	Mexico	Depression	Significant
Neuner, Schauer, Klaschik, Karunakara, and Elbert (2004)	Unable to determine	Pilot RCT	Uganda	Trauma	Significant
Neuner et al. (2008)	Unable to determine	RCT	Uganda	Trauma	Nonsignificant
Niu, Tan, Guan, Zhang, and Wang (2010)	Original	Pilot RCT	China	Neuropsychiatric symptoms	Significant
O'Callaghan, McMullen, Shannon, Rafferty, and Black (2013)	Original	RCT	Demographic Republic of Congo	Post-traumatic stress disorder, depression, and anxiety and conduct problems and increasing prosocial behavior	Significant
Ogel and Coskun (2011)	Original	RCT	Turkey	Substance use	Significant
Onyechi et al. (2016)	Adaptation	RCT	Nigeria	Depression	Significant
Onyechi et al. (2017)	Original	RCT	Nigeria	Cigarette smoking	Significant
Pan et al. (2015)	Original	RCT	China	Opiate use	Significant
Papas et al. (2011)	Adaptation	RCT	Kenya	Alcohol use	Significant
Park, Kwon, Seo, Lim, and Song (2009)	Original	RCT	South Korea	Depression and cognitive dysfunction	Nonsignificant

Continued

Table 5.1 Continued

Author	Adaptation	Study design	Location	Outcome(s)	Findings
Perez, Feldman, and Caballero (1999)	Original	RCT	Venezuela	Asthma	Significant
Phang, Mukhtar, Ibrahim, Keng, and Mohd Sidik (2015)	Adaptation	RCT	Malaysia	Stress	Significant
Pityaratstian et al. (2015)	Original	RCT	Thailand	Trauma	Significant
Qouta, Palosaari, Diab, and Punamaki (2012)	Original	RCT	Palestine	Trauma	Significant
Rabiei, Mulkens, Kalantari, Molavi, and Bahrami (2012)	Original	Pilot RCT	Iran	Body dysmorphic disorder	Significant
Rahman, Malik, Sikander, Roberts, and Creed (2008)	Original	RCT	Pakistan	Depression	Significant
Raj, Kumaraiah, and Bhide (2001)	Original	Pilot RCT	India	Self-harm	Significant
Rakitzi, Georgila, Efthimiou, and Mueller (2016)	Original	RCT	Greece	Schizophrenia	Significant
Ratanasiripong, Park, Ratanasiripong, and Kathalae (2015)	Original	RCT	Thailand	Stress and anxiety	Significant
Rodriguez-Martin, Moritz, Molerio-Perez, and Gil-Perez (2013)	Original	RCT	Cuba	OCD	Significant

Sabetnejad, Assarian, Omidi, and Najarzadegan (2016)	Original	RCT	Iran	Sexual function	Significant
Salehi, Pourasghar, Khalilian, and Shahhosseini (2016)	Original	RCT	Iran	Anxiety	Significant
Satyanarayana et al. (2016)	Original	RCT	India	Intimate partner violence	Significant
Sava, Yates, Lupu, Szentagotai, and David (2009)	Original	RCT	Chile	Depression	Nonsignificant
Shao, Gao, and Cao (2016)	Original	RCT	China	Psychological symptoms	Significant
Sharif et al. (2014)	Original	RCT	Iran	Depression	Significant
Shata, Amin, El-Kady, and Abu-Nazel (2017)	Original	RCT	Egypt	Depression, anxiety, burden of care	Significant
Shein-Szydlo et al. (2016)	Original	RCT	Mexico	Trauma	Significant
Sikander et al. (2015)	Original	RCT	Pakistan	Breastfeeding	Significant
Solati, Mousavi, Kheiri, and Hasanpour-Dehkordi (2017)	Adaptation	RCT	Iran	Psychological symptoms and quality of life	Significant
Song and Lindquist (2015)	Original	RCT	South Korea	Depression, anxiety, stress	Significant
Songprakun and McCann (2012a)[b]	Original	RCT	Thailand	Depression	Significant
Songprakun and McCann (2012b)[b]	Original	RCT	Thailand	Depression	Significant

Continued

Table 5.1 Continued

Author	Adaptation	Study design	Location	Outcome(s)	Findings
Stefanaki et al. (2015)	Original	RCT	Greece	Depression, anxiety, and stress	Significant
Sumathipala et al. (2008)	Original	RCT	Sri Lanka	General health	Nonsignificant
Sungur et al. (2011)	Original	RCT	Turkey	Schizophrenia	Significant
Thapinta, Skulphan, and Kittrattanapaiboon (2014)	Original	RCT	Thailand	Depression	Significant
Toledo, De Togni Muniz, Brito, de Abreu, and Tavares (2015)	Original	RCT	Brazil	Trichotillomania	Significant
Tulbure et al. (2015)	Original	RCT	Romania	Anxiety	Significant
Valencia, Rascon, Juarez, and Murow (2007)	Original	RCT	Mexico	Schizophrenia	Significant
Wang, Jian, et al. (2012)	Original	RCT	China	Pain	Significant
Wang, Ding, Xu, Zeng, and Xiao (2012)	Original	RCT	China	Anxiety	Nonsignificant
Wang, Wang, and Maercker (2013)[c]	Original	RCT	China	Trauma	Significant
Wang and Maercker (2014)[c]	Original	RCT	China	Trauma	Significant
Wang et al. (2014)	Original	RCT	China	Sleep	Significant
Wang et al. (2016)	Original	RCT	Kosovo	Trauma	Significant

Wechsberg et al. (2012)	Original	Pilot RCT	Russia	Drug use and sexual behavior	Significant
Wei et al. (2013)	Original	RCT	China	Depression, suicide, quality of life	Nonsignificant
Weiss et al. (2015)	Adaptation	RCT	Iraq	Trauma, depression, anxiety, dysfunction	Significant
Wu et al. (2012)	Original	RCT	China	Depression and anxiety	Significant
Yalcin, Unal, Pirdal, and Karahan (2014)	Original	RCT	Turkey	Anger and stress	Significant
Youngwanichsetha, Phumdoung, and Ingkathawornwong (2014)	Original	RCT	Thailand	Capillary fasting, plasma glucose, 2 h postprandial blood glucose, and hemoglobin A1c	Significant
Zhang et al. (2014)	Original	RCT	China	Schizophrenia	Significant
Y. Zhang et al. (2016)	Original	RCT	China	Cardiometabolic syndrome	Significant
Q. Zhang, Li, Zhang, Yu, and Cong (2017)	Original	RCT	China	Fatigue	Significant
Zhong et al. (2015)	Original	RCT	China	Opiate use	Significant
Zhuang, An, and Zhao (2014)	Original	RCT	China	Heroin use	Significant
Zu et al. (2014)	Original	RCT	China	Depression	Nonsignificant

[a, b, c] These citations represent the same set of intervention trials.

5.4 Considerations for transporting existing cognitive behavioral therapy evidence for use in low- and middle-income country settings

Transporting existing evidence-based CBT treatment models into LMIC without considering whether adaptation is needed may result in nonresponse and nonengagement. This is particularly the case in regard to CBT, which rests on cognitive and behavioral mechanisms of change, as compared with pharmacological treatment, which may be easier to transport across populations and settings because it engages molecular and synaptic mechanisms of change. Nonresponse may arise in nonadapted CBT models due to the unique social and structural determinants of mental health outcomes in a particular context. Nonengagement may also occur in the application of evidence-based CBT transported from one setting to another due to differences in population and characteristics of the target location compared with the population, and setting the original treatment was tested in.

Adaptations can be used to maintain the efficacy of interventions designed in one setting and transported to another setting for use. The goal of adaptation is to retain the efficacy and effectiveness of the evidence-based CBT treatment while maintaining and/or increasing response and engagement of the target population. To maintain efficacy and effectiveness, any changes made to the original evidence-based CBT protocol—whether additions, deletions, or modifications—should not alter the core components of the intervention tied to cognitive and behavioral change. Such an approach suggests that adaptation goes beyond language alterations. Rather, a theory-driven and systematic approach toward adaptation may be needed to guide the process of adaptation that takes into account contextual and cultural differences that might affect response and engagement. Thus, adaptation procedures should be designed to strike a delicate balance between the idea of CBT interventions being "universally applicable" to all populations, settings, cultures, and contexts with the notion that "custom tailoring" is always needed to address inevitable differences in populations, settings, cultures, and context.

5.5 Conceptual model for adaptation of cognitive behavioral treatments to low- and middle-income country settings: PROGRAM model

A search of PubMed was conducted to identify an existing conceptual model to guide the adaptation of psychological models—including CBT models—for transportation from high-income countries to LMIC settings or from low- and middle-income country contexts to other LMIC contexts. The search protocol involved the use of Boolean operators combining the following key terms: adapt; mental health (MeSH); and intervention, prevention, and treatment. This search did not yield any existing conceptual model. The majority of the literature focuses on cultural adaptations of interventions (see for example, reviews by Barrera, Castro, Strycker, & Toobert, 2013; Castro,

Barrera, & Holleran Steiker, 2010; Chowdhary et al., 2013; Gearing et al., 2012). The search also uncovered several existing models of processes for cultural adaptations (see, e.g., Barrera & Castro, 2006; Castro, Barrera, & Martinez, 2004; Hwang, 2010; A. S. Lau, 2006), but these models do not fully capture the scope of challenges entailed in adaptations of evidence-based interventions in high-income countries to LMIC settings. As such, existing models from the perspective of informing a systematic approach toward the adaptation of an evidence-based CBT model from one setting to another were reviewed (Barrera Jr et al., 2013; Barrera & Castro, 2006; Castro et al., 2010; Castro et al., 2004; Kumpfer, Alvarado, Smith, & Bellamy, 2002; Kumpfer, Pinyuchon, de Melo, & Whiteside, 2008).

Based on the absence of an existing model, this chapter details an approach to adaptation called the PROGRAM model, a conceptual model outlining six sequential steps for assessing and, if necessary, adapting existing psychological interventions in preparation for future efficacy or effectiveness trials of psychological interventions in LMIC. This conceptual model is designed to guide a cautious and careful methodological approach toward assessing the contextual and cultural factors that might necessitate adaptation to LMIC of empirically based interventions, such as CBT for mental health, and to increase the rigor of the adaptation process to ensure we appropriately and fully utilize existing evidence on empirically supported psychological interventions to address the global health treatment gap. The model is flexible, facilitating rigor for researchers, policy-makers, and practitioners as they move toward evaluating either efficacy or effectiveness of psychological interventions to meet the mental health treatment gap. The model proposes key principles in a sequential process for adaptation and, in so doing, offers a flexible rather than prescriptive guide toward adaptations in preparation for future efficacy or effectiveness trials. Such a model can be potentially applied to evaluate adaptation needs for CBT interventions designed in one setting but to be used in new settings.

Step 1: Psychological intervention models—What is the evidence for potentially promising existing psychological intervention models that address the target outcome(s)?

The first step in the **PROGRAM** model is to review the evidence on existing **psychological** intervention models in order to identify a candidate intervention for adaptation. Such a review can be conducted by searching for existing systematic reviews or metaanalyses or conducting one's own review. The review should focus on identifying existing psychological interventions that address the target outcome(s) (e.g., depression, anxiety, and PTSD). These candidate interventions have potential to be transported into the LMIC context or to be translated from one LMIC context to another in the pipeline from efficacy to effectiveness. Narrowing down choices to one candidate intervention can be accomplished by examining the depth of empirical evidence. Consulting criteria for evaluating empirically supported interventions versus evidence-based interventions is helpful (American Psychological Association, 2013). In choosing the final candidate model, it is helpful to evaluate evidence around efficacy (effects of treatment under controlled trial settings focused on high internal validity) and effectiveness (effects of treatment in real-world settings focused on high external validity) (Chambless & Ollendick, 2001) depending on whether the

PROGRAM model is being used to prepare for efficacy or effectiveness trials. Consider which populations the candidate intervention has been tested on previously. If possible, choose a candidate intervention that has been tested in multiple populations and adapted successfully to diverse populations and settings outside of the target LMIC setting. This may indicate promise in adaptation potential to the new target population and setting. If task shifting will be incorporated into the use of the candidate intervention in the new setting and population given the human resource and health system considerations described earlier, attention should be paid in particular to the complexity of the intervention and level of training needed to implement the intervention with integrity. A candidate intervention should only be chosen if it is possible to provide high-quality treatment in new settings and populations after adaptation, an ethical imperative to ensure that quality of care is not compromised.

Step 2: Retain core components—What are the core components of the candidate intervention that should be retained to ensure fidelity?

The next step in the P**R**OGRAM model is to identify and **retain** core components of the candidate intervention that will be used for adaptation. Core components are essential intervention elements thought to impact the target outcome(s). Core components typically align with the theoretical origins of the intervention, including the mechanisms of change thought to alter outcomes. These components could be composed of functions (e.g., psychoeducation to create an understanding of the illness), activities (e.g., frequent homework to strengthen behavioral skills for coping with illness), and principles (e.g., repetitively practicing coping skills will increase self-efficacy and result in improved outcomes). Identification of core components of the candidate intervention can be accomplished by contacting the original intervention designer, reviewing published literature, and if available consulting the intervention manual. Furthermore, core components may be yielded by publications of the intervention that identify mechanisms of change. Fidelity to core components of the intervention during adaptation will help ensure that the final intervention is an adaptation rather than a new intervention (La Roche & Christopher, 2008). Adaptation studies that eliminate core components of intervention models have resulted in reduced achievement in desired outcomes (Ickovics, Niccolai, Lewis, Kershaw, & Ethier, 2003).

Fidelity to core components of the candidate model is vital during adaptations regardless of whether the goal is to transport models from high-income settings to LMIC or to translate models from one LMIC context to another (McHugh, Murray, & Barlow, 2009). Understanding core components is especially vital in adaptations to settings where there is scarcity of mental health-care specialists, as noted previously. Honing in on core components allows better evaluation of whether task shifting might be appropriate and what level of training and supervision is needed for nonspecialists to deliver the adapted intervention with high quality and integrity. Others have eloquently written about the types of roles that specialists and nonspecialists might take on as one considers task shifting to address global mental health disparities in LMIC (Kakuma et al., 2011) and strategies for doing so including integration of mental health into primary care (Liu et al., 2016). Delineating core components prior to adaptation also allows the consideration of the costs for retaining core components not only from the perspective of intervention implementation but also from the perspective of engagement by the target population. Notable are recent data detailing the cost-effectiveness of mental health scale up in LMIC settings (Chisholm, Burman-Roy, et al., 2016) and substantial efficiency of return on investment at a cost ratio of 3.3–5.7 to 1 for mental health investment to address the mental health treatment gap (Chisholm, Sweeny, et al., 2016). Thus, core components help to evaluate the potential sustainability, scalability, and cost-effectiveness of candidate models from the perspective of intervention integrity and are vital when working in low-resource settings.

Step 3: Operator changers—What unique aspects related to the target population and settings are likely to negatively impact target outcomes?

The third step in the PROGRAM model is to identify unique aspects of the target population and setting that might negatively influence target **operators** if the intervention were to be delivered in an unadapted format. Whereas Step 2 of the PROGRAM model focuses on fidelity, this step in the model focuses on balancing fidelity with issues of fit. Some of the most important considerations in assessing whether psychological interventions need to be adapted from one context to another in order to ensure improved fit with the needs of the target population and context are highlighted here. Gathering information on how to create adaptations that balance the considerations of fidelity with fit is vital for ensuring adherence to core components of original intervention models (Lopez et al., 2004). The process of assessing adaptation needs should be data-driven to safeguard against "improvised" drift that could compromise fidelity or result in unwarranted changes to ensure fit (Lopez et al., 2004).

To gather data that can guide decisions to balance fidelity with fit, a variety of methods can be used including participatory methods, qualitative methods that gather data from both the target population and target operators, and consultations with experts providing services to the target population and with stakeholders such as clinic staff or community members who might be affected indirectly by the adapted intervention (through resource demands) or downstream (if the adapted intervention is found to be efficacious and scaled up). Regardless of approach, assessing adaptation needs should be data-driven and might affect the following aspects of the original intervention model: (1) changes to intervention materials including curriculum content, role-play, vignettes, examples, goals, and methods to increase salience with the target population; (2) integration of principles or metaphors unique to the study population that might affect the original intervention theory of change; and (3) changes to delivery modality including who delivers the intervention and the concomitant training and/or supervision needed for these interventionists to implement with integrity in the particular LMIC context. Ideally, data would be gathered in an iterative manner, in which formative data are used to create an initial adaptation of the intervention, this initial adapted version of the intervention is then demonstrated to the target population, and feedback is gathered from this demonstration to further refine adaptation. These considerations include linguistic and cultural considerations, which have been detailed within the literature on cultural adaptations of psychological interventions. These considerations also extend to the specific characteristics of low- and middle-income settings in regard to mental health, which have largely been under-explored within the extant literature.

Language

There may be a need to translate the intervention into a particular language. The most rigorous translation approach entails translation and back translation using a committee approach (Bhui, Mohamud, Warfa, Craig, & Stansfeld, 2003; Smit, van der Berg, Bekker, Seedat, & Stein, 2006). Here, attention must be paid not only toward accuracy of translation but also toward linguistic equivalence. A study of linguistic equivalence for commonly used mental health assessment tools among AmaXhosa language speakers in South Africa showed that the concept of "blues," a Western construct of depression, when translated literally, did not construe the same meaning. Rather "blue" was a Western construct of depression with no linguistically equivalent meaning in AmaXhosa (Smit et al., 2006).

Cultural considerations

Specific cultural factors, including but not limited to race and ethnicity, might also impact issues of intervention fit. A systematic review identified race as a salient factor in mental health outcomes (Paradies, 2006). Unique cultural characteristics of the target population are another important consideration. There may be culture-specific risk and protective factors for mental health unique to the study population; for example, Lopez et al. (2004) found that *famialismo* or a concept used to describe familial warmth served as a protective factor for schizophrenia relapse among Mexican Americans but not among Anglo-Americans. Similarly, Whitbeck (2009) noted that an intervention to address alcohol abuse among American Indians is needed to account for unique experiences of genocide and discrimination among this population. Another cultural consideration includes whether there is a need to embed culturally specific metaphors within the intervention to explain mental health concepts. For example, the term *ubuntu* is a cultural conception of human resilience that has been used to address mental health in South Africa (Sue, Zane, Nagayama Hall, & Berger, 2009). There are distinct forms of presentation that also might obscure both diagnosis and treatment of illness (Tomlinson, Swartz, Kruger, & Gureje, 2007). Also, cultures might posit unique explanatory models for the cause of mental illness that influence the acceptability of treatment and the type of stigma experienced by those participating in mental health treatment (Kleinman, 2008).

Taking into account these cultural considerations might result in a number of adaptations to the candidate intervention transported from high-income settings to LMIC or when translating the model from one LMIC setting to another LMIC setting. For example, adaptations might include content revisions to address unique risk and protective factors or to integrate culturally specific metaphors or explanatory models. Adaptations might include changes to the format of materials to reflect that target population needs including in images that reflect specific values, rituals, ethnic and racial groups, and other cultural practices (Ickovics et al., 2003). Adaptations might also include changing choice of an interventionist team to ensure culturally competent delivery of the intervention. Developing a culturally competent interventionist team is not simply matching the interventionist team to participants in regard to characteristics such as race, ethnicity, and cultural group. Rather, training must ensure delivery and engagement with participants that reflect a level of cultural knowledge around relevant beliefs, skills, and worldviews so as to facilitate the salience of the adapted intervention (Russell, Eaton, & Petersen-Williams, 2013).

Setting

The target setting for intervention delivery is also of great importance when considering whether adaptations are needed to meet the needs of the target population in LMIC. Whereas specialists in clinical settings deliver many psychological interventions in high-income countries, this is unlikely to be feasible in LMIC due to shortages in trained mental health specialists and the lack of existing mental health infrastructure. More likely than not, the intervention would need to be task-shifted to nonspecialists, highlighting the unique need for capacity building within adaptations of interventions for use in LMIC (Michaud & Kates, 2013). New methods are being developed to assess the competence of interventionists involved in task shifting (Kohrt et al., 2015). Similarly, the intervention will likely need to be offered in community-based settings or integrated into general health-care clinics; both of these strategies are being proposed by the World Health Organization in order to increase access to services, lower cost, and decrease stigma associated with accessing mental health care or living with a mental illness (2013). Operating in these settings often necessitates engagement with policy-makers and practitioners, whose support is essential to the effectiveness of the final adapted intervention. A stepped approach may be needed in adapted treatment models, where, for example, lay workers deliver an adapted intervention, but that robust linkage to specialized care is put into place to ensure high-quality delivery of services and responsiveness. This model of stepped care can only be implemented in settings that can accommodate treatment in regard to cost, access, and space.

Other important considerations regarding whether adaptations are needed include contextual issues that might impact upon engagement. Important contextual considerations in LMIC largely have to do with resources that affect delivery of the intervention, especially along the effectiveness and implementation spectrum. For example, the availability of electricity might affect the types of activities conducted within the intervention or the availability of road infrastructure and transport that would affect participant recruitment and engagement in the intervention. Poverty might also affect participants' ability to engage in the intervention if attendance undermines basic needs or if food security impacts upon cognitive engagement in intervention activities. Of course, these issues might also be present in high-income countries but likely to a far lesser degree. The key message is tailoring the adapted intervention to increase participant engagement that may require attention to contextual variables within LMIC settings.

Step 4: Generate a list of valid and reliable measurement tools—What are psychometrically valid tools for assessing outcomes with the target population?

The fourth step in the PROGRAM model is to **generate** a list of psychometrically valid tools to screen and evaluate target outcomes for the adapted intervention. The choice of psychometrically valid tools for screening and evaluating outcomes among diverse populations is a considerable issue in and of itself that might necessitate a related set of studies in addition to adaptation research (Briere & Elliott, 2003).

Indeed, few gold-standard tools have been fully validated, and even tools that have gone through an extensive process of validation such as the World Health Organization's Composite International Diagnostic Interview have exhibited potential problems with comparability across diverse global populations and settings (Ghimire, Chardoul, Kessler, Axinn, & Adhikari, 2013). Other commonly used tools for screening and assessment have been insufficiently adapted or have unknown psychometric performance in global settings (Sweetland, Belkin, & Verdeli, 2013; Uysal-Bozkir, Parlevliet, & de Rooij, 2013).

While we recognized the existing limitations in this area, ideally, psychometrically valid tools that have been previously tested with the population should be used. Another important consideration is how the equivalence of these tools might be affected by the process of translation. If translation is needed, this process must capture not only semantic equivalence but also conceptually equivalent theoretical constructs, culturally relevant content in each item of the tool, operational equivalence (e.g., procedures of administrating the instrument), and functional equivalence (Petersen, Lund, & Stein, 2011; Prince, 2008; Schwarz, 2003).

Step 5: **R**esearch acceptability and feasibility of the adapted intervention—Do initial adaptations have salience with the target population?

The fifth step in the PROG**R**AM model is to **research** acceptability and feasibility of the adapted intervention with the target population and with service providers operating in the target health system as an initial step in preparation for either efficacy testing or effectiveness testing of the adapted intervention. Assessing initial salience with the target population can be conducted using a number of approaches. Interviews or focus groups can be used to gather feedback on the acceptability of the intervention by the target population and their social ecosystem, alliance with interventionists, and satisfaction with the intervention materials and format. These assessments of salience should also investigate whether principles of the intervention (Step 2) need to be achieved through context-specific approaches. For example, perhaps, group-based behavioral practice is more appropriate for building self-efficacy in healthy coping skills in one setting, but individual behavioral practice to build self-efficacy in healthy coping skills is more appropriate in another context. Feasibility can also be examined and might include data on enrollment, attendance, and dropouts during piloting. Feasibility might also be examined regarding the modality of intervention delivery. For example, perhaps, activities need to be transitioned from electronic delivery to paper and pencil modes of delivery; perhaps, activities need to be delivered in visual formats that may meet the needs of populations with low literacy; perhaps, learning models might be more appropriate for groups versus individual modalities. Special attention may need to be paid to one particular aspect of feasibility—fidelity, especially if the adapted model task-shifts the role of delivery from specialists to nonspecialists in preparation for efficacy or effectiveness testing.

Step 6: **A**ssess **M**odel efficacy—What is the efficacy or effectiveness of the adapted intervention on the desired outcome?

The sixth and final step in the PROGR**AM** model is to **assess model** efficacy or effectiveness upon target outcomes. The PROGRAM model offers flexibility in steps 1 through 5 as to the direction in which the model is applied in Step 6. If the goal of the adaptation process is to prepare for efficacy testing—for example, if promising candidate psychological interventions were previously developed and showed efficacy outside of the LMIC setting—the principals of efficacy research models should be applied to evaluate the performance of the adapted intervention in controlled LMIC settings. The principles of efficacy testing include randomization, comparison with a control condition, and adequate power to assess effect sizes. While testing of the original intervention model likely identified active components of the model, one should not assume that the adapted intervention has the same active components. Additional steps should focus on gathering data on active components of the adapted intervention model. Specific attention should be focused on examining whether adaptations enhance or detract from existing active components and whether adaptations have created new active components. If the goal of the adaptation process was to prepare for effectiveness testing—for example, if promising candidate psychological interventions were previously developed and showed efficacy outside of the LMIC setting and now are being tested for effectiveness and future implementation—then effectiveness research designs may be more appropriate during Step 6. Testing for effectiveness and implementation can involve hybrid designs. Three commonly used designs include (1) a study design that is situated closer toward the effectiveness end of the spectrum where the main goal is to test the impact of the intervention on outcomes, often under less controlled conditions, while gathering information on implementation strategies; (2) a hybrid model that simultaneously examines the effectiveness of the intervention and implementation strategies; and (3) a study design that is situated closer toward the implementation end of the spectrum where the main goal is to test implementation strategies including adoption and fidelity to the intervention with the secondary goal of gathering information on the effectiveness of the intervention (Bernet, Willens, & Bauer, 2013; Curran, Bauer, Mittman, Pyne, & Stetler, 2012). In this summary of Step 6, efficacy and effectiveness are presented as two distinct steps, largely to simplify this within the proposed PROGRAM model. However, issues that might impact effectiveness should be considered at efficacy stages of research. This is because characteristics ubiquitous in LMIC—such as the limited availability of clinicians and other mental health specialists, resource scarcity that affects intervention delivery and population engagement, and low policy and financial prioritization of mental health—affect each step of adaptation and cannot be accounted for in the final process of the model, essential if we are to use adaptations of psychological interventions as a strategy for addressing global mental health disparities.

5.6 Conclusion

The evidence on CBT therapies continues to grow in strength. The existing evidence base is strong for the efficacy of CBTs for a diverse range of outcomes, populations, and settings. However, the current evidence based is geographically biased, with a relative paucity of evidence on the efficacy of CBTs in LMIC. To close the treatment gap, further evidence should be generated in LMIC settings for the efficacy and effectiveness of CBTs for diverse outcomes and populations. Adapting empirically based CBT interventions from high-income country settings or from one LMIC context to another offers one strategic approach for leveraging the existing evidence base to rapidly and rigorously address the global mental health treatment gap.

The PROGRAM model offers conceptual guidance for the process of assessing and, if necessary, guiding the adaptation of psychological interventions designed in one setting and being applied in a particular LMIC setting. The PROGRAM model involves six steps: (1) identification of candidate **P**sychological interventions for adaptation; (2) **R**etention of core active components of the intervention prior to adaptation changes; (3) identification of unique aspects of the target population and setting that might influence the **O**peration of the unadapted intervention—including language, culture, human resource capacity and health system financing and structure, and additional structural and social determinants of health including poverty and food security—and making adaptations to ensure fidelity and fit of the intervention to the new target setting and population; (4) **G**enerating a valid and reliable measures to assess outcomes of the adapted intervention; (5) **R**esearch to evaluate the acceptability and feasibility of the newly adapted intervention; and (6) **A**ssessing **M**odel efficacy or effectiveness upon target outcomes. Careful stepwise assessment and adaptation lays the groundwork for rigorous efficacy or effectiveness testing of CBT interventions. The model steps integrate research efforts that place considerations of context—bolstering health systems, training mental health providers, investment in mental health services and research, and combating stigma, among others—as central in the process of addressing global disparities in mental health treatment gaps. These contextual factors are acknowledged, explored, and integrated into the design of adapted intervention models as needed within the PROGRAM process.

An easily replicable conceptual model that guides the process of transporting existing empirically based intervention models to diverse contexts is crucial. Such a model may lend scientific rigor to the process of transporting empirically supported models from one context to another and, in so doing, help to broaden and diversify the use of the existing evidence base to help close the treatment gap in LMIC. However, this model should not be prescriptively applied. The use of the PROGRAM model should be iterative. It is possible that end users of this model will need to repeat steps in the PROGRAM model as new empirical evidence is uncovered and if they encounter challenges in the application process. For example, in the third step of the model, the operation of the adapted psychological intervention is unable to balance issues of fidelity with fit, when end users may need to revisit the first step of the model to identify another candidate intervention to use. The ideal application of the model involves flexibility in moving from step to step and if necessary revisiting previous steps to ensure that the final adapted psychological intervention delivers high-quality treatment that addresses the mental health treatment needs of the target population within their milieu. This model on the adaptation of existing psychological interventions aligns with current efforts to address the mental health treatment gap in LMIC, including task shifting, decentralization, integration, and deinstitutionalization (Eaton et al., 2011; Fairburn & Patel, 2014; Mendenhall et al., 2014; Petersen et al., 2015). The PROGRAM model complements innovative efforts to facilitate the delivery of evidence-based interventions such as the World Health Organization's Mental Health Gap Action Program (mhGAP) Guidelines, a practical guide for nonspecialist delivery of interventions for the most common disorders in LMIC (World Health Organization, 2013).

References

Abedi, M. R., & Vostanis, P. (2010). Evaluation of quality of life therapy for parents of children with obsessive-compulsive disorders in Iran. *European Child & Adolescent Psychiatry, 19* (7), 605–613. https://doi.org/10.1007/s00787-010-0098-4.

Aboulafia-Brakha, T., Suchecki, D., Gouveia-Paulino, F., Nitrini, R., & Ptak, R. (2014). Cognitive-behavioural group therapy improves a psychophysiological marker of stress in caregivers of patients with Alzheimer's disease. *Aging & Mental Health, 18*(6), 801–808. https://doi.org/10.1080/13607863.2014.880406.

Adelman, C. B., Panza, K. E., Bartley, C. A., Bontempo, A., & Bloch, M. H. (2014). A meta-analysis of computerized cognitive-behavioral therapy for the treatment of DSM-5 anxiety disorders. *Journal of Clinical Psychiatry, 75*(7), e695–e703.

Alavi, N., Hirji, A., Sutton, C., & Naeem, F. (2016). Online CBT is effective in overcoming cultural and language barriers in patients with depression. *Journal of Psychiatric Practice, 22*(1), 2–8. https://doi.org/10.1097/pra.0000000000000119.

American Psychological Association (2013). *Society of clinical psychology.* Retrieved from http://www.div12.org/PsychologicalTreatments/faq.html.

Araya, R., Fritsch, R., Spears, M., Rojas, G., Martinez, V., Barroilhet, S., … Montgomery, A. A. (2013). School intervention to improve mental health of students in Santiago, Chile: A randomized clinical trial. *JAMA Pediatrics, 167*(11), 1004–1010. https://doi.org/10.1001/jamapediatrics.2013.2361.

Arefnasab, Z., Babamahmoodi, A., Babamahmoodi, F., Noorbala, A. A., Alipour, A., Panahi, Y., … Ghanei, M. (2016). Mindfulness-based stress reduction (MBSR) and its effects on psychoimmunological factors of chemically pulmonary injured veterans. *Iranian Journal of Allergy, Asthma, and Immunology, 15*(6), 476–486.

Azhar, M. Z. (2000). Comparison of fluvoxamine alone, fluvoxamine and cognitive psychotherapy and psychotherapy alone in the treatment of panic disorder in Kelantan—Implications for management by family doctors. *Medical Journal of Malaysia, 55*(4), 402–408.

Barrera, M., Jr., Castro, F. G., Strycker, L. A., & Toobert, D. J. (2013). Cultural adaptations of behavioral health interventions: A progress report. *Journal of Consulting and Clinical Psychology, 81*(2), 196.

Barrera, M., & Castro, F. G. (2006). A heuristic framework for the cultural adaptation of interventions. *Clinical Psychology: Science and Practice, 13*(4), 311–316. https://doi.org/10.1111/j.1468-2850.2006.00043.x.

Bass, J. K., Annan, J., McIvor Murray, S., Kaysen, D., Griffiths, S., Cetinoglu, T., … Bolton, P. A. (2013). Controlled trial of psychotherapy for Congolese survivors of sexual violence. *New England Journal of Medicine, 368*(23), 2182–2191. https://doi.org/10.1056/NEJMoa1211853.

Beck, A. T. (1970). Cognitive therapy: Nature and relation to behavior therapy. *Behavior Therapy, 1*, 184–200.

Bello, A. I., Quartey, J., & Lartey, M. (2015). Efficacy of behavioural graded activity compared with conventional exercise therapy in chronic non-specific low back pain: Implication for direct health care cost. *Ghana Medical Journal, 49*(3), 173–180.

Bernet, A. C., Willens, D. E., & Bauer, M. S. (2013). Effectiveness-implementation hybrid designs: Implications for quality improvement science. *Implementation Science: IS*, *8* (Suppl. 1), S2. https://doi.org/10.1186/1748-5908-8-S1-S2.

Betancourt, T. S., McBain, R., Newnham, E. A., Akinsulure-Smith, A. M., Brennan, R. T., Weisz, J. R., & Hansen, N. B. (2014). A behavioral intervention for war-affected youth in Sierra Leone: A randomized controlled trial. *Journal of the American Academy of Child and Adolescent Psychiatry*, *53*(12), 1288–1297. https://doi.org/10.1016/j.jaac.2014.09.011.

Bhui, K., Mohamud, S., Warfa, N., Craig, T. J., & Stansfeld, S. A. (2003). Cultural adaptation of mental health measures: Improving the quality of clinical practice and research. *British Journal of Psychiatry*, *183*, 184–186.

Bolton, P., Bass, J. K., Zangana, G. A., Kamal, T., Murray, S. M., Kaysen, D., … Rosenblum, M. (2014). A randomized controlled trial of mental health interventions for survivors of systematic violence in Kurdistan, Northern Iraq. *BMC Psychiatry*, *14*. 360. https://doi.org/10.1186/s12888-014-0360-2.

Briere, J., & Elliott, D. M. (2003). Prevalence and psychological sequelae of self-reported childhood physical and sexual abuse in a general population sample of men and women. *Child Abuse & Neglect*, *27*(10), 1205–1222. https://doi.org/10.1016/j.chiabu.2003.09.008.

Bryant, R. A., Ekasawin, S., Chakrabhand, S., Suwanmitri, S., Duangchun, O., & Chantaluckwong, T. (2011). A randomized controlled effectiveness trial of cognitive behavior therapy for post-traumatic stress disorder in terrorist-affected people in Thailand. *World Psychiatry*, *10*(3), 205–209.

Castro, F. G., Barrera, M., Jr., & Holleran Steiker, L. K. (2010). Issues and challenges in the design of culturally adapted evidence-based interventions. *Annual Review of Clinical Psychology*, *6*, 213–239.

Castro, F. G., Barrera, M., Jr., & Martinez, C. R., Jr. (2004). The cultural adaptation of prevention interventions: Resolving tensions between fidelity and fit. *Prevention Science*, *5*(1), 41–45.

Chambless, D., & Ollendick, T. (2001). Empirically supported psychological interventions: Controversies and evidence. *Annual Review of Psychology*, *52*(1), 685–716. https://doi.org/10.1146/annurev.psych.52.1.685.

Chan, C. L., Ngai, E. K., Leung, P. K., & Wong, S. (2010). Effect of the adapted virtual reality cognitive training program among Chinese older adults with chronic schizophrenia: A pilot study. *International Journal of Geriatric Psychiatry*, *25*(6), 643–649. https://doi.org/10.1002/gps.2403.

Chen, Y., Shen, W. W., Gao, K., Lam, C. S., Chang, W. C., & Deng, H. (2014). Effectiveness RCT of a CBT intervention for youths who lost parents in the Sichuan, China, earthquake. *Psychiatric Services*, *65*(2), 259–262. https://doi.org/10.1176/appi.ps.201200470.

Chetty, D., & Hoque, M. E. (2013). Effectiveness of a nurse facilitated cognitive group intervention among mild to moderately-depressed-women in KwaZulu-Natal, South Africa. *African Journal of Psychiatry (Johannesbg)*, *16*(1), 29–34. https://doi.org/10.4314/ajpsy.v16i1.5.

Chiang, K. J., Tsai, J. C., Liu, D., Lin, C. H., Chiu, H., & Chou, K. R. (2017). Efficacy of cognitive-behavioral therapy in patients with bipolar disorder: A meta-analysis of randomized controlled trials. *PLoS ONE*, *12*(5). e0176849.

Chibanda, D., Mesu, P., Kajawu, L., Cowan, F., Araya, R., & Abas, M. (2011). Problem-solving therapy for depression and common mental disorders in Zimbabwe: Piloting a task-shifting primary mental health care intervention in a population with a high prevalence of people living with HIV. *BMC Public Health*, *11*(828). https://doi.org/10.1186/1471-2458-11-828.

Chien, W. T., & Thompson, D. R. (2014). Effects of a mindfulness-based psychoeducation programme for Chinese patients with schizophrenia: 2-year follow-up. *British Journal of Psychiatry*, *205*(1), 52–59. https://doi.org/10.1192/bjp.bp.113.134635.

Chisholm, D., Burman-Roy, S., Fekadu, A., Kathree, T., Kizza, D., Luitel, N. P., & Lund, C. (2016). Estimating the cost of implementing district mental healthcare plans in five low- and middle-income countries: The PRIME study. *The British Journal of Psychiatry*, *208* (s56), s71–s78. https://doi.org/10.1192/bjp.bp.114.153866.

Chisholm, D., Sweeny, K., Sheehan, P., Rasmussen, B., Smit, F., Cuijpers, P., & Saxena, S. (2016). Scaling-up treatment of depression and anxiety: A global return on investment analysis, *Lancet Psychiatry*. https://doi.org/10.1016/S2215-0366(16)30024-4.

Chowdhary, N., Jotheeswaran, A. T., Nadkarni, A., Hollon, S. D., King, M., Jordans, M. J., … Patel, V. (2013). The methods and outcomes of cultural adaptations of psychological treatments for depressive disorders: A systematic review. *Psychological Medicine*, *19*, 1–16.

Collins, P., Patel, V., Joestl, S., March, D., Insel, T., & Daar, A. (2011). Grand challenges in global mental health: A consortium of researchers, advocates and clinicians announces here research priorities for improving the lives of people with mental illness around the world, and calls for urgent action and investment. *Nature*, *475*(7354), 27–30. https://doi.org/10.1038/475027a.

Cuijpers, P., Cristea, I. A., Karyotaki, E., Reijnders, M., & Huibers, M. J. H. (2016). How effective are cognitive behavior therapies for major depression and anxiety disorders? A meta-analytic update of the evidence. *World Psychiatry*, *15*(3), 245–258. https://doi.org/10.1002/wps.20346.

Curran, G. M., Bauer, M., Mittman, B., Pyne, J. M., & Stetler, C. (2012). Effectiveness-implementation hybrid designs: Combining elements of clinical effectiveness and implementation research to enhance public health impact. *Medical Care*, *50*(3), 217–226. https://doi.org/10.1097/MLR.0b013e3182408812.

de Oliveira, I. R., Powell, V. B., Wenzel, A., Caldas, M., Seixas, C., Almeida, C., … Sudak, D. (2012). Efficacy of the trial-based thought record, a new cognitive therapy strategy designed to change core beliefs, in social phobia. *Journal of Clinical Pharmacy and Therapeutics*, *37*(3), 328–334. https://doi.org/10.1111/j.1365-2710.2011.01299.x.

Deng, X., Wang, G., Zhou, L., Zhang, X., Yang, M., Han, G., … Liu, B. (2014). Randomized controlled trial of adjunctive EEG-biofeedback treatment of obsessive-compulsive disorder. *Shanghai Archives of Psychiatry*, *26*(5), 272–279. https://doi.org/10.11919/j.issn.1002-0829.214067.

D'Souza, D. C., Radhakrishnan, R., Perry, E., Bhakta, S., Singh, N. M., Yadav, R., … Andrade, C. (2013). Feasibility, safety, and efficacy of the combination of D-serine and computerized cognitive retraining in schizophrenia: An international collaborative pilot study. *Neuropsychopharmacology*, *38*(3), 492–503. https://doi.org/10.1038/npp.2012.208.

Duarte, P. S., Miyazaki, M. C., Blay, S. L., & Sesso, R. (2009). Cognitive-behavioral group therapy is an effective treatment for major depression in hemodialysis patients. *Kidney International*, *76*(4), 414–421. https://doi.org/10.1038/ki.2009.156.

Eaton, J., McCay, L., Semrau, M., Chatterjee, S., Baingana, F., Araya, R., … Saxena, S. (2011). Scale up of services for mental health in low-income and middle-income countries. *Lancet*, *378*(9802), 1592–1603.

Edries, N., Jelsma, J., & Maart, S. (2013). The impact of an employee wellness programme in clothing/textile manufacturing companies: A randomised controlled trial. *BMC Public Health*. *13*. 25. https://doi.org/10.1186/1471-2458-13-25.

Ellis, A. (1957). Rational psychotherapy and individual psychology. *Journal of Individual Psychology*, *13*, 38–44.
Fabrizio, C. S., Lam, T. H., Hirschmann, M. R., Pang, I., Yu, N. X., Wang, X., & Stewart, S. M. (2015). Parental emotional management benefits family relationships: A randomized controlled trial in Hong Kong, China. *Behaviour Research and Therapy*, *71*, 115–124. https://doi.org/10.1016/j.brat.2015.05.011.
Fairburn, C. G., & Patel, V. (2014). The global dissemination of psychological treatments: A road map for research and practice. *American Journal of Psychiatry*, *171*(5), 495–498. https://doi.org/10.1176/appi.ajp.2013.13111546.
Fann, J. R., Bombardier, C. H., Vannoy, S., Dyer, J., Ludman, E., Dikmen, S., … Temkin, N. (2015). Telephone and in-person cognitive behavioral therapy for major depression after traumatic brain injury: A randomized controlled trial. *Journal of Neurotrauma*, *32*(1), 45–57. https://doi.org/10.1089/neu.2014.3423.
Faramarzi, M., Alipor, A., Esmaelzadeh, S., Kheirkhah, F., Poladi, K., & Pash, H. (2008). Treatment of depression and anxiety in infertile women: Cognitive behavioral therapy versus fluoxetine. *Journal of Affective Disorders*, *108*(1-2), 159–164. https://doi.org/10.1016/j.jad.2007.09.002.
Faramarzi, M., Yazdani, S., & Barat, S. (2015). A RCT of psychotherapy in women with nausea and vomiting of pregnancy. *Human Reproduction*, *30*(12), 2764–2773. https://doi.org/10.1093/humrep/dev248.
Farrer, L., Christensen, H., Griffiths, K. M., & Mackinnon, A. (2011). Internet-based CBT for depression with and without telephone tracking in a national helpline: Randomised controlled trial. *PLoS ONE*. *6*(11)e28099https://doi.org/10.1371/journal.pone.0028099.
Gaete, J., Martinez, V., Fritsch, R., Rojas, G., Montgomery, A. A., & Araya, R. (2016). Indicated school-based intervention to improve depressive symptoms among at risk Chilean adolescents: A randomized controlled trial. *BMC Psychiatry*. *16*, 276https://doi.org/10.1186/s12888-016-0985-4.
Gaudiano, B. A. (2008). Cognitive-behavioral therapies: Achievements and challenges. *Evidence-Based Mental Health*, *11*(1), 5–7. https://doi.org/10.1136/ebmh.11.1.5.
Gearing, R. E., Schwalbe, C. S., Mackenzie, M. J., Brewer, K. B., Ibrahim, R. W., Olimat, H. S., … Al-Krenawi, A. (2012). Adaptation and translation of mental health interventions in Middle Eastern Arab countries: A systematic review of barriers to and strategies for effective treatment implementation. *International Journal of Social Psychiatry*, *20*, 20.
Ghimire, D., Chardoul, S., Kessler, R., Axinn, W., & Adhikari, B. (2013). Modifying and validating the composite international diagnostic interview (CIDI) for use in Nepal. *International Journal of Methods in Psychiatric Research*, *22*(1), 71–81. https://doi.org/10.1002/mpr.1375.
Giasuddin, N. A., Nahar, J. S., Morshed, N. M., Balhara, Y. P., & Sobhan, M. A. (2013). Efficacy of combination of fluoxetine and cognitive behavioral therapy and fluoxetine alone for the treatment of obsessive compulsive disorder. *Pakistan Journal of Pharmaceutical Sciences*, *26*(1), 95–98.
Gohar, S. M., Hamdi, E., El Ray, L. A., Horan, W. P., & Green, M. F. (2013). Adapting and evaluating a social cognitive remediation program for schizophrenia in Arabic. *Schizophrenia Research*, *148*(1–3), 12–17. https://doi.org/10.1016/j.schres.2013.05.008.
Gomes, B. C., Abreu, L. N., Brietzke, E., Caetano, S. C., Kleinman, A., Nery, F. G., & Lafer, B. (2011). A randomized controlled trial of cognitive behavioral group therapy for bipolar disorder. *Psychotherapy and Psychosomatics*, *80*(3), 144–150. https://doi.org/10.1159/000320738.

Gorayeb, R., Borsari, A. C., Rosa-e-Silva, A. C., & Ferriani, R. A. (2012). Brief cognitive behavioral intervention in groups in a Brazilian assisted reproduction program. *Behavioral Medicine*, *38*(2), 29–35. https://doi.org/10.1080/08964289.2012.654834.

Gratzer, D., & Khalid-Khan, F. (2016). Internet-delivered cognitive behavioural therapy in the treatment of psychiatric illness. *CMAJ: Canadian Medical Association Journal*, *188*(4), 263–272. https://doi.org/10.1503/cmaj.150007.

Guo, X., Zhai, J., Liu, Z., Fang, M., Wang, B., Wang, C., … Zhao, J. (2010). Effect of antipsychotic medication alone vs combined with psychosocial intervention on outcomes of early-stage schizophrenia: A randomized, 1-year study. *Archives of General Psychiatry*, *67*(9), 895–904. https://doi.org/10.1001/archgenpsychiatry.2010.105.

Guo, Z. H., Li, Z. J., Ma, Y., Sun, J., Guo, J. H., Li, W. X., … Kingdon, D. (2017). Brief cognitive-behavioural therapy for patients in the community with schizophrenia: Randomised controlled trial in Beijing, China. *British Journal of Psychiatry*, *210*(3), 223–229. https://doi.org/10.1192/bjp.bp.116.183285.

Habib, N., Dawood, S., Kingdon, D., & Naeem, F. (2015). Preliminary evaluation of culturally adapted CBT for psychosis (CA-CBTp): Findings from developing culturally-sensitive CBT project (DCCP). *Behavioural and Cognitive Psychotherapy*, *43*(2), 200–208. https://doi.org/10.1017/s1352465813000829.

Hall, B. J., Bolton, P. A., Annan, J., Kaysen, D., Robinette, K., Cetinoglu, T., … Bass, J. K. (2014). The effect of cognitive therapy on structural social capital: Results from a randomized controlled trial among sexual violence survivors in the Democratic Republic of the Congo. *American Journal of Public Health*, *104*(9), 1680–1686. https://doi.org/10.2105/ajph.2014.301981.

Hamdan-Mansour, A. M., Puskar, K., & Bandak, A. G. (2009). Effectiveness of cognitive-behavioral therapy on depressive symptomatology, stress and coping strategies among Jordanian university students. *Issues in Mental Health Nursing*, *30*(3), 188–196. https://doi.org/10.1080/01612840802694577.

Henwood, K. S., Browne, K. D., & Chou, S. (2016). A randomized controlled trial exploring the effects of brief anger management on community-based offenders in malta. *International Journal of Offender Therapy and Comparative Criminology*. https://doi.org/10.1177/0306624x16666338.

Henwood, K. S., Chou, S., & Browne, K. D. (2015). A systematic review and meta-analysis on the effectiveness of CBT informed anger management. *Aggression and Violent Behavior*, *25*(Part B), 280–292. https://doi.org/10.1016/j.avb.2015.09.011.

Hofmann, S. G., Asnaani, A., Vonk, I. J. J., Sawyer, A. T., & Fang, A. (2012). The efficacy of cognitive behavioral therapy: A review of meta-analyses. *Cognitive Therapy and Research*, *36*(5), 427–440. https://doi.org/10.1007/s10608-012-9476-1.

Huang, F., Tang, Y. L., Zhao, M., Wang, Y., Pan, M., Wang, Y., & Qian, Q. (2017). Cognitive-behavioral therapy for adult ADHD: A randomized clinical trial in China. *Journal of Attention Disorders*. https://doi.org/10.1177/1087054717725874.

Husain, N., Afsar, S., Ara, J., Fayyaz, H., Rahman, R. U., Tomenson, B., … Chaudhry, I. B. (2014). Brief psychological intervention after self-harm: Randomised controlled trial from Pakistan. *British Journal of Psychiatry*, *204*(6), 462–470. https://doi.org/10.1192/bjp.bp.113.138370.

Husain, N., Chaudhry, N., Fatima, B., Husain, M., Amin, R., Chaudhry, I. B., … Creed, F. (2014). Antidepressant and group psychosocial treatment for depression: A rater blind exploratory RCT from a low income country. *Behavioural and Cognitive Psychotherapy*, *42*(6), 693–705. https://doi.org/10.1017/s1352465813000441.

Husain, N., Zulqernain, F., Carter, L. A., Chaudhry, I. B., Fatima, B., Kiran, T., … Rahman, A. (2017). Treatment of maternal depression in urban slums of Karachi, Pakistan: A randomized controlled trial (RCT) of an integrated maternal psychological and early child development intervention. *Asian Journal of Psychiatry*, *29*, 63–70. https://doi.org/10.1016/j.ajp.2017.03.010.

Hutchinson, G., Willner, P., Rose, J., Burke, I., & Bastick, T. (2017). CBT in a Caribbean context: A controlled trial of anger management in trinidadian prisons. *Behavioural and Cognitive Psychotherapy*, *45*(1), 1–15. https://doi.org/10.1017/s1352465816000266.

Hwang, W. (2010). The formative method for adapting psychotherapy (FMAP): A community-based developmental approach to culturally adapting therapy. *Professional Psychology: Research and Practice*, *40*(4), 369–377. https://doi.org/10.1037/a0016240.

Hyun, M. S., Chung, H. I., & Lee, Y. J. (2005). The effect of cognitive-behavioral group therapy on the self-esteem, depression, and self-efficacy of runaway adolescents in a shelter in South Korea. *Applied Nursing Research*, *18*(3), 160–166. https://doi.org/10.1016/j.apnr.2004.07.006.

Hyun, M. S., Nam, K. A., & Kim, M. A. (2010). Randomized controlled trial of a cognitive-behavioral therapy for at-risk Korean male adolescents. *Archives of Psychiatric Nursing*, *24*(3), 202–211. https://doi.org/10.1016/j.apnu.2009.07.005.

Ickovics, J., Niccolai, L., Lewis, J., Kershaw, T., & Ethier, K. (2003). High postpartum rates of sexually transmitted infections among teens: Pregnancy as a window of opportunity for prevention. *Sexually Transmitted Infections*, *79*, 469–473.

Iftene, F., Predescu, E., Stefan, S., & David, D. (2015). Rational-emotive and cognitive-behavior therapy (REBT/CBT) versus pharmacotherapy versus REBT/CBT plus pharmacotherapy in the treatment of major depressive disorder in youth; a randomized clinical trial. *Psychiatry Research*, *225*(3), 687–694. https://doi.org/10.1016/j.psychres.2014.11.021.

Ishola, A. G., & Chipps, J. (2015). The use of mobile phones to deliver acceptance and commitment therapy in the prevention of mother-child HIV transmission in Nigeria. *Journal of Telemedicine and Telecare*, *21*(8), 423–426. https://doi.org/10.1177/1357633x15605408.

Jakobsen, J. C., Lindschou Hansen, J., Storebø, O. J., Simonsen, E., & Gluud, C. (2011). The effects of cognitive therapy versus 'treatment as usual' in patients with major depressive disorder, *PLoS ONE*. *6*(8). e22890. https://doi.org/10.1371/journal.pone.0022890.

Jiang, X., & He, G. (2012). Effects of an uncertainty management intervention on uncertainty, anxiety, depression, and quality of life of chronic obstructive pulmonary disease outpatients. *Research in Nursing & Health*, *35*(4), 409–418. https://doi.org/10.1002/nur.21483.

Jones, C., Hacker, D., Cormac, I., Meaden, A., & Irving, C. B. (2012). Cognitive behavioural therapy versus other psychosocial treatments for schizophrenia. *Cochrane Database of Systematic Reviews*. *4*, CD008712https://doi.org/10.1002/14651858.CD008712.pub2.

Jordans, M. J., Komproe, I. H., Tol, W. A., Kohrt, B. A., Luitel, N. P., Macy, R. D., & de Jong, J. T. (2010). Evaluation of a classroom-based psychosocial intervention in conflict-affected Nepal: A cluster randomized controlled trial. *Journal of Child Psychology and Psychiatry*, *51*(7), 818–826. https://doi.org/10.1111/j.1469-7610.2010.02209.x.

Jung, H. Y., Lee, H., & Park, J. (2015). Comparison of the effects of Korean mindfulness-based stress reduction, walking, and patient education in diabetes mellitus. *Nursing & Health Sciences*, *17*(4), 516–525. https://doi.org/10.1111/nhs.12229.

Kaczkurkin, A. N., & Foa, E. B. (2015). Cognitive-behavioral therapy for anxiety disorders: An update on the empirical evidence. *Dialogues in Clinical Neuroscience*, *17*(3), 337–346.

Kakuma, R., Minas, H., van Ginneken, N., Dal Poz, M., Desiraju, K., Morris, J., … Scheffler, R. (2011). Human resources for mental health care: Current situation and strategies for action. *Lancet*, *378*(9803), 1654–1663. https://doi.org/10.1016/S0140-6736(11)61093-3.

Kalantari, M., Yule, W., Dyregrov, A., Neshatdoost, H., & Ahmadi, S. J. (2012). Efficacy of writing for recovery on traumatic grief symptoms of Afghani refugee bereaved adolescents: A randomized control trial. *Omega (Westport)*, *65*(2), 139–150. https://doi.org/10.2190/OM.65.2.d.

Karairmak, O., & Aydin, G. (2008). Reducing earthquake-related fears in victim and nonvictim children. *Journal of Genetic Psychology*, *169*(2), 177–185. https://doi.org/10.3200/gntp.169.2.177-186.

Khanlary, Z., Maarefvand, M., Biglarian, A., & Heravi-Karimooi, M. (2016). The effect of a family-based intervention with a cognitive-behavioral approach on elder abuse. *Journal of Elder Abuse & Neglect*, *28*(2), 114–126. https://doi.org/10.1080/08946566.2016.1141738.

Khodayarifard, M., Shokoohi-Yekta, M., & Hamot, G. E. (2010). Effects of individual and group cognitive-behavioral therapy for male prisoners in iran. *International Journal of Offender Therapy and Comparative Criminology*, *54*(5), 743–755. https://doi.org/10.1177/0306624x09344840.

Kim, S., Lee, H., Kim, H., Noh, D., & Lee, H. (2016). Effects of an integrated stress management program (ISMP) for psychologically distressed students: A randomized controlled trial. *Perspectives in Psychiatric Care*, *52*(3), 178–185. https://doi.org/10.1111/ppc.12114.

Kleinman, A. (2008). *Rethinking psychiatry: From cultural category to personal experience*. New York: Simon and Schuster.

Kohrt, B. A., Jordans, M. J. D., Rai, S., Shrestha, P., Luitel, N. P., Ramaiya, M. K., … Patel, V. (2015). Therapist competence in global mental health: Development of the ENhancing Assessment of Common Therapeutic factors (ENACT) rating scale. *Behaviour Research and Therapy*, *69*, 11–21. https://doi.org/10.1016/j.brat.2015.03.009.

Kraus-Schuman, C., Wilson, N. L., Amspoker, A. B., Wagener, P. D., Calleo, J. S., Diefenbach, G., … Stanley, M. A. (2015). Enabling lay providers to conduct CBT for older adults: Key steps for expanding treatment capacity. *Translational Behavioral Medicine*, *5* (3), 247–253. https://doi.org/10.1007/s13142-015-0306-3.

Kumpfer, K., Alvarado, R., Smith, P., & Bellamy, N. (2002). Cultural sensitivity and adaptation in family-based prevention interventions. *Prevention Science*, *3*(3), 241–246. https://doi.org/10.1023/a:1019902902119.

Kumpfer, K. L., Pinyuchon, M., de Melo, A. T., & Whiteside, H. O. (2008). Cultural adaptation process for international dissemination of the strengthening families program. *Evaluation & the Health Professions*, *31*(2), 226–239. https://doi.org/10.1177/0163278708315926.

La Roche, M., & Christopher, M. S. (2008). Culture and empirically supported treatments: On the road to a collision? *Culture & Psychology*, *14*(3), 333–356. https://doi.org/10.1177/1354067x08092637.

Lam, K. C., Ho, C. P., Wa, J. C., Chan, S. M., Yam, K. K., Yeung, O. S., … Balzan, R. P. (2015). Metacognitive training (MCT) for schizophrenia improves cognitive insight: A randomized controlled trial in a Chinese sample with schizophrenia spectrum disorders. *Behaviour Research and Therapy*, *64*, 38–42. https://doi.org/10.1016/j.brat.2014.11.008.

Lau, A. S. (2006). Making the case for selective and directed cultural adaptations of evidence-based treatments: Examples from parent training. *Clinical Psychology: Science and Practice*, *13*(4), 295–310. https://doi.org/10.1111/j.1468-2850.2006.00042.x.

Lau, W. Y., Chan, C. K., Li, J. C., & Au, T. K. (2010). Effectiveness of group cognitive-behavioral treatment for childhood anxiety in community clinics. *Behaviour Research and Therapy*, *48*(11), 1067–1077. https://doi.org/10.1016/j.brat.2010.07.007.

Lee, S. W., & Kwon, J. H. (2013). The efficacy of imagery rescripting (IR) for social phobia: A randomized controlled trial. *Journal of Behavior Therapy and Experimental Psychiatry*, *44*(4), 351–360. https://doi.org/10.1016/j.jbtep.2013.03.001.

Lee, W. K. (2013). Effectiveness of computerized cognitive rehabilitation training on symptomatological, neuropsychological and work function in patients with schizophrenia. *Asia-Pacific Psychiatry*, *5*(2), 90–100. https://doi.org/10.1111/appy.12070.

Lee, Y. M., & Yeun, Y. R. (2017). Effects of combined foot massage and cognitive behavioral therapy on the stress response in middle-aged women. *Journal of Alternative and Complementary Medicine*, *23*(6), 445–450. https://doi.org/10.1089/acm.2016.0421.

Lerma, A., Perez-Grovas, H., Bermudez, L., Peralta-Pedrero, M. L., Robles-Garcia, R., & Lerma, C. (2017). Brief cognitive behavioural intervention for depression and anxiety symptoms improves quality of life in chronic haemodialysis patients. *Psychology and Psychotherapy*, *90*(1), 105–123. https://doi.org/10.1111/papt.12098.

Li, Z. J., Guo, Z. H., Wang, N., Xu, Z. Y., Qu, Y., Wang, X. Q., … Kingdon, D. (2015). Cognitive-behavioural therapy for patients with schizophrenia: A multicentre randomized controlled trial in Beijing, China. *Psychological Medicine*, *45*(9), 1893–1905. https://doi.org/10.1017/s0033291714002992.

Lim, J. Y., Kim, M. A., Kim, S. Y., Kim, E. J., Lee, J. E., & Ko, Y. K. (2010). The effects of a cognitive-behavioral therapy on career attitude maturity, decision making style, and self-esteem of nursing students in Korea. *Nurse Education Today*, *30*(8), 731–736. https://doi.org/10.1016/j.nedt.2010.01.014.

Lin, Y., Xu, L., Huang, X., Jiang, F., Lin, F., Ye, Q., & Lin, J. (2016). Cardiac valve noise reduction by non-drug interventions improves the sleep quality of patients after mechanical cardiac valve implantation. *Annals of Thoracic and Cardiovascular Surgery*, *22*(2), 69–75. https://doi.org/10.5761/atcs.oa.15-00275.

Liu, G., Jack, H., Piette, A., Mangezi, W., Machando, D., Rwafa, C., … Abas, M. (2016). Mental health training for health workers in Africa: A systematic review. *Lancet Psychiatry*, *3*(1), 65–76. https://doi.org/10.1016/S2215-0366(15)00379-X.

Lopez, S., Nelson Hipke, K., Polo, A., Jenkins, J., Karno, M., Vaughn, C., & Snyder, K. (2004). Ethnicity, expressed emotion, attributions, and course of schizophrenia: Family warmth matters. *Journal of Abnormal Psychology*, *113*(3), 428–439.

Lou, P., Zhu, Y., Chen, P., Zhang, P., Yu, J., Zhang, N., … Zhao, J. (2013). Supporting smoking cessation in chronic obstructive pulmonary disease with behavioral intervention: A randomized controlled trial. *BMC Family Practice*, *14*. 91. https://doi.org/10.1186/1471-2296-14-91.

Lundgren, T., Dahl, J., & Hayes, S. C. (2008). Evaluation of mediators of change in the treatment of epilepsy with acceptance and commitment therapy. *Journal of Behavioral Medicine*, *31*(3), 225–235. https://doi.org/10.1007/s10865-008-9151-x.

Mahdizadeh, M., Peymam, N., Taghipour, A., Esmaily, H., & Mahdizadeh, S. M. (2013). Effect of health education program on promoting physical activity among diabetic women in Mashhad, Iran: Applying social cognitive theory. *Journal of Research in Health Sciences*, *13*(1), 90–97.

Maneesakorn, S., Robson, D., Gournay, K., & Gray, R. (2007). An RCT of adherence therapy for people with schizophrenia in Chiang Mai, Thailand. *Journal of Clinical Nursing*, *16*(7), 1302–1312. https://doi.org/10.1111/j.1365-2702.2007.01786.x.

Manjula, M., Prasadarao, P. S., Kumaraiah, V., & Raguram, R. (2014). Temporal patterns of change in panic disorder during cognitive behaviour therapy: An Indian study. *Behavioural and Cognitive Psychotherapy*, *42*(5), 513–525. https://doi.org/10.1017/s1352465813000635.

Mantell, J. E., Smit, J. A., Exner, T. M., Mabude, Z., Hoffman, S., Beksinska, M., … Stein, Z. A. (2015). Promoting female condom use among female university students in KwaZulu-Natal, South Africa: Results of a randomized behavioral trial. *AIDS and Behavior*, *19* (7), 1129–1140. https://doi.org/10.1007/s10461-014-0860-6.

McBain, R. K., Salhi, C., Hann, K., Kellie, J., Kamara, A., Salomon, J. A., … Betancourt, T. S. (2015). Improving outcomes for caregivers through treatment of young people affected by war: A randomized controlled trial in Sierra Leone. *Bulletin of the World Health Organization*, *93*(12), 834–841. https://doi.org/10.2471/blt.14.139105.

McCann, T. V., Songprakun, W., & Stephenson, J. (2015). Effectiveness of guided self-help in decreasing expressed emotion in family caregivers of people diagnosed with depression in Thailand: A randomised controlled trial. *BMC Psychiatry*, *15*. 258. https://doi.org/10.1186/s12888-015-0654-z.

McCann, T. V., Songprakun, W., & Stephenson, J. (2016). Efficacy of a self-help manual in increasing resilience in carers of adults with depression in Thailand. *International Journal of Mental Health Nursing*, *25*(1), 62–70. https://doi.org/10.1111/inm.12178.

McHugh, R. K., Murray, H. W., & Barlow, D. H. (2009). Balancing fidelity and adaptation in the dissemination of empirically-supported treatments: The promise of transdiagnostic interventions. *Behaviour Research and Therapy*, *47*(11), 946–953.

McMullen, J., O'Callaghan, P., Shannon, C., Black, A., & Eakin, J. (2013). Group trauma-focused cognitive-behavioural therapy with former child soldiers and other war-affected boys in the DR Congo: A randomised controlled trial. *Journal of Child Psychology and Psychiatry*, *54*(11), 1231–1241. https://doi.org/10.1111/jcpp.12094.

Mendenhall, E., De Silva, M. J., Hanlon, C., Petersen, I., Shidhaye, R., Jordans, M., … Lund, C. (2014). Acceptability and feasibility of using non-specialist health workers to deliver mental health care: Stakeholder perceptions from the PRIME district sites in Ethiopia, India, Nepal, South Africa, and Uganda. *Social Science & Medicine*, *118*, 33–42. https://doi.org/10.1016/j.socscimed.2014.07.057.

Michaud, J., & Kates, J. (2013). Global health diplomacy: Advancing foreign policy and global health interests. *Global Health: Science and Practice*, *1*(1), 24–28. https://doi.org/10.9745/ghsp-d-12-00048.

Min, Z., Xu, L., Chen, H., Ding, X., Yi, Z., & Mingyuang, Z. (2011). A pilot assessment of relapse prevention for heroin addicts in a Chinese rehabilitation center. *American Journal of Drug and Alcohol Abuse*, *37*(3), 141–147. https://doi.org/10.3109/00952990.2010.538943.

Momeni, J., Omidi, A., Raygan, F., & Akbari, H. (2016). The effects of mindfulness-based stress reduction on cardiac patients' blood pressure, perceived stress, and anger: A single-blind randomized controlled trial. *Journal of the American Society of Hypertension*, *10*(10), 763–771. https://doi.org/10.1016/j.jash.2016.07.007.

Mon, M. M., Liabsuetrakul, T., & Htut, K. M. (2016). Effectiveness of mindfulness intervention on psychological behaviors among adolescents with parental HIV Infection: A group-randomized controlled trial. *Asia-Pacific Journal of Public Health*, *28*(8), 765–775. https://doi.org/10.1177/1010539516675698.

Montero-Marin, J., Garcia-Campayo, J., López-Montoyo, A., Zabaleta-Del-Olmo, E., & Cuijpers, P. (2017). Is cognitive-behavioural therapy more effective than relaxation therapy in the treatment of anxiety disorders? A meta-analysis. *Psychological Medicine*, *17*, 1–12.

Moustafa, I. M., & Diab, A. A. (2015). The addition of upper cervical manipulative therapy in the treatment of patients with fibromyalgia: A randomized controlled trial. *Rheumatology International*, *35*(7), 1163–1174. https://doi.org/10.1007/s00296-015-3248-7.

Murray, C. J. L., Vos, T., Lozano, R., Naghavi, M., Flaxman, A. D., Michaud, C., … Lopez, A. D. (2012). Disability-adjusted life years (DALYs) for 291 diseases and injuries in 21 regions, 1990–2010: A systematic analysis for the global burden of disease study 2010. *Lancet*, *380*(9859), 2197–2223. https://doi.org/10.1016/S0140-6736(12)61689-4.

Murray, L. K., Skavenski, S., Kane, J. C., Mayeya, J., Dorsey, S., Cohen, J. A., … Bolton, P. A. (2015). Effectiveness of trauma-focused cognitive behavioral therapy among trauma-affected children in Lusaka, Zambia: A randomized clinical trial. *JAMA Pediatrics*, *169* (8), 761–769. https://doi.org/10.1001/jamapediatrics.2015.0580.

Naeem, F., Gul, M., Irfan, M., Munshi, T., Asif, A., Rashid, S., … Ayub, M. (2015). Brief culturally adapted CBT (CaCBT) for depression: A randomized controlled trial from Pakistan. *Journal of Affective Disorders*, *177*, 101–107. https://doi.org/10.1016/j.jad.2015.02.012.

Naeem, F., Saeed, S., Irfan, M., Kiran, T., Mehmood, N., Gul, M., … Kingdon, D. (2015). Brief culturally adapted CBT for psychosis (CaCBTp): A randomized controlled trial from a low income country. *Schizophrenia Research*, *164*(1-3), 143–148. https://doi.org/10.1016/j.schres.2015.02.015.

Naeem, F., Sarhandi, I., Gul, M., Khalid, M., Aslam, M., Anbrin, A., … Ayub, M. (2014). A multicentre randomised controlled trial of a carer supervised culturally adapted CBT (CaCBT) based self-help for depression in Pakistan. *Journal of Affective Disorders*, *156*, 224–227. https://doi.org/10.1016/j.jad.2013.10.051.

Naeem, F., Waheed, W., Gobbi, M., Ayub, M., & Kingdon, D. (2011). Preliminary evaluation of culturally sensitive CBT for depression in Pakistan: Findings from developing culturally-sensitive CBT project (DCCP). *Behavioural and Cognitive Psychotherapy*, *39*(2), 165–173. https://doi.org/10.1017/s1352465810000822.

Nance, D. C. (2012). Pains, joys, and secrets: Nurse-led group therapy for older adults with depression. *Issues in Mental Health Nursing*, *33*(2), 89–95. https://doi.org/10.3109/01612840.2011.624258.

Neuner, F., Onyut, P. L., Ertl, V., Odenwald, M., Schauer, E., & Elbert, T. (2008). Treatment of posttraumatic stress disorder by trained lay counselors in an African refugee settlement: A randomized controlled trial. *Journal of Consulting and Clinical Psychology*, *76*(4), 686–694. https://doi.org/10.1037/0022-006x.76.4.686.

Neuner, F., Schauer, M., Klaschik, C., Karunakara, U., & Elbert, T. (2004). A comparison of narrative exposure therapy, supportive counseling, and psychoeducation for treating post-traumatic stress disorder in an african refugee settlement. *Journal of Consulting and Clinical Psychology*, *72*(4), 579–587. https://doi.org/10.1037/0022-006x.72.4.579.

Ng, Q. X., Venkatanarayanan, N., & Kumar, L. (2017). A systematic review and meta-analysis of the efficacy of cognitive behavioral therapy for the management of pediatric migraine. *Headache*, *57*(3), 349–362.

Niu, Y. X., Tan, J. P., Guan, J. Q., Zhang, Z. Q., & Wang, L. N. (2010). Cognitive stimulation therapy in the treatment of neuropsychiatric symptoms in Alzheimer's disease: A randomized controlled trial. *Clinical Rehabilitation*, *24*(12), 1102–1111. https://doi.org/10.1177/0269215510376004.

O'Callaghan, P., McMullen, J., Shannon, C., Rafferty, H., & Black, A. (2013). A randomized controlled trial of trauma-focused cognitive behavioral therapy for sexually exploited, war-affected Congolese girls. *Journal of the American Academy of Child and Adolescent Psychiatry*, *52*(4), 359–369. https://doi.org/10.1016/j.jaac.2013.01.013.

Ogel, K., & Coskun, S. (2011). Cognitive behavioral therapy-based brief intervention for volatile substance misusers during adolescence: A follow-up study. *Substance Use & Misuse*, *46*(Suppl 1), 128–133. https://doi.org/10.3109/10826084.2011.580233.

Onyechi, K. C., Eseadi, C., Okere, A. U., Onuigbo, L. N., Umoke, P. C., Anyaegbunam, N. J., … Ugorji, N. J. (2016). Effects of cognitive behavioral coaching on depressive symptoms in a sample of type 2 diabetic inpatients in Nigeria. *Medicine (Baltimore)*, *95*(31). e4444. https://doi.org/10.1097/md. 0000000000004444.

Onyechi, K. C., Eseadi, C., Umoke, P. C., Ikechukwu-Ilomuanya, A. B., Otu, M. S., Obidoa, J. C., … Ugwuozor, F. O. (2017). Effects of a group-focused cognitive behavioral health education program on cigarette smoking in a sample of Nigerian prisoners. *Medicine (Baltimore)*, *96*(1). e5158. https://doi.org/10.1097/md.0000000000005158.

Ougrin, D. (2011). Efficacy of exposure versus cognitive therapy in anxiety disorders: Systematic review and meta-analysis. *BMC Psychiatry*, *11*, 200. https://doi.org/10.1186/1471-244X-11-200.

Pan, S., Jiang, H., Du, J., Chen, H., Li, Z., Ling, W., & Zhao, M. (2015). Efficacy of cognitive behavioral therapy on opiate use and retention in methadone maintenance treatment in China: A randomised trial. *PLoS ONE*. *10*(6). e0127598. https://doi.org/10.1371/journal.pone.0127598.

Papas, R. K., Sidle, J. E., Gakinya, B. N., Baliddawa, J. B., Martino, S., Mwaniki, M. M., … Maisto, S. A. (2011). Treatment outcomes of a stage 1 cognitive-behavioral trial to reduce alcohol use among human immunodeficiency virus-infected out-patients in western Kenya. *Addiction*, *106*(12), 2156–2166. https://doi.org/10.1111/j.1360-0443.2011.03518.x.

Paradies, Y. (2006). A systematic review of empirical research on self-reported racism and health. *International Journal of Epidemiology*, *35*(4), 888–901. https://doi.org/10.1093/ije/dyl056.

Park, M. H., Kwon, D. Y., Seo, W. K., Lim, K. S., & Song, M. S. (2009). The effects of cognitive training on community-dwelling elderly Koreans. *Journal of Psychiatric and Mental Health Nursing*, *16*(10), 904–909. https://doi.org/10.1111/j.1365-2850.2009.01467.x.

Patel, V., Chowdhary, N., Rahman, A., & Verdeli, H. (2011). Improving access to psychological treatments: Lessons from developing countries. *Behaviour Research and Therapy*, *49*(9), 523–528. https://doi.org/10.1016/j.brat.2011.06.012.

Patel, V., Weiss, H., Chowdhary, N., Naik, S., Pednekar, S., Chatterjee, S., … Kirkwood, B. (2010). Effectiveness of an intervention led by lay health counsellors for depressive and anxiety disorders in primary care in Goa, India (MANAS): A cluster randomised controlled trial. *Lancet*, *376*(9758).

Perez, M. G., Feldman, L., & Caballero, F. (1999). Effects of a self-management educational program for the control of childhood asthma. *Patient Education and Counseling*, *36*(1), 47–55.

Petersen, I., Fairall, L., Bhana, A., Kathree, T., Selohilwe, O., Brooke-Sumner, C., & Patel, V. (2015). Integrating mental health into chronic care in South Africa: The development of a district mental healthcare plan. *British Journal of Psychiatry*. https://doi.org/10.1192/bjp.bp.114.153726.

Petersen, I., Lund, C., & Stein, D. J. (2011). Optimizing mental health services in low-income and middle-income countries. *Current Opinion in Psychiatry*, *24*(4), 318–323.

Phang, C. K., Mukhtar, F., Ibrahim, N., Keng, S. L., & Mohd Sidik, S. (2015). Effects of a brief mindfulness-based intervention program for stress management among medical students: The Mindful-Gym randomized controlled study. *Advances in Health Sciences Education: Theory and Practice*, *20*(5), 1115–1134. https://doi.org/10.1007/s10459-015-9591-3.

Pityaratstian, N., Piyasil, V., Ketumarn, P., Sitdhiraksa, N., Ularntinon, S., & Pariwatcharakul, P. (2015). Randomized controlled trial of group cognitive behavioural therapy for post-traumatic stress disorder in children and adolescents exposed to tsunami in Thailand. *Behavioural and Cognitive Psychotherapy*, *43*(5), 549–561. https://doi.org/10.1017/s1352465813001197.

Prince, M. (2008). Measurement validity in cross-cultural comparative research. *Epidemiologia e Psichiatria Sociale*, *17*(3), 211–220.

Qouta, S. R., Palosaari, E., Diab, M., & Punamaki, R. L. (2012). Intervention effectiveness among war-affected children: A cluster randomized controlled trial on improving mental health. *Journal of Traumatic Stress*, *25*(3), 288–298. https://doi.org/10.1002/jts.21707.

Rabiei, M., Mulkens, S., Kalantari, M., Molavi, H., & Bahrami, F. (2012). Metacognitive therapy for body dysmorphic disorder patients in Iran: Acceptability and proof of concept. *Journal of Behavior Therapy and Experimental Psychiatry*, *43*(2), 724–729. https://doi.org/10.1016/j.jbtep.2011.09.013.

Rahman, A., Malik, A., Sikander, S., Roberts, C., & Creed, F. (2008). Cognitive behaviour therapy-based intervention by community health workers for mothers with depression and their infants in rural Pakistan: A cluster-randomised controlled trial. *Lancet*, *372* (9642), 902–909. https://doi.org/10.1016/s0140-6736(08)61400-2.

Raj, M. A., Kumaraiah, V., & Bhide, A. V. (2001). Cognitive-behavioural intervention in deliberate self-harm. *Acta Psychiatrica Scandinavica*, *104*(5), 340–345.

Rakitzi, S., Georgila, P., Efthimiou, K., & Mueller, D. R. (2016). Efficacy and feasibility of the integrated psychological therapy for outpatients with schizophrenia in Greece: Final results of a RCT. *Psychiatry Research*, *242*, 137–143. https://doi.org/10.1016/j.psychres.2016.05.039.

Ratanasiripong, P., Park, J. F., Ratanasiripong, N., & Kathalae, D. (2015). Stress and anxiety management in nursing students: Biofeedback and mindfulness meditation. *Journal of Nursing Education*, *54*(9), 520–524. https://doi.org/10.3928/01484834-20150814-07.

Rathod, S., Pinninti, N., Irfan, M., Gorczynski, P., Rathod, P., Gega, L., & Naeem, F. (2017). Mental health service provision in low- and middle-income countries. *Health Services Insights*, *10*. https://doi.org/10.1177/1178632917694350.

Rodriguez-Martin, B. C., Moritz, S., Molerio-Perez, O., & Gil-Perez, P. (2013). Effectiveness of association splitting in reducing unwanted intrusive thoughts in a nonclinical sample. *Behavioural and Cognitive Psychotherapy*, *41*(4), 433–440. https://doi.org/10.1017/s1352465812000513.

Russell, B. S., Eaton, L. A., & Petersen-Williams, P. (2013). Intersecting epidemics among pregnant women: Alcohol use, interpersonal violence, and HIV infection in South Africa. *Current HIV/AIDS Reports*, *10*(1), 103–110.

Sabetnejad, Z., Assarian, F., Omidi, A., & Najarzadegan, M. R. (2016). Effectiveness of cognitive behavioral therapy and fluoxetine on sexual function of women with obsessive compulsive disorder: A double-blind randomized controlled trial. *Electron Physician*, *8*(11), 3156–3163. https://doi.org/10.19082/3156.

Salehi, F., Pourasghar, M., Khalilian, A., & Shahhosseini, Z. (2016). Comparison of group cognitive behavioral therapy and interactive lectures in reducing anxiety during pregnancy: A quasi experimental trial. *Medicine (Baltimore)*, *95*(43). e5224. https://doi.org/10.1097/md.0000000000005224.

Saraceno, B., van Ommeren, M., Batniji, R., Cohen, A., Gureje, O., Mahoney, J., … Underhill, C. (2007). Barriers to improvement of mental health services in low-income and middle-income countries. *The Lancet*, *370*(9593), 1164–1174. https://doi.org/10.1016/S0140-6736(07)61263-X.

Satyanarayana, V. A., Nattala, P., Selvam, S., Pradeep, J., Hebbani, S., Hegde, S., & Srinivasan, K. (2016). Integrated cognitive behavioral intervention reduces intimate partner violence among alcohol dependent men, and improves mental health outcomes in their spouses: A clinic based randomized controlled trial from South India. *Journal of Substance Abuse Treatment*, *64*, 29–34. https://doi.org/10.1016/j.jsat.2016.02.005.

Sava, F. A., Yates, B. T., Lupu, V., Szentagotai, A., & David, D. (2009). Cost-effectiveness and cost-utility of cognitive therapy, rational emotive behavioral therapy, and fluoxetine (Prozac) in treating depression: A randomized clinical trial. *Journal of Clinical Psychology*, *65*(1), 36–52. https://doi.org/10.1002/jclp.20550.

Schwarz, N. (2003). Culture-sensitive context effects: A challenge for cross-cultural surveys. In J. Harkness, F. Van de Vijver, & M. P (Eds.), *Cross-cultural Survey Methods* (pp. 93–100). New York: John Wiley & Sons.

Seyffert, M., Lagisetty, P., Landgraf, J., Chopra, V., Pfeiffer, P. N., Conte, M. L., & Rogers, M. A. M. (2016). Internet-delivered cognitive behavioral therapy to treat insomnia: A systematic review and meta-analysis. *PLoS ONE*, *11*(2). e0149139. https://doi.org/10.1371/journal.pone.0149139.

Shao, D., Gao, W., & Cao, F. L. (2016). Brief psychological intervention in patients with cervical cancer: A randomized controlled trial. *Health Psychology*, *35*(12), 1383–1391. https://doi.org/10.1037/hea0000407.

Sharif, F., Masoudi, M., Ghanizadeh, A., Dabbaghmanesh, M. H., Ghaem, H., & Masoumi, S. (2014). The effect of cognitive-behavioral group therapy on depressive symptoms in people with type 2 diabetes: A randomized controlled clinical trial. *Iranian Journal of Nursing and Midwifery Research*, *19*(5), 529–536.

Shata, Z. N., Amin, M. R., El-Kady, H. M., & Abu-Nazel, M. W. (2017). Efficacy of a multicomponent psychosocial intervention program for caregivers of persons living with neurocognitive disorders, Alexandria, Egypt: A randomized controlled trial. *Avicenna Journal of Medicine*, *7*(2), 54–63. https://doi.org/10.4103/2231-0770.203610.

Shein-Szydlo, J., Sukhodolsky, D. G., Kon, D. S., Tejeda, M. M., Ramirez, E., & Ruchkin, V. (2016). A randomized controlled study of cognitive-behavioral therapy for posttraumatic stress in street children in Mexico City. *Journal of Traumatic Stress*, *29*(5), 406–414. https://doi.org/10.1002/jts.22124.

Sheriff, R., Adams, C., Tharyan, P., Jayaram, M., & Duley, L. (2008). Randomised trials relevant to mental health conductedin low and middle-income countries: A survey. *BMC Psychiatry*, *6*(1), 1–6. https://doi.org/10.1186/1471-244X-8-69.

Sikander, S., Maselko, J., Zafar, S., Haq, Z., Ahmad, I., Ahmad, M., … Rahman, A. (2015). Cognitive-behavioral counseling for exclusive breastfeeding in rural pediatrics: A cluster RCT. *Pediatrics*, *135*(2), e424–e431. https://doi.org/10.1542/peds.2014-1628.

Smit, J., van der Berg, C., Bekker, L., Seedat, S., & Stein, D. (2006). Translation and cross-cultural adaptation of a mental health battery in an African setting. *African Health Sciences*, *6*(4), 215–222.

Solati, K., Mousavi, M., Kheiri, S., & Hasanpour-Dehkordi, A. (2017). The effectiveness of mindfulness-based cognitive therapy on psychological symptoms and quality of life in systemic lupus erythematosus patients: A randomized controlled trial. *Oman Medical Journal*, *32*(5), 378–385. https://doi.org/10.5001/omj.2017.73.

Song, Y., & Lindquist, R. (2015). Effects of mindfulness-based stress reduction on depression, anxiety, stress and mindfulness in Korean nursing students. *Nurse Education Today*, *35*(1), 86–90. https://doi.org/10.1016/j.nedt.2014.06.010.

Songprakun, W., & McCann, T. V. (2012a). Evaluation of a bibliotherapy manual for reducing psychological distress in people with depression: A randomized controlled trial. *Journal of Advanced Nursing*, *68*(12), 2674–2684. https://doi.org/10.1111/j.1365-2648.2012.05966.x.

Songprakun, W., & McCann, T. V. (2012b). Evaluation of a cognitive behavioural self-help manual for reducing depression: A randomized controlled trial. *Journal of Psychiatric and Mental Health Nursing*, *19*(7), 647–653. https://doi.org/10.1111/j.1365-2850.2011.01861.x.

Stefanaki, C., Bacopoulou, F., Livadas, S., Kandaraki, A., Karachalios, A., Chrousos, G. P., & Diamanti-Kandarakis, E. (2015). Impact of a mindfulness stress management program on stress, anxiety, depression and quality of life in women with polycystic ovary syndrome: A randomized controlled trial. *Stress*, *18*(1), 57–66. https://doi.org/10.3109/10253890.2014.974030.

Sue, S., Zane, N., Nagayama Hall, G. C., & Berger, L. K. (2009). The case for cultural competency in psychotherapeutic interventions. *Annual Review of Psychology*, *60*, 525–548.

Sumathipala, A., Siribaddana, S., Abeysingha, M. R., De Silva, P., Dewey, M., Prince, M., & Mann, A. H. (2008). Cognitive-behavioural therapy v. structured care for medically unexplained symptoms: Randomised controlled trial. *The British Journal of Psychiatry*, *193*(1), 51–59. https://doi.org/10.1192/bjp.bp.107.043190.

Sungur, M., Soygur, H., Guner, P., Ustun, B., Cetin, I., & Falloon, I. R. (2011). Identifying an optimal treatment for schizophrenia: A 2-year randomized controlled trial comparing integrated care to a high-quality routine treatment. *International Journal of Psychiatry in Clinical Practice*, *15*(2), 118–127. https://doi.org/10.3109/13651501.2011.554987.

Sweetland, A. C., Belkin, G. S., & Verdeli, H. (2013). Measuring depression and anxiety in Sub-Saharan Africa. *Depression and Anxiety*, *18*(10)22142.

Thapinta, D., Skulphan, S., & Kittrattanapaiboon, P. (2014). Brief cognitive behavioral therapy for depression among patients with alcohol dependence in Thailand. *Issues in Mental Health Nursing*, *35*(9), 689–693. https://doi.org/10.3109/01612840.2014.917751.

The Cochrane Group (2012). *LMIC filters*. Retrieved from http://epoc.cochrane.org/lmic-filters.

Toledo, E. L., De Togni Muniz, E., Brito, A. M., de Abreu, C. N., & Tavares, H. (2015). Group treatment for trichotillomania: Cognitive-behavioral therapy versus supportive therapy. *Journal of Clinical Psychiatry*, *76*(4), 447–455. https://doi.org/10.4088/JCP.13m08964.

Tomlinson, M., Swartz, L., Kruger, L.-M., & Gureje, O. (2007). Manifestations of affective disturbance in sub-Saharan Africa: Key themes. *Journal of Affective Disorders*, *102*(1–3), 191–198. https://doi.org/10.1016/j.jad.2006.09.029.

Tulbure, B. T., Szentagotai, A., David, O., Stefan, S., Mansson, K. N., David, D., & Andersson, G. (2015). Internet-delivered cognitive-behavioral therapy for social anxiety disorder in Romania: A randomized controlled trial. *PLoS ONE*. *10*(5), e0123997. https://doi.org/10.1371/journal.pone.0123997.

Uysal-Bozkir, Ö., Parlevliet, J. L., & de Rooij, S. E. (2013). Insufficient cross-cultural adaptations and psychometric properties for many translated health assessment scales: A systematic review. *Journal of Clinical Epidemiology*, *66*(6), 608–618. https://doi.org/10.1016/j.jclinepi.2012.12.004.

Valencia, M., Rascon, M. L., Juarez, F., & Murow, E. (2007). A psychosocial skills training approach in Mexican out-patients with schizophrenia. *Psychological Medicine*, *37*(10), 1393–1402. https://doi.org/10.1017/s0033291707000657.

van Beugen, S., Ferwerda, M., Hoeve, D., Rovers, M. M., Spillekom-van Koulil, S., van Middendorp, H., & Evers, A. W. M. (2014). Internet-based cognitive behavioral therapy for patients with chronic somatic conditions: A meta-analytic review. *Journal of Medical Internet Research*, *16*(3). e88. https://doi.org/10.2196/jmir.2777.

van Straten, A., van der Zweerde, T., Kleiboer, A., Cuijpers, P., Morin, C. M., & Lancee, J. (2017). Cognitive and behavioral therapies in the treatment of insomnia: A meta-analysis. *Sleep Medicine Reviews*, *9*(17), 30034–30035.

Wang, J., Jian, F., Chen, J., Ye, N. S., Huang, Y. H., Wang, S., ... Lin, Y. F. (2012). Cognitive behavioral therapy for orthodontic pain control: A randomized trial. *Journal of Dental Research*, *91*(6), 580–585. https://doi.org/10.1177/0022034512444446.

Wang, J. P., & Maercker, A. (2014). Web-based interventions for traumatized people in mainland China. *European Journal of Psychotraumatology*. *5*, 26519. https://doi.org/10.3402/ejpt.v5.26519.

Wang, S. J., Bytyci, A., Izeti, S., Kallaba, M., Rushiti, F., Montgomery, E., & Modvig, J. (2016). A novel bio-psycho-social approach for rehabilitation of traumatized victims of torture and war in the post-conflict context: A pilot randomized controlled trial in Kosovo. *Conflict and Health*. *10*, 34. https://doi.org/10.1186/s13031-016-0100-y.

Wang, T., Ding, J. Y., Xu, G. X., Zeng, Y., & Xiao, S. R. (2012). Efficacy of Yiqiyangxin Chinese medicine compound combined with cognitive therapy in the treatment of generalized anxiety disorders. *Asian Pacific Journal of Tropical Medicine*, *5*(10), 818–822. https://doi.org/10.1016/s1995-7645(12)60150-3.

Wang, W. D., Li, G. X., Hong, L., Liu, Y. J., Zhao, Y., Lin, Y. N., ... Huang, Y. Y. (2014). Low Resistance Thought Induction Sleep-regulating Technique (TIP3-2) combined with medication for primary insomnia: A randomized controlled trial. *International Journal of Behavioral Medicine*, *21*(4), 618–628. https://doi.org/10.1007/s12529-014-9415-5.

Wang, Z., Wang, J., & Maercker, A. (2013). Chinese my trauma recovery, a web-based intervention for traumatized persons in two parallel samples: Randomized controlled trial. *Journal of Medical Internet Research*, *15*(9). e213. https://doi.org/10.2196/jmir.2690.

Wang, Z., Whiteside, S. P. H., Sim, L., Farah, W., Morrow, A., Alsawas, M., ... Murad, M. H. (2017). Comparative Effectiveness and safety of cognitive behavioral therapy and pharmacotherapy for childhood anxiety disorders: A systematic review and meta-analysis. *JAMA Pediatrics*, *171*(11), 1049–1056.

Wechsberg, W. M., Krupitsky, E., Romanova, T., Zvartau, E., Kline, T. L., Browne, F. A., ... Jones, H. E. (2012). Double jeopardy—drug and sex risks among Russian women who inject drugs: Initial feasibility and efficacy results of a small randomized controlled trial. *Substance Abuse Treatment, Prevention, and Policy*. *7*(1). https://doi.org/10.1186/1747-597x-7-1.

Wei, S., Liu, L., Bi, B., Li, H., Hou, J., Tan, S., ... Liu, Y. (2013). An intervention and follow-up study following a suicide attempt in the emergency departments of four general hospitals in Shenyang, China. *Crisis*, *34*(2), 107–115. https://doi.org/10.1027/0227-5910/a000181.

Weiss, W. M., Murray, L. K., Zangana, G. A., Mahmooth, Z., Kaysen, D., Dorsey, S., ... Bolton, P. (2015). Community-based mental health treatments for survivors of torture and militant attacks in Southern Iraq: A randomized control trial. *BMC Psychiatry*. *15*, 249. https://doi.org/10.1186/s12888-015-0622-7.

Whitbeck, L. (2009). Depressed affect and historical loss among North American indigenous adolescents. *American Indian and Alaska Native Mental Health Research*, *16*(3), 16. https://doi.org/10.5820/aian.1603.2009.16.

WHO (2013). *mhGAP intervention guide for mental, neurological and substance use disorders in non-specialized health settings*. Retrieved from Geneva.

World Health Organization (2009). *Mental health systems in selected low- and middle-income countries: A WHO-AIMS cross national analysis*. Retrieved from Geneva.

World Health Organization (2011). *Mental health atlas 2011*. Retrieved from Geneva.

World Health Organization (2017). *WHO mental health gap action program.* Retrieved from. http://www.who.int/mental_health/mhgap/en/.

Wu, D. Y., Guo, M., Gao, Y. S., Kang, Y. H., Guo, J. C., Jiang, X. L., … Li, M. (2012). Clinical effects of psychological intervention and drug therapy against peptic ulcer. *Asian Pacific Journal of Tropical Medicine*, *5*(10), 831–833. https://doi.org/10.1016/s1995-7645(12)60153-9.

Yalcin, B. M., Unal, M., Pirdal, H., & Karahan, T. F. (2014). Effects of an anger management and stress control program on smoking cessation: A randomized controlled trial. *Journal of American Board of Family Medicine*, *27*(5), 645–660. https://doi.org/10.3122/jabfm.2014.05.140083.

Youngwanichsetha, S., Phumdoung, S., & Ingkathawornwong, T. (2014). The effects of mindfulness eating and yoga exercise on blood sugar levels of pregnant women with gestational diabetes mellitus. *Applied Nursing Research*, *27*(4), 227–230. https://doi.org/10.1016/j.apnr.2014.02.002.

Zhang, Q., Li, F., Zhang, H., Yu, X., & Cong, Y. (2017). Effects of nurse-led home-based exercise & cognitive behavioral therapy on reducing cancer-related fatigue in patients with ovarian cancer during and after chemotherapy: A randomized controlled trial. *International Journal of Nursing Studies*. https://doi.org/10.1016/j.ijnurstu.2017.08.010.

Zhang, Y., Mei, S., Yang, R., Chen, L., Gao, H., & Li, L. (2016). Effects of lifestyle intervention using patient-centered cognitive behavioral therapy among patients with cardio-metabolic syndrome: A randomized, controlled trial. *BMC Cardiovascular Disorders*, *16*(1), 227. https://doi.org/10.1186/s12872-016-0398-9.

Zhang, Z., Zhai, J., Wei, Q., Qi, J., Guo, X., & Zhao, J. (2014). Cost-effectiveness analysis of psychosocial intervention for early stage schizophrenia in China: A randomized, one-year study. *BMC Psychiatry*. *14*, 212. https://doi.org/10.1186/s12888-014-0212-0.

Zhong, N., Yuan, Y., Chen, H., Jiang, H., Du, J., Sun, H., … Zhao, M. (2015). Effects of a randomized comprehensive psychosocial intervention based on cognitive behavioral therapy theory and motivational interviewing techniques for community rehabilitation of patients with opioid use disorders in Shanghai, China. *Journal of Addiction Medicine*, *9*(4), 322–330. https://doi.org/10.1097/adm.0000000000000139.

Zhuang, S. M., An, S. H., & Zhao, Y. (2014). Effect of cognitive behavioural interventions on the quality of life in Chinese heroin-dependent individuals in detoxification: A randomised controlled trial. *Journal of Clinical Nursing*, *23*(9–10), 1239–1248. https://doi.org/10.1111/jocn.12287.

Zu, S., Xiang, Y. T., Liu, J., Zhang, L., Wang, G., Ma, X., … Li, Z. J. (2014). A comparison of cognitive-behavioral therapy, antidepressants, their combination and standard treatment for Chinese patients with moderate-severe major depressive disorders. *Journal of Affective Disorders*, *152-154*, 262–267. https://doi.org/10.1016/j.jad.2013.09.022.

Caroline Kuo, DPhil, MPhil, is assistant professor and assistant dean at Brown University School of Public Health. She also holds an appointment as senior honorary lecturer at the University of Cape Town. Her research focuses on building evidence-based public health programs that can be deployed on a large scale and sustained in low-resource communities for youth and families affected by poor mental health, HIV, and violence.

Emerging models of psychotherapy

6

Maxine F. Spedding[*], *Dixon Chibanda*[†]
[*]Department of Psychiatry & Mental Health, Alan J. Flisher School for Public Mental Health, University of Cape Town, Cape Town, South Africa, [†]Department of Psychiatry, University of Zimbabwe, Harare, Zimbabwe

6.1 Introduction

Traditionally delivered by highly qualified specialists and often considered a luxury, psychotherapy—a highly effective treatment for a broad range of mental disorders (Barth et al., 2013; Wampold & Imel, 2015)—has long been the reserve of the wealthy. However, mental disorders are highly prevalent across all socioeconomic sectors, with a significant burden for societies to bear (Whiteford et al., 2013, 2015). The 2013 Global Burden of Disease Study found that mental and substance use disorders are the leading cause of years lived with disability (YLDs) (Whiteford et al., 2013), accounting for 21.1% of all YLDs and 11% of all disability-adjusted life years (DALYs) (Global Burden of Disease Study Collaborators, 2015). These findings generated increased recognition concerning the burden that mental disorders represent to communities, especially in under-resourced settings such as low- and middle-income countries (LMIC), where it has been found that up to 90% of people who require mental health treatment do not receive any (Kohn et al., 2004; Wang et al., 2007). The treatment gap is not limited to LMIC. The upsurge in forcibly displaced populations around the world has meant that even relatively well-resourced countries must reassess the ways in which mental health treatments are delivered (Sijbrandij et al., 2017; Silove, Ventevogel, & Rees, 2017), making room for the emergence of innovative approaches to psychotherapy.

The global mental health movement has advocated tirelessly for the development of accessible and equitable mental health-care services for all (Kakuma et al., 2011; Lancet Global Mental Health Group et al., 2007; Patel, 2012). It is not surprising then that some of the most important innovations in the field of mental health have focused on attending to the treatment gap crisis. As a result, novel approaches to psychotherapy must generally satisfy one overarching criteria: cost-effectiveness. This is attended to in several ways: first, ensuring the adaptability of the approach to different sociocultural settings; second, developing a scientifically sound evidence base; and third, using innovative delivery methods so as to maximize reach and ensure scalability. Increasing need for task-shifting/task-sharing approaches using nonspecialist health workers, such as lay counselors, has necessitated the development of therapies

Global Mental Health and Psychotherapy. https://doi.org/10.1016/B978-0-12-814932-4.00006-9

that are brief, manualized, portable, culturally sensitive, accessible, and grounded in rigorous evidence.

Task-shifting/task-sharing interventions are not designed to treat severe mental disorders and so do not negate the need for specialist care (WHO, 2007). However, where evidence-based specialist practice is concerned, the cost-effectiveness mandate applies just as rigorously. This is especially so given that—once deemed effective—innovations in specialist psychotherapies are often later adapted for use by nonspecialists, as has been seen with a range of cognitive behavioral therapeutic (CBT) practices (Singla et al., 2017). In this chapter, we will describe several emerging therapy modalities and provide a broad overview of the evidence for each. First, we will describe schema therapy as an emerging "third wave" psychotherapy that shows a great deal of promise. We then explore interpersonal psychotherapy (IPT), an important adaptation of integrated psychodynamic psychotherapies that has recently found significant traction among evidence-based therapies that can be task shifted to lay counselors. Thereafter, we provide an overview of problem-solving therapy (PST) as an important derivative of CBT that has made significant inroads where task-shifting interventions in LMIC are concerned. This is followed by a description of some of the innovative approaches promulgated by the World Health Organization in its *mhGAP Intervention Guide for mental, neurological and substance use disorders in non-specialized health settings, Version 2.0* (mhGAP-IG) (WHO, 2016). Novel methods of delivery are explored in the following section, with a focus on the employment of technology. We conclude by highlighting some of the gaps in the current research and make recommendations concerning the way forward.

6.2 Emerging therapy modalities

6.2.1 Schema therapy

Schema therapy is one of several emerging psychotherapies that falls under the banner of the "third wave" of cognitive behavioral therapies (Hayes & Hofmann, 2017). First described by Young (1990), schema therapy is a therapeutic modality that integrates cognitive behavioral approaches with a variety of techniques and elements from schools such as Gestalt, attachment, constructivist, and psychodynamic therapies (Young, Klosko, & Weishaar, 2003). It was developed for the treatment of chronic and entrenched psychological disorders that are typified by characterological problems and are frequently resistant to traditional CBT approaches or are prone to relapse (Farrell, Reiss, & Shaw, 2014; Young et al., 2003). According to Arntz and Jacob (2013), there are three main ways in which schema therapy differs from traditional CBT. First, it foregrounds problematic emotions, alongside the cognitive and behavioral facets of the patient's problem, using interventions that are emotion focused and experiential. Second, it pays far more attention to childhood experiences as the foundation of dysfunctional patterns than CBT does. Third, it centralizes the therapeutic relationship as a mechanism of change in its role as the source of "limited reparenting" (Arntz & Jacob, 2013).

In their book, *Schema Therapy: A Practitioner's Guide*, Young et al. (2003) describe the conceptual model and provide a guide on the various therapeutic techniques employed in the schema therapy process. In conceptualizing psychopathology, the authors identify 18 "early maladaptive schemas" (EMS) or schemas (used interchangeably) that are formed as a result of unmet core emotional needs during childhood and are thought to be at the heart of these difficult-to-treat conditions. In this model, an EMS is defined as "a broad, pervasive theme or pattern comprised of memories, emotions, cognitions, and bodily sensations, regarding oneself and one's relationships with others, developed during childhood or adolescence, elaborated throughout one's lifetime and dysfunctional to a significant degree" (Young et al., 2003, p. 7). Schemas are seen as organizing principles that impose patterns on experiences so as to make meaningful sense of them.

Young et al. (2003) posit that schemas develop as a result of repeated early childhood experiences in which one or more of the five identified core emotional needs are not met. These needs include the following: "(1) secure attachments to others (includes safety, stability, nurturance, and acceptance); (2) autonomy, competence, and sense of identity; (3) freedom to express valid needs and emotions; (4) spontaneity and play; and (5) realistic limits and self-control" (Young et al., 2003, p. 10). The 18 schemas are grouped in five categories of unmet needs called "schema domains." These are "disconnection and rejection" (which include schemas such as abandonment/instability and mistrust/abuse), "impaired autonomy and performance" (including schemas such as dependence/incompetence and enmeshment/undeveloped self), "impaired limits" (schemas included here are entitlement/grandiosity), "other directedness" (with schemas such as subjugation and self-sacrifice), and "overvigilance and inhibition" (schemas include negativity/pessimism and punitiveness). Maladaptive behavioral responses result when schemas are activated by experiences in the present that confirm the content of the schema. While driven by schemas, behaviors are not considered to be part of them, but rather components of the coping mechanisms employed by the individual to manage the difficult emotional and cognitive content that the maladaptive schema typically engenders. Young et al. (2003) identify three maladaptive coping styles: overcompensation, avoidance, and surrender. These are roughly equated with fight, flight, and freeze, respectively. These styles are expressed in specific behaviors known as coping responses (Young et al., 2003). Activated by an emotional event, a schema mode is the cognitive and emotional state that a person may find him- or herself in at any given moment, which can "flip" rapidly in people with severe personality problems (Dadomo et al., 2016; Young et al., 2003).

The primary goal of schema therapy is "schema healing," so as "to increase conscious control over schemas, working to weaken the memories, emotions, bodily sensations, cognitions, and behaviors associated with them" (Young et al., 2003, p. 29). Correspondingly, the treatment includes cognitive, affective, and behavioral interventions. It has no rigid therapeutic protocol, and the number of sessions is dependent on the client's needs. The therapeutic process is broadly divided into two phases: (1) the assessment and education phase and (2) the change phase. In the first phase, the patient is oriented to the model, helped to identify schemas and their childhood origins, and taught to recognize maladaptive coping responses that serve to perpetuate problematic schemas. A variety of tools might be used for assessment purposes, including a life history interview, schema questionnaires, and imagery exercises to trigger schemas. The therapist and patient work collaboratively to develop a conceptualization of the schema case and determine a schema-focused treatment plan that incorporates cognitive, behavioral, and emotional strategies, which are employed in the second phase. Cognitive strategies include evaluating the evidence for and against a particular schema so as to refute it. To access emotional content, experiential techniques are used, which might include the use of imagery or role-playing. Strategies to break behavioral patterns might include homework assignments in which the patient is required to practice replacing a maladaptive coping response with an adaptive one. As a backdrop to all techniques, the reparative nature of the therapeutic relationship is essential, especially as seen in two features: empathic confrontation and limited parenting (Young et al., 2003).

The evidence for schema therapy has grown substantially in the last decade. Given that the model was initially intended for the treatment of borderline personality disorder (PD), it's not surprising that the bulk of academic attention concerning this approach has focused on treating this condition (Jacob & Arntz, 2013; Sempértegui et al., 2013), with positive outcomes. In one of the earliest and most promising trials, Giesen-Bloo et al. (2006) compared the efficacy of schema therapy with transference-focused therapy to treat the disorder in 88 patients. After 3 years of biweekly psychotherapy, both groups showed significant reductions in borderline PD symptoms, general psychopathological dysfunction, and changes in associated personality features, along with increased quality of life. However, schema therapy was found to be superior in the reduction of symptoms, general pathological dysfunction, and effecting personality changes as conceptualized by the model (Giesen-Bloo et al., 2006).

Similar findings were demonstrated in a trial that randomized 32 patients with borderline PD to a schema therapy group combined with treatment as usual (TAU), while the control group received TAU (Farrell, Shaw, & Webber, 2009). After 30 weekly group therapy sessions over an 8-month period, results showed significant reductions in borderline PD symptoms and global severity of psychiatric symptoms, along with improved global functioning. Ninety-four percent of the treatment group no longer met the borderline PD criteria, compared with 16% of the TAU cohort (Farrell et al., 2009). Smaller uncontrolled pilot studies have shown similarly large treatment effects. Reiss et al. (2014) report on three independent uncontrolled pilot studies that combined inpatient individual and group schema therapy to treat borderline PD in a total of 92 patients. Their results showed significant reductions in severe borderline PD symptoms and global severity of psychopathology. Likewise, a pilot of two cohorts (combined $n=18$) who also received a combination of weekly group and individual schema therapy showed significantly reduced manifestations of borderline PD with large effect sizes and 77% recovery at 30 months (Dickhaut & Arntz, 2014). These findings are confirmed in a systematic review by Jacob and Arntz (2013), who found large treatment effect sizes in all the studies they reviewed that targeted borderline PD, with a pooled effect size of 2.38 at the 95% confidence interval (Jacob & Arntz, 2013).

High attrition rates among borderline PD patients is a frequent barrier to effective psychotherapy (Kellogg & Young, 2006; Reiss et al., 2014; Sempértegui et al., 2013). However, the results from schema therapy studies generally show high retention rates. The results from the metaanalysis undertaken by Jacob and Arntz (2013) showed attrition rates of just over 10% for schema therapy interventions to treat borderline PD, compared with an average of 25% demonstrated in a random effect metaanalysis for interventions of longer than 12 months in duration (Barnicot, Katsakou, Marougka, & Priebe, 2011, cited in Jacob & Arntz, 2013). In the Giesen-Bloo et al. (2006) study, survival analyses on the attrition rates showed a significantly larger risk of dropout among the transference-focused therapy group than the schema therapy group, while retention rates in the schema therapy group were 100% compared with 75% in the TAU group (Farrell et al., 2009). These are promising findings and suggest that the approach has a high level of acceptability among this population.

More recently, researchers have expanded the focus of schema therapy's effectiveness, targeting a range of other difficult-to-treat problems including other personality disorders (PD) (Bamelis et al., 2014; Bernstein et al., 2012; Jacob & Arntz, 2013), substance use disorders comorbid with PDs (Lee, Cameron, & Jenner, 2015), eating disorders (Linardon et al., 2017; Pugh, 2015), treatment-resistant depression and anxiety (Hawke & Provencher, 2011), and problems associated with emotional dysregulation (Dadomo et al., 2016; Fassbinder et al., 2016). Masley et al. (2012) conducted a systematic review of 12 trials that tested the efficacy of schema therapy to treat a range of psychiatric conditions including personality, eating, substance abuse, and posttraumatic stress disorders. The heterogeneity of methods and outcomes precluded metaanalysis of the data; however, in general, the results were positive. While treatment effect sizes differed, all studies showed symptom reduction. Similarly, Taylor, Bee, and Haddock (2017) reviewed 12 studies that measured the extent to which schema therapy changed both EMS and symptoms across mental disorders. Seven of these studies addressed borderline PD, while two targeted eating disorders, one focused on agoraphobia and personality disorders, one examined PTSD in war veterans, and the last investigated schema therapy's effect on depression. All but one of the eating disorder studies reported reductions in both EMS and symptoms. However, only three studies examined the correlation between EMS and symptom outcome measures. All three found positive correlations between symptom reduction and reductions in EMS (Taylor et al., 2017).

This growing body of evidence suggests that schema therapy represents a promising new approach to intervening with difficult-to-treat psychological and characterological problems. However, very few RCTs have contributed to the evidence base, with both the Masley et al. (2012) and the Taylor et al. (2017) reviews noting the low quality of the available evidence. Furthermore, to the best of our knowledge, there have been no systematic studies of schema therapy in LMIC. As such, the applicability of the modality to other contexts is not clear and needs to be explored.

6.2.2 Interpersonal psychotherapy

Like schema therapy, the contemporary model of interpersonal psychotherapy (IPT) draws on long-standing psychotherapeutic traditions. Grounded in the psychodynamic ideas of Harry Stack Sullivan and the psychobiological theory of Adolf Meyer, the manualized version of IPT was informed by the work of several psychotherapists and developed in the mid-1980s by Gerald Klerman, Myrna Weissman, and colleagues to treat depression (Markowitz & Weissman, 2004). However, as a therapeutic approach, the efficacy of the original was somewhat serendipitously "discovered." Devised as a therapeutic condition for a control group in a clinical trial for antidepressant medication in the 1970s, IPT unexpectedly demonstrated comparable efficacy with medication in the trial's outcomes (Klerman et al., 1984). For the purposes of the trial, Gerald Klerman, Myrna Weissman, and colleagues used the literature available at the time to develop a model that addressed the areas in people's lives that were most commonly affected by depression, which were largely interpersonal in nature (Robertson, Rushton, & Wurm, 2008). With significant evidence of its efficacy, Klerman and colleagues set about formalizing the approach by developing a comprehensive practitioner's guide that was influenced by a number of psychotherapeutic theories, including attachment and family system theory (Weissman, Markowitz, & Klerman, 2000). The result is a diagnosis-specific, time-limited therapy of 12–16 sessions that attends to patients' current interpersonal and psychosocial experiences.

Pragmatic in its approach, IPT is premised on two principals: First, depression is an illness and not the patient's fault, and second, depressive symptoms exist in the interpersonal context, such that clear connections between symptoms and life events can be drawn (Weissman et al., 2000). While it recognizes the influence of patients' histories on their current functioning, these are not the focus of the therapeutic process, according to the *Comprehensive Guide to Interpersonal Psychotherapy* (Weissman et al., 2000). Emphasizing the "here and now," the overarching treatment goal is adaptation to interpersonal situations and the mastery of current social roles, achieved in a process that is divided into three phases. The first phase of one to three sessions incorporates a psychiatric history-taking and diagnostic assessment and establishing the treatment framework. During this phase, the therapist allows the patient to assume Parsons's (1951) definition of the "sick role," which excuses the patient from overwhelming social obligations. Compiling an interpersonal inventory of the patient's social roles and current social functioning provides a framework for understanding the patient's interpersonal context within which the depressive symptoms have formed, allowing for the treatment focus to be clearly defined. Within this framework, one of four interpersonal problem areas is identified: (1) grief, (2) interpersonal role disputes, (3) role transitions, and (4) interpersonal deficits (Weissman et al., 2000).

According to the manual (Weissman et al., 2000), the second phase of treatment involves the application of strategies that are specific to the selected interpersonal problem area. Addressing *grief* or complicated bereavement, the therapist facilitates a process of mourning and works with the patient to find new relationships and activities that might compensate for the loss. When focusing on *interpersonal role disputes*, the patient and therapist explore the relationship and the nature of the dispute, with a view to developing options to resolve it if possible or ending the relationship if need be. Since *role transition* as a problem area concerns changes in life status, such as the ending of a relationship or career, the focus here is on developing recognition of the positive and negative aspects of the newly assumed role and those of the old role. When a patient is assessed as having significantly inadequate social skills, the problem area of *interpersonal deficits* takes priority. More focus is given to childhood relationships than in other problem areas, and the patient-therapist relationship assumes more of a central role in resolving problems associated with this area. The third and final phase of IPT is concerned with consolidating therapeutic gains and developing strategies to recognize and manage depressive symptoms should they recur in the future (Weissman et al., 2000).

Since its discovery, the evidence for IPT has grown significantly (Bernecker et al., 2017; Cuijpers et al., 2016), with IPT demonstrating comparable efficacy to CBT as an effective psychotherapeutic treatment (Jakobsen et al., 2012; Linardon et al., 2017). IPT has also shown promising outcomes for other psychiatric disorders, including eating and anxiety disorders (Cuijpers et al., 2016; Markowitz & Weissman, 2004). Given the diagnosis-specific design of IPT however, the bulk of the evidence in support of this treatment is for depression. Several systematic reviews and metaanalyses of data have been conducted to date, all of which generally show positive outcomes. Perhaps the largest review to date was a metaanalysis of 90 studies conducted by Cuijpers et al. (2016), which found that IPT may prevent the onset of depressive disorders in subclinical samples, while maintenance IPT had a significant impact on recurrence and relapse rates among clinically depressed samples. Overall, the analysis showed that IPT was not significantly more or less effective than other psychotherapies to treat depression, but combining IPT with pharmacological treatments was significantly more effective than intervening with medication alone (Cuijpers et al., 2016). These findings were echoed in a review by van Hees et al. (2013) of IPT among outpatients receiving IPT for depression.

Other systematic reviews have focused on the efficacy of IPT to treat depression among other special populations, such as perinatal women and adolescents. For example, Sockol (2018) reviewed 28 studies of IPT to treat depression during the perinatal period. She found that IPT effectively reduced depressive symptoms and the prevalence of depressive episodes in prevention studies. Among treatment studies, she found significantly reduced symptoms of both depression and anxiety, in addition to improvements in relationship quality, social adjustment, and social support (Sockol, 2018). Miniati et al. (2014) reviewed 11 clinical trials of IPT to treat postnatal depression and also found that IPT led to overall clinical improvement and often full recovery, as well as reducing the time to recovery and prolonging time spent in remission. Among adolescent populations, Mychailyszyn and Elson (2018) metaanalyzed data from 10 studies of IPT to treat depression in adolescents (IPT-A). They found that IPT-A significantly reduced depressive symptoms and was significantly more effective than control or treatment-as-usual groups in treating depression in this population (Mychailyszyn & Elson, 2018). Similarly, pooled data from a review of seven studies with a total of 538 adolescent participants found that IPT was significantly more effective than control conditions at reducing depressive symptoms at both posttreatment and follow-up intervals, in addition to increasing the posttreatment remission period (Pu et al., 2017).

Until recently, the evidence for IPT was limited to high-income countries such as the United States and Europe (Robertson et al., 2008). With the increasing urgency to cost-effectively address the mental health treatment gap in LMIC, IPT has emerged as a significant role-player in the development of evidence-based task-shifting and collaborative care intervention strategies, particularly in group format. One of the largest of these studies was a cluster randomized controlled trial conducted by Bolton et al. (2003). Thirty villages in rural Uganda were randomly selected; 15 were assigned to study men and 15 to study women. Of the 15 villages assigned to study men, 8 were randomized to the intervention arm and 7 to control conditions. Seven of the 15 female villages were randomized to the intervention and 8 to the control arm. A total of 224 people completed the study: 108 men and 116 women. The intervention comprised 16 weeks of 90 min weekly group IPT sessions delivered by a local lay person. Results showed that IPT was highly effective at reducing both depression symptoms and dysfunction, with 6.5% of all intervention participants and 54.7% of those in the control groups meeting the criteria for major depression post intervention, compared with 86% and 94%, respectively, at baseline. Data from a 6-month follow-up study (Bass et al., 2006) found that intervention's effects largely persisted, with the intervention groups continuing to show significantly lower depression and dysfunction scores than control groups and significantly lower rates of depression. Depression rates among those in the treatment arm were 11.7% compared with 54.9% among controls (Bass et al., 2006).

Other smaller studies of IPT delivered by nonspecialists in LMIC have similarly shown promising results. In Pakistan, Nusrat et al. (2016) randomly assigned 50 mothers assessed as mild to moderately depressed to IPT plus TAU and TAU groups. The intervention group received 10 sessions of IPT. The intervention group fared significantly better compared with control at both 3- and 6-month intervals. In South Africa, Petersen, Bhana, and Baillie (2012) piloted a 12-week, group-based IPT intervention delivered by community health workers to treat 60 primary healthcare patients who were assessed as having moderate-to-severe depression. The intervention group showed a significant reduction in depressive symptoms at both 12- and 24-week postbaseline assessment, compared with the control group. In Uganda, Mutamba et al. (2018) conducted a nonrandomized trial of a 12-session, group-based IPT intervention with 142 caregivers of children affected by nodding syndrome, to reduce both caregiver and child depression. Significantly greater reductions in depression risk among the intervention group were observed, from baseline to 1-month and 6-month postintervention, compared with the TAU group. Depression scores for the children of caregivers in the intervention group were also significantly lower compared with controls at both intervals. Psychological distress, stigma, and social support among caregivers also demonstrated significant effects (Mutamba et al., 2018).

There is a substantial body of evidence supporting the efficacy of specialist-delivered IPT to treat depression and, increasingly, a range of other psychiatric disorders. The evidence for task-shifting IPT to nonspecialist health workers is highly promising but very limited. Furthermore, the majority of the evidence from LMIC is for group-based interventions. More research is needed to establish the efficacy of the modality in these contexts.

6.2.3 Problem solving therapy

As one of the WHO *mhGAP*-recommended treatments (WHO, 2016), PST in particular has garnered significant support as an easily adaptable, user-friendly, and accessible modality (Chibanda et al., 2011; Cuijpers, van Straten, & Warmerdam, 2007; Gellis & Kenaley, 2007; Patel et al., 2009). PST is a brief, evidence-based, cognitive behavioral intervention designed to improve problem-solving skills and coping (D'Zurilla & Nezu, 1999). Since it follows clearly defined steps that are simple to teach and easy to manualize, the risk of intervention drift is decreased, and fidelity to the protocol is better facilitated. PST is grounded in D'Zurilla et al.'s (1998) theory of social problem-solving, where the term "social problem-solving" refers to "the process of problem solving as it occurs in the natural environment or 'real world'" (D'Zurilla, Nezu, & Maydeu-Olivares, 2004, p. 11). D'Zurilla and Goldfried (1971, cited in D'Zurilla et al., 2004) describe problem-solving as a cognitive behavioral process that generates a range of potential solutions to a problem, before increasing the likelihood of choosing one that will be the most effective.

According to D'Zurilla et al. (2004), the ability to problem-solve is composed of two components, namely, problem orientation and problem-solving skills (or problem-solving style). *Problem orientation* is defined as "a metacognitive process involving the operation of a set of relatively stable cognitive-emotional schemas that reflect a person's general beliefs, appraisals, and feelings about problems in living, as well as his or her own problem-solving ability" (D'Zurilla et al., 2004, p. 14). *Problem-solving skills* refer to the cognitive and behavioral activities used to understand a problem and find effective ways of coping with it, requiring five major processes: defining and formulating the problem, generating alternative solutions, deciding on the solution to implement, implementing the solution, and verifying the effectiveness of solution (Nezu & Nezu, 2001).

According to D'Zurilla et al. (2004), the model was further developed to classify individuals' problem-solving abilities according to their *problem-solving orientation* (either positive or negative) and by the dominant of three possible *problem-solving styles* (rational style, impulsivity-carelessness style, and avoidance style). Maladaptive problem-solving exists when individuals have a negative problem orientation and an impulsive-careless or avoidant style of problem-solving. A *rational* problem-solving style is defined as a constructive approach that is deliberate and systematic in its application of problem-solving skills. The *impulsivity-carelessness* style employs problem-solving strategies in hurried, careless, and inadequate ways. Generally, a person with this dominant style will consider very few solutions and often impulsively applies the first that comes to mind. An *avoidance* problem-solving style is typified by procrastination, passivity, and inaction. An individual with this dominant style frequently avoids problems in the hope that they will spontaneously resolve and may shift the responsibility for problem-solving to others (D'Zurilla et al., 2004).

Problem-solving therapy is based on the idea that the capacity for social problem-solving significantly mediates the relationship between stressful life events and experiences and psychological well-being (Bell & D'Zurilla, 2009). It is a strategy that teaches people more effective management of stressful life situations by focusing on changing the problem or the maladaptive response to the situation or both (Nezu & Nezu, 2001). D'Zurilla and Nezu (2007) present a comprehensive generic PST manual incorporating 14 modules that can be adapted and tailored for different populations and purposes. The manual's focus is on principles of general behavior change and resists a prescriptive approach to implementation (D'Zurilla & Nezu, 2010). These modules and their corresponding objectives and activities are summarized in D'Zurilla and Nezu (2010), with the first three modules concerned with introducing the model to the client, assessing the stressful areas of the client's life, and identifying the obstacles to effective problem-solving. The following six modules are concerned with problem orientation and are composed of objectives such as fostering self-efficacy and positive problem orientation, using feelings to recognize problems when they occur, challenging negative thinking and dysfunctional attitudes, developing an understanding of the role of emotions in problem-solving, teaching techniques that inhibit impulsivity and avoidance behaviors, and helping the client to develop more realist problem-solving goals and strategies. The next three modules are focused on fostering the client's creative capacity for generating possible solutions, effective decision-making, and ability to implement and evaluate the effectiveness of the chosen solution. The remaining two modules are focused on maximizing proficient problem-solving attitudes and skills and teaching the client a rapid problem-solving model that can quickly be implemented. Recommendations for how the modules might be incorporated into structured and time-limited formats are also provided, along with a variety of exercises and activities (D'Zurilla & Nezu, 2007, 2010).

A substantial base of empirical evidence supports the efficacy of this approach for the treatment of a wide range of mental health and health problems (Malouff, Thorsteinsson, & Schutte, 2007). Evidence suggests that PST is an effective treatment for several common mental disorders including mood (Bell & D'Zurilla, 2009; Cuijpers et al., 2007), anxiety (den Boer, Wiersma, & van den Bosch, 2004), psychological distress (van't Hof et al., 2011), and substance use disorders (Jaffee & D'Zurilla, 2009; Sorsdahl et al., 2014a, 2014b) in a broad range of sociocultural settings (Chowdhary et al., 2014; Pierce, 2012). It has also been used to support people who have cancer, diabetes, obesity, and chronic headaches (D'Zurilla & Nezu, 2010). It has been adapted for a wide range of populations and age groups, including the elderly, criminal offenders (Gellis & Kenaley, 2007), and pregnant women (Sampson, Villarreal, & Rubin, 2016), using different formats (groups, families, individuals, and couples) (D'Zurilla & Nezu, 2010). Several systematic reviews of PST have been conducted. A metaanalysis of 31 studies found that PST leads to significant reductions in mental health symptoms and is more effective in reducing these problems than treatment-as-usual or attention-control interventions (Malouff et al., 2007). A review of 22 studies of PST for depression in adults found mixed evidence for PST alone but more favorable outcomes when combined with antidepressant treatment (Gellis & Kenaley, 2007). Similarly, Cuijpers et al.'s (2007) metaanalysis of 13 studies of PST for depression found that most studies had results that supported this treatment, but effects varied considerably between studies. In a recent update of this metaanalysis, Cuijpers et al. (2018) reviewed 30 studies investigating the efficacy of PST to treat depression. An overall large effect size was found for PST compared with control groups. However, based on studies with low bias risk and after adjusting for publication bias, the analysis suggested a small effect size, comparable with other psychotherapeutic treatments for depression (Cuijpers et al., 2018).

In low- and middle-income settings, given its adaptability and portability, interest in PST as a cost-effective intervention that can readily be task shifted from specialist health professionals to nonspecialist staff has grown (Abas et al., 2016; Chibanda et al., 2011, 2014; Sorsdahl et al., 2014a, 2014b; van't Hof et al., 2011). While the evidence is still limited, it shows promise. For example, in Zimbabwe, Chibanda et al. (2011) trained 10 lay workers to deliver an adapted PST intervention to 320 adults who screened positive for CMD symptoms. A significant decrease in CMD symptoms was noted after three to six PST sessions. A subsequent cluster randomized trial among 573 randomized patients (286 in the PST intervention group and 287 in the control group) followed up for 6 months resulted in improved symptoms (Chibanda, Weiss, et al., 2016). A recent follow-up study of the same intervention found high acceptability among service users and workers (Abas et al., 2016), and the project is currently being scaled up to 60 primary health-care clinics in Zimbabwe (Chibanda, Verhey, et al., 2016). In South Africa, an adapted PST program was delivered to 103 participants in low-income communities who were experiencing psychological distress (van't Hof et al., 2011). Seventy-three participants completed a 5-week PST self-help program in either workshop or booklet format. Levels of psychological distress dropped significantly post intervention, and the program was positively evaluated. Sorsdahl et al. (2014a, 2014b) had peer counselors deliver a blended motivational interviewing and PST intervention to 20 South African participants screened as at risk for substance abuse. They found significantly reduced substance use at the 3-month follow-up. A study conducted by Chibanda et al. (2014) compared the depression outcomes in two treatment conditions for women living with HIV. Women were randomly assigned to a group PST intervention delivered by trained peer counselors or to a group receiving amitriptyline. At 6 weeks post intervention, the depression scores from the PST group were significantly lower than those receiving the antidepressant (Chibanda et al., 2014). The evidence base in support of PST as a psychotherapy that is adaptable to a range of settings is positive and growing. It is not surprising that the WHO draws on it considerably to inform its intervention packages (WHO, 2015).

6.2.4 The WHO's MhGAP interventions

In order to address the treatment gap in mental health, the WHO has developed a range of low-intensity psychological interventions that are suitable for delivery by nonspecialists (WHO, 2016). These interventions draw on the techniques of evidence-based therapies and are designed for the prevention of psychological problems and treatment of mild mental disorders. They are not intended to treat severe mental disorders. However, in settings where there are no specialist resources, these interventions are often the only means to relief available.

6.2.4.1 Disorder-specific interventions

The WHO recognition of the importance of using this empirical evidence to inform the development of programs that could effectively address the LMIC treatment gap crisis led to the development of the action program, known as *mhGAP* (WHO, 2008, 2015). Updated in 2015, *mhGAP* provided a set of guidelines for health planners and policy-makers, so as to accelerate the scaling up of services to treat MNS disorders. It identified priority conditions that require the most urgent attention in that they represent the largest burden in terms of mortality, morbidity, or disability, as well as those that are associated with elevated economic costs or human rights violations. These priority conditions are depression, psychosis, bipolar disorders, epilepsy, developmental and behavioral disorders in children and adolescents, dementia, alcohol use disorders, drug use disorders, self-harm/suicide, and other significant emotional or medically unexplained complaints (WHO, 2008, 2015).

Based on *mhGAP*, an integrated package of evidence-based interventions was developed for the prevention and management of each priority condition, and this took the form of the *mhGAP Intervention Guide for mental, neurological and substance use disorders in non-specialized health settings, Version 2.0* (mhGAP-IG) (WHO, 2016). In addition to promoting good clinical practice by presenting requirements for general principles of care, mhGAP-IG provides a master flow chart that allows the health worker to conduct an informed assessment of the service user and make logical decisions about condition treatment and management. Depending on various factors related to the condition, such as symptom severity, a range of evidence-based, cost-effective psychosocial interventions are recommended and described for implementation. The package provides templates of adaptable treatments and psychosocial interventions, taking context-related variances into account, including existing barriers. Where human resources are available, the guide recommends "advanced psychosocial interventions" (WHO, 2010, p. 83). These are interventions that are traditionally delivered by specialists but have been successfully implemented in task-shifted models by NHSWs. These include interpersonal psychotherapy (IPT), motivational enhancement therapy, contingency management therapy, social skills therapy, family therapy, and parenting skills, as well as a variety of cognitive behavioral therapies (CBT) and techniques such as behavioral activation, relaxation training, and problem-solving therapy (PST) (WHO, 2016).

The interventions described in mhGAP-IG are all grounded in sound evidence, which is the basis for their inclusion. However, most of that evidence comes from well-resourced countries that used specialists to deliver the interventions. The data supporting the adaptation of these interventions to other contexts, especially in task-shifted formats, are promising but still emerging (Singla et al., 2017). In Nigeria, a demonstration project was implemented in eight local government areas (Gureje et al., 2015). The project trained 198 primary care workers from 68 primary care clinics to deliver mhGAP-IG interventions to treat a range of priority conditions. They found a marked improvement in the care workers' knowledge of mental illness and skills and increased rates of detection and referral (Gureje et al., 2015). Several other ongoing studies are in the process of testing these interventions in low-resource settings. For example, the program for improving mental health care (PRIME) is an ongoing multinational research consortium operating in five LMIC (South Africa, Nepal, India, Ethiopia, and Uganda) (Lund et al., 2012). The overarching purpose of PRIME is to generate high-quality evidence for scaling up mental health interventions in primary health-care settings in LMIC, using interventions from mhGAP-IG to treat priority conditions (Davies & Lund, 2017; Mendenhall et al., 2014).

6.2.4.2 Problem management plus (PM+)

Problem management plus (PM+) was developed by the WHO as a transdiagnostic treatment for delivery by nonspecialist providers (NSP) (World Health Organization, 2016). It is a five-session manualized intervention that was designed for use in adversity-dense communities that typically do not have access to specialist care. It is not intended to treat severe mental illness, but rather to provide people with skill sets to better manage the stress and emotional strain associated with extreme adversity, such as humanitarian crises or natural disasters (Dawson et al., 2015). However, it is also applicable to the treatment of depression, anxiety and stress, whether or not these were caused by adversity. The transdiagnostic feature of the intervention is critical, as it reduces the need for NSPs to know how to make differential diagnoses and learn different interventions (Dawson et al., 2015). The approach deliberately avoids the term "problem-solving" so as to acknowledge the insolubility of certain adverse circumstances (Dawson et al., 2015; World Health Organization, 2016).

The content and procedures of this five-session intervention are clearly detailed in a treatment manual (World Health Organization, 2016). In addition to the intervention itself, the manual includes a range of information, such as basic counseling skills; guidelines for adapting the intervention to local cultures and contexts; information on referral options for those clients who are not suited to the intervention; assessment procedures, including suicide-risk assessment; case studies and dialogue examples; information on self-care; and handouts and aids pertaining to the intervention (World Health Organization, 2016). Sessions are 90 min long in duration and ideally take place on a weekly basis over 5 weeks. Along with psychoeducational and motivational interviewing components, PM+ incorporates four core therapeutic strategies, with an emphasis on behavioral rather than cognitive techniques so as to maximize providers' ability to learn the intervention (Dawson et al., 2015). These include "managing stress"; "managing problems"; "get going, keep doing"; and "strengthening social support" (World Health Organization, 2016). Under "managing stress," NSPs teach clients a technique to regulate breathing, which they are encouraged to practice in-session and in their own time. The "managing problem" component involves teaching clients problem-solving therapy techniques that begin with categorization of problems into solvable, unsolvable, and unimportant as proposed by Bowman, Scogin, and Lyrene (1995). Thereafter, clients are taken through the problem-solving steps of choosing a problem, defining the problem, brainstorming all possible solutions to the problem, choosing a solution along with an action plan to implement it, and reviewing the outcomes in the following session (World Health Organization, 2016). The "get going, keep doing" component is a behavioral activation strategy to address the inertia that frequently accompanies psychological distress. Having identified activities and tasks for the client to engage in (categories include pleasant, self-care, social connection, and exercise), the client and NSP break down the activities into smaller goals and develop a schedule for the activities. The "strengthening social support" component involves encouraging the client to draw on appropriate sources of support. The intervention concludes with relapse prevention strategies and a postintervention assessment (Dawson et al., 2015; World Health Organization, 2016).

While the evidence for the psychotherapeutic techniques that PM+ draws on is substantial, the program itself is relatively novel, and so, the evidence for it is still very limited. To date, two RCTs have been conducted to test the efficacy of the intervention. In Peshawar, Pakistan, Rahman et al. (2016) assessed the efficacy of the intervention at three primary care centers. In a single-blind RCT, 346 adult patients who were assessed by their physicians as having high levels of psychological distress and impaired functioning were assigned to either the PM+ treatment group or enhanced usual care. Three months after the intervention, the treatment group was found to have significantly improved on all primary and secondary outcomes, compared with the control group. The treatment group showed significantly reduced depression, anxiety, and posttraumatic stress symptoms and reduced functional impairment and problems for which the person sought help. At baseline, 94% of the treatment group and 89.7% of the control group met the criteria for depression according to the Patient Health Questionnaire (PHQ-9). *Post hoc* analysis revealed that, at 3-month follow-up, these rates had reduced to 27% for the treatment group and 59% for the control group (Rahman et al., 2016).

A second single-blind RCT in Kenya, conducted by Bryant et al. (2017), recruited 421 adult women who had experienced gender-based violence (GBV) and were identified through community screening as having high levels of psychological distress and functional impairment. The women were randomized to either receive the PM+ intervention delivered by a trained community worker at their home (or another safe place) or facility-based enhanced usual care. The study found that significantly fewer women from the treatment group met the criteria for psychological morbidity as measured by the General Health Questionnaire (GHQ-12) compared with the control group, at both the posttreatment and 3-month follow-up assessment intervals, with a moderate effect size in the intervention's favor. Small-to-moderate effect sizes were found for the intervention on the study's secondary outcomes, with significant reductions in posttraumatic stress symptoms, functional impairment, and problems for which the person sought help. While limited, the evidence delivered by both studies is promising for the scalability of an NSP-delivered intervention for communities that have high levels of adverse circumstances.

6.2.4.3 Thinking healthy

As another low-intensity WHO mhGAP intervention, Thinking Healthy (World Health Organization, 2015) was developed for the treatment of perinatal depression. It was designed for integration into maternal and child care programs in primary care settings and to be delivered by community health workers. It is a manualized intervention that is based on CBT principles and incorporates five modules that are timed to be delivered in accordance with the developmental stage of the infant, with the mother's needs in mind at each stage. Each module comprises three sessions, beginning in the second or third trimester and ending at approximately 1 year after the child's birth. Each session is of 45–60 min in duration and has "Three Steps to Thinking Healthy" that address one of three areas: the personal well-being of the mother, the mother-infant relationship, and the relationship with and support from significant others. These three steps are learning to identify unhealthy thinking, replacing unhealthy thinking with helpful thinking, and practicing thinking and acting healthy. The intervention makes use of illustrations and vignettes to optimize accessibility and includes psychoeducation and activities to be carried out between sessions. In addition to the intervention procedures, the manual contains information about the general principles of CBT, tips on communicating well, information about perinatal depression, training and supervision requirements, and guidelines on how to adapt the intervention to the context (World Health Organization, 2015).

The intervention was adapted from the study conducted by Rahman et al. (2008) in rural Pakistan. This cluster RCT assigned 903 women with major depressive disorder in their third trimester of pregnancy to either the intervention or the control arm. The intervention group received 16 sessions of the CBT intervention, delivered by trained community health workers in participants' homes. The control group received the same number of home visits from untrained community health workers. At 6 months, 23% of the intervention group and 53% of the control group met the criteria for major depression. These effects were sustained at 12 months. No significant difference in the infants' weight-for-age and height-for-age scores was found (Rahman et al., 2008). A follow-up study conducted 7 years later to assess the long-term effects of the intervention on child outcomes found no difference between the treatment and control groups on overall cognitive, socioemotional, or physical development outcomes (Maselko et al., 2015). Several trials are currently underway to develop the evidence base for the program, in India and Pakistan (Atif et al., 2017), Vietnam (Fisher et al., 2014), and Nepal (Jordans et al., 2016).

6.3 Emerging methods of delivery

The innovation of emerging psychotherapies lies not only in the development of effective therapeutic techniques but also in their capacity to reach as many people who need them as possible. To this end, therapies that are likely to gain the most traction in global mental health are those that, first, can be delivered by cadres of health workers other than specialists in the context of task shifting/sharing or collaborative care models (see Chapter 1) and, second, are compatible with technological advances and can be adapted for a variety of technological platforms.

6.3.1 Employing technology

With the invention of the internet and the rapid advent of accompanying technologies, psychotherapy is increasingly being delivered on electronic platforms or supplemented by technological innovations, collectively known as behavioral intervention technologies (BIT) (Mohr et al., 2013). BITs are mental health-specific products of *eHealth* (electronic health) and *mHealth* (mobile health), where *eHealth* broadly encompasses all web-based and electronic platforms and *mHealth* is a subcategory of *eHealth* and refers to applications that are employed on mobile devices such as smartphones and tablets (Clough & Casey, 2015). Perhaps, in part, due to the fact that electronic platforms lend themselves well to collecting data about a range of related matters (Bauer & Moessner, 2012) and, in part, as a result of the exponential rate at which technological developments occur, there is a substantial body of literature examining this topic (Wolf, 2011), despite its novelty. A number of systematic reviews have been conducted, with focus areas that are wide ranging and include the efficacy of technology-based interventions to reduce symptoms of mental disorders (Mohr et al., 2013; Rokicki & Fink, 2017), treatment adherence (Clough & Casey, 2011b; Kauppi et al., 2014; Välimäki et al., 2017), psychotherapy supervision and training (Barnett, 2011; Rousmaniere, Abbass, & Frederickson, 2014; Watkins, 2014; Wolf, 2011), technological adjuncts to psychotherapy (Clough & Casey, 2011a; Eonta et al., 2011; Imel et al., 2017; Lindhiem et al., 2015), and symptom monitoring (Bauer & Moessner, 2012; Dogan et al., 2017).

Remotely delivered psychotherapies, via telephone or internet, were perhaps the earliest endeavors to employ technology in the field. A review of 13 studies examined the clinical effectiveness of remotely communicated, therapist-delivered psychotherapy (Bee et al., 2008). Ten of the reviewed studies assessed psychotherapy by telephone, two investigated psychotherapy via the internet, and one by videoconference. Psychotherapies included CBT, PST, interpersonal therapy, and psychoeducation. For depression, medium pooled effect sizes were found for remote therapy versus control conditions, while for anxiety-related disorders, pooled effect sizes were large (Bee et al., 2008). However, several studies in this review did not compare remote therapy with face-to-face therapy but only with waiting-list control conditions, making it difficult to accurately determine how remote delivery of psychotherapy measures alongside face-to-face therapy. Another systematic review of 20 studies investigating evidence-based therapies delivered by videoconferencing to treat anxiety disorders found that these interventions are both effective at reducing symptoms and comparable with face-to-face psychotherapy (Rees & Maclaine, 2015). These findings were echoed by Backhaus et al. (2012) who reviewed 65 studies and found that using videoconferencing to deliver psychotherapy is feasible, generally associated with good user satisfaction, with similar clinical outcomes to face-to-face psychotherapy.

A broad-based review of research concerning behavioral intervention technologies beyond remote delivery methods was undertaken by an expert panel convened by the Agency for Healthcare Research and Quality and the National Institute of Mental Health (Mohr et al., 2013). They found that videoconferencing is generally effective and acceptable to clients and provides a unique way to extend specialized care to facilities in remote areas. In addition to reducing dropout rates, psychotherapy by telephone was found to be as effective as face-to-face therapy, while moderate effect sizes were found for instant messaging delivery methods. The same review showed that interventions operationalizing evidence-based psychotherapy frameworks for web delivery were effective in the treatment of depression, anxiety, substance use disorders, and insomnia, with promising outcomes for bipolar mood disorder and schizophrenia. However, effect size in these studies ranges between none at all to effect sizes comparable with those found in face-to-face interventions. The inclusion of human support through e-mail or telephone contact has been found to improve both the adherence to and outcomes for these interventions. Studies of mobile BITs have shown positive outcomes for a range of disorders including anxiety, eating disorders, bipolar mood disorder, and schizophrenia, although some studies were not effective at treating depression. The review also found that while internet support groups are frequently used as sources of support and information by patients, the quality of the studies is generally poor (Mohr et al., 2013).

Lindhiem et al. (2015) conducted a metaanalysis of 25 clinical trials to evaluate the benefits of using mobile technology to deliver psychotherapy. The trials targeted a range of problems including substance use disorders, depression, anxiety, post-traumatic stress disorder, and medical conditions such as diabetes or weight loss. Overall, the review found that mobile BITs, as supplements to or substitutions for psychotherapy, improve treatment outcomes more than no treatment at all, with a small-to-medium aggregate effect size that was found across the 25 studies (Lindhiem et al., 2015). However, the review provided no information on the interventions themselves, only the method of delivery, making it difficult to draw conclusions about the mechanisms underlying their effectiveness. Nevertheless, a more rigorous systematic review and metaanalysis of 9 RCTs designed to treat a range of problems that include anxiety symptoms as an outcome also showed generally positive results (Firth et al., 2017). This review found a small-to-moderate effect size of smartphone interventions using cognitive behavioral techniques to reduce total anxiety symptoms, compared with all control conditions. The largest treatment effects were seen in those studies that compared smartphone interventions with waiting-list control conditions. Studies that controlled for attention or user engagement by providing nontherapeutic applications showed significantly smaller benefits. However, smartphone interventions still reduced symptoms of anxiety significantly more than comparison conditions (Firth et al., 2017).

The role of technology to increase treatment adherence has also received some attention. A Cochrane review by Kauppi et al. (2014) concerning the effectiveness of technology-based prompting and support to increase treatment compliance among people with serious mental illness yielded mixed results. The review found that, while prompts showed small effect sizes for improving mental state, increasing levels of insight at 6 months compared with controls, and improving quality of life, there was no clear evidence that prompting improved treatment compliance (Kauppi et al., 2014). However, the review only included two studies, noting the absence of available evidence. The finding was echoed in a study by Clough and Casey (2014) that examined the impact of SMS reminders on appointment attendance among 140 outpatients at a psychology clinic. They found no difference in appointment attendance between patients who received SMS prompts and those who did not. In fact, the dropout rate among those who received prompts was significantly higher compared with controls (Clough & Casey, 2014).

The evidence for the application of technology to the practice of psychotherapy is generally promising. There are several ways in which the use of technology can address barriers to mental health care and contribute to reducing the global treatment gap. These include expanding access to services or treatments, the improved capacity for interventions to reduce stigma as a result of the privacy and anonymity that technology affords, and improving mental health literacy. However, most of the evidence has been generated from high-income countries, and so little is known about their treatment efficacy in resource-poor contexts (Seko et al., 2014), where the burden of mental disorders is particularly acute. While there are a handful of reviews examining mHealth for noncommunicable diseases in LMIC (DeRenzi et al., 2011; Opoku, Stephani, & Quentin, 2017), the evidence of their application to mental health in these settings is minimal (Tomlinson et al., 2013). One systematic review found just three articles that reported on RCTs of online mental health interventions in LMIC (Arjadi et al., 2015). Two of the studies showed reductions in target symptoms, while one did not. In addition to a small number of studies, all used waiting list instead of active controls resulting in the reviewers being unable to draw any firm conclusions regarding the efficacy of BITs in low- and middle-income settings (Arjadi et al., 2015). While the role of BITs in psychotherapy and mental health shows great potential in high-income countries, there is a stark lack of research using BITs in LMIC.

6.4 Conclusion

In this chapter, we described several emerging models of psychotherapy that provided a broad overview of the evidence to support them. First, we described schema therapy and highlighted the growing evidence of its efficacy to address a range of difficult-to-treat mental disorders, including borderline PD. Second, we explored PST as an important derivative of CBT that has generated relatively substantial evidence and made significant contributions to task-shifting intervention research in LMIC. Third, we outlined three of the innovative intervention packages promulgated by World Health Organization's mhGAP-IG. We concluded the chapter by outlining two novel methods of delivery: task shifting/sharing and the employment of technology.

There are several gaps in the research concerning these emerging therapeutic models and methods of delivery. First, it is clear that the evidence is not evenly distributed. The evidence base for schema therapy, for example, is quite substantial;

however, there is currently no evidence for its application to low- and middle-income settings. The same can be said of BITs as a method of delivery: the evidence for their application in high-income countries is considerable but somewhat absent in LMIC. Second, psychotherapies that can be employed in a task-shifting/task-sharing approach have focused on the therapies themselves, with less attention to the human resources required to deliver them. In this respect, core competencies required to deliver effective interventions are only starting to receive some attention (Kohrt et al., 2015). Third, models of supervision for task-shifting/task-sharing approaches have also not been adequately attended to in the current research (see also chapter by Kohrt). This is particularly relevant to the scaling up and integration of interventions into existing primary health-care settings. Future research might consider how technology might be combined with task-shifting interventions to optimize their effectiveness. The WHO recently launched an electronic application for mhGAP (http:/www.who.int/mental_health/mhgap/e_mhgap/en/), which has been used by a study in Kenya as a screening measure to determine the prevalence and determinants of depression (Musyimi et al., 2018). However, the utility of the application for intervention purposes is not yet known. The role that technology might play in the delivery of professional supervision and training for nonspecialist providers in remote settings has also yet to be fully explored.

References

Abas, M., et al. (2016). "Opening up the mind": Problem-solving therapy delivered by female lay health workers to improve access to evidence-based care for depression and other common mental disorders through the Friendship Bench Project in Zimbabwe. *International Journal of Mental Health Systems*, *10*, 39. https://doi.org/10.1186/s13033-016-0071-9.

Arjadi, R., et al. (2015). A systematic review of online interventions for mental health in low and middle income countries: A neglected field. *Global Mental Health*, *2*. e12. https://doi.org/10.1017/gmh.2015.10.

Arntz, A., & Jacob, G. (2013). *Schema therapy in practice: An introductory guide to the schema mode approach.* West Sussex: Wiley Blackwell.

Atif, N., et al. (2017). Mother-to-mother therapy in India and Pakistan: Adaptation and feasibility evaluation of the peer-delivered thinking healthy programme. *BMC Psychiatry*, *17* (1), 1–15. https://doi.org/10.1186/s12888-017-1244-z.

Backhaus, A., et al. (2012). Videoconferencing psychotherapy: A systematic review. *Psychological Services*, *9*(2), 111–131. https://doi.org/10.1037/a0027924.

Bamelis, L. L. M., et al. (2014). Results of a multicenter randomized controlled trial of the clinical effectiveness of schema therapy for personality disorders. *American Journal of Psychiatry*, *171*(3), 305–322. https://doi.org/10.1176/appi.ajp.2013.12040518.

Barnett, J. E. (2011). Utilizing technological innovations to enhance psychotherapy supervision, training, and outcomes. *Psychotherapy*, *48*(2), 103–108. https://doi.org/10.1037/a0023381.

Barth, J., et al. (2013). Comparative efficacy of seven psychotherapeutic interventions for patients with depression: A network meta-analysis. *PLoS Medicine*, *10*(5), e1001454. https://doi.org/10.1371/journal.pmed.1001454.

Bass, J., et al. (2006). Group interpersonal psychotherapy for depression in rural Uganda: 6-month outcomes. *British Journal of Psychiatry*, *188*, 567–573. https://doi.org/10.1192/bjp.188.6.567.

Bauer, S., & Moessner, M. (2012). Technology-enhanced monitoring in psychotherapy and e-mental health. *Journal of Mental Health*, *21*(4), 355–363. https://doi.org/10.3109/09638237.2012.667886.

Bee, P. E., et al. (2008). Psychotherapy mediated by remote communication technologies: A meta-analytic review. *BMC Psychiatry*, *8*(60), 1–14. https://doi.org/10.1186/1471-244X-8-60.

Bell, A. C., & D'Zurilla, T. J. (2009). The influence of social problem-solving ability on the relationship between daily stress and adjustment. *Cognitive Therapy and Research*, *33* (5), 439–448. https://doi.org/10.1007/s10608-009-9256-8.

Bernecker, S. L., et al. (2017). For whom does interpersonal psychotherapy work? A systematic review. *Clinical Psychology Review*, *56*(June), 82–93. https://doi.org/10.1016/j.cpr.2017.07.001.

Bernstein, D. P., et al. (2012). Schema therapy for forensic patients with personality disorders: Design and preliminary findings of a multicenter randomized clinical trial in the Netherlands. *International Journal of Forensic Mental Health*, *11*(4), 312–324. https://doi.org/10.1080/14999013.2012.746757.

Bolton, P., et al. (2003). Group interpersonal psychotherapy for depression in rural Uganda. *JAMA*, *289*(23), 3117–3124.

Bowman, D., Scogin, F., & Lyrene, B. (1995). The efficacy of self-examination therapy and cognitive bibliotherapy in the treatment of mild to moderate depression. *Psychotherapy Research*, *5*, 131–140.

Bryant, R. A., et al. (2017). Effectiveness of a brief behavioural intervention on psychological distress among women with a history of gender-based violence in urban Kenya: A randomised clinical trial. *PLoS Medicine*, *14*(8), 1–20. https://doi.org/10.1371/journal.pmed.1002371.

Chibanda, D., Verhey, R., et al. (2016). Scaling up interventions for depression in sub-Saharan Africa: Lessons from Zimbabwe. *Global Mental Health*, *3*. e13. https://doi.org/10.1017/gmh.2016.8.

Chibanda, D., Weiss, H., et al. (2016). Effect of a primary care-based psychological intervention on symptoms of common mental disorders in Zimbabwe: A randomized clinical trial. *Journal of American*, *316*(24), 2618–2626.

Chibanda, D., et al. (2011). Problem-solving therapy for depression and common mental disorders in Zimbabwe: Piloting a task-shifting primary mental health care intervention in a population with a high prevalence of people living with HIV. *BMC Public Health*, *11* (1), 828. https://doi.org/10.1186/1471-2458-11-828.

Chibanda, D., et al. (2014). Group problem-solving therapy for postnatal depression among HIV positive and HIV negative mothers in Zimbabwe. *Journal of the International Association of Providers of AIDS Care*, *13*(4), 335–341. https://doi.org/10.1177/2325957413495564.

Chowdhary, N., et al. (2014). The content and delivery of psychological interventions for perinatal depression by non-specialist health workers in low and middle income countries: A systematic review. *Best Practice & Research Clinical Obstetrics & Gynaecology*, *28*(1), 113–133. https://doi.org/10.1016/j.bpobgyn.2013.08.013.

Clough, B. A., & Casey, L. M. (2011a). Technological adjuncts to enhance current psychotherapy practices: A review. *Clinical Psychology Review*, *31*(3), 279–292. https://doi.org/10.1016/j.cpr.2010.12.008.

Clough, B. A., & Casey, L. M. (2011b). Technological adjuncts to increase adherence to therapy: A review. *Clinical Psychology Review*, *31*(5), 697–710. https://doi.org/10.1016/j.cpr.2011.03.006.

Clough, B. A., & Casey, L. M. (2014). Using SMS reminders in psychology clinics: A cautionary tale. *Behavioural and Cognitive Psychotherapy*, *42*(3), 257–268. https://doi.org/10.1017/S1352465813001173.

Clough, B. A., & Casey, L. M. (2015). The smart therapist: A look to the future of smartphones and mHealth technologies in psychotherapy. *Professional Psychology: Research and Practice*, *46*(3), 147–153. https://doi.org/10.1037/pro0000011.

Cuijpers, P., van Straten, A., & Warmerdam, L. (2007). Problem solving therapies for depression: A meta-analysis. *European Psychiatry: The Journal of the Association of European Psychiatrists*, *22*(1), 9–15. https://doi.org/10.1016/j.eurpsy.2006.11.001.

Cuijpers, P., et al. (2016). Interpersonal psychotherapy for mental health problems: A comprehensive meta-analysis. *American Journal of Psychiatry*, *173*(7), 680–687. https://doi.org/10.1176/appi.ajp.2015.15091141.

Cuijpers, P., et al. (2018). Problem-solving therapy for adult depression: An updated meta-analysis. *European Psychiatry*, *48*, 27–37. https://doi.org/10.1016/j.eurpsy.2017.11.006.

D'Zurilla, T. J., Chang, E. C., Nottingham, E. J., & Faccini, L. (1998). Social problem-solving deficits and hopelessness, depression, and suicidal risk in college students and psychiatric inpatients. *Journal of Clinical Psychology*, *54*(8), 1091–1107. https://doi.org/10.1002/(SICI)1097-4679(199812)54:8<1091::AID-JCLP9>3.0.CO;2-J.

D'Zurilla, T. J., & Nezu, A. M. (1999). *Problem-solving therapy: a social competence approach to clinical intervention*. New York: Springer Publishing.

D'Zurilla, T., & Nezu, A. (2010). Problem solving therapy. In K. S. Dobson (Ed.), *Handbook of cognitive behavioural therapies* (3rd ed., pp. 197–225). New York: New Guilford Press.

D'Zurilla, T. J., & Nezu, A. M. (2007). *Problem-solving therapy: A positive approach to clinical intervention* (3rd ed.). New York: Springer.

D'Zurilla, T. J., Nezu, A. M., & Maydeu-Olivares, A. (2004). Social problem solving: Theory and assessment. In E. C. Chang, T. D'Zurilla, & L. J. Sanna (Eds.), *Social problem solving: Theory, research, and training* (pp. 11–27). Washington, DC: American Psychological Association.

Dadomo, H., et al. (2016). Schema therapy for emotional dysregulation: Theoretical implication and clinical applications. *Frontiers in Psychology*, *7*(DEC), 1–16. https://doi.org/10.3389/fpsyg.2016.01987.

Davies, T., & Lund, C. (2017). Integrating mental health care into primary care systems in low- and middle-income countries: Lessons from PRIME and AFFIRM. *Global Mental Health*, *4*. e7. https://doi.org/10.1017/gmh.2017.3.

Dawson, K. S., et al. (2015). Problem management plus (PM+): A WHO transdiagnostic psychological intervention for common mental health problems. *World Psychiatry*, *14*(3), 354–357. https://doi.org/10.1002/wps.20255.

den Boer, P. C. A., Wiersma, D., & van den Bosch, R. J. (2004). Why is self-help neglected in the treatment of emotional disorders? A meta-analysis. *Psychological Medicine*, *34*(6), 959–971. https://doi.org/10.1017/S003329170300179X.

DeRenzi, B., et al. (2011). Mobile phone tools for field-based health care workers in low-income countries. *Mount Sinai Journal of Medicine*, *78*(3), 406–418.

Dickhaut, V., & Arntz, A. (2014). Combined group and individual schema therapy for borderline personality disorder: A pilot study. *Journal of Behavior Therapy and Experimental Psychiatry*, *45*(2), 242–251. https://doi.org/10.1016/j.jbtep.2013.11.004.

Dogan, E., et al. (2017). Smartphone-based monitoring of objective and subjective data in affective disorders: Where are we and where are we going? Systematic review. *Journal of Medical Internet Research*, *19*(7), 1–18. https://doi.org/10.2196/jmir.7006.

Eonta, A. M., et al. (2011). Using everyday technology to enhance evidence-based treatments. *Professional Psychology: Research and Practice*, *42*(6), 513–520. https://doi.org/10.1037/a0025825.

Farrell, J. M., Reiss, N., & Shaw, I. A. (2014). *The schema therapy clinician's guide*. West Sussex: Wiley Blackwell.

Farrell, J. M., Shaw, I. A., & Webber, M. A. (2009). A schema-focused approach to group psychotherapy for outpatients with borderline personality disorder: A randomized controlled trial. *Journal of Behavior Therapy and Experimental Psychiatry*, *40*(2), 317–328. https://doi.org/10.1016/j.jbtep.2009.01.002.

Fassbinder, E., et al. (2016). Emotion regulation in schema therapy and dialectical behavior therapy. *Frontiers in Psychology*, *7*(SEP), 1–19. https://doi.org/10.3389/fpsyg.2016.01373.

Firth, J., et al. (2017). Can smartphone mental health interventions reduce symptoms of anxiety? A meta-analysis of randomized controlled trials. *Journal of Affective Disorders*, *218*, 15–22. https://doi.org/10.1016/j.jad.2017.04.046.

Fisher, J., et al. (2014). Translation, cultural adaptation and field-testing of the thinking healthy program for Vietnam. *Globalization and Health*, *10*(1), 1–17.

Gellis, Z. D., & Kenaley, B. (2007). Problem-solving therapy for depression in adults: A systematic review. *Research on Social Work Practice*, *18*(2), 117–131. https://doi.org/10.1177/1049731507301277.

Giesen-Bloo, J., et al. (2006). Outpatient psychotherapy for borderline personality disorder. *Archives of General Psychiatry*, *63*, 649–658. https://doi.org/10.1001/archpsyc.63.6.649.

Global Burden of Disease Study Collaborators. (2015). Global, regional, and national incidence, prevalence, and years lived with disability for 301 acute and chronic diseases and injuries in 188 countries, 1990–2013: A systematic analysis for the global burden of disease study 2013. *Lancet*, *386*, 743–800.

Gureje, O., et al. (2015). Integrating mental health into primary care in Nigeria: Report of a demonstration project using the mental health gap action programme intervention guide. *BMC Health Services Research*, *15*(242), 1–8. https://doi.org/10.1186/s12913-015-0911-3.

Hawke, L. D., & Provencher, M. D. (2011). Schema theory and schema therapy in mood and anxiety disorders: A review. *Journal of Cognitive Psychotherapy*, *25*(4), 257–276. https://doi.org/10.1891/0889-8391.25.4.257.

Hayes, S. C., & Hofmann, S. G. (2017). The third wave of cognitive behavioral therapy and the rise of process-based care. *World Psychiatry*, *16*(3), 245–246. https://doi.org/10.1002/wps.20442.

Imel, Z. E., et al. (2017). Technology-enhanced human interaction in psychotherapy. *Journal of Counseling Psychology*, *64*(4), 385–393. https://doi.org/10.1037/cou0000213.

Jacob, G. A., & Arntz, A. (2013). Schema therapy for personality disorders—A review. *International Journal of Cognitive Therapy*, *6*(2), 171–185.

Jaffee, W. B., & D'Zurilla, T. (2009). Personality, problem solving, and adolescent substance use. *Behavior Therapy*, *40*(1), 93–101.

Jakobsen, J. C., et al. (2012). Effects of cognitive therapy versus interpersonal psychotherapy in patients with major depressive disorder: A systematic review of randomized clinical trials with meta-analyses and trial sequential analyses. *Psychological Medicine*, 1343–1357. https://doi.org/10.1017/S0033291711002236.

Jordans, M. J. D., et al. (2016). Development and pilot testing of a mental healthcare plan in Nepal. *British Journal of Psychiatry*, *208*, s21–s28. https://doi.org/10.1192/bjp.bp.114.153718.

Kakuma, R., et al. (2011). Human resources for mental health care: Current situation and strategies for action. *Lancet*, *378*(9803), 1654–1663. https://doi.org/10.1016/S0140-6736(11)61093-3.

Kauppi, K., et al. (2014). Information and communication technology based prompting for treatment compliance for people with serious mental illness. *Cochrane Database of Systematic Reviews*, *6*. https://doi.org/10.1002/14651858.CD009960.pub2.

Kellogg, S. H., & Young, J. E. (2006). Schema therapy for borderline personality disorder. *Journal of Clinical Psychology*, 445–458. https://doi.org/10.1002/jclp.20240.

Klerman, G. L., et al. (1984). *Interpersonal psychotherapy for depression*. New York: Basic Books.

Kohn, R., et al. (2004). The treatment gap in mental health care. *Bulletin of the World Health Organization*, *82*(3), 858–866.

Kohrt, B. A., et al. (2015). Therapist competence in global mental health: Development of the ENhancing Assessment of Common Therapeutic factors (ENACT) rating scale. *Behaviour Research and Therapy*, *69*, 11–21. https://doi.org/10.1016/j.brat.2015.03.009.

Lancet Global Mental Health Group, et al. (2007). Scale up services for mental disorders: A call for action. *Lancet*, *370*(9594), 1241–1252. https://doi.org/10.1016/S0140-6736(07)61242-2.

Lee, N. K., Cameron, J., & Jenner, L. (2015). A systematic review of interventions for co-occurring substance use and borderline personality disorders. *Drug and Alcohol Review*, *34*(6), 663–672. https://doi.org/10.1111/dar.12267.

Linardon, J., et al. (2017). The empirical status of the third-wave behaviour therapies for the treatment of eating disorders: A systematic review. *Clinical Psychology Review*, *58*(October), 125–140. https://doi.org/10.1016/j.cpr.2017.10.005.

Lindhiem, O., et al. (2015). Mobile technology boosts the effectiveness of psychotherapy and behavioral interventions: A meta-analysis. *Behavior Modification*, *39*(6), 785–804. https://doi.org/10.1177/0145445515595198.

Lund, C., et al. (2012). PRIME: A programme to reduce the treatment gap for mental disorders in five low- and middle-income countries. *PLoS Medicine*, *9*(12), 1–6. https://doi.org/10.1371/journal.pmed.1001359.

Malouff, J. M., Thorsteinsson, E. B., & Schutte, N. S. (2007). The efficacy of problem solving therapy in reducing mental and physical health problems: A meta-analysis. *Clinical Psychology Review*, *27*(1), 46–57. https://doi.org/10.1016/j.cpr.2005.12.005.

Markowitz, J. C., & Weissman, M. M. (2004). Interpersonal psychotherapy: Principles and applications. *World Psychiatry*, *3*(3), 136–139.

Maselko, J., et al. (2015). Impact of an early perinatal depression intervention on longer—Term child development. *Lancet*, *2*(7), 609–617. Available from http://repository.essex.ac.uk/13904/7/Lancet%2520Psychiatry%2520ACCEPTED%2520%25281%2529.pdf (accessed 29.01.18).

Masley, S., et al. (2012). A systematic review of the evidence base for schema therapy. *Cognitive Behaviour Therapy*, *41*(3), 185–202. https://doi.org/10.1080/16506073.2011.614274.

Mendenhall, E., et al. (2014). Acceptability and feasibility of using non-specialist health workers to deliver mental health care: Stakeholder perceptions from the PRIME district sites in Ethiopia, India, Nepal, South Africa, and Uganda. *Social Science & Medicine*, *118*, 33–42. https://doi.org/10.1016/j.socscimed.2014.07.057.

Miniati, M., et al. (2014). Interpersonal psychotherapy for postpartum depression: A systematic review. *Archives of Women's Mental Health*, *17*, 257–268. https://doi.org/10.1007/s00737-014-0442-7.

Mohr, D. C., et al. (2013). Behavioral intervention technologies: Evidence review and recommendations for future research in mental health. *General Hospital Psychiatry*, *35*(4), 332–338. https://doi.org/10.1016/j.genhosppsych.2013.03.008.

Musyimi, C. W., et al. (2018). Mobile based mhGAP-IG depression screening in Kenya. *Community Mental Health Journal*, *54*(1), 84–91. https://doi.org/10.1007/s10597-016-0072-9.

Mutamba, B. B., et al. (2018). Psychological treatments delivered by community health workers in low-resource government health systems: Effectiveness of group interpersonal psychotherapy for caregivers of children affected by nodding syndrome in Uganda. *Psychological Medicine*, 1–11. https://doi.org/10.1017/S0033291718000193.

Mychailyszyn, M. P., & Elson, D. M. (2018). Working through the blues: A meta-analysis on interpersonal psychotherapy for depressed adolescents (IPT-A). *Children and Youth Services Review*, *87*(March), 123–129. https://doi.org/10.1016/j.childyouth.2018.02.011.

Nezu, A. M., & Nezu, C. M. (2001). Problem solving therapy. *Journal of Psychotherapy Integration*, *11*(2), 187–205.

Nusrat, H., et al. (2016). Group interpersonal psychotherapy for maternal depression an exploratory randomized control trial. *European Psychiatry*, *33*, S413–S414.

Opoku, D., Stephani, V., & Quentin, W. (2017). A realist review of mobile phone-based health interventions for non-communicable disease management in sub-Saharan Africa. *BMC Medicine*, *15*(24), 1–12. https://doi.org/10.1186/s12916-017-0782-z.

Parsons, T. (1951). Illness and the role of the physician: A sociological persepctive. *American Journal of Orthopsychiatry*, *21*, 452–460.

Patel, V. (2012). Global mental health: From science to action. *Harvard Review of Psychiatry*, *20*(1), 6–12. https://doi.org/10.3109/10673229.2012.649108.

Patel, V., et al. (2009). Packages of care for depression in low- and middle-income countries. *PLoS Medicine*, *6*(10), e1000159. https://doi.org/10.1371/journal.pmed.1000159.

Petersen, I., Bhana, A., & Baillie, K. (2012). The feasibility of adapted group-based interpersonal therapy (IPT) for the treatment of depression by community health workers within the context of task shifting in South Africa. *Community Mental Health Journal*, *48*(3), 336–341. https://doi.org/10.1007/s10597-011-9429-2.

Pierce, D. (2012). Problem solving therapy: Use and effectiveness in general practice. *Australian Family Physician*, *41*(9), 676–679.

Pu, J., et al. (2017). Efficacy and acceptability of interpersonal psychotherapy for depression in adolescents: A meta-analysis of randomized controlled trials. *Psychiatry Research*, *253* (March), 226–232. https://doi.org/10.1016/j.psychres.2017.03.023.

Pugh, M. (2015). A narrative review of schemas and schema therapy outcomes in the eating disorders. *Clinical Psychology Review*, 30–41. https://doi.org/10.1016/j.cpr.2015.04.003.

Rahman, A., et al. (2008). Cognitive behaviour therapy-based intervention by community health workers for mothers with depression and their infants in rural Pakistan: A cluster-randomised controlled trial. *Lancet*, *372*(9642), 902–909. Available from http://www.ncbi.nlm.nih.gov/pmc/articles/PMC2603063/ (accessed 16.01.13).

Rahman, A., et al. (2016). Effect of a multicomponent behavioral intervention in adults impaired by psychological distress in a conflict-affected area of Pakistan: A randomized clinical trial. *Journal of the American Medical Association*, *316*(24), 2609–2617. https://doi.org/10.1001/jama.2016.17165.

Rees, C. S., & Maclaine, E. (2015). A systematic review of videoconference-delivered psychological treatment for anxiety disorders. *Australian Psychologist*, *50*(4), 259–264. https://doi.org/10.1111/ap.12122.

Reiss, N., et al. (2014). Responding to the treatment challenge of patients with severe BPD: Results of three pilot studies of inpatient schema therapy. *Behavioural and Cognitive Psychotherapy*, *42*(3), 355–367. https://doi.org/10.1017/S1352465813000027.

Robertson, M., Rushton, P., & Wurm, C. (2008). Interpersonal psychotherapy: An overview. *Psychotherapy in Australia*, *14*(3), 46–54. https://doi.org/10.1093/acprof.

Rokicki, S., & Fink, G. (2017). Assessing the reach and effectiveness of mHealth: Evidence from a reproductive health program for adolescent girls in Ghana. *BMC Public Health*, *17*(969), 1–14. https://doi.org/10.1186/s12889-017-4939-7.

Rousmaniere, T., Abbass, A., & Frederickson, J. (2014). New developments in technology-assisted supervision and training: A practical overview. *Journal of Clinical Psychology*, *70*(11), 1082–1093. https://doi.org/10.1002/jclp.22129.

Sampson, M., Villarreal, Y., & Rubin, A. (2016). A problem-solving therapy intervention for low-income, pregnant women at risk for postpartum depression. *Research on Social Work Practice*, *26*(3), 236–242. https://doi.org/10.1177/1049731514551143.

Seko, Y., et al. (2014). Youth mental health interventions via mobile phones: A scoping review. *Cyberpsychology, Behavior, and Social Networking*, *17*(9), 591–602. https://doi.org/10.1089/cyber.2014.0078.

Sempértegui, G. A., et al. (2013). Schema therapy for borderline personality disorder: A comprehensive review of its empirical foundations, effectiveness and implementation possibilities. *Clinical Psychology Review*, *33*(3), 426–447. https://doi.org/10.1016/j.cpr.2012.11.006.

Sijbrandij, M., et al. (2017). Strengthening mental health care systems for Syrian refugees in Europe and the Middle East: Integrating scalable psychological interventions in eight countries. *European Journal of Psychotraumatology*, *8*(Suppl. 2), 1388102. https://doi.org/10.1080/20008198.2017.1388102.

Silove, D., Ventevogel, P., & Rees, S. (2017). The contemporary refugee crisis: An overview of mental health challenges. *World Psychiatry*, *16*(2), 130–139. https://doi.org/10.1002/wps.20438.

Singla, D. R., et al. (2017). Psychological treatments for the world: Lessons from low- and middle-income countries. *Annual Review of Clinical Psychology*, *13*(1), 149–181. https://doi.org/10.1146/annurev-clinpsy-032816-045217.

Sockol, L. E. (2018). A systematic review and meta-analysis of interpersonal psychotherapy for perinatal women. *Journal of Affective Disorders*, *232*(August), 316–328. https://doi.org/10.1016/j.jad.2018.01.018.

Sorsdahl, K., et al. (2014a). Adapting a blended motivational interviewing and problem-solving intervention to address risky substance use amongst South Africans. *Psychotherapy Research*, 37–41. https://doi.org/10.1080/10503307.2014.897770.

Sorsdahl, K., et al. (2014b). Screening and brief interventions for substance use in emergency departments in the Western Cape province of South Africa: Views of health care professionals. *International Journal of Injury Control and Safety Promotion*, *21*(3), 236–243. https://doi.org/10.1080/17457300.2013.811267.

Taylor, C. D. J., Bee, P., & Haddock, G. (2017). Does schema therapy change schemas and symptoms? A systematic review across mental health disorders. *Psychology and Psychotherapy: Theory, Research and Practice*, *90*(3), 456–479. https://doi.org/10.1111/papt.12112.

Tomlinson, M., et al. (2013). Scaling up mHealth: Where is the evidence? *PLoS Medicine*, *10* (2), 1–5. https://doi.org/10.1371/journal.pmed.1001382.

Välimäki, M., et al. (2017). Short text messages to encourage adherence to medication and follow-up for people with psychosis (mobile.net): Randomized controlled trial in Finland. *Journal of Medical Internet Research*, *19*(7), 1–16. https://doi.org/10.2196/jmir.7028.

van Hees, M. L. J. M., et al. (2013). The effectiveness of individual interpersonal psychotherapy as a treatment for major depressive disorder in adult outpatients: A systematic review. *BMC Psychiatry*, *13*(22), 1–10. https://doi.org/10.1186/1471-244X-13-22.

van't Hof, E., et al. (2011). The effectiveness of problem solving therapy in deprived South African communities: Results from a pilot study. *BMC Psychiatry*, *11*(156), 1–8. https://doi.org/10.1186/1471-244X-11-156.

Wampold, B. E., & Imel, Z. E. (2015). *The great psychotherapy debate* (2nd ed.). New York: Routledge.

Wang, P. S., et al. (2007). Worldwide use of mental health services for anxiety, mood, and substance disorders: Results from 17 countries in the WHO world mental health (WMH) surveys. *Lancet*, *370*(9590), 841–850.

Watkins, C. E. (2014). Psychotherapy supervision developments and innovations for the new millennium: Contributions from the cutting edge. *American Journal of Psychotherapy*, *68*(2), 141–149.

Weissman, M. M., Markowitz, J. C., & Klerman, G. L. (2000). *Comprehensive guide to interpersonal psychotherapy*. New York: Basic Books.

Whiteford, H. A., et al. (2013). Global burden of disease attributable to mental and substance use disorders: Findings from the global burden of disease study 2010. *Lancet*, *382*(13), 1575–1586. https://doi.org/10.1016/S0140-6736(13)61611-6.

Whiteford, H. A., et al. (2015). The global burden of mental, neurological and substance use disorders: An analysis from the global burden of disease study 2010. *PLoS ONE*, *10*(2), 1–14. https://doi.org/10.1371/journal.pone.0116820.

WHO (2007). *Task shifting to tackle health worker shortages*: (pp. 1–12). Geneva: WHO. https://doi.org/10.1016/S0033-3506(01)00422-X.

WHO (2015). Mental health gap action programme. *mhGAP Newsletter*, *1*(9), 1–4. Available from http://www.who.int/about/licensing/copyright_.

WHO (2016). *mhGAP intervention guide version 2.0, mhGAP newsletter*. Geneva: World Health Organization. Available from*http://books.google.com/books?id=diAlkgAACAAJ*.

Wolf, A. W. (2011). Internet and video technology in psychotherapy supervision and training. *Psychotherapy*, *48*(2), 179–181. https://doi.org/10.1037/a0023532.

World Health Organization (2008). *mhGAP: Scaling up care for mental, neurological, and substance use disorders, mental health gap action programme*. Geneva: World Health Organization ISBN: 9789241596.

World Health Organization (2010). *mhGAP intervention guide for mental, neurological and substance use disorders in non-specialized health settings*. .

World Health Organization (2015). *Thinking healthy: A manual for psychosocial management of perinatal depression*. Geneva: World Health Organization.

World Health Organization (2016). *Problem management plus (PM+): Individual psychological help for adults impaired by distress in communities exposed to adversity*. Geneva: WHO.

Young, J. E. (1990). *Cognitive therapy for personality disorders: a schema-focused approach*. Sarasota: Professional Resource Exchange.

Young, J. E., Klosko, J. S., & Weishaar, M. E. (2003). *Schema therapy: A practitioner's guide*. New York: Guildford Publications.

Collaborative care models: A global perspective

7

Bradley H. Wagenaar, Inge Petersen†, Deepa Rao*,‡, Lydia Chwastiak‡*
*Department of Global Health, University of Washington, Seattle, WA, United States, †Centre for Rural Health, University of KwaZulu-Natal, Durban, South Africa, ‡Department of Psychiatry and Behavioral Sciences, School of Medicine, University of Washington, Seattle, WA, United States

7.1 Introduction

In well-resourced health-care systems, when health providers identify patients who need treatment from a mental health specialist, they typically provide a written or electronic referral to mental health specialists, for example, psychiatrists, psychologists, or other mental health providers such as social workers or psychiatric nurses located outside of a given clinic. Patients are expected to follow up and arrange separate specialist appointments as needed, and communication between the referring providers and mental health specialists is inconsistent, limited, or nonexistent. If patients fail to present for a given psychiatric referral, there is often no active follow-up from the referring clinic. An improvement on this "siloed" model has been the colocation of mental health specialists within primary care and other clinics—such as gynecologic, infectious disease, or noncommunicable disease clinics—which helps increase access to mental health specialists and facilitates communication and follow-up among diverse providers.

Collaborative care is an evidence-based model for mental health-care integration that goes beyond both of these models and is more than a simple colocation of mental health providers within a health-care center. Collaborative care is delivered by a fully integrated team of providers that includes mental health specialists, with the patient at the center, and a care manager who coordinates the patient's care across the team. This model of integrated mental health-care delivery has been shown to be both more effective and more cost-effective and to lead to greater patient satisfaction, compared with usual care (Archer et al., 2012; Coventry et al., 2014; Katon et al., 2001, 2005, 2012; Liu et al., 2003; Muntingh, van der Feltz-Cornelis, van Marwijk, Spinhoven, & van Balkom, 2016; Unutzer et al., 2002). Collaborative care is a multicomponent delivery model organized around four foundational principles: (1) patient-centered team-based care, (2) population-based care, (3) treatment to target with timely treatment modifications, and (4) use of evidence-based treatments. In collaborative care, there is a focus on quality improvement, and providers are accountable for patient outcomes.

This first principle—patient-centered team-based care—means (i) that care is centered on the patient and organized around a patient's health needs and expectations

Global Mental Health and Psychotherapy. https://doi.org/10.1016/B978-0-12-814932-4.00007-0

and (ii) that providers focus on their function within the care delivery system, rather than focusing on classical roles determined by clinical titles. This requires the integration of many providers (nurses, doctors, psychiatrists, and other mental health providers such as psychiatric nurses, psychologists, social workers, and administrative staff) with different "cultures" of practice to work together on a team. To achieve this goal of team-based care, all providers must work toward common goals, develop mutual trust, clarify roles and workflows, and develop and use active communication strategies. Collaborative care models utilize task-sharing principles whereby specific tasks are assigned, where appropriate, to health workers with less training and fewer qualifications than higher-level specialist providers. For example, in collaborative care models, the care manager who provides first-line mental health care could be a nurse, social worker, or even a lay counselor trained to provide evidence-based psychological/behavioral mental health interventions.

It is important to note this flexibility in collaborative care models—that the exact credentials and makeup of the team will differ based on the availability of specialist staff and the organization of the health system. However, while the credentials, training, and experience of members of the collaborative care team may differ, the four foundational principles should stay intact. For example, as is discussed later in the case studies, care managers in a collaborative care trial ongoing in India for comorbid depression and diabetes had a background in dietetics, diabetes education, and psychology and had experience working with diabetes patients, but were not members of the clinic staff and were not mental health providers.

In the collaborative care model, psychiatric experts do not often see patients directly, but instead provide a consultation service via telemedicine or in-person consultation to the health-care providers and care manager, the frequency of which depends on their availability. Psychiatric experts typically review patient progress and recommend treatment adjustments for patients that are not improving. In addition, psychiatric experts are engaged, where possible, at initiation of treatment to help health-care providers and care managers adopt an appropriate treatment plan. Patients who have severe illness or who have not improved in treatment with the health-care provider team can be "stepped up" to direct consultation with a mental health specialist, thus optimizing the use of scarce psychiatric, psychological, or other specialist time. This is especially important when considering implementing collaborative care in low- and middle-income countries (LMIC) due to scarce availability of mental health experts such as psychiatrists and psychologists. Most often, $<10\%$ of the patient population engaged in collaborative care requires direct mental health specialist consultation.

Most often in collaborative care models, the primary care provider is the initial "gatekeeper" who conducts initial screening and mental health assessment. If the patient needs additional assessment and/or treatment and the patient is willing to work with the collaborative care team, the health-care provider most often provides an in-person introduction to the provider who will provide direct mental health care at the time of that initial visit. The intake health-care team will conduct an assessment, including the use of validated screening tools of the patients' condition, as well as the use of psychoactive substances, previous experience of mental health treatment, and assessment of patient safety. Again, the exact makeup of which providers will do which tasks will vary depending on expertise, resources available, and local health system context and organization.

The health-care team will then collaboratively develop a provisional diagnosis and initial treatment plan. If needed, members of the health-care team may consult with the psychiatrist/psychologist to support the development of the treatment plan. If this treatment plan requires medications, these are prescribed and managed by the appropriate health-care provider, often a primary care doctor or psychiatric nurse. The care manager will then discuss the treatment plan in detail with the patient to address questions and concerns. The care manager coordinates patient care through medication management, referrals to other services, active patient and adherence tracking, and tracking patient outcomes on structured and validated symptom and functional impairment measures.

The second principle of the collaborative care model is population-based care, including active tracking of care and patient outcomes over time. Unlike care as usual where patients are responsible for coordinating their care including following up, scheduling, and organizing disparate referrals to mental health specialists, in collaborative care models, patients are entered into a registry to track all care and patient outcomes. Each patient is assigned to a specific care manager who tracks important dates, scores on mental health screening tools, and treatments. This is essential because the care manager can reach out to patients when they miss appointments, providing support for consistent engagement in care.

The third principle of collaborative care uses the patient registry and validated tools to track patient progress and adjust treatment as necessary. The health-care provider and the care manager use evidence-based guidelines/mental health tools to assess symptoms at each appointment. A common tool that has been used in diverse settings is the Patients Health Questionnaire-9 (PHQ-9) for tracking depressive symptoms (Kroenke, Spitzer, & Williams, 2001). These tools can be combined with structured assessment of functional impairment, response to treatment, or treatment side effects. If alcohol or substance use is a key concern, the use of these substances can also be tracked, along with other general health problems as managed by the health-care provider. Cases are reviewed by the care manager, preferably with a consulting mental health specialist at weekly meetings. If the tracking of outcomes does not suggest clinical improvement, treatment modifications, including stepped care to more intensive treatments, are initiated/recommended collaboratively with the health-care provider and care manager.

The fourth principle of collaborative care focuses on using evidence-based treatments. Care managers provide evidence-based brief behavioral or psychological treatments, such as problem-solving therapy, motivational interviewing, interpersonal psychotherapy, behavioral activation, or cognitive behavioral therapy, as relevant to a given context or patient population. The health-care provider focuses on initiating medication treatment as needed, for patients with severe illness or functional impairment, or if behavioral/psychological treatments have failed to provide sufficient clinical improvement as measured through patient tracking. Team members work together to deliver evidence-based treatment. The health-care provider or care manager can also provide adherence counseling, with the health-care provider often being the first to hear about negative medication side effects. The consulting mental health specialist provides supervision for the different components of the treatment plan: behavioral, psychological, and medication treatments, including the consideration of medical comorbidities (e.g., in the selection of medication).

Collaborative care emphasizes quality improvement and accountability. At the individual patient level, with the use of a registry and tools to track patient treatment outcomes, each provider is accountable to ensure their patients' treatments are adjusted until they achieve clinical improvements or illness remission. At the organizational level, each clinic or clinic group reviews all process and clinical indicators regularly and uses quality improvement methodologies to identify system weaknesses and propose solutions. For example, if a clinic notes low rates of follow-up among adolescent patients, they may add specific evidence-based programming to encourage adherence for adolescents. Or if a clinic group observes long waiting times for appointments, they might change the workflow around referral and then test to see whether this change improves waiting times.

7.2 Evidence for the effectiveness of collaborative care

The collaborative care model has been tested and evaluated in >80 randomized controlled trials (RCTs) in high-income and primarily United States-based settings (Archer et al., 2012). However, there is less high-quality evidence of the effectiveness of the collaborative care model in LMIC settings where the model is necessarily adapted due to a limited number of health-care providers able to prescribe medications for psychiatric illnesses, behavioral health experts trained in evidence-based brief psychological treatments, and mental health specialists to act as consultants on teams. The effectiveness of collaborative care has most often been tested for treating depression (Archer et al., 2012; Gilbody, Bower, Fletcher, Richards, & Sutton, 2006), although significant evidence is accumulating regarding the effectiveness of collaborative care for anxiety disorders (Archer et al., 2012; Muntingh et al., 2016). A systematic review in 2013 could not identify any studies relevant to the use of collaborative care for people with schizophrenia and called for more large well-designed trials testing collaborative care for patients with severe mental illness (Reilly et al., 2013).

One of the first and still the largest RCTs of collaborative care was the "Improving Mood—Promoting Access to Collaborative Treatment" (IMPACT) program, which was a multisite RCT of collaborative care for 1801 individuals 60 years or older with major depression, dysthymia, or both (Unutzer et al., 2001, 2002). This study included 18 primary care clinics across five states, in which collaborative care was introduced and nurses or psychologists were trained as depression care managers. Patient treatment responses were tracked using the PHQ-9—with recovery from depression operationalized as ≥50% reduction in PHQ-9 score and fewer than three of nine symptoms of major depression. At 12 months, 45% of individuals in the collaborative care arm had recovered from their depression, compared with only 19% of usual care participants, a highly statistically significant finding (Unutzer et al., 2002). One of the major intermediate findings was that patients who received collaborative care were significantly more likely to (1) use antidepressants (73% at 12 months compared with 57%), (2) use psychotherapy (43% at 12 months compared with 16%), and (3) be satisfied with their depression care (76% at 12 months compared with 47%). Patients in the collaborative care group also achieved significantly less functional impairment and reported better quality of life at 12 months compared with usual care (Unutzer et al., 2002).

Since this landmark IMPACT trial, numerous other RCTs have been conducted on collaborative care for depression that were first synthesized in a 2006 meta-analysis including 37 RCTs and a total of 12,355 patients (Gilbody et al., 2006). This initial synthesis found that collaborative care significantly improved depression outcomes at 6 months, with evidence of significant long-term benefit also up to 5 years. Analyses of heterogeneity in these initial 37 RCTs found that regular supervision of the care manager and the use of care managers with specific mental health background were associated with more positive clinical outcomes (Gilbody et al., 2006). A follow-up 2012 Cochrane systematic review and meta-analysis included 79 separate RCTs evaluating collaborative care for depression and/or anxiety, with 92% of studies from the United States, the United Kingdom, or other European countries and one study each from Chile, India, and Puerto Rico (Archer et al., 2012). This review found that collaborative care leads to significantly greater improvement in depression outcomes in the short and medium term, although the significance of effects waned after 2 years of follow-up. This systematic review also showed that collaborative care leads to significantly greater improvement in anxiety outcomes also up to 2 years of follow-up (Archer et al., 2012). However, it is important to note that at the time of the review, no RCTs of collaborative care had been completed in sub-Saharan Africa, with the only existing LMIC study coming from India.

There have also been a significant number of studies on costs and cost-effectiveness of collaborative care models in high-income countries. In general, studies have found that collaborative care is more expensive than care as usual, although the investment is comparable with many other widely accepted medical interventions. The cost per depression-free day has ranged from $21 to $24 (Katon et al., 2001; Liu et al., 2003), and incremental outpatient costs per quality-adjusted life year has ranged from $2519 to $5037 (Hay, Katon, Ell, Lee, & Guterman, 2012; Katon et al., 2005). Another large RCT in the United Kingdom suggested that collaborative care had a 54% likelihood to be cost-effective given a willingness to pay threshold of £20,000. In contrast, in studies of patients with comorbid diabetes or heart disease, collaborative care lowered outpatient health costs an average of $594 per patient (Katon et al., 2012).

More recently, RCTs have been conducted showing effectiveness and cost-effectiveness of collaborative care for adolescents with depression (Richardson et al., 2014). A recent 2016 RCT of collaborative care for depression among adolescents also showed cost-effectiveness even among the highest values in 95% confidence intervals (Wright et al., 2016). Additional trials have demonstrated the model's effectiveness for post-traumatic stress disorder (PTSD) (Zatzick et al., 2004). Despite this extensive evidence of effectiveness, there remain scant few studies on the effectiveness of collaborative care in LMIC.

7.3 Case studies of collaborative care studies from high-income countries

7.3.1 Collaborative care models in obstetric and gynecological settings—DAWN and MOMcare

Collaborative care has also shown promise when implemented in obstetric and gynecologic settings. In the Depression Attention for Women Now (DAWN) study, a physician (in this case an obstetrician gynecologist) prescribed psychiatric medications, a social worker served as the care manager and provided problem-solving therapy, and psychologists and psychiatrists provided consultation during weekly systematic caseload review meetings. This intervention had a greater impact on depression outcomes for socially disadvantaged women with no insurance or with public coverage, compared with women with commercial insurance (Katon et al., 2016).

Another model of collaborative care delivered in obstetric and gynecologic settings includes the "MOMcare" model that was a collaborative care model delivered within antenatal care settings, in which care managers used interpersonal psychotherapy (IPT) to treat pregnant women. Women in the trial were predominantly from low-income, ethnic/racial minority backgrounds. All women who participated in MOMcare met the criteria for major depressive disorder, and 65% had comorbid PTSD. In this study, IPT had the greatest effect on women with both major depression and PTSD, but psychotherapy effectiveness was transdiagnostic, benefitting women with PTSD diagnoses even though IPT was not specifically adapted to treat PTSD (Grote et al., 2014, 2015, 2016).

7.3.2 Collaborative care for diabetes settings—TEAMcare

Collaborative care has also been adapted to improve outcomes among patients with multiple chronic conditions such as diabetes or coronary heart disease and comorbid depression. TEAMcare is a collaborative care model in which a nurse provides care management for a population of patients whose outcomes are tracked in a registry. Specialist physicians (psychiatrists and diabetologists) provide clinical input through regular systematic case review meetings. The primary care physician or diabetologist who treats the patient prescribes all of the medications, including antidepressants. The care manager provides behavioral counseling, using techniques from problem-solving therapy, motivational interviewing, and behavioral activation. During the systematic caseload review meeting, the team reviews clinical data from patients in the caseload—including regularly administered Patient Health Questionnaire-9 item (PHQ-9) scores (Kroenke et al., 2001) and diabetes/cardiometabolic indicators—focusing on those patients who are not improving. The team uses data from this meeting to guide changes in treatment.

In a large clinical trial conducted in the United States, TEAMcare was associated with enhanced response to depression treatment and control of diabetes (Katon et al., 2010). In addition, patients reported greater satisfaction for depression care (35% higher), medical care (16% higher), and higher quality of life (15% higher). Furthermore, costing studies have shown that with little to no additional costs, the program was associated with improved quality-adjusted life years (QALYs) (Katon et al., 2012). Since these original trials, TEAMcare has been scaled in a large national demonstration project in the United States (Coleman et al., 2017) and also adapted for limited resource contexts and shown feasibility for public safety-net settings (Chwastiak et al., 2017).

7.4 Case studies of ongoing studies on collaborative care from low- and middle-income settings

7.4.1 Collaborative care for diabetes and comorbid depression in India: The INDEPENDENT study

INtegrating DEPrEssioN and Diabetes treatmENT (INDEPENDENT) care is a multicomponent collaborative care model that combines TEAMcare with decision support technology to provide population health management for patients with comorbid diabetes and depression living in India. INDEPENDENT care is based on the four core principles of collaborative care described in the introduction: person-centered team care, population-based care, evidence-based care, and measurement-based treatment to target. Care teams are composed of the patient's diabetes physician, a nonphysician care manager, and a consultant psychiatrist and diabetologist who review cases. In addition to treatment from their diabetes physician, care managers are central figures in the INDEPENDENT care model—they encourage and support patient self-care, monitor patient outcomes on key indicators, proactively (at least monthly) follow up with patients who are not improving, manage case review meetings, and coordinate care between the patient and their care team. To support effective depression and diabetes self-care, care managers engage patients in education about self-care, motivational interviewing, behavioral activation, and problem-solving treatment strategies.

The INDEPENDENT intervention is being evaluated in a pragmatic RCT comparing the care model with usual care. Participants are adults (age $\geq$ 35 years) with poorly controlled diabetes and comorbid moderate to severe depressive symptoms, defined as having a Patient Health Questionnaire-9 (PHQ-9) score $\geq$ 10 at initial screening (Kowalski et al., 2017). The intervention and patient education materials were extensively adapted from the abovementioned TEAMcare model for the Indian cultural context during a formative phase of the study. Cultural modifications included engaging families in the treatment process and the provision of clear written information to participants with nonjargon verbal information (Rao et al., 2016). The study has a 12-month active intervention phase followed by a 12-month observational follow-up period. The study is being conducted at four diabetes clinics in urban centers in India; a large public hospital outpatient clinic in Delhi; and private diabetes clinics in Bangalore, Chennai, and Visakhapatnam and will end in June 2018.

7.4.1.1 Intervention

Care manager role. In an effort to address the acute shortage of mental health professionals in India, locally based, bilingual allied health professionals were identified and trained as care managers. Care managers had backgrounds in dietetics, diabetes education, and psychology and had experience working with diabetes patients, but were not members of the clinic staff and were not mental health specialists. An initial 5-day in-person training session and 2-day refresher training at the coordinating site focused on identifying depressive symptoms; patient-centered depression and diabetes care; evidence-based brief behavioral interventions to support depression and diabetes self-care; patient outcome monitoring; and the use of the decision support system through a combination of didactic instruction, role play, and case studies. Care managers received ongoing support through regular coaching calls with investigators and clinicians experienced in collaborative care, individualized feedback on videotaped case review meetings, and annual refresher trainings. Additionally, the care managers formed and maintain a WhatsApp group that is used to pose questions to one another and the coaching team and problem-solve across sites.

Decision support for clinical team. Response to depression and diabetes treatment is monitored through repeat measures of clinical indicators collected at visits with the care manager and entered into a decision support-electronic health record (DS-EHR) system. The DS-EHR tool supports population health management within the clinic. Data entry into the system is managed by the care manager, and the display can be shared with the patient's diabetes physician and the team's caseload review specialists. The DS-EHR recommends guideline-based care prompts for glucose, blood pressure, lipid, and depression management. Care prompts are generated by programmed algorithms for each indicator that take a treat-to-target approach by considering the participant's most recent indicator values and current therapies with clinical targets.

Measurement-based care/treatment-to-target. Caseload review is a systematic process that operationalizes depression and diabetes population health management. Caseload reviews involve the care manager, a specialist psychiatrist, and a specialist diabetologist/endocrinologist at each clinic and occur twice monthly. Caseload review meetings prioritize discussion of patients with little or no improvement, those not consistently engaged in care, and new patients. The caseload review team reviews each patient's current care plan and recommends continuation or modification of the plan. Modifications and their justification are documented in the DS-EHR and communicated to the patient's diabetes physician. The patient's diabetes physician has full discretion over their patient's care and may accept or further modify the recommendations to the care plan put forth by the caseload review team but is asked to document justification. The care manager communicates the final care plan to the participant and helps them implement the recommendations. In addition to supporting participants' care, caseload review meetings also give the specialist physicians an opportunity to educate and support the care managers.

7.4.1.2 Program implementation

Key findings from the process evaluation of the INDEPENDENT study about how care managers and physicians utilize the DS-EHR and caseload review to operationalize measurement-based population health management have implications for the scaling of this collaborative care model. First, additional training and supervision needs were identified. Initially, care managers reported feeling pressure associated with being the primary source of patient information for the psychiatrist to determine patients' depression treatment plans. Regular meetings for caseload review with the team psychiatrist increased care manager confidence and self-efficacy, and specific content areas for education by the team psychiatrists were identified (e.g., management of comorbid anxiety or alcohol use disorder and treatment of grief). Similarly, diabetes physicians confirmed that psychiatrist oversight in case reviews provided support and additional training during the initial implementation months. Over time, they reported feeling less reliant on psychiatrist input and more confident recognizing depression and prescribing antidepressant medications based on the treatment algorithms. Second, the scaling of the intervention will likely require adaptations to the technology support for teams. While care managers reported satisfaction with the DS-EHR software, they continued to maintain paper records because of the uncertainty of internet connectivity. This inefficiency doubled their documentation burden and also slowed clinic flow. Delays in entering lab values, for example, sometimes resulted in physicians skipping decision prompts to expediently serve patients who were pressed for time.

7.4.1.3 Future directions for application of the intervention

There will be an estimated 5 million deaths due to cardiovascular disease annually in India by 2020. In 2008, the national government launched the National Programme for Prevention and Control of Diabetes, Cardiovascular Disease, and Stroke in 10 states (Directorate General of Health Services, Ministry of Health and Family Welfare, 2009). The current national policy includes universal screening for diabetes and hypertension among adults 30 and older and the provision of care for these chronic conditions in chronic disease clinics located in community health centers.

The INDEPENDENT study leverages existing infrastructure of the health-care system in India to integrate mental health treatment into diabetes clinical settings and may be an efficient and cost-effective strategy to increase the reach of effective mental health treatment. Future implementation research efforts will aim to scale the INDEPENDENT intervention in these chronic disease clinics created by this policy initiative. It will be important to address the unique needs of clinics in rural districts, given that 70% of the Indian population lives in rural communities.

In conclusion, the INDEPENDENT care model is an adaptation of the evidence-based collaborative care model for diabetes and depression augmented with decision support software and tailored for the Indian context (Rao et al., 2016). The multisite effectiveness trial will end in June 2018, and lessons learned from this trial will inform contextualization and implementation of the intervention in community health centers, which are at the intersection between primary (village health centers) and specialist care (district hospitals) within publicly funded rural health care in India.

7.4.2 Collaborative care for depression in patients with chronic physical diseases including HIV and hypertension in South Africa: The PRIME COBALT studies

The PRogramme for Improving Mental health carE (PRIME) is a multinational research consortium aimed at strengthening integrated primary care for priority mental health conditions in five LMIC (Ethiopia, India, Nepal, South Africa, and Uganda) (Lund et al., 2012). In South Africa, PRIME concentrated on strengthening integrated depression care for primary care patients with chronic physical conditions. This focus was driven by (i) the transition of HIV to a chronic illness as a result of the rapid roll-out of antiretroviral treatment (ART), as well as the rising noncommunicable disease (NCD) epidemic in South Africa (Mayosi et al., 2012), and (ii) the negative impact that comorbid depression has on health outcomes of these chronic conditions as a result of poorer treatment adherence (Gonzalez, Batchelder, Psaros, & Safren, 2011; Ngo et al., 2013). Intensive formative work in one district in South Africa resulted in a collaborative care model for depression comorbid with other chronic conditions (Petersen, Bhana, et al., 2016) that was tested in a nonrandomized trial in four large primary health-care facilities with good outcomes (Petersen, Fairall, et al., 2016) and is being evaluated for effectiveness through a pair of parallel pragmatic cluster RCTs. The PRIME trial is evaluating the impact on depression and blood pressure outcomes in service users on hypertensive treatment (Petersen et al., in press), and Comorbid Affective Disorders, AIDS/HIV, and Long-term Health (CobALT) (Fairall et al., 2018) is assessing the effectiveness of the model on depression and viral load suppression outcomes in ART patients. The PRIME and CobALT trials will be complete by June 2018.

The PRIME/CobALT collaborative care models leverage existing national scale-up of integrated clinical services management in South Africa, where the Department of Health is shifting from previously vertical services for chronic conditions (particularly HIV) to integrated care for all chronic conditions. At the facility level, decision support for multimorbid care is strengthened for nurse practitioners through the use of an integrated set of chronic care guidelines called "Adult Primary Care" (Fairall et al., 2015). In addition, ward-based outreach teams support clinically stable patients within the community, and health promotion and population screening are envisaged to promote an informed and activated population at the population level (Mahomed, Asmall, & Freeman, 2014). The collaborative care model for comorbid depression builds on this platform through providing nurse practitioners—who are the care managers—with additional technical skill training for the identification and management of comorbid depression and training in clinical communication skills, dealing with emotional self-care, and the promotion of patient self-management using motivational interviewing techniques. Referral pathways for counseling are strengthened through the training of facility-based lay counselors in structured manualized depression counseling for mild to moderate depression that draws on cognitive behavioral therapy techniques. The lay counselors also provide adherence counseling for all chronic conditions. Lay counselors and nurse care managers are supported by psychological counselors who have 4-year bachelors of psychology degree and who are registered with the South African Professional Board of Psychology. Existing referral pathways to primary health-care doctors and hospital/specialist care remain. The model adopts a stepped care approach, with moderate to severe conditions being referred to primary care doctors or to hospital care. Patients attending the counseling sessions are also required to be reassessed by the nurse case managers following termination of the lay counseling sessions. If symptoms still persist after lay counseling, these patients are referred onward for medical or specialist care as needed. Follow-up of patients in the community is provided through ward-based outreach teams composed of community health workers who conduct home visits and are able to trace nonadherent patients to reengage them in care.

7.4.2.1 Intervention

Use of theory of change in developing the collaborative care model. Theory of change is an approach that engages key stakeholders in a participatory method to identify causal pathways that lead to an effect. Stakeholders involved in managing, delivering, and receiving the program are typically engaged in identifying the intended impact and then working backward to identify outcomes along the causal pathway needed to achieve the intended impact (Anderson, 2004). An evaluation of the theory of change process in the development of the collaborative care model suggests that this approach helped to (i) ensure that the collaborative care model was contextually appropriate and synergistic with the functioning of existing systems; (ii) garner the buy-in and support of district management and service providers involved in supporting and delivering the collaborative services and clarifying roles and responsibilities of various service providers within the collaborative care model; and (iii) identify potential challenges and needs as well as potential solutions, for example, specialist resources to provide supervision within the collaborative care model (Breuer et al., 2014).

Leveraging existing decision support tools, indicators and community outreach infrastructure. The collaborative care model leverages an existing national scale-up of integrated clinical services management. Integrated clinical guidelines for the identification and management of multiple chronic diseases by nurse practitioners, called Adult Primary Care (also referred to as Practical Approach to Care Kit internationally), is a key component of the integrated clinical guidelines. These guidelines are aligned with the World Health Organization's Mental Health Gap Action Programme algorithms for mental disorders (World Health Organization, 2016). In this model, the training of professional nurses who are the care managers involves 12 sessions using case studies of patients with comorbid conditions. To optimize scale-up throughout the country, a cascade model of training is adopted whereby master trainers who are district-based are trained through regional training centers to provide training to facility-based trainers who then train nurses in their facilities. This model of training allows the training of new staff hires and refresher trainings to occur at the facility level in contrast to one-off specialist training that does not allow for ongoing retraining (Petersen et al., 2017). In the national guidelines, only two training sessions are explicitly devoted to mental health. An evaluation of Adult Primary Care in South

Africa found that this level of mental health training was insufficient to improve identification and management of depressive symptoms (Fairall et al., 2016). Given this, the PRIME collaborative care model includes four additional mental health training sessions leveraging the cascade model of training. An evaluation of these additional mental health training sessions using a repeat cross-sectional facility detection survey in three large facilities in the PRIME/CobALT research site showed a significant improvement in the detection of depression and alcohol use disorder from baseline to 12-month follow-up (Petersen, Bhana, et al., 2016).

Another key component of integrated clinical services management in South Africa is the development of ward-based outreach teams composed of community health workers who engage in health promotion and screening activities in the community, point-of-care monitoring, initiation of patient support groups and adherence clubs, and follow-up of nonadherent patients in the community (Mahomed et al., 2014). Within the PRIME collaborative care model, community health workers are engaged to assist in following up nonadherent patients and returning them to care (Petersen, Bhana, et al., 2016). In order to create a culture of using information for monitoring patient outcomes improving the quality of services provided, the PRIME collaborative care model includes a structured referral form for nurse care coordinators. Nurse care coordinators use this form to monitor patient progress and guide the assessment of whether treatment needs to be stepped up to more intensive care. Information generated by these forms is also used to monitor uptake of the intervention by service providers/facilities and identify bottlenecks and potential strategies to address bottlenecks using a continuous quality improvement framework.

7.4.2.2 PRIME collaborative care implementation challenges and opportunities

Key findings from the pilot implementation and initial case study data collection related to the PRIME collaborative care model revealed the need for broader system-level innovations to optimize the implementation of the model in the South African context. First, although the theory of change was used to contextualize implementation and generate buy-in, this was conducted at the district level, with insufficient attention to organizational readiness and implementation climate at the facility level. Increased attention at the facility level would have helped assure uptake of expanded roles and responsibilities of the various human resources involved in the collaborative care model. Second, throughout implementation, it became clear that routinely collected mental health indicators are insufficient and not prioritized for data collection, aggregation, or reporting. Therefore, efforts for tracking of model progress and continuous quality improvement embedded within the collaborative care model were not prioritized by facility managers.

7.4.2.3 Future directions for application of the intervention

The PRIME collaborative care model for depression comorbid with other chronic conditions was developed through formative and pilot work and is currently being evaluated through a pair of pragmatic cluster RCTs powered for detecting reductions in depressive symptoms and viral load suppression in patients with HIV/AIDS. Reduced blood pressure in hypertensive patients is a secondary outcome in the PRIME trial (Fairall et al., 2018; Petersen et al., in press). The PRIME collaborative care model leverages a number of the system changes that have accompanied the introduction of integrated chronic care through the integrated clinical service management in South Africa. However, as has been highlighted, a number of challenges to successful implementation remain. In particular, formative work is necessary to improve buy-in and engagement from facility-level staff prior to promoting organizational readiness, and efforts are needed to strengthen the routine collection of mental health indicators and targets to measure progress, inform data-driven decision-making, and promote continuous quality improvement.

7.5 Lessons learned from application of collaborative care in low- and middle-income settings

Collaborative care models show immense promise for improving access, effectiveness, cost-effectiveness, and patient satisfaction related to treating mental ill-health globally. Furthermore, these models allow for contextualization for a give patient population, culture or health system, provided that the four foundational principles outlined at the beginning of this chapter are maintained. These models have been tested in many best-evidence trials in high-income settings mostly in the United States and Europe with great success. At the time of writing this chapter, nascent evidence of feasibility, cost-effectiveness, and effectiveness is emerging from LMIC, including India and South Africa. We now aim to outline some lessons learned from these initial efforts to implement best-evidence collaborative care models in India and South Africa. These lessons include the following:

(i) Collaborative care models implemented in LMIC need intensive engagement with key stakeholders in the development of the collaborative care model so as to ensure that the reorganization of care pathways are feasible and sustainable and so that the modifications of roles and responsibilities of existing staff are acceptable. This may entail lengthy discussions with service managers and providers, ministries of health, and nongovernmental organizations about which cadres of workers are appropriate for the different roles within a task-sharing collaborative care approach. Specific efforts may be required for elucidating the best fit for who will provide mental health counseling, prescription of psychopharmaceuticals as needed, ongoing supervision, and mental health specialist care.

(ii) Diversification of roles to include the provision of mental health care among staff not previously oriented to this may be viewed as an additional burden and can lead to burnout and high staff turnover. To counter this, a focused approach to train providers in nontechnical skills such as clinical communication skills and emotional coping skills is recommended. These would be in addition to training and supervision in clinical technical skills related to mental health service provision.

(iii) Where service providers are required to take on an expanded scope of work, effort must be made to provide recognition through certification and higher pay to obtain buy-in and motivation.

(iv) Ongoing support and mental health specialist supervision of care managers and primary care providers within collaborative care models are particularly important and may require that identified supervisors are provided with additional supervision training. Supervision is widely recognized as necessary to foster the development of skills in mental health service delivery (Beidas, Koerner, Weingardt, & Kendall, 2011) (see also Chapter 3). A lack of ongoing supervision past the training phase can result in low intervention fidelity and clinician competency (Massatti, Sweeney, Panzano, & Roth, 2008). Without supervisory support, established programs experience significant declines in service delivery (Tibbits, Bumbarger, Kyler, & Perkins, 2010). Systematic reviews and cross-country studies of integrated care and task-sharing programs in LMIC settings emphasize the importance of ongoing supervision to help service providers meet patient needs (Mendenhall et al., 2014; Padmanathan & De Silva, 2013; van Ginneken et al., 2013). The collaborative care approach blends well with other models such as the apprenticeship model of layered supervision for psychotherapy (Murray et al., 2011).

7.6 Conclusion

The evidence from the global case studies in this chapter highlights that patient-centered collaborative team care is a promising approach for the treatment of common mental disorders in nonpsychiatric settings in both high-income and LMIC settings. However, at the time of writing, there are limited best-evidence studies showing the effectiveness and cost-effectiveness of collaborative care models in LMIC. In addition, given the need for adaptation to local cultural and health system contexts, it remains to be seen how different models for supervision and different cadres serving in the roles of care manager, primary care provider, and mental health specialist will affect effectiveness, cost-effectiveness, patient satisfaction, and the implementation of collaborative care models in global settings. The lessons learned through initial implementation of collaborative care models in India and South Africa highlight the need for high-quality implementation science related to optimal delivery of collaborative care in LMIC. Initial lessons learned focus on the need for intensive efforts around organizational readiness, role change, and managing the changing of roles, along with significant formative work to understand which cadres are best suited to provide the different essential collaborative care roles in diverse health system contexts. The inclusion of technologies for supervision and outcome tracking provides potential leapfrogging opportunities to ensure improved quality and effective services are provided for mental health in nonpsychiatric settings in LMIC. Challenges remain around cadres of workers involved, but patient-centered team-based collaborative care is a promising method for bringing essential mental health treatment to people in need in nonpsychiatric settings in areas with critical mental health workforce shortages.

References

Anderson, A. (2004). *A community builder's approach to theory of change: A practical guide to theory development*. New York: The Aspen Institute.

Archer, J., Bower, P., Gilbody, S., Lovell, K., Richards, D., Gask, L., et al. (2012). Collaborative care for depression and anxiety problems. *Cochrane Database of Systematic Reviews*, CD006525. https://doi.org/10.1002/14651858.CD006525.pub2www.cochranelibrary.com.

Beidas, R. S., Koerner, K., Weingardt, K. R., & Kendall, P. C. (2011). Training research: Practical recommendations for maximum impact. *Administration and Policy in Mental Health, 38*, 223–237. https://doi.org/10.1007/s10488-011-0338-z.

Breuer, E., De Silva, M. J., Fekadu, A., Luitel, N. P., Murhar, V., Nakku, J., et al. (2014). Using workshops to develop theories of change in five low and middle income countries: Lessons from the programme for improving mental health care (PRIME). *International Journal of Mental Health Systems, 8*, 15. https://doi.org/10.1186/1752-4458-8-15.

Chwastiak, L. A., Jackson, S. L., Russo, J., Dekeyser, P., Kiefer, M., Belyeu, B., et al. (2017). A collaborative care team to integrate behavioral health care and treatment of poorly-controlled type 2 diabetes in an urban safety net primary care clinic. *General Hospital Psychiatry, 44*, 10–15. https://doi.org/10.1016/j.genhosppsych.2016.10.005.

Coleman, K. J., Magnan, S., Neely, C., Solberg, L., Beck, A., Trevis, J., et al. (2017). The COMPASS initiative: Description of a nationwide collaborative approach to the care of patients with depression and diabetes and/or cardiovascular disease. *General Hospital Psychiatry, 44*, 69–76. https://doi.org/10.1016/j.genhosppsych.2016.05.007.

Coventry, P. A., Hudson, J. L., Kontopantelis, E., Archer, J., Richards, D. A., Gilbody, S., et al. (2014). Characteristics of effective collaborative care for treatment of depression: A systematic review and meta-regression of 74 randomised controlled trials. *PLoS ONE. 9*, e108114. https://doi.org/10.1371/journal.pone.0108114.

Directorate General of Health Services. (2009). *Ministry of Health and Family Welfare G of I. National Programme for Prevention and Control of Diabetes, Cardiovascular Diseases, and Stroke: A guide for health workers. Available from http:/www.searo.who.int/india/topics/cardiovascular_diseases/NCD_Resources_Training_module_for_NPDCS_for_health_workers.pdf (accessed January 26th, 2018).*

Fairall, L., Bateman, E., Cornick, R., Faris, G., Timmerman, V., Folb, N., et al. (2015). Innovating to improve primary care in less developed countries: Towards a global model. *BMJ Innovations, 1*, 196–203. https://doi.org/10.1136/bmjinnov-2015-000045.

Fairall, L., Petersen, I., Zani, B., Folb, N., Georgeu-Pepper, D., Selohilwe, O., … CobALT Research Team. (2018). Collaborative care for the detection and management of depression among adults receiving antiretroviral therapy in South Africa: study protocol for the CobALT randomised controlled trial. *Trials, 19*(1), 193. https://doi.org/10.1186/s13063-018-2517-7.

Fairall, L. R., Folb, N., Timmerman, V., Lombard, C., Steyn, K., Bachmann, M. O., et al. (2016). Educational outreach with an integrated clinical tool for nurse-led non-communicable chronic disease management in primary care in South Africa: A pragmatic cluster randomised controlled trial. *PLoS Medicine. 13*, e1002178. https://doi.org/10.1371/journal.pmed.1002178.

Gilbody, S., Bower, P., Fletcher, J., Richards, D., & Sutton, A. J. (2006). Collaborative care for depression: A cumulative meta-analysis and review of longer-term outcomes. *Archives of Internal Medicine, 166*, 2314–2321. https://doi.org/10.1001/archinte.166.21.2314.

Gonzalez, J., Batchelder, A., Psaros, C., & Safren, S. (2011). Depression and HIV/AIDS treatment nonadherence: A review and meta-analysis. *Journal of Acquired Immune Deficiency Syndromes, 58*, 1–13. https://doi.org/10.1097/QAI.0b013e31822d490a.Depression.

Grote, N. K., Katon, W. J., Lohr, M. J., Carson, K., Curran, M., Galvin, E., et al. (2014). Culturally relevant treatment services for perinatal depression in socio-economically disadvantaged women: The design of the MOMCare study. *Contemporary Clinical Trials*, *39*, 34–49. https://doi.org/10.1016/j.cct.2014.07.001.Culturally.

Grote, N. K., Katon, W. J., Russo, J. E., Lohr, M. J., Curran, M., Galvin, E., et al. (2015). Collaborative care for perinatal depression in socio-economically disadvantaged women: A randomized trial. *Depression and Anxiety*, *32*, 821–834. https://doi.org/10.1002/da.22405.Collaborative.

Grote, N. K., Katon, W. J., Russo, J. E., Lohr, M. J., Curran, M., Galvin, E., et al. (2016). A randomized trial of collaborative care for perinatal depression in socioeconomically disadvantaged women: The impact of comorbid posttraumatic stress disorder. *Journal of Clinical Psychiatry*, *77*, 1527–1537.

Hay, J. W., Katon, W. J., Ell, K., Lee, P., & Guterman, J. J. (2012). Cost-effectiveness analysis of collaborative care management of major depression among low-income, predominantly hispanics with diabetes. *Value Heal*, *15*, 249–254. https://doi.org/10.1016/j.jval.2011.09.008.

Katon, W., Russo, J., Lin, E. H. B., Schmittdiel, J., Ciechanowski, P., Ludman, E., et al. (2012). Cost-effectiveness of a multicondition collaborative care intervention: A randomized controlled trial. *Archives of General Psychiatry*, *69*, 1–18. https://doi.org/10.1001/archgenpsychiatry.2011.1548.

Katon, W., Russo, J., Reed, S. D., Croicu, C. A., Ludman, E., Larocco, A., et al. (2016). A randomized trial of collaborative depression care in obstetrics and gynecology clinics: Socioeconomic disadvantage and treatment response. *American Journal of Psychiatry*, *172*, 32–40. https://doi.org/10.1176/appi.ajp.2014.14020258.A.

Katon, W. J., Lin, E. H. B., Von Korff, M., Ciechanowski, P., Ludman, E. J., Young, B., et al. (2010). Collaborative care for patients with depression and chronic illnesses. *New England Journal of Medicine*, *363*, 2611–2620.

Katon, W. J., Schoenbaum, M., Fan, M.-Y., Callahan, C. M., Williams, J., Hunkeler, E., et al. (2005). Cost-effectiveness of improving primary care treatment of late-life depression. *Archives of General Psychiatry*, *62*.

Katon, W. J., Vonkorff, M., Sc, D., Unützer, J., Lin, E. H. B., Walker, E. A., et al. (2001). Cost-effectiveness of a collaborative care program for primary care patients with persistent depression. *American Journal of Psychiatry*, *158*, 1638–1644.

Kowalski, A. J., Poongothai, S., Chwastiak, L., Hutcheson, M., Tandon, N., Khadgawat, R., et al. (2017). The INtegrating DEPrEssioN and Diabetes treatmENT (INDEPENDENT) study: Design and methods to address mental healthcare gaps in India. *Contemporary Clinical Trials*, *60*, 113–124. https://doi.org/10.1016/j.cct.2017.06.013.

Kroenke, K., Spitzer, R. L., & Williams, J. B. W. (2001). The PHQ-9: Validity of a brief depression severity measure. *Journal of General Internal Medicine*, *16*, 606–613.

Liu, C.-F., Hedrick, S. C., Chaney, E., Heagerty, P., Felker, B., Hasenberg, N., et al. (2003). Cost-effectiveness of collaborative care for depression in a primary care veteran population. *Psychiatric Services*, *54*, 698–704.

Lund, C., Tomlinson, M., De Silva, M., Fekadu, A., Shidhaye, R., Jordans, M., et al. (2012). PRIME: A programme to reduce the treatment gap for mental disorders in five low- and middle-income countries. *PLoS Medicine*, *9*, e1001359. https://doi.org/10.1371/journal.pmed.1001359.

Mahomed, O. H., Asmall, S., & Freeman, M. (2014). An integrated chronic disease management model: A diagonal approach to health system strengthening in South Africa. *Journal of Health Care for the Poor and Underserved*, *25*, 1723–1729. https://doi.org/10.1353/hpu.2014.0176.

Massatti, R. R., Sweeney, H. A., Panzano, P. C., & Roth, D. (2008). The de-adoption of innovative mental health practices (IMHP): Why organizations choose not to sustain an IMHP. *Administration and Policy in Mental Health*, *35*, 50–65. https://doi.org/10.1007/s10488-007-0141-z.

Mayosi, B. M., Lawn, J. E., van Niekerk, A., Bradshaw, D., Abdool Karim, S. S., & Coovadia, H. M. (2012). Health in South Africa: Changes and challenges since 2009. *Lancet (London, England)*, *380*, 2029–2043. https://doi.org/10.1016/S0140-6736(12)61814-5.

Mendenhall, E., De Silva, M. J., Hanlon, C., Petersen, I., Shidhaye, R., Jordans, M., et al. (2014). Acceptability and feasibility of using non-specialist health workers to deliver mental health care: Stakeholder perceptions from the PRIME district sites in Ethiopia, India, Nepal, South Africa, and Uganda. *Social Science & Medicine*, *118*, 33–42. https://doi.org/10.1016/j.socscimed.2014.07.057.

Muntingh, A. D., van der Feltz-Cornelis, C. M., van Marwijk, H. W., Spinhoven, P., & van Balkom, A. J. (2016). Collaborative care for anxiety disorders in primary care: A systematic review and meta-analysis. *BMC Family Practice*, *17*, 62. https://doi.org/10.1186/s12875-016-0466-3.

Murray, L. K., Dorsey, S., Bolton, P., Jordans, M. J., Rahman, A., Bass, J., et al. (2011). Building capacity in mental health interventions in low resource countries: An apprenticeship model for training local providers. *International Journal of Mental Health Systems*, *5*, 30. https://doi.org/10.1186/1752-4458-5-30.

Ngo, V. K., Rubinstein, A., Ganju, V., Kanellis, P., Loza, N., Rabadan-Diehl, C., et al. (2013). Grand challenges: Integrating mental health care into the non-communicable disease agenda. *PLoS Medicine*, *10*, e1001443. https://doi.org/10.1371/journal.pmed.1001443.

Padmanathan, P., & De Silva, M. J. (2013). The acceptability and feasibility of task-sharing for mental healthcare in low and middle income countries: A systematic review. *Social Science & Medicine*, *97*, 82–86. https://doi.org/10.1016/j.socscimed.2013.08.004.

Petersen, I., Bhana, A., Fairall, L., Selohilwe, O., Kathree, T., Baron, E., et al. (2016). Increasing access and health outcomes for chronic care patients with comorbid common mental disorders in South Africa: Preliminary outcomes from the PRIME study in South Africa. In: *World Psychiatr. Assoc. Conf., Cape Town, South Africa*.

Petersen I, Bhana A, Folb N, Thornicroft G, Zani B, Selohilwe O, et al. Collaborative care for the detection and management of depression among adults with hypertension in South Africa (PRIME-SA): Study protocol for the PRIME-SA randomised controlled trial. Trials (in press).

Petersen, I., Fairall, L., Bhana, A., Kathree, T., Selohilwe, O., Brooke-sumner, C., et al. (2016). Integrating mental health into chronic care in South Africa: The development of a district mental healthcare plan. *British Journal of Psychiatry*, *101*, s29–s39. https://doi.org/10.1192/bjp.bp.114.153726.

Petersen, I., Marais, D., Abdulmalik, J., Ahuja, S., Alem, A., Chisholm, D., et al. (2017). Strengthening mental health system governance in six low- and middle-income countries in Africa and South Asia: Challenges, needs and potential strategies. *Health Policy and Planning*, *32*, 699–709. https://doi.org/10.1093/heapol/czx014.

Rao, D., Lipira, L., Kumar, S., Mohanraj, R., Poongothai, S., Tandon, N., et al. (2016). Input of stakeholders on reducing depressive symptoms and improving diabetes outcomes in India: Formative work for the INDEPENDENT study. *International Journal of Non-communicable Diseases*, *1*, 65–75. https://doi.org/10.4103/2468-8827.191979.

Reilly, S., Planner, C., Gask, L., Hann, M., Knowles, S., Druss, B., et al. (2013). Collaborative care approaches for people with severe mental illness. *Cochrane Database of Systematic Reviews*. https://doi.org/10.1002/14651858.CD009531.pub2www.cochranelibrary.com.

Richardson, L. P., Ludman, E., Mccauley, E., Lindenbaum, J., Larison, C., Zhou, C., et al. (2014). Collaborative care for adolescents with depression in primary care a randomized clinical trial. *JAMA, 98121*, 809–816. https://doi.org/10.1001/jama.2014.9259.

Tibbits, M. K., Bumbarger, B. K., Kyler, S. J., & Perkins, D. F. (2010). Sustaining evidence-based interventions under real-world conditions: Results from a large-scale diffusion project. *Prevention Science, 11*, 252–262. https://doi.org/10.1007/s11121-010-0170-9.

Unutzer, J., Katon, W., Callahan, C. M., Williams, J. W., Hunkeler, E., Harpole, L., et al. (2002). Collaborative care management of late-life depression in the primary care setting. *JAMA, 288*, 2836–2845.

Unutzer, J., Katon, W., WIlliams, J. W., Callahan, C., Harpole, L., Hunkeler, E. M., et al. (2001). Improving primary care for depression in late life: The design of a multicenter randomized trial. *Medical Care, 39*, 785–799.

van Ginneken, N., Tharayan, P., Lwein, S., Rao, G., Meera, S., Pian, J., et al. (2013). Non-specialist health worker interventions for the care of mental, neurological and substance-abuse disorders in low- and middle-income countries. *Cochrane Database of Systematic Reviews*. (11), CD009149. https://doi.org/10.1002/14651858.CD009149.pub2 (Review).

World Health Organization. (2016). *mhGAP intervention guide. Vol. 2*, Available from http://www.who.int/mental_health/mhgap/mhGAP_intervention_guide_02/en/ (accessed26.01.18).

Wright, D., Haaland, W. L., Ludman, E., McCauley, E., Lindenbaum, J., & Richardson, L. P. (2016). The costs and cost-effectiveness of collaborative care for adolescents with depression in primary care settings: A randomized clinical trial. *JAMA Pediatrics, 170*, 1048–1054. https://doi.org/10.1001/jamapediatrics.2016.1721.

Zatzick, D., Roy-Byrne, P., Russo, J., Rivara, F., Droesch, R., Wagner, A., et al. (2004). A randomized effectiveness trial of stepped collaborative care for acutely injured trauma survivors. *JAMA Psychiatry, 61*, 498–506.

Section C

Clinical Disorders

Psychotherapy for depression and anxiety in low- and middle-income countries

8

Pim Cuijpers, Ozlem Eylem*, Eirini Karyotaki*, Xinyu Zhou†, Marit Sijbrandij**
*Department of Clinical, Neuro and Developmental Psychology, Amsterdam Public Health Research Institute, Vrije Universiteit Amsterdam, Amsterdam, Netherlands, †Department of Psychiatry, First Affiliated Hospital of Chongqing Medical University, Chongqing Medical University, Chongqing, China

8.1 Introduction

Depression and anxiety are highly prevalent, disabling, and costly disorders that are linked with considerably diminished role functioning and quality of life, medical comorbidity, and mortality (Cuijpers, Koole, et al., 2014; Cuijpers, Sijbrandij, et al., 2014; Cuijpers, Vogelzangs, et al., 2014; Spijker et al., 2004; Steel, Marnane, Iranpour, et al., 2014). It is estimated that every year, almost one in five persons among the general population suffers from a common mental disorder (Steel et al., 2014). Not only these disorders do cause considerable personal suffering in patients and their families, but also they are associated with huge economic costs, in terms of both work productivity loss and health and social care expenditures (Bloom, Cafiero, Jane-Llopis, et al., 2011; Chisholm, Sweeny, Sheehan, et al., 2016; Hu, 2006; Whiteford, Degenhardt, Rehm, et al., 2010).

Several evidence-based treatments are available for depression and anxiety disorders, including not only several antidepressant medications and several types of psychotherapy but also other therapies, such as bright light therapy, electroconvulsive therapy, transcranial magnetic stimulation, and herbal treatment. Many patients suffering from depression and anxiety receive antidepressant medications as their main treatment. Pharmacotherapy is currently the first-line treatment for depression in most countries, although the majority of patients with depression prefer psychotherapy to medications (McHugh, Whitton, Peckham, Welge, & Otto, 2013). However, research on patients' preferences has largely been conducted in Western countries, and therefore, it is not clear whether this is also the case in low- and middle-income countries (LMIC). Psychological treatments are also as effective as these medications and probably have longer lasting effects than medications when these are discontinued (Karyotaki, Riper, et al., 2016; Karyotaki, Smit, et al., 2016). Furthermore, the effects of acute-phase psychotherapy on depression are considerable over the long term, and these effects are comparable with those of maintenance medication (Cuijpers, Hollon, et al., 2013; Cuijpers, Sijbrandij, et al., 2013).

Global Mental Health and Psychotherapy. https://doi.org/10.1016/B978-0-12-814932-4.00008-2

Although hundreds of randomized trials have examined the effects of treatments of depression and anxiety disorders, by far, the majority of these trials have been conducted in Western, high-income countries, and only a few have been conducted in LMIC. In this chapter, we will give an overview of the field of psychotherapies for depression and anxiety disorders in LMIC. We will first focus on the prevalence of depression and anxiety in LMIC. Then, we will describe the different types of psychotherapy that have been developed for the treatment of depression and anxiety disorders. We will also discuss the question if and how therapies should be adapted to local conditions and populations. Moreover, we will describe examples of therapies that have been developed in LMIC and discuss how psychotherapies can be combined with other treatments. Finally, we will describe the results of randomized trials on psychotherapies for depression and anxiety in LMIC.

8.2 Depression and anxiety in low- and middle-income countries

In this chapter, we will focus on depression, including major depressive disorders and chronic types of depression, and on anxiety disorders, such as generalized anxiety, panic disorder, and social anxiety disorder. These disorders together are often called "common mental disorders," although this term can also include substance-use-related disorders. Because depression and anxiety disorders often go together and because it is not clear if the concepts of depression and anxiety are comparable in LMIC, many studies focus on general "distress," rather than depressive and anxiety disorders. Although this concept of distress is not very clearly defined, we will focus on these studies as well. We will not focus on obsessive compulsive disorders or on post-traumatic stress disorder (PTSD) and other trauma-related disorders, such as acute stress disorder (ASD) (see chapter by Sikkema). Although these disorders were in the past classified as anxiety disorders, they are now widely considered as a separate cluster of disorders. Most research on PTSD in LMIC has been conducted in crisis and war-affected populations, and it is clearly a different field from the depression field because of the focus on trauma exposure. However, depression, PTSD, and anxiety disorders are all grouped under the common mental disorders, and war-affected populations may present with symptoms related to depression, PTSD, and anxiety or a combination of these symptoms (Steel et al., 2009).

A popular idea is that depression and anxiety are less prevalent in non-Western countries and are typically Western diseases that are related to the demands of modern Western societies. However, the evidence is very clear that this is not true. The prevalence rates of major depressive disorders and anxiety differ per country, but on average, these rates are comparable in high-income countries and in LMIC. Data from the World Mental Health Survey, which is an international collaborative project examining the prevalence of mental disorders across countries, showed very comparable 12-month prevalence estimates in high-income countries (5.5%) and LMIC (5.9%) (Kessler et al., 2010; Kessler & Bromet, 2013). However, the 12-month prevalence across the 18 examined countries differed considerably, ranging from 2.2% in Japan to 10.4% in Brazil (see also Ferrari et al., 2013). WHO estimates that the total number of people with depression in the world is 322 million (WHO, 2017). Nearly half of the people with depression live in the Southeast Asia Region and Western Pacific Region. In China, for example, 54 million people suffer from depression, which is more than the total population of Spain. The 12-month prevalence of anxiety disorders ranges from 2.4 to 29.8% across 44 countries (with an average of 11.6%) (Baxter, Scott, Vos, & Whiteford, 2013). The prevalence rates in the United States are higher than in other regions of the world (WHO, 2017). There are clear indications that the prevalence rates of anxiety disorders are higher in conflict areas compared with other areas (Baxter et al., 2013).

The average age of onset of most anxiety disorders is in childhood and adolescence, while the age of onset of major depression is in the early to mid-twenties. These ages of onset can differ per country (Kessler et al., 2007; Kessler & Bromet, 2013). For example, in high-income countries, the age ranges from 23 in the United States to 30 in Spain and Japan. In LMIC, the age of onset ranges from 19 years in Shenzhen to 28 years in Ukraine, to 32 years in Pondicherry.

Women are twice as likely as men to develop depressive disorders in most of the high-income countries (Kessler & Bromet, 2013; Van de Velde, Bracke, & Levecque, 2010). The same is true for anxiety disorders (Baxter et al., 2013). Similar research from LMIC is scarce, but the small number of studies that have been conducted so far confirms the findings that women have a higher chance for depression than men. Overall, the prevalence of depression and anxiety disorders decreases with age (Baxter et al., 2013; Kessler & Bromet, 2013), but that is not true in all countries. In some countries, the prevalence of depression among younger age groups (18–34) is up to 5.5 times higher than the oldest age group, while in other countries, young age is associated with low risk. There are indications, however, that the association between (higher) age and (lower) depression is stronger in high-income compared with LMIC (Kessler & Bromet, 2013).

8.3 Psychotherapies for depression and anxiety

Psychotherapies (or psychological treatments) can be defined as interventions with a primary focus on language-based communication between a patient and a therapist. There are hundreds of different types of psychotherapy. Most of these have been developed in Western countries, although there are also several therapies that have been developed in LMIC and high-income countries outside the Western world, such as Japan. However, only a small part of all therapies have been examined in well-designed randomized controlled trials. Without such trials, it is uncertain whether these therapies are indeed effective in reducing mental health problems. In this chapter, we will focus mostly on evidence-based therapies that have been tested in randomized trials and have proved to be effective.

In the following, we will describe the psychotherapies that have been tested in trials. We will limit this to those that have been tested in depression and anxiety disorders. Then, we will give an overview of the effects of these therapies on depression and anxiety. Finally, we will give an overview of therapies in LMIC and research on these therapies and the research on Western therapies that are applied in LMIC.

There are three broad, generic types of therapies: cognitive behavioral, psychodynamic, and humanistic categories of psychotherapy (Wampold & Imel, 2015). These categories are, however, not well delineated, and there are all kinds of therapies that are not easily captured in one of these categories, such as interpersonal psychotherapy or couple therapy. Psychotherapies can be applied in different formats, including individual, group, telephone-based, internet-based, or as guided self-help in which the patient works through a self-help book more or less independently and is only supported by brief telephone calls with a professional coach. In this chapter, we do not consider the Internet or mobile interventions without any human support for the patient as psychotherapy. Most of the therapies that have been tested in trials are brief, but there is still a large variation in the number of treatment sessions, which ranges from 4 to more than 30, and in treatment duration.

8.4 Cognitive and behavioral therapies for depression and anxiety

By far, the most examined type of therapy is cognitive behavioral therapy (CBT). In CBT, it is assumed that patients get depressed because of dysfunctional thoughts about themselves, their environment, and their future (Cuijpers, 2017). In this therapy, these dysfunctional thoughts are evaluated, challenged, and modified, which is assumed to result in a reduction of depression and anxiety. This technique is called cognitive restructuring. In CBT, there is a strong focus on the current situation of the patient, on psychoeducation about depression and anxiety, and on the role of dysfunctional thoughts and homework.

Behavioral therapies are usually considered to be part of the broader "family" of cognitive behavioral therapies. They focus more on actual behavior and less on cognitions and thoughts. The most important types of behavioral therapies are behavioral activation for depression and graded exposure for phobias and anxiety disorders. In graded exposure, the patient makes a hierarchy of situations that are increasingly anxious. Subsequently, the patient enters into the situation that is somewhat frightening and remains there until the anxiety diminishes and disappears (Cuijpers & Schuurmans, 2007). Then, a more frightening situation is chosen, and the procedure is repeated until the anxiety has disappeared completely. There is evidence that exposure is effective in all phobias (agoraphobia, social phobia, and specific phobias). In most therapies, exposure is applied together with cognitive restructuring or other cognitive behavioral techniques.

Behavioral activation is a behavioral therapy that is used for the treatment of depression. It is aimed at increasing positive interactions between a person and his or her environment (Dimidjian, Barrera, Martell, Munoz, & Lewinsohn, 2011). During therapy, the patient learns that activities improve his or her mood and how the patient can more often undertake these activities. Behavioral activation is usually integrated into CBT, but it can also be used as a stand-alone treatment. There is evidence that behavioral activation also works as stand-alone treatment (Ekers et al., 2014).

Cognitive and behavioral therapies focus on the current situation of the patient and how this can be changed in order to improve the symptoms of depression or anxiety. These also focus on concrete behaviors and cognitions that have a strong focus on psychoeducation and on homework so that skills are trained in real life outside of therapy. From this perspective, other therapies can also be considered to be part of the broader family of cognitive behavioral therapies. One example is problem-solving therapy (see also chapter by Spedding). The basic idea of problem-solving therapy is that patients learn how to handle the problems in their life, thereby reducing or solving the mental health problems. Patients make an overview of their problems (from any domain of their life) and prioritize them. Then, they solve each of the most important ones by first defining the problem in the best possible way. The next step is to generate multiple solutions, then select the best solution, work out of a systematic plan for this solution, and finally do it. After that, it is evaluated whether the solution has resolved the problem, and if not, the second best solution is tried in the same way and so on. Problem-solving therapy works not only for depression but also for generalized anxiety.

Another type of therapy that is often considered to belong to the family of cognitive behavioral therapies is social skill training. In this therapy, patients are taught skills that help in building and retaining of social and interpersonal relationships (Cuijpers, van Straten, Andersson, & van Oppen, 2008; Cuijpers, van Straten, Warmerdam, & Smits, 2008). In most versions of SST, patients are trained in assertiveness, meaning that the patient is taught to stand up for his or her rights by expressing feelings in an honest and respectful way, without insulting other people.

Relaxation techniques are used in the treatment of anxiety disorders. Several of these techniques have been developed systematically over the years, with applied relaxation (developed by Öst, 1986) being the most widely used. With these techniques, the patient learns to relax his or her body systematically and then to relax while entering anxious situations. Relaxation has been found to be effective in generalized anxiety, panic disorder, social anxiety disorder, and specific phobias. A recent meta-analysis found that overall, the effects of relation only are somewhat less effective than cognitive behavioral therapies, but this difference was not significant for generalized anxiety disorder, panic disorder, and social anxiety disorder (Montero-Marin, Garcia-Campayo, López-Montoyo, Zabaleta-del-Olmo, & Cuijpers, 2018).

In the last two decades, the so-called third-wave cognitive behavioral therapies have introduced several new techniques to the broader family of cognitive and behavioral therapies. This heterogeneous group of therapies has in common that they abandon or only cautiously use content-oriented cognitive interventions and use skill-deficit models to delineate the core maintaining mechanisms of the addressed disorders (Kahl, Winter, & Schweiger, 2012). One important third-wave therapy is acceptance and commitment therapy (ACT). ACT focuses on decreasing experiential avoidance and increasing value-based behavior (Hayes, Strosahl, & Wilson, 1999).

In ACT, acceptance and mindfulness strategies are used in different ways to increase psychological flexibility. Another important third-wave therapy is mindfulness-based CBT (MBCT). MBCT combines mindfulness exercises with cognitive restructuring techniques. Mindfulness exercises are derived from Eastern meditation techniques. MBCT was originally developed for the prevention of relapse in people with recurrent depression (Segal, Williams, & Teasdale, 2002), but an increasing number of studies now examine the effects of MBCT in acute depression.

8.5 Other types of psychotherapy for depression and anxiety disorders

Although cognitive and behavioral therapies are by far the best examined psychotherapies for depression and anxiety disorders and most guidelines give them as first-line treatments for these disorders, several other types of psychotherapy exist. We already indicated that in addition to cognitive and behavioral therapies, there are two other broad, generic types of therapies, the psychodynamic and humanistic categories of psychotherapy (Wampold & Imel, 2015). Both have been well examined in depression but less so in anxiety disorders.

In the humanistic category, nondirective supportive counseling has been examined in many randomized trials (Cuijpers et al., 2012). This is an unstructured therapy without specific psychological techniques other than those common to all approaches, such as helping people to talk about their experiences and emotions and offering empathy. It is based on the assumption that relief from personal problems can be achieved through discussion with a therapist who offers unconditional support (Cuijpers, van Straten, Andersson, et al., 2008; Cuijpers, van Straten, Warmerdam, et al., 2008), while acquiring new skills is not the primary goal.

In the category of psychodynamic therapies, brief therapies for depression have been developed (Driessen et al., 2015). These therapies aim to enhance the patient's understanding, awareness, and insight about repetitive conflicts. The therapist focuses on the past of the patient, the unresolved conflicts, earlier relationships, and the impact that these have on a patient's current functioning. The therapy assumes that patient's current life situation is affected by his or her childhood experiences, past unresolved conflicts, and earlier relationships.

Although most therapies can be categorized into one of the three broad categories of cognitive behavioral, psychodynamic, and humanistic therapies, there are many other forms of therapies that do not fit into one of these categories. It is beyond the scope of this chapter to describe all of these therapies, but we must mention one of these, interpersonal psychotherapy (IPT; Klerman, Weissman, Rounsaville, & Chevron, 1984) (see also chapter by Verdeli). IPT is a brief, structured psychotherapy that was developed for the treatment of depression, but it has also been tested for the treatment of anxiety disorders in some trials (Cuijpers, Cristea, Karyotaki, Reijnders, & Huibers, 2016; Cuijpers, Donker, Weissman, Ravitz, & Cristea, 2016). In IPT, interpersonal issues are addressed, and it focuses on the relationships between a person and significant others. It is not assumed that these relationships cause depression or anxiety disorders, but these disorders always happen in an interpersonal context, and changing this context can help to resolve the mental health problems.

8.6 The effects of psychotherapies for depression

The effects of psychotherapies for depression have been examined in more than 550 randomized trials, and several hundreds of trials have examined the effects of therapies for anxiety disorders. The trials focused on depression have shown that psychotherapies are effective. The sizes of the effects are usually given in terms of effect sizes, indicating the difference between a treatment and a comparison condition in terms of the standard deviation. This effect size is also called "Cohen's d," "Hedges' g" (that has a slightly different way of calculating the difference), or the "standardized mean difference." Effect sizes of $d=0.2$ are considered to be small, $d=0.5$ moderate, and $d=0.8$ large (Cohen, 1988).

The pooled effect sizes found in randomized trials in which psychotherapies for depression are compared with control conditions are about $d=0.70$ (Cuijpers, Karyotaki, Reijnders, & Huibers, 2018). Control conditions are, for example, waiting lists, care as usual, or placebo. However, this effect size is probably overestimated because the quality of many trials is suboptimal, and studies with lower quality typically find higher effect sizes than studies with higher quality (Cuijpers, Donker, van Straten, Li, & Andersson, 2010; Cuijpers, van Straten, Bohlmeijer, Hollon, & Andersson, 2010). Furthermore, many studies showing no effect of treatment are not published, resulting in an overestimate of the true effect size when this is based on published studies only. When the pooled effect size for psychotherapies for depression is adjusted for publication bias and low study quality, the effect size is considerably smaller (but still significant).

Most trials have focused on the effects of therapies from the CBT family of therapies, but several other therapies have also been tested in enough trials to conclude that they are effective for depression. There is evidence that cognitive behavioral therapy with cognitive restructuring as the core element is effective, and that is also true for behavioral activation, problem-solving therapy, interpersonal psychotherapy, brief psychodynamic therapies, and supportive counseling. All these therapies seem to be equally effective or about equally effective. There are also indications that the effects of therapies last over time, at least for a year (Cuijpers, Hollon, et al., 2013; Cuijpers, Sijbrandij, et al., 2013). This has been mostly examined for CBT.

There is no indication that the treatment format is related to the effects of therapies, as long as there is a therapist or coach involved. Individual, group, guided self-help, and guided internet-based therapies are all effective, and there is no indication that one format is more effective than another (Cuijpers, Donker, et al., 2010; Cuijpers, van Straten, et al., 2010; Cuijpers, van Straten, Andersson, et al., 2008; Cuijpers, van Straten, Warmerdam, et al., 2008). These therapies have found to be effective not only in adults in general but also in more specific target groups, such as older adults, women with postpartum depression, and patient with general medical disorders, such as heart disease, cancer, or diabetes (Cuijpers et al., 2018) (see also chapter by Magidson). There are also no indications that the effects of therapy are lower in patients from ethnic minority groups (Unlu Ince, Riper, van't Hof, & Cuijpers, 2014). If patients have subthreshold depressive symptoms without a full major depressive disorder, it has been found that psychotherapy can prevent the onset of a full depressive disorder in the next year (Cuijpers, Koole, et al., 2014; Cuijpers, Sijbrandij, et al., 2014; Cuijpers, Vogelzangs, et al., 2014).

Sometimes, it is assumed that psychotherapies are only effective in mild and moderate depression, while in severe depression, pharmacotherapy should be given (preferably in combination with psychotherapy). However, research has shown that the short-term effects of CBT and pharmacotherapy are comparable, without clinically or statistically significant differences (Cuijpers, Hollon, et al., 2013; Cuijpers, Sijbrandij, et al., 2013), and that is also true in severe depression (Weitz et al., 2015). The combination of psychotherapy and pharmacotherapy is more effective than either pharmacotherapy alone (Cuijpers, Koole, et al., 2014; Cuijpers, Sijbrandij, et al., 2014; Cuijpers, Vogelzangs, et al., 2014) or psychotherapy alone (Cuijpers, van Straten, Warmerdam, & Andersson, 2009). Over the longer term, combined therapy has also been found to be more effective than pharmacotherapy (Karyotaki, Riper, et al., 2016; Karyotaki, Smit, et al., 2016). No significant difference has been found between combined treatment and psychotherapy alone, although this may be related to the small number of studies that have examined this issue (Karyotaki, Riper, et al., 2016; Karyotaki, Smit, et al., 2016).

When a patient is recovering from a depressive disorder or is currently recovering, psychological interventions can prevent the patient to relapse (Biesheuvel-Leliefeld et al., 2015). These relapse prevention therapies are usually based on CBT or on mindfulness-based CBT.

8.7 The effects of psychotherapies for anxiety disorders

Psychotherapies are also effective in the treatment of anxiety disorders. In anxiety disorders, by far, the most studies have examined the effects of cognitive and behavioral therapies; very few studies have examined other types of therapies. The effects of CBT for generalized anxiety disorder, panic disorder, and social anxiety disorder are large, with effect sizes of $d=0.80$, 0.81, and 0.88, respectively (Cuijpers, Cristea, et al., 2016; Cuijpers, Donker, et al., 2016). However, the majority of these trials have at least some risk of bias, suggesting that these results are uncertain. Furthermore, many of these trials use waiting-list control groups, and these control groups probably overestimate the effects of treatments (Cuijpers & Cristea, 2016; Furukawa et al., 2014). The effects of meta-analyses in which studies with waiting-list control groups are excluded are much smaller ($d=0.27$–0.47). The number of studies with low risk of bias that do not use waiting-list control groups is so small that the actual effects of these therapies are very uncertain.

We conducted a meta-analysis in which we included trials in which CBT was directly compared with relaxation and found no significant difference for generalized anxiety disorders, panic disorders, and social anxiety disorders (Montero-Marin et al., 2018). When all comparative trials were pooled across all anxiety disorders, however, a small effect in favor of CBT was found ($d=0.27$).

Studies in which therapies are directly compared with antidepressant medication indicate that both treatments are about equally effective in panic disorder and social anxiety disorder (Cuijpers, Hollon, et al., 2013; Cuijpers, Sijbrandij, et al., 2013). There are not enough comparative studies in generalized anxiety disorder to indicate how they compare with each other. Combined treatment is more effective than pharmacotherapy alone in panic disorder ($d=0.54$), but in social anxiety disorder and generalized anxiety disorder, too few studies are available (Cuijpers, Koole, et al., 2014; Cuijpers, Sijbrandij, et al., 2014; Cuijpers, Vogelzangs, et al., 2014).

8.8 Psychotherapies in low- and middle-income countries

As indicated earlier, almost all evidence-supported psychotherapies for depression and anxiety disorders have been developed in Western countries. However, there are some psychotherapies that have been developed in non-Western countries. For example, Morita therapy is a systematic psychological therapy based on Eastern philosophy that was developed in Japan and has been used for the treatment of anxiety disorders for decades (Wu et al., 2015). It has been tested in several trials, although they were small and the quality was suboptimal. Another therapy that was recently developed outside the Western world is the Chinese Dejian mind-body intervention, which is based on the principle of the Shaolin Temple and consists of psychosocial education, mind-body exercises, and diet modification (Chan et al., 2012a, 2012b). A small trial found that this therapy may have positive effects on depression (Chan et al., 2012a, 2012b). Some therapies mix non-Western ideas and philosophies with Western therapies, such as Taoist cognitive therapy (Zhang et al., 2012). Mind-body interventions are, for example, considered to be compatible with Chinese holistic beliefs, and there are several trials examining the effects of this therapy in depression (Bo, Mao, & Lindsey, 2017). The effects found for this therapy are large, although there is considerable risk of bias in the majority of trials. Mindfulness-based therapies, such as mindfulness-based CBT and dialectical behavior therapy also mix non-Western with Western approaches. However, the majority of studies in non-Western countries use psychotherapies that have been developed in Western countries. In a recent meta-analysis of trials of psychotherapies for adult depression in non-Western countries (Cuijpers et al., 2018), we only included one type of therapy that was not developed in Western countries (Chan et al., 2012a, 2012b).

These therapies can be considered to be the result of a "bottom-up" approach (Hwang, 2006). However, in most studies, a "top-down" approach is used. In this approach, therapies that have been developed in Western countries and found to be effective in trials are adapted to other cultures. Cultural adaptation has been defined as "the systematic modification of an evidence-based treatment or intervention protocol to consider language, culture, and context in such a way that it is compatible with the individual's cultural patterns, meanings, and values"

(Bernal, Jimenez-Chafey, & Domenech Rodriguez, 2009). This adaptation is usually assumed to be needed in order for a therapy to be effective (Xu & Tracey, 2016), especially when there are community-specific cultural contexts of risk and resilience that influence disorders (Forehand & Kotchick, 1996; Hall, Ibaraki, Huang, Marti, & Stice, 2016; Lau, 2006). For instance, high rates of common mental disorders, including depression, have been observed in the South Sudanese refugee population, locally described and prioritized as "overthinking" (Adaku et al., 2016) or Kufungisisa in Zambia (Patel, Simunyu, & Gwanzura, 1995).

While there is an increasing realization of the need for cultural adaptation of psychological interventions for mental and physical health problems, the lack of standardized terminologies and theoretical frameworks provides poor guidance for the real-world cultural adaptations (Chu & Leino, 2017; Koslofsky & Rodriguez, 2017; Rathod, Kingdon, Pinninti, Turkington, & Phiri, 2015). One of the most well-known theoretical frameworks is known as the "Bernal framework" (Bernal, Bonilla, & Bellido, 2015). Accordingly, cultural adaptations can be done on several dimensions, including language, people, metaphors, content, concepts, goals, methods, and context (Bernal et al., 2015). There are several limitations with the Bernal framework that restrict its implication in LMIC. For instance, mental health workers often report that the language used in the Bernal framework is difficult to follow for lay people (Koslofsky & Rodriguez, 2017). Additionally, the framework was based on an expert opinion rather than tried and tested, and some of the elements overlap (Chu & Leino, 2017). In the light of these limitations, the WHO is developing a protocol for adapting psychological interventions in LMIC (not yet published). This protocol is based on the bottom-up approach and suggests a number of steps: (1) contextual research (i.e., rapid qualitative community assessment), (2) literal translation into local language, (3) pretesting (i.e., focus group interviews to check the relevance, understandability, and appropriateness). (4) accuracy check (i.e., back translation to the original language to check whether the adapted version has the same meaning as the original), and (5) adaptation during the use of the materials (i.e., further adaptation as a result of the use of the intervention within the community). Most studies suggest that culturally adapted interventions are more effective than interventions that have not been adapted (Hall et al., 2016; Harper Shehadeh, Heim, Chowdhary, Maercker, & Emiliano, 2016), although that is not confirmed in all studies (Cuijpers et al., 2018; Rathod et al., 2017).

There is growing evidence that psychological treatments are effective in non-Western countries. In a recent meta-analysis of 32 controlled trials examining the effects of psychotherapies conducted in non-Western countries, significant effects of these therapies were found (Cuijpers et al., 2018). A comparison with 253 trials in Western countries indicated that these therapies may even be more effective than in Western countries. This association remained significant after adjusting for quality of the trials and other characteristics of the studies, patients, and therapies. Although this finding may be related to other factors, this study does suggest that psychological treatments are probably no less effective and can therefore also be used in non-Western countries, regardless of the income level of the country.

Some of the largest studies in LMIC are not only exclusively aimed at depression but also focused on anxiety disorders (Patel et al., 2003, 2010; Van't Hof, Cuijpers,

Waheed, & Stein, 2011). Relatively few studies in non-Western countries have focused specifically on anxiety disorders, although there is some research on, for example, social anxiety disorder (D'El Rey, Lacava, Cejkinski, & Mello, 2007; Knijnik, Kapczinski, Chachamovich, Margis, & Eizirik, 2004) and panic disorder (Ito et al., 2001). Overall, these studies support the conclusion that psychotherapies are at least as effective in non-Western countries as in Western countries.

The number of studies on psychotherapy in non-Western countries is increasing. For example, of the 32 trials that we included in our recent meta-analysis of studies on depression, 20 were conducted in 2010 or later, and only three were conducted before 2005 (Cuijpers et al., 2018). However, one source of concern is the quality of these studies. Although there are several trials that meet all the quality criteria and can be considered to belong to the best research in the field of psychotherapy research (Patel et al., 2010, 2017; Rahman, Malik, Sikander, Roberts, & Creed, 2008a, 2008b), the quality of many other trials is suboptimal. For example, in our metaanalysis of 32 trials on psychotherapy for depression, only five studies met all the criteria for low risk of bias.

8.9 Implementation of psychotherapies in low- and middle-income countries

Implementation of psychotherapies in LMIC is complicated for several reasons. Because of the considerable disease burden, the huge economic costs, and the enormous personal suffering related to depression and anxiety, treatment of these disorders is a highly important and urgent public health issue. In most LMIC, the large majority of patients suffering from a depression or anxiety disorder do not receive any treatment (Chisholm et al., 2016). In low-income countries, it is estimated that only 7% of depressed patients receive treatment and 5% of anxiety patients (Chisholm et al., 2016; Thornicroft et al., 2017). Psychotherapies could play a role in reducing this disease burden both in high-income countries and in LMIC.

However, the reason why most LMIC do not provide psychotherapies in their health systems or provide psychotherapies only to a limited extent is that the financial resources for health care are very limited. If countries with low resources do invest in health care, they usually invest in basic physical care with a focus on severe physical disorders and do not prioritize mental health care for common mental disorders. That means that interventions for mental health care have to be highly scalable; otherwise, they will not be implemented at all. Scalable means that the interventions have to be cheap, and the resources, in this case therapists or other people who deliver the interventions, must be available in the country where it is implemented. In LMIC, specialized mental health-care workers such as psychotherapists and psychiatrists are usually scarce, which hampers scaling-up of mental health interventions.

One method to make therapies more scalable is to make use of the principle of "task shifting" or "task sharing." According to the WHO, task shifting is "the rational redistribution of tasks among health workforce teams" (WHO, 2008). It means that specific functions are shifted from highly qualified health workers to nonprofessional or lay health workers with shorter training and fewer qualifications. In mental health research, task shifting has been used in several well-designed, large trials (Bryant et al., 2017; Patel et al., 2010; 2017; Rahman et al., 2008a, 2008b, 2016). In these trials, nonprofessional counselors without a background in mental health care are locally recruited and received a training to deliver psychological treatments and care management to people with common mental disorders. Task-shifting protocols have been developed based on CBT (Rahman et al., 2008a, 2008b), behavioral activation (Patel et al., 2017), and multimodal protocols based on CBT and problem-solving techniques (Bryant et al., 2017; Rahman et al., 2016). Task shifting is one of the important ways in which psychological treatments can be made scalable for implementation in LMIC. A systematic review of trials in task shifting in noncommunicable diseases, including mental disorders, found positive effects, including for depression, although the number of studies is still relatively small (Joshi et al., 2014; van Ginneken et al., 2013).

Another possibility to reach and treat more individuals with mental disorders in LMIC is through the Internet and mobile technologies. There is considerable evidence that Internet-based therapies are effective in the treatment of depression and anxiety (Andrews, Cuijpers, Craske, McEvoy, & Titov, 2010; Richards & Richardson, 2012). Although the best effects are realized when there is some support from a professional coach or therapist (Richards & Richardson, 2012), the effects are also significant when there is no support related to the therapeutic content (Koslofsky & Rodriguez, 2017). Furthermore, the time spent by a professional coach on the treatment of a patient is much less than the time spent in a face-to-face therapy. Guided and unguided interventions through the Internet or mobile phones are therefore a good option for building an infrastructure in low-resourced countries. Furthermore, the training of therapists to deliver psychological treatments can also greatly be enhanced and facilitated by Internet-based approaches. A recent systematic review showed that there are not yet many randomized trials examining the effects of these interventions in mental health care in LMIC (Naslund et al., 2017), but there are several dozens of pilot and feasibility studies testing the use of these technologies in mental health care in LMIC. There are, however, also important potential barriers to the implementation of such intervention in LMIC, such as limited access to technology and the Internet and the lack of resources.

Recently, more personalized and tailor-made strategies to engage with the target populations have been proposed as viable solutions to address the mental health treatment gap in LMIC (Arjadi, Nauta, Chowdhary, & Bockting, 2015). Thus, adapting e-mental health interventions according to the cultural context of the potential users can increase their effectiveness and efficacy (Harper Shehadeh et al., 2016). There are several advantages with this form of service delivery over the face-to-face psychological therapies. It is relatively easy to tailor the content of the interventions linguistically and culturally according to various ethnic groups in an online setting (Eylem, van Straten, Bhui, & Kerkhof, 2015; Munoz-Sanchez, Dergado, Sanchez-Prada, De Leo, & Franco-Martin, 2017). Thus, culturally adapted e-mental health interventions are appealing especially for some cultural groups who are concerned about stigma and shame associated with help-seeking from their formal and informal networks (Eylem et al., 2015, 2016). On the part of the service providers, such interventions promise to tackle the issue of cultural mismatch between the service provider and the service user and distance or transport issues that are restricting the provision of psychological therapies in LMIC (Munoz-Sanchez et al., 2017).

The effectiveness and efficacy of culturally adapted e-mental health interventions have been mostly tested in Western context (Harper Shehadeh et al., 2016; Tulbure, Månsson, & Andersson, 2012; Unlu Ince et al., 2014), and only a few RCTs have been conducted in non-Western countries (Arjadi et al., 2015; Ip et al., 2016; Wang, Wang, & Maercker, 2013). For instance, a recent RCT in a school sample of 257 Chinese adolescents in China showed that culturally adapted e-mental health intervention resulted in reductions of depressive symptoms at the 12-month follow-up in comparison with the control group with a medium effect size ($d=0.36$) (Ip et al., 2016).

Overall, although the current evidence is preliminary, it promises that the culturally adapted e-mental health interventions can address the treatment gap and increase the impact of the culturally adapted psychological interventions in LMIC. However, participant engagement still remains as the main challenge (Clarke, Kuosmanen, & Barry, 2015) highlighting the necessity for further adaptations in recruitment strategies and the delivery of psychological interventions.

Recently, the WHO has taken the initiative to develop brief interventions that can be implemented on a large scale in conflict-affected areas and other low-resourced settings (see also chapter by Spedding). The Problem Management Plus (PM+) programs and its related programs are delivered by lay health workers in five weekly 90 min individual sessions and include strategies of problem-solving, behavioral activation, strengthening social support, and stress management (WHO, 2016). The PM+ programs are available in an individual format and group format. Individual PM+ has been evaluated in primary care patients in Pakistan (Rahman et al., 2016) and women affected by gender-based violence in Kenya (Bryant et al., 2017). The results show improvements in terms of depression, anxiety (Rahman et al., 2016), and psychological distress (Bryant et al., 2017). Group PM+ is under evaluation in Swat, Pakistan, and pilot results are also promising (Khan et al., 2017). An e-health intervention to reduce symptoms of psychological distress is currently developed by WHO and awaits formal trial evaluation (see Sijbrandij, Acarturk, Bird, et al., 2017).

8.10 Conclusion

Depression and anxiety disorders are important public health problems in all parts of the world, including LMIC. They are highly prevalent, disabling, and costly and are linked with considerably diminished role functioning and quality of life, medical comorbidity, and mortality. Reducing the disease burden of these burdens is a major challenge for public health across the world. Although evidence-based treatments are available, access to services is low because of stigma, low resources, and insufficient political support. Psychological treatments for depression and anxiety disorders could play a major role in reducing the disease burden of these disorders, although access to these treatments is almost nonexistent in LMIC. Most psychological treatments that are evidence-based have been developed in Western countries, and these include a range of cognitive behavioral therapies, interpersonal psychotherapy, psychodynamic approaches, and counseling. A growing number of studies show that these therapies are at least as effective in non-Western countries as they are in Western countries. Adaptation of the interventions to other cultures is needed in order for therapies to be effective. Implementation of therapies may be facilitated through the use of lay health counselors instead of fully trained psychotherapists. New technologies may also offer new opportunities to reduce the disease burden of depression and anxiety disorders in LMIC.

References

Adaku, A., Okello, J., Lowry, B., Kane, J. C., Alderman, S., Musisi, S., & Tol, W. (2016). Mental health and psychological support for South Sudanese refugees in Northern Uganda: A needs and resource assessment. *Conflict and Health*, *10*, 1–10.

Andrews, G., Cuijpers, P., Craske, M. G., McEvoy, P., & Titov, N. (2010). Computer therapy for the anxiety and depressive disorders is effective, acceptable and practical health care: A meta-analysis and pilot implementation. *PLoS ONE*, *5*, e13196.

Arjadi, R., Nauta, M., Chowdhary, N., & Bockting, C. (2015). A systematic review of online interventions for mental health in low and middle income countries: A neglected field. *Global Mental Health*, *2*, 1–6.

Baxter, A. J., Scott, K. M., Vos, T., & Whiteford, H. A. (2013). Global prevalence of anxiety disorders: A systematic review and meta-regression. *Psychological Medicine*, *43*, 897–910.

Bernal, G., Bonilla, J., & Bellido, C. (2015). Ecological validity and cultural sensitivity for outcome research: Issues for the cultural adaptation and development of psychosocial treatments with Hispanics. *Journal of Abnormal Child Psychology*, *23*, 67–82.

Bernal, G., Jimenez-Chafey, M. I., & Domenech Rodriguez, M. M. (2009). Cultural adaptation of treatments: A resource for considering culture in evidence-based practice. *Professional Psychology: Research and Practice*, *40*, 361–368.

Biesheuvel-Leliefeld, K. E., Kok, G. D., Bockting, C. L., Cuijpers, P., Hollon, S. D., van Marwijk, H. W., & Smit, F. (2015). Effectiveness of psychological interventions in preventing recurrence of depressive disorder: Meta-analysis and meta-regression. *Journal of Affective Disorders*, *174*, 400–410.

Bloom, D. E., Cafiero, E., Jane-Llopis, E., et al. (2011). *The global economic burden of noncommunicable diseases*. Geneva: World Economic Forum.

Bo, A., Mao, W., & Lindsey, M. A. (2017). Effects of mind-body interventions on depressive symptoms among older Chinese adults: A systematic review and meta-analysis. *International Journal of Geriatric Psychiatry*, *32*, 509–521.

Bryant, R. A., Schafer, A., Dawson, K. S., Anjuri, D., Mulili, C., Ndogoni, L., & van Ommeren, M. (2017). Effectiveness of a brief behavioural intervention on psychological distress among women with a history of gender-based violence in urban Kenya: A randomized clinical trial. *PLoS Medicine*, *14*, e1002371.

Chan, A. S., Wong, Q. Y., Sze, S. L., Kwong, P. P. K., Han, Y. M. Y., & Cheung, M. C. (2012a). A Chinese Chan-based mind-body intervention improves sleep on patients with depression: A randomized controlled trial. *Scientific World Journal*, *235206*, .

Chan, A. S., Wong, Q. Y., Sze, S. L., Kwong, P. P. K., Han, Y. M. Y., & Cheung, M. C. (2012b). A Chinese Chan-based mind–body intervention for patients with depression. *Journal of Affective Disorders*, *15*(142), 283–289.

Chisholm, D., Sweeny, K., Sheehan, P., et al. (2016). Scaling-up treatment of depression and anxiety: A global return on investment analysis. *Lancet Psychiatry*, *3*, 415–424.
Chu, J., & Leino, A. (2017). Advancement in the maturing science of cultural adaptations of evidence based interventions. *Journal of Consulting and Clinical Psychology*, *85*, 47–57.
Clarke, A. M., Kuosmanen, T., & Barry, M. M. (2015). A systematic review of online youth mental health promotion and prevention interventions. *Journal of Youth and Adolescence*, *44*, 90–113.
Cohen, J. (1988). *Statistical power analysis for the behavioral sciences* (2nd ed.). Hillsdale, NJ: Erlbaum.
Cuijpers, P. (2017). Treatment of depression. In *SAGE encyclopedia of abnormal and clinical psychology* (pp. 1063–1066). .
Cuijpers, P., & Cristea, I. A. (2016). How to prove that your therapy is effective, even when it is not: A guideline. *Epidemiology and Psychiatric Sciences*, *25*, 428–435.
Cuijpers, P., Cristea, I. A., Karyotaki, E., Reijnders, M., & Huibers, M. J. H. (2016). How effective are cognitive behavior therapies for major depression and anxiety disorders? A meta-analytic update of the evidence. *World Psychiatry*, *15*, 245–258.
Cuijpers, P., Donker, T., van Straten, A., Li, J., & Andersson, G. (2010). Is guided self-help as effective as face-to-face psychotherapy for depression and anxiety disorders? A systematic review and meta-analysis of comparative outcome studies. *Psychological Medicine*, *40*, 1943–1957.
Cuijpers, P., Donker, T., Weissman, M. M., Ravitz, P., & Cristea, I. A. (2016). Interpersonal psychotherapy for mental health problems: A comprehensive meta-analysis. *The American Journal of Psychiatry*, *173*, 680–687.
Cuijpers, P., Driessen, E., Hollon, S. D., van Oppen, P., Barth, J., & Andersson, G. (2012). The efficacy of non-directive supportive therapy for adult depression: A meta-analysis. *Clinical Psychology Review*, *32*, 280–291.
Cuijpers, P., Hollon, S. D., van Straten, A., Bockting, C., Berking, M., & Andersson, G. (2013). Does cognitive behaviour therapy have an enduring effect that is superior to keeping patients on continuation pharmacotherapy? A meta-analysis. *BMJ Open*, *3*, https://doi.org/10.1136/bmjopen-2012-002542.
Cuijpers, P., Karyotaki, E., Reijnders, M., & Huibers, M. J. H. (2018). Who benefits from psychotherapies for adult depression? A meta-analytic update of the evidence. *Cognitive Behaviour Therapy*, [epub ahead of print].
Cuijpers, P., Koole, S. L., van Dijke, A., Roca, M., Li, J., & Reynolds, C. F. (2014). Psychotherapy for subclinical depression: A meta-analysis. *British Journal of Psychiatry*, *205*, 268–274.
Cuijpers, P., & Schuurmans, J. (2007). Self-help interventions for anxiety disorders: An overview. *Current Psychiatry Reports*, *9*, 284–290.
Cuijpers, P., Sijbrandij, M., Koole, S. L., Andersson, G., Beekman, A. T., & Reynolds, C. F., III (2013). The efficacy of psychotherapy and pharmacotherapy in treating depressive and anxiety disorders: A meta-analysis of direct comparisons. *World Psychiatry*, *12*, 137–148.
Cuijpers, P., Sijbrandij, M., Koole, S. L., Andersson, G., Beekman, A. T., & Reynolds, C. F., III (2014). Adding psychotherapy to antidepressant medication in depression and anxiety disorders: A meta-analysis. *World Psychiatry*, *13*, 56–67.
Cuijpers, P., van Straten, A., Andersson, G., & van Oppen, P. (2008). Psychotherapy for depression in adults: A meta-analysis of comparative outcome studies. *Journal of Consulting and Clinical Psychology*, *76*, 909–922.
Cuijpers, P., van Straten, A., Bohlmeijer, E., Hollon, S. D., & Andersson, G. (2010). The effects of psychotherapy for adult depression are overestimated: A meta-analysis of study quality and effect size. *Psychological Medicine*, *40*, 211–223.

Cuijpers, P., van Straten, A., Warmerdam, L., & Andersson, G. (2009). Psychological treatment versus combined treatment of depression: A meta-analysis. *Depression and Anxiety*, *26*, 279–288.

Cuijpers, P., van Straten, A., Warmerdam, L., & Smits, N. (2008). Characteristics of effective psychological treatments of depression; a meta-regression analysis. *Psychotherapy Research*, *18*, 225–236.

Cuijpers, P., Vogelzangs, N., Twisk, J., Kleiboer, A., Li, J., & Penninx, B. (2014). Comprehensive meta-analysis of excess mortality in depression in the general community versus patients with specific illnesses. *American Journal of Psychiatry*, *171*, 453–462.

D'El Rey, G. J. F., Lacava, J. P. L., Cejkinski, A., & Mello, S. L. (2007). Cognitive-behavioral group treatment in social phobia: 12-week outcome. *Revista de Psiquiatria Clínica*, *35*, 79–83.

Dimidjian, S., Barrera, M., Martell, C., Munoz, R. F., & Lewinsohn, P. M. (2011). The origins and current status of behavioral activation treatments for depression. *Annual Review of Clinical Psychology*, *7*, 1–38.

Driessen, E., Hegelmaier, L. M., Abbass, A. A., Barber, J. P., Dekker, J. J., Van, H. L., … Cuijpers, P. (2015). The efficacy of short-term psychodynamic psychotherapy for depression: A meta-analysis update. *Clinical Psychology Review*, *42*, 1–15.

Ekers, D., Webster, L., Van Straten, A., Cuijpers, P., Richards, D., & Gilbody, S. (2014). Behavioural activation for depression: An update of meta-analysis of effectiveness and sub group analysis. *PLoS ONE*, *9*, e100100.

Eylem, O., van Bergen, D. D., Rathod, S., van Straten, A., Bhui, K., & Kerkhof, A. J. F. M. (2016). Canına Kıymak 'crushing life energy': A qualitative study on lay and professional understandings of suicide and help-seeking among Turkish migrants in the UK and in the Netherlands. *International Journal of Culture and Mental Health*, *9*, 1–16.

Eylem, O., van Straten, A., Bhui, K., & Kerkhof, A. J. F. M. (2015). Protocol: Reducing suicidal thinking among Turkish migrants in the Netherlands and in the UK: Effectiveness of an online intervention. *International Review of Psychiatry*, *27*, 72–81.

Ferrari, A. J., Somerville, A. J., Baxter, A. J., Norman, R., Patten, S. B., Vos, T., & Whiteford, H. A. (2013). Global variation in the prevalence and incidence of major depressive disorder: A systematic review of the epidemiological literature. *Psychological Medicine*, *43*, 471–481.

Forehand, R., & Kotchick, B. A. (1996). Cultural diversity: Awake-up call for parent training. *Behavior Therapy*, *27*, 187–206.

Furukawa, T. A., Noma, H., Caldwell, D. M., Honyashiki, M., Shinohara, K., Imai, H., … Churchill, R. (2014). Waiting list may be a nocebo condition in psychotherapy trials: A contribution from network meta-analysis. *Acta Psychiatrica Scandinavica*, *130*, 181–192.

Hall, G. C. N., Ibaraki, A. Y., Huang, E. R., Marti, C. N., & Stice, E. (2016). A meta-analysis of cultural adaptations of psychological interventions. *Behavior Therapy*, *47*, 993–1014.

Harper Shehadeh, M., Heim, E., Chowdhary, N., Maercker, A., & Emiliano, A. (2016). Cultural adaptation of minimally guided interventions for common mental disorders: A systematic review and meta-analysis. *JMIR Mental Health*, *3*, 1–13.

Hayes, S. C., Strosahl, K. D., & Wilson, K. G. (1999). *Acceptance and commitment therapy: An experiential approach to behavior change*. New York: Guilford Press.

Hu, T.-W. (2006). Perspectives: An international review of the national cost estimates of mental illness, 1990–2003. *Journal of Mental Health Policy and Economics*, *9*, 3–13.

Hwang, W. (2006). The psychotherapy adaptation and modification framework: Application to Asian Americans. *American Psychologist*, *61*, 702–715.

Ip, P., Chim, D., Chan, K. L., Li, T. M., Ho, F. K., Van Voorhees, B. W., … Wong, W. H. (2016). Effectiveness of a culturally attuned internet-based depression prevention program for Chinese adolescents: A randomized controlled trial. *Depression and Anxiety, 33*, 1123–1131.

Ito, L. M., de Araujo, L. A., Tess, V. L. C., de Barros-Neto, T. P., Asbahr, F. R., & Marks, I. (2001). Self-exposure therapy for panic disorder with agoraphobia: Randomised controlled study of external v. interoceptive self-exposure. *British Journal of Psychiatry, 178*, 331–336.

Joshi, R., Alim, M., Kengne, A. P., Jan, S., Maulik, P. K., Peiris, D., & Patel, A. A. (2014). Task shifting for non-communicable disease management in low and middle income countries; a systematic review. *PLoS ONE, 9*, e103754.

Kahl, K. G., Winter, L., & Schweiger, U. (2012). The third wave of cognitive behavioural therapies: What is new and what is effective? *Current Opinion in Psychiatry, 25*, 522–528.

Karyotaki, E., Riper, H., Twisk, J., Hoogendoorn, A., Kleiboer, A., Mira, A., … Cuijpers, P. (2016). Efficacy of self-guided internet-based cognitive behavioral therapy (iCBT) in treatment of depressive symptoms: An individual participant data meta-analysis. *JAMA Psychiatry, 74*, 351–359.

Karyotaki, E., Smit, Y., Holdt Henningsen, K., Huibers, M. J., Robays, J., de Beurs, D., & Cuijpers, P. (2016). Combining pharmacotherapy and psychotherapy or monotherapy for major depression? A meta-analysis on the long-term effects. *Journal of Affective Disorders, 194*, 144–152.

Kessler, R. C., Amminger, G. P., Aguilar-Gaxiola, S., Alonso, J., Lee, S., & Ustun, T. B. (2007). Age of onset of mental disorders: A review of recent literature. *Current Opinion in Psychiatry, 20*, 359–364.

Kessler, R. C., Birnbaum, H. G., Shahly, V., Bromet, E., Hwang, I., et al. (2010). Age differences in the prevalence and co-morbidity of DSM-IV major depressive episodes: Results from the WHO World Mental Health Survey Initiative. *Depression and Anxiety, 27*, 351–364.

Kessler, R. C., & Bromet, E. J. (2013). The epidemiology of depression across cultures. *Annual Review of Public Health, 34*, 119–138.

Khan, M. N., Hamdani, S. U., Chiumento, A., Dawson, K., Bryant, R. A., Sijbrandij, M., & Rahman, A. (2017). Evaluating feasibility and acceptability of a group WHO transdiagnostic intervention for women with common mental disorders in rural Pakistan: A cluster randomized controlled feasibility trial. *Epidemiology and Psychiatric Sciences*, 1–11. https://doi.org/10.1017/S2045796017000336.

Klerman, G. L., Weissman, M. M., Rounsaville, B. J., & Chevron, E. S. (1984). *Interpersonal psychotherapy of depression: A brief, focused, specific strategy* (1st ed.). Northvale, NJ: Jason Aronson, Incorporated.

Knijnik, D. Z., Kapczinski, F., Chachamovich, E., Margis, R., & Eizirik, C. L. (2004). Psychodynamic group treatment for generalized social phobia. *Revista Brasileira de Psiquiatria, 26*, 77–81.

Koslofsky, S., & Rodriguez, D. M. M. (2017). Cultural adaptations to psychotherapy: Real-world applications. *Clinical Case Studies, 16*, 3–8.

Lau, A. S. (2006). Making the case for selective and directed cultural adaptations of evidence-based treatments: Examples from parent training. *Clinical Psychology: Science and Practice, 13*, 295–310.

McHugh, R. K., Whitton, S. W., Peckham, A. D., Welge, J. A., & Otto, M. W. (2013). Patient preference for psychological vs pharmacological treatment of psychiatric disorders: A meta-analytic review. *Journal of Clinical Psychiatry, 74*, 595–602.

Montero-Marin, J., Garcia-Campayo, J., López-Montoyo, A., Zabaleta-del-Olmo, E., & Cuijpers, P. (2018). Is cognitive behavioral therapy more effective than relaxation therapy in the treatment of anxiety disorders? A meta-analysis. *Psychological Medicine*, *48*, 1427–1436.

Munoz-Sanchez, J. L., Dergado, C., Sanchez-Prada, A., De Leo, D., & Franco-Martin, M. A. (2017). Facilitating factors and barriers to the use of new technologies for suicide prevention in Europe: A multi-country exploratory study. *JMIR Mental Health*, *4*(2), e23.

Naslund, J. A., Aschbrenner, K. A., Araya, R., Marsch, L. A., Unützer, J., Patel, V., & Bartels, S. J. (2017). Digital technology for treating and preventing mental disorders in low-income and middle-income countries: A narrative review of the literature. *Lancet Psychiatry*, *4*, 486–500.

Öst, L. G. (1986). Applied relaxation: Description of a coping technique and review of controlled studies. *Behaviour Research and Therapy*, *25*, 397–409.

Patel, V., Chrisholm, D., Rabe-Hesketh, S., Dias-Saxena, F., Andrew, G., & Mann, A. (2003). Efficacy and cost-effectiveness of drug and psychological treatments for common mental disorders in general health care in Goa, India: A randomised, controlled trial. *Lancet*, *361*, 33–39.

Patel, V., Simunyu, E., & Gwanzura, F. K. (1995). Thinking too much: A Shona idiom for non-psychotic mental illness. *Central African Journal of Medicine*, *41*, 209–215.

Patel, V., Weiss, H. A., Chowdhary, N., Naik, S., Pednekar, S., Chatterjee, S., … Kirkwood, B. R. (2010). Effectiveness of an intervention led by lay health counsellors for depressive and anxiety disorders in primary care in Goa, India (MANAS): a cluster randomised controlled trial. *Lancet*, *376*, 2086–2095.

Patel, V., Weobong, B., Weiss, H. A., Anand, A., Bhat, B., Katti, B., … Fairburn, C. G. (2017). The Healthy Activity Program (HAP), a lay counsellor-delivered brief psychological treatment for severe depression, in primary care in India: A randomised controlled trial. *Lancet*, *389*, 176–185.

Rahman, A., Hamdani, S. U., Awan, N. R., Bryant, R. A., Dawson, K. S., Khan, M. F., … van Ommeren, M. (2016). Effect of a multicomponent behavioral intervention in adults impaired by psychological distress in a conflict-affected area of Pakistan: A randomized clinical trial. *JAMA*, *316*, 2609–2617.

Rahman, A., Malik, A., Sikander, S., Roberts, C., & Creed, F. (2008a). Cognitive behaviour therapy-based intervention by community health workers for mothers with depression and their infants in rural Pakistan: A cluster-randomised controlled trial. *Lancet*, *372*, 902–909.

Rahman, A., Malik, A., Sikander, S., Roberts, C., & Creed, F. (2008b). Cognitive behaviour therapy-based intervention by community health workers for mothers with depression and their infants in rural Pakistan: A cluster-randomised controlled trial. *Lancet*, *372*, 902–909.

Rathod, S., Gega, L., Degnan, A., Pikard, J., Khan, T., Hussain, N., … Naeem, F. (2017). The current status of culturally adapted mental health interventions: A practice-focused review of meta-analyses. *Neuropsychiatric Disease and Treatment*, *13*, 1–14.

Rathod, S., Kingdon, D., Pinninti, N., Turkington, D., & Phiri, P. (2015). *Cultural adaptation of CBT for serious mental illness: A guide for training and practice*. Wiley – Blackwell.

Richards, D., & Richardson, T. (2012). Computer-based psychological treatments for depression: A systematic review and meta-analysis. *Clinical Psychology Review*, *32*, 329–342.

Segal, Z. V., Williams, J. M. G., & Teasdale, J. D. (2002). *Mindfulness-based cognitive therapy for depression: A new approach to relapse prevention*. New York: Guilford Press.

Sijbrandij, M., Acarturk, C., Bird, M., et al. (2017). Strengthening mental health care systems for Syrian refugees in Europe and the Middle East: Integrating scalable psychological interventions in eight countries. *European Journal of Psychotraumatology*, *8*(Suppl. 2), 1388102.

Spijker, J., Graaf, R., Bijl, R. V., Beekman, A. T., Ormel, J., & Nolen, W. A. (2004). Functional disability and depression in the general population. Results from the Netherlands mental health survey and incidence study (NEMESIS). *Acta Psychiatrica Scandinavica*, *110*, 208–214.

Steel, Z., Chey, T., Silove, D., Marnane, C., Bryant, R. A., & van Ommeren, M. (2009). Association of torture and other potentially traumatic events with mental health outcomes among populations exposed to mass conflict and development. *JAMA*, *302*, 537–549.

Steel, Z., Marnane, C., Iranpour, C., et al. (2014). The global prevalence of common mental disorders: A systematic review and meta-analysis 1980–2013. *International Journal of Epidemiology*, *43*, 476–493.

Thornicroft, G., Chatterji, S., Evans-Lacko, S., Gruber, M., Sampson, N., Aguilar-Gaxiola, S., … Kessler, R. C. (2017). Undertreatment of people with major depressive disorder in 21 countries. *The British Journal of Psychiatry*, *210*, 119–124.

Tulbure, B. T., Månsson, K. N., & Andersson, G. (2012). Internet treatment for social anxiety disorder in Romania: Study protocol for a randomized controlled trial. *Trials*, *13*, 1–19.

Unlu Ince, B., Riper, H., van't Hof, E., & Cuijpers, P. (2014). The effects of psychotherapy on depression among racial-ethnic minority groups: A meta-regression analysis. *Psychiatric Services*, *65*, 612–617.

Van de Velde, S., Bracke, P., & Levecque, K. (2010). Gender differences in depression in 23 European countries. Cross-national variation in the gender gap in depression. *Social Science & Medicine*, *71*, 305–313.

van Ginneken, N., Tharyan, P., Lewin, S., Rao, G. N., Meera, S. M., Pian, J., & Patel, V. (2013). Non-specialist health worker interventions for the care of mental, neurological and substance-abuse disorders in low- and middle-income countries. *Cochrane Database of Systematic Reviews*, *11*, CD009149.

Van't Hof, E., Cuijpers, P., Waheed, W., & Stein, D. J. (2011). Psychological treatments for depression and anxiety disorders in low- and middle- income countries: A meta-analysis. *African Journal of Psychiatry*, *14*, 200–207.

Wampold, B. E., & Imel, Z. E. (2015). *The great psychotherapy debate: The evidence for what makes psychotherapy work* (2nd ed.). New York: Routledge.

Wang, Z., Wang, J., & Maercker, A. (2013). Chinese my trauma recovery, a web-based intervention for traumatized persons in two parallel samples: Randomized controlled trial. *Journal of Medical Internet Research*, *15*, 1–14.

Weitz, E. S., Hollon, S. D., Twisk, J., van Straten, A., Huibers, M. J. H., David, D., … Cuijpers, P. (2015). Does baseline depression severity moderate depression outcomes between CBT versus pharmacotherapy? An individual patient data meta-analysis. *JAMA Psychiatry*, *72*, 1102–1109.

Whiteford, H. A., Degenhardt, L., Rehm, J., et al. (2010). Global burden of disease attributable to mental and substance use disorders: Findings from the global burden of disease study. *Lancet*, *382*, 1575–86, 2013.

WHO/MSD/MER/2017. (2017). *2 – Depression and other common mental disorders: Global health estimates*. Geneva: World Health Organization. License: CC BY-NC-SA 3.0 IGO.

World Health Organization. (2008). *Treat train retain. Task shifting: Global recommendations and guidelines*. Geneva: WHO.

World Health Organization. (2016). *Problem management plus (PM+): individual psychological help for adults impaired by distress in communities exposed to adversity (generic field-trial version 1.0).* Geneva, Switzerland: World Health Organization.

Wu, H., Yu, D., He, Y., Wang, J., Xiao, Z., & Li, C. (2015). Morita therapy for anxiety disorders in adults. *Cochrane Database of Systematic Reviews*, CD008619.

Xu, H., & Tracey, T. J. G. (2016). Cultural congruence with psychotherapy efficacy: A network meta-analytic examination in China. *Journal of Counseling Psychology*, *63*, 359–365.

Zhang, Y., Young, D., Lee, S., Li, L., Zhang, H., Xiao, Z., ... Chang, D. F. (2012). Chinese taoist cognitive psychotherapy in the treatment of generalized anxiety disorder in contemporary China. *Transcultural Psychiatry*, *39*, 115–129.

Psychotherapy for PTSD and stress disorders

9

Kathleen J. Sikkema, Jessica N. Coleman
Department of Psychology and Neuroscience, Duke Global Health Institute, Duke University, Durham, NC, United States

Traumatic events are defined as "exposure to actual or threatened death, serious injury, or sexual violence" in the fifth edition of the *Diagnostic and Statistical Manual of Mental Disorders* (DSM-5) (American Psychiatric Association, 2013). Common traumatic events include assault, sexual trauma, intimate partner violence, exposure to violence, accidents, and natural disasters. Direct or indirect exposure to traumatic events can have deleterious effects on mental and physical health, particularly if resulting symptoms of traumatic stress are chronic and untreated (Brief, Bollinger, Vielhauer, et al., 2004; Scott, Koenen, Aguilar-Gaxiola, et al., 2013; Turner & Lloyd, 1995). While many survivors exhibit tremendous resilience in response to traumatic events and utilize resources such as adaptive coping and social support to overcome adversity, others may experience severe adjustment difficulties.

Distress related to traumatic events is most often measured by assessing posttraumatic stress symptoms. If symptom severity meets a threshold, a diagnosis of posttraumatic stress disorder (PTSD) can be made. Symptoms of PTSD include (1) reexperiencing (e.g., intrusive thoughts, nightmares, and flashbacks); (2) avoidance of trauma-related thoughts, feelings, or reminders; (3) negative thoughts or feelings (e.g., inability to recall details of the traumatic event, negative affect, and self-blame); and (4) trauma-related arousal or reactivity (e.g., irritability or aggression, risky behavior, difficulty concentrating, and hypervigilance) (U.S. Department of Veterans Affairs, 2017). PTSD is related to poor psychosocial outcomes, such as depression and anxiety (Betancourt, Agnew-Blais, Gilman, Williams, & Ellis, 2010; Fox & Tang, 2000; Gelaye, Arnold, Williams, Goshu, & Berhane, 2009). Worldwide PTSD prevalence varies considerably but has been reported as high as 40% of the general population in conflict-affected countries (Peterson, Togun, Klis, Menten, & Colebunders, 2012). There are few studies of general population PTSD rates in low- and middle-income countries (LMIC) (Koenen, Ratanatharathorn, Ng, et al., 2017). Rather, the focus of most research has been on populations designated as high risk for trauma, such as soldiers and veterans, refugees, and survivors of natural disasters. Many LMIC are affected by serious issues that contribute to the development of traumatic stress, such as war and conflict, internal displacement, poverty, food insecurity, and disease (Smigelsky, Aten, Gerberich, et al., 2014).

Psychological trauma can result in community- and society-level impacts. The World Health Organization (WHO) conducted surveys on mental and physical

Global Mental Health and Psychotherapy. https://doi.org/10.1016/B978-0-12-814932-4.00009-4

disorders in 24 countries (not specific to LMIC) to examine their effect on society (Alonso, Petukhova, Vilagut, et al., 2011). Over two-thirds of participants reported exposure to a traumatic event, and approximately 30% reported four or more events (Benjet, Bromet, Karam, et al., 2016). PTSD ranked third in terms of negative impact on productivity, and data indicated a greater negative impact on low-income countries. People living in settings with intersecting and compounding stressors would benefit greatly from evidence-based treatments targeting traumatic stress, and the social and economic damage of trauma on countries can be offset by scaling up mental health-care services. However, there is a sizable global mental health treatment gap, and LMIC fare the worst (Kazlauskas, 2017). LMIC are underequipped to respond to the demand for mental health services, and lack of infrastructure, funding, and trained professionals are barriers to service delivery (Morina, Malek, Nickerson, & Bryant, 2017a; Morina, Rushiti, Salihu, & Ford, 2010). Studies have estimated the mental health services needed to address population needs in LMIC (Chisholm, Lund, & Saxena, 2007; Lund, Boyce, Flisher, Kafaar, & Dawes, 2009), suggesting the cost would be reasonable when compared with costs of other major contributors to global disease. However, these studies excluded PTSD, which may require more time-intensive treatments and thus more resources (Smigelsky et al., 2014).

Evidence-based psychological treatments for PTSD have been developed and tested in high-income countries such as the United States, Europe, and Canada (Schnyder, Ehlers, Elbert, et al., 2015), and research indicates that they are the most effective PTSD treatments (Bisson, Roberts, Andrew, Cooper, & Lewis, 2013). Approaches for treating trauma are primarily cognitive behavioral such as trauma-focused cognitive behavioral therapy (TF-CBT) and include psychoeducation, exposure techniques (prolonged exposure and narrative exposure therapy (NET)), cognitive processing therapy (CPT), and stress management (e.g., coping skills development) (Bisson, 2010; Bradley, McCourt, Rayment, & Parmar, 2016; Cukor, Olden, Lee, & Difede, 2010; Ponniah & Hollon, 2009). Less research has been conducted in LMIC to examine if similar treatments for PTSD are efficacious in various cultural contexts and within a range of delivery settings. For example, a review of 70 studies of psychological treatments for chronic PTSD found only seven studies in LMIC (Bisson et al., 2013). There is an urgent need to address traumatic stress in LMIC due to its impact on well-being and health outcomes, comorbidity with other conditions, and contribution to the global burden of disease.

9.1 Identification of global evidence

In this chapter, we review psychological interventions for PTSD and stress disorders that have been evaluated in LMIC, provide an overview of their efficacy, synthesize the strengths and weaknesses of empirical work to date, and discuss future directions for research and treatment implementation. A literature search was conducted to identify studies that met the following criteria: described a trial (randomized controlled, quasi-experimental, or noncontrolled) evaluating a psychological intervention; were conducted in an LMIC (The World Bank Group, 2015) assessed posttraumatic stress disorder, symptoms of posttraumatic stress, or psychological distress; and assessed outcomes at both pre- and postintervention. Studies unavailable in English, qualitative exploratory studies, and studies not published in a peer-reviewed journal were excluded from this review. Systematic reviews and meta-analyses of interventions that met the above criteria were also included.

PubMed and PsycINFO were searched in October 2017. Limits to time period were not applied to the search. Standardized search terms and key words related to the constructs of (a) PTSD, (b) LMIC, and (c) psychological intervention were used in all databases. For example, within PubMed, terms used to capture the construct of PTSD included the following: PTSD, posttraumatic stress disorder, trauma, stress disorders, and distress. Search terms for LMIC were derived from the World Bank's classification of low-income, lower-middle-income, and upper-middle-income economies (The World Bank Group, 2015).

Resulting studies were organized by population stressor into the following sections: conflict and violence, natural disasters, and gender-based violence, including comorbid medical conditions. Studies focused on youth are integrated in these sections and then briefly summarized. Given the number of systematic reviews and meta-analyses identified (Lipinski, Liu, & Wong, 2016; Lopes, Macedo, Coutinho, Figueira, & Ventura, 2014; Morina et al., 2017a; Morina, Malek, Nickerson, & Bryant, 2017b; Tol, Patel, Tomlinson, et al., 2011; Verhey, Chibanda, Brakarsh, & Seedat, 2016; Weiss, Ugueto, Mahmooth, et al., 2016; Yatham, Sivathasan, Yoon, da Silva, & Ravindran, 2017), we have framed each section around these reviews and identified additional relevant studies in Table 9.1. Categorizations of stressors related to trauma and promising treatments are visually depicted in Fig. 9.1.

9.2 Conflict and violence

Conflict is currently the highest it has been since 1999 on a global scale, with 40 armed conflicts in more than 25 locations (Pettersson & Wallensteen, 2015). Most research on psychological treatments for conflict-related traumatic stress has focused on war veterans and refugees living in Western countries (Morina et al., 2017a, 2017b). However, civilians comprise the majority of war survivors (Bartov, 2000), and most of them live in LMIC (Pettersson & Wallensteen, 2015), creating a vast need for resources in countries where there are few, if any, mental health services. There is a high prevalence of PTSD and depression in these settings (de Jong, Komproe, Van Ommeren, et al., 2001; Steel et al., 2009), and rates are higher than in regions with no recent conflict (Steel et al., 2009). More than 10 million people worldwide were displaced in 2016 (The UN Refugee Agency, 2016), and 95% of refugees and internally displaced people live in LMIC (The World Bank, 2017). A systematic review and meta-analysis estimated the overall prevalence of PTSD among refugee and conflict-affected populations at 30% (Steel et al., 2009). The high rates of civilians, soldiers, and veterans affected by conflict and violence and their resulting psychological trauma have significant implications for the global burden of disease if their symptoms are not adequately treated (Kessler, Aguilar-Gaxiola, Alonso,

Table 9.1 PTSD treatment studies not identified in reviews and meta-analyses

Study	Population	Country	Study design	Sample size in outcome	Study conditions	Modality	Experimental treatment interventionist	Follow-up posttreatment (all have pre-post)	PTSD measure	Outcomes * = statistically significant
Conflict and violence										
Chiumento, Hamdani, Khan, et al. (2017)	Adults (women only)	Pakistan	cRCT	612 (1:1)	PM+, 5 sessions *Control:* EUC	Group	Female community health workers	4 months	PCL-5 *secondary outcome*	Protocol paper
Hinsberger, Holtzhausen, Sommer, et al. (2017)	Adults (men only, age 16–49)	South Africa	RCT (pilot)	39 (1:1:1)	FORNET, 8 sessions "TFAC" CBT intervention, 7 sessions *Control:* wait list	Individual	Local counselors	8 months	PSS-I	Reduction of PTSD symptoms in FORNET sample only*
Kalantari, Yule, Dyregrov, Neshatdoost, and Ahmadi (2012)	Youth (age 12–18)	Iran (Afghani refugees)	RCT	61 (1:1)	"Writing for Recovery," 6 sessions *Control:* no treatment	Group	Not specified	1 week post only	TGIC	Reduction of traumatic grief in experimental group*
Khan, Hamdani, Chiumento, et al. (2017)	Adults (women only)	Pakistan	cRCT (pilot)	112 (1:1)	PM+, 5 sessions *Control:* EUC	Group	Nonspecialist female health workers	2 weeks post only	PCL-5 *secondary outcome*	Greater reduction of PTSD symptoms in PM+ group
Nakimuli-Mpungu, Okello, Kinyanda, et al. (2013)	Adults	Uganda	Quasi-experimental	613 (69 GC, 544 non)	Group counseling, 5 sessions *Comparison:* nonparticipants at the clinic	Group	Trauma counselor, social worker	1 month	HTQ	Reduction of PTSD symptoms in whole sample*, similar rate among groups
Onyut, Neuner, Schauer, et al. (2005)	Youth (age 12–17)	Uganda (Somali refugees)	Noncontrolled (pilot)	6	KIDNET (child version of NET), 4–6 sessions	Individual	Expert clinicians	9 months	CIDI	Reduction of PTSD symptoms*
Sijbrandij, Farooq, Bryant, et al. (2015)	Adults	Pakistan	RCT	346 (1:1)	PM+, 5 sessions *Control:* TAU	Individual	Lay counselors	13 weeks	HTQ, PCL-5 *secondary outcome*	Protocol paper

Talbot, Uwihorcyc, Kamen, et al. (2013)	Youth (orphans, age 15–25)	Rwanda	Noncontrolled (pilot)	120	HIV prevention plus existing mental health services, 1 year	Both	NGO staff, psychologists, and adult mentors	Post only	PCL	Reduction of PTSD symptoms at 12 months*, increased use of counseling services associated with decline in symptoms*
Natural disasters										
Chen et al. (2014)	Youth (adolescents who lost a parent in earthquake)	China	RCT (pilot)	32 (1:1:1)	Short-term CBT, 6 sessions General supportive intervention No treatment	Group Individual	Not specified Local volunteers with basic training	3 months	CRIES-13	Greater reduction in PTSD symptoms in CBT group*
Jiang et al. (2014)	Adults (earthquake survivors)	China	RCT (pilot)	41 (1:1)	IPT + TAU, 12 sessions *Control:* TAU	Individual	Trained local mental health personnel	3 months (comparison only at post)	CAPS	Greater reduction in PTSD symptoms in IPT group, post only*
Wang, Wang, and Maercker (2013)	Adults	China	RCT	90 urban (1:1), 93 rural (1:1)	CMTR self-help trauma intervention program, 6 online modules *Control:* wait list	Individual (online)	Rural intervention assisted by volunteers	3 months (comparison only at post)	PDS *primary outcome* PCC, CSE *secondary outcomes*	Reduction in PTSD symptoms post only (both urban and rural)*, group-time interaction*
Wu, Zhu, Zhang, et al. (2012)	Adults (Chinese military rescuers)	China	RCT	1267 (1:1:1)	"512 PIM," 1 session Standard postdisaster debriefing *Control:* no intervention *Control:* supportive counseling, 12 sessions	Group	Clinical psychologists	1, 2, 4 months	SI-PTSD	Reduction in the severity of PTSD over time for all groups*, lower PTSD scores in 512 PIM group (2 and 4 months)*

Continued

Table 9.1 Continued

Study	Population	Country	Study design	Sample size in outcome	Study conditions	Modality	Experimental treatment interventionist	Follow-up posttreatment (all have pre-post)	PTSD measure	Outcomes * = statistically significant
Gender-based violence										
Allon (2015)	Adults (women only, sexual assault)	DR Congo	Quasi-experimental	37 (8 individual, 29 group)	EMDR therapy, 2 sessions EMDR-IGTP procedure, 2 sessions	Individual Group	Psychologists and psychiatric nurse	2 weeks post only	SUD	Reduction of distress in both groups*, greater improvements in EDMR therapy group than EDMR-IGTP*
Bass, Annan, McIvor Murray, et al. (2013)	Adults (women only, sexual violence)	DR Congo	RCT	405 (157 CPT, 248 control)	CPT, 1 individual and 11 group sessions *Control:* access to individual support	Both	Experienced psychosocial assistants	1 and 6 months	HTQ	Reduction of PTSD symptoms in both groups*, greater improvements in CPT group*
Bryant, Schafer, Dawson, et al. (2017)	Adults (women only, GBV)	Kenya	RCT	421 (1:1)	PM+, 5 sessions *Control:* EUC	Individual	Lay community workers	3 months	PCL-5 *secondary outcome*	Greater reduction in PTSD symptoms in PM+ group than EUC*
Hustache, Moro, Roptin, et al. (2009)	Adults (women only, sexual violence)	DR Congo	Noncontrolled	64	Psychological intervention, median of 2 sessions	Individual	Psychologist	12–24 months	TSQ	TSQ not administered at pretest, but results suggest long-term positive impact of psychosocial support
O'Callaghan, McMullen, Shannon, Rafferty, and Black (2013)	Youth (girls only, sexual violence, age 12–17)	DR Congo	RCT	52 (1:1)	Culturally modified TF-CBT, 15 sessions	Group	Nonclinical facilitators (social workers)	3 months (intervention only, comparison only at post)	UCLA PTSD-RI (Revised)	Greater reduction in PTSD symptoms post only in TF-CBT group compared with control group*

Gender-based violence and HIV										
Onu, Ongeri, Bukusi, et al. (2016)	Adults (women only, GBV and HIV)	Kenya	RCT (pilot)	200 (1:1)	IPT + TAU, 12 sessions *Control:* TAU (offered IPT at post)	Individual	Nonspecialists	3, 6, 9 months for all IPT (RCT post only)	MINI 5.0, PCL-C	Protocol paper
Sikkema et al. (2018)	Adults (women only, sexual trauma and HIV)	South Africa	RCT (pilot)	64 (1:1)	ImpACT coping intervention, 4 individual and 3 group sessions (plus SoC)	Both	Nonspecialists	6 months	PCL-5	Greater reduction of avoidance and arousal symptoms of PTSD in ImpACT group at post (3 months), with clinically significant decreases in overall PTSD symptoms

Key: Study conditions: WHO problem management plus (PM+), enhanced usual care (EUC), forensic offender rehabilitation narrative exposure therapy (FORNET), thinking for a change (TFAC), cognitive behavioral therapy (CBT), narrative exposure therapy adapted for children (KIDNET), treatment as usual (TAU), eye movement desensitization and reprocessing (EMDR), EMDR integrative group treatment protocol (EMDR-IGTP), cognitive processing therapy (CPT), trauma-focused cognitive behavioral therapy (TF-CBT), interpersonal therapy (IPT), improving AIDS care after trauma (ImpACT), standard of care (SoC), Chinese version of the my trauma recovery (CMTR), 512 psychological intervention model (512 PIM).

PTSD measures: PTSD Checklist for DSM-5 (PCL-5), PTSD Symptom Scale-Interview (PSS-I), Traumatic Grief Inventory for Children (TGIC), Harvard Trauma Questionnaire (HTQ), Composite International Diagnostic Interview (CIDI), PTSD Checklist (PCL), Subjective Units of Disturbance (SUD), Trauma Screening Questionnaire (TSQ), UCLA PTSD-RI Revised (Reaction Index), Mini International Neuropsychiatric Interview (MINI 5.0), PTSD Checklist—Civilian (PCL-C), Children's Revised Impact of Events Scale (CRIES-13), Clinician-Administered PTSD Scale (CAPS), Posttraumatic Diagnostic Scale (PDS), Posttraumatic Cognitive Changes (PCC), Trauma Coping Self-Efficacy Scale (CSE), Structured Interview for PTSD (SI-PTSD).

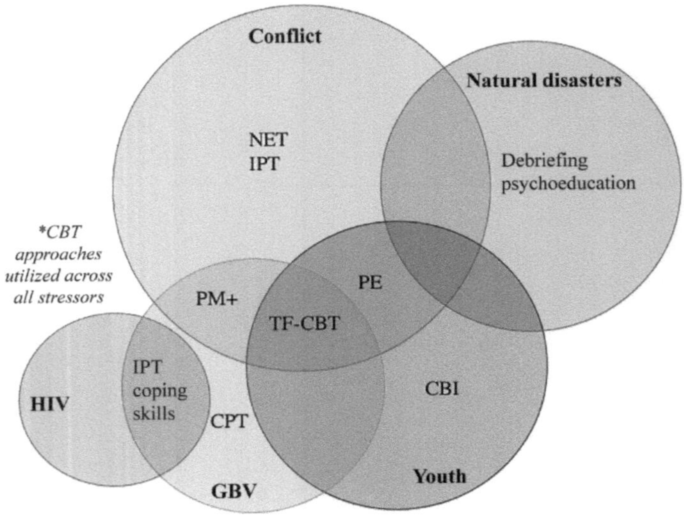

Fig. 9.1 Promising PTSD treatments for stressors in LMIC.

et al., 2009; Morina, Wicherts, Lobbrecht, & Priebe, 2014; Sabes-Figuera, McCrone, Bogic, et al., 2012).

Research on PTSD and traumatic stress in Western countries, particularly among war veterans and refugees, indicates the efficacy of empirically supported psychological interventions in improving mental health outcomes (Bisson et al., 2013). LMIC struggle with significant barriers to the implementation of these interventions such as the lack of mental health infrastructure, paucity of trained practitioners, and issues with attrition in settings with ongoing conflict and violence. However, a number of controlled trials have evaluated the efficacy of psychological interventions on PTSD outcomes in LMIC affected by conflict and violence. Two meta-analyses and two reviews have outlined psychological interventions for PTSD among survivors of conflict and mass violence, systematic violence, and torture in LMIC (Morina et al., 2017a, 2017b; Tol et al., 2011; Weiss et al., 2016). Tol et al. (2011) reviewed mental health and psychosocial support in humanitarian settings related to conflict, natural disasters, and technological disasters. Weiss et al. (2016) conducted a review of psychological interventions for survivors of torture and systematic violence. Morina et al. (2017a, 2017b) cited issues with these reviews (e.g., limitations in study design, not applying meta-analytic approaches, and not specifically focusing on LMIC) and therefore assessed the empirical support for psychological interventions for PTSD and depression among both adult and youth survivors of mass violence in LMIC in two meta-analyses to more clearly determine treatment efficacy (Morina et al., 2017a, 2017b). Our literature search yielded eight studies that were not included in these meta-analyses and reviews (see Table 9.1) (Chiumento et al., 2017; Hinsberger et al., 2017; Kalantari et al., 2012; Khan et al., 2017; Nakimuli-Mpungu et al., 2013; Onyut et al., 2005; Sijbrandij et al., 2015; Talbot et al., 2013).

9.2.1 Summary of interventions

Various types of cognitive behavioral therapy (CBT), including NET, have been the most frequently studied psychological treatments for PTSD in the conflict literature in LMIC, with limited use of interpersonal therapy (IPT) (Betancourt, McBain, Newnham, et al., 2014; Jacob, Neuner, Maedl, Schaal, & Elbert, 2014; Schaal, Elbert, & Neuner, 2009). In the youth PTSD intervention literature from conflict-afflicted settings, TF-CBT and classroom-based interventions (CBIs) are among the most commonly studied treatments (Morina et al., 2017a). CBTs are a broad category of psychological treatments that focus on cognitions, emotions, and behaviors as well as their intersections. TF-CBT typically focuses on addressing traumatic memories and their meaning among children and their caregivers using cognitive and behavioral approaches and exposure and stress management skills. NET is an example of a manualized CBT-based treatment that incorporates exposure (Hinsberger et al., 2017). IPT is a 10–12-session treatment that addresses issues in social functioning, in order to reduce symptoms of depression. IPT is considered a first-line treatment for depression (Markowitz & Weissman, 2004) and has been found to be comparable in efficacy with exposure-based treatments for PTSD (Markowitz, Petkova, Neria, et al., 2015). Additionally, WHO developed Problem Management Plus (PM+) and initially found support for the program from a trial in Pakistan, which consists of strategies such as behavioral activation (BA), problem-solving, utilizing social support, and stress reduction (Chiumento et al., 2017; Khan et al., 2017). Other treatments that have been tested are CPT (Bolton, Bass, Zangana, et al., 2014), BA (Bolton, Bass, et al., 2014; Rahman, Hamdani, Awan, et al., 2016), eye movement desensitization and reprocessing (EMDR) (Acarturk, Konuk, Cetinkaya, et al., 2015), meditation-relaxation and mind–body treatments (Catani et al., 2009), thought field therapy (Connolly & Sakai, 2011), dialogic exposure, transdiagnostic interventions (Bolton, Lee, Haroz, et al., 2014), and psychosocial support. Several trials have combined multiple types of treatments (e.g., CBT and IPT (Betancourt et al., 2014) and NET and IPT (Jacob et al., 2014)). The eight additional studies yielded from our search contained the following types of interventions: 3 PM+, two NET, a writing intervention, group counseling, and a multidisciplinary program.

The number of sessions in existing interventions ranged from 1 to 18, aside from a few interventions consisting of several full-day workshops (Morina et al., 2017a, 2017b). Most psychological interventions for conflict-afflicted adult populations utilized an individual rather than group format, while most interventions for youth were group- and classroom-based. Many of the study interventionists were paraprofessionals (e.g., lay counselors and community health workers), and others were counselors, social workers, and psychologists. Some published trials have reported on training of study interventionists, and among these trials, the amount of training ranged from 1 day to 1 month (Morina et al., 2017b). Weiss et al. (2016) note that manuscripts in this area of research infrequently provide details about training and supervision processes and fidelity to the intervention but these factors are important to report in order to understand the implementation of these treatments.

9.2.2 *Methodological approaches and treatment effects*

The Morina et al. (2017a, 2017b) metaanalyses included only RCTs, and the eight additional studies in Table 9.1 included five RCTs (Chiumento et al., 2017; Hinsberger et al., 2017; Kalantari et al., 2012; Khan et al., 2017; Sijbrandij et al., 2015), one quasi-experimental study (Nakimuli-Mpungu et al., 2013), and two non-controlled studies (Onyut et al., 2005; Talbot et al., 2013). Most of the RCTs compared a randomized intervention arm with a control arm, typically a wait list control or treatment as usual control condition, but there were limited active comparison conditions. The duration of follow-up among all studies varied considerably, ranging from 1 to 24 months (Morina et al., 2017a, 2017b).

The majority of studies assessed PTSD by self-report and often using standardized measures administered by an interviewer. A limited number of studies utilized structured clinical interviews to measure PTSD (e.g., Clinician-Administered PTSD Scale, CAPS). The most commonly cited self-report measures were the PTSD Checklist for DSM-5 (PCL-5), Harvard Trauma Questionnaire (HTQ), Posttraumatic Diagnostic Scale (PDS), Impact of Event Scale (IES), and the UCLA PTSD Reaction Index (RI). Less than half the studies reported the number of participants that met diagnostic criteria for PTSD at pretreatment or PTSD prevalence rates (Morina et al., 2017a, 2017b). Studies that reported prevalence rates indicated rates of 45%–94% before treatment (Morina et al., 2017a, 2017b). Attrition rates differed across studies, ranging from 0% to 40.5%, with an average of 11.5%.

Evidence indicates that psychological interventions can reduce symptoms of PTSD among conflict- and violence-exposed populations in LMIC, and CBT interventions that address memories of the traumatic event or include exposure components are particularly effective (Morina et al., 2017a; Weiss et al., 2016). The meta-analyses suggest that psychological interventions, when compared with control conditions, yielded small to medium effect sizes for PTSD (Morina et al., 2017a, 2017b). Morina et al. (2017b) found that the trials had similar effect sizes, regardless of the type of treatment. Another notable finding was that effect sizes for depression were large at posttreatment and follow-up, even in instances when trials were designed to intervene on PTSD and not depression. This suggests that trauma-focused interventions can have discernable secondary effects on other comorbid conditions such as depression and functional impairment.

9.2.3 *Discussion and future directions*

Psychological interventions may be efficacious in treating PTSD among adults and youth who have been exposed to conflict and violence in LMIC. Many treatment approaches have been utilized and adapted for different cultural settings. There is little empirical support to suggest that a particular treatment approach works best, but evidence indicates CBT, CBT with exposure, CBT with biofeedback, NET, IPT, and CPT can be effective. These interventions require further evidence from randomized controlled trials, including hybrid effectiveness-implementation models (Curran, Bauer, Mittman, Pyne, & Stetler, 2012).

There are several limitations of intervention trials for conflict-affected populations that have been published to date. First, most RCTs utilized a wait list or treatment as usual control condition, which often involves little to no intervention. Second, most studies had small sample sizes. Third, most studies do not include PTSD diagnosis as part of their inclusion criteria, which makes it difficult to assess and compare the level of PTSD severity among participants in each trial. Fourth, historically few trials have reported on intent-to-treat analyses (e.g., all randomized subjects are analyzed regardless of attrition) and instead have reported results from only treatment completers, which makes interpreting results difficult and subject to biases (e.g., related to recruitment, loss to follow-up, and symptom severity). Fifth, there is variability in the types of self-report measures and structured clinical interviews used to assess PTSD symptoms. Additionally, these measures have been used to assess PTSD across many countries with varying cultural norms (some of which have limited cross-cultural validity). Lastly, there is a risk of publication bias in the field, as apparent in funnel plots from meta-analyses (Morina et al., 2017a, 2017b) suggesting that similar psychological intervention trials with nonsignificant treatment results may not have been published. In order to establish which treatments are most efficacious and effective in LMIC, all trials should be published and available.

In recent years, research on systematic violence (Weiss et al., 2016) has explored transdiagnostic or common element approaches. Transdiagnostic interventions can address several mental health problems by selecting assorted combinations of elements of empirically supported treatments, suggesting that CBT elements can be used flexibly. Future research in LMIC could study components of interventions to identify empirically supported mechanisms of change and further test transdiagnostic interventions for PTSD. These interventions could support implementation, as they may be able to address a range of issues and may require fewer sessions.

9.3 Natural disasters

The occurrence of natural disasters and the number of people affected have continually increased over the past decades (Strömberg, 2007). Natural disasters can have devastating psychological consequences, in addition and related to mass casualties, destruction of property, and displacement. Among survivors of natural disasters, estimates of PTSD range from 3% to 60% (Neria, Nandi, & Galea, 2008). Interventions to address and treat PTSD among survivors of natural disasters have most commonly been conducted following earthquakes and more recently, the Indian Ocean tsunami. The studies reviewed that were conducted following earthquakes are not specific to LMIC, but are representative of worldwide efforts in disaster situations where resources are low and mental health services limited. Empirically supported guidelines for postdisaster psychosocial care (e.g., promoting sense of safety, calming, self-efficacy and community efficacy, social connectedness, and hope) have been established and disseminated as well (Hobfoll, Watson, Bell, et al., 2007).

Three relevant systematic reviews were identified that addressed psychological treatment of PTSD following natural disasters (Lipinski et al., 2016; Lopes et al.,

2014; Tol et al., 2011). In the broader context of humanitarian assistance, Tol et al. (2011) reviewed mental health and psychosocial support across both conflict settings and natural disasters, which was discussed above. Lopes et al. (2014) evaluated the evidence base for CBT utilized in natural disaster settings (primarily earthquakes), and Lipinski and authors specifically examined the effectiveness of psychological interventions following the Indian Ocean tsunami. Through our literature search, four studies were identified (Chen et al., 2014; Jiang et al., 2014; Wang et al., 2013; Wu et al., 2012) that were not captured in these systematic reviews (see Table 9.1). Interestingly, each of these studies examined distinct psychological treatments for PTSD following the earthquake in Sichuan, China.

9.3.1 Summary of interventions

Psychological treatment of PTSD among earthquake survivors (based on 10 of 11 studies that met the Lopes et al. review criteria) was primarily cognitive behavioral in approach, with the majority using exposure techniques and more limited use of problem-solving (Lopes et al., 2014). As shown in Table 9.1, other treatment approaches included IPT and broader cognitive behavioral techniques such as coping and cognitive reframing. Innovative intervention techniques such as self-directed, web-based approaches and an integrated model of stress debriefing and cohesion training for military rescuers have also been described. Session frequency ranged from 1 to 12 sessions and included interventions for children and adults. Details on interventionists, training, supervision, and fidelity are limited.

The Lipinski et al. (2016) review of psychosocial interventions implemented after the Indian Ocean tsunami identified a range of treatment approaches, described as 10 different psychological interventions to address PTSD or psychological well-being more broadly. While the intervention approaches did vary, the majority were either psychoeducational, cognitive behavioral, or stress debriefing and crisis intervention. Session frequency varied from 1 to 12 sessions, not only were typically individual in format but also included group sessions, and were delivered in a variety of settings including schools. These interventions were delivered by a wide range of providers, including nonspecialists in mental health (e.g., community health workers, teachers, and volunteers) and mental health professionals (e.g., clinical psychologists and counselors), and were considered culturally tailored and adapted to local context (Lipinski et al., 2016).

9.3.2 Methodological approaches and treatment effects

Most studies identified in the systematic reviews specific to natural disasters (Lipinski et al., 2016; Lopes et al., 2014) were not RCTs. In Lipinski et al.'s review of CBT approaches (10 earthquakes and 1 hurricane), three were RCTs, three were quasi-experimental studies, and six were noncontrolled studies. In the systematic review of interventions following the tsunami (10 studies), none of the studies were RCTs, although there was a combination of quasi-experimental designs and pre-/posttest uncontrolled studies. Among the studies listed in Table 9.1, all four were RCTs; two were pilot trials. Of the seven RCTs identified across all studies, most utilized wait list or treatment as usual control conditions. Two of those trials (Chen et al., 2014; Wu et al., 2012) (see Table 9.1) compared the experimental treatment with an active treatment. The use of wait list and treatment as usual control conditions was also common across the quasi- and nonexperimental design studies.

Among the total of 25 studies from the two systematic reviews (Lipinski et al., 2016; Lopes et al., 2014) and identified in Table 9.1, all but two reported a reduction in PTSD symptoms following treatment. The five RCTs (Başoglu, Salcioglu, & Livanou, 2007; Başoğlu, Salcioğlu, Livanou, Kalender, & Acar, 2005; Chen et al., 2014; Zang, Hunt, & Cox, 2013) that evaluated traditional CBT approaches (exposure techniques, IPT, and short-term CBT) among earthquake survivors demonstrated significant reductions in PTSD in comparison with the control conditions. Standardized and widely used measures of PTSD (e.g., CAPS, Impact of Event Scale-Revised (IES-R), PCL, and UCLA PTSD Index) were used in the large majority of studies, and a diagnosis of PTSD was an inclusion criteria for the RCTs. Outcomes in the exposure and short-term CBT therapy studies were based on symptom reduction, while the IPT pilot trial reported on reduction in PTSD diagnoses. However, sample sizes were small, even in the RCTs (sample size range 22–59), and effects were not consistently maintained at 3- or 6-month follow-up assessments.

9.3.3 Discussion and future directions

The evidence base for psychological treatment of PTSD among natural disaster survivors is limited, although brief exposure therapy and IPT have demonstrated short-term effectiveness in small RCTs and merit further evaluation in full-scale trials. In addition, a number of studies with less rigorous methodology support the potential effectiveness of PTSD treatment in these settings but underscore the need for more rigorous designs that include intervention comparison conditions. This is especially important given the improvement shown in quasi-experimental and noncontrolled trials among participants not receiving a PTSD treatment, which could be due to natural recovery over time. In research on treatment effectiveness in natural disasters, this is further complicated by the need to intervene and conduct research soon after the traumatic event. Mental health treatment in LMIC is usually not readily available beyond debriefing and crisis intervention. Thus, future research could better address the delivery of PTSD treatment by nonspecialists in mental health, strategies to ensure cultural adaptation, and enhancing the capacity of local mental health providers to deliver short-term cognitive behavioral treatment post natural disasters. Future research on the treatment of PTSD following natural disasters must also address issues of small sample size and assess readiness of the field to compare treatment effectiveness.

9.4 Gender-based violence

Gender-based violence (GBV) is a significant global public health issue, and approximately one in three women will experience GBV in their lifetime (World Health Organization, 2013). Violence against women is defined by the United Nations as "any act of gender-based violence that results in, or is likely to result in, physical, sexual, or mental harm or suffering to women, including threats of such acts, coercion or arbitrary deprivation of liberty, whether occurring in public or in private life" (United Nations, 1993). GBV encompasses domestic and interpersonal violence, sexual abuse and assault, and genital mutilation. GBV can result in adverse outcomes including psychological distress (e.g., posttraumatic stress, depression, and anxiety) (Rees, Silove, Chey, et al., 2011) and physical health problems (e.g., injuries, sexually transmitted infections, unintended pregnancy, and vaginal and rectal fistulas) (Chivers-Wilson, 2006; World Health Organization, 2013). Women and girls are disproportionately affected, but the impact transcends individuals and greatly affects communities and societies.

Several evidence-based treatments for trauma related to interpersonal and sexual violence have demonstrated efficacy in high-income countries (Vickerman & Margolin, 2009). However, few treatments have been tested in low-income and/or high-conflict settings, which have high rates of GBV (Decker, Latimore, Yasutake, et al., 2015; World Health Organization, 2013). For example, sub-Saharan Africa's lifetime prevalence range for GBV is 56%–71% (Garcia-Moreno, Jansen, Ellsberg, Heise, & Watts, 2006). This high risk for exposure to violence in LMIC, many of which are also conflict-affected, intersects with limited availability of mental health services. Those who experience GBV are vulnerable to social stigma, which can further impede the utilization of services following a traumatic event (García-Moreno et al., 2015). Research suggests that women with a history of GBV infrequently disclose these experiences to providers, which is a barrier to obtaining appropriate treatment for trauma (Watt, Dennis, Choi, et al., 2017). This indicates a serious need for psychological treatments that can be implemented in LMIC to reach this vulnerable group.

An emerging area of research in GBV and PTSD treatment is the intersection of traumatic stress and comorbid medical conditions, primarily in HIV/AIDS. Individuals living with HIV, women in particular, report disproportionately higher levels of trauma and interpersonal violence and higher rates of PTSD than the general population (Machtinger, Haberer, Wilson, & Weiss, 2012; Seedat, 2012). An HIV diagnosis may be experienced as a traumatic event itself, which can exacerbate the psychological impact of past traumas (Martin & Kagee, 2011; Myer et al., 2008). For example, among women attending HIV clinics in South Africa, PTSD prevalence ranges from 19% to 70% (Martin & Kagee, 2011; Myer et al., 2008; Olley, Gxamza, Seedat, et al., 2003; Peltzer et al., 2012; Yemeke et al., 2017). Yet, the evidence base for trauma-focused interventions among HIV-infected populations is limited (Applebaum et al., 2015; McLean & Fitzgerald, 2016; Verhey et al., 2016), with few intervention trials conducted with rigorous methodology (Ironson, O'Cleirigh, Leserman, et al., 2013; Pacella, Armelie, Boarts, et al., 2012; Sikkema et al., 2013).

9.4.1 Summary of interventions

No systematic reviews of psychological interventions for women and girls who have experienced GBV in LMIC were identified, and few studies have been published in peer-reviewed journals (Allon, 2015; Hustache et al., 2009; Bass et al., 2013; Bryant et al., 2017; Onu et al., 2016; O'Callaghan et al., 2013; Sikkema et al., 2018). Our search yielded five RCTs (Bass et al., 2013; Bryant et al., 2017; O'Callaghan et al., 2013; Onu et al., 2016; Sikkema et al., 2018), one quasi-experimental study (Allon, 2015), and one noncontrolled study (Hustache et al., 2009). As shown in Table 9.1, intervention trials targeting GBV and sexual violence among women living in LMIC also intersect with those focused on women living with HIV. Existing interventions tested in RCTs utilize several approaches, including CBT (e.g., TF-CBT, PM+, and coping skills) and IPT. The interventions utilized either individual or group formats, and a few trials incorporated both formats in the intervention design (Bass et al., 2013; O'Callaghan et al., 2013; Sikkema et al., 2018). The number of sessions ranged from 2 to 15. The two additional studies tested EMDR and a postrape psychosocial support program.

Two of the RCTs referenced above are randomized pilot intervention trials addressing PTSD and GBV or sexual violence among women living with HIV (Onu et al., 2016; Sikkema et al., 2018). In South Africa, a brief coping intervention for women living with HIV and a history of sexual trauma was developed and culturally adapted based on a US evidence-based intervention (Meade et al., 2010; Sikkema et al., 2013; Sikkema, Hansen, Kochman, et al., 2007; Sikkema, Kochman, van den Berg, Hansen, & Watt, 2009; Sikkema, Wilson, Hansen, et al., 2008). In addition to reducing traumatic stress, the intervention also focused on improving HIV treatment adherence and care engagement (Sikkema et al., 2017). A trial underway in Kenya evaluates the preliminary effectiveness and feasibility of 12 individual sessions of IPT on PTSD and major depression among women living with HIV who have experienced GBV (Onu et al., 2016). Both interventions are delivered by nonspecialists in HIV clinic settings.

Intervention providers consisted of nonspecialists in five of the studies and psychologists or social workers in two of the studies (level of psychological intervention expertise not specified). Several trials had extensive training processes and ongoing supervision. In one study, interventionists were provided a manual before each session and had opportunities to ask questions or suggest ideas for cultural adaptation beforehand (O'Callaghan et al., 2013). Two trials assessed interventionist competency before the study began and excluded those who did not meet the competency threshold to ensure fidelity to the intervention (Bryant et al., 2017; Onu et al., 2016). The manuscripts that included details about how the intervention fidelity was monitored stated that protocol adherence was assessed by supervisors completing fidelity checklists or transcribing and translating audio files of sessions and rating them afterward.

9.4.2 Methodological approaches and treatment effects

Most studies were randomized trials that conducted a priori power analyses to determine sample size. One study utilized a cluster randomized design, grouping 16 villages into blocks of 2–4 based on proximity and shared language and then randomizing them to provide CPT or individual support (Bass et al., 2013). A trial currently underway has an effectiveness-implementation hybrid type I design, in which both short-term clinical effectiveness and potential for scale-up are evaluated (Onu et al., 2016).

Among the RCTs, the control conditions were individual support, enhanced usual care, treatment as usual/standard of care, and wait list control. Follow-up assessment periods ranged from 3 to 6 months.

Some studies used inclusion criteria requiring a PTSD diagnosis, some required that participants met a threshold for symptom severity, and others only required experiencing GBV or sexual violence regardless of trauma symptoms. Every trial used self-report measures (e.g., HTQ, PCL-5, and PTSD-RI) and reported moderate to high internal consistency in their samples, and one trial utilized a diagnostic interview (Mini International Neuropsychiatric Interview, MINI 5.0) (Onu et al., 2016). All four completed RCTs used an intent-to-treat analysis and found that the experimental intervention was more effective than the control condition in reducing PTSD symptoms at follow-up when delivered by local facilitators.

9.4.3 Discussion and future directions

There is a significant need for psychological interventions for women who have experienced GBV, but few treatments have been developed and tested for this population. A few trials have found promising effects of treatment on PTSD outcomes, with sustained gains several months after the end of treatment. There are several strengths of these interventions that have implications for scale-up of implementation in low-resource settings. The first is that interventions in RCTs to date have been delivered by local paraprofessionals that mostly receive training and supervision throughout the intervention. Second, the interventions are adapted to cultural context and utilize measures that have been validated in these settings (O'Callaghan et al., 2013; Sikkema et al., 2018). Third, some trials incorporate a group format, utilize less than half the standard number of sessions for currently used interventions (Bryant et al., 2017), and adapt the treatment to low-literacy population in settings with ongoing conflict (Bass et al., 2013). Fourth, retention has been relatively high despite conducting interventions in settings with ongoing conflict (Bass et al., 2013). The demonstration of treatment success in improving mental health while promoting implementation indicates promise for sustaining these treatments in settings with limited mental health service resources and participant availability. Additionally, the O'Callaghan et al. (2013) and Sikkema et al. (2018) trials are examples of how psychological interventions can be integrated into existing infrastructure, such as vocational training programs and primary care clinics.

Several limitations of these studies should be considered. Most of the treatments were resource-intensive, requiring a great amount of participant, interventionist, and supervisor time to complete. Further study is needed to evaluate treatments in terms of effectiveness and potential for scale-up in LMIC. For example, the trials of CPT and IPT involve a greater number of sessions than the trial of PM+. The brevity of the PM+, even if not as effective as CPT, could make it a more cost-effective and therefore more scalable option to integrate into local services. However, more resource-intensive psychological treatments may be needed due to the symptom severity exhibited by this population. These findings make a strong case for future investigations of trials in LMIC using a stepped-care framework to evaluate interventions, in which patient progress is monitored to identify when it is necessary to transition to a more intensive treatment. Almost all interventions to date have been in the Democratic Republic of the Congo or Kenya, and there is a need to test these interventions in other cultural contexts to investigate if the results generalize across settings. Additionally, future trials should continue to test treatments that have yielded promising results. For example, it is noteworthy that few studies have tested CPT, given how effective it is, and that it was developed for female survivors of sexual assault (Bass et al., 2013; Sikkema et al., 2018).

A recent systematic review (Verhey et al., 2016) calls attention to this lack of rigorously evaluated interventions for PTSD among people living with HIV/AIDS in resource-poor settings. Only seven studies were identified that met the search criteria. Six RCTs were conducted in resource-limited settings in the United States; all utilized a form of cognitive behavioral treatment and assessed outcomes using standardized measures of PTSD symptoms, and the majority utilized mental health professionals for treatment delivery. One observational prospective cohort study utilizing trauma counselors in postgenocidal Rwanda reported high PTSD prevalence rates over time. Thus, no intervention trials evaluating PTSD interventions for people living with HIV/AIDS in LMIC were reported. Since the publication of the systematic review, the Onu et al. (2016) and Sikkema et al. (2018) trials addressing HIV and GBV or sexual violence have been published. Future research should move toward conducting large-scale RCTs in this area to examine effects on PTSD- and HIV-related outcomes, including adherence to antiretroviral therapy (ART) and HIV viral suppression.

The integration of PTSD treatment into primary care settings in low-resource settings provides an opportunity to screen and intervene with individuals who otherwise may not seek mental health treatment and could also enhance care engagement for comorbid medical conditions. This is especially appropriate for HIV/AIDS populations, in which GBV and PTSD are more common than general populations and are associated with other health risk behaviors including substance use, sexual transmission risk behavior, and ART nonadherence. Challenges in integrating PTSD treatment into HIV clinic settings include the lack of resources for screening; availability of referral sources and trained providers; and concern related to the dual stigma of HIV infection and trauma, especially GBV. However, with a small but increasing number of promising mental health intervention trials that address depression and anxiety among people living with HIV (Sikkema et al., 2015), lessons learned related to trial methodology and implementation approaches can inform PTSD intervention trials.

9.5 Vulnerable youth

The prevalence of PTSD among youth in LMIC is substantially higher than youth in high-income countries (Yatham et al., 2017). Interventions for children and adolescents and their findings are represented in the conflict, natural disasters, and GBV sections above (see also Chapter 13). One of the meta-analyses conducted by Morina et al. (2017a, 2017b) focused on psychological interventions for PTSD and depression in youth survivors of mass violence in LMIC. Yatham et al. (2017) also published a review of prevalence studies and 21 randomized and cluster randomized controlled intervention studies addressing PTSD, depression, and anxiety among youth in LMIC. The interventions consisted of psychological, psychoeducational, and supportive approaches and were delivered in community- and school-based settings. Most trials were conducted in locations with armed conflict, and two studies targeted orphaned youth who lost their parents to HIV/AIDS.

In conflict settings, several studies have implemented some form of CBT such as teaching recovery techniques (TRT), a group TF-CBT intervention (Barron, Abdallah, & Smith, 2013; Qouta, Palosaari, Diab, & Punamäki, 2012), and CBIs that included CBT and creative expression approaches (Jordans, Komproe, Tol, et al., 2010; Tol et al., 2008; Tol, Komproe, Jordans, et al., 2012; Tol, Komproe, Jordans, et al., 2014). Yatham et al. (2017) noted that these interventions yielded mixed results. Studies in nonconflict settings employed various techniques, including CBT, peer-based support groups, writing interventions, psychoeducation, and mind-body skills. For example, Murray et al. (2015) conducted a full-scale RCT and found significant improvements in PTSD symptomatology among children who received a TF-CBT intervention delivered by nonspecialists. In line with findings from Yatham et al., recent pilot studies have tested TF-CBT for orphaned children (O'Donnell, Dorsey, Gong, et al., 2014) and an innovative approach to prolonged exposure for adolescents with favorable results (Rossouw, 2017).

Study findings indicate that psychological or supportive interventions can effectively reduce PTSD symptoms among youth in LMIC. Approaches with empirical support, such as TF-CBT, provide the strongest evidence to date, although often with small to medium effects. Reviews and meta-analyses (Morina et al., 2017a; Tol et al., 2011; Yatham et al., 2017) have found great variability in intervention efficacy, which may be attributed in part to the heterogeneity of the study population (e.g., age, gender, socioeconomic status, diagnoses, and comorbidities), varied study settings (e.g., armed conflicts and nonconflict), utilizing different outcome measures, and significant limitations in study designs. While research suggests the promise of psychological interventions for vulnerable youth, more rigorous community- and school-based intervention trials that can be delivered by teachers and nonspecialists are needed in order to determine the most efficacious approaches and promote dissemination (see also Chapter 13).

9.6 Conclusion

The purpose of this chapter was to review psychological interventions for PTSD and stress disorders related to diverse stressors in LMIC, synthesize strengths and weaknesses of studies to date, and discuss implications for future research. Over the past couple of decades, a number of studies have demonstrated the efficacy of evidence-based psychological treatments when delivered by nonspecialists in LMIC. While these treatments are promising, PTSD outcome research in resource-limited countries is relatively limited compared with high-income countries. Additionally, the field is largely still focused on the first stage of translational research, including pilot trials, a limited number of rigorous treatment trials, and a growing but limited number of effectiveness and implementation trials in existing clinical care systems. The urgency to address the enormous burden of PTSD in LMIC warrants further research in this area and research oriented toward both efficacy and effectiveness in order to scale up implementation and meet the need for mental health-care services.

Existing interventions have several methodological strengths, such as numerous studies utilizing empirically supported approaches, group-based intervention structures, and intervention delivery via nonspecialists in mental health (e.g., lay counselors or community health workers). The treatments evaluated are on a continuum of tradition from treatments in the CBT framework such as TF-CBT and NET to broader psychological treatments such as problem-solving, IPT, and BA. A potential direction for future research may be conducting component analysis of these evidence-based interventions and then creating brief interventions consisting of empirically supported principles of change. This could potentially promote scalability by yielding shorter, more flexible treatments that would be more feasible to implement in low-resource settings where both providers and patients have competing demands. However, treatments may need to be of longer duration or utilize maintenance sessions to address complex or multiple traumas. Additionally, group-based psychological interventions are a promising approach for LMIC because of their potential to reach many people and their lower cost (e.g., less facilitator time and fewer facilitators needed). Hiring local nonspecialists to deliver interventions in community organizations or existing health-care systems can also increase access in settings with few mental health specialists, and studies have demonstrated that training and ongoing supervision systems can be implemented successfully (Bass et al., 2013).

A dilemma in PTSD treatment research conducted in low-resource settings and global mental health research more broadly involves trial methodology and ethical concerns. Experimental and control treatments in LMIC trials commonly differ with respect to intervention content, length, clinical experience of facilitators, amount of training and supervision, and group or individual format. Trials have largely compared treatments with a wait list control, no-treatment control, or treatment-as-usual (e.g., referral in context of limited services) condition, although attention-matched treatment controls are considered the most rigorous design. Therefore, for many PTSD trials, the extent of the effect attributable to treatment is not clear. For ethical reasons, studies that utilize a wait list or no-treatment control often use a short-term follow-up and offer the treatment to control participants. While this is ethically important, it contributes to the need for trials with longer follow-up to assess the maintenance of treatment effects. A question that must be addressed for both study design and ethical reasons is whether control participants with PTSD should receive psychological services beyond crisis intervention. The field must address whether the standard for trials in LMIC should compare experimental and attention-matched treatments (e.g., matched on the number of sessions; time per session; and type of facilitator, training, and supervision) to determine the most efficacious treatments. For example, in a study among women experiencing GBV, participants in the control condition (e.g., enhanced usual care) improved markedly on every measure and speculated that their control facilitators (e.g., nurses) were better qualified than the intervention facilitators (e.g., community health workers), because they had more years of education on average and prior HIV counseling experience (Bryant et al., 2017). The authors speculated that this comparison condition was too rigorous and suggested that another control condition, such as home visits without the psychological intervention, would have been a better comparison. Other researchers believe that these control conditions are too low of a reference to compare with an active treatment because they are essentially a null treatment, so they could potentially exaggerate the effect size of the intervention (Cunningham, Kypri, & McCambridge, 2013; Mohr, Spring, Freedland, et al., 2009). However, trials have also found reductions in distress among participants in the wait list conditions (Devilly & McFarlane, 2009; Hesser, Weise, Rief, & Andersson, 2011). Reasons for this are unclear, but participants may experience psychological benefits from completing assessments with an interviewer or spontaneous resolution of symptoms (Morina et al., 2014; Poston & Hanson, 2010). In resource-limited settings where patients have no mental health resources available to them, having any contact with a provider may have a positive effect on mental health. Thus, more rigorous trial designs are needed to support the evidence base for specific PTSD treatment approaches, especially with the need for broader implementation.

A potentially significant limitation of existing interventions is that they consist of many sessions (often more than 10) and require extensive training and supervision of the facilitator to ensure intervention fidelity. If a large time commitment is needed from both patients and providers to improve psychological outcomes, various barriers could interfere with treatment adherence in these settings (e.g., transportation, inability to take time off work, conflict, and managing medical conditions). Patients who live in communities that are experiencing ongoing conflict and violence or displacement may also find it difficult to sustain a long-term psychological treatment. To be consistent with principles of global mental health, further research is needed on cost-effectiveness and scalability of interventions for PTSD, including effective task-sharing models of delivery by nonspecialists.

Lastly, many PTSD intervention trials did not include threshold symptomatology as inclusion criteria for participation. While youth and adults who have experienced a traumatic event may benefit from psychological interventions regardless of PTSD diagnosis, severity may vary greatly among individuals. It is important to consider how distress may manifest differently in populations experiencing unique stressors and the implications of this on selecting treatments and delivery strategies. Cultural sensitivity is also imperative to future work in PTSD treatment (Kazlauskas, 2017). More studies adapting measures and intervention content to cultural context are needed to validate psychological treatments for PTSD in LMIC, and these approaches should be documented in publications.

9.7 Cross-cutting recommendations for future research

As a field, global mental health researchers should work toward efficacious, culturally adapted interventions that can be delivered by local nonspecialists as a more cost-effective option to reduce untreated PTSD in low-resource settings. Integrating PTSD screening and interventions into medical settings such as primary care, HIV care, and perinatal care by means of a collaborative stepped-care framework may be a sustainable approach to disseminate mental health care and reach many patients who could benefit from these services. Home-based interventions may also promote implementation, especially among the most psychologically and physically vulnerable patients, and community- and school-based approaches to reach those who do not routinely access health care. Additionally, intervention guides such as the recent addition of PM+ (Bryant et al., 2017) to the WHO Mental Health Gap Action Programme (mhGAP), an action plan to scale up mental health services in LMIC, can be major steps toward dissemination.

Future research to investigate the extent to which task-sharing models are best utilized across stressors and settings is needed, as specialists may be needed in complex and severe cases (e.g., patients with multiple traumatic experiences in settings with ongoing violence). Another direction for future research is to differentiate how subpopulations of interest may benefit from specific treatment approaches. For example, the context of providing mental health care related to stressors such as natural disasters, displacement, conflict, sexual violence, and HIV/AIDS differs. The effectiveness of social programs, group interventions, brief and structured psychotherapy, or long-term treatment may be specific to setting (e.g., NGO, school, and primary care) and delivery agents. As noted (Morina et al., 2017b), it is debated whether PTSD treatment should center on past traumatic experiences or address current stressors and adversity that are common in LMIC, such as war, poverty, the lack of infrastructure, overcrowding, and discrimination (Miller & Rasmussen, 2010). Further investigation is needed to understand if one approach is more effective in reducing PTSD symptoms than the other, and innovative approaches are needed to address the intersection of traumatic experiences such as GBV, HIV/AIDS, and conflict settings.

Alternate models of care, such as interventions delivered via Internet or mobile phone applications, should also be studied. Developing online platforms with multi-language assessments, treatment sessions, and personalized features could improve access for patients in rural, remote, and underserved areas and reduce costs of PTSD treatments. However, identified barriers to the dissemination of these services such as high attrition rates, ethical issues related to referrals, and cultural factors that influence the utilization of online interventions need to be addressed in order to promote successful implementation (Wang, Tang, Wang, & Maercker, 2012).

While the current empirical data are not sufficiently robust to provide a clear path forward for a gold-standard psychological treatment of PTSD in LMIC, available data from published trials identify several task-sharing approaches (e.g., cognitive behavioral interventions, exposure therapy, and group interventions) that may be key to disseminating both efficacious and effective interventions widely in resource-limited settings. Future directions should include testing mechanisms of change in treatment, developing brief and scalable interventions that have been culturally tailored, and using attention-matched control comparisons to elucidate effective treatment components. It is unclear if global mental health should prioritize efficacy-style trials that also investigate underlying psychobiological mechanisms of change or make assumptions of effect and pursue implementation designs that compare factors related to scalability. Given the expansive reach that trauma has on worldwide public health outcomes, it is imperative that the field continues to work toward identifying efficacious treatments that can be scaled up so that effective, culturally appropriate interventions can be disseminated.

References

Acarturk, C., Konuk, E., Cetinkaya, M., et al. (2015). EMDR for Syrian refugees with post-traumatic stress disorder symptoms: Results of a pilot randomized controlled trial. *European Journal of Psychotraumatology*, *6*, 27414.

Allon, M. (2015). EMDR group therapy with women who were sexually assaulted in the Congo. *Journal of EMDR Practice and Research*, *9*(1), 28–34. https://doi.org/10.1891/1933-3196.9.1.28.

Alonso, J., Petukhova, M., Vilagut, G., et al. (2011). Days out of role due to common physical and mental conditions: Results from the WHO world mental health surveys. *Molecular Psychiatry*, *16*(12), 1234–1246. https://doi.org/10.1038/mp.2010.101.

American Psychiatric Association. (2013). *Diagnostic and statistical manual of mental disorders* (5th ed.). Washington, DC: American Psychiatric Publishing.

Applebaum, A. J., Bedoya, C. A., Hendriksen, E. S., Wilkinson, J. L., Safren, S. A., & O'Cleirigh, C. (2015). Future directions for interventions targeting PTSD in HIV-infected adults. *Journal of the Association of Nurses in AIDS Care*, *26*(2), 127–138. https://doi.org/10.1016/j.jana.2014.11.001.

Barron, I. G., Abdallah, G., & Smith, P. (2013). Randomized control trial of a CBT trauma recovery program in Palestinian schools. *Journal of Loss and Trauma*, *18*(4), 306–321. https://doi.org/10.1080/15325024.2012.688712.

Bartov, O. (2000). *Mirrors of destruction: War, genocide and modern identity*. Oxford University Press.

Başoglu, M., Salcioglu, E., & Livanou, M. (2007). A randomized controlled study of single-session behavioural treatment of earthquake-related post-traumatic stress disorder using an earthquake simulator. *Psychological Medicine*, *37*(2), 203–213. https://doi.org/10.1017/S0033291706009123.

Başoğlu, M., Salcioğlu, E., Livanou, M., Kalender, D., & Acar, G. (2005). Single-session behavioral treatment of earthquake-related posttraumatic stress disorder: A randomized waiting list controlled trial. *Journal of Traumatic Stress*, *18*(1), 1–11. https://doi.org/10.1002/jts.20011.

Bass, J. K., Annan, J., McIvor Murray, S., et al. (2013). Controlled trial of psychotherapy for Congolese survivors of sexual violence. *New England Journal of Medicine*, *368*(23), 2182–2191. https://doi.org/10.1056/NEJMoa1211853.

Benjet, C., Bromet, E., Karam, E. G., et al. (2016). The epidemiology of traumatic event exposure worldwide: Results from the World Mental Health Survey Consortium. *Psychological Medicine*, *46*(2), 327–343. https://doi.org/10.1017/S0033291715001981.

Betancourt, T. S., Agnew-Blais, J., Gilman, S. E., Williams, D. R., & Ellis, B. H. (2010). Past horrors, present struggles: The role of stigma in the association between war experiences and psychosocial adjustment among former child soldiers in Sierra Leone. *Social Science & Medicine 1982*, *70*(1), 17–26. https://doi.org/10.1016/j.socscimed.2009.09.038.

Betancourt, T. S., McBain, R., Newnham, E. A., et al. (2014). A behavioral intervention for war-affected youth in Sierra Leone: A randomized controlled trial. *Journal of the American Academy of Child and Adolescent Psychiatry*, *53*(12), 1288–1297. https://doi.org/10.1016/j.jaac.2014.09.011.

Bisson, J. I. (2010). Post-traumatic stress disorder. *Occupational Medicine*, *57*(6), 399–403.

Bisson, J. I., Roberts, N. P., Andrew, M., Cooper, R., & Lewis, C. (2013). Psychological therapies for chronic post-traumatic stress disorder (PTSD) in adults. *Cochrane Database of Systematic Reviews*, *12*. CD003388. https://doi.org/10.1002/14651858.CD003388.pub4.

Bolton, P., Bass, J. K., Zangana, G. A. S., et al. (2014). A randomized controlled trial of mental health interventions for survivors of systematic violence in Kurdistan, Northern Iraq. *BMC Psychiatry*, *14*, 360. https://doi.org/10.1186/s12888-014-0360-2.

Bolton, P., Lee, C., Haroz, E. E., et al. (2014). A transdiagnostic community-based mental health treatment for comorbid disorders: Development and outcomes of a randomized controlled trial among Burmese refugees in Thailand. *PLoS Medicine*, *11*(11). e1001757. https://doi.org/10.1371/journal.pmed.1001757.

Bradley, S., McCourt, C., Rayment, J., & Parmar, D. (2016). Disrespectful intrapartum care during facility-based delivery in sub-Saharan Africa: A qualitative systematic review and thematic synthesis of women's perceptions and experiences. *Social Science & Medicine*, *169*(Suppl. C), 157–170. https://doi.org/10.1016/j.socscimed.2016.09.039.

Brief, D. J., Bollinger, A. R., Vielhauer, M. J., et al. (2004). Understanding the interface of HIV, trauma, post-traumatic stress disorder, and substance use and its implications for health outcomes. *AIDS Care*, *16*(Suppl. 1), 97–120. https://doi.org/10.1080/09540120412301315259.

Bryant, R. A., Schafer, A., Dawson, K. S., et al. (2017). Effectiveness of a brief behavioural intervention on psychological distress among women with a history of gender-based violence in urban Kenya: A randomised clinical trial. *PLoS Medicine*, *14*(8). e1002371. https://doi.org/10.1371/journal.pmed.1002371.

Catani, C., Kohiladevy, M., Ruf, M., Schauer, E., Elbert, T., & Neuner, F. (2009). Treating children traumatized by war and Tsunami: A comparison between exposure therapy and meditation-relaxation in North-East Sri Lanka. *BMC Psychiatry*, *9*, 22. https://doi.org/10.1186/1471-244X-9-22.

Chen, Y., Shen, W. W., Gao, K., Lam, C. S., Chang, W. C., & Deng, H. (2014). Effectiveness RCT of a CBT intervention for youths who lost parents in the Sichuan, China, earthquake. *Psychiatric Services*, *65*(2), 259–262. https://doi.org/10.1176/appi.ps.201200470.

Chisholm, D., Lund, C., & Saxena, S. (2007). Cost of scaling up mental healthcare in low- and middle-income countries. *British Journal of Psychiatry: The Journal of Mental Science*, *191*, 528–535. https://doi.org/10.1192/bjp.bp.107.038463.

Chiumento, A., Hamdani, S. U., Khan, M. N., et al. (2017). Evaluating effectiveness and cost-effectiveness of a group psychological intervention using cognitive behavioural strategies for women with common mental disorders in conflict-affected rural Pakistan: Study protocol for a randomised controlled trial. *Trials*, *18*(1), 190. https://doi.org/10.1186/s13063-017-1905-8.

Chivers-Wilson, K. A. (2006). Sexual assault and posttraumatic stress disorder: A review of the biological, psychological and sociological factors and treatments. *McGill Journal of Medicine*, *9*(2), 111–118.

Connolly, S., & Sakai, C. (2011). Brief trauma intervention with Rwandan genocide-survivors using thought field therapy. *International Journal of Emergency Mental Health*, *13*(3), 161–172.

Cukor, J., Olden, M., Lee, F., & Difede, J. (2010). Evidence-based treatments for PTSD, new directions, and special challenges. *Annals of the New York Academy of Sciences*, *1208*, 82–89. https://doi.org/10.1111/j.1749-6632.2010.05793.x.

Cunningham, J. A., Kypri, K., & McCambridge, J. (2013). Exploratory randomized controlled trial evaluating the impact of a waiting list control design. *BMC Medical Research Methodology*, *13*, 150. https://doi.org/10.1186/1471-2288-13-150.

Curran, G. M., Bauer, M., Mittman, B., Pyne, J. M., & Stetler, C. (2012). Effectiveness-implementation hybrid designs: Combining elements of clinical effectiveness and implementation research to enhance public health impact. *Medical Care*, *50*(3), 217–226. https://doi.org/10.1097/MLR.0b013e3182408812.

de Jong, J. T., Komproe, I. H., Van Ommeren, M., et al. (2001). Lifetime events and posttraumatic stress disorder in 4 postconflict settings. *Journal of the American Medical Association, 286*(5), 555–562.

Decker, M. R., Latimore, A. D., Yasutake, S., et al. (2015). Gender-based violence against adolescent and young adult women in low- and middle-income countries. *Journal of Adolescent Health, 56*(2), 188–196. https://doi.org/10.1016/j.jadohealth.2014.09.003.

Devilly, G. J., & McFarlane, A. C. (2009). When wait lists are not feasible, nothing is a thing that does not need to be done. *Journal of Consulting and Clinical Psychology, 77*(6), 1159–1168. https://doi.org/10.1037/a0016878.

Fox, S. H., & Tang, S. S. (2000). The Sierra Leonean refugee experience: Traumatic events and psychiatric sequelae. *Journal of Nervous and Mental Disease, 188*(8), 490–495.

García-Moreno, C., Hegarty, K., d'Oliveira, A. F. L., Koziol-McLain, J., Colombini, M., & Feder, G. (2015). The health-systems response to violence against women. *Lancet, 385* (9977), 1567–1579. https://doi.org/10.1016/S0140-6736(14)61837-7.

Garcia-Moreno, C., Jansen, H. A., Ellsberg, M., Heise, L., & Watts, C. H. (2006). Prevalence of intimate partner violence: Findings from the WHO multi-country study on women's health and domestic violence. *Lancet, 368*(9543), 1260–1269. https://doi.org/10.1016/S0140-6736(06)69523-8.

Gelaye, B., Arnold, D., Williams, M. A., Goshu, M., & Berhane, Y. (2009). Depressive symptoms among female college students experiencing gender-based violence in Awassa, Ethiopia. *Journal of Interpersonal Violence, 24*(3), 464–481. https://doi.org/10.1177/0886260508317173.

Hesser, H., Weise, C., Rief, W., & Andersson, G. (2011). The effect of waiting: A meta-analysis of wait-list control groups in trials for tinnitus distress. *Journal of Psychosomatic Research, 70*(4), 378–384. https://doi.org/10.1016/j.jpsychores.2010.12.006.

Hinsberger, M., Holtzhausen, L., Sommer, J., et al. (2017). Feasibility and effectiveness of narrative exposure therapy and cognitive behavioral therapy in a context of ongoing violence in South Africa. *Psychological Trauma Theory Research Practice and Policy, 9*(3), 282–291. https://doi.org/10.1037/tra0000197.

Hobfoll, S. E., Watson, P., Bell, C. C., et al. (2007). Five essential elements of immediate and mid-term mass trauma intervention: Empirical evidence. *Psychiatry, 70*(4), 283–315. discussion 316-369. https:/doi.org/10.1521/psyc.2007.70.4.283.

Hustache, S., Moro, M.-R., Roptin, J., et al. (2009). Evaluation of psychological support for victims of sexual violence in a conflict setting: Results from Brazzaville, Congo. *International Journal of Mental Health Systems, 3*, 7. https://doi.org/10.1186/1752-4458-3-7.

Ironson, G., O'Cleirigh, C., Leserman, J., et al. (2013). Gender-specific effects of an augmented written emotional disclosure intervention on posttraumatic, depressive, and HIV-disease-related outcomes: A randomized, controlled trial. *Journal of Consulting and Clinical Psychology, 81*(2), 284–298. https://doi.org/10.1037/a0030814.

Jacob, N., Neuner, F., Maedl, A., Schaal, S., & Elbert, T. (2014). Dissemination of psychotherapy for trauma spectrum disorders in postconflict settings: A randomized controlled trial in Rwanda. *Psychotherapy and Psychosomatics, 83*(6), 354–363. https://doi.org/10.1159/000365114.

Jiang, R. F., Tong, H. Q., Delucchi, K. L., Neylan, T. C., Shi, Q., & Meffert, S. M. (2014). Interpersonal psychotherapy versus treatment as usual for PTSD and depression among Sichuan earthquake survivors: A randomized clinical trial. *Conflict and Health, 8*, 14. https://doi.org/10.1186/1752-1505-8-14.

Jordans, M. J. D., Komproe, I. H., Tol, W. A., et al. (2010). Evaluation of a classroom-based psychosocial intervention in conflict-affected Nepal: A cluster randomized controlled trial.

Journal of Child Psychology and Psychiatry, *51*(7), 818–826. https://doi.org/10.1111/j.1469-7610.2010.02209.x.

Kalantari, M., Yule, W., Dyregrov, A., Neshatdoost, H., & Ahmadi, S. J. (2012). Efficacy of writing for recovery on traumatic grief symptoms of Afghani refugee bereaved adolescents: A randomized control trial. *Omega*, *65*(2), 139–150. https://doi.org/10.2190/OM.65.2.d.

Kazlauskas, E. (2017). Challenges for providing health care in traumatized populations: Barriers for PTSD treatments and the need for new developments. *Global Health Action*, *10*(1). https://doi.org/10.1080/16549716.2017.1322399.

Kessler, R. C., Aguilar-Gaxiola, S., Alonso, J., et al. (2009). The global burden of mental disorders: An update from the WHO world mental health (WMH) surveys. *Epidemiologia e Psichiatria Sociale*, *18*(1), 23–33.

Khan, M. N., Hamdani, S. U., Chiumento, A., et al. (2017). Evaluating feasibility and acceptability of a group WHO trans-diagnostic intervention for women with common mental disorders in rural Pakistan: A cluster randomised controlled feasibility trial. *Epidemiology and Psychiatric Sciences*, 1–11. https://doi.org/10.1017/S2045796017000336.

Koenen, K. C., Ratanatharathorn, A., Ng, L., et al. (2017). Posttraumatic stress disorder in the World Mental Health Surveys. *Psychological Medicine*, *47*(13), 2260–2274. https://doi.org/10.1017/S0033291717000708.

Lipinski, K., Liu, L. L., & Wong, P. W. C. (2016). The effectiveness of psychosocial interventions implemented after the Indian Ocean Tsunami: A systematic review. *International Journal of Social Psychiatry*, *62*(3), 271–280. https://doi.org/10.1177/0020764015623807.

Lopes, A. P., Macedo, T. F., Coutinho, E. S. F., Figueira, I., & Ventura, P. R. (2014). Systematic review of the efficacy of cognitive-behavior therapy related treatments for victims of natural disasters: A worldwide problem. *PLoS ONE*, *9*(10). e109013. https://doi.org/10.1371/journal.pone.0109013.

Lund, C., Boyce, G., Flisher, A. J., Kafaar, Z., & Dawes, A. (2009). Scaling up child and adolescent mental health services in South Africa: Human resource requirements and costs. *Journal of Child Psychology and Psychiatry*, *50*(9), 1121–1130. https://doi.org/10.1111/j.1469-7610.2009.02078.x.

Machtinger, E. L., Haberer, J. E., Wilson, T. C., & Weiss, D. S. (2012). Recent trauma is associated with antiretroviral failure and HIV transmission risk behavior among HIV-positive women and female-identified transgenders. *AIDS and Behavior*, *16*(8), 2160–2170. https://doi.org/10.1007/s10461-012-0158-5.

Markowitz, J. C., Petkova, E., Neria, Y., et al. (2015). Is exposure necessary? A randomized clinical trial of interpersonal psychotherapy for PTSD. *American Journal of Psychiatry*, *172*(5), 430–440. https://doi.org/10.1176/appi.ajp.2014.14070908.

Markowitz, J. C., & Weissman, M. M. (2004). Interpersonal psychotherapy: Principles and applications. *World Psychiatry*, *3*(3), 136–139.

Martin, L., & Kagee, A. (2011). Lifetime and HIV-related PTSD among persons recently diagnosed with HIV. *AIDS and Behavior*, *15*(1), 125–131. https://doi.org/10.1007/s10461-008-9498-6.

McLean, C. P., & Fitzgerald, H. (2016). Treating posttraumatic stress symptoms among people living with HIV: A critical review of intervention trials. *Current Psychiatry Reports*, *18*(9), 83. https://doi.org/10.1007/s11920-016-0724-z.

Meade, C. S., Drabkin, A. S., Hansen, N. B., Wilson, P. A., Kochman, A., & Sikkema, K. J. (2010). Reductions in alcohol and cocaine use following a group coping intervention for HIV-positive adults with childhood sexual abuse histories. *Addiction*, *105*(11), 1942–1951. https://doi.org/10.1111/j.1360-0443.2010.03075.x.

Miller, K. E., & Rasmussen, A. (2010). War exposure, daily stressors, and mental health in conflict and post-conflict settings: Bridging the divide between trauma-focused and psychosocial frameworks. *Social Science & Medicine*, *70*(1), 7–16. https://doi.org/10.1016/j.socscimed.2009.09.029.

Mohr, D. C., Spring, B., Freedland, K. E., et al. (2009). The selection and design of control conditions for randomized controlled trials of psychological interventions. *Psychotherapy and Psychosomatics*, *78*(5), 275–284. https://doi.org/10.1159/000228248.

Morina, N., Malek, M., Nickerson, A., & Bryant, R. A. (2017a). Psychological interventions for post-traumatic stress disorder and depression in young survivors of mass violence in low- and middle-income countries: Meta-analysis. *British Journal of Psychiatry: The Journal of Mental Science*, *210*(4), 247–254. https://doi.org/10.1192/bjp.bp.115.180265.

Morina, N., Malek, M., Nickerson, A., & Bryant, R. A. (2017b). Meta-analysis of interventions for posttraumatic stress disorder and depression in adult survivors of mass violence in low- and middle-income countries. *Depression and Anxiety*, *34*(8), 679–691. https://doi.org/10.1002/da.22618.

Morina, N., Rushiti, F., Salihu, M., & Ford, J. D. (2010). Psychopathology and well-being in civilian survivors of war seeking treatment: A follow-up study. *Clinical Psychology & Psychotherapy*, *17*(2), 79–86. https://doi.org/10.1002/cpp.673.

Morina, N., Wicherts, J. M., Lobbrecht, J., & Priebe, S. (2014). Remission from post-traumatic stress disorder in adults: A systematic review and meta-analysis of long term outcome studies. *Clinical Psychology Review*, *34*(3), 249–255. https://doi.org/10.1016/j.cpr.2014.03.002.

Murray, L. K., Skavenski, S., Kane, J. C., Mayeya, J., Dorsey, S., Cohen, J. A., … Bolton, P. A. (2015). Effectiveness of trauma-focused cognitive behavioral therapy among trauma-affected children in Lusaka, Zambia: a randomized clinical trial. *JAMA Pediatrics*, *169* (8), 761–769.

Myer, L., Smit, J., Le Roux, L., Parker, S., Stein, D. J., & Seedat, S. (2008). Common mental disorders among HIV-infected individuals in South Africa: Prevalence, predictors, and validation of brief psychiatric rating scales. *AIDS Patient Care and STDs*, *22*(2), 147–158. https://doi.org/10.1089/apc.2007.0102.

Nakimuli-Mpungu, E., Okello, J., Kinyanda, E., et al. (2013). The impact of group counseling on depression, post-traumatic stress and function outcomes: A prospective comparison study in the Peter C. Alderman trauma clinics in northern Uganda. *Journal of Affective Disorders*, *151*(1), 78–84. https://doi.org/10.1016/j.jad.2013.05.055.

Neria, Y., Nandi, A., & Galea, S. (2008). Post-traumatic stress disorder following disasters: A systematic review. *Psychological Medicine*, *38*(4), 467–480. https://doi.org/10.1017/S0033291707001353.

O'Callaghan, P., McMullen, J., Shannon, C., Rafferty, H., & Black, A. (2013). A randomized controlled trial of trauma-focused cognitive behavioral therapy for sexually exploited, war-affected Congolese girls. *Journal of the American Academy of Child and Adolescent Psychiatry*, *52*(4), 359–369. https://doi.org/10.1016/j.jaac.2013.01.013.

O'Donnell, K., Dorsey, S., Gong, W., et al. (2014). Treating maladaptive grief and post-traumatic stress symptoms in orphaned children in Tanzania: Group-based trauma-focused cognitive-behavioral therapy. *Journal of Traumatic Stress*, *27*(6), 664–671. https://doi.org/10.1002/jts.21970.

Olley, B. O., Gxamza, F., Seedat, S., et al. (2003). Psychopathology and coping in recently diagnosed HIV/AIDS patients—The role of gender. *African Medical Journal*, *93*(12), 928–931.

Onu, C., Ongeri, L., Bukusi, E., et al. (2016). Interpersonal psychotherapy for depression and posttraumatic stress disorder among HIV-positive women in Kisumu, Kenya: Study protocol for a randomized controlled trial. *Trials*, *17*, 64. https://doi.org/10.1186/s13063-016-1187-6.

Onyut, L. P., Neuner, F., Schauer, E., et al. (2005). Narrative exposure therapy as a treatment for child war survivors with posttraumatic stress disorder: Two case reports and a pilot study in an African refugee settlement. *BMC Psychiatry*, *5*, 7. https://doi.org/10.1186/1471-244X-5-7.

Pacella, M. L., Armelie, A., Boarts, J., et al. (2012). The impact of prolonged exposure on PTSD symptoms and associated psychopathology in people living with HIV: A randomized test of concept. *AIDS and Behavior*, *16*(5), 1327–1340. https://doi.org/10.1007/s10461-011-0076-y.

Peltzer, K., Naidoo, P., Matseke, G., Louw, J., McHunu, G., & Tutshana, B. (2012). Prevalence of post-traumatic stress symptoms and associated factors in tuberculosis (TB), TB retreatment and/or TB-HIV co-infected primary public health-care patients in three districts in South Africa. *Psychology, Health & Medicine*, *18*(4), 387–397. https://doi.org/10.1080/13548506.2012.726364.

Peterson, K., Togun, T., Klis, S., Menten, J., & Colebunders, R. (2012). Depression and posttraumatic stress disorder among HIV-infected Gambians on antiretroviral therapy. *AIDS Patient Care and STDs*, *26*(10), 589–596. https://doi.org/10.1089/apc.2012.0089.

Pettersson, T., & Wallensteen, P. (2015). Armed conflicts, 1946–2014. *Journal of Peace Research*, *52*(4), 536–550. https://doi.org/10.1177/0022343315595927.

Ponniah, K., & Hollon, S. D. (2009). Empirically supported psychological treatments for adult acute stress disorder and posttraumatic stress disorder: A review. *Depression and Anxiety*, *26*(12), 1086–1109. https://doi.org/10.1002/da.20635.

Poston, J. M., & Hanson, W. E. (2010). Meta-analysis of psychological assessment as a therapeutic intervention. *Psychological Assessment*, *22*(2), 203–212. https://doi.org/10.1037/a0018679.

Qouta, S. R., Palosaari, E., Diab, M., & Punamäki, R.-L. (2012). Intervention effectiveness among war-affected children: A cluster randomized controlled trial on improving mental health. *Journal of Traumatic Stress*, *25*(3), 288–298. https://doi.org/10.1002/jts.21707.

Rahman, A., Hamdani, S. U., Awan, N. R., et al. (2016). Effect of a multicomponent behavioral intervention in adults impaired by psychological distress in a conflict-affected area of Pakistan: A randomized clinical trial. *Journal of the American Medical Association*, *316*(24), 2609–2617. https://doi.org/10.1001/jama.2016.17165.

Rees, S., Silove, D., Chey, T., et al. (2011). Lifetime prevalence of gender-based violence in women and the relationship with mental disorders and psychosocial function. *Journal of the American Medical Association*, *306*(5), 513–521. https://doi.org/10.1001/jama.2011.1098.

Rossouw, J. (2017). *Results and experiences of stakeholders in a taskshifted community-based prolonged exposure and supportive counselling randomized control trial of post-traumatic stress disorder*. In: *Presented at the: 1st Pan-African Psychology Congress; Durban, South Africa*. http:/papu2017.com/wp-content/uploads/2017/08/PAPU-Durban-abstracts-30-August-2017_31-Aug.pdf (accessed 23.01.18).

Sabes-Figuera, R., McCrone, P., Bogic, M., et al. (2012). Long-term impact of war on healthcare costs: An eight-country study. *PLoS ONE*, *7*(1). e29603. https://doi.org/10.1371/journal.pone.0029603.

Schaal, S., Elbert, T., & Neuner, F. (2009). Narrative exposure therapy versus interpersonal psychotherapy. A pilot randomized controlled trial with Rwandan genocide orphans. *Psychotherapy and Psychosomatics*, *78*(5), 298–306. https://doi.org/10.1159/000229768.

Schnyder, U., Ehlers, A., Elbert, T., et al. (2015). Psychotherapies for PTSD: What do they have in common? *European Journal of Psychotraumatology*, *6*, 28186.

Scott, K. M., Koenen, K. C., Aguilar-Gaxiola, S., et al. (2013). Associations between lifetime traumatic events and subsequent chronic physical conditions: A cross-national, cross-sectional study. *PLoS ONE*, *8*(11). e80573. https://doi.org/10.1371/journal.pone.0080573.

Seedat, S. (2012). Interventions to improve psychological functioning and health outcomes of HIV-infected individuals with a history of trauma or PTSD. *Current HIV/AIDS Reports*, *9* (4), 344–350. https://doi.org/10.1007/s11904-012-0139-3.

Sijbrandij, M., Farooq, S., Bryant, R. A., et al. (2015). Problem management plus (PM+) for common mental disorders in a humanitarian setting in Pakistan; study protocol for a randomised controlled trial (RCT). *BMC Psychiatry*, *15*, 232. https://doi.org/10.1186/s12888-015-0602-y.

Sikkema, K. J., Dennis, A. C., Watt, M. H., Choi, K. W., Yemeke, T. T., & Joska, J. A. (2015). Improving mental health among people living with HIV: A review of intervention trials in low- and middle-income countries. *Global Mental Health*, *2*. https://doi.org/10.1017/gmh.2015.17.

Sikkema, K. J., Hansen, N. B., Kochman, A., et al. (2007). Outcomes from a group intervention for coping with HIV/AIDS and childhood sexual abuse: Reductions in traumatic stress. *AIDS and Behavior*, *11*(1), 49–60. https://doi.org/10.1007/s10461-006-9149-8.

Sikkema, K. J., Joska, J. A., Choi, K. W., et al. (2017). *ImpACT: Improving AIDS care after trauma—Intervention manual*. Duke University and University of Cape Town.

Sikkema, K. J., Kochman, A., van den Berg, J. J., Hansen, N. B., & Watt, M. H. (2009). *LIFT: Living in the face of trauma—An intervention for coping with HIV and trauma*. Duke University.

Sikkema, K. J., Mulawa, M. I., Robertson, C., Watt, M. H., Ciya, N., Stein, D. J., … Joska, J. A. (2018). Improving AIDS Care After Trauma (ImpACT): Pilot outcomes of a coping intervention among HIV-infected women with sexual trauma in South Africa. *AIDS and Behavior*, *22*(3), 1039–1052.

Sikkema, K. J., Ranby, K. W., Meade, C. S., Hansen, N. B., Wilson, P. A., & Kochman, A. (2013). Reductions in traumatic stress following a coping intervention were mediated by decreases in avoidant coping for people living with HIV/AIDS and childhood sexual abuse. *Journal of Consulting and Clinical Psychology*, *81*(2), 274–283. https://doi.org/10.1037/a0030144.

Sikkema, K. J., Wilson, P. A., Hansen, N. B., et al. (2008). Effects of a coping intervention on transmission risk behavior among people living with HIV/AIDS and a history of childhood sexual abuse. *Journal of Acquired Immune Deficiency Syndromes*, *47*(4), 506–513. https://doi.org/10.1097/QAI.0b013e318160d727.

Smigelsky, M. A., Aten, J. D., Gerberich, S., et al. (2014). Trauma in Sub-Saharan Africa: Review of cost, estimation methods, and interventions. *International Journal of Emergency Mental Health and Human Resilience*, *16*(4). https://www.omicsonline.org/open-access/trauma-in-subsaharan-africa-review-of-cost-estimation-methods-and-interventions-1522-4821-16-129.php?aid=31891 (accessed 09.12.17).

Steel, Z., Chey, T., Silove, D., Marnane, C., Bryant, R. A., & van Ommeren, M. (2009). Association of torture and other potentially traumatic events with mental health outcomes among populations exposed to mass conflict and displacement: A systematic review and meta-analysis. *Journal of the American Medical Association*, *302*(5), 537–549. https://doi.org/10.1001/jama.2009.1132.

Strömberg, D. (2007). Natural disasters, economic development, and humanitarian aid. *Journal of Economic Perspectives*, *21*(3), 199–222.

Talbot, A., Uwihoreye, C., Kamen, C., et al. (2013). Treating psychological trauma among Rwandan orphans is associated with a reduction in HIV risk-taking behaviors: A pilot study. *AIDS Education and Prevention Official Publication International Society of AIDS Educcation*, *25*(6), 468–479. https://doi.org/10.1521/aeap.2013.25.6.468.

The UN Refugee Agency. (2016). *Global trends: Forced displacement in 2016*. United Nations. http://www.unhcr.org/5943e8a34.pdf (accessed 17.01.18).

The World Bank. (2017). *Fragility, conflict and violence*. The World Bank. http://www.worldbank.org/en/topic/fragilityconflictviolence/overview (accessed 17.01.18).

The World Bank Group. (2015). *Country and lending groups*. http://data.worldbank.org/about/country-and-lending-groups (accessed 16.10.17).

Tol, W. A., Komproe, I. H., Jordans, M. J., et al. (2012). Outcomes and moderators of a preventive school-based mental health intervention for children affected by war in Sri Lanka: A cluster randomized trial. *World Psychiatry*, *11*(2), 114–122. https://doi.org/10.1016/j.wpsyc.2012.05.008.

Tol, W. A., Komproe, I. H., Jordans, M. J. D., et al. (2014). School-based mental health intervention for children in war-affected Burundi: A cluster randomized trial. *BMC Medicine*, *12*, 56. https://doi.org/10.1186/1741-7015-12-56.

Tol, W. A., Komproe, I. H., Susanty, D., Jordans, M. J. D., Macy, R. D., & Jong, J. T. V. M. D. (2008). School-based mental health intervention for children affected by political violence in Indonesia: A cluster randomized trial. *Journal of the American Medical Association*, *300* (6), 655–662. https://doi.org/10.1001/jama.300.6.655.

Tol, W. A., Patel, V., Tomlinson, M., et al. (2011). Research priorities for mental health and psychosocial support in humanitarian settings. *PLoS Medicine*, *8*(9). e1001096. https://doi.org/10.1371/journal.pmed.1001096.

Turner, R. J., & Lloyd, D. A. (1995). Lifetime traumas and mental health: The significance of cumulative adversity. *Journal of Health and Social Behavior*, *36*(4), 360–376.

U.S. Department of Veterans Affairs. (2017). *PTSD and DSM-5*. PTSD: National Center for PTSD. https://www.ptsd.va.gov/professional/PTSD-overview/dsm5_criteria_ptsd.asp (accessed 17.01.18).

United Nations. (1993). *Declaration on the elimination of violence against women*. United Nations. *http://www.un.org/documents/ga/res/48/a48r104.htm* (accessed 17.01.18).

Verhey, R., Chibanda, D., Brakarsh, J., & Seedat, S. (2016). Psychological interventions for post-traumatic stress disorder in people living with HIV in resource poor settings: A systematic review. *Tropical Medicine & International Health*, *21*(10), 1198–1208. https://doi.org/10.1111/tmi.12756.

Vickerman, K. A., & Margolin, G. (2009). Rape treatment outcome research: Empirical findings and state of the literature. *Clinical Psychology Review*, *29*(5), 431–448. https://doi.org/10.1016/j.cpr.2009.04.004.

Wang, Z., Tang, S., Wang, J., & Maercker, A. (2012). Foundations and future application of internet-based interventions for PTSD in PR China. *International Journal of Electronic Healthcare*, *7*(1), 19–35. https://doi.org/10.1504/IJEH.2012.048667.

Wang, Z., Wang, J., & Maercker, A. (2013). Chinese my trauma recovery, a web-based intervention for traumatized persons in two parallel samples: Randomized controlled trial. *Journal of Medical Internet Research*, *15*(9). e213. https://doi.org/10.2196/jmir.2690.

Watt, M. H., Dennis, A. C., Choi, K. W., et al. (2017). Impact of sexual trauma on HIV care engagement: Perspectives of female patients with trauma histories in Cape Town, South Africa. *AIDS and Behavior*, *21*(11), 3209–3218. https://doi.org/10.1007/s10461-016-1617-1.

Weiss, W. M., Ugueto, A. M., Mahmooth, Z., et al. (2016). Mental health interventions and priorities for research for adult survivors of torture and systematic violence: A review of the literature. *Torture Q J Rehabil Torture Vict Prev Torture*, *26*(1), 17–44.

World Health Organization (2013). *Global and regional estimates of violence against women: Prevalence and health effects of intimate partner violence and non-partner sexual violence*. World Health Organization. http://apps.who.int/iris/bitstream/10665/85239/1/9789241564625_eng.pdf?ua=1 (accessed 17.01.17).

Wu, S., Zhu, X., Zhang, Y., et al. (2012). A new psychological intervention: "512 psychological intervention model" used for military rescuers in Wenchuan earthquake in China. *Social Psychiatry and Psychiatric Epidemiology*, *47*(7), 1111–1119. https://doi.org/10.1007/s00127-011-0416-2.

Yatham, S., Sivathasan, S., Yoon, R., da Silva, T. L., & Ravindran, A. V. (2017). Depression, anxiety, and post-traumatic stress disorder among youth in low and middle income countries: A review of prevalence and treatment interventions. *Asian Journal of Psychiatry*, https://doi.org/10.1016/j.ajp.2017.10.029.

Yemeke, T. T., Sikkema, K. J., Watt, M. H., Ciya, N., Robertson, C., & Joska, J. A. (2017). Screening for traumatic experiences and mental health distress among women in HIV care in Cape Town, South Africa. *Journal of Interpersonal Violence*, https://doi.org/10.1177/0886260517718186. 0886260517718186.

Zang, Y., Hunt, N., & Cox, T. (2013). A randomised controlled pilot study: The effectiveness of narrative exposure therapy with adult survivors of the Sichuan earthquake. *BMC Psychiatry*, *13*, 41. https://doi.org/10.1186/1471-244X-13-41.

Psychotherapy for schizophrenia and bipolar disorder

10

Muhammad Irfan, Saadia Muzaffar*[†], *David Kingdon*[‡], *Shanaya Rathod*[‡,§], *Farooq Naeem*[¶]

*Department of Mental Health, Psychiatry and Behavioural Sciences, Peshawar Medical College, Riphah International University, Islamabad, Pakistan, [†]Southern Health NHS Foundation Trust, Hampshire, United Kingdom, [‡]Clinical Trials Facility, Tom Rudd Unit, Southern Health NHS Foundation Trust, Hampshire, United Kingdom, [§]Portsmouth-Brawijaya Centre for Global Health, Population, and Policy, University of Portsmouth, Portsmouth, United Kingdom, [¶]University of Toronto and Centre for Addiction and Mental Health, Toronto, Canada

The majority (more than 85%) of the world's population resides in low- and middle-income countries (LMIC) (Jacob, Sharan, Mirza, et al., 2007). A breakdown of the total disease burden contribution for low-income and lower-middle-income countries provides figures of 8.8% for mental illness and 16.6% for substance misuse (World Health Organization, 2008, 2004). In these countries alone, the number of people suffering from schizophrenia is more than that in the whole North America (Adams, Tharyan, Coutinho, et al., 2006). There is therefore clearly a need for better treatments for these conditions.

Psychosocial interventions are recommended in the national treatment guidelines of some high-income countries. The National Institute of Health and Care Excellence guidelines (NICE, 2014a, 2014b) recommend high-intensity psychological interventions for schizophrenia such as cognitive behavioral therapy (CBT) (at least 16 sessions), art therapy, and family interventions, while for bipolar disorder, the NICE guidelines recommend interpersonal therapy, CBT, or behavioral couple therapy (NICE, 2014a, 2014b) individually, in groups or family therapy setting. An immediate question is the value of such therapies in LMIC.

This chapter explores psychotherapeutic interventions for schizophrenia and bipolar disorder and considers the evidence base for their use in LMIC. We also outline barriers to and challenges of implementation and provide some suggestions on how to overcome them.

10.1 Modalities used in high-income countries

10.1.1 Cognitive behavioral therapy

CBT for psychosis focuses on reducing the distress caused by positive symptoms including hallucinations. There is evidence that such CBT helps in decreasing symptoms of depression and anxiety (including the lack of motivation) and assists in

Global Mental Health and Psychotherapy. https://doi.org/10.1016/B978-0-12-814932-4.00010-0

developing social, problem-solving, coping, and decision-making skills and planning of relapse prevention (Wykes, Steel, Everitt, et al., 2008). Indeed, CBT is recognized as an evidence-based treatment for schizophrenia in clinical guidelines in the United States (Lehman, Lieberman, Dixon, et al., 2004) and in the United Kingdom (NICE, 2014). NICE guidelines suggest that "cognitive behavioral therapy (CBT) should be offered to people with schizophrenia either during the acute phase or later, including inpatient settings."

Despite this guidance, reports from the United Kingdom suggest that only about 50% of those suffering from schizophrenia have access to CBT (Kingdon & Kirschen, 2006). Naeem, Johal, McKenna, et al. (2016) and Naeem, Farooq, and Kingdon (2014) suggest offering guided self-help or brief CBT that might be able to bridge this gap. These authors also reported a RCT in which brief CBT was found efficacious in reducing symptoms of schizophrenia against care as usual (Naeem, Saeed, Irfan, et al., 2015). They defined brief as 6–10 sessions delivered in less than 4 months' period as opposed to a standard CBT lasting nearly 16 sessions delivered over 4–6 months. Similarly, studies have suggested that mobile phone-based applications can be used to deliver evidence-based interventions for patients with schizophrenia and bipolar disorder (Menon, Rajan, & Sarkar, 2017; Watts, Mackenzie, Thomas, et al., 2013).

Naeem, Kingdon, and Turkington (2008) concluded that insight was the most important predictor of response to CBT in schizophrenia due to its role in better engagement and improved adherence. Those with higher levels of psychopathology surprisingly reported more improvement with CBT. One of the largest multicenter randomized trial of brief insight-focused CBT for schizophrenia, delivered by trained nurses, showed clinical and cost-effectiveness in the medium term on a number of outcome measures (Turkington, Kingdon, Rathod, et al., 2006). Studies such as these will be a helpful indicator of outcomes when designing research and interventions in LMIC.

Medication adherence can also be improved by using cognitive therapy as an adjunct (Kingdon, Rathod, Hansen, et al., 2007). This can be done using an individualized and collaborative approach for psychoeducation about schizophrenia and available treatments including modifying automatic thoughts and core beliefs about the medication along with examining the evidence for the maladaptive belief. While the evidence remains sparse for CBT alone without pharmacotherapy, elements of CBT such as developing a strong therapeutic alliance and open discussions allow maintained contact with the therapist and might ultimately lead to revisiting the option of medication (Kingdon et al., 2007). CBT allows the therapist to take an exploratory view while agreeing to disagree.

The data for the use of CBT in bipolar disorder are comparatively limited. However, a recent meta-analysis consisting of 19 RCTs, published between 2000 and 2015, involving 1384 patients showed that CBT could lower the relapse rate and improve depressive symptoms, mania severity, and psychosocial functioning in patients with bipolar disorder proving the efficacy of CBT in bipolar disorder (Chiang, Tsai, Liu, et al., 2017).

10.1.2 Cognitive remediation therapy

This is an emerging behavioral treatment for treating adults and children with schizophrenia and adults with bipolar disorder (Dickstein, Cushman, Kim, et al., 2015). It was initially used for patients with rehabilitation from stroke or a traumatic brain injury. In children, the focus is on face processing, response inhibition, frustration, and cognitive flexibility. It is based on being able to assess and treat different cognitive domains independently; using the brain's neuroplasticity and change to respond to drill-and-practice learning, such as improvements in working memory in schizophrenia allowing personalization of the treatment to the individual's needs; and improving these skills to reduce functional impairment and, in turn, reduce the burden of the disease.

Cognitive processes that are altered in patients with schizophrenia include working memory, verbal memory, processing speed, and reasoning and so are focused on in cognitive remediation (Garrido, Barrios, Penades, et al., 2013). A systematic review of cognitive remediation in early schizophrenia, including 11 trials with 615 participants, showed a significant positive effect on verbal learning and memory, an almost significant effect on social cognition, and approached significance on working memory (Revell, Neill, Harte, et al., 2015).

Cognitive remediation is a cost-effective approach for adults with schizophrenia (Patel, Knapp, Romeo, et al., 2010), with effects chiefly on cognitive functioning, as well as quality of life and self-esteem (Rathod & Kingdon, 2009). One meta-analysis revealed that cognitive remediation may lead to improvements in functioning (Wykes, Huddy, Cellard, et al., 2011), while another meta-analysis demonstrated a medium effect size for cognitive performance, a smaller effect size for psychosocial functioning, and a small effect size for symptoms (McGurk, Twamley, Sitzer, et al., 2007). A study by Dickstein et al. (2015) evaluated cognitive remediation for executive function and working memory in adolescents presenting with early-onset schizophrenia, compared with those randomized to receive treatment as usual; this revealed improvement in working memory and executive function and improved daily living skills and global functioning.

The results from the first randomized controlled trial assessing the effect of cognitive remediation for adults with continued cognitive difficulties in full or partial remission from bipolar disorder concluded that individual and long-term cognitive remediation therapy may be needed to achieve an improvement in cognition. Although this RCT did not lead to a significant change in psychosocial and cognitive functioning in the treatment group, by week 12, there were reports of improved verbal fluency and quality of life (Demant, Vinberg, Kessing, et al., 2015).

The literature continues to demonstrate a number of inconsistencies. Sole, Bonnin, Mayoral, et al. (2014) have reported a significant improvement in overall psychosocial functioning for patients with bipolar disorder, after 21 weeks of a group adapted cognitive remediation, but Veeh, Kopf, Kittel-Schneider, et al. (2017) in a naturalistic study did not report any change in psychosocial functioning and quality of life. Further work is therefore needed to assess the impact of cognitive remediation in bipolar disorder.

10.1.3 Family interventions

In schizophrenia, there is evidence that family-focused psychosocial interventions are useful, with especially good outcomes in families with high expressed emotion as overinvolvement, criticism, and hostility (Amaresha & Venkatasubramanian, 2012). Attachments to primary caregivers are taken into consideration; these attachments may remain of an anxious or ambivalent nature due to the impact of the illness. Robust peer supervision for family therapists is essential to maintain objectivity and deal with resistance to work undertaken. It has been suggested that outcomes in LMIC are better due to the role of extended families and a partly tolerant attitude of families (Kuipers, Leff, & Lam, 1992). However, this view has now been challenged, and Cohen, Patel, Thara, et al. (2008) and Farooq, Large, Nielssen, et al. (2009) have provided data to suggest otherwise.

For bipolar disorder, family interventions when delivered as an adjunct to psychopharmacological interventions have shown a delayed treatment effect and little effect on acute treatment response or remission (Mansfield, Dealy, & Keitner, 2012). However, given that medication is the mainstay of treatment, demonstrating the additional benefit of family interventions has been difficult. Families are often left to deal with various sequelae of the illness such as debts, social disruption, strained relationships, and impulsive and risky behaviors; in this context, family work can prove to be a crucial aspect of not only intervention but also prevention of relapse. In their review, Vieta, Pacchiarotti, Valentí, et al. (2009) concluded that family interventions based on a psychoeducational model are effective in bipolar disorder. Reinares, Vieta, Colom, et al. (2002) noted that family interventions also reduce the impact of the disorder on families, while Miklowitz, Simoneau, George, et al. (2000) found that family interventions helped mainly families with high expressed emotions. Such interventions have also served to improve treatment adherence and increased the gap to next admission (Miklowitz, George, Richards, et al., 2003), both of which are of significant clinical relevance in bipolar disorder.

10.1.4 Other therapies

There are a number of other therapies that may have a role in the treatment of schizophrenia and bipolar disorder, but currently there is not enough evidence to recommend them.

Acceptance and commitment therapy (ACT), focusing on the reduction of the believability of negative thoughts and unacceptability of negative feelings associated with the mental disorder, has possible efficacy in psychotic symptoms (Ost, 2014). Pankey and Hayes (2003) describe this as altering the *"function of undesirable thoughts, feelings and bodily sensations" to develop a new relationship with these experiences and to shift focus to "overt behavior that furthers one's values and purposes even in the presence of challenging experiences."* A randomized controlled trial reported significantly less rehospitalization in the group of patients given ACT as compared with the treatment as usual group (Bach & Hayes, 2002).

Basal exposure therapy (BET) was developed for use in inpatient settings and is based on the notion that patients with treatment-resistant illnesses have an innate fear and live under an existential threat (Heggdal, Lillelien, Johnsrud, et al., 2013). The therapy promotes autonomy and personal responsibility in the patient, use of solution-based approaches, validation, and normalizing interactions while helping them face their fears of avoidance behaviors. With BET, inpatients who previously had not responded to repeated treatments showed improvement in symptoms and functioning (Heggdal, Foose, & Hammer, 2016).

Based on the view that disrupted circadian rhythm leads to the development of affective episodes, interpersonal and social rhythm therapy (IPSRT) was studied in bipolar disorder and reported to reduce recurrences of the illness, with patients in the treatment group remaining well during a 2-year maintenance period (Frank, Kupfer, Thase, et al., 2005). However, one RCT of 100 participants receiving IPSRT versus treatment as usual and supportive counseling did not reveal any significant differences between these psychotherapies (Inder, Crowe, Luty, et al., 2015). In a 1-year prepost finding of an efficacy study, IPSRT was effective in reducing depressive symptoms and hospital admissions (Bouwkamp, de Kruiff, van Troost, et al., 2013).

10.2 Modalities used in low- and middle-income countries

A lack of financial resources and trained professional staff and geographic distance from urban centers or hospitals are some of the many important factors to be considered when designing psychotherapeutic interventions for psychotic disorders in LMIC. That said, despite limited financial resources, it is possible to creatively overcome these barriers through differential allocation and utilization of available resources.

An example of an innovative approach is that of the National Institute of Mental Health And Neuro Sciences (NIMHANS) in Bangalore and Christian Medical College in Vellore; this allows families to live with patients, granting them participation in therapeutic programs (Thara, Padmavati, & Srinivasan, 2004). This potentially allows patients to overcome the problem of a lack of availability of trained mental health professionals while providing psychoeducation to families about relapse prevention and symptom monitoring. This is a practical solution considering that in many LMIC, for example, India, 90% of people with mental illness live with their families, and involvement of families can potentially improve outcomes (Rathod, Pinninti, Irfan, et al., 2017; Thara, Henrietta, Joseph, et al., 1994).

The supervised treatment in outpatients for schizophrenia (STOPS) intervention (Farooq, Nazar, Irfan, et al., 2011) is a good example of employing a brief focused psychoeducational intervention in Pakistan to deal with medication adherence in schizophrenia. A family member's help was enlisted to monitor and administer medication regularly after they were educated about the trajectory of the illness, the importance of adherence to treatment and other aspects of the illness. This had promising results in STOPS (67.3% fully concordant) versus 45.5% (TAU group).

The use of brief culturally adapted CBT for psychosis (six sessions) versus TAU in patients with schizophrenia in Karachi, Pakistan, resulted in better carer engagement and led to low dropout rate (Naeem et al., 2015). The results from this bio-psycho-spiritual-social novel approach were encouraging as the treatment group demonstrated not only statistically significant improvement across all psychopathology domains in comparison with the TAU group but also an improvement in insight. This is an example of adapting CBT in a low-income country, albeit in a major urbanized city.

Qualitative studies were undertaken to explore the views of professionals and patients with psychosis alike and their carers in Pakistan, to design an adapted approach to CBT for psychosis (Naeem, Habib, Gul, et al., 2016). Professionals stated that an intervention that favors psychoeducation about the illness is the most useful. The professionals noted expectations of a directive style by the patient from the therapist and attribution of illness to biological or spiritual/supernatural causes as obstacles to therapy. Such attributions lead to seeking help in half of patients from different types of faith healers before coming to the trained mental health professional (Naeem, Ayub, McGuire, et al., 2010; Naeem, Phiri, Rathod, et al., 2010).

An extension of this work was conducted in a teaching hospital in China where qualitative interviews were conducted to gather information that would help design and culturally inform CBT for psychosis in China, a country where psychosis is viewed along the lines of a bio-psycho-spiritual-social model (Li, Zaung, Xuerong, et al., 2017). Carers, patients, and professionals emphasized the importance of adapting the use of language, being cognizant of Eastern cultural and spiritual values, and the positive influence of involving carers in treatment. Among the barriers, social stigma was significant, and the majority of the patients did not know the cause of illness but had seen faith healers. The number of dropouts was high (80%), engagement was a problem, traveling distance and travel expenses were a barrier, and there was a reported lack of knowledge about psychotherapy and its relevance to psychosis.

More randomized controlled trials of psychotherapies for schizophrenia and bipolar disorders are needed in LMIC. There is a need to include patients from a range of different socioeconomic classes as factors such as lower level of literacy and decreased knowledge of psychotherapy may lead to worse outcomes. It may be particularly useful to explore self-help groups, given the evidence of their value in high-income countries (Kingdon, Murray, & Doyle, 2004).

10.3 Barriers/challenges in low- and middle-income countries

10.3.1 Legislation/organization and planning

In LMIC, recognition of mental health disorders and their treatment is poor. Policymakers may lack an understanding of mental health needs, and more emphasis may be put on physical health disorders (World Health Organization, 2001). Use of evidence-based approaches to treatment and adequate research training and facilities for professionals may only be available in urban areas. The workforce of psychiatrists, social workers, nurses, and psychologists is often inadequate and highlights the scarcity of resources allocated to mental health. The majority of psychiatrists in LMIC are based in hospitals in urban cities, so limiting limits access to the majority of the population (Gadit & Khalid, 2002). According to the Ministry of Health (2012), China had a reported average of only 1.55% psychiatrists per 100,000 people as compared with a global average of 3.96 psychiatrists per 100,000 people.

Allocation of health-care budgets needs to focus on programs that can reach out to rural communities or a secondment opportunity of the urban psychiatrists to work in the rural areas, incentivized possibly by financial support and further opportunities for training and research. Integration of such services with primary care may be a good way to make mental health more accessible while reducing stigma. An example of this is seen in India, where mental health teams trained primary health-care physicians in some districts (Rathod et al., 2017).

Increased budgets for mental health research with more focus on schizophrenia and bipolar disorder are required, along with increasing the publications on mental health in medical journals. A good example is that of South Africa (Stein & Seedat, 2007) where despite mental disorders being prevalent, South African medical research allocates a very small part of its budget to mental health research. Likewise, there may be a bias in publications such as the South African Medical Journal, which publishes more articles on physical health disorders than mental health disorders as compared with their counterparts in the West (Ipser & Stein, 2007).

10.3.2 Training programes

Training programs focused on severe mental illness are lengthy and expensive to run. Moreover, in LMIC, there is a relative lack of facilities, of qualified mentors, and of research scholarships. Institutions may not do enough to promote or encourage medical students or other undergraduate students to choose the field of psychiatry and mental health. It is important to include psychiatry and mental health in the undergraduate degree curriculum and to encourage curriculum reform to ensure an adequate focus on mental disorders. It is also important to increase training of nonclinical staff.

10.3.3 Supervision

Since psychotherapies for psychosis have not been developed and therapists trained in psychosis are scarce in LMIC, inadequate supervision has been a big challenge in the provision of services. Where there is good supervision of CBT for psychosis, there is evidence of a positive impact on client outcomes (Ng & Cheung, 2007). Murray, Dorsey, Bolton, et al. (2011) recommend their "apprenticeship model," which may be effective in overcoming supervision and feedback barriers in LMIC (see also Chapter 2).

In the modern age, barriers to inadequate supervision by trained psychotherapists can be overcome with the use of the Internet (Fishkin, Fishkin, Leli, et al., 2011). The China American Psychoanalytic Alliance (CAPA), for example, arranges Internet supervision for therapists in psychoanalysis and psychodynamic psychotherapy. This training is provided from the United States via Skype by using an encryption protocol for confidentiality and to overcome third-party interception. This has been successful, despite some challenges such as access to high-speed Internet (Fishkin et al., 2011).

10.3.4 Research and evidence base

There is a paucity of research in the LMIC on psychotherapy interventions for schizophrenia and bipolar disorder. This may be due to the lack of funding and a cultural perception of mental illnesses as not having tangible enough outcomes as compared with physical health disorders. Nevertheless, growing work on public mental health is occurring in LMIC. PRogramme for Improving Mental health carE (PRIME) is a good example of implementing evidence-based policy in low-income countries. Its objective is to scale up integrated care packages for mental health disorders in Ethiopia, India, Nepal, South Africa, and Uganda (Lund, Tomlinson, De Silva, et al., 2012).

10.3.5 Pathways to care

Usual pathways to care depend upon beliefs of attribution regarding the illness and explanatory models of psychosis (Joel, Sathyaseelan, Jayakaran, et al., 2006). Care pathways are complicated and may involve frequenting faith healers, spiritual leaders, or community religious leaders first. In LMIC, religion is an important part of everyday life and society. In some instances, patients report that their faith helps them make sense of their mental health experiences and alleviates their distress. Rathod and Kingdon (2009) speak of South Asian Muslim cultures where families ward off evil spirits by reciting Koranic verses and wearing a talisman or an armband from a faith healer. To clarify these beliefs, Naeem, Phiri, et al. (2010) recommend asking the patient to contact their religious scholar or Imam of the mosque to explain the relationship between their faith and the illness.

Some South Asian Muslims believe that witchcraft, evil spirits, or the evil eye has affected them by someone jealous in their family or that "jinn" or spirits are responsible for psychosis, while South Asian Hindus may believe in spirits of ancestors. It is interesting how a similar attribution model is shared across the globe: being termed the usog, in the Philippines, this is blamed on a stranger that has cast an "evil eye," while in Egypt, this is given the name of the "eye of horus," "ojear" in South America, or evil eye in South Asian Muslims. Some Mexican cultures such as Sal Si Puedes also believe in the power of the evil spirits and supernatural forces (Rathod, Kingdon, Pinninti, et al., 2015). Local cultural knowledge can help gain an inner window into the beliefs of the patient and contribute to building a therapeutic alliance.

Studies exploring the beliefs of patients regarding their diagnosis of schizophrenia found that more than half of the patients preferred faith healers and medication to be their chosen treatment (Awan, Jehangir, Irfan, et al., 2017; Awan, Zahoor, Irfan, et al., 2015). While visiting the psychiatrist, many may still be visiting the faith healer, who may even have recommended a referral to the health professional. In such instances, it is important to check if the family has already been to see a faith healer or a spiritual or religious leader as repetitions of religious mantras "wird or wazifa" may bring reassurance and hope; working in conjunction with their religious leaders as an integrated approach may promote trust and also improve outcomes (Rathod et al., 2015). On the other hand, structured educational interventions that target the beliefs and attribution of illness to supernatural causes have been reported to lessen these beliefs (Das, Saravanan, Karunakaran, et al., 2016; Joel et al., 2006).

Awan et al. reported that in Pakistan, majority of patients did not know the name of their illness as schizophrenia per se, but were acutely aware that what they experienced was a mental disorder. They attributed the leading causes of this ailment to be stress, witchcraft, and evil spirits (Awan et al., 2015, 2017). It is important, however, not to stereotype because even within the same cultures, help- seeking behavior may differ across individuals. Edgerton (1966) described four apparently similar East African societies but noted that in one community, 60% attributed psychosis to witchcraft, as compared with 1% in another community. One believed psychosis to be an illness; in the other, two-thirds attributed its occurrence to a worm in the brain when under stress (Edgerton, 1966).

10.3.6 Role of stigma and shame

The stigma of being diagnosed with a mental illness in LMIC can have far-reaching repercussions on an individual's standing in his/her society, marital prospects, respect and authority, and employment. Hence, it is important to be aware of cultural perceptions regarding the illness, as this will significantly influence engagement and treatment. Stigma is multiplied when the mental illness is psychotic in nature.

In some countries, having a mental disorder is perceived as a contagious disease, which may especially affect marital prospects especially of young females, in India and Pakistan. In these cultures, there is an inherent belief that mental illnesses are genetic disorders that are passed to the next generation (Rathod, Kingdon, Phiri, et al., 2010). The gender of the professional, such as a preference for a female professional, may also be important to the patient and their family, as eye contact with the opposite gender may be considered immodest or too forward especially in Muslim females.

Families can, however, be a source of strength in many cohesive cultures of the LMIC. Many individuals as stated above live with families and adhere to hierarchical structures of respect toward elders of the families. There may be an overinvolvement from the family in terms of the family knowing best; however, this can be used by the therapist to gain more information, help support the patient, and act as a cotherapist while attending with patient for follow-up appointments and tracking and reporting progress (Naeem, Phiri, et al., 2010).

The respect culturally ingrained for figures of authority may be helpful in medication adherence; however, with psychotherapy approaches, this may prove a double-edged sword as such intervention may be considered less effective in some cultures. There also may be an expectation of a directive style of working rather than collaborative, as in their view the professional knows best. Patients' expectations and preferences may differ in diverse cultures, and hence, a patient may have more faith in the therapist or professional if he or she uses a directive approach.

10.3.7 Family structure and hierarchy

Families in LMIC may be nuclear or extended units with a strong patriarchal influence in all aspects of decisions about life. Such families may accompany patients to appointments and influence beliefs and decision-making about treatments. Family work may prove to be useful as part of the clinical work in LMIC due to the strong influence of the extended family on the individual patient. This influence may be particularly useful if the patient is having a psychotic illness involving the lack of insight.

The age of independence may be later in these countries; children may not have left the nest after getting married due to tradition and a sense of duty of looking after their parents in old age resulting in cohabitation in the same household. Families may have a tendency to resist any external interventions due to their own ideas on how best to support the patient (Kuipers et al., 1992). The family's view of treatment has an impact on how the patient perceives his/her care or trusts the professional. The therapist may have to deeply examine their own beliefs about a family's role and learn to be aware of the transference it may sometimes elicit in order to manage their anxieties in dealing with an especially "overinvolved family."

In some families, where the wife suffers from schizophrenia, this work may be complicated by the guilt of a *husband who may be physically or emotionally absent*. He may deal with the guilt of leaving the first family by continuing to be a good provider after having a second marriage and a second family. In some Muslim countries, this may be more acceptable, without any due guilt either due to the men being allowed to have four wives at a time according to their religion. The impact of this nevertheless on the children in the first family may be multifold. For the family therapist, involving the husband may prove to be particularly difficult as they must focus on retaining involvement through chiefly avoidance of any blame and judgment and maintaining focus on psychoeducation of the illness, its management, and its outcomes for the patient and the children.

Cultural aspects of *marital prospects* of young adults, males and especially females, will need to be a consideration in treatment approaches. The families may be anxious and have a realistic fear of being ostracized from their wider social circle and the extended family. Due to a lack of awareness of mental health disorders in such cultures, these patients are at times deemed contagious or "dangerous" by their condition (Cowan, Raja, Nail, et al., 2012). The therapist may have to preempt such fears and perceived stigmas while tactfully exploring these fears and not dismissing them.

10.3.8 Geographical distance to treatment facilities

In rural populations in LMIC, it may be difficult to convince a psychotic patient with the lack of insight to travel to the hospital for a single treatment session, let alone to engage in any form of psychotherapy. Financial constraints may further contribute to treatment barriers. In these instances, the role of local community leaders and religious leaders may be crucial in helping the patients and their families engage with treatment. This may require psychoeducation for the former. The following practical strategies can be employed:

(i) Financial incentives could be offered to therapists in rural areas with supervision via the Internet, or providing this incentive to local lay health workers would be a cost-effective option.
(ii) Involvement of carers by psychoeducating them first.
(iii) Increasing trend toward a growing appreciation of the involvement and role of peer support workers and people with experience of mental health disorders that can work alongside patients while sharing their own personal narratives of their recovery and offering and instilling hope to those who are acutely unwell.

These peer workers are usually people within the local community and can be trained by professional staff and eventually employed as mental health workers. Due to their local community knowledge, they may also improve follow-up rates and avoid dropouts from treatment by preempting any obstacles to this at the designing stage of service. The stigma in certain cultures, however, may prevent people from disclosing their mental health condition, and this may require a wider change of culture first. A drawback of this approach without robust supervision arrangements for the peer workers is that if the choice of peer workers did not occur at the right stage of recovery and if the former is still fragile and not fully recovered, it could have a detrimental impact on the patient.

Training lay health workers has certainly overcome the scarcity of resources in one of these countries; for example, Rahman, Hamdani, Awan, et al. (2016) report a randomized control trial delivering behavioral interventions via lay health workers to adults experiencing psychological distress in conflict affected area of Pakistan (Rathod et al., 2017). These included 90min sessions for 5weeks and resulted in an improvement in depressive and anxiety symptoms. Although this may incur initial costs of training, however long term, this could prove to be a cost-effective approach.

Lady health workers were also employed and trained to deliver CBT in rural Pakistan that has not only improved postnatal depression but also benefited the health of children of these mothers; they had reduced episodes of diarrhea and an increased likelihood of receiving immunizations (Rahman, Malik, Sikander, et al., 2008). Similarly, in Nairobi, Kenya, an intervention for women with gender-based violence was evaluated after 3months and was found to lessen their psychological distress (Bryant, Schafer, Dawson, et al., 2017).

10.3.9 Cultural adaptation

As a result of globalization, the West has witnessed a substantial increase in immigration figures and the rise of multicultural societies. This highlights an even greater need for mental health professionals to be able to respond to the cultural and diverse needs of this growing population. It is well known that people from minority ethnic groups with schizophrenia have been more likely to be misunderstood as compared with their White counterparts and treated more with ECT and medication than psychotherapy (Fernando, 1998). Research evidence demonstrates that despite an apparent efficacy of CBT for schizophrenia within large study samples, the outcomes for minority ethnic group are not as good as compared with the White population (Rathod, Kingdon, Smith, et al., 2005).

Rathod and Kingdon (2009) believe that due to CBT's extensive evidence base, its pragmatic and personalized approach allows it to work in an integrated way with Eastern cultures and other philosophies. The strength of this approach is that it enables incorporation of language, tradition, and an encouragement in the use of personal and cultural resources to increase self-awareness. Degnan, Baker, Edge, et al. (2017) in their meta-analysis showed significant posttreatment effects in favor of adapted interventions for total symptom severity while describing the nature and efficacy of culturally adapted psychosocial interventions for schizophrenia. A recent meta-review of culturally adapted interventions also concluded a moderate benefit of culturally adapted interventions (Rathod et al., 2017).

Rathod et al. (2010) developed an adaptation framework using existing literature and the coproduction model (2010) that was tested through a randomized controlled trial (RCT) of CBT in psychosis. The RCT showed promising results in minority ethnic groups (Rathod, Phiri, Harris, et al., 2013). Naeem, Phiri, Nasar, et al. (2016) described an evidence-based framework to culturally adapted CBT for psychosis that has been used in Pakistan; England; and recently in the Middle East, Morocco, and China. This holistic approach took into consideration the triad of philosophical, practical, and theoretical constructs and an awareness of the pertinent cultural issues in anticipation of preparation for therapy. This was achieved through a process, which involved taking views of the stakeholders into account along with field testing and was found to be effective in trials (Irfan, Saeed, Awan, et al., 2017).

10.4 Conclusion

The view that psychotherapeutic approaches in the field of psychosis from HIC are not transferrable or generalizable to LMIC is an incorrect one, especially so in the light of a detailed review of successful and creative ways that have been employed in LMIC to overcome these challenges and barriers. We hope that with careful attention to legislation, planning, training, and involvement of carers and patients alike, this will not be an insurmountable battle in the future. Further research is needed to develop and evaluate the outcomes of the work done while maintaining an emphasis on understanding the thoughts and feelings of patients and their carers about their symptoms, exploring their relationship with their symptoms, and striving to maintain respect for their culture and identity.

References

Adams, C. E., Tharyan, P., Coutinho, E. S., et al. (2006). The schizophrenia drug treatment paradox: Pharmacological treatment based on best possible evidence may be hardest to practise in high-income countries. *British Journal of Psychiatry*, *189*(5), 391–392.

Amaresha, A. C., & Venkatasubramanian, G. (2012). Expressed emotion in schizophrenia: An overview. *Indian Journal of Psychological Medicine*, *34*(1), 12–20.

Awan, N. R., Jehangir, S. F., Irfan, M., et al. (2017). Explanatory model of illness of the patients with schizophrenia and the role of educational intervention. *Schizophrenia Research, 190*, 68–73.

Awan, N. R., Zahoor, N., Irfan, M., et al. (2015). Beliefs about illness of patients with schizophrenia. *Journal of Postgraduate Medical Institute, 29*(2), 67–71.

Bach, P., & Hayes, S. C. (2002). The use of acceptance and commitment therapy to prevent the rehospitalization of psychotic patients: A randomized controlled trial. *Journal of Consulting and Clinical Psychology, 70*(5), 1129–1139.

Bouwkamp, C. G., de Kruiff, M. E., van Troost, T. M., et al. (2013). Interpersonal and social rhythm group therapy for patients with bipolar disorder. *International Journal of Group Psychotherapy, 63*(1), 97–115.

Bryant, R., Schafer, A., Dawson, K., et al. (2017). Effectiveness of a brief behavioural intervention on psychological distress among women with a history of gender-based violence in urban Kenya: A randomised clinical trial. *PLoS Medicine, 14*(8), 1–20.

Chiang, K.-J., Tsai, J.-C., Liu, D., et al. (2017). Efficacy of cognitive-behavioral therapy in patients with bipolar disorder: A meta-analysis of randomized controlled trials. *PLoS ONE, 12*(5) e0176849.

Cohen, A., Patel, V., Thara, R., et al. (2008). Questioning an axiom: Better prognosis for schizophrenia in the developing world? *Schizophrenia Bulletin, 34*(2), 229–244.

Cowan, J., Raja, S., Nail, A., et al. (2012). Knowledge and attitudes of doctors regarding the provision of mental health care in Doddaballapur Taluk, Bangalore rural district, Karnataka. *International Journal of Mental Health Systems, 6*, 21–28.

Das, S., Saravanan, B., Karunakaran, K. P., et al. (2016). Effect of a structured educational intervention on explanatory models of relatives of patients with schizophrenia: Randomised controlled trial. *British Journal of Psychiatry, 188*(3), 286–287.

Degnan, A., Baker, S., Edge, D., et al. (2017). The nature and efficacy of culturally-adapted psychosocial interventions for schizophrenia: A systematic review and meta-analysis. *Psychological Medicine, 1-14*, https://doi.org/10.1017/S0033291717002264.

Demant, K. M., Vinberg, M., Kessing, L. V., et al. (2015). Effects of short-term cognitive remediation on cognitive dysfunction in partially or fully remitted individuals with bipolar disorder: Results of a randomized controlled trial. *PLoS ONE, 10*(6), 1–17.

Dickstein, D. P., Cushman, G. K., Kim, K. L., et al. (2015). Cognitive remediation: Potential novel brain-based treatment for bipolar disorder in children and adolescents. *Paedia Neuroimag, 20*(4), 382–390.

Edgerton, R. B. (1966). Conceptions of psychosis in four East African societies. *American Anthropologist, 68*(2), 408–425.

Farooq, S., Large, M., Nielssen, O., et al. (2009). The relationship between the duration of untreated psychosis and outcome in low and middle income countries. *Schizophrenia Research, 109*, 15–23.

Farooq, S., Nazar, Z., Irfan, M., et al. (2011). Schizophrenia medication adherence in a resource-poor setting: Randomized controlled trial of supervised treatment in out-patients for schizophrenia (STOPS). *British Journal of Psychiatry, 199*(6), 467–472.

Fernando, S. (1998). *Race and culture in psychiatry*. London: Billing and Sons Ltd.

Fishkin, R., Fishkin, L., Leli, U., et al. (2011). Psychodynamic treatment, training, and supervision using internet-based technologies. *Journal of the American Academy of Psychoanalysis and Dynamic Psychiatry, 39*(1), 155–168.

Frank, E., Kupfer, J. D., Thase, M., et al. (2005). Two-year outcomes for interpersonal and social rhythm therapy in individuals with bipolar I disorder. *Archives of General Psychiatry, 62*(9), 996–1004.

Gadit, A., & Khalid, N. (2002). *State of mental health in Pakistan: Service, education and research*. Karachi, Pakistan: Hamdard Foundation.
Garrido, G., Barrios, M., Penades, R., et al. (2013). Computer-assisted cognitive remediation therapy: Cognition, self-esteem and quality of life in schizophrenia. *Schizophrenia Research*, *150*(2–3), 563–569.
Heggdal, D., Foose, R., & Hammer, J. (2016). Basal exposure therapy: A new approach for treatment-resistant patients with severe and composite mental disorders. *Frontiers in Psychiatry*, *7*, 198–209.
Heggdal, D., Lillelien, A., Johnsrud, S. S., et al. (2013). Basal eksponerings-terapi: En vei inn til seg selv og ut til et liv det går an å leve [Basal exposure therapy – A way into oneself and out to a life possible to live]. *Dialog*, *23*(4), 7–19.
Inder, M. L., Crowe, M. T., Luty, S. E., et al. (2015). Randomized, controlled trial of interpersonal and social rhythm therapy for young people with bipolar disorder. *Bipolar Disorders*, *17*(2), 128–138.
Ipser, J. C., & Stein, D. J. (2007). Little mental disorder research in general medical journals in low- and middle-income countries. *South African Medical Journal*, *97*, 110–111.
Irfan, M., Saeed, S., Awan, N. R., et al. (2017). Psychological healing in Pakistan: From Sufism to culturally adapted cognitive behaviour therapy. *Journal of Contemporary Psychotherapy*, *47*, 119–124.
Jacob, K., Sharan, P., Mirza, I., et al. (2007). Mental health systems in countries: Where are we now. *Lancet*, *370*(9592), 1061–1077.
Joel, D. D., Sathyaseelan, M., Jayakaran, R., et al. (2006). A biomedical educational intervention to change explanatory models of psychosis among community health workers in South India. *Indian Journal of Psychiatry*, *48*(3), 138–142.
Kingdon, D., & Kirschen, H. (2006). Who does not get cognitive behavioral therapy for schizophrenia when therapy is readily available. *Psychiatric Services*, *57*(12), 1792–1794.
Kingdon, D., Murray, P., & Doyle, E. (2004). Reading about self-help for schizophrenia. *Psychiatric Bulletin*, *28*(9), 349–351.
Kingdon, D., Rathod, S., Hansen, L., et al. (2007). Combining cognitive therapy and pharmacotherapy for schizophrenia. *Journal of Cognitive Psychotherapy*, *21*(1), 28–36.
Kuipers, L., Leff, J., & Lam, D. (1992). *Family work for schizophrenia: A practical guide*. London: Gaskell.
Lehman, A., Lieberman, J. A., Dixon, L. B., et al. (2004). American Psychiatric Association practice guideline for the treatment of patients with schizophrenia. *American Journal of Psychiatry*, *161*(2), 1–56.
Li, W., Zaung, L., Xuerong, L., et al. (2017). A qualitative study to explore views of patients', carers' and mental health professionals' to inform cultural adaptation of CBT for psychosis (CBTp) in China. *BMC Psychiatry*, *17*, 131–139.
Lund, C., Tomlinson, M., De Silva, M., et al. (2012). PRIME: A programme to reduce the treatment gap for mental disorders in five low- and middle-income countries. *PLoS Medicine*, *9*(12), e1001359–e1001364.
Mansfield, A. K., Dealy, J. A., & Keitner, G. I. (2012). Family interventions for bipolar disorder: A review of the literature. *Neuropsychiatry*, *2*(3), 1–8.
McGurk, S. R., Twamley, E. W., Sitzer, D. I., et al. (2007). A meta-analysis of cognitive remediation in schizophrenia. *American Journal of Psychiatry*, *164*(12), 1791–1802.
Menon, V., Rajan, T. M., & Sarkar, S. (2017). Psychotherapeutic applications of Mobile phone-based technologies: A systematic review of current research and trends. *Indian Journal of Psychological Medicine*, *39*(1), 4–11.

Miklowitz, D. J., George, E. L., Richards, J. A., et al. (2003). A randomized study of family-focused psychoeducation and pharmacotherapy in the outpatient management of bipolar disorder. *Archives of General Psychiatry*, *60*(9), 904–912.

Miklowitz, D. J., Simoneau, T. L., George, E. L., et al. (2000). Family-focused treatment of bipolar disorder: One year effects of a psychoeducational program in conjunction with pharmacotherapy. *Biological Psychiatry*, *48*(6), 582–592.

Murray, L. K., Dorsey, S., Bolton, P., et al. (2011). Building capacity in mental health interventions in low resource countries: An apprenticeship model for training local providers. *International Journal of Mental Health Systems*, *5*(1), 1–12.

Naeem, F., Ayub, M., McGuire, N., et al. (2010). *Culturally adapted CBT (CaCBT) for depression: Therapy manual.* Lahore: Pakistan Association of Cognitive Therapists.

Naeem, F., Farooq, S., & Kingdon, D. (2014). Cognitive behavioural therapy (brief versus standard duration) for schizophrenia. *Cochrane Database of Systematic Reviews*, *4*.

Naeem, F., Habib, N., Gul, M., et al. (2016). A qualitative study to explore patients, career and health professionals, views to culturally adapt CBT for psychosis (CBT p) in Pakistan. *Behavioural and Cognitive Psychotherapy*, *44*(1), 43–55.

Naeem, F., Johal, R., McKenna, C., et al. (2016). Cognitive behaviour therapy for psychosis based guided self-help (CBTp-GSH) delivered by frontline mental health professionals: Results of a feasibility study. *Schizophrenia Research*, *173*, 69–74.

Naeem, F., Kingdon, D., & Turkington, D. (2008). Predictors of response to cognitive behaviour therapy in the treatment of schizophrenia: A comparison of brief and standard intervention. *Cognitive Therapy and Research*, *32*(5), 651–656.

Naeem, F., Phiri, P., Nasar, A., et al. (2016). An evidence-based framework for cultural adaptation of cognitive behaviour therapy: Process, methodology and foci of adaptation. *World Cultural Psychiatry Research Review*, *11*(1/2), 61–70.

Naeem, F., Phiri, P., Rathod, S., et al. (2010). Using CBT with diverse patients: Working with South Asian Muslims. In M. Mueller, H. Kennerley, & F. McManus et al. (Eds.), *Oxford guide to surviving as a CBT therapist.* Oxford: Oxford University Press.

Naeem, F., Saeed, S., Irfan, M., et al. (2015). Brief culturally adapted CBT for psychosis (CaCBTp): A randomized controlled trial from a low income country. *Schizophrenia Research*, *164*(1–3), 143–148.

National Institute for Health and Care Excellence. (2014a). *Psychosis and schizophrenia in adults: Prevention and management (website). https://www.nice.org.uk/guidance/cg178/ifp/chapter/psychological-therapy* (accessed 02.12.17).

National Institute for Health and Care Excellence. (2014b). *Bipolar disorder: Assessment and management (website). https://www.nice.org.uk/guidance/cg185/chapter/1-recommendations* (accessed 02.12.17).

Ng, R., & Cheung, M. (2007). Supervision of cognitive behavioural therapy for psychosis: A Hong Kong experience. *Hong Kong Journal of Psychiatry*, *17*(4), 124–130.

Ost, L. G. (2014). The efficacy of acceptance and commitment therapy: An updated systematic review and meta-analysis. *Behaviour Research and Therapy*, *61*, 105–121.

Pankey, J., & Hayes, S. C. (2003). Acceptance and commitment therapy for psychosis. *International Journal of Psychology and Psychological Therapy*, *3*(2), 311–328.

Patel, A., Knapp, M., Romeo, R., et al. (2010). Cognitive remediation therapy in schizophrenia: Cost-effectiveness analysis. *Schizophrenia Research*, *120*(1–3), 217–224.

Rahman, A., Hamdani, S. U., Awan, N. R., et al. (2016). Effect of a multicomponent behavioural intervention in adults impaired by psychological distress in a conflict-affected area of Pakistan: A randomized clinical trial. *JAMA*, *316*(24), 2609–2617.

Rahman, A., Malik, A., Sikander, S., et al. (2008). Cognitive behaviour therapy-based intervention by community health workers for mothers with depression and their infants in rural Pakistan: A cluster-randomised controlled trial. *Lancet, 372*(9642), 902–909.

Rathod, S., & Kingdon, D. (2009). Cognitive behavioural therapy across cultures. *Psychiatry, 8*(9), 370–371.

Rathod, S., Kingdon, D., Phiri, P., et al. (2010). Developing culturally sensitive cognitive behaviour therapy for psychosis for ethnic minority patients by exploration and incorporation of service users and health professional's views and opinions. *Behavioural and Cognitive Psychotherapy, 38*(5), 511–533.

Rathod, S., Kingdon, D., Pinninti, N., et al. (2015). *Cultural adaptation of CBT for serious mental illness: A guide for training and practice* (1st ed.). Oxford: Wiley and Sons, Ltd.

Rathod, S., Kingdon, D., Smith, P., et al. (2005). Insight into schizophrenia: The effects of cognitive behavioural therapy on the components of insight and association with socio-demographics-data on a previously published randomised controlled trail. *Schizophrenia Research, 74*(2–3), 211–219.

Rathod, S., Phiri, P., Harris, S., et al. (2013). Cognitive behaviour therapy for psychosis can be adapted for minority ethnic groups: A randomized controlled trial. *Schizophrenia Research, 143*, 319–326.

Rathod, S., Pinninti, N., Irfan, M., et al. (2017). Mental health service provision in low and middle income countries. *Health Services Insights, 10*, 1–7.

Reinares, M., Vieta, E., Colom, F., et al. (2002). Intervencion familiar de tipo psicoeducativo en al trastorno bipolar (Psychoeducational family intervention in bipolar disorder). *Revista de Psiquiatría de la Facultad de Medicina de Barcelona, 29*(2), 97–105.

Revell, E. R., Neill, J. C., Harte, M., et al. (2015). A systematic review and meta-analysis of cognitive remediation in early schizophrenia. *Schizophrenia Research, 168*(1–2), 213–222.

Sole, B., Bonnin, C. M., Mayoral, M., et al. (2014). Functional remediation for patients with bipolar II disorder: Improvement of functioning and subsyndromal symptoms. *European Neuropsychopharmacology, 25*(2), 257–264.

Stein, D. J., & Seedat, S. (2007). From research methods to clinical practice in psychiatry: Challenges and opportunities in the developing world. *International Review of Psychiatry, 19*(5), 573–581.

Thara, R., Henrietta, M., Joseph, A., et al. (1994). Ten-year course of schizophrenia—The Madras longitudinal study. *Acta Psychiatrica Scandinavica, 90*(5), 329–336.

Thara, R., Padmavati, R., & Srinivasan, T. N. (2004). Focus on psychiatry in India. *British Journal of Psychiatry, 184*, 366–373.

The Ministry of Health of the People's Republic of China. (2012). *The China health statistical yearbook in 2012, Beijing*. China Statistics Press.

Turkington, D., Kingdon, D., Rathod, S., et al. (2006). An effectiveness trial of a brief cognitive behavioural intervention by mental health nurses in schizophrenia: Clinically important outcomes in the medium term. *British Journal of Psychiatry, 189*(1), 31–35.

Veeh, J., Kopf, J., Kittel-Schneider, S., et al. (2017). Cognitive remediation for bipolar patients with objective cognitive impairment: A naturalistic study. *International Journal of Bipolar Disorders, 5*(1), 8–20.

Vieta, E., Pacchiarotti, I., Valentí, M., et al. (2009). A critical update on psychological interventions for bipolar disorders. *Current Psychiatry Reports, 11*, 494–502.

Watts, S., Mackenzie, A., Thomas, C., et al. (2013). CBT for depression: A pilot RCT comparing mobile phone vs. computer. *BMC Psychiatry, 13*, 49–57.

World Health Organization (2001). *The world health report 2001—Mental health: New understanding, new hope*. Geneva: World Health Organization.

World Health Organization. (2004). *Disease and injury regional estimates for 2004 (website). www.who.int/healthinfo/global_burden_disease/estimates_regional/en/index.html* (accessed 12.12.17).

World Health Organization. (2008). *The global burden of disease: 2004 update*. Geneva: World Health Organization.

Wykes, T., Huddy, V., Cellard, C., et al. (2011). A meta-analysis of cognitive remediation for schizophrenia: Methodology and effect sizes. *American Journal of Psychiatry*, *168*(5), 472–485.

Wykes, T., Steel, C., Everitt, B., et al. (2008). Cognitive behavior therapy for schizophrenia: Effect sizes, clinical models, and methodological rigor. *Schizophrenia Bulletin*, *34*(3), 523–537.

Psychotherapy for substance use disorders

11

Bronwyn Myers
Alcohol, Tobacco and Other Drug Research Unit, South African Medical Research Council and Division of Addiction Psychiatry, Department of Psychiatry and Mental Health, University of Cape Town, Cape Town, South Africa

11.1 Introduction

Substance use disorders (SUDs) range on a continuum from mild to severe. These disorders are highly prevalent, with the World Health Organization (WHO, 2014) estimating that there are more than 208 million people with alcohol use disorders, globally. In addition, recent global estimates suggest there are at least 29.5 million people living with a drug use disorder, with the global incidence of these disorders increasing over the last few years (United Nations Office on Drugs and Crime, 2017). Substance use disorders (SUDs) are characterized by a cluster of cognitive, behavioral, and physical symptoms related to the recurrent and maladaptive use of a psychoactive substance (American Psychiatric Association, 2013). On the more severe end of the spectrum, core symptoms include increased desire and craving for substance use, impaired self-control, emotional dysregulation (negative mood), and increased stress reactivity. These symptoms lead to significant psychological distress and impairment in social, interpersonal, and occupational functioning (Lee, An, Levin, et al., 2015). From a public health perspective, it is imperative to ensure effective treatment is available for SUDs, given that they are, together with other mental disorders, the leading cause of years lost to disability and the fifth leading cause of death and disability globally (Degenhardt, Whiteford, Ferrari, et al., 2013; Whiteford, Degenhardt, Rehm, et al., 2013). To illustrate, the harmful use of alcohol is among the top five risk factors for disease, disability, and mortality (Lim, Vos, Flaxman, et al., 2012). Alcohol use disorders are estimated to cause around 3.3 million deaths per year (accounting for 5.9% of all deaths globally) and account for 5.1% of the global burden of disease and injury (WHO, 2014).

While the prevalence of SUDs and associated burden of disease vary from region to region, the substance-attributable burden of disease appears to be greater in high-income than low- and middle-income countries (LMIC; Degenhardt et al., 2013; Whiteford et al., 2013). However, in recent years, there has been a growth in the prevalence and burden of disease associated with SUDs in LMIC, suggesting shifts in the global epidemiology of substance use (UNODC, 2017). These findings, along with the assumption that the provision of evidence-based SUD treatment can avert much of

Global Mental Health and Psychotherapy. https://doi.org/10.1016/B978-0-12-814932-4.00011-2

the substance-attributable burden of disease and associated costs, underline the importance of LMIC ensuring access to evidence-based treatment for people with SUDs.

In recent years, our knowledge of the etiology of substance use disorders has grown. This improved understanding has led to advances in psychotherapy for SUDs, with several evidence-based treatment approaches available for implementation. Within established substance abuse treatment systems in high-income countries, adoption of evidence-based psychotherapies has been slower than anticipated (Bradley & Kivlahan, 2014). In LMIC, SUD treatment is still in its infancy (Pasche, Kleintjes, Wilson, et al., 2015). As these systems evolve, there is an opportunity to influence service planners and providers to adopt effective psychotherapeutic treatments for SUDs. With this goal in mind, this chapter provides an overview of the development of SUDs and implications for treatment. The chapter then describes the major evidence-based psychotherapies for SUDs, reviews evidence in support of their effectiveness, and discusses considerations for their implementation in LMIC. The chapter ends with a discussion of the importance of patient preferences for the choice of psychotherapy.

11.2 Development of substance use disorders and implications for treatment

Understanding how SUDs develop is key to advancing psychotherapies for the treatment of these disorders. Both positive and negative reinforcement processes play a role in the cycle of substance use. During the initial stages of experimentation, substance use generally results in pleasurable experiences with little or no adverse consequences—this positively reinforces continued use (Rutherford, Mayes, & Potenza, 2010). However, continued and regular substance use results in adaptations to the motivational and reward circuitry of the brain. As tolerance for the substance develops, the pleasurable effects associated with substance use diminish, and the person has to increase the quantity and frequency of substance use in order to experience the same level of reward (Potenza, Sofuoglu, Carroll, et al., 2011). As substance use becomes more habitual, positive pleasure-related motivations for substance use decrease, while negative reinforcement motivations increase. For instance, some people are motivated to continue or increase substance use to avoid experiencing unpleasant and uncomfortable withdrawal symptoms that may occur when a person reduces or stops using particular types of substances after a period of protracted use. The desire to avoid stress and negative mood states is also a powerful negative reinforcer of continued substance use. Regular substance use is now known to change the brain circuitry implicated in emotional regulation, stress responsiveness, and cognitive control, rendering people with substance use problems more reactive and less able to manage external triggers for substance use and internal cues such as stressors and negative mood states (Potenza et al., 2011; Sinha, 2018).

Given this understanding, effective treatment should address motivation for change; find ways of interrupting the negative reinforcing relationship between external triggers, internal emotional cues, and substance use; and find substance-free alternatives for positive reinforcement (Potenza et al., 2011). Over time, various evidence-based psychotherapies have evolved to address either the motivational, positive reinforcement, or negative reinforcement aspects of SUDs. The following section provides an overview of each of these types of psychotherapy along with evidence in support of their effectiveness. It is important to note that these therapies are often combined or used sequentially in the treatment of SUDs in order to ensure that both the motivational and reinforcement aspects of SUDs are addressed.

11.3 Evidence-based psychotherapy for substance use disorders

11.3.1 Motivational therapies

Motivational therapies hold that individuals need to be ready and willing and have sufficient self-efficacy to change their use of substances (DiClemente, Corno, & Graydon, 2017). Initially developed by Miller and Rollnick (1992) for the treatment of alcohol use disorders, motivational interviewing (MI) and its structured derivative, motivational enhancement therapy (MET), is now applied to the treatment of other drug use disorders, behavioral addictions, and health concerns where there is a motivational component (DiClemente et al., 2017). These brief psychotherapies comprise one to four counseling sessions with an MI-trained therapist, either as a stand-alone SUD treatment (often in settings where people present for other health services such as an emergency room) or as the first part of a multicomponent substance use treatment program that includes other psychotherapies to ensure adequate motivation for change and to facilitate engagement in treatment (Ball, Martino, Nich, et al., 2009; Simpson, 2004).

The goal of MI/MET is to enhance intrinsic motivation to change through resolving the person's ambivalence and improving their self-efficacy to change (Miller & Rollnick, 2002; Smedslund, Berg, Hammerstrøm, et al., 2011). MI has two active components. First, there is a relational component in which the therapist adopts a collaborative, client-centered counseling style that is positive and encouraging and uses this relationship to express empathy for the client and affirm decisions and actions toward behavior change (Apodaca & Longabaugh, 2009; Miller & Rose, 2009). Second, there is a technical component where the therapist uses MI-specific strategies and techniques to build self-efficacy and elicit "change talk" (Miller & Rose, 2009). "Change talk" reflects intention to change, whereas "sustain talk" reflects intention to remain the same (Apodaca & Longabaugh, 2009; Miller & Rose, 2009). One strategy used include "rolling with resistance," where instead of challenging resistance to change, the therapist uses the resistance as an opportunity to better understand the client's position (Miller, 1996). Another strategy is to develop discrepancies between current behavior and future goals as a means to enhance motivation for change (Miller & Rose, 2009; Smedslund et al., 2011). Systematic reviews provide support for these mechanisms of action. For instance, more "change talk" seems to enhance readiness for change, self-efficacy, and result in better substance use outcomes (Jiang, Wu, & Gao, 2017; Magill, Apodaca, Borsari, et al., 2017). In contrast, therapist behaviors inconsistent with an MI style are associated with worse outcomes (Apodaca & Longabaugh, 2009; Magill et al., 2017; Pace, Dembe, Soma, et al., 2017).

In terms of effectiveness, systematic reviews show that stand-alone MI/MET is superior to no treatment for reduced substance use (Burke, Arkowitz, & Menchola, 2003; Hettema, Steele, & Miller, 2005; DiClemente et al., 2017; Dunn, Deroo, & Rivara, 2001; Jiang et al., 2017; Smedslund et al., 2011). However, MI/MET is as, but no more, effective than other psychotherapies for reducing substance use (DiClemente et al., 2017; Smedslund et al., 2011). Given this finding, it may be valuable to combine MI/MET with other evidence-based treatments that address drivers of substance use other than motivation. Further, while there is strong evidence in support of MI/MET for alcohol, tobacco, and cannabis use disorder treatment (DiClemente et al., 2017; Joseph & Basu, 2017; O'Donnell, Anderson, Newbury-Birch, et al., 2014) across a range of cultural contexts, there is limited evidence of its efficacy for methamphetamine and opiate use disorders (DiClemente et al., 2017). Therefore, treatment providers should proceed with caution when using MI/MET as the sole therapeutic approach for methamphetamine and opiate use disorders.

Evidence for the efficacy of this brief psychotherapy has led to increased implementation in treatment systems in the United States (Drapkin, Wilbourne, Manuel, et al., 2016) and calls for implementation in primary health-care systems in LMIC (Myers & Sorsdahl, 2014). In these contexts, MI/MET holds appeal as it is brief, posing minimal burden to busy service providers. Second, it is transportable to primary care services (Joseph & Basu, 2017), thereby addressing availability and geographic access barriers that predominate when substance use services are limited to stand-alone facilities (Myers, Louw, & Pasche, 2010). Emerging evidence that MI/MET can be effectively delivered through mobile technologies suggests a further avenue for enhancing access to this psychotherapy in low-resource and remote settings (Jiang et al., 2017). Finally, as MI/MET can be task shifted to generalist health providers with adequate training and ongoing supervision (Smedslund et al., 2011), it enhances the likelihood of implementation in low-resource systems where there are few SUD providers. Should MI/MET be adopted and implemented in these settings, it will be important to assess whether the counselor is using an MI style or reverting back to a traditional therapeutic approach (Myers, Sorsdahl, Morojele, et al., 2016; Myers, Williams, Johnson, et al., 2016). Evaluations of the dissemination of MI/MET in high-income countries emphasize the importance of fidelity checking and ongoing therapist training to build capacity for MI/MET delivery (Schwalbe, Oh, & Zweben, 2014) and enhance the likelihood of positive effects (Hallgren, Dembe, Pace, et al., 2018).

11.3.2 Providing alternative rewards through contingency management

Contingency management is a behavioral therapy based on the theory of operant conditioning (Skinner, 1938). As such, CM's core belief is that the reinforcement of abstinence through the provision of positive rewards can interrupt the cycle of substance use (Dutra, Stathopoulou, Basden, et al., 2008; Lussier, Heil, Mongeon, et al., 2006). In practice, CM involves the provision of concrete financial rewards to reinforce reductions in or abstinence from substance use during the course of SUD treatment. These rewards generally escalate in value and are contingent on objective evidence of behavior change such as drug-free urine samples. Rewards may include store vouchers, cash, access to educational or employment services, or other desirable items (Ainscough, McNeill, Strang, et al., 2017).

CM appears efficacious for a wide range of substance use disorders. Multiple systematic reviews have shown that CM is superior to treatment as usual for alcohol, tobacco, and illicit drug use (Ainscough et al., 2017; Davis, Kurti, Skelly, et al., 2016; Dutra et al., 2008; Lussier et al., 2006; Prendergast, Podus, Finney, et al., 2006). These systematic reviews found moderate to large effect sizes for CM, with effect sizes being somewhat larger for opiate use disorders (Prendergast et al., 2006). These reviews have taught us several lessons for the implementation of CM in SUD treatment settings. First, CM treatment that provides immediate incentives, of greater monetary value, and that appeal to the patient population appears most effective (Lussier et al., 2006), suggesting that the rewards provided must be sufficiently valued by the treatment population. Second, findings show diminishing effects on substance use posttreatment (Davis et al., 2016; Prendergast et al., 2006). Consequently, CM may be most effective when combined with other psychotherapies (McKay, Lynch, Coviello, et al., 2010). More specifically, CM may be an aid to attaining abstinence during early treatment, enabling patients to benefit from other psychotherapies that prevent relapse to substance use (Prendergast et al., 2006).

While the empirical support for CM has led to calls for its nationwide use in the United Kingdom (Pilling, Strang, & Gerada, 2007) and the United States (Petry, DePhilippis, Rash, et al., 2014), the SUD treatment community's interest in implementing CM has been limited in both high-income (Hartzler, Lash, Roll, et al., 2012) and LMIC contexts. Barriers to implementation include limited knowledge of evidence in support of CM's efficacy, poor understanding of how to integrate CM with other treatments, and concerns about the costs of providing incentives (Hartzler et al., 2012; Shearer, Tie, & Byford, 2015). Convincing the treatment community to introduce CM may require the development of clinical guidelines for CM's application in LMIC settings that is accompanied by substance abuse workforce training. Questions about how to contain CM-related costs (through providing interventions of a short duration or incentives of a smaller value) while maintaining effectiveness will also need to be answered.

11.3.3 Addressing negative reinforcers through cognitive behavioral therapy (CBT)

As CBT has been thoroughly described in other chapters in this volume, this chapter focuses on describing relapse prevention (RP), the most commonly used CBT intervention for the treatment of SUDs (Morin, Harris, & Conrod, 2017). Initially developed to assist people who had achieved abstinence from substance use after a brief period of treatment maintain this abstinence by avoiding a relapse to old patterns of behavior, the RP model is now offered as a first-line treatment—sometimes not only as a monotherapy but also in combination with other motivational and behavioral treatment strategies (Irvin, Bowers, Dunn, et al., 1999; Marlatt & Donovan, 2005). RP programs typically comprise between 14 and 20 counseling sessions and therefore are typically longer than other forms of psychotherapy for SUD. RP can be provided in group or individual settings (Morin et al., 2017).

This model holds that continued or relapse to substance use occurs when internal and external triggers for substance use are managed using problematic coping skills and expectancies that increase the propensity to use substances as a way of coping with high-risk situations (Morin et al., 2017). As a result, RP uses a combination of behavioral skill training, cognitive intervention, and lifestyle change procedures to help individuals identify their internal (emotional) and external (situational) high-risk situations and triggers, teach them new skills and coping strategies for addressing these triggers and situations, and enhance their self-efficacy to achieve and maintain abstinence through the provision of opportunities for practicing these new skills (Marlatt & Donovan, 2005; Witkiewitz & Marlatt, 2004, 2007). RP typically comprises five elements. First, the therapist conducts a functional analysis of the patient's substance use and high-risk situations for substance use. Second, the patient identifies thoughts, negative moods, and external events (people, places, and objects) that trigger thoughts, urges, and cravings for substance use (Morin et al., 2017; Witkiewitz & Marlatt, 2007). Third, patients are taught behavioral mechanisms for avoiding these triggers. Fourth, where avoidance is not possible, patients are taught cognitive strategies for enhancing self-control and for coping with high-risk situations (Marlatt & Donovan, 2005; Morin et al., 2017; Witkiewitz & Marlatt, 2007). Fifth, patients are assisted in identifying and increasing pleasurable and rewarding activities that are unrelated to substance use (Morin et al., 2017). Through these elements, RP is thought to help patients achieve and maintain abstinence through helping them improve their cognitive control over substance use and by reducing the reward salience associated with substance use. Emerging evidence from neuroimaging studies that RP treatment results in reduced recruitment of brain regions associated with impulse control and reward sensitivity provides some support for this hypothesis (Zilverstand, Parvaz, Moeller, et al., 2016).

The efficacy of CBT approaches for the treatment of SUDs has been extensively evaluated. Systematic reviews have shown that CBT approaches (including RP) are superior to treatment as usual for alcohol, tobacco, and illicit drug use (Dutra et al., 2008; Hides, Samet, & Lubman, 2010; Magill & Ray, 2009; McHugh, Hearon, & Otto, 2018). These reviews found small to moderate treatment effects that varied according to the substance being targeted. Larger treatment effects were found for alcohol and cannabis use disorder, followed by cocaine and opioids, with the smallest effects for polysubstance dependence (Magill & Ray, 2009; McHugh et al., 2018). However, there is little evidence that RP or other forms of CBT are more efficacious than other evidence-based psychotherapies for reducing substance use (Carroll, 1996; Farronato, Dürsteler-Macfarland, Wiesbeck, et al., 2013; Kadden, Carroll, Donovan, et al., 2003; Morin et al., 2017). This suggests that RP is as effective but not superior to other forms of evidence-based psychotherapy for treating SUDs. Nonetheless, in comparison with other evidence-based psychotherapies, RP and other forms of CBT appear to have more durable effects posttreatment (Carroll, Rounsaville, Nich, et al., 1994; Rawson, Huber, McCann, et al., 2002). Instead of the common pattern of diminishing effects posttreatment, several studies have demonstrated sustained and sometimes enhanced treatment effects for RP therapy (Carroll, 2018; McHugh et al., 2018). Together, these findings suggest that RP is an effective approach for reducing barriers to achieving and maintaining abstinence. However, as RP does not address the motivational components of engagement in treatment and readiness for change, it may be most effective to offer this psychotherapy in combination with MI/MET.

11.3.4 Contextual cognitive behavioral treatment

In recent years, contextual CBTs have been applied to the treatment of SUDs. Unlike traditional CBT that focuses on controlling or changing the content of feelings, thoughts, and beliefs, contextual CBTs focus on changing the influence of these internal triggers on propensity to use substances (Lee et al., 2015; Tang, Tang, & Posner, 2016). Various contextual CBTs exist, of which mindfulness-based approaches have received the most attention (Lee et al., 2015) and consequently will be the focus of this section.

First developed for the treatment of depression, mindfulness therapies were applied to the treatment of SUDs after findings that mindfulness meditation improves self-control by enhancing emotion regulation and stress reactivity—some of the key drivers of continued substance use (Tang et al., 2016). Mindfulness-based treatments for SUDs include approaches that focus solely on mindfulness meditation (e.g., Bowen, Witkiewitz, Dillworth, et al., 2016) and those that combine mindfulness practices with other evidence-based psychotherapies, such as mindfulness-based relapse prevention (Witkiewitz, Marlatt, & Walker, 2005) and mindfulness-oriented recovery enhancement (Garland, Froeliger, & Howard, 2014; Garland, Manusov, Froeliger, et al., 2014). Mindfulness-based treatments involve coaching patients in mindfulness meditation and other body awareness techniques in order to enhance their cognitive awareness and improve the regulation of thoughts, feelings, and bodily sensations that may lead to substance use or psychological distress (Garland, Gaylord, Boettiger, et al., 2010). Mindfulness-based treatments also focus on developing alternative coping responses to internal triggers, through enhancing acceptance of negative cognitions and emotions rather than trying to avoid or control them (Tapper, 2018). Patients are encouraged to develop daily mindfulness practices in which they apply these techniques.

Mindfulness-based treatments appear to work through disrupting two of the key cognitive and affective mechanisms that underpin continued substance use (Garland, Froeliger, et al., 2014; Garland, Manusov, et al., 2014; Witkiewitz, Bowen, Harrop, et al., 2014). First, patients are likely to become more conscious of their internal triggers and less reactive to substance-related cues with regular mindfulness practice (Garland, Froeliger, et al., 2014; Garland, Manusov, et al., 2014;

Witkiewitz et al., 2014). As such, this approach may enhance cognitive control. Second, mindfulness practice appears to improve patients' response to stress through enhancing emotional regulation, thereby reducing the likelihood of stress-precipitated relapse to substance use (Garland, Froeliger, et al., 2014). Evidence that mindfulness-based training leads to increased connectivity in the regions of the brain implicated in emotional regulation and cognitive control (Tang et al., 2016) provides support for these proposed mechanisms of action.

Emerging evidence suggests that mindfulness treatments hold promise for reducing substance use. Recent systematic reviews suggest that mindfulness-based treatments perform somewhat better (with a significant but small effect) compared with comparison conditions without mindfulness practice for reducing substance use posttreatment (Chiesa & Serretti, 2014; Katz & Toner, 2013; Li, Howard, Garland, et al., 2017). Despite their promise, the quality of evidence in support of mindfulness-based treatment remains poor, with most studies characterized by small sample sizes and other methodological limitations (Goldberg, Tucker, Greene, et al., 2018). Further, well-designed studies are needed to strengthen the evidence-based in support of the effectiveness (and cost-effectiveness) of this psychotherapeutic approach.

In addition, the transportability of this psychotherapy to LMIC and non-Western cultural settings is unclear as almost all studies on mindfulness-based treatment for SUDs have occurred in high-income countries. On the one hand, Western-based mindfulness treatments have been criticized for extracting meditative practices out of their sociocultural contexts and possibly changing their meaning (Kirmayer, 2015). On the other hand, Rathod, Pinninto, Irfan, et al. (2017) argue that many Eastern and Asian cultures are familiar with meditative practices and thus may find mindfulness techniques easy to accept and practice. Further research is needed to establish the feasibility and cultural acceptability of mindfulness-based treatments in LMIC contexts, including countries where meditation does not form part of cultural practice.

11.3.5 Combining psychotherapies for the treatment of SUDs

This chapter has focused largely on describing evidence-based monotherapies for SUDs. While there are several effective psychotherapies now available for the treatment of SUDs, none of these treatments are completely effective when used as a single therapeutic approach (Carroll & Onken, 2005). As a result, using combinations of therapies has been proposed as a way of enhancing treatment effects. Three key strategies have been proposed for combining psychotherapies: (i) combining two treatments that are different but complementary, thereby allowing weakness in either therapeutic approach to be addressed; (ii) using two efficacious treatments that target the same underlying mechanisms but in different ways, thereby having an additive effect; and (iii) using treatments that on their own are not particularly efficacious but when combined can catalyze each other (Potenza et al., 2011). The first strategy is most often used in the treatment of SUDs.

For example, MI/MET approaches are often combined with other evidence-based psychotherapies, such as CBT, in order to enhance intrinsic motivation for behavior change while providing patients with the necessary tools in achieving and maintaining reductions in substance use (Moyers & Houck, 2011). There are several examples of SUD treatment programs that combine MI/MET with CBT including the matrix model. This 16-week program combines behavioral skill training, cognitive interventions, lifestyle changes, and a motivational interviewing therapeutic style to engage and retain individuals in treatment, facilitate early abstinence from substance use, and prevent relapse through equipping patients with behavioral skills and coping strategies (Obert, London, & Rawson, 2002; Rawson, Shoptaw, Obert, et al., 1995). Findings from evaluations of the matrix program demonstrate better treatment retention and completion rates and greater reductions in drug use, better abstinence rates, and longer periods of abstinence for individuals assigned to the matrix model compared with individuals assigned to treatment as usual (Obert, Hamilton Brown, Zweben, et al., 2005; Rawson, Marinelli-Casey, & Anglin, 2004). The matrix model has been implemented in several LMIC, including South Africa, where outcomes comparable with those reported by research studies in high-income settings have been reported (Gouse, Magidson, Burnhams, et al., 2016; Magidson, Gouse, Burnhams, et al., 2017). However, this operational research has shown low rates of treatment completion, raising questions about the feasibility of implementing such a lengthy and intensive treatment program in low-resource treatment settings when retention in care is such a concern (Gouse et al., 2016; Magidson et al., 2017). Apart from rigorously controlled trials, implementation studies that explore the environmental, social, and clinical requirements for the effective and cost-effective implementation of these interventions are needed to enhance the feasibility and utility of this and other combined psychotherapies in LMIC. In particular, concerns around (i) how to contain costs through novel delivery mechanisms and (ii) how to abbreviate lengthy programs while maintaining effectiveness will need to be examined.

For the former concern, there has been some promising evidence that combined MI/RP treatments are equally effective in group and individual formats (Schmitz, Oswald, Jacks, et al., 1997)—this may be a way of containing costs and increasing service coverage in LMIC. In this vein, there is also promising evidence that MI-RP and other CBT-based interventions can be delivered using web platforms and mobile technology. While this guided self-administration of CBT appears as effective as standard care in reducing substance use problems (Carroll, 2014), more trials are needed to establish whether these technology-delivered interventions are as effective as face-to-face modalities (Morin et al., 2017). For the treatment duration concern, there is evidence that brief MI-CBT interventions are effective treatments for mild and moderate SUDs. These brief treatments may be more feasible to implement in low-resource settings than treatments of longer duration that are more resource-intensive. Evidence from South Africa that four sessions of blended MI and problem-solving therapy, a form of CBT, are feasible and acceptable to implement from both a patient (Myers, Sorsdahl, et al., 2016; Myers, Williams, et al., 2016; Sorsdahl, Myers, Ward, et al., 2014) and provider perspective (Sorsdahl, Myers, Ward, et al., 2015) and effective for reducing substance use (Sorsdahl, Stein, Corrigall, et al., 2015) provides some support for this claim.

11.4 Considering patient preferences in choice of psychotherapy

As there are sometimes options for treating SUDs, several decisions (including which level of care (inpatient vs. outpatient) and type of treatment modality) need to be made when seeking care. In the past, clinicians and treatment providers have been largely responsible for this decision-making. In recent years, the emphasis has shifted to shared decision-making around choice of treatment modality, where patients have an active role in choosing the type of SUD treatment that appeals to them (Friedrichs, Spies, Harter, et al., 2016). When available treatment options are equally effective, patient preferences and perceived treatment needs should be the deciding factor. Shared decision-making is important given findings that patients who play an active role in the choice of drug treatment are more invested and engaged with services and have greater satisfaction with treatment and better substance use outcomes than those who have limited choice in their treatment program (Brener, Resnick, Ellard, et al., 2009; Rieckmann, Daley, Fuller, et al., 2017). Given the important role that patient preference for treatment plays in engagement and retention in SUD treatment and consequently treatment outcomes (Friedrichs et al., 2016), SUD treatment systems should strive to provide a menu of evidence-based treatment approaches for patients to select, as far as this is feasible (Morin et al., 2017). Previous literature has suggested that treatment providers tend to offer a particular evidence-based psychotherapy with the majority of programs offering limited treatment options (Bradley & Kivlahan, 2014). Where limited options exist, treatment providers should consider expanding their menu of treatment modalities. Encouraging programs to offer a diverse set of evidence-based practices may enable greater patient choice while increasing the chance of addressing the multiple and complex service needs of patients.

11.5 Conclusion: Ensuring the quality of psychotherapy for substance use disorders

This chapter has reviewed several efficacious psychotherapies for the treatment of SUDs. Despite the availability of efficacious treatments, SUDs continue to be difficult to treat. Reviews suggest that abstinence from substance use is achieved in only 30%–50% of cases, treatments have a small overall effect size (Prendergast, Podus, Chang, et al., 2002), and treatment effects are often not long-lasting (Benishek, Dugosh, Kirby, et al., 2014). Therefore, there is room to improve the outcomes and quality of substance abuse treatment through ensuring the adoption and implementation of evidence-based therapies. Emerging evidence suggests that provider training in the psychotherapies outlined in this chapter along with ongoing coaching in these methods is essential for ensuring the sustained implementation of these evidence-based practices in LMIC (Rawson, Rataemane, Raetamane, et al., 2013) (see Chapter 3). This ongoing coaching may also help ensure intervention fidelity and the provision of quality services.

In addition to the broad dissemination of evidence-based psychotherapies, ensuring the quality of SUD treatment will require international and national treatment standards to be defined and operationalized, quality assurance processes to be developed, and compliance to these standards to be monitored. A recent initiative to develop global standards for SUD treatment quality, accompanied by quality assurance tools, may help countries realize these objectives (United Nations Office on Drugs and Crime, 2016). At a national level, these efforts to improve SUD treatment quality can be aided further by implementing performance measurement systems for SUD treatment. These systems collect data on a standardized set of indicators to monitor treatment quality, identify areas for treatment strengthening, and evaluate efforts to improve service functioning (Ferri & Griffiths, 2015; Garnick, Horgan, Acevedo, et al., 2012; Myers, Sorsdahl, et al., 2016; Myers, Williams, et al., 2016). Most LMIC currently lack performance measurement systems for SUD treatment. An exception is South Africa that has developed and implemented a system for assessing the outcomes and quality of publicly funded SUD treatment services (Myers, Williams, Johnson, et al., 2017). The South African experience has demonstrated that such systems are feasible to implement, acceptable, and appropriate for use in low-resource treatment settings. It has also demonstrated that these systems generate clinically useful data that can guide the design of treatment improvement interventions (Myers, Williams, Govender, et al., 2018). Given these promising findings, this system may provide a useful template for other LMIC to use when developing their own national performance measurement system for SUD treatment. In conclusion, efforts to disseminate and implement the evidence-based treatment approaches to SUD treatment described in this chapter should be accompanied by adequate training of providers in these practices, clear treatment standards, and ongoing monitoring of the outcomes and quality of treatment.

References

Ainscough, T. S., McNeill, A., Strang, J., et al. (2017). Contingency management interventions for non-prescribed drug use during treatment for opiate addiction: A systematic review and meta-analysis. *Drug and Alcohol Dependence*, *178*, 318–339.

American Psychiatric Association. (2013). *Diagnostic and statistical manual of mental disorders* (5th ed.). Washington, DC: American Psychiatric Association.

Apodaca, T. R., & Longabaugh, R. (2009). Mechanisms of change in motivational interviewing: A review and preliminary evaluation of the evidence. *Addiction*, *104*, 705–715.

Ball, S. A., Martino, S., Nich, C., et al. (2009). Site matters: Multisite randomized trial of motivational enhancement therapy in community drug abuse clinics. *Journal of Consulting and Clinical Psychology*, *77*, 336–345.

Benishek, L. A., Dugosh, K. L., Kirby, K. C., et al. (2014). Prize-based contingency management for the treatment of substance abusers: A meta-analysis. *Addiction*, *109*, 1426–1436.

Bowen, S., Witkiewitz, K., Dillworth, T., et al. (2016). Mindfulness meditation and substance use in an incarcerated population. *Psychology of Addictive Behaviors*, *20*, 343–347.

Bradley, K. A., & Kivlahan, D. R. (2014). Bringing patient-centered care to patients with alcohol use disorders. *Journal of the American Medical Association*, *311*, 1861–1862.

Brener, L., Resnick, I., Ellard, J., et al. (2009). Exploring the role of consumer participation in drug treatment. *Drug and Alcohol Dependence*, *105*, 172–175.

Burke, B. L., Arkowitz, H., & Menchola, M. (2003). The efficacy of motivational interviewing: A meta-analysis of controlled clinical trials. *Journal of Consulting and Clinical Psychology*, *71*, 843–861.

Carroll, K. M. (1996). Relapse prevention as a psychosocial treatment: A review of controlled clinical trials. *Experimental and Clinical Psychopharmacology*, *4*, 46–54.

Carroll, K. M. (2018). *A cognitive-behavioral approach: Treating cocaine addiction.* Rockville, MD: National Institute on Drug Abuse (NIH Publication 98-4308).

Carroll, K. M. (2014). Computerized cognitive-behavioral therapy. *Alcohol Research: Current Reviews*, *36*, 12–130.

Carroll, K. M., & Onken, L. S. (2005). Behavioral therapies for drug abuse. *American Journal of Psychiatry*, *162*, 1452–1460.

Carroll, K. M., Rounsaville, B. J., Nich, C., et al. (1994). One-year follow-up of psychotherapy and pharmacotherapy for cocaine dependence. Delayed emergence of psychotherapy effects. *Archives of General Psychiatry*, *51*, 989–997.

Chiesa, A., & Serretti, A. (2014). Are mindfulness-based interventions effective for substance use disorders? A systematic review of the evidence. *Substance Use & Misuse*, *49*, 492–512.

Davis, D. R., Kurti, A. N., Skelly, J. M., et al. (2016). A review of the literature on contingency management in the treatment of substance use disorders. *Preventive Medicine*, 2009–2014.

Degenhardt, L., Whiteford, H. A., Ferrari, A. J., et al. (2013). The global burden of disease attributable to illicit drug use: Results from the GBD 2010 study. *Lancet*, *382*, 1562–1574.

DiClemente, C., Corno, C. M., & Graydon, M. M. (2017). Motivational interviewing, enhancement, and brief interventions over the last decade: A review of reviews of efficacy and effectiveness. *Psychology of Addictive Behaviors*, *31*, 862–887.

Drapkin, M. L., Wilbourne, P., Manuel, J. K., et al. (2016). National dissemination of motivation enhancement therapy in the veterans health administration: Training program design and initial outcomes. *Journal of Substance Abuse Treatment*, *65*, 83–87.

Dunn, C., Deroo, L., & Rivara, F. P. (2001). The use of brief interventions adapted from motivational interviewing across behavioral domains: A systematic review. *Addiction*, *96*, 1725–1742.

Dutra, L., Stathopoulou, G., Basden, S. L., et al. (2008). A meta-analytic review of psychosocial interventions for substance use disorders. *American Journal of Psychiatry*, *165*, 179–187.

Farronato, N. S., Dürsteler-Macfarland, K. M., Wiesbeck, G. A., et al. (2013). A systematic review comparing cognitive-behavioral therapy and contingency management for cocaine dependence. *Journal of Addictive Diseases*, *32*, 274–287.

Ferri, M., & Griffiths, P. (2015). Good practice and quality standards. In N. el-guebaly et al. (Eds.), *Textbook of addiction treatment: International perspectives* (pp. 1337–1359). Italy: Springer-Verlag.

Friedrichs, A., Spies, M., Harter, M., et al. (2016). Patient preferences and shared decision making in the treatment of substance use disorders: A systematic review of the literature. *PLoS ONE*, *11*, e0145817.

Garland, E. L., Froeliger, B., & Howard, M. O. (2014). Effects of mindfulness-oriented recovery enhancement on reward responsiveness and opioid cue-reactivity. *Psychopharmacology*, *231*, 3229–3238.

Garland, E. L., Gaylord, S. A., Boettiger, C. A., et al. (2010). Mindfulness training modifies cognitive, affective, and physiological mechanisms implicated in alcohol dependence: Results of a randomized controlled pilot trial. *Journal of Psychoactive Drugs*, *82*, 177–192.

Garland, E. L., Manusov, E., Froeliger, B., et al. (2014). Mindfulness-oriented recovery enhancement for chronic pain and prescription opioid misuse: Results from an early-stage randomized controlled trial. *Journal of Consulting and Clinical Psychology*, *82*, 448–459.

Garnick, D. W., Horgan, C. M., Acevedo, A., et al. (2012). Performance measures for substance use disorders—What research is needed? *Addiction Science & Clinical Practice*, *7*, 18.

Goldberg, S. B., Tucker, R. P., Greene, P. A., et al. (2018). Mindfulness-based interventions for psychiatric disorders: A systematic review and meta-analysis. *Clinical Psychology Review*, *59*, 52–60.

Gouse, H., Magidson, J. F., Burnhams, W., et al. (2016). Implementation of cognitive-behavioral substance abuse treatment in Sub-Saharan Africa: Treatment engagement and abstinence at treatment exit. *PLoS ONE*, *11*, e0147900.

Hallgren, K. A., Dembe, A., Pace, B. T., et al. (2018). Variability in motivational interviewing adherence across sessions, providers, sites, and research contexts. *Journal of Substance Abuse Treatment*, *84*, 30–41.

Hartzler, B., Lash, S., Roll, J., et al. (2012). Contingency management in substance abuse treatment: A structured review of the evidence for its transportability. *Drug and Alcohol Dependence*, *122*, 1–10.

Hettema, J., Steele, J., & Miller, W. R. (2005). Motivational interviewing. *Annual Review of Clinical Psychology*, *1*, 91–111.

Hides, L., Samet, S., & Lubman, D. I. (2010). Cognitive behaviour therapy (CBT) for the treatment of co-occurring depression and substance use: Current evidence and directions for future research. *Drug and Alcohol Review*, *29*, 508–517.

Irvin, J. E., Bowers, C. A., Dunn, M. E., et al. (1999). Efficacy of relapse prevention: A meta-analytic review. *Journal of Consulting and Clinical Psychology*, *67*, 563–570.

Jiang, S., Wu, L., & Gao, X. (2017). Beyond face-to-face individual counseling: A systematic review on alternative modes of motivational interviewing in substance abuse treatment and prevention. *Addictive Behaviors*, *73*, 216–235.

Joseph, J., & Basu, D. (2017). Efficacy of brief interventions in reducing hazardous or harmful alcohol use in middle-income countries: Systematic review of randomized controlled trials. *Alcohol and Alcoholism*, *52*, 56–64.

Kadden, R., Carroll, K., Donovan, D., et al. (2003). *Volume 3: Cognitive-behavioral coping skills therapy manual: A clinical research guide for therapists treating individuals with alcohol abuse and dependence*. National Institute on Alcohol Abuse and Alcoholism Project MATCH Monograph Series: Rockville, MD.

Katz, D., & Toner, B. (2013). A systematic review of gender differences in the effectiveness of mindfulness-based treatments for substance use disorders. *Mindfulness*, *4*, 318–331.

Kirmayer, L. J. (2015). Mindfulness in cultural context. *Transcultural Psychiatry*, *52*, 447–469.

Lee, E. B., An, W., Levin, M. E., et al. (2015). An initial meta-analysis of acceptance and commitment therapy for treating substance use disorders. *Drug and Alcohol Dependence*, *155*, 1–7.

Li, W., Howard, M. O., Garland, E. L., et al. (2017). Mindfulness treatment for substance misuse: A systematic review and meta-analysis. *Journal of Substance Abuse Treatment*, *75*, 62–96.

Lim, S. S., Vos, T., Flaxman, A. D., et al. (2012). A comparative risk assessment of burden of disease and injury attributable to 67 risk factors and risk factor clusters in 21 regions, 1990–2010: A systematic analysis for the global burden of disease study 2010. *Lancet*, *380*, 2224–2260.

Lussier, J. P., Heil, S. H., Mongeon, J. A., et al. (2006). A meta-analysis of voucher-based reinforcement therapy for substance use disorders. *Addiction*, *101*, 192–203.

Magidson, J. F., Gouse, H., Burnhams, W., et al. (2017). Beyond methamphetamine: Documenting the implementation of the Matrix model of substance use treatment for opioid users in a South African setting. *Addictive Behaviors, 66*, 132–137.

Magill, M., Apodaca, T. R., Borsari, B., et al. (2017). A meta-analysis of motivational interviewing process: Technical, relational and conditional process models of change. *Journal of Consulting and Clinical Psychology*. https://doi.org/10.1037/ccp0000250.

Magill, M., & Ray, L. A. (2009). Cognitive-behavioral treatment with adult alcohol and illicit drug users: A meta-analysis of randomized controlled trials. *Journal of Studies on Alcohol and Drugs, 70*(4), 516–527.

Marlatt, G., & Donovan, J. R. (2005). *Relapse prevention: Maintenance strategies in the treatment of addictive behaviors* (2nd ed.). New York: Guilford Press.

McHugh, R. K., Hearon, B., & Otto, M. (2018). Cognitive-behavioral therapy for substance use disorders. *The Psychiatric Clinics of North America, 33*, 511–525.

McKay, J. R., Lynch, K. G., Coviello, D., et al. (2010). Randomized trial of continuing care enhancements for cocaine dependent patients following initial engagement. *Journal of Consulting and Clinical Psychology, 78*, 111–120.

Miller, W. R. (1996). Motivational interviewing: Research, practice and puzzles. *Addictive Behaviors, 61*, 835–842.

Miller, W. R., & Rollnick, S. (1992). In *Motivational interviewing: Preparing people to change addictive behavior*. New York: Guildford Press.

Miller, W. R., & Rollnick, S. (2002). *Motivational interviewing: Preparing people for change* (2nd ed.). Guilford Press.

Miller, W. R., & Rose, G. S. (2009). Towards a theory of motivational interviewing. *American Psychologist, 64*, 527–537.

Morin, J. F. G., Harris, M., & Conrod, P. J. (2017). *A review of CBT treatments for substance use disorders*. Oxford: Oxford University Press.

Moyers, T. B., & Houck, J. (2011). Combining motivational interviewing with cognitive-behavioural treatments for substance abuse: Lessons from the COMBINE research project. *Cognitive and Behavioural Practice, 18*, 38–45.

Myers, B., Louw, J., & Pasche, S. (2010). Inequitable access to substance abuse treatment services in Cape Town, South Africa. *Substance Abuse Treatment, Prevention, and Policy, 5*, 28.

Myers, B., & Sorsdahl, K. (2014). Addressing substance use within primary health care settings in South Africa: Opportunities and challenges. *Addicta: The Turkish Journal on Addictions, 1*, 80–94.

Myers, B., Sorsdahl, K., Morojele, N. K., et al. (2016). "In this thing I have everything I need": Perceived acceptability of a brief alcohol-focused intervention for people living with HIV. *AIDS Care, 19*, 1–5.

Myers, B., Williams, P. P., Govender, R., et al. (2018). A mixed methods evaluation of a performance measurement system for South Africa's substance abuse treatment services. *Journal of Studies on Alcohol and Drugs*.

Myers, B., Williams, P. P., Johnson, K., et al. (2016). Providers' perceptions of the implementation of a performance measurement system for substance abuse treatment: A process evaluation of the Service Quality Measures initiative. *South African Medical Journal, 106*, 308–311.

Myers, B., Williams, P. P., Johnson, K., et al. (2017). Readiness to adopt a performance measurement system for substance abuse treatment: Findings from the Service Quality Measures Initiative. *South African Medical Journal, 107*, 160–164.

Obert, J. L., Hamilton Brown, A., Zweben, J., et al. (2005). When treatment meets research: Clinical perspectives from the CSAT methamphetamine treatment project. *Journal of Substance Abuse Treatment, 28*, 231–237.

Obert, J. L., London, E. D., & Rawson, R. A. (2002). Incorporating brain research findings into standard treatment: An example using the Matrix Model. *Journal of Substance Abuse Treatment*, *23*, 107–113.

O'Donnell, A., Anderson, P., Newbury-Birch, D., et al. (2014). The impact of brief alcohol interventions in primary healthcare: A systematic review of reviews. *Alcohol and Alcoholism*, *49*, 66–78.

Pace, B. T., Dembe, A., Soma, C. S., et al. (2017). A multivariate meta-analysis of motivational interviewing process and outcome. *Psychology of Addictive Behaviors*, *31*, 524–533.

Pasche, S., Kleintjes, S., Wilson, D., et al. (2015). Improving addiction care in South Africa: Development and challenges to implementing training in addictions care at the University of Cape Town. *International Journal of Mental Health and Addiction*, *13*, 322–332.

Petry, N. M., DePhilippis, D., Rash, C. J., et al. (2014). Nationwide dissemination of contingency management: The Veterans Administration initiative. *American Journal on Addictions*, *23*, 205–210.

Pilling, S., Strang, J., & Gerada, C. (2007). NICE: Psychosocial interventions and opioid detoxification for drug misuse: Summary of NICE guidance. *BMJ*, *335*, 203–205.

Potenza, M. N., Sofuoglu, M., Carroll, K. M., et al. (2011). Neuroscience of behavioral and pharmacological treatments for addictions. *Neuron*, *69*, 695–710.

Prendergast, M., Podus, D., Chang, E., et al. (2002). The effectiveness of drug abuse treatment: A meta-analysis of comparison group studies. *Drug and Alcohol Dependence*, *67*, 53–72.

Prendergast, M., Podus, D., Finney, J., et al. (2006). Contingency management for treatment of substance use disorders: A meta-analysis. *Addiction*, *101*, 1546–1560.

Rathod, S., Pinninto, N., Irfan, M., et al. (2017). Mental health service provision in low- and middle-income countries. *Health Service Insights*, *10*, 1178632917694350.

Rawson, R., Shoptaw, S., Obert, J. L., et al. (1995). An intensive outpatient approach for cocaine abuse: The Matrix model. *Journal of Substance Abuse Treatment*, *12*, 117–127.

Rawson, R. A., Huber, A., McCann, M., et al. (2002). A comparison of contingency management and cognitive-behavioral approaches during methadone maintenance treatment for cocaine dependence. *Archives of General Psychiatry*, *59*, 817–824.

Rawson, R. A., Marinelli-Casey, P. J., & Anglin, M. D. (2004). A multi-site comparison of psychosocial approaches for the treatments of methamphetamine dependence. *Addiction*, *99*, 708–717.

Rawson, R. A., Rataemane, S., Raetamane, L., et al. (2013). Dissemination and implementation of cognitive behavioral therapy for stimulant dependence: A randomized trial comparison of 3 approaches. *Substance Abuse*, *34*, 108–117.

Rieckmann, T., Daley, M., Fuller, B. E., et al. (2017). Client and counselor attitudes toward the use of medications for treatment of opioid dependence. *Journal of Substance Abuse Treatment*, *32*, 207–215.

Rutherford, H. L. V., Mayes, L. C., & Potenza, M. N. (2010). Neurobiology of adolescent substance use disorders: Implications for prevention and treatment. *Child and Adolescent Psychiatric Clinics of North America*, *19*, 479–492.

Schmitz, J. M., Oswald, L. M., Jacks, S. D., et al. (1997). Relapse prevention treatment for cocaine dependence: Group vs. individual format. *Addictive Behaviors*, *22*, 405–418.

Schwalbe, C. S., Oh, H. Y., & Zweben, A. (2014). Sustaining motivational interviewing: A meta-analysis of training studies. *Addiction*, *109*, 1287–1294.

Shearer, J., Tie, H., & Byford, S. (2015). Economic evaluations of contingency management in illicit drug misuse programmes: A systematic review. *Drug and Alcohol Review*, *34*, 289–296.

Simpson, D. D. (2004). A conceptual framework for drug treatment process and outcomes. *Journal of Substance Abuse Treatment*, *27*, 99–121.

Sinha, R. (2018). Chronic stress, drug use and vulnerability to addiction. *Addiction Reviews, 1141*, 105–130.

Skinner, B. F. (1938). *The behavior of organisms: An experimental analysis.* New York: Appleton-Century.

Smedslund, G., Berg, R. C., Hammerstrøm, K. T., et al. (2011). Motivational interviewing for substance abuse. *Cochrane Database of Systematic Reviews. 11*, CD008063. https://doi.org/10.1002/14651858.CD008063.pub2.

Sorsdahl, K., Myers, B., Ward, C., et al. (2014). Screening and brief interventions for substance use in emergency departments in the Western Cape province of South Africa: Views of health care professionals. *International Journal of Injury Control and Safety Promotion, 21*, 236–243.

Sorsdahl, K., Myers, B., Ward, C. L., et al. (2015). Adapting a blended motivational interviewing and problem-solving intervention to address risky substance use amongst South Africans. *Psychotherapy Research*, (4), 435–444.

Sorsdahl, K., Stein, D. J., Corrigall, J., et al. (2015). The efficacy of a blended motivational interviewing and problem solving therapy intervention to reduce substance use among patients presenting for emergency services in South Africa: A randomized controlled trial. *Substance Abuse Treatment, Prevention, and Policy, 10*(46).

Tang, Y., Tang, R., & Posner, M. I. (2016). Mindfulness meditation improves emotional regulation and reduces drug abuse. *Drug and Alcohol Dependence, 163*, s13–s18.

Tapper, K. (2018). Mindfulness and craving: Effects and mechanisms. *Clinical Psychology Review, 59*, 101–117.

United Nations Office on Drugs and Crime. (2016). *International quality standards for the treatment of drug use disorders. Available from https://www.unodc.org/documents/commissions/CND/CND_Sessions/CND_59/ECN72016_CRP4_V1601463.pdf (accessed 16.09.17).*

United Nations Office on Drugs and Crime. (2017). *World drug report 2017.* Vienna: United Nations Office on Drugs and Crime. Available from *http:/www.unodc.org/documents/wdr2017/World_Drug_Report_2014_exsexsum.pdf* (accessed 16.01.18).

Whiteford, H. A., Degenhardt, L., Rehm, J., et al. (2013). The global burden of mental and substance use disorders. *The Lancet, 382*, 1575–1586.

Witkiewitz, K., Bowen, S., Harrop, N., et al. (2014). Mindfulness-based treatment to prevent addictive behavior relapse: Theoretical models and hypothesized mechanisms of change. *Substance Use & Misuse, 49*, 513–524.

Witkiewitz, K., & Marlatt, G. A. (2004). Relapse prevention for alcohol and drug problems: That Was Zen, this is Tao. *American Psychologist, 59*, 224–235.

Witkiewitz, K., & Marlatt, G. A. (2007). Overview of relapse prevention. In *Therapist's guide to evidence-based relapse prevention* (pp. 3–17).

Witkiewitz, K., Marlatt, G. A., & Walker, D. (2005). Mindfulness-based relapse prevention for alcohol and substance use disorders. *Journal of Cognitive Psychotherapy, 19*, 211–228.

World Health Organization. (2014). *Global status report on alcohol and health 2014.* Geneva: World Health Organization. Available from *http:/www.who.int/substance_abuse/publications/alcohol_2014/en/* (accessed 16.01.18).

Zilverstand, A., Parvaz, M. A., Moeller, S. J., et al. (2016). Cognitive interventions for addiction medicine: Understanding the underlying neurobiological mechanisms. *Progress in Brain Research, 224*, 285–304.

Section D

Clinical populations

Chronic physical diseases

12

Jessica F. Magidson, Kristen S. Regenauer*[†], *Lena S. Andersen*[‡], *Steven A. Safren*[§]

*Department of Psychology, University of Maryland, College Park, MD, United States, [†]Behavioral Medicine Service, Department of Psychiatry, Massachusetts General Hospital, Boston, MA, United States, [‡]HIV Mental Health Research Unit, Department of Psychiatry and Mental Health, University of Cape Town, Cape Town, South Africa, [§]Department of Psychology, University of Miami, Coral Gables, FL, United States

12.1 Introduction

12.1.1 Global burden of disease

Chronic diseases, defined as conditions that are incurable, have a long duration (National Health Council, 2014), are slow in progression, and require medical treatment, account for a growing proportion of the global disease burden (Bernell & Howard, 2016; World Health Organization, 2017a) and are among the top leading causes of deaths and disability worldwide (Kassebaum, Arora, Barber, et al., 2016; WHO, 2014). Noncommunicable chronic diseases, including cardiovascular diseases, cancer, chronic respiratory diseases, and diabetes, are responsible for the greatest number of noncommunicable disease deaths globally (WHO, 2014). In the Unites States, almost half of the adult population lives with a chronic disease, and just over 30% lives with multiple chronic diseases. Yet, the total global burden of disease is borne mostly by countries in the African and Southeast Asian regions of the world, in large part due to the chronic health burden of HIV/AIDS and tuberculosis (TB).

12.1.2 Importance of adherence in chronic conditions

Managing chronic conditions is typically lifelong and requires a range of different and, at times, complex behaviors, including medication adherence and continued engagement in medical care. Suboptimal medication adherence can compromise the effectiveness of treatment and result in adverse health outcomes including medication resistance and mortality (DiMatteo, Giordani, Lepper, et al., 2002; Gonzalez, Batchelder, Psaros, et al., 2011; Gonzalez, Peyrot, McCarl, et al., 2008; Uthman, Magidson, Safren, et al., 2014). To reduce the global burden of chronic disease, behavioral interventions are needed to improve nonadherence, especially in the context of psychiatric comorbidity.

Global Mental Health and Psychotherapy. https://doi.org/10.1016/B978-0-12-814932-4.00012-4

12.1.3 Self-management in chronic disease care

Unlike acute conditions, the majority of chronic illness management occurs outside of formal health-care settings (Swendeman, Ingram, & Rotheram-Borus, 2009). Individuals living with chronic diseases must take an active role in disease management, including adhering to medication, monitoring and interpreting chronic disease symptoms, coping with new social and economic challenges, and altering behaviors on a daily basis to improve length and quality of life (Swendeman et al., 2009; Turner & Kelly, 2000; White, 2001). These responsibilities, in addition to physical limitations associated with living with a chronic disease, are factors that contribute to psychological distress and point to the need for addressing psychiatric comorbidity in the context of integrated behavioral interventions.

12.1.4 Role of psychotherapy in chronic disease management

Evidence-based psychological interventions have been tailored to focus on people living with chronic diseases (Safren, Gonzalez, & Soroudi, 2007; Vranceanu, Safren, & Greer, 2017). Adapting treatment to the needs of these individuals is important because (a) those with chronic diseases may have unique struggles that lead to added psychological distress and (b) requirements of chronic disease self-management may be disrupted in the context of psychological distress, further exacerbating physical symptoms of a chronic condition. Developing and adapting evidence-based psychotherapies for patients with chronic diseases are important to improving both mental and physical health.

Psychotherapies for chronic diseases can be disease-specific or integrated, such that the therapy may address universal self-management skills across chronic conditions (i.e., skills to treat depression, communication with providers, problem-solving, and goal setting; Swendeman et al., 2009). While integrated programs have been effective in different parts of the world, for instance, the United Kingdom (Kennedy, Reeves, Bower, et al., 2007), Australia (Swerissen, Belfrage, Weeks, et al., 2006), China (Fu, Ding, McGowan, et al., 2006), and Cambodia (Janssens, Van Damme, Raleigh, et al., 2007), chronic disease management also benefits from disease-specific skills (Swendeman et al., 2009). Certain conditions may have unique self-care needs, for instance, the importance of on-time adherence to antiretroviral therapy (ART) for the treatment of HIV/AIDS, which is especially crucial in settings where ART regimen options are limited, as we focus on later in this chapter.

12.1.5 Chapter overview

In this chapter, we first provide a framework for understanding the outcomes and the role of psychotherapy in chronic disease management, including the application to low- and middle-income countries (LMIC). Next, we highlight lessons learned from the HIV epidemic and how they can be leveraged across chronic conditions. Specifically, we address task sharing models for adherence support that have now been utilized broadly for global mental health. We also provide examples of implementing evidence-based psychotherapies for adherence for HIV/AIDS in sub-Saharan Africa (SSA) using a task sharing model and demonstrate how this can be integrated into other evidence-based interventions to address co-occurring psychiatric disorders. Finally, we end this chapter with future directions, including the role of technology to support adherence across chronic conditions.

12.2 Framework for conceptualizing outcomes in chronic disease management

When evaluating the effectiveness of psychotherapies in chronic disease management, several outcomes can be considered. For instance, effectiveness can be based on physical factors (e.g., does one's physical health improve after the intervention?), psychological factors (e.g., do psychological symptoms comorbid with the chronic disease reduce after the intervention?), behavioral factors (e.g., does medication adherence improve after the intervention?), social factors (e.g., does communication with one's health-care provider improve after the intervention?), and structural factors (e.g., is an individual more easily able to access the appropriate health-care services after the intervention?). An established framework to evaluate psychotherapy for chronic disease management groups these factors into three broad types of outcomes: improvements in physical health and physical health support, improvements in psychological functioning, and improvements in social relationships (Swendeman et al., 2009; White, 2001).

12.2.1 Physical health

Improvements in physical health and physical health support focus on patients' abilities to manage physical factors associated with their chronic disease. This may include patients' understanding of how their behaviors impact their diseases; participation in health-supporting behaviors (e.g., exercising, eating healthy, and avoiding substance use); adherence to their treatment regimen (e.g., medication adherence); ability to correctly monitor their physical health status and make decisions based on this monitoring (e.g., checking one's insulin and taking proper steps if one's insulin levels are too high or too low); knowledge of available and appropriate treatments and services; and ability to prevent transmission of chronic disease (Swendeman et al., 2009).

12.2.2 Psychological functioning

Improvements in psychological functioning focus on improving the psychological states and well-being of individuals living with a chronic condition. Outcomes may include patients' feelings of self-efficacy in managing their chronic condition, cognitive skills of disease management (e.g., cognitive ability to plan, make decisions, and problem-solve around barriers to adherence), identity (e.g., how well they integrate health-promoting behaviors with their values), and psychological distress (e.g., reducing their levels of anxiety or depression) (Swendeman et al., 2009). Psychotherapies focusing on psychological functioning often emphasize the unique struggles and psychiatric symptom manifestation that individuals living with chronic disease may experience (e.g., depression in chronic conditions) (Vranceanu et al., 2017).

12.2.3 Social relationships

Improvements in social relationships focus on how individuals with chronic diseases interact with their health-care providers, families, friends, and communities. For instance, studies may measure how collaborative patients are with health-care professionals (e.g., how active they are in disease decision-making or how strong their communication skills are), how patients feel about disclosing that they have a chronic disease to others, how patients cope with the stigma often associated with chronic diseases, how supportive patients' social and familial relationships are (e.g., how their relationships contribute to healthy decision-making or help them cope with stress), and how strong their social support networks are (Swendeman et al., 2009). Interventions may include peer leaders, or people living successfully with a chronic disease, in order to create healthy social relationships and model healthy social behavior (e.g., Lorig, Ritter, & Plant, 2005).

12.3 Chronic disease management psychotherapies in low- and middle-income countries

While several studies have examined the effect of psychotherapy on many types of chronic disease management in high-income countries (HIC), such as the United States (e.g., Safren, Gonzalez, Wexler, et al., 2014), there has been more limited research evaluating a range of chronic disease management strategies in LMIC. There are many important considerations when adapting chronic disease interventions from HIC to LMIC, including who should deliver the program, the cost of the program, and necessary cultural adaptations. A robust literature around the development and expansion of chronic disease management programs for HIV/AIDS in LMIC and especially in SSA can guide future efforts for adapting and scaling other evidence-based chronic disease self-management interventions in LMIC. Next, we provide a brief overview of chronic disease management related to HIV/AIDS in SSA and how these scale-up efforts can inform approaches to other chronic conditions in LMIC.

12.3.1 Lessons learned from the HIV epidemic

In SSA, the scale-up of HIV biomedical and behavioral health services represents the largest scale chronic disease infrastructure to incorporate attention to integrated models of care and behavioral adherence support. There are numerous lessons learned from this framework that can be a model for addressing other chronic diseases in resource-limited settings (e.g., Rabkin & El-Sadr, 2011). As such, we focus the next part of this chapter on the scale-up of HIV services in SSA, the area with the highest burden in the world.

Then, we highlight the ways in which lessons learned from these care models are models for addressing behavioral health needs across other conditions.

12.4 HIV epidemic in sub-Saharan Africa

SSA bears the greatest burden of the HIV epidemic in the world, with approximately 70% of all people living with HIV/AIDS (PLWH) (UNAIDS, 2017). Likewise, of the approximate 5000 new HIV infections in the world each day, 64% of these are in SSA (UNAIDS, 2017). Within SSA, South Africa (SA) has the greatest number of PLWH: approximately 7.1 million or about 20% of all PLWH in the world (UNAIDS, 2017). In 2006, the WHO called attention to the health-care workforce shortages in SSA and the need to expand and upskill the workforce to appropriately address the disease management needs related to the HIV epidemic in SSA (WHO, 2008).

12.4.1 Task shifting HIV treatment has changed the HIV epidemic in SSA

Universal access to HIV treatment and appropriate adherence support for ART rely heavily on "task shifting" or "task sharing" models of care (WHO, 2006). The WHO defines task shifting as the "process of delegation whereby tasks are moved, where appropriate, to less specialized health workers" (WHO, 2008). In response to the HIV epidemic in SSA, task shifting efforts are allocated for trained nurses, who are in greater supply than physicians, to prescribe ART rather than exclusively physicians. Further, less specialized health-care workers, such as lay adherence counselors and community health workers (CHWs), have also been incorporated into HIV care models to deliver a wide range of clinical services to support HIV treatment outcomes and further reduce the burden on more specialized professionals. More recently, task shifting models have been reconceptualized and often relabeled as "task sharing," that is, task *sharing* structures more specialized clinical teams around the lower level care workers to provide adequate training, support, and supervision. In task sharing, specific roles and responsibilities are delineated for each member of a clinical team and even for family members and the patients themselves (Padmanathan & De Silva, 2013). Further, care delivery is often structured so that resources are allocated where they are needed most: physicians and skilled nurses can attend to the most complex patients and provide ongoing supervision and training to other members of the care team.

Since 2005, there has been a significant decline in AIDS-related deaths in SSA due to the rapid increase in PLWH on treatment (UNAIDS, 2017). In fact, by 2016, SA alone had approximately 3.9 million people on ART (UNAIDS, 2017). This significant decline in deaths is largely accounted for by the increased availability and wide dissemination of ART via task sharing efforts. Additionally, task sharing has enabled patients to receive the behavioral support necessary for successful HIV treatment outcomes.

12.4.2 Importance of adherence for treatment and prevention

Medication adherence is essential across numerous chronic medical conditions and arguably most impactful on health outcomes in HIV/AIDS. Nonadherence and inconsistent patterns of adherence (e.g., interruptions in treatment and breaks from medication) are associated with increased likelihood of medication-resistant HIV strains, greater health complications, failure to achieve full viral suppression (Bangsberg, Perry, Charlebois, et al., 2001), increased risk of death (García de Olalla, Knobel, Carmona, et al., 2002), and greater likelihood of transmitting HIV to others (Cohen, Chen, McCauley, et al., 2011; Safren, Mayer, Ou, et al., 2015). In 2006, a meta-analysis (Mills, Nachega, Buchan, et al., 2006) looking at ART adherence in SSA found that approximately 23% of patients did not achieve optimal adherence (Mills et al., 2006). This is especially problematic given the limited availability of different ART regimens in SSA; if a patient develops resistance to their ART regimen, they may not have other treatments available to them (Palombi, Marazzi, Guidotti, et al., 2009).

12.4.3 Task sharing HIV adherence support

In HIV care in SSA, nurses and/or CHWs distribute HIV medication, provide ongoing adherence counseling, facilitate engagement in care among those who are struggling, and can increase patient access to other behavioral health services. Specifically, ART adherence counseling has been task shared to lay health counselors (Callaghan, Ford, & Schneider, 2010; Mdege, Chindove, & Ali, 2013; Mwai, Mburu, Torpey, et al., 2013), who provide psychoeducation, preparation support for patients initiating ART, and ongoing adherence support for patients engaged in HIV care. Importantly, this support can be intensified when someone is struggling with adherence. Like other CHWs, adherence counselors typically do not have formal training or education, and their training is often supported by nongovernmental intermediaries (Lewin, Dick, Pond, et al., 2005). However, many CHW programs have faced sustainability and quality of care difficulties (Berman, Gwatkin, & Burger, 1987; Gilson, Walt, Heggenhougen, et al., 1989; Hermann, Van Damme, Pariyo, et al., 2009; Mwai et al., 2013), and few studies have described or evaluated task sharing adherence counseling in routine clinical services (Dewing, Mathews, Schaay, et al., 2013). Continued efforts are needed to evaluate how to best use task sharing models to deliver empirically supported interventions across chronic conditions in resource-limited settings.

12.4.3.1 Empirical support for task sharing to improve behavioral HIV outcomes

Uptake of HIV treatment, engagement in HIV care, and optimal ART adherence are three of the most important factors required for long-term success of HIV treatment (and thereby prevention). Each of these behavioral factors appears to benefit from task sharing models (Mwai et al., 2013). To date, task sharing in HIV care has been shown to improve clinical care, including reducing loss to follow-up and maintaining the same survival rates over 1 year as physician-led models (Iwu & Holzemer, 2014). Further, there is evidence that task sharing may aid physician time savings (Callaghan et al., 2010; Mdege et al., 2013; Mwai et al., 2013; Price & Binagwaho, 2010) and cost savings. CHW involvement also has been shown to improve retention in care and quality of life among PLWH (Ledikwe, Kejelepula, Maupo, et al., 2013; Mwai et al., 2013). One study found that individuals with CHW adherence support picked up their medication 95% of the time versus 67% for individuals without CHW support (Igumbor, Scheepers, Ebrahim, et al., 2011).

12.4.4 Addressing co-occurring psychiatric conditions in HIV to improve self-care

Globally, psychiatric conditions commonly co-occur among PLWH and can significantly interfere with HIV-related self-care. This has been documented in SSA, namely, with major depressive disorder and alcohol use disorders (AUDs) (Nakimuli-Mpungu, Bass, Alexandre, et al., 2012; Uthman, Magidson, Safren, et al., 2014). In fact, a meta-analysis focused on depression and AUDs among PLWH in SSA found an 18% pooled estimate rate of major depression, and 31% of individuals across studies had elevated depressive symptoms (Nakimuli-Mpungu et al., 2012). Although documented less frequently than depression, rates of AUDs also reach up to 31% (Nakimuli-Mpungu et al., 2012).

12.4.5 Task sharing for mental health in HIV to improve self-care

Task sharing efforts initially used to expand access to HIV services have now been applied to expand access to mental health treatment (Magidson, Gouse, Psaros, et al., 2017). Low-income countries more typically have less than one psychiatric specialist per 100,000 people across all provider types (Saxena, Thornicroft, Knapp, et al., 2007). Behavioral health task sharing models may be used to specifically address the ways in which psychiatric symptoms interfere with self-care in chronic conditions, for instance, integrated, cognitive behavioral therapy (CBT) treatment models to improve adherence to HIV/AIDS.

12.5 Empirical support for cognitive behavioral therapy for chronic disease management

Several types of psychotherapies have been evaluated to support individuals manage and cope with the stressors of living with a chronic condition, including CBT, dialectical behavioral therapy (DBT), positive psychology, mindfulness meditation (Purdy, 2013), and acceptance and commitment therapy (ACT) (Graham, Gouick, Krahé, et al., 2016; Purdy, 2013). CBT-based treatments have the strongest empirical support for supporting chronic disease management compared with other psychotherapies (for instance, Dickens, Cherrington, Adeyemi, et al., 2013; Lett, Davidson, & Blumenthal, 2005; Li, Xu, Hu, et al., 2017), especially in LMIC (Magidson et al., 2017).

12.5.1 CBT for adherence

CBT, as introduced elsewhere in this volume, has strong empirical support as a brief type of psychological therapy to improve medication adherence across chronic medical conditions (Safren et al., 2007; Vranceanu et al., 2017), including diabetes (Safren et al., 2014) and HIV/AIDS (Safren & Otto, 1999). In HIV, a meta-analysis of randomized controlled trials (RCTs) evaluating behavioral medication adherence interventions (74% US-based trials) conducted by Simoni et al. found that most interventions (79%) featured components of CBT (Simoni, Pearson, Pantalone, et al., 2006). Specifically, many of these trials included psychoeducation, motivational interviewing, healthy coping strategies, or cognitive restructuring, as well as behavioral CBT strategies (activity scheduling and cue reminders), and 58% of these studies included at least three CBT components. Further, interventions that included CBT components demonstrated greater improvements in adherence than the interventions that did not. Yet, in a review of HIV medication adherence RCTs in SSA (Bärnighausen, Chaiyachati, Chimbindi, et al., 2011), very few, if any, studies used evidence-based CBT approaches.

12.5.1.1 Integrated CBT interventions for adherence and co-occurring conditions

CBT also has empirical support for improving adherence in combination with other evidence-based CBT interventions for co-occurring conditions. Prior research (e.g., Safren, Otto, Worth, et al., 2001) has demonstrated that to achieve improvements in adherence when co-occurring psychiatric symptoms, such as depression, are present, it is important to also address the symptoms of depression. There is support for treatment approaches that integrate CBT for adherence and depression in diabetes (Safren et al., 2014), HIV/AIDS (Safren et al., 2009, 2016), and among individuals with co-occurring depression, substance use, and HIV (Daughters, Magidson, Schuster, et al., 2010; Safren, O'Cleirigh, Bullis, et al., 2012). Empirical support also has accumulated for this integrated CBT approach to address adherence and depression simultaneously in sub-Saharan Africa (Abas, Nyamayaro, Bere, et al., 2018; Andersen, Magidson, O'Cleirigh, et al., 2016).

12.5.2 CBT appealing for task sharing

Meta-analyses show that the majority of the empirical support for CBT for adherence has come from studies in which interventionists were highly trained. For example, Simoni et al. (2006) found that approximately half of studies used medical providers (i.e., physicians or nurses), and 26% of studies used trained psychologists, with the majority of these providers being designated research staff. That being said, there is accumulating empirical support for task sharing models of CBT for adherence. CBT's structured, time-limited approach is appealing for the demands of task sharing to improve ease of training and supervision (Papas, Sidle, Martino, et al., 2010).

Further, CBT offers a clear model for structured training and support to facilitate task sharing, which is important for successful task sharing models. In the next section, we provide a "case example" of adapting CBT for HIV/AIDS self-care in SSA to demonstrate how this work can inform efforts across other chronic conditions and settings.

12.5.3 Case example: Adapting "Life-Steps" to improve ART adherence in South Africa

South Africa (SA) has one of the highest HIV/AIDS burdens in the world. To support ART adherence, lay counselors have been integrated into primary HIV care as "adherence counselors." Adherence counselors receive several weeks of training from the People Development Center (PDC) (Western Cape Government, 2017). Historically, counselors had been trained in Egan's "skilled helper" model of counseling. However, this approach brought some challenges, including a lack of structure to the counseling sessions and the tendency for counselors to give advice rather than identifying potential barriers to adherence and problem-solving ways to overcome them (Dewing et al., 2013). There was a need for an evidence-based, structured adherence intervention to be implemented, tested, and disseminated by adherence counselors in primary HIV care.

Life-Steps is an evidence-based, structured adherence intervention that has accumulated empirical support in the United States (Safren & Otto, 1999) and abroad (e.g., Abas et al., 2018; Andersen et al., 2016; Bere, Nyamayaro, Magidson, et al., 2016; Simoni, Chen, Huh, et al., 2011). It consists of 10 informational, problem-solving, and cognitive behavioral steps. Each step addresses a potential barrier to adherence using a standardized format: (1) set the goal, (2) identify potential barriers to reaching the goal, and (3) formulate a plan and backup plan to overcome the barrier.

Formative research was initiated in 2009 to culturally adapt Life-Steps for PLWH in SA. Based on research and in consultation with local and international health providers and stakeholders, cultural adaptations were made. Modifications included using comprehensible language, using culturally appropriate examples, and adding locally relevant adherence barriers, such problem-solving around social support (i.e., identifying someone to support them in their treatment) and alcohol/substance use (i.e., finding ways to adhere to ART while using substances) (Andersen et al., 2016).

To improve the retention rates without compromising postinitiation adherence rates, a working group led by Médecins Sans Frontières designed a revised counseling model that integrated TB counseling and reduced time taken to initiate ART. The team piloted the model, consisting of the Life-Steps intervention, at a primary care clinic run by the City of Cape Town. Over 96% of patients were initiated on ART, and most were initiated less than a week after being deemed eligible. Of those initiated, 85.9% were retained in care after 6 months, and 94.4% were virally suppressed. These rates are higher than previous rates documented in this community (Wilkinson, Duvivier,

Patten, et al., 2015). Consequently, in 2015, this new counseling model became official Western Province policy and was endorsed in the national adherence guidelines (Médecins Sans Frontières, 2015). This example depicts a local adaptation of an evidence-based CBT intervention to support adherence that included plans for sustainability and scale-up.

12.5.4 Summary and considerations for task shifting CBT interventions

Research on task shifting CBT for behavioral health needs is still in its early phases. However, the above case example suggests that it may be a feasible, sustainable solution for addressing adherence in resource-limited settings. In the future, lay counselors' abilities to deliver more complicated integrated interventions that focus on both psychiatric symptoms and self-care outcomes in chronic conditions should be examined, for this will clarify the interventions that paraprofessionals are best suited to deliver. Intervention decisions will likely need to weigh the advantages and disadvantages of incorporating multiple treatment targets into an integrated treatment protocol (i.e., improved efficiency yet also added complexity that may hinder feasibility or acceptability for training and supervision).

12.6 Application of cognitive behavioral therapy for other chronic diseases

As mentioned above, lessons learned from HIV/AIDS adherence support can be translated to other chronic conditions, including diabetes and cardiovascular diseases (CVDs), which also require intensive adherence and behavioral support (Rabkin & El-Sadr, 2011). The subsequent sections outline the application of CBT for diabetes management and cardiovascular disease more broadly and the limited empirical support to date in LMIC.

12.6.1 CBT for diabetes management

Diabetes mellitus is one of the most common chronic diseases across virtually all countries, and by 2030, it is predicted that 552 million people will be living with diabetes (Whiting, Guariguata, Weil, et al., 2011). Additionally, people living with diabetes are about twice as likely to have depression as people without diabetes (Anderson, Freedland, Clouse, et al., 2001). This is problematic on many levels, as depression is associated with poor physical health outcomes in people living with diabetes (e.g., De la Roca-Chiapas, Hernandez-Gonzalez, Candelario, et al., 2013; Egede, 2005; Lustman & Clouse, 2005).

There is evidence that CBT can effectively reduce depression and fasting glucose in diabetic participants with depression (Li et al., 2017). For instance, CBT for adherence and depression (CBT-AD) includes Life-Steps plus CBT for depression to improve adherence and depression among patients with uncontrolled type 2 diabetes in the

United States (Safren et al., 2014). In an RCT evaluating CBT-AD to treatment as usual plus Life-Steps only, CBT-AD resulted in significantly better adherence, lower depression, and better glycemic control following treatment compared with treatment as usual plus Life-Steps only (Safren et al., 2014). At a 12-month follow-up, participants in CBT-AD continued to show better adherence and glycemic control than enhanced treatment as usual (ETAU); however, there were no differences in depression.

A 2017 systematic review and meta-analysis of RCTs of CBT for diabetes and depression identified 10 relevant RCTs, for a total of 998 participants, and found that participants who received a CBT-based intervention had significant, long-term improvements in depression, quality of life, fasting glucose, and anxiety when compared with participants in control conditions (Li et al., 2017). Yet, participants in the CBT-based intervention groups did not have significant improvements in glycemic control or diabetes-related distress when compared with the control condition participants (Li et al., 2017). More research is needed to evaluate how to optimally deliver a CBT intervention to improve adherence, physical health outcomes, and psychological distress among individuals with diabetes.

12.6.1.1 Applications in LMIC

Diabetes is an important public health issue in LMIC; by 2030, it is predicted that the rate of diabetes will increase more greatly in LMIC than HIC, with the number of people over 60 years old living with diabetes more than doubling in LMIC (Whiting et al., 2011). Yet, despite these estimations, very few studies have examined the effect of CBT-based interventions to improve diabetes outcomes in LMIC (Li et al., 2017). In one study identified that was conducted in Iran, Sharif, Masoudi, Ghanizadeh, et al. (2014) randomized 60 patients living with type 2 diabetes into either a CBT group or a diabetes care as usual group. The CBT group included 10 patients in each group who met for an hour and a half twice per week for 4 weeks. CBT participants showed significant improvements in their depression from baseline at 2-week, 4-week, and 2-month postintervention, while control participants did not see this improvement. However, the intervention had no significant effect on participant's glycosylated hemoglobin levels (Sharif et al., 2014). As the number of people with diabetes grows (Whiting et al., 2011), more research is needed on evidence-based psychotherapies, such as CBT, to improve diabetes outcomes in LMIC.

12.6.2 CBT for cardiovascular disease management

Globally, CVDs are the number one cause of death (World Health Organization, 2017b). Concurrently, depression is common in people with CVDs, such as coronary heart disease, and is associated with factors such as mortality and poor health-related quality of life (Barth, Schumacher, & Herrmann-Lingen, 2004; Dickens et al., 2013; Nicholson, Kuper, & Hemingway, 2006; Stafford, Berk, Reddy, et al., 2007; Van Melle, De Jonge, Spijkerman, et al., 2004). Similarly, depression itself may be a risk factor for CVDs such as coronary heart disease (Carney, Freedland, Sheline, et al., 1997; Lett et al., 2005; Lett, Blumenthal, Babyak, et al., 2004).

Research suggests that CBT may be effective in helping people with CVDs. For instance, a systematic review and meta-regression of psychological interventions for depression in people with coronary heart disease found that only CBT was significantly associated with decreased depression in high-quality studies, although the effect size was small (Dickens et al., 2013). Likewise, other reviews have concluded that CBT may be the most effective way to treat depression in patients with coronary heart disease (Lett et al., 2005); other studies have found that participants with CVDs who received CBT-based therapies have significantly improved in depression over participants who did not receive CBT-based therapies (Berkman, Blumenthal, Burg, et al., 2003; Friedman, Thoresen, Gill, et al., 1986). One study found that cardiac patients who received a CBT-based intervention had reduced ischemia and were less likely to have a cardiac event during the study than cardiac patients who did not receive CBT (Blumenthal, Jiang, Babyak, et al., 1997). However, the evidence for CBT for physical health outcomes has been mixed (Berkman et al., 2003; Richards, Anderson, Jenkinson, et al., 2017) and may not be generalizable to diverse patient populations (Dickens et al., 2013; Lett et al., 2005; Schneiderman, Saab, Catellier, et al., 2004).

12.6.2.1 Low- and middle-income countries

Currently, very limited research has been done on evidence-based behavioral interventions such as CBT for CVDs in LMIC. In fact, a recent systematic review and meta-analysis examining RCTs of psychological interventions for coronary heart disease only identified 34 studies in the United States, Europe, and Australia and one study in China (Richards et al., 2017). With increasing rates of obesity in LMIC, including in SSA (Price, Crampin, Amberbir, et al., 2018), building evidence for the application of evidence-based behavioral interventions to address CVDs is imperative.

12.6.3 Use of technology to support task sharing for adherence in chronic conditions

Technology has the capacity to support the implementation of evidence-based behavioral health strategies for chronic conditions in resource-limited settings, for instance, using mobile health (mHealth). mHealth can potentially improve access to chronic illness management and self-care interventions by providing a platform that is universally accessible (Hartzler & Wetter, 2014). There are more than 7 billion mobile phone subscribers worldwide, and many of these reside in LMIC (International Telecommunications Union, 2017). Mobile phones can support patients in the management of their chronic illness by providing access to doctors or other health-care providers who are located elsewhere; by transmitting beneficial health information and/or supportive messages; and by sending medication, clinic appointment, and medication refill reminders (Hurt, Walker, Campbell, et al., 2016). Mobile phones also have the potential to improve the services provided by health-care providers by providing automated follow-up reminders, receiving alerts when patient's results are concerning, and providing access to specialists for expert advice and/or supervision (Hurt et al., 2016).

Promising research exists on the use of mHealth in supporting chronic illness management in HIV and hypertension in LMIC. In Kenya, an RCT found SMS adherence reminders to significantly improve self-reported adherence and viral suppression rates in patients initiating ART (Lester, Ritvo, Mills, et al., 2010). In Uganda, clinic attendance rates improved when ART users were contacted immediately after a missed appointment (Kunutsor, Walley, Katabira, et al., 2010). In Mexico and Honduras, patients who received automated weekly telephone calls from a server with reminders to check their blood pressure (BP) and to refill their medication experienced a greater decrease in their systolic blood pressure and reported better general health compared with the control condition (Piette, Datwani, Gaudioso, et al., 2012). In this study, health-care providers also received alerts when patients reported high BPs, poor adherence, or a nearly depleted supply of medication. Innovative mHealth approaches such as these show the enormous potential for mobile phones to be used for the implementation of behavioral health strategies in chronic conditions in regions of the world with significant resource limitations.

More extensive research is needed on mHealth interventions in LMIC (Hurt et al., 2016). High-quality research will be needed to foster government support and funding in mHealth systems (Tomlinson, Rotheram-Borus, Swartz, et al., 2013). Finally, technology may also facilitate task sharing of evidence-based mental health strategies by providing platforms to increase fidelity to intervention delivery (Remien, Mellins, Robbins, et al., 2013; Robbins, Mellins, Leu, et al., 2015). Additional research is needed to demonstrate how multimedia-based platforms may be a potentially useful strategy to promote sustainable implementation of task sharing models for self-care among individuals living with chronic conditions in resource-poor settings.

12.7 Conclusion

In conclusion, CBT interventions to address self-care in chronic conditions and co-occurring psychiatric symptoms that interfere with self-care are promising and essential strategy for managing chronic conditions in resource-limited settings. Task sharing models may be feasible and acceptable in the context of provider shortages. Addressing adherence and the prevalent, co-occurring mental health problems that interfere with adherence are key to the success of biomedical treatment options across chronic conditions, with implications for both treatment and prevention in conditions such as HIV/AIDS. Task shifting of biomedical treatment options, such as ART, can only succeed in the context of also addressing behavioral health needs and promoting adherence using task sharing models for evidence-based interventions. Future work evaluating technology-enhanced models of care may support the dissemination and implementation of evidence-based task sharing models for chronic disease management.

References

Abas, M., Nyamayaro, P., Bere, T., et al. (2018). Feasibility and acceptability of a task-shifted intervention to enhance adherence to HIV medication and improve depression in people living with HIV in Zimbabwe, a low income country in sub-Saharan Africa. *AIDS and Behavior*, *22*(1), 86–101.

Andersen, L. S., Magidson, J. F., O'Cleirigh, C., et al. (2016). A pilot study of a nurse-delivered cognitive behavioral therapy intervention (Ziphamandla) for adherence and depression in HIV in South Africa. *Journal of Health Psychology*.

Anderson, R. J., Freedland, K. E., Clouse, R. E., et al. (2001). The prevalence of comorbid depression in adults with diabetes: A meta-analysis. *Diabetes Care*, *24*(6), 1069–1078.

Bangsberg, D. R., Perry, S., Charlebois, E. D., et al. (2001). Non-adherence to highly active antiretroviral therapy predicts progression to AIDS. *AIDS*, *15*(9), 1181–1183.

Bärnighausen, T., Chaiyachati, K., Chimbindi, N., et al. (2011). Interventions to increase antiretroviral adherence in sub-Saharan Africa: A systematic review of evaluation studies. *The Lancet Infectious Diseases*, *11*(12), 942–951.

Barth, J., Schumacher, M., & Herrmann-Lingen, C. (2004). Depression as a risk factor for mortality in patients with coronary heart disease: A meta-analysis. *Psychosomatic Medicine*, *66*(6), 802–813.

Bere, T., Nyamayaro, P., Magidson, J. F., et al. (2016). Cultural adaptation of a cognitive-behavioural intervention to improve adherence to antiretroviral therapy among people living with HIV/AIDS in Zimbabwe: Nzira Itsva. *Journal of Health Psychology*, *22*(10), 1265–1276.

Berkman, L. F., Blumenthal, J., Burg, M., et al. (2003). Effects of treating depression and low perceived social support on clinical events after myocardial infarction: The enhancing recovery in coronary heart disease patients (ENRICHD) randomized trial. *JAMA*.

Berman, P. A., Gwatkin, D. R., & Burger, S. E. (1987). Community-based health workers: Head start or false start towards health for all? *Social Science & Medicine*, *25*(5), 443–459.

Bernell, S., & Howard, S. W. (2016). Use your words carefully: What is a chronic disease? *Front Public Health*, *4*.

Blumenthal, J. A., Jiang, W., Babyak, M. A., et al. (1997). Stress management and exercise training in cardiac patients with myocardial ischemia: Effects on prognosis and evaluation of mechanisms. *Archives of Internal Medicine*, *157*(19), 2213–2223.

Callaghan, M., Ford, N., & Schneider, H. (2010). A systematic review of task-shifting for HIV treatment and care in Africa. *Human Resources for Health*, *8*, 8.

Carney, R. M., Freedland, K. E., Sheline, Y. I., et al. (1997). Depression and coronary heart disease: A review for cardiologists. *Clinical Cardiology*, *20*(3), 196–200.

Cohen, M. S., Chen, Y. Q., McCauley, M., et al. (2011). Prevention of HIV-1 infection with early antiretroviral therapy. *New England Journal of Medicine*, *365*(6), 493–505.

Daughters, S. B., Magidson, J. F., Schuster, R. M., et al. (2010). ACT HEALTHY: A combined cognitive-behavioral depression and medication adherence treatment for HIV-infected substance users. *Cognitive and Behavioral Practice*, *17*(3), 309–321.

De la Roca-Chiapas, J. M., Hernandez-Gonzalez, M., Candelario, M., et al. (2013). Association between depression and higher glucose levels in middle-aged Mexican patients with diabetes. *Revista de Investigación Clínica*, *65*(3), 209–213.

Dewing, S., Mathews, C., Schaay, N., et al. (2013). It's important to take your medication everyday okay? An evaluation of counselling by lay counsellors for ARV adherence support in the Western Cape, South Africa. *AIDS and Behavior*, *17*(1), 203–212.

Dickens, C., Cherrington, A., Adeyemi, I., et al. (2013). Characteristics of psychological interventions that improve depression in people with coronary heart disease: A systematic review and meta-regression. *Psychosomatic Medicine*, *75*(2), 211–221.

DiMatteo, M. R., Giordani, P. J., Lepper, H. S., et al. (2002). Patient adherence and medical treatment outcomes a meta-analysis. *Medical Care*, *40*(9), 794–811.

Egede, L. E. (2005). Effect of depression on self-management behaviors and health outcomes in adults with type 2 diabetes. *Current Diabetes Reviews*, *1*(3), 235–243.

Friedman, M., Thoresen, C. E., Gill, J. J., et al. (1986). Alteration of type A behavior and its effect on cardiac recurrences in post myocardial infarction patients: Summary results of the recurrent coronary prevention project. *American Heart Journal*, *112*(4), 653–665.

Fu, D., Ding, Y., McGowan, P., et al. (2006). Qualitative evaluation of chronic disease self management program (CDSMP) in Shanghai. *Patient Education and Counseling*, *61*(3), 389–396.

García de Olalla, P., Knobel, H., Carmona, A., et al. (2002). Impact of adherence and highly active antiretroviral therapy on survival in HIV-infected patients. *Journal of Acquired Immune Deficiency Syndromes*, *30*(1), 105–110.

Gilson, L., Walt, G., Heggenhougen, K., et al. (1989). National community health worker programs: How can they be strengthened? *Journal of Public Health Policy*, *10*(4), 518–532.

Gonzalez, J., Batchelder, A., Psaros, C., et al. (2011). Depression and HIV/AIDS treatment nonadherence: A review and meta-analysis. *Journal of Acquired Immune Deficiency Syndromes*, *58*(2).

Gonzalez, J., Peyrot, M., McCarl, L., et al. (2008). Depression and diabetes treatment nonadherence: A meta-analysis. *Diabetes Care*, *31*(12), 2398–2403.

Graham, C. D., Gouick, J., Krahé, C., et al. (2016). A systematic review of the use of acceptance and commitment therapy (ACT) in chronic disease and long-term conditions. *Clinical Psychology Review*, *46*(Suppl. C), 46–58.

Hartzler, A., & Wetter, T. (2014). Engaging patients through mobile phones: Demonstrator services, success factors, and future opportunities in low and middle-income countries. *Yearbook of Medical Informatics*, *9*(1), 182–194.

Hermann, K., Van Damme, W., Pariyo, G. W., et al. (2009). Community health workers for ART in sub-Saharan Africa: Learning from experience—Capitalizing on new opportunities. *Human Resources for Health*, *7*, 31.

Hurt, K., Walker, R. J., Campbell, J. A., et al. (2016). mHealth interventions in low and middle-income countries: A systematic review. *Global Journal of Health Science*, *8*(9), 183–193.

Igumbor, J. O., Scheepers, E., Ebrahim, R., et al. (2011). An evaluation of the impact of a community-based adherence support programme on ART outcomes in selected government HIV treatment sites in South Africa. *AIDS Care*, *23*(2), 231–236.

International Telecommunications Union: ITU-D webpages (website); 2017. https:/www.itu.int/en/ITU-D/Statistics/Documents/statistics/2017/Stat_page_all_charts_2017.xls (accessed 01.02.18).

Iwu, E. N., & Holzemer, W. L. (2014). Task shifting of HIV management from doctors to nurses in Africa: Clinical outcomes and evidence on nurse self-efficacy and job satisfaction. *AIDS Care*, *26*(1), 42–52.

Janssens, B., Van Damme, W., Raleigh, B., et al. (2007). Offering integrated care for HIV/AIDS, diabetes and hypertension within chronic disease clinics in Cambodia. *Bulletin of the World Health Organization*, *85*(11), 880–885.

Kassebaum, N. J., Arora, M., Barber, R. M., et al. (2016). Global, regional, and national disability-adjusted life-years (DALYs) for 315 diseases and injuries and healthy life expectancy (HALE), 1990–2015: A systematic analysis for the global burden of disease study 2015. *Lancet*, *388*(10053), 1603–1658.

Kennedy, A., Reeves, D., Bower, P., et al. (2007). The effectiveness and cost effectiveness of a national lay-led self care support programme for patients with long-term conditions: A pragmatic randomised controlled trial. *Journal of Epidemiology and Community Health*, *61*(3), 254–261.

Kunutsor, S., Walley, J., Katabira, E., et al. (2010). Using mobile phones to improve clinic attendance amongst an antiretroviral treatment cohort in rural Uganda: A cross-sectional and prospective study. *AIDS and Behavior*, *14*(6), 1347–1352.

Ledikwe, J. H., Kejelepula, M., Maupo, K., et al. (2013). Evaluation of a well-established task-shifting initiative: The lay counselor cadre in Botswana. *PLoS ONE*, *8*(4).

Lester, R. T., Ritvo, P., Mills, E. J., et al. (2010). Effects of a mobile phone short message service on antiretroviral treatment adherence in Kenya (WelTel Kenya1): A randomised trial. *Lancet*, *376*(9755), 1838–1845.

Lett, H. S., Blumenthal, J. A., Babyak, M. A., et al. (2004). Depression as a risk factor for coronary artery disease: Evidence, mechanisms, and treatment. *Psychosomatic Medicine*, *66*(3), 305–315.

Lett, H. S., Davidson, J., & Blumenthal, J. A. (2005). Nonpharmacologic treatments for depression in patients with coronary heart disease. *Psychosomatic Medicine*, *67*, S58–S62.

Lewin, S. A., Dick, J., Pond, P., et al. (2005). Lay health workers in primary and community health care. *Cochrane Database of Systematic Review*, *1*.

Li, C., Xu, D., Hu, M., et al. (2017). A systematic review and meta-analysis of randomized controlled trials of cognitive behavior therapy for patients with diabetes and depression. *Journal of Psychosomatic Research*, *95*(Suppl. C), 44–54.

Lorig, K., Ritter, P. L., & Plant, K. (2005). A disease-specific self-help program compared with a generalized chronic disease self-help program for arthritis patients. *Arthritis Care and Research*, *53*(6), 950–957.

Lustman, P. J., & Clouse, R. E. (2005). Depression in diabetic patients: The relationship between mood and glycemic control. *Journal of Diabetes and its Complications*, *19*(2), 113–122.

Magidson, J. F., Gouse, H., Psaros, C., et al. (2017). Task shifting and delivery of behavioral medicine interventions in resource-poor global settings: HIV/AIDS treatment in sub-Saharan Africa. In A. M. Vranceanu, J. A. Greer, & S. A. Safren (Eds.), *The Massachusetts general hospital handbook of behavioral medicine*. Humana Press.

Mdege, N. D., Chindove, S., & Ali, S. (2013). The effectiveness and cost implications of task-shifting in the delivery of antiretroviral therapy to HIV-infected patients: A systematic review. *Health Policy and Planning*, *28*(3), 223–236.

Médecins Sans Frontières (Doctors Without Borders) (2015). *ART/TB/PMTCT initiation patient education and counselling model: Report and toolkit*. South Africa: Khayelitsha. 1/21.

Mills, E. J., Nachega, J. B., Buchan, I., et al. (2006). Adherence to antiretroviral therapy in sub-Saharan Africa and North America: A meta-analysis. *JAMA*, *296*(6), 679–690.

Mwai, G. W., Mburu, G., Torpey, K., et al. (2013). Role and outcomes of community health workers in HIV care in sub-Saharan Africa: A systematic review. *Journal of the International AIDS Society*, *16*(1).

Nakimuli-Mpungu, E., Bass, J. K., Alexandre, P., et al. (2012). Depression, alcohol use and adherence to antiretroviral therapy in sub-Saharan Africa: A systematic review. *AIDS and Behavior*, *6*(8), 2101–2118.

National Health Council (2014). *About chronic disease, Washington, DC. Retrieved from* http://www.nationalhealthcouncil.org/sites/default/files/NHC_Files/Pdf_Files/AboutChronicDisease.pdf.

Nicholson, A., Kuper, H., & Hemingway, H. (2006). Depression as an aetiologic and prognostic factor in coronary heart disease: A meta-analysis of 6362 events among 146 538 participants in 54 observational studies. *European Heart Journal*, *27*(23), 2763–2774.

Padmanathan, P., & De Silva, M. J. (2013). The acceptability and feasibility of task-sharing for mental healthcare in low and middle income countries: A systematic review. *Social Science & Medicine*, *97*, 82–86.

Palombi, L., Marazzi, M. C., Guidotti, G., et al. (2009). Incidence and predictors of death, retention, and switch to second-line regimens in antiretroviral-treated patients in sub-Saharan African sites with comprehensive monitoring availability. *Clinical Infectious Diseases*, *48* (1), 115–122.

Papas, R. K., Sidle, J. E., Martino, S., et al. (2010). Systematic cultural adaptation of cognitive-behavioral therapy to reduce alcohol use among HIV-infected outpatients in western Kenya. *AIDS and Behavior*, *14*(3), 669–678.

Piette, J. D., Datwani, H., Gaudioso, S., et al. (2012). Hypertension management using mobile technology and home blood pressure monitoring: Results of a randomized trial in two low/middle-income countries. *Telemedicine Journal and E-Health*, *18*(8), 613–620.

Price, A. J., Crampin, A. C., Amberbir, A., et al. (2018). Prevalence of obesity, hypertension, and diabetes, and cascade of care in sub-Saharan Africa: A cross-sectional, population-based study in rural and urban Malawi. *Lancet Diabetes & Endocrinology*.

Price, J., & Binagwaho, A. (2010). From medical rationing to rationalizing the use of human resources for AIDS care and treatment in Africa: A case for task shifting. *Developing World Bioethics*, *10*(2), 99–103.

Purdy, J. (2013). Chronic physical illness: A psychophysiological approach for chronic physical illness. *Yale Journal of Biology and Medicine*, *86*(1), 15–28.

Rabkin, M., & El-Sadr, W. M. (2011). Why reinvent the wheel? Leveraging the lessons of HIV scale-up to confront non-communicable diseases. *Global Public Health*, *6*(3), 247–256.

Remien, R. H., Mellins, C. A., Robbins, R. N., et al. (2013). Masivukeni: Development of a multimedia based antiretroviral therapy adherence intervention for counselors and patients in South Africa. *AIDS and Behavior*, *17*(6), 1979–1991.

Richards, S. H., Anderson, L., Jenkinson, C. E., et al. (2017). Psychological interventions for coronary heart disease: Cochrane systematic review and meta-analysis. *European Journal of Preventive Cardiology*, *25*(2), 247–259.

Robbins, R. N., Mellins, C. A., Leu, C. S., et al. (2015). Enhancing lay counselor capacity to improve patient outcomes with multimedia technology. *AIDS and Behavior*, *19*(2), 163–176.

Safren, S. A., Bedoya, C. A., O'Cleirigh, C., Biello, K. B., Pinkston, M. M., Stein, M. D., & Mayer, K. H. (2016). Cognitive behavioural therapy for adherence and depression in patients with HIV: a three-arm randomised controlled trial. *The Lancet HIV*, *3*(11), e529–e538. https://doi.org/10.1016/S2352-3018(16)30053-4.

Safren, S., Gonzalez, J., & Soroudi, N. (2007). *Coping with chronic illness: A cognitive-behavioral approach for adherence and depression therapist guide*. New York: Oxford University Press.

Safren, S. A., Gonzalez, J. S., Wexler, D. J., et al. (2014). A randomized controlled trial of cognitive behavioral therapy for adherence and depression (CBT-AD) in patients with uncontrolled type 2 diabetes. *Diabetes Care*, *37*(3), 625–633.

Safren, S. A., Mayer, K. H., Ou, S. S., et al. (2015). Adherence to early antiretroviral therapy: Results from HPTN 052, a phase III, multinational randomized trial of ART to prevent HIV-1 sexual transmission in serodiscordant couples. *Journal of Acquired Immune Deficiency Syndromes*, *69*(2), 234.

Safren, S. A., O'Cleirigh, C. M., Bullis, J. R., et al. (2012). Cognitive behavioral therapy for adherence and depression (CBT-AD) in HIV-infected injection drug users: A randomized controlled trial. *Journal of Consulting and Clinical Psychology*, *80*(3), 404–415.

Safren, S. A., O'Cleirigh, C., Tan, J., Raminani, S., Reilly, L. C., Otto, M. W., & Mayer, K. H. (2009). A randomized controlled trial of cognitive behavioral therapy for adherence and depression (CBT-AD) in HIV-infected individuals. *Health Psychology: Official Journal of the Division of Health Psychology, American Psychological Association*, *28*(1), 1–10. http://doi.org/10.1037/a0012715.

Safren, S. A., & Otto, W. M. (1999). Worth: Life-steps: Applying cognitive behavioral therapy to HIV medication adherence—ScienceDirect. *Cognitive and Behavioral Practice*, *6*(4), 332–341.

Safren, S. A., Otto, W. M., Worth, J. L., et al. (2001). Two strategies to increase adherence to HIV antiretroviral medication: Life-steps and medication monitoring. *Behaviour Research and Therapy*, *39*(10), 1151–1162.

Saxena, S., Thornicroft, G., Knapp, M., et al. (2007). Resources for mental health: Scarcity, inequity, and inefficiency. *Lancet*, *370*(9590), 878–889.

Schneiderman, N., Saab, P. G., Catellier, D. J., et al. (2004). Psychosocial treatment within sex by ethnicity subgroups in the enhancing recovery in coronary heart disease clinical trial. *Psychosomatic Medicine*, *66*(4), 475–483.

Sharif, F., Masoudi, M., Ghanizadeh, A., et al. (2014). The effect of cognitive-behavioral group therapy on depressive symptoms in people with type 2 diabetes: A randomized controlled clinical trial. *Iranian Journal of Nursing and Midwifery Research*, *19*(5), 529–536.

Simoni, J. M., Chen, W. T., Huh, D., et al. (2011). A preliminary randomized controlled trial of a nurse-delivered medication adherence intervention among HIV-positive outpatients initiating antiretroviral therapy in Beijing, China. *AIDS and Behavior*, *15*(5), 919–929.

Simoni, J. M., Pearson, C. R., Pantalone, D. W., et al. (2006). Efficacy of interventions in improving highly active antiretroviral therapy adherence and HIV-1 RNA viral load. *Journal of Acquired Immune Deficiency Syndromes*, *43*(Suppl. 1), S23–S35.

Stafford, L., Berk, M., Reddy, P., et al. (2007). Comorbid depression and health-related quality of life in patients with coronary artery disease. *Journal of Psychosomatic Research*, *62*(4), 401–410.

Swendeman, D., Ingram, B. L., & Rotheram-Borus, M. J. (2009). Common elements in self-management of HIV and other chronic illnesses: An integrative framework. *AIDS Care*, *21*(10), 1321–1334.

Swerissen, H., Belfrage, J., Weeks, A., et al. (2006). A randomised control trial of a self-management program for people with a chronic illness from Vietnamese, Chinese, Italian and Greek backgrounds. *Patient Education and Counseling*, *64*(1), 360–368.

Tomlinson, M., Rotheram-Borus, M. J., Swartz, L., et al. (2013). Scaling up mHealth: Where is the evidence? *PLoS Medicine*, *10*(2). e1001382.

Turner, J., & Kelly, B. (2000). Emotional dimensions of chronic disease. *Western Journal of Medicine*, *172*(2), 124–128.

UNAIDS (2017). *UNAIDS data 2017, Joint United Nations Programme on HIV/AIDS (UNAIDS)*. Retrieved from http://www.unaids.org/sites/default/files/media_asset/20170720_Data_book_2017_en.pdf.

Uthman, O. A., Magidson, J. F., Safren, S. A., et al. (2014). Depression and adherence to antiretroviral therapy in low-, middle- and high-income countries: A systematic review and meta-analysis. *Current HIV/AIDS Reports*, *11*(3), 291–307.

Van Melle, J. P., De Jonge, P., Spijkerman, T. A., et al. (2004). Prognostic association of depression following myocardial infarction with mortality and cardiovascular events: A meta-analysis. *Psychosomatic Medicine*, *66*(6), 814–822.

Vranceanu AM, Safren SA, Greer JA, ed.: The Massachusetts general hospital handbook of behavioral medicine, 2017, Humana Press.

Western Cape Government (2017). *People development centre: Overview (website).* https://www.westerncape.gov.za/your_gov/185 *(accessed 30.01.18).*

White, C. A. (2001). Cognitive behavioral principles in managing chronic disease. *Western Journal of Medicine*, *175*(5), 338–342.

Whiting, D. R., Guariguata, L., Weil, C., et al. (2011). IDF diabetes atlas: Global estimates of the prevalence of diabetes for 2011 and 2030. *Diabetes Research and Clinical Practice*, *94*(3), 311–321.

WHO (2006). *Working together for health: The world health report 2006.*

WHO (2008). *Task shifting: Rational redistribution of tasks among health workforce teams: Global recommendations and guidelines.* Geneva: WHO Press.

WHO (2014). *Global status report on noncommunicable diseases 2014.* Geneva: WHO.

Wilkinson, L., Duvivier, H., Patten, G., et al. (2015). Outcomes from the implementation of a counselling model supporting rapid antiretroviral treatment initiation in a primary healthcare clinic in Khayelitsha, South Africa. *Southern African Journal of HIV Medicine*, *16*(1), 1–7.

World Health Organization (2017a). *Noncommunicable diseases (Fact Sheet).* WHO.

World Health Organization (2017b). *Cardiovascular diseases (CVDs) (Fact Sheet).* WHO.

Psychotherapy adaptation for children and adolescents

13

Shannon Dorsey, Leah Lucid*, Jessica Leith†, Laura M. Eise*, Cyrilla Amanya‡, Lucy X. Dong§*
*Department of Psychology, University of Washington, Seattle, WA, United States,
†Psychiatry and Behavioral Sciences, University of Washington School of Medicine, Seattle, WA, United States, ‡Ace Africa, Bungoma, Kenya, §School of Public Health, University of Washington, Seattle, WA, United States

13.1 Introduction

Neuropsychiatric disorders are ranked as the most prominent cause of years lost because of disability for young people (Gore et al., 2011). Specifically, global prevalence of mental health disorders in children and adolescents runs from 13.4% to 23.4% (Kessler et al., 2012; Polanczyk, Salum, Sugaya, Caye, & Rohde, 2015). Promisingly, there is a robust evidence base documenting effective psychosocial treatments for children and adolescents, primarily conducted in high-income countries (HIC). Yet very limited child- and adolescent-focused mental health research has focused on youth in low- to middle-income countries (LMIC). The available research suggests that the treatment gap for children and adolescents in LMIC is higher than that of almost any other subpopulation, with estimates that fewer than 1% of children and adolescents with mental health need will receive treatment (Saxena, Thornicroft, Knapp, & Whiteford, 2007). In addition to this substantial treatment gap, if we can generalize from emerging research documenting the undertreatment of depression worldwide (e.g., 1 in 27 individuals in LMIC receives minimally adequate treatment; Thornicroft et al., 2017), we might assume that when care is received, it is unlikely to be effective. With more than 80% of the world's children and adolescents living in LMIC, more attention is critical to relieve the global burden of disease (Patel, Flisher, Hetrick, & McGorry, 2007). Taken together, these findings suggest that rapid advancement in treating mental health needs of children and adolescents in LMIC is needed to improve the lives and well-being of those impacted by mental health problems.

In this chapter, we review the empirical literature on psychotherapy treatments for four primary mental health problems among children and adolescents: anxiety, depression, behavior problems, and posttraumatic stress (PTS). Given the limited empirical base globally, we first broadly review treatment outcome research for each presenting problem, most of which is from HIC. We then review studies conducted in LMIC and, in some instances, research currently underway that may yield important

Global Mental Health and Psychotherapy. https://doi.org/10.1016/B978-0-12-814932-4.00013-6

findings once it is completed. Following these reviews, we conclude with an example of a study focused on child and adolescent mental health and implementation science, Building and Sustaining Interventions for Children (BASIC) in Kenya (NIMH-funded R01 MH108551). This study illustrates the use of a psychotherapy treatment with evidence in LMIC, task sharing (in which interventions are delivered by paraprofessionals or nonspecialists, often with limited or no prior mental health training or experience), limited resources, and a plan for scale-up and sustainment.

13.2 Overview: Effectiveness of mental health treatment for children and adolescents from HIC studies

There is no shortage of treatment approaches. By the year 2000, there were more than 500 different psychosocial treatment protocols for children and adolescents (Kazdin, 2000). Weisz, Kuppens, et al. (2017) and Weisz, Bearman, Santucci, and Jensen-Doss (2017) recently conducted a rigorous meta-analysis that takes advantage of a variety of analytic advancements to more accurately assess treatment effectiveness from 447 studies over 50 years, involving over 30,000 youth. The authors found an overall psychosocial treatment effect size of 0.46 (Cohen's *d*, approaching Cohen's threshold of 0.5 for a medium effect). The problem the treatment targeted was related to therapy effectiveness, with the strongest effect for anxiety-focused treatments (0.61) and the weakest effect for depression (0.29), with a nonsignificant effect when the treatment focus was multiproblem (0.15). A few factors played a role in the size of the effect, including the comparison condition type, informant for outcomes (youth, parent, and teacher), and type of treatment. Behavioral therapy treatment types, which included cognitive behavioral therapies, showed the most robust and consistent effects across informants, but were not consistently superior to other treatments.

Evidence for existing protocols continues to accumulate (published trials have nearly tripled since 1995; Weisz, Bearman, et al., 2017; Weisz, Kuppens, et al., 2017), and new treatments are still being developed and tested. Yet the research-to-practice gap in low-resource contexts, both in HIC (e.g., rural areas) and in most LMIC, is still substantial. As we address at the end of the chapter, solutions to improve mental health outcomes for children and adolescents will require attention that goes beyond the treatments themselves; further research is needed that focuses on how to best support the implementation of treatments in LMIC (e.g., how to optimize supervision when using task sharing and what organizational and system-level supports are needed), where resources for implementation will be limited. However, we begin with reviewing the literature on psychotherapies by problem area, capitalizing on a series of recent reviews for the *Journal of Clinical Child and Adolescent Psychology* that utilized a common rating system across problem areas (Southam-Gerow & Prinstein, 2014). We provide a narrative description for each area summarizing the evidence base for younger children and for adolescents.

13.3 Anxiety

Anxiety disorders are the most common mental health challenges facing children and adolescents (Cartwright-Hatton, McNicol, & Doubleday, 2006; Merikangas et al., 2010). Worldwide prevalence is estimated to be between 6.5% and 10% of the population (Essau & Gabhidon, 2013; Polanczyk et al., 2015). These disorders typically emerge in mid to late childhood; result in considerable distress; and have an adverse impact on the child's familial, social, and academic interactions (Grills-Taquechel & Ollendick, 2013). Furthermore, they frequently persist into adulthood and are oftentimes associated with other negative mental health outcomes (e.g., major depression and substance abuse; Creswell, Waite, & Cooper, 2014).

In a literature review spanning 50 years, Higa-McMillan, Francis, Rith-Najarian, and Chorpita (2016) identified cognitive behavioral therapy (CBT), including exposure-based approaches, as effective for youth with anxiety disorders. Specifically, CBT, exposure, CBT with parents, and CBT with medication have been shown to reduce symptoms and improve functional impairment. These approaches have a strong and diverse evidence base. They improved anxiety symptoms across participants of 10 different ethnicities[1] and a broad range of ages. The treatments could also be used regardless of therapist education levels, delivery format (e.g., individual, group, and electronic), or physical settings (e.g., day cares and hospitals).

Exposure techniques address a patient's avoidance of feared stimuli by providing safe, anxiety-provoking experiences to face stimuli in real time (i.e., in vivo), either within the therapy session or in the natural environment. Depending on the patient's anxiety, a fear hierarchy (e.g., a fear ladder) may be developed in order to work up to the highest anxiety-provoking stimuli. Exposure is a key component of CBT for anxiety, and treatment outcomes vary based on time and tasks associated with it. For example, more time spent on exposure exercises is linked with greater reduction in anxiety (Peris et al., 2017). Also, fewer exposure tasks per session paired with greater time processing exposure tasks are tied to better treatment outcomes. Practicing more challenging exposure tasks also predicts better treatment outcomes (Hedtke, Kendall, & Tiwari, 2009; Tiwari, Kendall, Hoff, Harrison, & Fizur, 2013).

In addition, working with family can enhance effectiveness: CBT with parents, family psychoeducation, and CBT approaches that include the child and parent are found to reduce anxiety symptoms. In particular, high parental involvement and supporting parents in using the same contingency management strategies used by therapists resulted in *gains* from posttreatment to a 1-year follow-up (Manassis et al., 2014).

Despite research substantiating effective treatments for anxiety disorders in children and adolescents, many children suffer from unmet mental health needs, even in HIC, such that the majority of children and adolescents either do not have access to or do not receive evidence-based treatments (EBT; Higa-McMillan et al., 2016).

[1] Aboriginal (Australia), American Indian or Alaska Native, Asian, African American, Caucasian, Dutch, Hindu, Hispanic or Latino/a, Indonesian, Multiethnic, and others

Anxiety disorders were found to be higher in certain LMIC, as well, which further exacerbates the problem (Fleitlich-Bilyk & Goodman, 2004; Visagie, Loxton, & Silverman, 2015). "Poverty, civil conflict, and environmental stressors tend to be endemic in [LMIC] and contribute to significant psychiatric morbidity, including depression, anxiety, and post-traumatic stress disorder" (Yatham, Sivathasan, Yoon, da Silva, & Ravindran, 2017, p. 1). As such, early intervention has greater potential to significantly reduce the personal and societal impacts (Collins et al., 2011). Although CBT has grown to be one of the most researched and empirically supported forms of psychotherapy, limited research has occurred to substantiate these claims for children and adolescents in LMIC (de Souza et al., 2013). Most of the existing research for LMIC was carried out in the past 5 years. This includes a pilot study assessing modular CBT and cognitive behavioral hypnotherapy for treating anxiety in Iranian girls. Results showed that both treatments significantly reduced anxiety (Ebesutani, Helmi, Fierstein, Taghizadeh, & Chorpita, 2016). In addition, de Souza et al. (2013) conducted a small open trial ($N=20$) evaluating a group CBT protocol for youth in a community sample in Brazil. The results showed improvement for anxiety and reduction of externalizing symptoms over time. In an effort to examine the long-term effectiveness, Davis, Mansur De Souza, Rigatti, and Heldt (2015) conducted a 2-year follow-up, finding no additional improvement for anxiety symptoms, but improvement in general quality of life.

While research is scarce, there are several reasons that CBT may be considered a useful treatment in LMIC. For example, CBT is goal-oriented and symptom-focused, which helps children and adolescents develop skills and techniques to handle their difficulties. It is also briefer than other forms of psychotherapy, and there are specific, measurable target goals. Another advantage is that "therapeutic models of CBT in children and adolescents lend themselves to adjustments to fit and cohere with various cultural and language differences" (Rosenstein & Seedat, 2011, p. 70). For example, a study in Japan demonstrated that CBT significantly decreased anxiety in children and adolescents both immediately after treatment and 3 months later (Ishikawa et al., 2012).

Overall, the research indicates that CBT has significant potential to treat anxiety disorders in both HIC and LMIC. However, the current studies are limited, and the majority of LMIC studies to date focus on assessing anxiety disorders versus treating them. While CBT- and exposure-based approaches appear to be an appropriate first-line treatment, they may require cultural modification. For example, Huey and Polo (2008) reviewed research on EBT for ethnic minority youth. While they did not discover any well-established treatments for anxiety disorders, their research uncovered two studies that indicate that group CBT is possibly efficacious for Hispanic/Latino and African American youth with anxiety disorders (Ginsburg & Drake, 2002; Silverman et al., 1999).

It is worth considering alternative treatment if children and adolescents do not respond well to CBT (Higa-McMillan et al., 2016). For example, cultural storytelling has shown evidence of helping Hispanic inner-city youth significantly decrease anxiety (Costantino, Malgady, & Rogler, 1994). Anxiety management training, study skill training, and the combination of both were found to be possibly efficacious in the treatment of African American youth with testing anxiety (Huey & Polo, 2008; Wilson & Rotter, 1986). As such, research into treatments, including CBT and alternatives, has the potential to improve the quality of life of youth with mental health problems who are residing in LMIC.

13.4 Depression

Depression remains one of the leading causes of disability worldwide and is associated with impaired relationships, education and socioeconomic status, and an increased risk of suicide (Patel, Simon, Chowdhary, Kaaya, & Araya, 2009; Weersing, Jeffreys, Do, Schwartz, & Bolano, 2017). The typical onset for depression is in adolescence during puberty, with "nearly one in five youth experiencing a clinically significant episode before the end of puberty" (Weersing, Rozenman, & Gonzalez, 2009, p. 26). Furthermore, adolescent onset is associated with a higher risk for chronic recurrence and functional impairment throughout the life span than adult onset, making early intervention critical (Weersing et al., 2017). Cognitive behavioral therapy and interpersonal psychotherapy (IPT) have the greatest evidence of effectiveness in treating adolescent depression (Klasen & Crombag, 2013; Zhou et al., 2015), including evidence cross-culturally with Latino populations (Rosselló, Bernal, & Rivera-Medina, 2008). Group CBT, individual CBT, and individual IPT have earned a level 1 rating as *well-established* interventions, and group IPT earned a level 2 rating as *probably efficacious* (Weersing et al., 2017). CBT for depression targets cognitive styles and maladaptive coping behaviors, while IPT focuses on lessening interpersonal stress and improving behavioral responses specific to relationship problems (Weersing et al., 2009). It is worth noting that CBT and IPT share the active elements of problem-solving, social skill building, and assertiveness training (Weersing et al., 2017).

While currently no EBT meets the criteria of *well-established* or *probably efficacious* intervention for treating depression in prepubertal children (i.e., younger than age 13), CBT obtained a level 3 rating as a *possibly efficacious* intervention. Weersing et al. (2017) note that there are data suggesting that childhood depression may be categorically separate from the strongly linked adolescent depression and adult recurrent mood disorder, and that childhood environmental influences may have a higher impact on depression when children are younger. This may necessitate unique approaches to intervention for depression in children and is an area in need of further research (Weersing et al., 2017).

In a systematic review of the literature up to January 2017, Yatham and colleagues found youth prevalence rates of depressive symptoms in LMIC varied between 0 and 28%, which is comparable with rates of depressive disorders among youth in HIC (2%–25%; Yatham et al., 2017). However, because of the large population base in LMIC, these prevalence rates translate into huge numbers of affected youth in LMIC (Yatham et al., 2017). No randomized controlled trials (RCTs) specifically designed to treat major depressive disorder among youth in LMIC have been conducted (Klasen & Crombag, 2013), though several studies have attempted to reduce depression symptoms. Yatham et al. (2017) reviewed 21 randomized and cluster-randomized controlled trials targeting depression, anxiety, and/or PTSD symptoms in LMIC; most of the rigorous interventions utilized some form of CBT. A majority of these trials ($n = 15$) occurred in armed conflict-affected regions (e.g., Palestine, Nepal, and Sri Lanka) and focused primarily on PTS symptoms (see also Chapter 9). Many studies focused on traumatized youth have included measures of depression, but these trauma-focused treatments have, perhaps unsurprisingly, had small or nonsignificant effect sizes for depression symptoms (Morina, Malek, Nickerson, & Bryant, 2017), which is consistent with the relatively weak effect sizes for depression seen more generally across youth mental health intervention studies (Weisz, Kuppens, et al., 2017). To date, only one RCT has focused on utilizing IPT to treat youth depression symptoms in LMIC. Bolton and colleagues studied group-based IPT for adolescents living in camps for internally displaced persons in Uganda ($n = 314$) and found that group-based IPT was effective for reducing depression symptoms among adolescent girls affected by war and displacement, but not boys (Bolton et al., 2007). They posited that the gender differences found may reflect that boys were "less willing to talk about emotional problems, particularly in a group format" and that the higher rates of comorbid substance use and PTS symptoms among the boys may have rendered IPT less effective (Bolton et al., 2007, p. 526). Based on these results, it is possible that interventions may need some gender-specific modifications in LMIC, particularly if specific gender roles and cultural norms would make a group format unsuitable for boys to talk about their emotions.

Studies in nonarmed conflict settings that used a mixture of cognitive, interpersonal, and educational content found significant reductions in depression symptoms (Yatham et al., 2017). An RCT in China found that CBT-based Penn Optimism Program (POP) groups led by teachers with children ages 8–15 resulted in significantly reduced depressive symptoms in a subclinically depressed group of children ($n = 220$; Yu & Seligman, 2002). Yu and Seligman found that teaching children in China a more optimistic explanatory style showed promise as a possible mechanism for preventing clinically significant depression (Yu & Seligman, 2002). Rivet-Duval and colleagues employed the Resourceful Adolescent Program (RAP), which combines CBT and IPT components, delivered by teachers in an RCT with adolescents ($n = 160$) in Mauritius (Rivet-Duval, Heriot, & Hunt, 2011). They found that RAP decreased depression symptoms posttreatment but not at a 6-month follow-up, though youth in the RAP intervention did have increased self-esteem and adaptive coping skills at follow-up (Rivet-Duval et al., 2011). More research is needed to determine how to maintain decreased depression symptoms among youth in LMIC.

Currently, additional work is underway seeking to treat youth depression in LMIC. This includes research on the common elements treatment approach for youth (CETA-Youth), a transdiagnostic intervention that builds on work by Weisz and Chorpita (Chorpita, Daleiden, & Weisz, 2005; Weisz et al., 2012), and includes active treatment ingredients for depression, anxiety, posttraumatic stress, and behavioral symptoms. As with the adult version that has evidence of effectiveness from two large RCTs in LMIC (Bolton et al., 2014; Weiss et al., 2015), CETA-Youth treats depressive symptoms using behavioral activation and cognitive techniques. CETA-Youth was tested in an open trial with refugee youth on the Ethiopian/Somali border and demonstrated positive effects on internalizing, externalizing, and PTS symptoms (Murray et al., 2018). Further dissemination of interventions based on the proven principles of CBT and IPT in LMIC is recommended (Klasen & Crombag, 2013), as results of the limited studies to date suggest that these strategies can be effective for alleviating depression symptoms among youth in LMIC.

13.5 Behavior problems

Disruptive behavior problems are characterized by a range of externalizing behaviors (e.g., aggression/defiance) in children and adolescents that are consistent and pervasive over time. Youth experiencing these symptoms are commonly diagnosed with oppositional defiant disorder (ODD) or conduct disorder (CD). ODD is more prevalent among children aged 12 and younger, as they generally exhibit milder versions of these behaviors, while CD is more characteristic of antisocial tendencies that often escalate to law-breaking behavior in adolescence. Studies estimate that 4.6% of children aged 3–17 have had a history of parent-reported behavioral or conduct problems, while other estimates indicate that 3.5% are currently experiencing these behaviors (Kaminski & Claussen, 2017). Children and adolescents who exhibit these behaviors experience a high degree of impairment in their overall functioning, which can persist into adulthood without proper intervention (McCart & Sheidow, 2016).

Parent management training (PMT) is considered to be the most effective treatment for reducing disruptive behavior for children 12 and under, earning a level 1 rating as a well-established mode of intervention (Kaminski & Claussen, 2017). PMT, a primarily parent-mediated treatment conducted either individually or in groups (Kazdin, 2018), is a parent behavior training that teaches parents skills for managing child behaviors. Due to the many "name brand" interventions with similar content overlap, efforts have been made to identify the specific elements of PMT interventions most associated with positive outcomes (Chorpita & Daleiden, 2009; Garland, Hawley, Brookman-Frazee, & Hurlburt, 2008). These include caregiver use of rewards/consequences, praise, differential reinforcement, giving instructions in an effective way, encouraging parent-child relationship building, and problem-solving skills to increase the occurrence of positive or desired behaviors (e.g., complying with an instruction).

Different versions of PMT vary some in specific content and mode of delivery for these elements. For example, in parent-child interaction therapy (PCIT; Eyberg & Robinson, 1982), the counselor teaches PMT to the parent and then spends most of the sessions coaching the parent in interactions with their child, with homework in between sessions. In The Incredible Years (IY), parenting skills are taught in a group format (i.e., groups of parents meeting with a counselor); the children do not participate in these group parent sessions, but they may participate in a concurrently delivered child-focused group ("Dinosaur School") that strengthens social, emotional, and academic (e.g., school readiness) skills.

Interventions targeting adolescents (ages 12–19) with disruptive behaviors continue to place an emphasis on the parent/child relationship and interactions while also taking into consideration the youth's increased cognitive capacity and the importance of positive peer relationships. Programs with the highest level of empirical support (i.e., level 1) for this population include programs with a combination of behavioral therapy, CBT, and family therapy and are typically accessed through involvement with the juvenile justice system (i.e., Multisystemic Therapy (MST) and Treatment Foster Care Oregon (TFCO)). Treatments that are classified as level 2 (probably efficacious treatment) include programs just focused on CBT (Solution-Focused Group Program (SFGP) and Aggression Replacement Training (ART)) and MST when used as a primary intervention for treating disruptive behaviors with nonjuvenile justice-involved youth (McCart & Sheidow, 2016).

PMT treatments have demonstrated positive outcomes in the reduction of disruptive behaviors among youth in Europe, North America, and Australia (Leijten, Melendez-Torres, Knerr, & Gardner, 2016) and the improvement in parent-child relationships (Gardner, Montgomery, & Knerr, 2016); however, it is not as clearly understood if these outcomes can be replicated in LMIC. Implementation and efficacy studies of PMT in LMIC are scarce, yet results are promising among studies conducted in LMIC. Leijten et al.'s (2016) meta-analysis of PMT interventions tested globally (i.e., IY, Positive Parenting Program (Triple P), and PCIT) showed a reduction in disruptive behaviors with families in Iran, China (Hong Kong), and Panama. One of the studies conducted in Indonesia did not result in a significant reduction in disruptive behaviors, which may indicate that the intervention needed to be more culturally adapted to the target population.

Many parenting interventions have been adapted to fit the cultural context of a new population while maintaining the primary treatment elements (i.e., flexibility within fidelity; Kendall & Beidas, 2007). For example, PCIT was adapted for families in Puerto Rico (Matos, Torres, Santiago, Jurado, & Rodriguez, 2006), and parental feedback from this preliminary study reported a decrease in child externalizing behaviors. Evidence is mixed as to whether these culturally adapted PMT interventions are more effective (Gardner et al., 2016; Hasson, Sundell, Beelmann, & von Thiele Schwarz, 2014), but as with other interventions, PMT treatments should be assessed for cultural fit before implementation in any new cultural context (Lau, 2006). Research findings appear to support the effectiveness both of evidence-based PMTs, standardly delivered, and of those culturally adapted or developed specifically for the setting, as long as the intervention includes effective elements (Leijten et al., 2016; Mejia, Leijten, Lachman, & Parra-Cardona, 2017). One intervention developed specifically for use in LMIC, CETA-Youth (Murray et al., 2018), included the common elements of PMT in an open trial with Somali refugees in Ethiopia, with a reported reduction in externalizing behaviors from both child and caregiver perspectives.

In our review of the PMT literature in LMIC, PMT interventions were more commonly used for the purpose of preventing child abuse, which is often correlated with the presence of disruptive behaviors (Vlahovicova, Melendez-Torres, Leijten, Knerr, & Gardner, 2017). This is not surprising, given that some (e.g., PCIT, IY, and Triple P) have been used in HIC to prevent maltreatment or decrease recidivism of maltreatment (Chaffin, Funderburk, Bard, Valle, & Gurwitch, 2011). Many of these studies target maladaptive parenting as a primary measure of outcome, with externalizing child behavior often tracked as a secondary outcome. Annan, Sim, Puffer, Salhi, and Betancourt (2017) conducted an RCT in which they adapted a group-based PMT program, *Happy Families* (Strengthening Families), for Burmese migrants who were displaced in Thailand and saw a reduction in child externalizing behaviors and attention problems and an increase in prosocial behaviors (Puffer, Annan, Sim, Salhi, & Betancourt, 2017). A similar RCT study conducted in Liberia using PMT demonstrated a decrease in child conduct problems, as reported by their caregivers (Puffer et al., 2015).

Overall, interventions including the core elements of PMT and well-established name-brand programs show promise for use as a parenting intervention in LMIC with younger children, but more research is needed to determine the extent of its impact on reducing disruptive behaviors in Africa, SE Asia, and Latin America. The limited studies that do exist focus heavily on younger children (ages 12 and younger), with little known about PMT effectiveness with adolescents in LMIC. Whittle et al. (2017) found that positive parenting moderated the negative effects that socioeconomic disadvantage typically has on adolescent populations as it relates to executive functioning, further reinforcing the importance of disseminating these interventions in LMIC for older youth as well.

13.6 Posttraumatic stress

Children and adolescents are often exposed to trauma. For example, studies indicate that nearly two-thirds of youth in the United States will experience a traumatic event before their 18th birthday (Copeland, Keeler, Angold, & Costello, 2007; McLaughlin et al., 2013). Although comparable epidemiological global data are not available, other high- (e.g., Trocmé & Wolfe, 2001) and low-income (e.g., Benjet, Borges, Medina-Mora, Zambrano, & Aguilar-Gaxiola, 2009) countries also present significant rates of trauma exposure during childhood and adolescence. Specifically, recent community studies indicate that trauma exposure is higher in lower-income countries compared with high-income countries (Atwoli, Stein, Koenen, & McLaughlin, 2015; Koenen et al., 2017).

Maltreatment and other traumatic experiences have a variety of impacts on children and adolescents. In the short term, youth who experience abuse and other traumatic experiences show adjustment problems such as posttraumatic stress (PTS), depression, and conduct problems (Arseneault et al., 2011). In the long term, PTS puts children and adolescents at greater risk of health challenges later in life (e.g., mood, anxiety, and substance use disorders; Dunn, Nishimi, Powers, & Bradley, 2017; McLaughlin et al., 2010). As such, early detection and intervention has the potential to greatly improve quality of life for affected children and adolescents.

Compared with the other three problem areas (i.e., anxiety, depression, and behavioral disorders), there have been more global studies examining treatments for trauma-related mental health sequelae, primarily focused on alleviating PTS and post-traumatic stress disorder (PTSD; Dorsey et al., 2017; see also Chapter 9). In general, cognitive behavioral therapy (CBT)-based approaches have the greatest evidence of effectiveness in treating posttraumatic stress in children and adolescents, rated as level 1 (Dorsey et al., 2017). Specifically, individual CBT (with and without parent involvement) and group CBT are deemed well established (Dorsey et al., 2017; Wethington et al., 2008). Group CBT with parent involvement and eye movement desensitization and reprocessing (EMDR) have been deemed probably efficacious (level 2). Looking at name-brand protocols within CBT, trauma-focused CBT (TF-CBT; Cohen, Deblinger, & Mannarino, 2006), cognitive behavioral intervention for schools (CBITS; Kataoka et al., 2003), and narrative exposure therapy (KIDNET; Ruf et al., 2010) are among those with the most evidence of effectiveness. Looking across these treatment approaches, common elements include psychoeducation, exposure (usually imaginal, often also in vivo), coping skill development, and cognitive restructuring of trauma-related maladaptive or unhelpful thinking (Dorsey et al., 2017).

A few studies have tested TF-CBT in LMIC, with all studies using a task sharing approach. Studies include small, open, pilot studies in Zambia (Murray et al., 2013) and Tanzania (O'Donnell et al., 2014); small RCTs in the Democratic Republic of Congo (DRC; McMullen, O'Callaghan, Shannon, Black, & Eakin, 2013; O'Callaghan, McMullen, Shannon, Rafferty, & Black, 2013); and two large RCTs, one in Zambia (Murray et al., 2015) and one in Tanzania and Kenya (Dorsey et al., in preparation). Studies also have examined counselor and child/guardian acceptability and how counselors deliver TF-CBT in a culturally acceptable way (Murray et al., 2014; Woods-Jaeger, Kava, Akiba, Lucid, & Dorsey, 2017). In the largest global trial to date ($n = 257$), conducted in Lusaka, Zambia, TF-CBT was compared with treatment as usual (TAU) for children and adolescents (ages 5–18) who had experienced a wide range of traumatic events and had PTS symptoms (Murray et al., 2015). Children, adolescents, and one of their guardians received TF-CBT individually for 10–16 sessions. TF-CBT outperformed TAU, with a large effect for PTS and a small effect for functioning.

Although to our knowledge CBITS has not been tested in LMIC, it is likely a good candidate for application with culturally and ethnically diverse children and adolescents, given that it was developed for and originally tested with culturally diverse youth in Los Angeles County, many of whom were immigrants. In one RCT, Mexican and Central American youths showed significant reduction in PTS and depressive symptoms (Kataoka et al., 2003; Stein et al., 2003). Similar positive effects were found in other communities, including urban African American, Native American, and rural communities (Morsette et al., 2009; Ngo et al., 2008).

In KIDNET, the main intervention element is the child's construction of a trauma narrative, with the provider focused on providing empathetic understanding, active listening, congruency, and unconditional positive regard (Schauer, Neuner, & Elbert, 2017). KIDNET has evidence of effectiveness in LMIC from a pilot study and two RCTs, including for child war survivors in Somalia and traumatized refugee children (Onyut et al., 2005; Ruf et al., 2010) and former child soldiers in Northern Uganda (Ertl, Pfeiffer, Schauer, Elbert, & Neuner, 2011). Importantly, KIDNET is relatively brief (i.e., 4–8 sessions). A major challenge for global mental health is to "develop more low-intensity interventions that can still achieve reasonable effect sizes but simultaneously provide cost-effective solutions to LMIC" (Morina et al., 2017, p. 247). This makes KIDNET a useful tool for resource-strapped communities.

Other versions of CBT approaches that include trauma-specific exposure have also shown effectiveness in Bosnia (Layne et al., 2001, 2008) and China (Chen et al., 2014). The Youth Readiness Intervention (YRI), a behavioral intervention less explicitly focused on trauma exposure and more on reducing functional impairment, has demonstrated some evidence of effectiveness for PTS in two RCTs (Betancourt et al., 2014; Newnham et al., 2015), with comparatively greater effects, perhaps unsurprisingly, on functional impairment. More eclectic treatments have shown less consistent evidence of effectiveness, which is important for our understanding of how to approach treating PTS and other trauma exposure-related impacts. Among the most rigorously tested, Tol and colleagues tested an intervention for children exposed to armed conflict in Indonesia (2008) and Burundi (2014), designed for group-based delivery in schools in 15 sessions over 5 weeks. The intervention included some CBT trauma-processing elements, in addition to cooperative play and creative-expressive elements, and was compared with a wait list control (WLC). Outcomes across the two trials varied. In the Tol et al. (2008) study (Indonesia), girls in the treatment group had a moderate reduction in PTS symptoms and functional impairment and greater hope; boys had greater hope. In the Tol et al. (2014) study, there were no main effects between treatment and WLC, but there were a number of significant moderators (e.g., household size and orphan status).

As a cautionary note, Morina and colleagues' review of psychological interventions for PTSD (and depression) among children and adolescents exposed to mass violence found imputed effect sizes for PTS were medium (for uncontrolled studies) and small (for controlled studies) after adjusting for publication bias (Morina et al., 2017). The strongest effects were seen for treatments that focused on the memories of the traumatic events in some way (e.g., imaginal exposure) versus those that were CBT with a more general focus. This review points out the need to be cautious about enthusiasm, given that in the area of mass violence, the promise of interventions for trauma exposure may have been somewhat overstated when looking at effect sizes across studies and making necessary adjustments for publication bias (i.e., that studies finding no differences may not be published).

13.7 Future directions

We see a few areas that are critical for advancing the field of child and adolescent global mental health. Given the research reviewed here, clearly more studies of psychotherapies in LMIC are needed, particularly those with larger samples or more rigorous evaluation methods (e.g., RCTs). However, we also need more research that provides direction for how to advance knowledge about *how* to implement and support effective psychotherapies in LMIC (Betancourt & Chambers, 2016). We address each of these in turn.

13.7.1 Child and adolescent psychotherapy treatment research in LMIC

While more research is needed, ideally, treatment research in LMIC would build on recent advancements in psychotherapy research. Increasingly, adaptations to existing treatments and newly developed treatments are more in line with the World Health Organization's mandate to "begin with the end in mind" by including attention to potential scale-up and sustainment early and not only after effectiveness is established (World Health Organization, 2011; see also Chapter 1). Some recent research has included a greater focus on treatments that are briefer and lower in complexity and/or include stepped care or lower-intensity options (Salloum et al., 2014), although not all of these efforts are child- and adolescent-focused (Dawson et al., 2015). Recent advancements also include transdiagnostic approaches for children and adolescents that are modular and flexible in nature, including Modular Approach to Therapy for Children with Anxiety, Depression, Trauma, or Conduct Problems (MATCH-ADTC) (33 elements; Weisz et al., 2012) and FIRST, which is an intervention based on just five principles of practice (Weisz, Bearman, et al., 2017; see also Chapter 2). To simplify the understanding of the growing empirical knowledge base, treatment researchers have increasingly moved away from a focus on name-brand interventions and toward a focus on classes or families of interventions (Southam-Gerow & Prinstein, 2014). This move is supported by research in the area of behavior problems cited earlier, which documents that whether "homegrown" or name brand, the "ingredients" or elements of an intervention are what matter for client outcomes (Leijten et al., 2016).

13.7.2 Greater focus on implementation

Addressing the mental health treatment gap will depend on attention to factors beyond a treatment's effectiveness, to factors like feasibility, penetration, and sustainment (see also Chapter 4). Unfortunately, there are few examples of interventions for child and adolescent mental health that have been scaled up or sustained in either HIC or LMIC. Research clearly documents that simply training providers—without other supports—is not an effective approach to implementation (Beidas & Kendall, 2010; Rawson et al., 2013). Attention to other implementation supports (e.g., supervision/consultation and workflow adjustments), organizations themselves (Weiner, Lewis, & Linnan, 2009), and implementation climate (i.e., the degree to which any innovation is expected, supported, and rewarded; Klein & Sorra, 1996) is necessary. While this chapter focuses on interventions to improve mental health for children and adolescents, attention to the broader array of determinants of implementation at multiple levels (provider and organization) will be needed.

The National Institute of Mental Health (NIMH) has been calling for implementation science research that focuses on scale-up and sustainment of mental health treatments in LMIC (National Institutes of Health, 2016). With the urgent need for research in this area—identifying treatments that are effective in LMIC and how we can best scale-up and sustain them—hybrid effectiveness and implementation studies are needed (Curran, Bauer, Mittman, Pyne, & Stetler, 2012). In a study by our research group (Dorsey & Whetten, MPIs; MH108551; Authors Dorsey, Lucid, and Amanya), Building and Sustaining Interventions for Children (BASIC), we are testing approaches to scaling up and sustaining an EBT (TF-CBT; Cohen, Mannarino, & Deblinger, 2006) that has evidence in LMIC and in Kenya, specifically (Dorsey et al., in preparation).

As in other works, we use a task sharing approach, but we advance task sharing efforts. Experienced former lay counselors at a nongovernmental organization in Bungoma, Kenya, Ace Africa, are "promoted" and serve as trainers and supervisors for new lay counselors—teachers and community health volunteers (CHVs) who will deliver TF-CBT (called Pamoja Tunaweza, or "Together We Can" in Kiswahili) in the education and health sectors, respectively, to increase population reach. Although the local trainers still receive some support from mental health professionals, they provide all of the direct training and supervision. Given that 2% or less of health budgets in most LMIC are dedicated to mental health (Thornicroft et al., 2010), the potential promise of task sharing for closing the mental health treatment gap goes unrealized if evidence-based guidance for pursuing low-cost delivery solutions is unavailable. BASIC is a partnership between Ace Africa and the Ministries of Education and Health, focusing on urban and rural areas, and leverages a large country-wide volunteer network (e.g., the CHVs). The study builds on Kenya's National Mental Health Policy (launched May 2016; Kenya Mental Health Policy 2015–30), which includes priority actions such as increasing the budgetary allocation of mental health services to WHO minimum standards at the county and national levels, public-private partnerships, and multisectoral approaches for service provision, promoting equity, and targeted interventions for more vulnerable groups, including children and adolescents. BASIC focuses on implementation practices and policies that support successful implementation (i.e., adoption, fidelity, and sustainment) in both the health and education sectors, applying Weiner and colleagues' theory of organizational effectiveness (Weiner et al., 2009). In schools, Pamoja Tunaweza is being delivered over game time (a period for athletics and extracurricular activities), with the hope of making it a part of a club regularly incorporated in the curriculum. We hope that BASIC yields information to inform Kenyan policies around how to best provide and support mental health care for young people.

13.8 Conclusion

The science for children's mental health globally has advanced substantially in the last 10–15 years, and we expect greater testing of potentially effective approaches in LMIC in the coming years. We hope these studies include implementation-level questions, as in BASIC, that allow us to rapidly generate new knowledge that can inform efforts to bridge the mental health treatment gap in LMIC and improve the lives of children.

References

Annan, J., Sim, A., Puffer, E. S., Salhi, C., & Betancourt, T. S. (2017). Improving mental health outcomes of Burmese migrant and displaced children in Thailand: A community-based randomized controlled trial of a parenting and family skills intervention. *Prevention Science*, *18*(7), 793–803. https://doi.org/10.1007/s11121-016-0728-2.

Arseneault, L., Cannon, M., Fisher, H. L., Polanczyk, G., Moffitt, T. E., & Caspi, A. (2011). Childhood trauma and children's emerging psychotic symptoms: A genetically sensitive longitudinal cohort study. *American Journal of Psychiatry*, *168*(1), 65–72. https://doi.org/10.1176/appi.ajp.2010.10040567.

Atwoli, L., Stein, D. J., Koenen, K. C., & McLaughlin, K. A. (2015). Epidemiology of post-traumatic stress disorder: Prevalence, correlates and consequences. *Current Opinion in Psychiatry*, *28*(4), 307–311. https://doi.org/10.1097/YCO.0000000000000167.

Beidas, R. S., & Kendall, P. C. (2010). Training therapists in evidence-based practice: A critical review of studies from a systems-contextual perspective. *Clinical Psychology: Science and Practice*, *17*(1), 1–30. https://doi.org/10.1111/j.1468-2850.2009.01187.x.

Benjet, C., Borges, G., Medina-Mora, M. E., Zambrano, J., & Aguilar-Gaxiola, S. (2009). Youth mental health in a populous city of the developing world: Results from the mexican adolescent mental health survey. *Journal of Child Psychology and Psychiatry and Allied Disciplines*, *50*(4), 386–395. https://doi.org/10.1111/j.1469-7610.2008.01962.x.

Betancourt, T. S., & Chambers, D. A. (2016). Optimizing an era of global mental health implementation science. *JAMA Psychiatry*, *73*(2), 99–100. https://doi.org/10.1001/jamapsychiatry.2015.2705.

Betancourt, T. S., McBain, R., Newnham, E. A., Akinsulure-Smith, A. M., Brennan, R. T., Weisz, J. R., & Hansen, N. B. (2014). A behavioral intervention for war-affected youth in Sierra Leone: A randomized controlled trial. *Journal of the American Academy of Child & Adolescent Psychiatry*, *53*(12), 1288–1297. https://doi.org/10.1016/j.jaac.2014.09.011.

Bolton, P., Bass, J., Betancourt, T., Speelman, L., Onyango, G., Clougherty, K. F., … Verdeli, H. (2007). Interventions for depression symptoms among adolescent survivors of war and displacement in northern Uganda: A randomized controlled trial. *Journal of the American Medical Association*, *298*(5), 519–527. https://doi.org/10.1001/jama.298.5.519.

Bolton, P., Lee, C., Haroz, E. E., Murray, L., Dorsey, S., Robinson, C., … Bass, J. (2014). A transdiagnostic community-based mental health treatment for comorbid disorders: Development and outcomes of a randomized controlled trial among Burmese refugees in Thailand. *PLoS Medicine*, *11*(11), 1–16. https://doi.org/10.1371/journal.pmed.

Cartwright-Hatton, S., McNicol, K., & Doubleday, E. (2006). Anxiety in a neglected population: Prevalence of anxiety disorders in pre-adolescent children. *Clinical Psychology Review*, *26*(7), 817–833. https://doi.org/10.1016/j.cpr.2005.12.002.

Chaffin, M., Funderburk, B., Bard, D., Valle, L.-A., & Gurwitch, R. (2011). A combined motivation and parent-child interaction therapy package reduces child welfare recidivism in a randomized dismantling field trial. *Journal of Consulting and Clinical Psychology*, *79*(1), 84–95. https://doi.org/10.1037/a0021227.

Chen, Y., Shen, W. W., Gao, K., Lam, C. S., Chang, W. C., & Deng, H. (2014). Effectiveness RCT of a CBT intervention for youths who lost parents in the Sichuan, China, earthquake. *Psychiatric Services*, *65*(2), 259–262. https://doi.org/10.1176/appi.ps.201200470.

Chorpita, B. F., & Daleiden, E. L. (2009). Mapping evidence-based treatments for children and adolescents: application of the distillation and matching model to 615 treatments from 322 randomized trials. *Journal of Consulting and Clinical Psychology*, *77*(3), 566–579. https://doi.org/10.1037/a0014565.

Chorpita, B. F., Daleiden, E. L., & Weisz, J. R. (2005). Identifying and selecting the common elements of evidence based interventions: A distillation and matching model. *Mental Health Services Research*, *7*(1), 5–20. https://doi.org/10.1007/s11020-005-1962-6.

Cohen, J. A., Deblinger, E., & Mannarino, A. P. (2006). Trauma-focused cognitive-behavioral therapy for sexually abused children. In E. D. Hibbs & P. S. Jensen (Eds.), *Psychosocial treatments for child and adolescent disorders: Empirically based strategies for clinical practice* (pp. 743–765). (2nd ed.). Washington, DC: American Psychological Association.

Cohen, J. A., Mannarino, A. P., & Deblinger, E. (2006). *Treating trauma and traumatic grief in children and adolescents*. New York City, NY: Guilford Press.

Collins, Y., Patel, V., Joestl, S., March, D., Insel, T., & Daar, A. (2011). Grand challenges in global mental health. *Nature*, *475*, 27–30. https://doi.org/10.1038/475027a.Grand.

Copeland, W. E., Keeler, G., Angold, A., & Costello, E. J. (2007). Traumatic events and posttraumatic stress in childhood. *Archives of General Psychiatry*, *64*(5), 577–584. https://doi.org/10.1001/archpsyc.64.5.577.

Costantino, G., Malgady, R. G., & Rogler, L. H. (1994). Storytelling through pictures: Culturally sensitive psychotherapy for Hispanic children and adolescents. *Journal of Clinical Child Psychology*, *23*(1), 13–20. https://doi.org/10.1207/s15374424jccp2301_3.

Creswell, C., Waite, P., & Cooper, P. J. (2014). Assessment and management of anxiety disorders in children and adolescents. *Archives of Disease in Childhood*, *99*(7), 674–678. https://doi.org/10.1136/archdischild-2013-303768.

Curran, G. M., Bauer, M., Mittman, B., Pyne, J. M., & Stetler, C. (2012). Effectiveness-implementation hybrid designs: Combining elements of clinical effectiveness and implementation research to enhance public health impact. *Medical Care*, *50*(3), 217–226. https://doi.org/10.1097/MLR.0b013e3182408812.

Davis, R., Mansur De Souza, M. A., Rigatti, R., & Heldt, E. (2015). Two-year outcome following group cognitive behavioural therapy for adolescents with anxiety disorders in low- and middle-income Country. *Journal of Psychology and Behavioral Science*, *3*(1), 71–77. https://doi.org/10.15640/jpbs.v3n1a8.

Dawson, K. S., Bryant, R. A., Harper, M., Kuowei Tay, A., Rahman, A., Schafer, A., & van Ommeren, M. (2015). Problem management plus (PM+): A WHO transdiagnostic psychological intervention for common mental health problems. *World Psychiatry*, *14*(3), 354–357. https://doi.org/10.1002/wps.20255.

de Souza, M. A., Salum, G. A., Jarros, R. B., Isolan, L., Davis, R., Knijnik, D., … Heldt, E. (2013). Cognitive-behavioral group therapy for youths with anxiety disorders in the community: Effectiveness in low and middle income countries. *Behavioural & Cognitive Psychotherapy*, *41*(3), 255–264. https://doi.org/10.1017/S1352465813000015.

Dorsey, S., Lucid, L., Martin, P. M., King, K., O'Donnell, K., Murray, K., … Whetten, R. (in preparation). Task-shared trauma-focused cognitive behavioral therapy for orphaned children: A randomized trial in Kenya and Tanzania.

Dorsey, S., McLaughlin, K. A., Kerns, S. E. U., Harrison, J. P., Lambert, H. K., Briggs, E. C., … Amaya-Jackson, L. (2017). Evidence base update for psychosocial treatments for children and adolescents exposed to traumatic events. *Journal of Clinical Child & Adolescent Psychology*, *46*(3), 303–330. https://doi.org/10.1080/15374416.2016.1220309.

Dunn, E. C., Nishimi, K., Powers, A., & Bradley, B. (2017). Is developmental timing of trauma exposure associated with depressive and post-traumatic stress disorder symptoms in adulthood? *Journal of Psychiatric Research*, *84*, 119–127. https://doi.org/10.1016/j.jpsychires.2016.09.004.

Ebesutani, C. K., Helmi, K., Fierstein, M., Taghizadeh, M. E., & Chorpita, B. F. (2016). A pilot study of modular cognitive-behavioral therapy and cognitive-behavioral hypnotherapy for treating anxiety in Iranian girls. *International Journal of Cognitive Therapy*, *9*(1), 13–37. https://doi.org/10.1521/ijct_2016_09_01.

Ertl, V., Pfeiffer, A., Schauer, E., Elbert, T., & Neuner, F. (2011). Community-implemented trauma therapy for former child soldiers in northern Uganda. *JAMA*, *306*(5), 503–512. https://doi.org/10.1001/jama.2011.1060.

Essau, C. A., & Gabhidon, J. (2013). Epidemiology, comorbidity and mental health services utilization. In *The Wiley-Blackwell handbook of the treatment of childhood and adolescent anxiety*. Hoboken, NJ: Wiley.

Eyberg, S. M., & Robinson, E. A. (1982). Parent-child interaction training: Effects on family functioning. *Journal of Clinical Child & Adolescent Psychology*, *11*(2), 130–137. https://doi.org/10.1080/15374418209533076.

Fleitlich-Bilyk, B., & Goodman, R. (2004). Prevalence of child and adolescent psychiatric disorders in Southeast Brazil. *Journal of the American Academy of Child and Adolescent Psychiatry*, *43*(6), 727–734. https://doi.org/10.1097/01.chi.0000120021.14101.ca.

Gardner, F., Montgomery, P., & Knerr, W. (2016). Transporting evidence-based parenting programs for child problem behavior (age 3–10) between countries: Systematic review and meta-analysis. *Journal of Clinical Child & Adolescent Psychology*, *45*(6), 749–762. https://doi.org/10.1080/15374416.2015.1015134.

Garland, A. F., Hawley, K. M., Brookman-Frazee, L., & Hurlburt, M. S. (2008). Identifying common elements of evidence-based psychosocial treatments for children's disruptive behavior problems. *Journal of the American Academy of Child and Adolescent Psychiatry*, *47*(5), 505–514. https://doi.org/10.1097/CHI.0b013e31816765c2.

Ginsburg, G. S., & Drake, K. L. (2002). School-based treatment for anxious African-American adolescents: A controlled pilot study. *Journal of the American Academy of Child and Adolescent Psychiatry*, *41*(7), 768–775. https://doi.org/10.1097/00004583-200207000-00007.

Gore, F. M., Bloem, P. J. N., Patton, G. C., Ferguson, J., Joseph, V., Coffey, C., … Mathers, C. D. (2011). Global burden of disease in young people aged 10-24 years: A systematic analysis. *Lancet*, *377*(9783), 2093–2102. https://doi.org/10.1016/S0140-6736(11)60512-6.

Grills-Taquechel, A. E., & Ollendick, T. H. (2013). *Phobic and anxiety disorders in children and adolescents*. Göttingen, Germany: Hogrefe Publishing.

Hasson, H., Sundell, K., Beelmann, A., & von Thiele Schwarz, U. (2014). Novel programs, international adoptions, or contextual adaptations? Meta-analytical results from German and Swedish intervention research. *BMC Health Services Research*, *14*(2), O32. https://doi.org/10.1186/1472-6963-14-S2-O32.

Hedtke, K. A., Kendall, P. C., & Tiwari, S. (2009). Safety-seeking and coping behavior during exposure tasks with anxious youth. *Journal of Clinical Child and Adolescent Psychology*, *38*(1), 1–15. https://doi.org/10.1080/15374410802581055.

Higa-McMillan, C. K., Francis, S. E., Rith-Najarian, L., & Chorpita, B. F. (2016). Evidence base update: 50 years of research on treatment for child and adolescent anxiety. *Journal of Clinical Child & Adolescent Psychology*, *45*(2), 91–113. https://doi.org/10.1080/15374416.2015.1046177.

Huey, S. J., & Polo, A. J. (2008). Evidence-based psychosocial treatments for ethnic minority youth. *Journal of Clinical Child and Adolescent Psychology*, *37*(1), 262–301. https://doi.org/10.1080/15374410701820174.

Ishikawa, S.-I., Motomura, N., Kawabata, Y., Tanaka, H., Shimotsu, S., Sato, Y., & Ollendick, T. H. (2012). Cognitive behavioural therapy for Japanese children and adolescents with anxiety disorders: A pilot study. *Behavioural and Cognitive Psychotherapy*, *40*(3), 271–285. https://doi.org/10.1017/S1352465811000713.

Kaminski, J. W., & Claussen, A. H. (2017). Evidence base update for psychosocial treatments for disruptive behaviors in children. *Journal of Clinical Child & Adolescent Psychology*, *46*(4), 477–499. https://doi.org/10.1080/15374416.2017.1310044.

Kataoka, S. H., Stein, B. D., Jaycox, L. H., Wong, M., Escudero, P., Tu, W., … Fink, A. (2003). School-based mental health program for traumatized Latino immigrant children. *Journal of the American Academy of Child & Adolescent Psychiatry*, *42*(3), 311–318. https:/doi.org/doi:10.1097/00004583-200303000-00011.

Kazdin, A. E. (2000). *Psychotherapy for children and adolescents: Directions for research and practice*. New York, NY: Oxford University Press.

Kazdin, A. E. (2018). Implementation and evaluation of treatments for children and adolescents with conduct problems: Findings, challenges, and future directions. *Psychotherapy Research*, *28*(1), 3–17. https://doi.org/10.1080/10503307.2016.1208374.

Kendall, P. C., & Beidas, R. S. (2007). Smoothing the trail for dissemination of evidence-based practices for youth: Flexibility within fidelity. *Professional Psychology: Research and Practice*, *38*(1), 13–20. https://doi.org/10.1037/0735-7028.38.1.13.

Kessler, R. C., Avenevoli, S., Costello, E. J., Georgiades, K., Green, J. G., Gruber, M. J., … Petukhova, M. (2012). Prevalence, persistence, and sociodemographic correlates of DSM-IV disorders in the National Comorbidity Survey Replication Adolescent Supplement. *Archives of General Psychiatry*, *69*(4), 372–380. https://doi.org/10.1001/archgenpsychiatry.2011.160.

Klasen, H., & Crombag, A.-C. (2013). What works where? A systematic review of child and adolescent mental health interventions for low and middle income countries. *Social Psychiatry and Psychiatric Epidemiology*, *48*(4), 595–611. https://doi.org/10.1007/s00127-012-0566-x.

Klein, K. J., & Sorra, J. S. (1996). The challenge of innovation implementation. *The Academy of Management Review*, *21*(4), 1055–1080. https://doi.org/10.5465/AMR.1996.9704071863.

Koenen, K. C., Ratanatharathorn, A., Ng, L., McLaughlin, K. A., Bromet, E. J., Stein, D. J., … Kessler, R. C. (2017). Posttraumatic stress disorder in the world mental health surveys. *Psychological Medicine*, *47*, 2260–2274. https://doi.org/10.1017/S0033291717000708.

Lau, A. S. (2006). Making the case for selective and directed cultural adaptations of evidence-based treatments: Examples from parent training. *Clinical Psychology: Science and Practice*, *13*(4), 295–310. https://doi.org/10.1111/j.1468-2850.2006.00042.x.

Layne, C. M., Pynoos, R. S., Saltzman, W. R., Arslanagic, B., Black, M., Savjak, N., … Houston, R. (2001). Trauma/grief-focused group psychotherapy: School-based postwar intervention with traumatized Bosnian adolescents. *Group Dynamics: Theory, Research, and Practice*, *5*(4), 277–290.

Layne, C. M., Saltzman, W. R., Poppleton, L., Burlingame, G. M., Pašalić, A., Duraković, E., … Pynoos, R. S. (2008). Effectiveness of a school-based group psychotherapy program for war-exposed adolescents: A randomized controlled trial. *Journal of the American Academy of Child & Adolescent Psychiatry*, *47*(9), 1048–1062. https://doi.org/10.1097/CHI.0b013e31817eecae.

Leijten, P., Melendez-Torres, G. J., Knerr, W., & Gardner, F. (2016). Transported versus homegrown parenting interventions for reducing disruptive child behavior: A multilevel meta-regression study. *Journal of the American Academy of Child & Adolescent Psychiatry*, *55* (7), 610–617. https://doi.org/10.1016/j.jaac.2016.05.003.

Manassis, K., Changgun Le, T., Bennett, K., Zhao, X. Y., Mendlowitz, S., Duda, S., … Wood, J. J. (2014). Types of parental involvement in CBT with anxious youth: A preliminary meta-analysis. *Journal of Consulting and Clinical Psychology*, *82*(6), 1163–1172. https://doi.org/10.1037/a0036969.

Matos, M., Torres, R., Santiago, R., Jurado, M., & Rodriguez, I. X. A. (2006). Adaptation of parent–child interaction therapy for Puerto Rican families: A preliminary study. *Family Process*, *45*(2), 205–222. https://doi.org/10.1111/j.1545-5300.2006.00091.x.

McCart, M. R., & Sheidow, A. J. (2016). Evidence-based psychosocial treatments for adolescents with disruptive behavior. *Journal of Clinical Child & Adolescent Psychology*, *45*(5), 529–563. https://doi.org/10.1080/15374416.2016.1146990.

McLaughlin, K. A., Green, J. G., Gruber, M. J., Sampson, N. A., Zaslavsky, A. M., & Kessler, R. C. (2010). Childhood adversities and adult psychiatric disorders in the national comorbidity survey replication II: Associations with persistence of DSM-IV disorders. *Archives of General Psychiatry*, *67*(2), 113–123. https://doi.org/10.1001/archgenpsychiatry.2009.187.

McLaughlin, K. A., Koenen, K., Hill, E., Petukhova, M., Sampson, N., Zaslavsky, A., & Kessler, R. (2013). Trauma exposure and posttraumatic stress disorder in a national sample of adolescents. *Journal of the American Academy of Child and Adolescent Psychiatry*, *52* (8), 815–830. https://doi.org/10.1124/dmd.107.016501.CYP3A4-Mediated.

McMullen, J., O'Callaghan, P., Shannon, C., Black, A., & Eakin, J. (2013). Group trauma-focused cognitive-behavioural therapy with former child soldiers and other war-affected boys in the DR Congo: A randomised controlled trial. *Journal of Child Psychology and Psychiatry*, *54*(11), 1231–1241. https://doi.org/10.1111/jcpp.12094.

Mejia, A., Leijten, P., Lachman, J. M., & Parra-Cardona, J. R. (2017). Different strokes for different folks? Contrasting approaches to cultural adaptation of parenting interventions. *Prevention Science*, *18*(6), 630–639. https://doi.org/10.1007/s11121-016-0671-2.

Merikangas, K. R., He, J., Burstein, M., Swanson, S. A., Avenevoli, S., Cui, L., … Swendsen, J. (2010). Lifetime prevalence of mental disorders in US adolescents: Results from the National Comorbidity Survey Replication–Adolescent Supplement (NCS-A). *Journal of the American Academy of Child & Adolescent Psychiatry*, *49*(10), 980–989. https://doi.org/10.1016/j.jaac.2010.05.017.

Morina, N., Malek, M., Nickerson, A., & Bryant, R. A. (2017). Psychological interventions for post-traumatic stress disorder and depression in young survivors of mass violence in low- and middle-income countries: Meta-analysis. *British Journal of Psychiatry*, *210*(4), 247–254. https://doi.org/10.1192/bjp.bp.115.180265.

Morsette, A., Swaney, G., Stolle, D., Schuldberg, D., van den Pol, R., & Young, M. (2009). Cognitive behavioral intervention for trauma in schools (CBITS): School-based treatment on a rural American Indian reservation. *Journal of Behavior Therapy and Experimental Psychiatry*, *40*(1), 169–178. https://doi.org/10.1016/j.jbtep.2008.07.006.

Murray, L. K., Familiar, I., Skavenski, S., Jere, E., Cohen, J., Imasiku, M., … Bolton, P. (2013). An evaluation of trauma focused cognitive behavioral therapy for children in Zambia. *Child Abuse & Neglect*, *37*(12), 1175–1185. https://doi.org/10.1016/j.chiabu.2013.04.017.

Murray, L. K., Hall, B. J., Dorsey, S., Ugueto, A. M., Puffer, E. S., Sim, A., … Bolton, P. A. (2018). An evaluation of a common elements treatment approach for youth in Somali refugee camps. *Global Mental Health*, *5*(16), 1–15. https://doi.org/10.1017/gmh.2018.7.

Murray, L. K., Skavenski, S., Kane, J. C., Mayeya, J., Dorsey, S., Cohen, J. A., … Bolton, P. A. (2015). Effectiveness of trauma-focused cognitive behavioral therapy among trauma-affected children in Lusaka, Zambia: A randomized clinical trial. *JAMA Pediatrics*, *169*(8). https://doi.org/10.1001/jamapediatrics.2015.0580.

Murray, L. K., Skavenski, S., Michalopoulos, L. M., Bolton, P. A., Bass, J. K., Familiar, I., … Cohen, J. (2014). Counselor and client perspectives of trauma-focused cognitive behavioral therapy for children in Zambia: A qualitative study. *Journal of*

Clinical Child & Adolescent Psychology, *43*(6), 1–13. https://doi.org/10.1080/15374416.2013.859079.

National Institutes of Health (2016). *Implementation science for the prevention and treatment of mental and/or substance use disorders in low- and middle-income countries (U01)*. .

Newnham, E. A., McBain, R. K., Hann, K., Akinsulure-Smith, A. M., Weisz, J., Lilienthal, G. M., … Betancourt, T. S. (2015). The youth readiness intervention for war-affected youth. *Journal of Adolescent Health*, *56*(6), 606–611. https://doi.org/10.1016/j.jadohealth.2015.01.020.

Ngo, V., Langley, A., Kataoka, S. H., Nadeem, E., Escudero, P., & Stein, B. D. (2008). Providing evidence-based practice to ethnically diverse youths: Examples from the cognitive behavioral intervention for trauma in schools (CBITS) program. *Journal of the American Academy of Child and Adolescent Psychiatry*, *47*(8), 858–862. https://doi.org/10.1097/CHI.0b013e3181799f19.

O'Callaghan, P., McMullen, J., Shannon, C., Rafferty, H., & Black, A. (2013). A randomized controlled trial of trauma-focused cognitive behavioral therapy for sexually exploited, war-affected Congolese girls. *Journal of the American Academy of Child & Adolescent Psychiatry*, *52*(4), 359–369. https://doi.org/10.1016/j.jaac.2013.01.013.

O'Donnell, K., Dorsey, S., Gong, W., Ostermann, J., Whetten, R., Cohen, J. A., … Whetten, K. (2014). Treating maladaptive grief and posttraumatic stress symptoms in orphaned children in Tanzania: Group-based trauma-focused cognitive-behavioral therapy. *Journal of Traumatic Stress*, *27*(6). https://doi.org/10.1002/jts.21970.

Onyut, L. P., Neuner, F., Schauer, E., Ertl, V., Odenwald, M., Schauer, M., & Elbert, T. (2005). Narrative exposure therapy as a treatment for child war survivors with posttraumatic stress disorder: Two case reports and a pilot study in an African refugee settlement. *BMC Psychiatry*, *5*(1), 1–9. https:/doi.org/10.1186/1471-244X-5-7.

Patel, V., Flisher, A. J., Hetrick, S., & McGorry, P. (2007). Mental health of young people: A global public-health challenge. *Lancet*, *369*(9569), 1302–1313. https://doi.org/10.1016/S0140-6736(07)60368-7.

Patel, V., Simon, G., Chowdhary, N., Kaaya, S., & Araya, R. (2009). Packages of care for depression in low- and middle-income countries. *PLoS Medicine*, *6*(10). https://doi.org/10.1371/journal.pmed.1000159.

Peris, T. S., Caporino, N. E., O'Rourke, S., Kendall, P. C., Walkup, J. T., Albano, A. M., … Compton, S. N. (2017). Therapist-reported features of exposure tasks that predict differential treatment outcomes for youth with anxiety. *Journal of the American Academy of Child and Adolescent Psychiatry*, *56*(12), 1043–1052. https://doi.org/10.1016/j.jaac.2017.10.001.

Polanczyk, G. V., Salum, G. A., Sugaya, L. S., Caye, A., & Rohde, L. A. (2015). Annual research review: A meta-analysis of the worldwide prevalence of mental disorders in children and adolescents. *Journal of Child Psychology & Psychiatry & Allied Disciplines*, *56* (3), 345–365. https:/doi:10.1111/jcpp.12381.

Puffer, E. S., Annan, J., Sim, A. L., Salhi, C., & Betancourt, T. S. (2017). The impact of a family skills training intervention among Burmese migrant families in Thailand: A randomized controlled trial. *PLoS ONE*, *12*(3), 1–19. https://doi.org/10.1371/journal.pone.0172611.

Puffer, E. S., Green, E. P., Chase, R. M., Sim, A. L., Zayzay, J., Friis, E., … Boone, L. (2015). Parents make the difference: A randomized-controlled trial of a parenting intervention in Liberia. *Global Mental Health*, *2*, 1–13. https://doi.org/10.1017/gmh.2015.12.

Rawson, R. A., Rataemane, S., Rataemane, L., Ntlhe, N., Fox, R. S., McCuller, J., & Brecht, M.-L. L. (2013). Dissemination and implementation of cognitive behavioral therapy for stimulant dependence: A randomized trial comparison of 3 approaches. *Substance Abuse*, *34*(2), 108–117. https://doi.org/10.1080/08897077.2012.691445.

Rivet-Duval, E., Heriot, S., & Hunt, C. (2011). Preventing adolescent depression in Mauritius: A universal school-based program. *Child and Adolescent Mental Health*, *16*(2), 86–91. https://doi.org/10.1111/j.1475-3588.2010.00584.x.

Rosenstein, D., & Seedat, S. (2011). Child and adolescent cognitive behaviour therapy in South Africa: An editorial review. *Journal of Child and Adolescent Mental Health*, *23*(2), 69–73. https://doi.org/10.2989/17280583.2011.644447.

Rosselló, J., Bernal, G., & Rivera-Medina, C. (2008). Individual and group CBT and IPT for Puerto Rican adolescents with depressive symptoms. *Cultural Diversity and Ethnic Minority Psychology*, *14*(3), 234–245. https://doi.org/10.1037/1099-9809.14.3.234.

Ruf, M., Schauer, M., Neuner, F., Catani, C., Schauer, E., & Elbert, T. (2010). Narrative exposure therapy for 7- to 16-year-olds: A randomized controlled trial with traumatized refugee children. *Journal of Traumatic Stress*, *23*(4), 437–445. https://doi.org/10.1002/jts.20548.

Salloum, A., Robst, J., Scheeringa, M. S., Cohen, J. A., Wang, W., Murphy, T. K., … Storch, E. A. (2014). Step one within stepped care trauma-focused cognitive behavioral therapy for young children: A pilot study. *Child Psychiatry & Human Development*, *45*(1), 65–77.

Saxena, S., Thornicroft, G., Knapp, M., & Whiteford, H. (2007). Resources for mental health: Scarcity, inequity, and inefficiency. *Lancet*, *370*(9590), 878–889. https://doi.org/10.1016/S0140-6736(07)61239-2.

Schauer, M., Neuner, F., & Elbert, T. (2017). Narrative exposure therapy for children and adolescents (KIDNET). In M. Landolt, M. Cloitre, & U. Schnyder (Eds.), *Evidence-based treatments for trauma related disorders in children and adolescents* (pp. 227–250). Cham: Springer International Publishing. https://doi.org/10.1007/978-3-319-46138-0_11.

Silverman, W. K., Kurtines, W. M., Ginsburg, G. S., Weems, C. F., Lumpkin, P. W., & Carmichael, D. H. (1999). Treating anxiety disorders in children with group cognitive-behavioral therapy: A randomized clinical trial. *Journal of Consulting and Clinical Psychology*, *67*(6), 995–1003. https://doi.org/10.1037/0022-006X.67.6.995.

Southam-Gerow, M. A., & Prinstein, M. J. (2014). Evidence base updates: The evolution of the evaluation of psychological treatments for children and adolescents. *Journal of Clinical Child & Adolescent Psychology*, *43*(1), 1–6. https://doi.org/10.1080/15374416.2013.855128.

Stein, B. D., Jaycox, L. H., Kataoka, S. H., Wong, M., Tu, W., Elliott, M. N., & Fink, A. (2003). A mental health intervention for schoolchildren exposed to violence: A randomized controlled trial. *Journal of the American Medical Association*, *290*(5), 603–611. https://doi.org/10.1001/jama.290.5.603.

Thornicroft, G., Alem, A., Dos Santos, R. A., Barley, E., Drake, R. E., Gregorio, G., … Wondimagegn, D. (2010). WPA guidance on steps, obstacles and mistakes to avoid in the implementation of community mental health care. *World Psychiatry*, *9*(2), 67–77. https://doi.org/10.1002/j.2051-5545.2010.tb00276.x.

Thornicroft, G., Chatterji, S., Evans-Lacko, S., Gruber, M., Sampson, N., Aguilar-Gaxiola, S., … Kessler, R. C. (2017). Undertreatment of people with major depressive disorder in 21 countries. *British Journal of Psychiatry*, *210*(2), 119–124. https://doi.org/10.1192/bjp.bp.116.188078.

Tiwari, S., Kendall, P. C., Hoff, A. L., Harrison, J. P., & Fizur, P. (2013). Characteristics of exposure sessions as predictors of treatment response in anxious youth. *Journal of Clinical Child and Adolescent Psychology*, *42*(1), 34–43. https://doi.org/10.1080/15374416.2012.738454.

Tol, W. A., Komproe, I. H., Jordans, M. J. D., Ndayisaba, A., Ntamutumba, P., Sipsma, H., … de Jong, J. T. V. M. (2014). School-based mental health intervention for children in war-affected Burundi: A cluster randomized trial. *BMC Medicine*, *12*(1), 56. https://doi.org/10.1186/1741-7015-12-56.

Tol, W. A., Komproe, I. H., Susanty, D., Jordans, M. J. D., Macy, R. D., & De Jong, J. T. V. M. (2008). School-based mental health intervention for children affected by political violence in Indonesia: A cluster randomized trial. *JAMA*, *300*(6), 655–662. https://doi.org/10.1001/jama.300.6.655.

Trocmé, N., & Wolfe, D. (2001). Child maltreatment in Canada: Selected results from the Canadian incidence study of reported child abuse and neglect. Ottawa, Ontario: Minister of Public Works and Government Services Canada (retrieved 15.05.13).

Visagie, L., Loxton, H., & Silverman, W. K. (2015). Research protocol: Development, implementation and evaluation of a cognitive behavioural therapy-based intervention programme for the management of anxiety symptoms in South African children with visual impairments. *African Journal of Disability*, *4*(1), 1–10. https://doi.org/10.4102/ajod.v4i1.160.

Vlahovicova, K., Melendez-Torres, G. J., Leijten, P., Knerr, W., & Gardner, F. (2017). Parenting programs for the prevention of child physical abuse recurrence: A systematic review and meta-analysis. *Clinical Child and Family Psychology Review*, *20*(3), 351–365. https://doi.org/10.1007/s10567-017-0232-7.

Weersing, V. R., Jeffreys, M., Do, M.-C. T., Schwartz, K. T. G., & Bolano, C. (2017). Evidence base update of psychosocial treatments for child and adolescent depression. *Journal of Clinical Child & Adolescent Psychology*, *46*(1), 11–43. https://doi.org/10.1080/15374416.2016.1220310.

Weersing, V. R., Rozenman, M., & Gonzalez, A. (2009). Core components of therapy in youth: Do we know what to disseminate? *Behavior Modification*, *33*(1), 24–47. https://doi.org/10.1177/0145445508322629.

Weiner, B. J., Lewis, M. A., & Linnan, L. A. (2009). Using organization theory to understand the determinants of effective implementation of worksite health promotion programs. *Health Education Research*, *24*(2), 292–305. https://doi.org/10.1093/her/cyn019.

Weiss, W. M., Murray, L. K., Zangana, G. A. S., Mahmooth, Z., Kaysen, D., Dorsey, S., … Bolton, P. (2015). Community-based mental health treatments for survivors of torture and militant attacks in Southern Iraq: A randomized control trial. *BMC Psychiatry*, *15*(1), 249. https://doi.org/10.1186/s12888-015-0622-7.

Weisz, J. R., Bearman, S. K., Santucci, L. C., & Jensen-Doss, A. (2017). Initial test of a principle-guided approach to transdiagnostic psychotherapy with children and adolescents. *Journal of Clinical Child and Adolescent Psychology*, *46*(1), 44–58. https://doi.org/10.1080/15374416.2016.1163708.

Weisz, J. R., Chorpita, B. F., Palinkas, L. A., Schoenwald, S. K., Miranda, J., Bearman, S. K., … Martin, J. (2012). Testing standard and modular designs for psychotherapy treating depression, anxiety, and conduct problems in youth: A randomized effectiveness trial. *Archives of General Psychiatry*, *69*(3), 274–282. https://doi.org/10.1001/archgenpsychiatry.2011.147.

Weisz, J. R., Kuppens, S., Ng, M. Y., Eckshtain, D., Ugueto, A. M., Vaughn-Coaxum, R., … Fordwood, S. R. (2017). What five decades of research tells us about the effects of youth psychological therapy: A multilevel meta-analysis and implications for science and practice. *American Psychologist*, *72*(2), 79–117. https://doi.org/10.1037/a0040360.

Wethington, H. R., Hahn, R. A., Fuqua-Whitley, D. S., Sipe, T. A., Crosby, A. E., Johnson, R. L., … Chattopadhyay, S. K. (2008). The effectiveness of interventions to reduce psychological harm from traumatic events among children and adolescents: A systematic review.

American Journal of Preventive Medicine, *35*(3), 287–313. https://doi.org/10.1016/j.amepre.2008.06.024.

Whittle, S., Vijayakumar, N., Simmons, J. G., Dennison, M., Schwartz, O., Pantelis, C., … Allen, N. B. (2017). Role of positive parenting in the association between neighborhood social disadvantage and brain development across adolescence. *JAMA Psychiatry*, *74*(8), 824–832. https://doi.org/10.1001/jamapsychiatry.2017.1558.

Wilson, N. H., & Rotter, J. C. (1986). Anxiety management training and study skills counseling for students on self-esteem and test anxiety and performance. *The School Counselor*, *34*(1), 18–31. https://www.jstor.org/stable/23900379.

Woods-Jaeger, B. A., Kava, C. M., Akiba, C. F., Lucid, L., & Dorsey, S. (2017). The art and skill of delivering culturally responsive trauma-focused cognitive behavioral therapy in Tanzania and Kenya. *Psychological Trauma: Theory, Research, Practice, and Policy*, *9*(2). https://doi.org/10.1037/tra0000170.

World Health Organization. (2011). Beginning with the end in mind: Planning pilot projects and other programmatic research for successful scaling up. Geneva, Switzerland: WHO.

Yatham, S., Sivathasan, S., Yoon, R., da Silva, T. L., & Ravindran, A. V. (2017). Depression, anxiety, and post-traumatic stress disorder among youth in low and middle income countries: A review of prevalence and treatment interventions. *Asian Journal of Psychiatry*. Advance online publication. https://doi.org/10.1016/j.ajp.2017.10.029.

Yu, D. L., & Seligman, M. E. P. (2002). Preventing depressive symptoms in Chinese children. *Prevention & Treatment*, *5*(1). https://doi.org/10.1037/1522-3736.5.1.59a.

Zhou, X., Hetrick, S. E., Cuijpers, P., Qin, B., Barth, J., Whittington, C. J., … Michael, K. D. (2015). Comparative efficacy and acceptability of psychotherapies for depression in children and adolescents: A systematic review and network meta-analysis. *World Psychiatry*, *14*(2), 207–222. https://doi.org/10.1002/wps.20217.

Psychotherapy for perinatal mental disorders in low- and middle-income countries

14

*Thandi Davies**, *Atif Rahman*†, *Crick Lund**,‡
*Alan J Flisher Centre for Public Mental Health, Department of Psychiatry and Mental Health, University of Cape Town, Cape Town, South Africa, †Institute for Psychological Health and Society, University of Liverpool, Liverpool, United Kingdom, ‡Centre for Global Mental Health, Department of Health Service and Population Research, Institute of Psychiatry, Psychology and Neuroscience, King's College London, London, United Kingdom

14.1 Perinatal mental disorders

Mental, neurological, and substance use disorders now account for over 10% of all burden of disease (GBD 2015 DALYs and Hale Collaborators, 2016), with mental and substance use disorders specifically being the leading cause of years lived with disability (YLD) in 2010 (Whiteford et al., 2013). Increasingly, perinatal mental disorders are being brought into the spotlight. The latest pooled prevalence estimates of depression in pregnancy and the postpartum period in low- and middle-income countries (LMIC) are 19.2% and 18.7%, respectively, which is almost double that of high-income countries, at 9.2% prenatally and 9.5% postnatally (Woody, Ferrari, Siskind, Whiteford, & Harris, 2017).

Perinatal mental disorders occur in the perinatal period, which is generally understood as the period from conception until an infant is 1 year old. The most common perinatal mental disorders are depression and anxiety disorders. Others include post-traumatic stress disorder (PTSD), somatic disorders, and obsessive-compulsive disorder (OCD). These are generally known as perinatal common mental disorders (PCMDs). Less common but more serious conditions include postpartum psychosis and suicidal behavior.

It is particularly important to address and treat PCMDs, not only because of the disability they cause for women but also because of the wide-ranging impacts they have on infants. Pregnant mothers with common mental disorders (CMDs) are at risk of neglecting prenatal care, missing check-ups, having inappropriate diet, poor weight gain, and low baby birth weight, using harmful substances, and self-harm and suicide (Stewart, 2011). The presence of a CMD in pregnancy also increases the risk of depression and other CMDs postnatally (Rahman & Creed, 2007). Postnatal depression has been found to predict poor mother-infant relationships and slower child growth, affect child temperament, and impair behavioral and cognitive development (Cooper et al., 2009; Surkan, Kennedy, Hurley, & Black, 2011). This condition can

Global Mental Health and Psychotherapy. https://doi.org/10.1016/B978-0-12-814932-4.00014-8

also affect appropriate attachment and bonding in infants and children and can lead to social difficulties later on (Murray, Fiori-Cowley, Hooper, & Cooper, 1996). At a very early age, young infants are already able to observe and interpret their mothers' affect and interaction and can modify their own responses accordingly (Cohn, Matias, Tronick, Connell, & Lyons-Ruth, 1986). If a mother is detached and unresponsive to cues put out by the infant, this can cause withdrawal and discontent (Murray, Cooper, & Stein, 1991), with appreciable difficulties for children later in life.

Despite the high rates of PCMDs, they are still largely unrecognized in LMIC (Rahman et al., 2013) and do not receive the research attention or service personnel they deserve (Saxena, Thornicroft, Knapp, & Whiteford, 2007). Where services are provided, they are usually led by nongovernmental organizations or research institutions. There is consequently an enormous treatment gap, referring to the gap between the number of women suffering from PCMDs and the number who receive evidence-based care.

In order to try and address this treatment gap, task sharing has been recommended to provide a degree of health service provision where previously it has been poor or absent. Task sharing involves employing nonspecialist health workers such as community health workers (CHWs) to deliver mental health care through routine healthcare delivery systems but trained and supervised by mental health specialists. The focus of most mental health research innovations in LMIC in recent years has been on testing the effectiveness of task sharing for mental health care (see Chapter 1).

14.2 Risk factors and social determinants of perinatal common mental disorders

With the high rates of PCMDs in LMIC, it is helpful to examine the factors that increase the risk of women suffering from these illnesses in pregnancy or after birth. Risk factors vary across contexts but do have commonalities in the majority of populations in LMIC, particularly in adverse socioeconomic conditions. These populations often have inadequate health service provision, high levels of crime and violence, high presence of communicable diseases, poor sanitation and access to basic services, and overcrowded houses and communities.

Within the context of adverse socioeconomic situations, there are more specific risk factors that make it more likely for women to experience a PCMD. These include unintended or unwanted pregnancies, being a younger age, not having a partner, feeling inadequately supported by family or friends, experiencing intimate partner violence, and having a history of mental health problems (Fisher et al., 2012). In the postnatal period particularly, women are temporarily excluded from a cash economy while at the same time having an extra mouth to feed (Hanlon, Whitley, Wondimagegn, Alem, & Prince, 2009). The presence of a new and significant stressor such as pregnancy and all the worries that come with it are exacerbated by these risk factors.

On a broader level, social and environmental determinants can also predispose people to mental disorders. These are more generalized factors, such as the relative deprivation of a neighborhood or the social capital a person possesses (Ehsan & De Silva, 2015; Lund, Stansfeld, & Silva, 2014; Truong & Ma, 2006). These in turn influence mental health and resilience and can compound risk factors for PCMDs.

For example, being a member of an ethnic minority may predispose this population to poorer support structures and less political attention, through being neglected, displaced, and undersupported (Lund, Stansfeld, et al., 2014; Veling, 2013). Likewise, being a victim of gender stereotyping or experiencing hostility that restricts women's social participation may increase likelihood of developing a CMD, as would social instability and neighborhood violence (Rahman et al., 2013).

Extreme poverty sets women at many disadvantages, given its links to substandard education and high unemployment. Chronic poverty also affects women's ability to engage in acts of reciprocity, which can exclude women from the social networks vital in the perinatal period (Hanlon et al., 2009). It has been shown that there is in fact a cyclical relationship between poverty and mental illness, whereby having a mental illness can cause a "drift" toward poverty, and poverty, with its related implications, can increase likelihood and severity of mental illness (Lund et al., 2011).

Conversely, a few factors have been identified that protect against developing PCMDs. These include education, permanent employment, being an ethnic majority, and having a trustworthy intimate partner (Fisher et al., 2012). Sadly, these factors are not easy to change. However, increasing social support and having a supportive community can assist in protecting against developing or worsening mental illnesses.

In examining these risk and protective factors, we can see that treatment options for PCMDs need to address or negotiate these factors, particularly because PCMDs can be more contextually influenced, compared with other more genetically or neurologically determined disorders.

14.3 Detection

PCMDs are relatively easy to detect and diagnose with screening or diagnosis tools, although causes for the disorders can differ in pregnancy and postnatally. Cox et al. designed a tool to specifically detect postnatal depression: the Edinburgh Postnatal Depression Scale (EPDS) (Cox, Holden, & Sagovsky, 1987). This is used worldwide and has subsequently been validated for prenatal use (Cox & Holden, 1994; Murray & Cox, 1990) and for use in LMIC (Chibanda et al., 2010; De Bruin, Swartz, Tomlinson, Cooper, & Molteno, 2004; Ghubash, Abou-Saleh, & Daradkeh, 1997). The EPDS is the most commonly used perinatal-specific screening tool. Other tools used for screening are those used for general CMDs. These include the Hopkins Symptom Checklist (Derogatis, Lipman, Rickels, Uhlenhuth, & Covi, 1974), the Harvard Trauma Questionnaire (Mollica et al., 1992), the Center for Epidemiological Studies-Depression Scale (Radloff, 1977), the Patient Health Questionnaire (Kroenke, Spitzer, & Williams, 2001), the Beck Depression Inventory (Beck, Steer, & Carbin, 1988), the General Health Questionnaire (Goldberg & Hillier, 1979), the Hamilton Depression Rating Scale (Hamilton, 1960), and the Kessler 10 (Kessler et al., 2002).

14.4 Psychotherapies for PCMDs in low- and middle-income countries: An overview of research

Pharmaceutical treatments for women with CMDs in the perinatal period have not always been found to be safe for the fetus or for breastfeeding infants. This intensifies the importance of implementing psychotherapies for women during this period, unless pharmacotherapy is deemed unavoidable. In the LMIC context, the term psychotherapy can be defined as any intervention where the active ingredient involves "talking" to the client, her family members or significant others to achieve an improvement in both maternal and child health outcomes.

Three systematic reviews have reported the majority of research trials that conducted interventions for PCMDs in LMIC in the last decade (Chowdhary et al., 2014; Clarke, King, & Prost, 2013; Rahman et al., 2013). The reviews identified controlled trials that provided psychological interventions specifically for PCMDs and health promotion interventions that largely focused on promoting maternal and child health but measured PCMD outcomes. Most of these interventions used task sharing, employing the use of nonspecialist health-care workers to provide therapeutic services to the women.

The reviews by Rahman et al. and Clarke et al. found effect sizes of −0.38 (95% CI: −0.56 and −0.21) and −0.34 (95% CI: −0.53 and −0.16) respectively, compared to routine care. These effect sizes suggest that interventions for PCMDs using nonspecialist health care workers are effective in primary care and community settings. The few purely psychological interventions report much stronger results, with pooled effect sizes of −0.46 (95% CI: −0.58 and −0.33).

Including subsequent published and unpublished trials, approximately 27 trials examining psychosocial interventions for PCMDs have been conducted in LMIC in total. Compared with the number of trials conducted in high-income countries, this number is very low. The following sections describe the types of interventions that have been implemented for PCMDs in LMIC to date.

14.4.1 Psychological interventions

Of all published trials for PCMDs in LMIC, the largest proportion uses psychoeducation as the basis for their interventions (Aracena et al., 2009; Ho et al., 2009; Hughes, 2009; Lara, Navarro, & Navarrete, 2010; Rojas et al., 2007). Psychoeducation is used both as a treatment class in its own right and also as a technique in other forms of therapy. This intervention covers a wide range of issues but is based on the concept of increasing knowledge, awareness, and identification of CMDs and providing basic strategies to manage and cope with these CMDs, including steps to promote personal agency and maximize chances of recovery (Hanlon, Fekadu, & Patel, 2014). It can include elements of problem-solving, behavior change, communication, and relaxation skills.

In the perinatal period, psychoeducation includes information about pregnancy, birth, and infant development, with the aim of reducing anxiety around pregnancy, increasing bonding with the fetus and infant, and providing information for new mothers on how to care for their infants. The frequency of use of psychoeducation may be in part because it uses fewer human resources, is less time-consuming, may be easier to train lay health workers, and is easier to implement across more general populations.

In both PCMD and adult CMD, cognitive behavioral therapy (CBT)-based interventions appear to be the most effective in improving mental health outcomes across low-and high-income countries (Cuijpers, Karyotaki, Reijnders, Purgato, & Barbui, 2018; Dennis & Hodnett, 2007; Singla et al., 2017; Van't Hof, Cuijpers, Waheed, & Stein, 2011). CBT addresses the premise that negative or maladaptive thinking patterns lead to maladaptive emotional and behavioral responses to situations. CBT techniques aim to teach clients to recognize and monitor these cognitions, examine the evidence for the thoughts, replace them with more reality-oriented interpretations, and ultimately alter the dysfunctional beliefs leading to the behavioral responses (Beck, 1979) (see Chapter 5).

Three published trials have implemented effective CBT-based interventions for PCMD in LMIC (Hou et al., 2014; Mao, Li, Chiu, Chan, & Chen, 2012; Rahman, Malik, Sikander, Roberts, & Creed, 2008), and one pilot study found reductions in depressive scores (Futterman et al., 2010). Another trial is also underway, using the "Thinking Healthy" adapted CBT program (Sikander et al., 2015). The downside to CBT is that it is human-resource intensive and requires a great deal of training, supervision, and therapy hours with the client, which is not always possible in LMIC settings.

Two studies have employed group problem-solving therapy for postnatal women (Chibanda et al., 2014; Tezel & Gozum, 2006). Problem-solving therapy works on the assumption that practical problems are often at the basis of depression and anxiety symptoms (see Chapter 7). It is a relatively brief treatment that focuses on establishing the link between the symptoms the client experiences and the external problems they face and then identifying practical strategies, tasks, and goals to work through these problems to resolution (Mynors-Wallis, 2005).

One trial has employed interpersonal therapy-oriented groups for postnatal women (Gao, Chan, Li, Chen, & Hao, 2010). Interpersonal psychotherapy (IPT) is an acute, time-limited treatment that works with current interpersonal relationships, focusing on the client's immediate social context. It examines symptom formation and the social dysfunction associated with depression (Klerman & Weissman, 1994). Therapy involves getting clients to examine the interpersonal context of their depression, find the links between the depression and their environment, and make changes in their interactions (Verdeli et al., 2003) (see Chapter 6).

Lastly, two recent trials employed multiple techniques for perinatal depression, with results yet to be published (Gureje et al., 2015; Lund, Schneider, et al., 2014). Both these trials used psychoeducation, problem solving and parenting skills, and the second included CBT and relaxation training as well (Lund, Schneider, et al., 2014).

In their review of 27 trials of psychotherapies for adult CMD in LMIC, Singla et al. (2017) also found psychoeducation to be the most common treatment class, with 33% of trials using this method. This was followed by problem-solving therapy

(23.1%), cognitive behavioral therapy (17.9%), and behavioral activation or interpersonal psychotherapy (12.8%). An important consideration in choosing a therapeutic method is the amount of resources it requires for training, supervision, and delivery by nonspecialist health workers to women with PCMDs. The socioeconomic context of the intervention would thus need to influence the type of intervention most suitable for each situation.

14.4.2 Health promotion interventions

Health promotion interventions have also been shown to have beneficial effects on PCMDs. These interventions include developing skills to improve perinatal health, teaching women about infant development, engaging and stimulating infants, and encouraging sensitivity and responsiveness toward infants. These types of interventions aim to improve mother-infant interaction and maternal self-efficacy and satisfaction (Rahman et al., 2013) and often give women an opportunity to share concerns and feelings, and receive social support from a group (Clarke et al., 2013).

The systematic reviews of PCMD treatment reported that health promotion interventions brought about improvements in PCMDs compared with usual care but with smaller effect sizes than the psychological interventions (Clarke et al., 2013). These studies included those conducted by Cooper et al. (2002, 2009), Baker-Henningham, Powell, Walker, and Grantham-McGregor (2005), Rahman, Iqbal, Roberts, and Husain (2009), Tripathy et al. (2010), Morris et al. (2012), Langer et al. (1996), le Roux et al. (2013), Robledo-Colonia, Sandoval-Restrepo, Mosquera-Valderrama, Escobar-Hurtado, and Ramírez-Vélez (2012), and Aracena et al. (2009). Clarke et al. examined seven of these health promotion interventions and reported a pooled effect size of −0.15; (95% CI: −0.27 and −0.02) on PCMDs. This effect size is much smaller than for psychological interventions but still larger than for no treatment.

In the context of LMIC, Clarke et al. (2013) identify some benefits of health promotion interventions over psychological interventions. When implemented at primary care level, they increase health knowledge and awareness among all pregnant women and postnatal mothers and not just those diagnosed with PCMDs. They also ensure that women with potential CMDs would be included in treatment programs, and not be missed by the lack of screening or diagnosis for PCMDs in busy public clinics. This would have the benefit of detecting mental disorders earlier, which would have positive impacts on the mother, fetus, infant, and on mother-infant bonding. Health promotion interventions also attempt to address some of the determinants of PCMDs, such as poor maternal health, infant mortality, and the lack of social support (Clarke et al., 2013). Lastly, training and supervision of health workers in generalized maternal and child health may be more resource efficient than specific psychological counseling.

While noting that health promotion and risk factor prevention are very necessary for the general perinatal population, effect sizes indicate that it is more beneficial to those with mental illnesses to receive more specialized *psychological* services, and evidence has shown that it is possible to train nonspecialist health workers to effectively provide these services, provided that they are supervised.

14.5 Key issues in implementing psychotherapies in low- and middle-income countries

A number of key issues arise when implementing psychotherapies in low-resource settings in LMIC. These include acknowledging contextual factors and local understandings of PCMDs, identifying effective elements of therapeutic interventions, and incorporating practical considerations in implementation into primary care.

14.5.1 Paying attention to contextual factors

In their Consolidated Framework for Implementation Research, Damschroder et al. (2009) discuss two types of contexts: the outer and inner setting (see also Chapter 2). The outer setting involves the "economic, political, and social context within which an organization resides," and the inner setting involves "structural, political, and cultural contexts through which the implementation process will proceed" (p. 55), both of which always need to be taken into account for the implementation of psychosocial interventions for PCMD.

Although shown to be effective, mental health services provided by nonspecialists need to be relevant to the local context, using strategies identified by or acceptable to both service users and those who will deliver the services. This includes structural and causal attributions of PCMDs and local understandings and interpretations of them.

14.5.1.1 Addressing social adversity

Studies have found that many women perceive mental illness to be associated with and attributed to social adversity such as financial difficulties, unemployment, poor partner relationships, unwanted pregnancies, food insecurity, and inadequate social support, rather than psychiatric illnesses per se (Davies, Schneider, Nyatsanza, & Lund, 2016; Hanlon et al., 2009; Rahman, Iqbal, & Harrington, 2003; Rodrigues, Patel, Jaswal, & De Souza, 2003; Selim, 2010). Interventions therefore need to include practical means of addressing the social conditions that women face, such as identifying resources to access food, potential jobs, and safe homes. Addressing domestic violence is also an important contextual element in preventing and addressing mental illness (Chowdhary et al., 2014).

Many authors also recommend the culturally appropriate involvement of the family and significant others into the process of treatment, which not only increases support but also can mitigate some of the risk factors for depression (Abas, Broadhead, Mbape, & Khumalo-Sakatukwa, 1994; Chibanda et al., 2014; Patel, Chowdhary, Rahman, & Verdeli, 2011). This acknowledges the "salience of social and family connectedness in many developing countries" (Chowdhary et al., 2014, p. 124).

In Pakistan, Rahman (2007) found that women expressed the desire for information on infant health over the need for psychological therapy, and that this would be more acceptable and less stigmatizing than attending pure "talk therapy." The subsequent research trial used infant health as a motivator to mobilize and include women in group therapeutic programs (Rahman et al., 2008). Other examples of including local strategies for improving mental health include attending religious activities, involving traditional healers, employing yoga and breathing exercises, and exploring community resources and support systems (Aggarwal et al., 2014).

This evidence emphasizes the need to work collaboratively with women in the development of interventions and not impose external solutions or ideas of healing that are foreign to women. Counseling guidelines and manuals need to be nonspecific enough to encourage ideas from the women themselves, while counselors keep the background knowledge of the context in mind to formulate realistic and achievable treatment goals and collaborative plans for healing, as well as resource identification where needs be.

It is thus also important that counselors are recruited from the area the women live in, for them to be better prepared for the issues that are raised by women, and collaboratively find ways to problem-solve and heal, within the lived context. It would be unrealistic, for example, to suggest specific types of job seeking for a poorly educated woman or to suggest leaving a partner, when a woman's only source of income and housing comes from their partner.

14.5.1.2 Local understandings of mental illness

PCMDs need to be treated from within a deep understanding and use of the local culture and language specific to the population. A good amount of work has been done on identifying and including local idioms of depression and anxiety in some LMIC, as described in other chapters. In relation to PCMDs, specific examples include "ukudakumba" (sadness) and "ucingakakhulu" (thinking too much) in South Africa (Andersen, Kagee, O'Cleirigh, Safren, & Joska, 2015; Davies et al., 2016) and "tension" or "stress" in South Asia (Aggarwal et al., 2014; Rahman, 2007). The use of these idioms assists to avoid the medicalization of mental illness where it is not seen as such and develop interventions that are congruent with local culture and experience.

Understanding local idioms also assists in the identification and screening for CMDs. An example of this is the development of a "Community Informant Detection Tool" (CIDT) in Nepal, for detecting mental health problems by nonspecialist health workers. This tool incorporates locally identified cultural concepts of distress and manifestations of mental health problems that are commonly understandable and uses vignettes rather than a checklist of symptoms, with good accuracy (Jordans, Kohrt, Luitel, Komproe, & Lund, 2015). Similarly, the Shona Symptom Questionnaire was developed and validated in Zimbabwe to identify CMDs (Patel, Simunyu, Gwanzura, Lewis, & Mann, 1997) and is now widely used in the country.

Knowing the local understandings of CMDs is important particularly in psychoeducation. For example, Rojas et al.'s (2007) study in Chile involved teaching women to recognize and understand the symptoms of depression in order to treat and manage it, and this could not have been done through an imposition of western understandings of depression onto Chilean women.

In Zimbabwe, Chibanda and colleagues developed an intervention that has proved to be effective and acceptable to the local population, known as the "Friendship Bench" (see Chapter 7). This project involves local women health workers providing problem-solving therapy (PST) to clients with CMDs on benches in the grounds of local clinics (Chibanda et al., 2016). For this intervention, the health workers conceived of and developed local terms to describe components and processes of the PST so that it could be acceptable and feasible for use in primary care facilities. These concepts included opening the mind, uplifting, strengthening, and strengthening further.

Patel et al. (2011) note the modifications that had to be made to three mental health trial interventions to improve their acceptability for use by nonspecialists in LMIC (Bolton et al., 2003; Patel et al., 2010; Rahman et al., 2008). These included simplifying the language and content of interventions, using pictorial materials for demonstrations, and using contextually appropriate metaphors and methods for the interventions.

14.5.2 Identifying effective elements of psychotherapies

Essential elements of psychotherapies vary widely across cultures and countries. However, there are a few therapeutic elements that are effective across settings and treatment types. Rahman et al. identified the importance of the therapeutic relationship with the health worker, particularly involving trust and listening skills, and the ability of health workers to be nonjudgmental, empathic, and supportive (Rahman et al., 2013). This supports evidence for "Client-centered therapy" (Rogers, 2012) as an important base for all therapeutic methods for PCMDs. The core tenets of this therapy involve providing empathy, unconditional positive regard, congruence, and genuineness to the client. This is particularly relevant in the perinatal period when mothers may feel unsure, anxious, and insecure.

In their review of CMDs in LMIC, Singla et al. (2017) identified the common and effective therapeutic elements used in 27 research trials. Almost half of the studies included in the review targeted mothers or parents, with a focus on child care. As with Rahman et al.'s (2013) review, the essential "nonspecific" elements identified were empathy, collaboration, active listening, normalizing, and involving family members or a significant other. More specific elements within the therapy involve identifying social support, problem-solving techniques, identifying or eliciting affect, linking affect to events, and identifying thoughts (Singla et al., 2017). Lastly, the most common in-session techniques identified were psychoeducation, providing direct suggestions, assigning homework, giving praise, and goal setting (Singla et al., 2017). Table 14.1 summarizes the most used treatment elements of the 27 studies, all of which are relevant for therapies for PCMDs.

14.5.3 Practical considerations for implementation

While the content of therapeutic interventions is important, the nature of the delivery can be equally significant in ensuring interventions are effective. LMIC are significantly different in context to high-income countries, where there are many more qualified mental health specialists and generally better resources, as well as fewer social and economic risk factors that come into play. Practical considerations of delivering

Table 14.1 The most commonly used treatment elements from 27 psychotherapy trials in adult CMD in LMIC

Psycho-therapy Type:	Psycho-education (33%)	Problem Solving (23%)	Cognitive behavioural therapy (CBT) (18%)	Behavioural activation or interpersonal therapy (13%)	
Specific elements in therapy:	Eliciting or identifying social support	Engaging in problem solving	Identifying or eliciting affect	Linking affect to events	Identifying thoughts
Nonspecific elements in therapy:	Empathy	Collaboration	Active listening	Normalizing treatment or aspects of the illness	Involving family members or a significant other
In-session techniques:	Psycho-education	Providing direct suggestions	Assigning homework	Giving praise	Goal setting

perinatal interventions in LMIC include factors such as whether therapy be provided individually or in groups, by specialists or nonspecialist health workers, and at households or in clinics and duration and intensity of the therapy itself.

14.5.3.1 Individual versus group therapy

Clarke et al. (2013) found that group-based interventions had greater impact on PCMDs than individual ones. However, this depends on the context: often, groups are more effective in rural areas and less so in urban ones, and group meetings can be more resource effective than individual ones but less specific in intensity and focus.

Individual home visits to women can benefit them by engaging the extended family in caring for the infant and mother, increasing knowledge of maternal and infant health (Clarke et al., 2013), increasing family support, reducing women's reticence, and encouraging longer-term behavior change (Rahman et al., 2013).

Groups, however, can assist women to share information and concerns, gather support, and increase their social networks (Clarke et al., 2013). They can also encourage continuation of meetings after interventions are complete, as has been seen in countries such as Zimbabwe after the "Friendship Bench" project (Chibanda et al., 2016). As Rahman (2007) showed, by focusing on maternal and child health, groups can provide an opportunity by which mothers (and their families) could be accessed for interventions to improve both maternal mood *and* infant health.

Group interventions can also be integrated into other health programs and treatment services, such as maternal and child health, HIV care, and nutrition, and can be useful when resources are scarce. This has the benefit of reducing stigma associated with mental illness and reducing the costs of service provision. For instance, in South

Africa, HIV care has become well integrated into primary care, to the degree that HIV support groups provide important support systems for people with this illness. CMDs are nowhere near as recognized as HIV, even though the burden of these illnesses is increasing rapidly.

14.5.3.2 Timing and targeting of interventions

It appears that interventions delivered during pregnancy and/or after birth (and not just during pregnancy) are most effective (Clarke et al., 2013). It is important that prenatal CMDs are addressed because of their tendency to increase postnatal CMDs, but often, more support and care are needed in the postnatal period for assistance in recovering from birth, caring for newborn babies, and ultimately resuming normal routines and activities (Clarke et al., 2013). Further research is needed in LMIC to identify optimal timing of psychotherapy interventions during the prenatal and postnatal period.

14.5.3.3 Setting

Past interventions have most commonly been delivered at women's homes and integrated into other health-care home visit programs. However, clinic interventions can be helpful when there are high levels of resistance from family members to women receiving mental health care at home or concerns about confidentiality. These could be aligned with well-baby checkups. The perinatal period is also an optimal time to provide interventions at clinics because pregnant women and women with new babies come to clinic checkups more regularly than other women. In most LMIC, uptake of prenatal services is relatively good and thus provides a good window of opportunity to access these populations. Other community areas for interventions include schools, community halls, and even outdoors.

14.5.3.4 Delivery agent

More and more research is being conducted to test the effectiveness of using "task sharing" with nonspecialist health workers to reduce the mental disorder treatment gap. There is evidence (shown above) to support the use of nonspecialists specifically in the management of PCMDs. Aside from reducing burden on mental health specialists, other reasons for involving nonspecialists in mental health care include that they have frequent contact with women, can be seen as "peers" for peer support, and can be more sustainable than scarce specialists (Singla et al., 2017). Local health-care workers would also have an intimate understanding of the local socioeconomic circumstances and cultural concepts of mental illness. This assists with the therapy being more relevant to the women and reduces judgment or difference within the therapeutic relationship between counselor and client.

However, task sharing can only work when there is adequate and regular supervision from a mental health specialist (see Chapter 3). Evidence across all studies has shown that this is vital for task sharing to be effective. The current authors conducted a randomized controlled trial (RCT) examining the cost-effectiveness of task sharing with CHWs for perinatal depression in Khayelitsha, South Africa (Lund,

Schneider, et al., 2014). In this context, trauma is common, with high levels of crime, interpersonal violence, HIV, unplanned pregnancies, insecure housing, and poor health and sanitation services. Often, the screening and provision of basic mental health services for these women were the first they had ever had, and past trauma was often revisited. This required careful and sensitive counseling from the CHWs but likewise equally careful supervision and guidance from the mental health specialist supervisor. The CHWs required debriefing and support in dealing with this trauma on a regular basis.

14.5.3.5 Duration

The length of interventions varies widely across programs, depending on the type of intervention. They range from once off contact information sessions to regular weekly sessions for a few months. The most effective intervention identified in the systematic reviews was the "Thinking Healthy" project (Rahman et al., 2008), which ran a total of 16 sessions for participants.

There is also a small body of evidence that screening itself can be influential on mood in pregnant women simply because of the interest taken in them, which they felt they had never had before. This was reported in anecdotal evidence in the author's RCT and endorsed in other studies in South Africa and England (Darwin, McGowan, & Edozien, 2013; Marsay, Manderson, & Subramaney, 2018).

14.6 Integration into primary care

Chibanda et al. (2014) recommend that screening and mental health services by nonspecialist health workers be integrated into all perinatal health services. With the particularly high rates of PMCDs in LMIC, we recommend a stepped care methodology for treating PCMDs. Stepped care would involve all pregnant women/new mothers receiving psychoeducation at primary care facilities. Within these groups, women who are identified with moderate-to-severe disorders would receive psychosocial interventions from nonspecialist health workers. Only women with suicidality or severe and unmanageable disorders would be referred to mental health specialists. Supervision of nonspecialist workers would still be key in this approach. An example of this technique, used for adult populations with depression and anxiety, was the MANAS trial in India (Patel et al., 2010). The stepped-care model improves efficiency and therefore increases capacity to treat more women in resource-constrained environments (Hanlon et al., 2014).

In line with the above, the World Health Qrganization (WHO) launched the Mental Health Gap Action Program (mhGAP) in 2008 (WHO, 2008) and the mhGAP implementation guide in 2010 (WHO, 2010), for management of mental, neurological, and substance use disorders by nonspecialist health workers at primary care level. The WHO has now published a specific evidence-based training manual for the management of perinatal depression, based on the successful RCT conducted by Rahman and colleagues in Pakistan, using the "Thinking Healthy" CBT-based intervention mentioned earlier (WHO, 2015). The manual contains explanations about perinatal depression, CBT core concepts, and the "Thinking Healthy" adaptation, with a step-by-step guide on how to conduct sessions throughout pregnancy and into the postnatal period. This is a generalized manual and can be applied across different cultures and contexts.

This is an important development in increasing service provision to women with perinatal depression in areas that do not have the resources for specialist mental health services but have double the need. However, there are still many factors to consider in implementing mental health care for perinatal populations in LMIC. There is no "one-size-fits-all" formula, and all manuals and interventions need to be adapted and contextualized to the population, culture, and country they are being used in.

14.7 Conclusion

This chapter has examined evidence for psychotherapies for PCMDs in LMIC. The evidence provides some key recommendations for practitioners, researchers, and policymakers alike, in moving forward with research and scaling up of psychotherapies in LMIC.

Firstly, given the implications of PCMDs on both women and their infants, there is an urgent need for policymakers to address and scale up psychotherapies for PCMDs in LMIC. Perinatal mental health care benefits not only the women themselves but importantly their infants too, with positive impacts on rates of diarrhea, immunizations, weight, and height (Cooper et al., 2002; Rahman et al., 2008).

Secondly, in developing and implementing psychotherapies for PCMDs, practitioners need to ensure that these interventions are contextually and culturally appropriate, taking into account the socioeconomic circumstances of the women involved. This should be explored through extensive formative research and consultation with all stakeholders before any form of implementation occurs. This consultation will also ensure that the right issues are addressed for those in need.

As many descriptions and attributions of mental illness are ascribed by women to socioeconomic factors and context-specific risk factors (e.g., interpersonal violence and poor partner support, unemployment, food insecurity, and poor social support), interventions need to address the risk factors faced by the women, in language acceptable and understandable to women and care providers alike. Consistently, the lack of social support has been emphasized by researchers as a factor associated with depression. Social network building is something that should be built into future interventions, along with other protective factors such as encouraging intimate partner support and finding employment (Fisher et al., 2012).

Having incorporated culturally relevant and local idioms and language, interventions can then be built on well-established theoretical models of therapy and grounded on evidence-based approaches that have shown to be effective, such as the "Thinking Healthy" approach (Rahman et al., 2008), the Friendship Bench (Chibanda et al., 2016), and interpersonal therapy (Bolton et al., 2003; Patel et al., 2010). Within these structures, the providers of counseling interventions need to embody the essential elements of client-centered therapy, including empathy, normalizing, collaboration, trust, and active listening.

Lastly, evidence has shown that nonspecialist health workers can be employed in a task-sharing approach to increase coverage of mental health services in low-resource, understaffed areas, but all research emphasizes the absolute importance of regular and qualified supervision of the health workers, to both support and train them in what can be a very stressful and demanding position. Going forward, researchers need to take into consideration the availability of local resources and the various challenges mentioned above so that research conducted is focused on efficacy and replicability into everyday settings where there is the greatest need. This may include testing simple, manualized interventions integrated into existing health-care programs focusing on maternal and child health.

References

Abas, M., Broadhead, J. C., Mbape, P., & Khumalo-Sakatukwa, G. (1994). Defeating depression in the developing world: A Zimbabwean Model: One country's response to the challenge. *British Journal of Psychiatry*, *164*(3), 293–296.

Aggarwal, N. K., Balaji, M., Kumar, S., Mohanraj, R., Rahman, A., Verdeli, H., et al. (2014). Using consumer perspectives to inform the cultural adaptation of psychological treatments for depression: A mixed methods study from South Asia. *Journal of Affective Disorders*, *163*, 88–101. https://doi.org/10.1016/j.jad.2014.03.036.

Andersen, L., Kagee, A., O'Cleirigh, C., Safren, S., & Joska, J. (2015). Understanding the experience and manifestation of depression in people living with HIV/AIDS in South Africa. *AIDS Care*, *27*(1), 59–62. https://doi.org/10.1080/09540121.2014.951306.

Aracena, M., Krause, M., Perez, C., Mendez, M. J., Salvatierra, L., Soto, M., et al. (2009). A cost-effectiveness evaluation of a home visit program for adolescent mothers. *Journal of Health Psychology*, *14*(7), 878–887. https://doi.org/10.1177/1359105309340988.

Baker-Henningham, H., Powell, C., Walker, S., & Grantham-McGregor, S. (2005). The effect of early stimulation on maternal depression: A cluster randomised controlled trial. *Archives of Disease in Childhood*, *90*(12), 1230–1234. https://doi.org/10.1136/adc.2005.073015.

Beck, A. (1979). *Cognitive therapy of depression*. Guilford Press.

Beck, A. T., Steer, R. A., & Carbin, M. G. (1988). Psychometric properties of the Beck Depression Inventory: Twenty-five years of evaluation. *Clinical Psychology Review*, *8*(1), 77–100. https://doi.org/10.1016/0272-7358(88)90050-5.

Bolton, P., Bass, J., Neugebauer, R., Verdeli, H., Clougherty, K. F., Wickramaratne, P., et al. (2003). Group interpersonal psychotherapy for depression in rural Uganda: A randomized controlled trial. *JAMA*, *289*(23), 3117–3124. https://doi.org/10.1001/jama.289.23.3117.

Chibanda, D., Mangezi, W., Tshimanga, M., Woelk, G., Rusakaniko, P., Stranix-Chibanda, L., et al. (2010). Validation of the Edinburgh postnatal depression scale among women in a high HIV prevalence area in urban Zimbabwe. *Archives of Women's Mental Health*, *13*(3), 201–206.

Chibanda, D., Shetty, A. K., Tshimanga, M., Woelk, G., Stranix-Chibanda, L., & Rusakaniko, S. (2014). Group problem-solving therapy for postnatal depression among HIV-positive and HIV-negative mothers in Zimbabwe. *Journal of the International Association of Providers of AIDS Care*, *13*(4), 335–341. https://doi.org/10.1177/2325957413495564.

Chibanda, D., Weiss, H. A., Verhey, R., Simms, V., Munjoma, R., Rusakaniko, S., et al. (2016). Effect of a primary care-based psychological intervention on symptoms of common mental disorders in Zimbabwe: A randomized clinical trial. *JAMA*, *316*(24), 2618–2626. https://doi.org/10.1001/jama.2016.19102.

Chowdhary, N., Sikander, S., Atif, N., Singh, N., Ahmad, I., Fuhr, D. C., et al. (2014). The content and delivery of psychological interventions for perinatal depression by non-specialist health workers in low and middle income countries: A systematic review. *Best Practice & Research Clinical Obstetrics & Gynaecology*, *28*(1), 113–133. https://doi.org/10.1016/j.bpobgyn.2013.08.013.

Clarke, K., King, M., & Prost, A. (2013). Psychosocial interventions for perinatal common mental disorders delivered by providers who are not mental health specialists in low- and middle-income countries: A systematic review and meta-analysis. *PLoS Medicine*. *10* (10)e1001541https://doi.org/10.1371/journal.pmed.1001541.

Cohn, J., Matias, R., Tronick, E. Z., Connell, D., & Lyons-Ruth, K. (1986). Face-to-face interactions of depressed mothers and their infants. *New Directions for Child and Adolescent Development*, *1986*(34), 31–45. https://doi.org/10.1002/cd.23219863405.

Cooper, P., Landman, M., Tomlinson, M., Molteno, C., Swartz, L., & Murray, L. (2002). Impact of a mother–infant intervention in an indigent peri-urban South African context: Pilot study. *British Journal of Psychiatry*, *180*(1), 76–81.

Cooper, P., Tomlinson, M., Swartz, L., Landman, M., Molteno, C., Stein, A., et al. (2009). Improving quality of mother-infant relationship and infant attachment in socioeconomically deprived community in South Africa: Randomised controlled trial. *BMJ*. *338*, https://doi.org/10.1136/bmj.b974.

Cox, J., & Holden, J. (1994). *Perinatal psychiatry: Use and misuse of the Edinburgh Postnatal Depression Scale*. Gaskell.

Cox, J., Holden, J., & Sagovsky, R. (1987). Detection of postnatal depression: development of the 10-item Edinburgh postnatal depression scale. *British Journal of Psychiatry*, *150*(6), 782–786.

Cuijpers, P., Karyotaki, E., Reijnders, M., Purgato, M., & Barbui, C. (2018). Psychotherapies for depression in low-and middle-income countries: A meta-analysis. *World Psychiatry*, *17* (1), 90–101.

Damschroder, L. J., Aron, D. C., Keith, R. E., Kirsh, S. R., Alexander, J. A., & Lowery, J. C. (2009). Fostering implementation of health services research findings into practice: A consolidated framework for advancing implementation science. *Implementation Science*, *4*, 50. https://doi.org/10.1186/1748-5908-4-50.

Darwin, Z., McGowan, L., & Edozien, L. C. (2013). Assessment acting as intervention: Findings from a study of perinatal psychosocial assessment. *Journal of Reproductive and Infant Psychology*, *31*(5), 500–511. https://doi.org/10.1080/02646838.2013.834042.

Davies, T., Schneider, M., Nyatsanza, M., & Lund, C. (2016). "The sun has set even though it is morning": Experiences and explanations of perinatal depression in an urban township, Cape Town. *Transcultural Psychiatry*, *53*(3), 286–312. https://doi.org/10.1177/1363461516632389.

De Bruin, G. P., Swartz, L., Tomlinson, M., Cooper, P. J., & Molteno, C. (2004). The factor structure of the Edinburgh postnatal depression scale in a South African peri-urban settlement. *South Africa Journal of Psychology*, *34*(1), 113–121.

Dennis, C. L., & Hodnett, E. (2007). Psychosocial and psychological interventions for treating postpartum depression. *Cochrane Database of Systematic Reviews*. *4*, CD006116https://doi.org/10.1002/14651858.CD006116.pub2.

Derogatis, L. R., Lipman, R. S., Rickels, K., Uhlenhuth, E. H., & Covi, L. (1974). The Hopkins Symptom Checklist (HSCL): A self-report symptom inventory. *Behavioral Science*, *19*(1), 1–15.

Ehsan, A. M., & De Silva, M. J. (2015). Social capital and common mental disorder: A systematic review. *Journal of Epidemiology and Community Health*, jech-2015-205868.

Fisher, J., Cabral de Mello, M., Patel, V., Rahman, A., Tran, T., Holton, S., et al. (2012). Prevalence and determinants of common perinatal mental disorders in women in low- and lower-middle-income countries: A systematic review. *Bulletin of the World Health Organization*, *90*(2), 139G–149G. https://doi.org/10.2471/BLT.11.091850.

Futterman, D., Shea, J., Besser, M., Stafford, S., Desmond, K., Comulada, W. S., et al. (2010). Mamekhaya: A pilot study combining a cognitive-behavioral intervention and mentor mothers with PMTCT services in South Africa. *AIDS Care*, *22*(9), 1093–1100. https://doi.org/10.1080/09540121003600352.

Gao, L.-l., Chan, S. W.-c., Li, X., Chen, S., & Hao, Y. (2010). Evaluation of an interpersonal-psychotherapy-oriented childbirth education programme for Chinese first-time childbearing women: A randomised controlled trial. *International Journal of Nursing Studies*, *47*(10), 1208–1216.

GBD 2015 DALYs and Hale Collaborators. (2016). Global, regional, and national disability-adjusted life-years (DALYs) for 315 diseases and injuries and healthy life expectancy (HALE), 1990-2015: A systematic analysis for the Global Burden of Disease Study 2015. *Lancet*, *388*(10053), 1603–1658. https://doi.org/10.1016/S0140-6736(16)31460-X.

Ghubash, R., Abou-Saleh, M., & Daradkeh, T. (1997). The validity of the Arabic Edinburgh postnatal depression scale. *Social Psychiatry and Psychiatric Epidemiology*, *32*(8), 474–476.

Goldberg, D. P., & Hillier, V. F. (1979). A scaled version of the general health questionnaire. *Psychological Medicine*, *9*(1), 139–145.

Gureje, O., Oladeji, B. D., Araya, R., Montgomery, A. A., Kola, L., Kirmayer, L., et al. (2015). Expanding care for perinatal women with depression (EXPONATE): Study protocol for a randomized controlled trial of an intervention package for perinatal depression in primary care. *BMC Psychiatry*. *15*, 136. https://doi.org/10.1186/s12888-015-0537-3.

Hamilton, M. (1960). A rating scale for depression. *Journal of Neurology, Neurosurgery, and Psychiatry*, *23*, 56–62.

Hanlon, C., Fekadu, A., & Patel, V. (2014). Interventions for mental disorders. In V. Patel, H. Minas, A. Cohen, & M. Prince (Eds.), *Global mental health: Principles and practices* (pp. 252–278). New York: Oxford University Press.

Hanlon, C., Whitley, R., Wondimagegn, D., Alem, A., & Prince, M. (2009). Postnatal mental distress in relation to the sociocultural practices of childbirth: An exploratory qualitative study from Ethiopia. *Social Science & Medicine*, *69*(8), 1211–1219. https://doi.org/10.1016/j.socscimed.2009.07.043.

Ho, S.-M., Heh, S.-S., Jevitt, C. M., Huang, L.-H., Fu, Y.-Y., & Wang, L.-L. (2009). Effectiveness of a discharge education program in reducing the severity of postpartum depression: A randomized controlled evaluation study. *Patient Education and Counseling*, *77*(1), 68–71.

Hou, Y., Hu, P., Zhang, Y., Lu, Q., Wang, D., Yin, L., et al. (2014). Cognitive behavioral therapy in combination with systemic family therapy improves mild to moderate postpartum depression. *Revista Brasileira de Psiquiatria*, *36*(1), 47–52. https://doi.org/10.1590/1516-4446-2013-1170.

Hughes, M. (2009). *Randomised, controlled trial of a perinatal psycho-social intervention for postnatal depression in Goa, India*. [thesis].

Jordans, M. J., Kohrt, B. A., Luitel, N. P., Komproe, I. H., & Lund, C. (2015). Accuracy of proactive case finding for mental disorders by community informants in Nepal. *British Journal of Psychiatry*, *207*(6), 5. https://doi.org/10.1192/bjp.bp.113.141077.

Kessler, R. C., Andrews, G., Colpe, L. J., Hiripi, E., Mroczek, D. K., Normand, S. L., et al. (2002). Short screening scales to monitor population prevalences and trends in non-specific psychological distress. *Psychological Medicine*, *32*(6), 959–976.

Klerman, G. L., & Weissman, M. M. (1994). *Interpersonal psychotherapy of depression: A brief, focused, specific strategy*. Jason Aronson Incorporated.

Kroenke, K., Spitzer, R. L., & Williams, J. B. (2001). The PHQ-9: Validity of a brief depression severity measure. *Journal of General Internal Medicine*, *16*(9), 606–613.

Langer, A., Farnot, U., Garcia, C., Barros, F., Victora, C., Belizan, J. M., et al. (1996). The Latin American trial of psychosocial support during pregnancy: Effects on mother's wellbeing and satisfaction. *Social Science & Medicine*, *42*(11), 1589–1597.

Lara, M. A., Navarro, C., & Navarrete, L. (2010). Outcome results of a psycho-educational intervention in pregnancy to prevent PPD: A randomized control trial. *Journal of Affective Disorders*, *122*(1-2), 109–117. https://doi.org/10.1016/j.jad.2009.06.024.

le Roux, I. M., Tomlinson, M., Harwood, J. M., O'Connor, M. J., Worthman, C. M., Mbewu, N., et al. (2013). Outcomes of home visits for pregnant mothers and their infants: A cluster randomised controlled trial. *AIDS (London, England)*, *27*(9), 1461.

Lund, C., De Silva, M., Plagerson, S., Cooper, S., Chisholm, D., Das, J., et al. (2011). Poverty and mental disorders: Breaking the cycle in low-income and middle-income countries. *Lancet*, *378*(9801), 1502–1514. https://doi.org/10.1016/s0140-6736(11)60754-x.

Lund, C., Schneider, M., Davies, T., Nyatsanza, M., Honikman, S., Bhana, A., et al. (2014). Task sharing of a psychological intervention for maternal depression in Khayelitsha, South Africa: Study protocol for a randomized controlled trial. *Trials*. *15*, 457. https://doi.org/10.1186/1745-6215-15-457.

Lund, C., Stansfeld, S., & De Silva, M. (2014). Social determinants of mental health. In V. Patel, H. Minas, A. Cohen, & M. Prince (Eds.), *Global mental health: Principles and practices* (pp. 116–136). New York: Oxford University Press.

Mao, H. J., Li, H. J., Chiu, H., Chan, W. C., & Chen, S. L. (2012). Effectiveness of antenatal emotional self-management training program in prevention of postnatal depression in Chinese women. *Perspectives in Psychiatric Care*, *48*(4), 218–224.

Marsay, C., Manderson, L., & Subramaney, U. (2018). Changes in mood after screening for antenatal anxiety and depression. *Journal of Reproductive and Infant Psychology*, 1–16. https://doi.org/10.1080/02646838.2018.1453601.

Mollica, R. F., Caspi-Yavin, Y., Bollini, P., Truong, T., Tor, S., & Lavelle, J. (1992). The Harvard trauma questionnaire. Validating a cross-cultural instrument for measuring torture, trauma, and posttraumatic stress disorder in Indochinese refugees. *Journal of Nervous and Mental Disease*, *180*(2), 111–116.

Morris, J., Jones, L., Berrino, A., Jordans, M. J., Okema, L., & Crow, C. (2012). Does combining infant stimulation with emergency feeding improve psychosocial outcomes for displaced mothers and babies? A controlled evaluation from northern Uganda. *American Journal of Orthopsychiatry*, *82*(3), 349–357.

Murray, D., & Cox, J. L. (1990). Screening for depression during pregnancy with the Edinburgh Depression Scale (EDDS). *Journal of Reproductive and Infant Psychology*, *8*(2), 99–107.

Murray, L., Cooper, P. J., & Stein, A. (1991). Postnatal depression and infant development. *British Medical Journal*, *302*(6783), 978.

Murray, L., Fiori-Cowley, A., Hooper, R., & Cooper, P. (1996). The Impact of Postnatal Depression and Associated Adversity on Early Mother-Infant Interactions and Later Infant Outcome. *Child Development*, *67*(5), 2512–2526. https://doi.org/10.1111/j.1467-8624.1996.tb01871.x.

Mynors-Wallis, L. (2005). *Problem-solving treatment for anxiety and depression: A practical guide*. OUP Oxford.

Patel, V., Chowdhary, N., Rahman, A., & Verdeli, H. (2011). Improving access to psychological treatments: Lessons from developing countries. *Behaviour Research and Therapy*, *49*(9), 523–528. https://doi.org/10.1016/j.brat.2011.06.012.

Patel, V., Simunyu, E., Gwanzura, F., Lewis, G., & Mann, A. (1997). The Shona symptom questionnaire: The development of an indigenous measure of common mental disorders in Harare. *Acta Psychiatrica Scandinavica*, *95*(6), 469–475.

Patel, V., Weiss, H. A., Chowdhary, N., Naik, S., Pednekar, S., Chatterjee, S., et al. (2010). Effectiveness of an intervention led by lay health counsellors for depressive and anxiety disorders in primary care in Goa, India (MANAS): A cluster randomised controlled trial. *The Lancet*, *376*(9758), 2086–2095. https://doi.org/10.1016/s0140-6736(10)61508-5.

Radloff, L. S. (1977). The CES-D scale: A self-report depression scale for research in the general population. *Applied Psychological Measurement*, *1*(3), 385–401. https://doi.org/10.1177/014662167700100306.

Rahman, A. (2007). Challenges and opportunities in developing a psychological intervention for perinatal depression in rural Pakistan-a multi-method study. *Archives of Women's Mental Health*, *10*(5), 211–219. https://doi.org/10.1007/s00737-007-0193-9.

Rahman, A., & Creed, F. (2007). Outcome of prenatal depression and risk factors associated with persistence in the first postnatal year: Prospective study from Rawalpindi, Pakistan. *Journal of Affective Disorders*, *100*(1-3), 115–121. https://doi.org/10.1016/j.jad.2006.10.004.

Rahman, A., Fisher, J., Bower, P., Luchters, S., Tran, T., Yasamy, M. T., et al. (2013). Interventions for common perinatal mental disorders in women in low- and middle-income countries: A systematic review and meta-analysis. *Bulletin of the World Health Organization*, *91*(8), 593–601I. https://doi.org/10.2471/BLT.12.109819.

Rahman, A., Iqbal, Z., & Harrington, R. (2003). Life events, social support and depression in childbirth: Perspectives from a rural community in the developing world. *Psychological Medicine*, *33*(7), 1161–1167. https://doi.org/10.1017/s0033291703008286.

Rahman, A., Iqbal, Z., Roberts, C., & Husain, N. (2009). Cluster randomized trial of a parent-based intervention to support early development of children in a low-income country. *Child: Care, Health and Development*, *35*(1), 56–62. https://doi.org/10.1111/j.1365-2214.2008.00897.x.

Rahman, A., Malik, A., Sikander, S., Roberts, C., & Creed, F. (2008). Cognitive behaviour therapy-based intervention by community health workers for mothers with depression and their infants in rural Pakistan: A cluster-randomised controlled trial. *Lancet*, *372*(9642), 902–909. https://doi.org/10.1016/s0140-6736(08)61400-2.

Robledo-Colonia, A. F., Sandoval-Restrepo, N., Mosquera-Valderrama, Y. F., Escobar-Hurtado, C., & Ramírez-Vélez, R. (2012). Aerobic exercise training during pregnancy reduces depressive symptoms in nulliparous women: A randomised trial. *Journal of Physiotherapy*, *58*(1), 9–15.

Rodrigues, M., Patel, V., Jaswal, S., & De Souza, N. (2003). Listening to mothers: Qualitative studies on motherhood and depression from Goa, India. *Social Science & Medicine*, *57*(10), 1797–1806.

Rogers, C. (2012). *Client centred therapy (New Ed)*. Hachette UK.

Rojas, G., Fritsch, R., Solis, J., Jadresic, E., Castillo, C., González, M., et al. (2007). Treatment of postnatal depression in low-income mothers in primary-care clinics in Santiago, Chile: A randomised controlled trial. *Lancet*, *370*(9599), 1629–1637. https://doi.org/10.1016/s0140-6736(07)61685-7.

Saxena, S., Thornicroft, G., Knapp, M., & Whiteford, H. (2007). Resources for mental health: Scarcity, inequity, and inefficiency. *The Lancet*, *370*(9590), 878–889.

Selim, N. (2010). Cultural dimensions of depression in Bangladesh: A qualitative study in two villages of Matlab. *Journal of Health, Population, and Nutrition*, *28*(1), 95.

Sikander, S., Lazarus, A., Bangash, O., Fuhr, D. C., Weobong, B., Krishna, R. N., et al. (2015). The effectiveness and cost-effectiveness of the peer-delivered Thinking Healthy Programme for perinatal depression in Pakistan and India: The SHARE study protocol for randomised controlled trials. *Trials. 16*, 534. https://doi.org/10.1186/s13063-015-1063-9.

Singla, D. R., Kohrt, B. A., Murray, L. K., Anand, A., Chorpita, B. F., & Patel, V. (2017). Psychological treatments for the world: Lessons from low- and middle-income countries. *Annual Review of Clinical Psychology*, *13*, 149–181. https://doi.org/10.1146/annurev-clinpsy-032816-045217.

Stewart, D. E. (2011). Depression during pregnancy. *New England Journal of Medicine*, *365* (17), 1605–1611. https://doi.org/10.1056/NEJMcp1102730.

Surkan, P. J., Kennedy, C. E., Hurley, K. M., & Black, M. M. (2011). Maternal depression and early childhood growth in developing countries: Systematic review and meta-analysis. *Bulletin of the World Health Organization*, *89*(8), 608–615. https://doi.org/10.2471/BLT.11.088187.

Tezel, A., & Gozum, S. (2006). Comparison of effects of nursing care to problem solving training on levels of depressive symptoms in post partum women. *Patient Education and Counseling*, *63*(1-2), 64–73. https://doi.org/10.1016/j.pec.2005.08.011.

Tripathy, P., Nair, N., Barnett, S., Mahapatra, R., Borghi, J., Rath, S., et al. (2010). Effect of a participatory intervention with women's groups on birth outcomes and maternal depression in Jharkhand and Orissa, India: A cluster-randomised controlled trial. *The Lancet*, *375*(9721), 1182–1192. https://doi.org/10.1016/s0140-6736(09)62042-0.

Truong, K. D., & Ma, S. (2006). A systematic review of relations between neighborhoods and mental health. *Journal of Mental Health Policy and Economics*, *9*(3), 137–154.

Van't Hof, E., Cuijpers, P., Waheed, W., & Stein, D. J. (2011). Psychological treatments for depression and anxiety disorders in low- and middle- income countries: A meta-analysis. *African Journal of Psychiatry*. *14*(3). https://doi.org/10.4314/ajpsy.v14i3.2.

Veling, W. (2013). Ethnic minority position and risk for psychotic disorders. *Current Opinion in Psychiatry*, *26*(2), 166–171.

Verdeli, H., Clougherty, K., Bolton, P., Speelman, L., Lincoln, N., Bass, J., et al. (2003). Adapting group interpersonal psychotherapy for a developing country: Experience in rural Uganda. *World Psychiatry*, *2*(2), 114.

Whiteford, H. A., Degenhardt, L., Rehm, J., Baxter, A. J., Ferrari, A. J., Erskine, H. E., et al. (2013). Global burden of disease attributable to mental and substance use disorders: Findings from the global burden of disease study 2010. *The Lancet*, *382*(9904), 1575–1586. https://doi.org/10.1016/S0140-6736(13)61611-6.

WHO (2008). *mhGAP: Mental health gap action programme: Scaling up care for mental, neurological and substance use disorders*. Retrieved from http:/www.who.int/mental_health/evidence/mhGAP/en/.

WHO (2010). *Mental health gap action programme implementation guide (mhGAP-IG) for mental, neurological and substance use disorders in non-specialized health settings*. Retrieved from https:/www.who.int/mental_health/publications/mhGAP_intervention_guide/en/.

WHO (2015). *Thinking healthy: A manual for psychosocial management of perinatal depression, WHO generic field-trial version 1.0, 2015 (9754004110)*. Retrieved from http:/apps.who.int/iris/handle/10665/152936.

Woody, C. A., Ferrari, A. J., Siskind, D. J., Whiteford, H. A., & Harris, M. G. (2017). A systematic review and meta-regression of the prevalence and incidence of perinatal depression. *Journal of Affective Disorders*, *219*, 86–92. https://doi.org/10.1016/j.jad.2017.05.003.

Psychotherapy adaptation in aging populations

15

Engelina Groenewald, John Joska*†*, Ricardo Araya*‡*

*Department of Psychiatry, University of Stellenbosch and Stikland Hospital, Cape Town, South Africa, †Department of Psychiatry and Mental Health, University of Cape Town, Cape Town, South Africa, ‡Centre of Global Mental Health, Institute of Psychiatry, Psychology and Neurosciences, King's College London, London, United Kingdom

15.1 Aging and global mental health

The elderly (defined as people aged 60 years and older) are often excluded from research on psychotherapy and global mental health (Kok & Reynolds, 2017; Reynolds et al., 2012). Yet the aging of the global population represents a major mental health concern. In 2015, 12% of the world's population was >60 years old. By 2050, this number will rise to 22% (World Health Organization, 2018a). The demographic transition is not a phenomenon that is unique to high-income countries (de Lima, Leibing, & Buschfort, 2008; Reynolds et al., 2012). It is estimated that 80% of the elderly will live in low- and middle-income countries (LMIC) by 2050 (World Health Organization, 2018a).

With increasing age, mental disorders become more prevalent. Approximately 20% of people over the age of 60 suffer from a mental disorder (World Health Organization, 2018b), and it is projected that by 2030, the number of older adults living with mental disorders will double (Reynolds et al., 2012). Mental disorders contribute to nearly 7% of the total disability-adjusted life years (DALY) of the world population older than 60 (World Health Organization, 2018b). Common mental disorders in the elderly include dementia, depression, anxiety disorders, and substance disorders (World Health Organization, 2018b).

In 2017, 50 million people in the world were living with dementia (also known as major neurocognitive disorder) (World Health Organization, 2018b). It is projected that this number will increase to 82 million in 2030 and 152 million by 2050 (World Health Organization, 2018b). The greatest burden (60%) of dementia is concentrated in LMIC (World Health Organization, 2018b). Dementia causes significant impairment in the quality of life of patients, their caregivers, and their family members. The impact on the family of patients with dementia is especially significant in LMIC where family members often have to take the full responsibility of caregiving, where there is limited financial and medical support, and where patients often live in households with extended family (Brodaty & Donkin, 2009; Cohen et al., 2016; Dias et al., 2004; Patel, Chowdhary, Rahman, & Verdeli, 2011; Patel & Prince, 2001).

Global Mental Health and Psychotherapy. https://doi.org/10.1016/B978-0-12-814932-4.00015-X

Depression is also common in the elderly with prevalence estimates of 7% in the general elderly population (World Health Organization, 2018b), 6%–10% in primary care settings, and 30% in medical inpatients and long-term care settings (Reynolds et al., 2012). Major depressive disorder is slightly less prevalent in the elderly than in the young (Kok & Reynolds, 2017). However, the less severe forms of depression (dysthymia, minor depression, and subsyndromal depression) occur more frequently in the elderly (Ciechanowski et al., 2004) and cause significant impairment in functioning, exacerbate the disability associated with other medical conditions, and result in increased utilization of health services (World Health Organization, 2018b).

Despite the magnitude of the problem, the treatment gap is likely much larger in the elderly than in the young. In the general population, inadequate investment in mental health care, stigma associated with mental illness, and a lack of skilled human resources who are able to provide a cultural perspective on psychotherapeutic treatments contribute to the mental illness treatment gap (Patel et al., 2011). These factors are even more significant in the elderly than in the young, especially in LMIC (de Lima et al., 2008).

15.2 Psychotherapy in the elderly

Since the advent of psychotherapy, the elderly have often been excluded from the benefits of this treatment modality. Freud believed that the elderly did not have the capacity to change and that psychotherapy should therefore not be attempted (Garner, 2013; Stern & Lovestone, 2000). Even today, many psychotherapists perceive the elderly as not being suitable candidates for psychotherapy and therefore choose not to offer psychotherapy to elderly individuals (Lewis & Johansen, 1982; Zivian, Larsen, Knox, Gekoski, & Hatchette, 1992). In addition, there are often patient-related barriers to psychotherapy in this age group, including decreased mobility, medical comorbidities, and cognitive symptoms. Yet, there is conclusive evidence that older persons can benefit from psychotherapy, especially when these challenges are accommodated (Cuijpers, Karyotaki, Pot, Park, & Reynolds, 2014; Karel & Hinrichsen, 2000; Pinquart, Duberstein, & Lyness, 2007).

15.2.1 The benefits of psychotherapy in the elderly

Contrary to the idea that the elderly are not suitable for psychotherapy, older individuals may be able to engage particularly well and benefit immensely (Karel & Hinrichsen, 2000). Older patients may be more introspective than the young, they are often clear about their values and beliefs, and they may have a lifetime of relationships and coping mechanisms to draw upon in psychotherapeutic work (Karel & Hinrichsen, 2000; Lewis & Johansen, 1982).

The psychosocial stressors that occur commonly in the elderly present both a challenge and an opportunity. These stressors make the elderly more prone to mental disorders, but they may also render psychotherapy more effective (Reynolds et al., 2012). Psychosocial stressors that occur commonly in the elderly include loneliness, stressful life events such as the loss of a partner, functional impairment, and medical comorbidities (Kok & Reynolds, 2017; Patel & Prince, 2001; Wetherell et al., 2004). The elderly in LMIC experience similar concerns, but they also have additional stressors such as poverty, the lack of care or abuse by the family, and a fear of abandonment and rejection (Cohen et al., 2016; Patel & Prince, 2001). These stressors can be addressed by psychotherapeutic treatments and lead to symptom reduction and an increase in the quality of life.

In LMIC, older persons often live with family members and are responsible for decision-making as head of households (Cohen et al., 2016; Patel & Prince, 2001; Statistics South Africa, 2014). Treatment of mental disorders, with pharmacotherapy and/or psychotherapy, is therefore potentially beneficial for both the patient and family members.

There is ample evidence for psychotherapy as an adjunct to pharmacotherapy for mental disorders in the elderly (Areán & Cook, 2002). However, psychotherapy can also be a useful alternative to pharmacotherapy. This is important in the elderly, who are frequently on many other medications with potentially dangerous drug-drug interactions. The elderly often develop debilitating side effects such as hyponatremia, bone demineralization, falls, cataracts, and memory problems on psychotropic medication (Ayers, Sorrell, Thorp, & Wetherell, 2007; Kok & Reynolds, 2017; Reynolds et al., 2012). In addition, psychotherapy is the treatment of choice in the "less severe depressive disorders" (minor depression and dysthymia) that occur commonly in the elderly and in which there is less evidence for the value of pharmacotherapy (Ciechanowski et al., 2004; Kok & Reynolds, 2017; Thomas, 2014). Lastly, many elderly prefer psychotherapy to the use of psychotropic medication (Ayers et al., 2007; Wetherell et al., 2004). This could be explained by the perception of side effects and an unwillingness to add additional medication to existing treatment regimens (Wetherell et al., 2004).

15.2.2 The barriers to psychotherapy in the elderly

Despite the evidence that psychotherapy is beneficial in the elderly, there may be significant challenges that result in older individuals being excluded from this therapeutic modality.

The elderly often have decreased mobility and debilitating medical comorbidities that might make it difficult to attend a clinic. Clinic settings, where patients are expected to come for psychotherapy, are frequently not very accommodating toward the needs of the elderly, especially in LMIC (Dias et al., 2008). For example, in a clinic in South Africa where the mean waiting time was >9h, a frail elderly patient with multiple medical comorbidities would find it extremely difficult to see a health-care practitioner (Rauf, Blitz, Geyser, & Rauf, 2008). The elderly are often poor, especially in LMIC (Cohen et al., 2016; Statistics South Africa, 2014), which makes it difficult for them to visit clinics and attend psychotherapy on a regular basis.

Cognitive disorders are more common in the elderly and could make psychotherapy more challenging (Kok & Reynolds, 2017). Limited research has been done on the efficacy of psychological therapies in individuals with cognitive disorders (Areán & Cook, 2002; NICE, 2006). There is a pervasive belief among health-care practitioners and society in general that cognitive deterioration is inevitable and occurs in all people as they age, despite evidence to the contrary (Lewis & Johansen, 1982; Patel & Prince, 2001). There is also a lack of awareness that cognitive impairment occurs on a spectrum and that patients with mild cognitive impairment can benefit from psychotherapy, even if it is supportive in nature, or utilizes simpler problem-solving approaches.

Patient and practitioner perceptions of psychotherapy are an important barrier to the delivery of this treatment. The elderly often do not present for psychotherapy due to the stigma against psychiatric or mental health treatments. The elderly are often not familiar with the "talking treatments" and may find these less acceptable (Patel et al., 2011; Zank, 1998). In primary health-care clinics in the United States, many older adults had a strong belief in self-reliance and were of the opinion that mental health treatment effects should be visible within 1 month (Wetherell et al., 2004). These opinions made them reluctant to present for psychotherapy, where benefits accrue over a longer period of time. On the other hand, psychotherapists often decide not to offer psychotherapy to the elderly due to the perception that psychotherapy is not beneficial in this age group (Lewis & Johansen, 1982; Zivian et al., 1992).

Many elderly patients with mental illness present with physical complaints such as fatigue, weight loss, pain, or other unexplained medical symptoms (the so-called masked depression) (Kok & Reynolds, 2017). As such, primary health-care practitioners often do not recognize mental disorders in the elderly and, therefore, do not refer these patients for psychotherapy (Patel et al., 2010; Wetherell et al., 2004). This could be attributed to ageism, negative views of mental health services, and the complicated comorbidity of medical and psychiatric disorders in the elderly (Mickus, Colenda, & Hogan, 2000).

Even in research on psychotherapy, the elderly are often omitted. Most studies of psychotherapy, including those done in LMIC, excluded patients over the age of 65. In studies where the elderly were included, age is often limited to 75 years (Kok & Reynolds, 2017). Furthermore, participants with medical comorbidities, cognitive impairment, psychosocial risk factors and those who live in rural areas or are homebound are often excluded from research on psychotherapy (Areán & Cook, 2002; Cuijpers et al., 2014; Kok & Reynolds, 2017; Reynolds et al., 2012). Assessment batteries that are used in psychotherapy research are often not culturally relevant or suitable for the elderly with little formal education (Reynolds et al., 2012). Due to these factors, the evidence for psychotherapeutic treatments in the elderly is limited in applicability and often not generalizable to other clinical or cultural contexts.

15.2.3 Adaptation of psychotherapy to overcome these barriers

The barriers to psychotherapy in the elderly can be overcome with some creativity and should be seen as a challenge and not an obstacle. To make clinics more accessible to the elderly, waiting times should be reduced, and general efficiency at primary health-care level should be improved. Home-based therapy should also be considered for those with decreased mobility or medical comorbidities (Ciechanowski et al., 2004).

Cognitive deficits are not a reason to exclude patients from psychotherapy. Psychotherapeutic interventions can be delivered to those with mild cognitive deficits and may even improve cognition or delay further cognitive decline (Areán & Cook, 2002). In those with more severe deficits, psychotherapy with the caregiver can decrease the neuropsychiatric symptoms of dementia in the patient and improve the quality of life of the caregiver and the patient (Brodaty, Green, & Koschera, 2003; Dias et al., 2008; Schulz et al., 2003).

Comorbid medical conditions are also not a valid contraindication to psychotherapy in the elderly. Untreated psychiatric disorders in patients with medical comorbidities may exacerbate the clinical manifestations of these disorders, lead to poor adherence to medication, and result in a poor outcome (Kok & Reynolds, 2017). Anxiety and depression related to medical conditions may lead to increased disability if not treated appropriately with psychotherapy (Wilkinson, 2014a). However, certain adaptations may have to be made for the patient with medical comorbidities. These adaptations could include shorter therapy sessions and delivery of psychotherapy at the patient's home (Dias et al., 2008; Karel & Hinrichsen, 2000).

The negative perceptions of health-care providers toward psychotherapy in the elderly should also be addressed. Given the high prevalence of mental disorders in the elderly and their comorbidity with medical conditions, primary health-care providers should be educated to recognize mental health problems, manage these conditions at the appropriate level, and refer those with complicated disorders (Mickus et al., 2000). The provision of mental health education for older persons may facilitate health literacy, health seeking, and utilization of available treatments. Another approach would be to develop mental health services that are framed around the needs and preferences of elderly patients (Wetherell et al., 2004). These services would collectively deal with structural barriers (such as access), reduce waiting times, improve detection through increased provider knowledge and skills, and reduce stigma through patient and provider education.

An attempt should be made to include generally representative participants in psychotherapy research. Elderly with medical comorbidities and frailty and those who are homebound should ideally not be omitted from psychotherapy research. These studies may call for an implementation science approach, with more emphasis on feasibility and acceptability, rather than on quantitative outcomes.

Perhaps the most important adaptation to psychotherapy in this age group is to remember that the elderly are individuals and not a homogeneous group. Even though cognitive symptoms, sensory deficits, and medical comorbidities are common in the elderly, not all elderly people experience these challenges. The administration of psychotherapy should, therefore, be adapted to the individual patient, not provided to the elderly as a homogenous group.

15.3 Psychological treatments for older adults

Evidence-based psychological treatments for older adults can broadly be divided into two groups: those that were developed for the elderly, specifically for those with dementia, and those developed for younger people and later adapted for use with older people (Wilkinson, 2014b).

15.3.1 Psychological treatments specific for the elderly

15.3.1.1 Reminiscence therapy

Reminiscence therapy comprises the discussion of past experiences and activities with the help of triggers such as photographs, familiar objects from the past, and music (Woods, Spector, Jones, Orrell, & Davies, 2009). Reminiscence therapy is an umbrella term that refers to discussions of life events in an individual or group context with the aim of enhancing personal well-being (Pinquart et al., 2007; Wilkinson, 2014b; Woods et al., 2009). It includes life-review therapy, where autobiographical memories are discussed in a therapeutic, one-to-one setting. Reminiscence therapy was specifically developed for older adults and is based on Erikson's theories of aging (Areán & Cook, 2002; Karel & Hinrichsen, 2000).

Unfortunately, very few randomized controlled trials on reminiscence therapy have been conducted, and the existing trials are small, with insufficient power and a lack of formal diagnostic testing (Areán & Cook, 2002; Woods et al., 2009). These randomized controlled trials suggest that reminiscence therapy results in an improvement in cognitive (Baines, Saxby, & Ehlert, 1987; Goldwasser, Auerbach, & Harkins, 1987; Wang, 2007), affective (Goldwasser et al., 1987; Wang, 2007), and behavioral symptoms (Baines et al., 1987; Goldwasser et al., 1987) in patients with dementia. Reminiscence therapy improves depressive symptoms in patients with depressive disorders (Areán & Cook, 2002; Cuijpers et al., 2014; Peng, Huang, Chen, & Lu, 2009). Participants in the randomized controlled trials were from diverse cultural and ethnic backgrounds. Where caregivers were involved in reminiscence therapy, it reduced the strain on the caregivers significantly (Woods et al., 2009).

15.3.1.2 Caregiver therapy

Psychoeducation, problem-solving therapy, and support groups have been shown to improve the quality of life of the caregiver, decrease caregiver burden, and improve the neuropsychiatric symptoms in the patient with dementia (Brodaty et al., 2003; Dias et al., 2008; Schulz et al., 2003). Caregiver therapy is most effective when the patient with dementia is actively involved in the treatment (Schulz et al., 2003). Caregiver interventions have a similar outcome in LMIC where they have been shown to be beneficial in patients with dementia and their caregivers (Dias et al., 2008).

15.3.2 Psychological treatments adapted for older people

15.3.2.1 Cognitive behavioral therapy

The premise of cognitive behavioral therapy (CBT) is that emotional states arise from people's beliefs about themselves and the world and that these beliefs can be changed (Wilkinson, 2014a) (see Chapter 5). Dysfunctional beliefs are common in the elderly and may arise from the self and society. A personal belief that may have been helpful in the past may become dysfunctional with a change in life circumstances (James, Kendell, & Reichelt, 1999). For example, when an elderly person who believes that meaning in life comes from hard work and making a contribution to society is forced to retire, he appraises his life as meaningless and becomes depressed. Dysfunctional beliefs often arise from society where negative perceptions about aging persist and the elderly are viewed as a burden (de Lima et al., 2008; Patel & Prince, 2001). In CBT, these underlying dysfunctional beliefs are identified and modified through the process of therapy.

In the elderly with depressive disorders, there is evidence that CBT improves depressive symptoms and results in enduring benefits (Cuijpers et al., 2014; Gould, Coulson, & Howard, 2012; Kok & Reynolds, 2017; Wilkinson, 2014a; Wilson, Mottram, & Vassilas, 2008). In the elderly, CBT is an effective treatment modality for anxiety disorders (Ayers et al., 2007; Stanley et al., 2009) and anxiety symptoms associated with a fear of falling (Zijlstra et al., 2009). Medical conditions in the elderly often lead to anxiety and depression that may exacerbate the disability associated with these conditions (Ayers et al., 2007). CBT can decrease the associated anxiety and depression and therefore reduce the disability associated with these conditions (Ayers et al., 2007; Beltman, Oude Voshaar, & Speckens, 2010). CBT is also effective for the treatment of insomnia in the elderly (Montgomery & Dennis, 2009). In adults with dementia, CBT may be helpful in treating the anxiety and depression associated with memory loss (Koder, 2017; Teri & Gallagher-Thompson, 1991), but little conclusive evidence exists. CBT for the caregiver of the patient with dementia has been shown to improve the mental state of the patient and delay the onset of institutional care (NICE, 2006; Wilkinson, 2014a).

CBT seems to be cross-culturally applicable, and evidence exists for the efficacy of CBT in LMIC (Patel et al., 2011). Cognitive behavioral interventions in LMIC were effective for the treatment of harmful drinking patterns (Nadkarni et al., 2017), perinatal depression (Rahman, Malik, Sikander, Roberts, & Creed, 2008), and depression in women attending primary care clinics (Araya et al., 2003). These studies provide support for the breadth of the applicability of CBT in LMIC; however, most of the research on CBT in LMIC excluded participants older than 65.

15.3.2.2 Interpersonal therapy

Interpersonal therapy (IPT) follows the premise that depression has a negative impact on the patient's relationships and that the origin of the depression is often in these relationships (see Chapter 7). Intervention therefore needs to be in the interpersonal domain (Wilkinson, 2014c). IPT addresses four areas of conflict: complicated bereavement, role transition, interpersonal disputes, and interpersonal deficits (Areán & Cook, 2002; Wilkinson, 2014c). IPT was initially developed for the treatment of depression but has been adapted for numerous other disorders.

IPT is effective for the treatment of depression in older adults (Van Schaik, Van Marwijk, Ader, Van Dyck, & De Haan, 2006) and decreases suicidal ideation in older patients with depression (Bruce et al., 2004). IPT has been adapted for the treatment of depression in patients with cognitive impairment (Miller & Iii, 2007) and often involves the caregivers of these patients. IPT is effective for the treatment of anxiety disorders and grief in the elderly (Wilkinson, 2014c). It can be provided in group format or by lay counselors (Bass et al., 2003; Bolton, Bass, Verdeli, Clougherty, & Ndogoni, 2003; Patel et al., 2010; Scocco, De Leo, & Frank, 2002). IPT is cross-culturally applicable, and there is evidence for the efficacy of IPT in LMIC (Bass et al., 2003; Bolton et al., 2003; Patel et al., 2010, 2011). The studies on IPT done in LMIC did not, however, include elderly participants. While there is good reason to suspect that this approach might also be effective in the elderly, robust data would provide a solid basis for recommendation.

15.3.2.3 Problem-solving therapy

Problem-solving therapy (PST) is based on the assumption that problems of daily life cause and perpetuate depressive symptoms (Ciechanowski et al., 2004) (see Chapter 7). Depressive symptoms can be decreased by helping the patient to systematically identify and address these problems (Ciechanowski et al., 2004). PST consists of a combination of skill building and cognitive restructuring and focuses on improving problem-resolution skills (Areán & Cook, 2002). PST has been shown to be effective in the treatment and prevention of depression in the elderly (Cuijpers et al., 2014; Reynolds et al., 2012). There is no available evidence on the efficacy of PST in elderly persons in LMIC (Cuijpers, van Straten, & Warmerdam, 2007; Patel, Simon, Chowdhary, Kaaya, & Araya, 2009).

15.3.2.4 Behavioral therapy

Behavioral therapy focuses on skill building and presupposes that changes in information processing are achieved through positive experiences with new behavior (Areán & Cook, 2002). The largest evidence base for behavioral therapy in the elderly is for the treatment of depression (Areán & Cook, 2002; Gilbody et al., 2017) and insomnia (Buysse et al., 2011; Germain et al., 2006; Reynolds et al., 2012). Behavioral therapy also resulted in decreased depressive symptoms in patients with dementia and their caregivers (Teri, Logsdon, Uomoto, & McCurry, 1997). Although there is currently no available evidence on the efficacy of behavioral therapy in the elderly in LMIC, a proposed randomized controlled trial in India will explore behavioral therapy as part of a depression prevention strategy in the elderly (Dias et al., 2017).

15.3.2.5 Dynamic psychotherapy

Brief dynamic psychotherapy (BDT) may be effective for treating depression in older adults (Thompson, Gallagher, & Breckenridge, 1987) although other therapies may result in a greater reduction in symptoms (Areán & Cook, 2002). BDT is better than no treatment (Thompson et al., 1987), but not more efficacious than CBT (Gallagher-Thompson & Steffen, 1994). Outcomes for major depression seem to be maintained over a 2-year period (Gallagher-Thompson, Hanley-Peterson, & Thompson, 1990). There is no evidence available on the efficacy of dynamic psychotherapy in the elderly in LMIC.

15.4 Scaling up of psychological treatments for the elderly

The magnitude of the treatment gap in the elderly is unknown. It is reasonable to believe that it is even larger than in the young and that the majority of elderly who require psychiatric treatment do not receive it (Cole & Yaffe, 1996; Eaton et al., 2011; Joling et al., 2011). Psychiatrists and psychologists are scarce human resources, especially in the field of old-age psychiatry. This is particularly problematic in LMIC where the mental health care of the elderly is not prioritized and resources are allocated to combat diseases prevalent in the young (de Lima et al., 2008; van Heerden, Uwakwe, & Potochnick, 2011). For example, South Africa, a middle-income country with a population of 55 million people, has only three old-age psychiatrists, one training unit where clinicians can be trained in old-age psychiatry, and no formal national dementia care plan (Statistics South Africa, 2014; van Heerden et al., 2011). In order to expand evidence-based psychological treatments to the elderly who need it, we will have to use creative approaches that accommodate the unique needs of this age group. There are several therapeutic approaches that aim to close the treatment gap in the elderly.

15.4.1 Group therapy

Group therapy was one of the first approaches used as an attempt to close the psychotherapy treatment gap. Group therapy was adopted as a treatment approach in the period after the second world war when there were suddenly an increased number of clients who required mental health services but not enough practitioners to provide these services (Parham, Priddy, McGovern, & Richman, 1982). It is still an efficient and cost-effective mode of therapy as a small number of practitioners are able to provide psychotherapy to a large number of patients (Karel & Hinrichsen, 2000).

Group therapy may be particularly suitable for the treatment of depression in the elderly. Elderly patients often struggle with loneliness, low self-esteem, and the feeling that their life has no meaning (Karel & Hinrichsen, 2000). The therapeutic group may provide a space where older adults can give and receive support, and it may address low self-esteem through the admiration and feedback of group members (Karel & Hinrichsen, 2000). Elderly patients seem to do well in a group setting, but the therapist might have to make certain adaptions such as making an effort to include group members with sensory impairment or cognitive deficits (Karel & Hinrichsen, 2000). Some research has shown that elderly patients treated in a primary care setting preferred individual therapy to group therapy (Areán, Alvidrez, Barrera, Robinson, & Hicks, 2002). However, these patients were never exposed to psychotherapy, either in a group or individual setting, prior to the study. They also indicated a preference for group psychoeducational classes.

Group therapy and individual therapy seem to be equally effective (Areán & Cook, 2002; Pinquart, Duberstein, & Lyness, 2006) even though there is a higher dropout rate with group interventions (Pinquart & Duberstein, 2007). CBT, IPT, PST, and psychodynamic therapy can be delivered in a group format (Karel & Hinrichsen, 2000; Wilkinson, 2014a, 2014c). Group therapy can be administered by lay counselors, and there is ample evidence for the efficacy of group therapy in multiple cultural contexts and in LMIC (Araya et al., 2003; Bass et al., 2003; Bolton et al., 2003).

15.4.2 Self-help interventions

Self-help interventions include bibliotherapy and internet-based therapy. With the guidance of a therapist, patients are encouraged to read disorder-specific manuals. Self-help interventions appear to be a useful treatment modality to close the treatment gap in the elderly. A major advantage is accessibility, as these therapies are within reach of the elderly who are homebound or those with decreased mobility due to frailty or comorbid medical conditions. There is some evidence that such interventions are cost-effective and require few human resources, which makes them advantageous in LMIC (Cuijpers & Schuurmans, 2007). Bibliotherapy is perceived by elderly individuals to be a more acceptable form of psychotherapy (Wetherell et al., 2004).

However, the evidence for bibliotherapy in the elderly is limited. Three randomized controlled trials showed bibliotherapy to be an effective and enduring treatment for mild to moderate depression in the elderly (Floyd, Scogin, McKendree-Smith, Floyd, & Rokke, 2004; McKendree-Smith, Floyd, & Scogin, 2003; Scogin, Hamblin, & Beutler, 1987; Scogin, Jamison, & Gochneaur, 1989). Nevertheless, sample sizes of these trials were small. A randomized controlled trial of bibliotherapy in very old adults with subthreshold depression showed no effect (Joling et al., 2011). Still, a stepped-care intervention that included bibliotherapy prevented depressive and anxiety symptoms in elderly individuals (van't Veer-Tazelaar et al., 2009).

Bibliotherapy is suitable for a limited group of patients because those with a low level of education and cognitive deficits would not benefit from this treatment modality. This might be problematic in certain LMIC where the elderly have a low level of education (Statistics South Africa, 2014). There are no randomized controlled trials on bibliotherapy in the elderly in LMIC.

Internet-guided interventions are effective for the treatment of depression and anxiety in younger patients (Cuijpers & Schuurmans, 2007; Spek et al., 2007). However, there are as yet no randomized controlled trials on the effect of internet-based interventions in the elderly with these disorders. Internet-guided interventions have been shown to improve the quality of life of patients with dementia and their caregivers when administered to the caregivers (Martínez-Alcalá, Pliego-Pastrana, Rosales-Lagarde, Lopez-Noguerola, & Molina-Trinidad, 2016).

Internet-based interventions are accessible to the elderly from a mobility perspective. However, many elderly are uncertain on how to use the internet and may even be afraid to use the internet (Martínez-Alcalá et al., 2016; van't Hof, Cuijpers, & Stein, 2009). The elderly with visual impairment and cognitive deficits are excluded from internet-based interventions. Furthermore, internet access is severely limited in certain LMIC (van't Hof et al., 2009).

15.4.3 Telephone-based interventions

Telephone-delivered psychotherapy is advantageous from an accessibility perspective. In a randomized clinical trial of 141 elderly adults with generalized anxiety disorder, telephone-delivered CBT was superior to nondirective supportive therapy in reducing anxiety and depressive symptoms (Brenes, Danhauer, Lyles, Hogan, & Miller, 2015). A telephone-based intervention reduced distress in the caregivers of patients with dementia (Schulz et al., 2003).

15.4.4 Task-sharing

Task sharing is currently the most popular approach to scale up psychological treatments in LMIC (see Chapter 2). Task sharing includes the delivery of psychological treatments by community health workers or peers who are not specialists in mental health (Eaton et al., 2011; Singla et al., 2017). Several randomized controlled trials have demonstrated that psychotherapeutic treatments are effective when administered by lay councillors with no mental health training (Patel et al., 2011).

There is a dearth of research on the efficacy of task sharing in elderly patients. Even though several authors (Patel et al., 2007, 2011) emphasize the importance of adapting psychotherapy to the relevant cultural context, there is almost no evidence-based guidance on how task sharing should be adapted to meet the needs of the elderly.

Another problem with task sharing is that this necessitates a considerable amount of training and with high staff turnover, this investment might draw considerable resources (Eaton et al., 2011). Task sharing with families, carers, and volunteers might be a better and more enduring investment. This form of task sharing enables caregivers to be more informed when caring for community members with mental illness (Eaton et al., 2011) and showed promising results in the elderly (Brodaty et al., 2003; Dias et al., 2008; Schulz et al., 2003; Teri et al., 1997). In high-income countries, empowering caregivers of patients with dementia resulted in less behavioral and psychological symptoms of dementia (BPSD) in the patients and a better quality of life in caregivers (Brodaty et al., 2003; Teri et al., 1997). Similar results have been demonstrated in diverse cultural and ethnic groups (Belle et al., 2006; Schulz et al., 2003) and in LMIC (Dias et al., 2008). Despite the efficacy of these task-sharing interventions, they have not been integrated into policies or implemented in clinical practice in LMIC (Eaton et al., 2011).

15.5 Evidence-based psychotherapy for specific disorders in the elderly in a global mental health context

15.5.1 Dementia

There is a perception that psychotherapy is not beneficial in a patient with cognitive deficits (Lewis & Johansen, 1982). However, psychotherapy could improve both the cognitive deficits and the symptoms associated with cognitive impairment. Cognitive symptoms are often a consequence of other psychiatric disorders, such as depression or anxiety disorders (Miller & Iii, 2007; Pinquart & Duberstein, 2007). In these cases, proper treatment of the underlying disorder, which may include psychotherapy, may improve the cognitive deficits (Areán & Cook, 2002). In patients where cognitive deficits are the result of dementia, it is important to remember that cognitive impairment exists on a spectrum from mild to severe. Psychotherapy could be beneficial in all stages of dementia, but the mode of psychotherapy should be tailored to where the patient falls on this spectrum.

Patients with mild cognitive impairment can benefit from any evidence-based psychotherapy that addresses their specific symptoms, such as depression, anxiety, or insomnia. Reminiscence therapy could be applied in all stages of dementia and may lead to improved quality of life and improvement in the behavioral and psychological symptoms of dementia (Baines et al., 1987; Bohlmeijer, Roemer, Cuijpers, & Smit, 2007; Goldwasser et al., 1987; Peng et al., 2009). However, the evidence for the value of reminiscence therapy for dementia patients is still limited (Bohlmeijer et al., 2007).

In patients with moderate to severe dementia, psychotherapy should focus on the caregiver of the patient with dementia. Caring for a patient with dementia can be extremely stressful, may lead to mental disorders, and come at an immense personal and financial cost (Brodaty & Donkin, 2009). The demands on caregivers are often much higher in LMIC, where family members are expected to care for patients with dementia with very little support (Dias et al., 2004, 2008). Caregiver psychotherapy not only relieves distress in the caregiver but also relieves the neuropsychiatric symptoms of dementia in the patient (Brodaty et al., 2003; Teri et al., 1997). Caregiver psychotherapy may lead to an improved quality of life of both the patient and the caregiver (Brodaty et al., 2003; Schulz et al., 2003).

Several psychotherapeutic interventions administered to the caregiver of the patient with dementia may have a beneficial effect. Psychoeducation, family therapy, support groups, and problem-solving therapy decrease psychological morbidity in the caregiver and improve caregiver knowledge, coping skills, and support (Brodaty et al., 2003). The most significant factor that predicted success of a caregiver intervention was the involvement of the patient with dementia (Brodaty et al., 2003). In Goa, India, a randomized controlled trial compared a caregiver intervention consisting of psychoeducation, problem-solving treatment, and support with waiting-list control (Dias et al., 2008). The stepped-care intervention was provided by lay counselors, delivered at patients' homes, and consisted of the following components: education about dementia, education about the common behavioral symptoms of dementia and the management of these symptoms, support for the caregiver, referral to doctors when severe behavioral problems warranted medication, and networking with other families and advice about government schemes for the elderly. The intervention drastically improved caregiver mental health and perceived burden of care.

15.5.2 Depression

The efficacy of psychotherapy in the treatment of depression in the elderly has been extensively researched. CBT, IPT, PST, and brief psychodynamic therapy have immediate and enduring effects in the treatment of the depressive disorders in the elderly

(Areán & Cook, 2002; Cuijpers et al., 2014; Gould et al., 2012; Karel & Hinrichsen, 2000). CBT is an effective treatment for the depressive symptoms associated with medical illnesses in elderly patients (Beltman et al., 2010). There is no difference between the mode of delivery of these therapies, and group therapy is just as effective as individual therapy (Areán & Cook, 2002; Karel & Hinrichsen, 2000). These therapies are equally effective when administered by clinicians who are not specialists in mental health. In the Program to Encourage Active, Rewarding Lives for Seniors (PEARL), PST was administered by social workers and reduced depressive symptoms in a group of medically ill, low-income, and homebound elderly (Ciechanowski et al., 2004). The intervention consisted of eight 50min sessions administered at patients' homes during which patients also had to select a pleasant activity to engage in before the next session. The PST sessions were modified to provide more emphasis on social and physical activation.

Psychotherapy can also be used to prevent depressive disorders and the consequences of depression in the elderly. A stepped-care program that included bibliotherapy and PST prevented the onset of depression in elderly patients (van't Veer-Tazelaar et al., 2009). In the CollAborative care for Screen-Positive EldeRs (CASPER) randomized clinical trial, a collaborative care program that included behavioral activation, the intervention reduced depressive symptoms and prevented more severe depression in elderly patients with subthreshold depression (Gilbody et al., 2017). PST was an effective intervention to prevent depressive symptoms in patients with strokes (Robinson et al., 2008) and macular degeneration (Rovner, Hegel, Leiby, & Tasman, 2007). The PROSPECT trial demonstrated that a combination of the antidepressant Citalopram and IPT resulted in a reduction of suicidal ideation in depressed elderly patients (Bruce et al., 2004). The psychotherapeutic intervention (IPT) was administered by social workers, nurses, and psychologists (Bruce et al., 2004).

The depression in later life (DIL) trial will be the first randomized controlled trial to address the prevention of depressive disorders in a LMIC (Dias et al., 2017). This trial will be conducted on older adults attending rural and primary health-care clinics in Goa, India. A combination of problem-solving therapy and brief behavioral treatment of sleep disturbances will be administered by lay councillors for the indicated prevention of depression in later life (Dias et al., 2017).

15.5.3 Anxiety disorders

There is strong evidence for the efficacy of CBT, relaxation training, and supportive therapy in the treatment of generalized anxiety disorder in elderly patients (Ayers et al., 2007; Pinquart & Duberstein, 2007; Stanley et al., 2003; Stanley et al., 2009). The effects of CBT on anxiety symptoms were maintained at 1 year follow-up (Stanley et al., 2003). However, the evidence is limited for late-life anxiety disorders other than GAD (Ayers et al., 2007). CBT has immediate and enduring benefits in decreasing the fear of falling in elderly patients (Zijlstra et al., 2009). CBT programs for late-life anxiety typically include education about anxiety, self-monitoring, relaxation training, systematic desensitization, and cognitive restructuring (Ayers et al., 2007). There is a dearth of evidence for the treatment of late-life anxiety disorders using a psychotherapeutic approach in LMIC.

15.5.4 Insomnia

Brief behavioral treatment for insomnia (BBTI) has been shown to be an effective treatment for insomnia in two randomized controlled trials in the elderly (Buysse et al., 2011; Germain et al., 2006). BBTI focuses on behavioral aspects of insomnia treatment but includes education about sleep and sleep physiology (Buysse et al., 2011). Patients are encouraged to spend less time in bed, get up at the same time every day, not to go to bed unless tired, and not to stay in bed unless asleep (Buysse et al., 2011). In both of these trials, the behavioral intervention was administered by nurse practitioners. The DIL trial in Goa, India, will use the brief behavioral intervention for insomnia as part of their depression prevention strategy (Dias et al., 2017).

15.6 Conclusion

Despite potential barriers to the delivery of psychotherapy in elderly individuals, data specific to the elderly in LMIC are limited. There is support for a range of effective psychotherapies—such as IPT and CBT—in high-income countries and in younger individuals. While these represent plausible opportunities to intervene in LMIC settings, empirical data should be sought. Elderly patients can benefit immensely from these treatments, especially in LMIC. In addition to effective psychotherapies for individual common mental disorders, there are approaches that may be used to manage caregiver distress and burden in those caring for persons living with dementia. These too require replication in LMIC. With the growing number of elderly, especially in LMIC, the need to acquire the evidence and improve service delivery is urgent.

References

Araya, R., Rojas, G., Fritsch, R., Gaete, J., Rojas, M., Simon, G., et al. (2003). Treating depression in primary care in low-income women in Santiago, Chile: A randomised controlled trial. *Lancet*, *361*, 995–1000. https://doi.org/10.1016/S0140-6736(03)12825-5.

Areán, P., & Cook, B. (2002). Psychotherapy and combined psychotherapy/pharmacotherapy for late life depression. *Society of Biological Psychiatry*, *52*, 293–303.

Areán, P. A., Alvidrez, J., Barrera, A., Robinson, G. S., & Hicks, S. (2002). Would older medical patients use psychological services? *Gerontologist*, *42*, 392–398.

Ayers, C. R., Sorrell, J. T., Thorp, S. R., & Wetherell, J. L. (2007). Evidence-based psychological treatments for late-life anxiety. *Psychology and Aging*, *22*, 8–17. https://doi.org/10.1037/0882-7974.22.1.8.

Baines, S., Saxby, P., & Ehlert, K. (1987). Reality orientation and reminiscence therapy. A controlled cross-over study of elderly confused people. *British Journal of Psychiatry*, *151*, 222–231. https://doi.org/10.1192/bjp.151.2.222.

Bass, J., Neugebauer, R., Clougherty, K. F., Verdeli, H., Wickramaratne, P., Atne, W., et al. (2003). Group interpersonal psychotherapy for depression in rural Uganda: 6-month outcomes randomised controlled trial. *Depression*. https://doi.org/10.1192/bjp.188.6.567.

Belle, S. H., Burgio, L., Burns, R., Coon, D., Czaja, S. J., Gallagher-Thompson, D., et al. (2006). Enhancing the quality of life of dementia caregivers from different ethnic or racial groups:

A randomized, controlled trial. *Annals of Internal Medicine*, *145*, 727–738. https://doi.org/10.1016/0022-2836(89)90001-6.

Beltman, M. W., Oude Voshaar, R. C., & Speckens, A. E. (2010). Cognitive-behavioural therapy for depression in people with a somatic disease: Meta-analysis of randomised controlled trials. *British Journal of Psychiatry*, *197*, 11–19. https://doi.org/10.1192/bjp.bp.109.064675.

Bohlmeijer, E., Roemer, M., Cuijpers, P., & Smit, F. (2007). The effects of reminiscence on psychological well-being in older adults: A meta-analysis. *Aging & Mental Health*, *11*, 291–300. https://doi.org/10.1080/13607860600963547.

Bolton, P., Bass, J., Verdeli, H., Clougherty, K. F., & Ndogoni, L. (2003). For depression in rural Uganda. *JAMA*, *289*, 3117–3124.

Brenes, G. A., Danhauer, S. C., Lyles, M. F., Hogan, P. E., & Miller, M. E. (2015). Telephone-delivered cognitive behavioral therapy and telephone-delivered nondirective supportive therapy for rural older adults with generalized anxiety disorder: A randomized clinical trial. *JAMA Psychiatry*, *72*, 1012–1020. https://doi.org/10.1001/jamapsychiatry.2015.1154.

Brodaty, H., & Donkin, M. (2009). Family caregivers of people with dementia. *Dialogues in Clinical Neuroscience*, *11*, 217–228. https://doi.org/10.1038/jid.2015.269.

Brodaty, H., Green, A., & Koschera, A. (2003). Meta-analysis of psychosocial interventions for caregivers of people with dementia. *Journal of the American Geriatrics Society*, *51*, 657–664. https://doi.org/10.1034/j.1600-0579.2003.00210.x.

Bruce, M. L., Have, T. R., Charles, F. R., Katz, I., Schulberg, H. C., Mulsant, B. H., et al. (2004). Reducing suicidal ideation and depressive symptoms in depressed older primary care patients. *JAMA*, *291*, 1081–1091.

Buysse, D. J., Germain, A., Moul, D. E., Franzen, P. L., Brar, L. K., Fletcher, M. E., et al. (2011). Efficacy of brief behavioral treatment for chronic insomnia in older adults. *Archives of Internal Medicine*, *171*, 887–895. https://doi.org/10.1001/archinternmed.2010.535.

Ciechanowski, P., Wagner, E., Schmaling, K., Schwartz, S., Williams, B., Diehr, P., et al. (2004). Community-integrated home-based depression treatment in older adults. *JAMA*, *291*, 1569. https://doi.org/10.1001/jama.291.13.1569.

Cohen, A., Dias, A., Azariah, F., Krishna, R. N., Sequeira, M., Abraham, S., et al. (2016). Aging and well-being in Goa, India: A qualitative study. *Aging & Mental Health*, *7863*, 1–7. https://doi.org/10.1080/13607863.2016.1236239.

Cole, M. G., & Yaffe, M. J. (1996). Pathway to psychiatric care of the elderly with depression. *International Journal of Geriatric Psychiatry*, *11*, 157–161. https://doi.org/10.1002/(SICI)1099-1166(199602)11:2<157::AID-GPS304>3.0.CO;2-S.

Cuijpers, P., Karyotaki, E., Pot, A. M., Park, M., & Reynolds, C. F. (2014). Managing depression in older age: Psychological interventions. *Maturitas*, *79*, 160–169. https://doi.org/10.1016/j.maturitas.2014.05.027.

Cuijpers, P., & Schuurmans, J. (2007). Self-help interventions for anxiety disorders: An overview. *Current Psychiatry Reports*, *9*, 284–290. https://doi.org/10.1007/s11920-007-0034-6.

Cuijpers, P., van Straten, A., & Warmerdam, L. (2007). Problem solving therapies for depression: A meta-analysis. *European Psychiatry*, *22*, 9–15. https://doi.org/10.1016/j.eurpsy.2006.11.001.

de Lima, C. A. M., Leibing, A., & Buschfort, R. (2008). Ageing and mental health resources for older persons in the African region of the World Health Organization. *South African Journal of Psychiatry*, *14*, 8–11.

Dias, A., Azariah, F., Cohen, A., Anderson, S., Morse, J., Cuijpers, P., et al. (2017). Intervention development for the indicated prevention of depression in later life: The "DIL" protocol in

Goa, India. *Contemporary Clinical Trials Communications*, *6*, 131–139. https://doi.org/10.1016/j.conctc.2017.04.006.

Dias, A., Dewey, M. E., D'Souza, J., Dhume, R., Motghare, D. D., Shaji, K. S., et al. (2008). The effectiveness of a home care program for supporting caregivers of persons with dementia in developing countries: A randomised controlled trial from Goa, India. *PLoS ONE*, *3*. https://doi.org/10.1371/journal.pone.0002333.

Dias, A., Samuel, R., Patel, V., Prince, M., Parameshwaran, R., & Krishnamoorthy, E. S. (2004). The impact associated with caring for a person with dementia: A report from the 10/66 dementia research Group's Indian network. *International Journal of Geriatric Psychiatry*, *19*, 182–184. https://doi.org/10.1002/gps.1016.

Eaton, J., McCay, L., Semrau, M., Chatterjee, S., Baingana, F., Araya, R., et al. (2011). Scale up of services for mental health in low-income and middle-income countries. *Lancet*, *378*, 1592–1603. https://doi.org/10.1016/S0140-6736(11)60891-X.

Floyd, M., Scogin, F., McKendree-Smith, N. L., Floyd, D. L., & Rokke, P. D. (2004). Cognitive therapy for depression: A comparison of individual psychotherapy and bibliotherapy for depressed older adults. *Behavior Modification*, *28*, 297–318. https://doi.org/10.1177/0145445503259284.

Gallagher-Thompson, D., Hanley-Peterson, P., & Thompson, L. W. (1990). Maintenance of gains versus relapse following brief psychotherapy for depression. *Journal of Consulting and Clinical Psychology*, *58*, 371–374.

Gallagher-Thompson, D., & Steffen, A. M. (1994). Comparative effects of cognitive-behavioral and brief psychodynamic psychotherapies for depressed family caregivers. *Journal of Consulting and Clinical Psychology*, *62*, 543–549. https://doi.org/10.1037/0022-006X.62.3.543.

Garner, J. (2013). Psychodynamic psychotherapy. In T. Dening & A. Thomas (Eds.), *Oxford textb. old age psychiatry* (pp. 247–257). (2nd ed.). Oxford: Oxford University Press.

Germain, A., Moul, D. E., Franzen, P. L., Miewald, J. M., Reynolds, C. F., 3rd, Monk, T. H., & Buysse, D. J. (2006). Effects of a brief behavioral treatment for late-life insomnia: Preliminary findings. *Journal of Clinical Sleep Medicine*, *15*, 403–406.

Gilbody, S., Lewis, H., Adamson, J., Atherton, K., Bailey, D., Birtwistle, J., et al. (2017). Effect of collaborative care vs usual care on depressive symptoms in older adults with subthreshold depression: The CASPER randomized clinical trial. *JAMA*. https://doi.org/10.1001/jama.2017.0130.

Goldwasser, A. N., Auerbach, S. M., & Harkins, S. W. (1987). Cognitive, affective and behavioral effects of reminiscence group therapy on demented elderly. *International Journal of Aging & Human Development*, *25*, 209–222.

Gould, R. L., Coulson, M. C., & Howard, R. J. (2012). Cognitive behavioral therapy for depression in older people: A meta-analysis and meta-regression of randomized controlled trials. *Journal of the American Geriatrics Society*, *60*, 1817–1830. https://doi.org/10.1111/j.1532-5415.2012.04166.x.

James, I. A., Kendell, K., & Reichelt, F. K. (1999). Conceptualizations of depression in older people: The interaction of positive and negative beliefs. *Behavioural and Cognitive Psychotherapy*, *27*, 285–290.

Joling, K. J., Van Hout, H. P. J., van't Veer-Tazelaar, P. J., van der Horst, H. E., Cuijpers, P., van de Ven, P. M., et al. (2011). How effective is bibliotherapy for very old adults with subthreshold depression? A randomized controlled trial. *American Journal of Geriatric Psychiatry*, *19*, 256–265. https://doi.org/10.1097/JGP.0b013e3181ec8859.

Karel, M. J., & Hinrichsen, G. (2000). Treatment of depression in late life: Psychotherapeutic interventions. *Clinical Psychology Review*, *20*, 707–729.

Koder, D. (2017). Treatment of anxiety in the cognitively impaired elderly: Can cognitive-behavior therapy help? *International Psychogeriatrics*, *10*, 173–182.

Kok, R. M., & Reynolds, C. F. (2017). Management of depression in older adults. *JAMA*, *317*, 2114–2122.

Lewis, J. M., & Johansen, K. H. (1982). Resistances to psychotherapy with the elderly. *American Journal of Psychotherapy*, *36*, 497–504.

Martínez-Alcalá, C. I., Pliego-Pastrana, P., Rosales-Lagarde, A., Lopez-Noguerola, J., & Molina-Trinidad, E. M. (2016). Information and communication technologies in the care of the elderly: Systematic review of applications aimed at patients with dementia and caregivers. *JMIR Rehabilitation and Assistive Technologies*. *3*, e6https://doi.org/10.2196/rehab.5226.

McKendree-Smith, N. L., Floyd, M., & Scogin, F. R. (2003). Self-administered treatments for depression: A review. *Journal of Clinical Psychology*, *59*, 275–288. https://doi.org/10.1002/jclp.10129.

Mickus, M., Colenda, C. C., & Hogan, A. J. (2000). Knowledge of mental health benefits and preferences for type of mental health providers among the general public. *Psychiatric Services*, *51*, 199–202. https://doi.org/10.1176/appi.ps.51.2.199.

Miller, M. D., & Iii, C. F. R. (2007). Expanding the usefulness of interpersonal psychotherapy (IPT) for depressed elders with co-morbid cognitive impairment. *International Journal of Geriatric Psychiatry*, 101–105. https://doi.org/10.1002/gps.

Montgomery, P., & Dennis, J. (2009). Cognitive behavioural interventions for sleep problems in adults aged 60+. *Cochrane Database of Systematic Reviews*, 1–39. https://doi.org/10.1002/14651858.CD003161.

Nadkarni, A., Weobong, B., Weiss, H. A., McCambridge, J., Bhat, B., Katti, B., et al. (2017). Counselling for alcohol problems (CAP), a lay counsellor-delivered brief psychological treatment for harmful drinking in men, in primary care in India: A randomised controlled trial. *Lancet*, *389*, 186–195. https://doi.org/10.1016/S0140-6736(16)31590-2.

NICE (2006). *Dementia: Supporting people with dementia and their carers in health and social care*. *Clinical guideline* (pp. 1–53). vol. 42, (pp. 1–53). https://www.nice.org.uk/guidance/cg42/resources/dementia-supporting-people-with-dementia-and-their-carers-in-health-and-social-care-pdf-975443665093 [accessed 02.01.18].

Parham, I. A., Priddy, J. M., McGovern, T. V., & Richman, C. M. (1982). Group psychotherapy with the elderly: Problems and prospects. *Psychotherapy Theory Research & Practice*, *19*, 437–443.

Patel, V., Araya, R., Chatterjee, S., Chisholm, D., Cohen, A., De Silva, M., et al. (2007). Treatment and prevention of mental disorders in low-income and middle-income countries. *Lancet*, *370*, 991–1005. https://doi.org/10.1016/S0140-6736(07)61240-9.

Patel, V., Chowdhary, N., Rahman, A., & Verdeli, H. (2011). Improving access to psychological treatments: Lessons from developing countries. *Behaviour Research and Therapy*, *49*, 523–528. https://doi.org/10.1016/j.brat.2011.06.012.

Patel, V., & Prince, M. (2001). Ageing and mental health in a developing country: Who cares? Qualitative studies from Goa, India. *Psychological Medicine*, *31*, 29–38. https://doi.org/10.1017/S0033291799003098.

Patel, V., Simon, G., Chowdhary, N., Kaaya, S., & Araya, R. (2009). Packages of care for depression in low- and middle-income countries. *PLoS Medicine*. *6*, https://doi.org/10.1371/journal.pmed.1000159.

Patel, V., Weiss, H. A., Chowdhary, N., Naik, S., Pednekar, S., Chatterjee, S., et al. (2010). Effectiveness of an intervention led by lay health counsellors for depressive and anxiety disorders in primary care in Goa, India (MANAS): A cluster randomised controlled trial. *Lancet*, *376*, 2086–2095. https://doi.org/10.1016/S0140-6736(10)61508-5.

Peng, X. D., Huang, C. Q., Chen, L. J., & Lu, Z. C. (2009). Cognitive behavioural therapy and reminiscence techniques for the treatment of depression in the elderly: A systematic review. *Journal of International Medical Research*, *37*, 975–982.

Pinquart, M., & Duberstein, P. R. (2007). Treatment of anxiety disorders in older adults: A meta-analytic comparison of behavioral and pharmacological interventions. *The American Journal of Geriatric Psychiatry*, *15*, 639–651. https://doi.org/10.1097/JGP.0b013e31806841c8.

Pinquart, M., Duberstein, P. R., & Lyness, J. M. (2006). Treatments for later-life depressive conditions: A meta-analytic comparison of pharmacotherapy and psychotherapy. *American Journal of Psychiatry*, *163*, 1493–1501. https://doi.org/10.1176/appi.ajp.163.9.1493.

Pinquart, M., Duberstein, P. R., & Lyness, J. M. (2007). Effects of psychotherapy and other behavioral interventions on clinically depressed older adults: A meta-analysis. *Aging & Mental Health*, *11*, 645–657. https://doi.org/10.1080/13607860701529635.

Rahman, A., Malik, A., Sikander, S., Roberts, C., & Creed, F. (2008). Cognitive behaviour therapy-based intervention by community health workers for mothers with depression and their infants in rural Pakistan: A cluster-randomised controlled trial. *Lancet*, *372*, 902–909. https://doi.org/10.1016/S0140-6736(08)61400-2.

Rauf, W., Blitz, J., Geyser, M., & Rauf, A. (2008). Quality improvement cycles that reduced waiting times at Tshwane District Hospital Emergency Department. *South African Family Practice*, *50*, 43e. https://doi.org/10.1080/20786204.2008.10873781.

Reynolds, C. F., Cuijpers, P., Patel, V., Cohen, A., Dias, A., Chowdhary, N., et al. (2012). Early intervention to reduce the global health and economic burden of major depression in older adults. *Annual Review of Public Health*, *33*, 123–135. https://doi.org/10.1146/annurev-publhealth-031811-124544.

Robinson, R. G., Jorge, R. E., Moser, D. J., Acion, L., Solodkin, A., Small, S. L., et al. (2008). Escitalopram and problem-solving therapy for prevention of poststroke depression. *Journal of the American Medical Association*, *299*, 2391–2400. https://doi.org/10.1001/jama.299.20.2391.

Rovner, B. W., Casten, R. J., Hegel, M. T., Leiby, B. E., & Tasman, W. S. (2007). Preventing depression in age-related macular degeneration. *Archives of General Psychiatry*, *64*, 886–892. https://doi.org/10.1016/j.bbi.2008.05.010.

Schulz, R., Burgio, L., Burns, R., Eisdorfer, C., Gallagher-Thompson, D., Gitlin, L. N., et al. (2003). Resources for enhancing Alzheimer's caregiver health (REACH): Overview, site-specific outcomes, and future directions. *Gerontologist*, *43*, 514–520.

Scocco, P., De Leo, D., & Frank, E. (2002). Report psychotherapy in group format a therapeutic option in late-life depression? *Clinical Psychology & Psychotherapy*, *75*, 68–75.

Scogin, F., Hamblin, D., & Beutler, L. (1987). Bibliotherapy for depressed older adults: A self-help alternative. *Gerontologist*, *27*, 383–387.

Scogin, F., Jamison, C., & Gochneaur, K. (1989). Comparative efficacy of cognitive and behavioral bibliotherapy for mildly and moderately depressed older adults. *Journal of Consulting and Clinical Psychology*, *57*, 403–407. https://doi.org/10.1037/0022-006X.57.3.403.

Singla, D. R., Kohrt, B. A., Murray, L. K., Anand, A., Chorpita, B. F., & Patel, V. (2017). Psychological treatments for the world: Lessons from low- and middle-income countries. *Annual Review of Clinical Psychology*, *13*, 149–181.

Spek, V., Cuijpers, P., Nyklícek, I., Riper, H., Keyzer, J., & Pop, V. (2007). Internet-based cognitive behaviour therapy for symptoms of depression and anxiety: A meta-analysis. *Psychological Medicine*, *37*, 319. https://doi.org/10.1017/S0033291706008944.

Stanley, M. A., Beck, J. G., Novy, D. M., Averill, P. M., Swann, A. C., Diefenbach, G. J., et al. (2003). Cognitive-behavioral treatment of late-life generalized anxiety disorder. *Journal of*

Consulting and Clinical Psychology, *71*, 309–319. https://doi.org/10.1037/0022-006X.71.2.309.

Stanley, M. A., Wilson, N. L., Novy, D. M., Rhoades, H. M., Wagener, P. D., Greisinger, A. J., et al. (2009). Cognitive behavior therapy for generalized anxiety disorder among older adults in primary care. *JAMA*, *301*, 1460. https://doi.org/10.1001/jama.2009.458.

Statistics South Africa (2014). *Profile of older persons in South Africa, Pretoria*.

Stern, J. M., & Lovestone, S. (2000). Therapy with the elderly: Introducing psychodynamic psychotherapy to the multi-disciplinary team. *International Journal of Geriatric Psychiatry*. https://doi.org/10.1002/1099-1166(200006)15:6<500::AID-GPS145>3.0.CO;2-F.

Teri, L., & Gallagher-Thompson, D. (1991). Cognitive-behavioral interventions for treatment of depression in Alzheimer's patients. *Gerontologist*, *31*, 413–416.

Teri, L., Logsdon, R. G., Uomoto, J., & McCurry, S. M. (1997). Behavioral treatment of depression in dementia patients: A controlled clinical trial. *Journals of Gerontology. Series B, Psychological Sciences and Social Sciences*, *52B*, P159–P166. https://doi.org/10.1093/geronb/52B.4.P159.

Thomas, A. (2014). Depression in older people. In T. Dening & A. Thomas (Eds.), *Oxford textb. old age psychiatry* (pp. 545–569). (2nd ed.). Oxford: Oxford University Press.

Thompson, L. W., Gallagher, D., & Breckenridge, J. S. (1987). Comparative effectiveness of psychotherapies for depressed elders. *Journal of Consulting and Clinical Psychology*, *55*, 385–390.

van Heerden, S., Uwakwe, R., & Potochnick, F. (2011). The future of old age psychiatry in Africa. *African Journal of Psychiatry*, *14*, 343–345. https://doi.org/10.4314/ajpsy.v14i5.1.

Van Schaik, A., Van Marwijk, H., Ader, H., Van Dyck, R., & De Haan, M. (2006). Interpersonal psychotherapy for elderly patients in primary care. *The American Journal of Geriatric Psychiatry*, *14*, 777–786.

van't Hof, E., Cuijpers, P., & Stein, D. J. (2009). Self-help and internet-guided interventions in depression and anxiety disorders: A systematic review of meta-analyses. *CNS Spectrums*, *14*, 34–40. https://doi.org/10.1017/S1092852900027279.

van't Veer-Tazelaar, P. J., Van Marwijk, H. W. J., van Oppen, P., van Hout, H. P. J., van der Horst, H. E., Cuijpers, P., et al. (2009). Stepped-care prevention of anxiety and depression in late life. *Archives of General Psychiatry*, *66*, 297–304. https://doi.org/10.1001/archgenpsychiatry.2008.555.

Wang, J. J. (2007). Group reminiscence therapy for cognitive and affective function of demented elderly in Taiwan. *International Journal of Geriatric Psychiatry*, *22*, 1235–1240.

Wetherell, J. L., Kaplan, R. M., Kallenberg, G., Dresselhaus, T. R., Sieber, W. J., & Lang, A. J. (2004). Mental health treatment preferences of older and younger primary care patients. *International Journal of Psychiatry in Medicine*, *34*, 219–234. https://doi.org/10.2190/qa7y-tx1y-wm45-kgv7.

Wilkinson, P. (2014a). Cognitive behaviour therapy. In T. Dening & A. Thomas (Eds.), *Oxford textb. old age psychiatry*. (2nd ed., pp. 233–241). Oxford: Oxford University Press.

Wilkinson, P. (2014b). Psychological treatments. In T. Dening & A. Thomas (Eds.), *Oxford textb. old age psychiatry*. (2nd ed., pp. 229–232). Oxford: Oxford University Press.

Wilkinson, P. (2014c). Interpersonal psychotherapy. In T. Dening & A. Thomas (Eds.), *Oxford textb. old age psychiatry*. (2nd ed.). Oxford: Oxford University Press.

Wilson, K., Mottram, P. G., & Vassilas, C. (2008). Psychotherapeutic treatments for older depressed people. *Cochrane Database of Systematic Reviews*, *51*, 1–32. https://doi.org/10.1002/14651858.CD004853.pub2. https:/www.cochranelibrary.com.

Woods, B., Spector, A. E., Jones, C. A., Orrell, M., & Davies, S. P. (2009). Reminiscence therapy for dementia (review). *Maturitas*, *72*, 1–36. https://doi.org/10.1016/j.maturitas.2012.04.008.

World Health Organization (2018a). *Ageing and health—Fact sheet. World heal organ media cent* 2015. http://www.who.int/mediacentre/factsheets/fs404/en/ [accessed 02.01.18].

World Health Organization (2018b). *Mental health of older adults—Fact sheet. World heal organmedia cent* 2017. http://www.who.int/mediacentre/factsheets/fs381/en/ [accessed 02.01.18].

Zank, S. (1998). Psychotherapy and aging: Results of two empirical studies between psychotherapists and elderly people. *Psychotherapy*, *35*, 531–536. https://doi.org/10.1037/h0087806.

Zijlstra, G. A. R., Van Haastregt, J. C. M., Ambergen, T., Van Rossum, E., Van Eijk, J. T. M., Tennstedt, S. L., et al. (2009). Effects of a multicomponent cognitive behavioral group intervention on fear of falling and activity avoidance in community-dwelling older adults: Results of a randomized controlled trial. *Journal of the American Geriatrics Society*, *57*, 2020–2028. https://doi.org/10.1111/j.1532-5415.2009.02489.x.

Zivian, M. T., Larsen, W., Knox, V. J., Gekoski, W. L., & Hatchette, V. (1992). Psychotherapy for the elderly: Psychotherapists' preferences. *Psychotherapy*, *29*, 668–674. https://doi.org/10.1037/0033-3204.29.4.668.

Engelina Groenewald is a neuropsychiatrist and consultant in geriatric psychiatry at Stikland Hospital and the University of Stellenbosch.

John Joska is a professor of psychiatry and a neuropsychiatrist in the Department of Psychiatry and Mental Health at the University of Cape Town. His research and clinical interests include assessment and screening of HIV-associated neuropsychiatric and neurocognitive disorders, interventions for persons living with HIV and neuropsychiatric disorders, mental health services, and mental health of the elderly.

Ricardo Araya is professor of Global Mental Health and director of the Centre of Global Mental Health at the Institute of Psychiatry, Psychology and Neuroscience, King's College London. His main research interest is to develop and test innovative interventions to treat mental disorders in low-resource settings.

Psychotherapy for refugees and other populations exposed to conflict

16

Derrick Silove, Alvin Tay†, Susan Rees**

*Psychiatry Research and Teaching Unit, School of Psychiatry, University of New South Wales, Sydney, NSW, Australia, †Perdana University-Royal College of Surgeons in Ireland School of Medicine, Early Career Research Fellow, National Health & Medical Research Council (NHMRC), School of Psychiatry, University of New South Wales, Sydney, NSW, Australia

16.1 Introduction

The refugee mental health field has made major advances in recent decades, a major development being the formulation and testing of brief psychotherapies for survivors of torture and other forms of trauma (Silove, Ventevogel, & Rees, 2017). These interventions were specifically designed to be implemented in low-resource environments by lay counselors drawn from the respective refugee communities (Silove, Ventevogel, et al., 2017). Concerns persist, however, that brief psychotherapies may not be sufficiently culturally grounded or address the complexities of the experiences and psychological responses of all refugees, especially those with chronic or complex traumatic stress disorders. In considering these questions, we draw on some of the key issues that continue to confront the modern refugee and postconflict mental health field. For ease of expression, we use the term "refugee" in a generic manner to include the range of populations displaced by persecution, war, and other forms of mass violence. When relevant, we extend our overview to the larger populations exposed to mass conflict but who are not displaced. We focus on issues of general importance to the field, encouraging the reader to refer to the specialized literature focusing on interventions for vulnerable subpopulations such as women, child soldiers, and torture survivors.

16.2 History of the modern field of refugee mental health

The formative period of the modern refugee mental health movement spanned a 30-year period commencing in the 1980s. During that time, dedicated torture and trauma rehabilitation services for refugees were established in high-income resettlement countries of Europe, North America, and Australasia. Models of service development supported by emerging theoretical frameworks set the stage for the principles of practice that are largely adhered to today. Prior to this period, research studies

Global Mental Health and Psychotherapy. https://doi.org/10.1016/B978-0-12-814932-4.00016-1

involved small samples based on clinic populations, for example, survivors of the Nazi concentration camps (Eitinger, 1980). From the 1980s onward, research based on clinic and population samples aimed to identify the prevalence of mental disorders and the risk factors associated with these morbid outcomes, especially exposure to torture and trauma (Steel, Bateman Steel, & Silove, 2009).

In relation to interventions, the publication of an account of testimony therapy represented a turning point in that it outlined a specific approach to treatment for torture survivors, in this instance, political activists during the time of the military dictatorship in Chile (Cienfuegos & Monelli, 1983; Rasmussen, Dam, & Nielsen, 1977). The authors were obliged to use pseudonyms, underscoring the risks that clinicians and patients confronted when engaging in therapy in settings of ongoing oppression. Testimony therapy involved the detailed recording of the survivor's experience of torture and other human rights abuses (Cienfuegos & Monelli, 1983), the dual objectives being to record evidence for potential use in future prosecutions (the legal and human rights aim) and the provision of a safe environment for survivors to ventilate repressed feelings of anger, shame, and self-doubt (the psychotherapeutic function). Although a combination of human rights and psychoanalytic principles guided the treatment, the actual procedure followed was broadly consistent with the technique of prolonged exposure, applied in behavioral therapy to overcome fears and phobias (Foa, Steketee, & Rothbaum, 1989). The convergence between the two approaches (testimony and exposure) has continued to influence the evolution of therapies ever since

In the 1970s and early 1980s, a combination of factors shaped the establishment and direction of the first specialist mental health services for refugee survivors of torture and trauma. Psychiatrists and psychologists who played leading roles in the worldwide campaign against torture (United Nations Convention Against, 2006) took a lead in promoting the establishment of dedicated mental health services to assist survivors, who, in high-income countries, were most often refugees. The number of refugee-specific services grew, first in economically developed countries of North America, Europe, and Australasia and then in low- and middle-income countries directly or indirectly affected by mass conflict and displacement.

The cultural backgrounds and historical affinity for psychotherapeutic interventions to some extent shaped the development of services. In Europe, educated South American political exiles were familiar with the process of psychotherapy, encouraging its use as the centerpiece of interventions. Early impressions suggested that brief psychotherapy involving the systematic recall of torture experiences was successful in overcoming traumatic symptoms among these torture survivors (Somnier & Genefke, 1986). Nevertheless, some commentators cautioned that some torture survivors were unable to recall the details of their trauma and that pressure should be avoided in encouraging them to do so (Silove, Tarn, Bowles, & Reid, 1991). Clinical experience suggested that many torture survivors employed rigid defenses of repression and avoidance to ward off overwhelming feelings of distress when confronted by past experiences of abuse (Weine, Kulenovic, Pavkovic, & Gibbons, 1998) so that it often required an extended period of trust building for survivors to be able to confront memories of abuse, and some patients never reached that point.

In North America, where it was evident that Southeast Asian refugees faced challenges in adapting to the new environment, the emphasis of services was on supporting acculturation and resettlement in addition to attending to general mental health needs (Beiser & Wickrama, 2004; Mollica et al., 1990; Mollica, Wyshak, & Lavelle, 1987; Wickrama, Beiser, & Kaspar, 2002). Although exploration of past trauma remained an important component of counseling, it was recognized that the recounting of the trauma story needed to unfold naturally over time and at the pace that the survivor could tolerate (Beiser, Turner, & Ganesan, 1989; Mollica, 2001, 2011; Westermeyer & Janca, 1997).

In these early years, the few naturalistic follow-up studies that were undertaken suggested that a range of psychotherapeutic interventions, including testimony therapy, were effective in reducing symptoms of posttraumatic stress, depression, and anxiety among refugees (Drozdek, 1997; Dzubur-Kulenović, Weine, & Pavković, 2001; Mollica et al., 2001; Weine et al., 1998). Randomized controlled trials (RCTs) proved difficult to initiate within busy service settings largely because of the pressures involved in establishing these agencies and the ethical concerns relating to the allocation of help-seeking refugees to inactive control groups.

Many services adopted a broad-based, comprehensive model of psychosocial service provision for refugee survivors of trauma, in which psychotherapy was regarded as only one, albeit important, intervention (Silove et al., 1991). Close attention was given to the milieu of services, the focus being on creating environments that would counteract the dehumanizing conditions in which torture was commonly practiced. The emphasis was on creating informal, welcoming, community-based environments in which the service culture actively reflected the aim of restoring the survivor's sense of dignity, humanity, and belonging. Practical assistance was given a high priority in order to facilitate acculturation, resettlement, and integration into the new society. In all aspects of the service model, cultural factors were central, with many services employing and training bicultural counselors drawn from the relevant refugee communities.

16.3 Influence of mainstream psychiatry

Major shifts in mainstream psychiatry influenced the early development of the modern refugee mental health movement. The introduction of posttraumatic stress disorder (PTSD) in DSM-III (American Psychiatric Association, 1980) led to the rapid adoption of that diagnosis as the central focus of clinical assessment and research in the refugee field (see also Chapter 10). Contemporary cross-national studies undertaken among the general population justify this focus. For example, there is strong evidence that persons exposed to sequential traumas, an experience typical of the refugee experience, are at greatest risk of developing PTSD (Karam et al., 2014). In addition, the traumas that are central to the refugee experience, such as exposure to organized violence, physical violence, rape, and other sexual assaults, are most clearly associated with risk of PTSD (Liu et al., 2017).

Prior to the adoption of PTSD, terms such as the torture and concentration camp (KZ) syndromes (Chodoff, 1968; Eitinger, 1980; Wagenaar & Groeneweg, 1990) were used to characterize the psychological responses of survivors to these forms of human rights abuses. The introduction of the category of PTSD raised concerns in the general field of psychiatric traumatology that the limited array of symptoms included in the definition of that diagnosis failed to encompass the full range of maladaptive responses observed among survivors of prolonged or repetitive exposure to interpersonal abuses such as torture, childhood sexual abuse, and rape (Herman, 1992). What became known as complex PTSD was broadly characterized as a long-term maladaptive response to chronic abuse, including features such as loss of trust, suspiciousness, and paranoia; difficulties regulating emotions especially anger; profound and pervasive feelings of hopelessness and despair; shame and guilt; feelings of isolation and alienation; and prominent symptoms of dissociation and somatization (Herman, 1992; Silove et al., 1991). Underlying these diverse responses was a profound shift in the existential vantage point of survivors, representing a loss of faith and trust in the benevolence of life and humanity. Some of these characteristics were incorporated in the ICD-10 category of enduring personality change after catastrophic experiences (EPCACE), but the diagnosis received little clinical or research attention (Beltran, Silove, & Llewellyn, 2009; The ICD-10, 1992). In the United States, the category of disorder of extreme stress not otherwise specified (DESNOS) was proposed but omitted from the final draft of DSM-IV (Van Der Kolk, Roth, Pelcovitz, Sunday, & Spinazzola, 2005) after field trials failed to support its validity (American Psychiatric Association, 1994). Nevertheless, a reformulated category of complex PTSD (CPTSD) will be included in ICD-11 (Maercker et al., 2013). PTSD has to be present to consider the addition diagnosis of CPTSD among persons exposed to prolonged, repeated interpersonal abuses; systematic violence; and related forms of extreme trauma. A disturbance of self-organization (DSO) is regarded as the core psychopathology, represented by three domains of symptoms of emotional dysregulation, interpersonal difficulties, and negative self-concept

Preliminary research in the refugee field has provided some support for the factor structure of CPTSD (Nickerson et al., 2016; Silove, Tay, Kareth, & Rees, 2017; Tay, Rees, Chen, Kareth, & Silove, 2015d). Importantly, in one recent study, CPTSD appeared to be the dominant disorder with relatively few refugees manifesting PTSD alone (Silove, Tay, Kareth, et al., 2017; Tay et al., 2015d). Consistent with theory, CPTSD is associated with extensive exposure to traumas arising from human rights abuses, and the disorder leads to high levels of disability (Tay et al., 2015d). Together, these findings raise important questions whether the focus of interventions in refugee mental health needs to shift from PTSD to the more complex form of traumatic stress response represented by CPTSD.

16.4 Other complexities in the mental health presentations of refugees

Recent epidemiological studies reveal further complexity in the psychiatric presentations observed among refugees. PTSD is commonly comorbid with other diagnoses (Palic & Elklit, 2011) not only depression (Steel et al., 2009) but also various manifestations of anxiety including the adult form of separation anxiety disorder (Silove, Momartin, Marnane, Steel, & Manicavasagar, 2010; Tay, Rees, Chen, Kareth, & Silove, 2015c; Tay, Rees, Kareth, & Silove, 2016), prolonged or complicated bereavement (Boehnlein, 1987; Momartin, Silove, Manicavasagar, & Steel, 2004; Nickerson et al., 2011; Tay, Rees, Chen, Kareth, & Silove, 2015b), explosive forms of anger (including intermittent explosive disorder) (Oruc et al., 2008; Rees et al., 2013; Rees & Silove, 2011; Tay, Rees, Chen, Kareth, & Silove, 2015a), somatic symptom disorder (Lin, Carter, & Kleinman, 1985; Van Ommeren et al., 2002; Westermeyer, Bouafuely, Neider, & Callies, 1989), and in some communities drug and alcohol abuse (Ezard et al., 2011).

These observations suggest that a transdiagnostic approach (where persons exhibit components of multiple disorders) may better suit the approach to assessment in the refugee field than a rigid focus on one diagnosis, particularly PTSD (see also Chapter 2). Defining transdiagnostic constellations of symptoms that map onto specific profiles of psychosocial disruptions and traumas experienced by refugees may generate a novel typology of mental health responses among refugees. For example, research has shown that persisting feelings of injustice following exposure to extensive traumatic losses arising from atrocities, extrajudicial killings, and disappearances can produce a combination of symptoms of complicated bereavement and extreme anger (Tay et al., 2015b, 2016). Identifying patterns such as these may assist in tailoring psychotherapies to the specific constellation experiences and responses of subpopulations of refugees.

A further consideration is whether the focus of psychotherapeutic interventions should be on the individual, the family, or the group. The traumas of mass conflict can lead to a cascade effect within families, impacting on intimate partners and children and potentially initiating long-term transgenerational effects (Rees, Thorpe, Tol, Fonseca, & Silove, 2015; Silove, Tay, Steel, et al., 2017; Tay et al., 2017). In recognition of these multiplier effects, specialized refugee services often extend interventions beyond the individual to include the partner and children, although, as will be seen, few of these approaches have been subjected to scientific evaluation.

16.5 The importance of culture

Although cultural change is accelerated by mass conflict and displacement, many resettled refugee communities retain aspects of their core traditional values and concepts of suffering and healing. In general, these societies tend to adhere to a holistic worldview in which physical, mental, and spiritual elements of health and suffering are intertwined. Distress commonly is expressed in somatic complaints, and the source of the malady often is attributed to spiritual or supernatural influences. In some societies, traumatic stress reactions are expressed in culture-specific syndromes. For example, among West Papuan refugees, sakit hati (sick heart) refers to overwhelming feelings of resentment and helplessness arising from conditions of prolonged persecution, manifesting in symptoms of withdrawal, brooding, distress, hostility, and angry outbursts (Rees & Silove, 2011). The confluence of political, cultural, familial, and personal factors in the genesis of sakit hati is well recognized in the community.

In collectivist societies, the sense of identity is grounded in systems of mutual interdependence and obligation that bind family and kinship groups together. The sense of belonging is inextricably connected to the land, the family, and the wider kinship group, bonds that are expressed by terms such as *wontok* in Melanesian culture and *ubuntu* in South Africa. It is not surprising, therefore, that some cultural groups initially may regard psychotherapies that focus primarily on the individual and personal as somewhat alien

In general, there is evidence that the cultural adaptation of psychotherapy adds to its efficacy when applied to a diversity of immigrant and refugee groups (Hall, Ibaraki, Huang, Marti, & Stice, 2016). Although greater attention is being given to adapting trauma-focused CBT approaches for use among refugees (Hinton & Patel, 2017), the extent to which culture is given priority varies across practitioners and services. A consensus is needed, therefore, in delineating the practical steps to be taken to ensure a thorough cultural adaptation of psychotherapies offered to refugees from a diversity of backgrounds.

16.6 The global mental health imperative

Meta-analyses and reviews of the growing body of epidemiological studies in the field estimate that a minimum of 15% of refugees experience PTSD or depression or both disorders (Charlson et al., 2016; Steel, Chey, et al., 2009). In relation to PTSD, the prevalence is roughly tenfold higher than observed in societies not exposed to mass trauma or displacement (Creamer, Burgess, & McFarlane, 2001; Kessler, Sonnega, Bromet, Hughes, & Nelson, 1995; Steel, Chey, et al., 2009). These figures underscore the large gap that exists between the mental health status of refugees and the global resources available to meet their needs in an equitable manner (Patel et al., 2010). The challenge is all the more daunting given that the majority of the world's 65 million refugees are distributed across low- and lower-middle-income countries where resources in mental health remain rudimentary. A large proportion of these persons lives in inaccessible or complex environments. These include the internally displaced who do not fall under the responsibility of the United Nations High Commissioner for Refugees (UNHCR, 2018) and those displaced to remote locations, dispersed across densely populated and deprived urban settings, or held in places of confinement and detention.

16.7 The psychosocial context

These considerations make it imperative that scarce mental health resources are allocated to those refugees with the highest priority needs. Defining subpopulations according to relative needs remains a difficult task, particularly in predicting which of the distressed subpopulation will respond to broad-based psychosocial programs and which require individual psychotherapeutic or general mental health interventions to recover. Epidemiological studies provide a broad indicator that many refugees will recover from periods of distress if provided favorable psychosocial conditions. Resettlement patterns in Australia illustrate this point. Vietnamese refugees afforded permanent residency and access to the full range of resettlement and psychosocial support services exhibited low rates of PTSD and related symptoms of anxiety and depression (Steel, Silove, Chey, Bauman, & Phan, 2005). In contrast, asylum seekers living in the same environment but in a state of constant fear of forced repatriation and facing restrictions in accessing basic services, income support, and work opportunities continued to experience high levels of posttraumatic symptoms, when compared with permanently resettled compatriots exposed to similar levels of premigration trauma (Steel et al., 2006, 2011). These and other observations support the contention that the overall ecology of the posttraumatic environment is critical to shaping the trajectory of PTSD and related symptoms of distress at a population level.

For these reasons, the psychosocial recovery environment is given a central focus in evolving ecological models of refugee trauma (Silove, Steel, & Psychol, 2006). All leading models draw on a multisystem framework in which a cascade of influences determines the balance between adaptation and mental health incapacity at a population level. At the macrocosmic level, international and regional refugee policies and their implementation play a key role in the way refugees are supported or treated with neglect; at the microcosmic level, key influences include the level of xenophobia and hostility in the host community, the extent of internecine conflict within the displaced population itself, the integrity and cohesion of families and kinship groups, and the effectiveness of agencies and institutions in providing support (Betancourt, 2005; Kohrt et al., 2010; Miller & Rasmussen, 2010; Silove, 2013).

Leading ecological theories converge in many respects but vary somewhat in emphasis. In his conservation of resources theory, Hobfoll identifies massive losses (interpersonal, material, and existential) as a key determinant of adverse mental health outcomes (Hobfoll et al., 2007). Psychosocial programs that promote the capacity to restore lost resources can prove pivotal to building resilience that in turn assists in overcoming mental health problems at a population level. Miller and colleagues emphasize the role of daily stressors in the genesis and maintenance of mental distress among refugees (Miller & Rasmussen, 2010). Examples of ongoing difficulties include living in unsafe environments, meeting basic survival needs (food, water, shelter, and health care), obstacles to pursuing income-generating activities, and isolation from family and traditional social supports. According to this model, psychosocial programs that address these immediate challenges and deprivations play a crucial role in maintaining the mental stability of the population.

The adaptation and development after persecution and trauma (ADAPT) model postulates that five psychosocial systems that support stable societies are fundamentally disrupted among refugee populations, including systems that support safety and security, justice, identities and roles, and a sense of meaning, whether political, social, cultural, ideological, or religious (Silove, 2013; Tay & Silove, 2016). The extent to which these support systems are maintained or undermined influences the capacity of individuals and collectives to adapt to the traumas and ongoing living difficulties they experience through the phases of the refugee experience. The more effectively the ADAPT pillars are restored, the less the need will be for individual-focused psychotherapy programs for traumatic stress reactions, although there will always be a minority who are too disabled to benefit from social support alone to achieve recovery (Silove, 2013).

16.8 Recent trends in developing, testing and implementing psychotherapies in the refugee mental health field

Until the turn of the century, only a small number of naturalistic studies had been undertaken to evaluate outcomes of psychosocial and psychotherapy interventions in the refugee field. In general, practitioners largely depended on theory, experience, and the adaptation of techniques borrowed from the general field of psychotherapy to guide their practices (van Wyk & Schweitzer, 2014). Over the past two decades, there has been greater scientific rigor in the formulation and outcome evaluation of brief psychotherapies in the field. Most of these programs share core characteristics: They draw on established principles and techniques of modern trauma-focused psychotherapies, interventions are designed to be brief and require relatively low levels of funding and other resources, procedures are clearly specified and manualized, and they are implemented by local lay or community workers following brief training. These characteristics increase the capacity to upscale and roll out therapies across a wider population.

Common components of therapies include psychoeducation (raising awareness of the nature and causes of stress-related reactions); stress management or dearousal techniques (relaxation and mindfulness); problem-solving, focusing on effective ways of dealing with key life challenges; the systematic review of trauma histories whether by use of testimony, narrative, or prolonged exposure; cognitive techniques such as thought restructuring to address negative attitudes and attributions; engagement with social supports; and behavioral activation methods to increase the person's engagement with pleasurable and productive pursuits. In addition, a minority of studies have included eye movement desensitization and retraining (EMDR) with some positive results (Acarturk et al., 2015; Ter Heide, Mooren, Kleijn, de Jongh, & Kleber, 2011; Ter Heide, Mooren, van de Schoot, de Jongh, & Kleber, 2016).

Several interventions have been subjected to systematic evaluation in both single arm and naturalistic follow-up studies and, in some instances, in randomized controlled trials (RCTS) (Nicholl & Thompson, 2004; Weiss et al., 2015). Most reviews of extant therapies have noted substantial variability in the content of interventions, in the methodologies for evaluating them, and in outcomes (Crumlish & O'Rourke, 2010; Nickerson, Bryant, Silove, & Steel, 2011; Palic & Elklit, 2011). In general, however, most studies support the efficacy of variants of trauma-focused cognitive behavioral therapies (CBT), especially when compared with waiting-list controls, unstructured supportive therapy, or treatment-as-usual (TAU) conditions. PTSD symptoms show the most consistent improvement, whereas changes in depression and broader psychosocial outcomes are less clear-cut (Morina, Malek, Nickerson, & Bryant, 2017a). A review of the literature of intervention studies among children and adolescents came to similar conclusions in that active psychotherapeutic interventions were superior to control conditions in ameliorating common mental health symptoms and improving functioning in these age groups (Morina, Malek, Nickerson, & Bryant, 2017b).

Most studies are of low methodological quality if judged by strict contemporary standards governing the conduct of RCTs (Morina et al., 2017a). Few studies compare two or more treatments that are expected to be effective, relying instead on waiting-list control comparisons. Most interventions are conducted by the originators of the therapy or their trainees, creating a potential commitment bias in which enthusiasm for the index intervention is conveyed to the counselors, even if inadvertently. Second-generation studies implemented by independent researchers are needed to overcome this limitation. Other constraints of contemporary studies include small samples, biases in concealing group allocation and blinding, and the relatively short follow-up periods, a constraint that is difficult to overcome given the mobility of refugee populations. Studies that recruit participants directly from the community, for example, based on preceding epidemiological surveys, have the advantage of assessing rates of uptake of therapy at a population level, but they do not produce findings that reflect outcomes among patients attending services.

Caution is needed, however, in applying unrealistically stringent criteria in judging the quality of intervention studies among refugees, given the special obstacles in undertaking research in this field. These include, among others, issues relating to access and recruitment, language, culture, educational levels, and the community's affinity for psychotherapy. In addition, there are major logistic obstacles in undertaking trials in remote, underresourced and, in some circumstances, insecure environments. Growing recognition of these challenges has prompted the formulation of more pragmatic guidelines for conducting outcome research among populations exposed to complex forms of trauma, notably those recently produced by the International Society for Traumatic Stress (Cloitre et al., 2011).

16.9 Examples of contemporary brief psychotherapies

Of the many variants of psychotherapy applied in the refugee field, three are chosen as representative of the progress made to date. All three approaches are explicitly derived from well-established models or principles applied to the treatment of common mental disorders such as that related to anxiety, depression, and posttraumatic stress. Narrative exposure therapy (NET) (Neuner, Schauer, Klaschik, Karunakara, & Elbert, 2004) is the most extensively assessed model (Bichescu, Neuner, Schauer, & Elbert, 2007; Ehntholt & Yule, 2006; Gwozdziewycz & Mehl-Madrona, 2013; Neuner et al., 2010), drawing on a combination of methods, particularly testimony and cognitive behavioral therapies. Using a visual timeline, lay workers support survivors in tracing their life histories prior to and through the period of trauma and displacement.

Survivors are encouraged to explore and express their thoughts, feelings, and interpretations of the sequential traumas and conditions of adversity they have experienced as they recount their narratives. The aim is to normalize and integrate trauma memories by locating them in a chronological and meaningful sequence of the individual life story. With the patient's consent, written documentation of the history of abuse may be forwarded to human rights agencies to assist in identifying and prosecuting perpetrators.

Reviews and meta-analyses of the substantial body of research into NET indicate broad support for the efficacy of the method in reducing symptoms of PTSD and possibly depression (Gwozdziewycz & Mehl-Madrona, 2013). Translation studies have demonstrated that the method can be integrated into real-life service settings. In addition, NET has been adapted for use among a range of populations, including children and asylum seekers.

The Common Elements Treatment Approach (CETA) addresses some of the limitations of NET (Murray et al., 2014). CETA adopts an explicitly transdiagnostic approach in which counselors are given flexibility to match the modalities of intervention to patient's primary presenting problems that may involve various combinations of depression, anxiety, PTSD, and drug and alcohol misuse (Murray et al., 2014). The development of a local group of supervisors ensures that counselors are provided ongoing support (Murray et al., 2011). RCTs support the efficacy of CETA in several postconflict settings in both reducing mental health symptoms and improving functioning, although less impact has been achieved on drug and alcohol problems (Bass et al., 2013; Bolton et al., 2014; Weiss et al., 2015).

Problem Management Plus (PM+) is a short, low-intensity, generic intervention developed by the World Health Organization for use in low-resource settings in general (Dawson et al., 2015). The intervention is designed to be suitable for persons with a range of common mental health symptoms including depression, anxiety, stress and grief, reactions that are commonly associated with social problems of unemployment, and interpersonal conflict. PM+ includes four therapeutic strategies of managing stress, problem-solving, behavioral activation, and strengthening social support. Early studies have provided preliminary support for the general effectiveness of PM+ in transcultural settings (Bryant et al., 2017; Dawson et al., 2016; Rahman et al., 2016).

16.10 Pragmatic trials in service settings

As indicated, most RCTs in the field have been undertaken as dedicated research projects, that is, the therapy has been initiated primarily to test its efficacy. The "laboratory" effect, that is, the creation of conditions to facilitate the methodology of the study, raises questions whether the same efficacy can be achieved when the method has been translated into real-life clinical settings.

A series of studies conducted in Denmark stand out because they were undertaken within a specialist mental health service for refugees, the Competence Center for Transcultural Psychiatry (Carlsson, Mortensen, & Kastrup, 2005; Carlsson, Olsen, Kastrup, & Mortensen, 2010). It is noteworthy, therefore, that despite the multidisciplinary clinical skills of the team, the outcomes of multimodal therapy have been modest. For example, in a large and well-designed RCT among refugees, a comprehensive package of interventions involving a combination of trauma-focused CBT techniques, general support, and medical consultations with the flexible use of psychotropic medications failed to produce improvement in PTSD symptoms over the course of a year (Buhmann, Nordentoft, Ekstroem, Carlsson, & Mortensen, 2016).

These findings stand in stark contrast to the uniformly positive findings of much briefer, packaged therapies applied among refugees in low- and lower-middle-income countries. One key difference in the two bodies of studies may lie in the characteristics of patients recruited to trials. Refugees in high-resource countries such as Denmark are more likely to have received extensive therapy prior to being referred to specialist services. As a result, specialist services concentrate cases that have already exhibited a degree of treatment resistance. An examination of the patient characteristics involved in studies in the Competence Center for Transcultural Psychiatry offers support for this explanation in that many participants had characteristics that may signify a poor prognosis, such as histories of exposure to extensive premigration trauma including torture; head injury, chronic pain, and other somatic complaints; failed previous treatments including psychopharmacology; and poor social supports, limited language acquisition and acculturation in spite of long residency in the host country, and longstanding unemployment.

It seems probable therefore that referral patterns in high-income countries may result in a bias toward the most complex cases attending specialist services. This small subpopulation of refugees may reflect the minority found to manifest chronic and disabling disorders in epidemiological studies (Steel, Silove, Phan, & Bauman, 2002). A series of vicious cycles may prevent recovery among this minority group of refugees. Biological factors such as head injury and consequent subtle cognitive impairment may limit the capacity of some torture survivors to process trauma memories that are perpetuated by symptoms of physical injury and chronic pain. Social factors such as poverty, isolation, acculturation difficulties, and insecure residency may inhibit the refugee in engaging with social supports and activities such as education and employment that are known to enhance mental health. Identifying refugees trapped in these vicious cycles may assist in designing tailored interventions to overcome these blockages to recovery. In general, future intervention studies need to characterize the samples included in a more comprehensive manner, a step that may help in explaining the variability in outcomes evident in the existing body of research.

16.11 Other approaches to psychotherapy

Given the stage of development of the field, it is important to try a range of credible psychotherapies for refugees, beyond the standard trauma-focused CBT approach. A potentially fruitful direction is to focus on therapies that explicitly aim to strengthen interpersonal bonds and social networks that are undermined during the refugee experience. For example, a small study among Sudanese refugees found that interpersonal therapy (IPT) achieved improvements in posttraumatic stress, depression, anger, and aggression (Meffert et al., 2011). Further studies of this type are needed.

Studies should also focus on primary outcomes other than PTSD. For example, a study drawing on the ADAPT model in Timor-Leste applying a culturally grounded approach to psychotherapy focused on explosive anger as a response to a persisting sense of injustice that survivors of persecution experienced following the prolonged period of persecution (Hewage et al., 2017). All participants in the active treatment arm exhibited a substantial improvement in anger, whereas the pattern continued in the majority of persons on the waiting-list control condition. A more comprehensive approach to psychotherapy based on the ADAPT model is undergoing trials among refugees from Myanmar in Malaysia. Preliminary qualitative data undertaken by the authorship team indicate that there is a high degree of affinity and receptivity for Integrated Adapt Therapy (IAT) among lay counselors and refugees participating in the program, but further work is needed to establish the efficacy of the approach in promoting the capacity of refugees to cope with the psychosocial challenges they confront.

16.12 Group and family therapies

In principle, group therapies are attractive options for refugees because they are consistent with the notion of collective trauma and shared suffering within many communities and are cost saving in terms of counselor time. Challenges remain, however, in determining the culturally appropriate mix of participants taking into consideration gender, age, status, political affiliations, etc. and in ensuring that facilitators are capable of dealing with complex group dynamics and ethical issues such as confidentiality.

In the only study of its kind, Drozdek and coworkers completed a naturalistic (single arm) 7-year follow-up of a multicomponent group treatment program for asylum seekers in the Netherlands (Drozdek, Kamperman, Tol, Knipscheer, & Kleber, 2014). Participants maintained their initial improvements in a range of symptoms over a prolonged period. Although not focused on refugees, a group IPT approach was shown to be effective in treating depression in Uganda, a country exposed to prolonged mass violence (Bolton et al., 2003). However, a small RCT comparing groups NET and IPT among orphans of the Rwandan genocide found the former approach to be more effective on a range of outcomes, including PTSD and depressive symptoms (Schaal, Elbert, & Neuner, 2009).

Sociotherapy was established in Rwanda following the genocide and has been applied among other refugee groups (Verduin, Smid, Wind, & Scholte, 2014). Groups share ways of dealing with daily problems ranging from interpersonal disputes, feelings of marginalization, and strategies to deal with gender-based violence and poverty at the community level. Preliminary research suggests that sociotherapy can have the dual effect of improving civic participation and individual mental health (Scholte et al., 2011; Verduin et al., 2014).

Classroom-based group therapy for adolescents in a conflict-affected region of Indonesia reduced posttraumatic stress and helped maintain hope but made no impact on depression, anxiety, and functioning (Tol et al., 2008). A similar intervention in Nepal produced positive effects in mental health symptoms and aggression in boys but not in girls, where only prosocial behaviors showed positive changes (Jordans et al., 2010). Overall, however, psychosocial interventions appear to be effective in reducing PTSD among children and adolescents in refugee and postconflict populations (Purgato et al., 2018).

As indicated, little attention has been given to evaluating family-based interventions for refugees, even though these approaches are used extensively in services. The exception is a multifamily intervention undertaken among refugees from the former Yugoslavia in which several families shared experiences of traumatic stress and chronic adversity. The approach led to improvements in self-confidence, social isolation, and utilization of mental health services (Van Ee, Mooren, & Kleber, 2014; Weine et al., 2008).

In summary, family- and group-based interventions show promise for use in the refugee field. Much further work is needed, however, to define selection criteria, group processes, and a consistent approach to evaluation prior to drawing any conclusions about the utility and relative efficacy of these methods, especially compared with individual approaches.

16.13 Conclusion

Substantial progress has been made in the development and testing of various approaches to psychotherapy in the refugee mental health field. In the past two decades, researchers have adopted systematic approaches to specifying both the content and procedures involved in applying brief, manualized approaches to psychotherapy designed to allow implementation by local workers following brief training. Most RCTs have supported the efficacy of trauma-focused, CBT-based interventions. Only a small number of studies have assessed other approaches to individual psychotherapy, group therapies, and family-oriented therapies. Yet, there is a dearth of studies evaluating novel interventions that are consistent with contemporary models that address the specific challenges of the refugee experience. Also, logistic and methodological challenges have limited the rigor with which broad-based psychosocial programs of assistance to refugees have been evaluated.

In general, important theoretical, scientific, and practical challenges remain to be addressed regarding the role of psychotherapy in the overall mental health service provision for refugees. In addition, there needs to be a greater consensus and consistency with respect to the process to be pursued to ensure that therapies are culturally grounded (Hinton & Patel, 2017). From a pragmatic perspective, more attention is needed to ensure the sustainability of psychotherapeutic interventions. Showing that they work is only relevant if they can be integrated and sustained within broader programs of psychosocial recovery offered to refugees. Within mental health, there are competing demands, including the imperative to provide generic services for those with severe mental illness. At a wider level, addressing the physical health and social well-being of refugees must be given the highest priority. In the context of severely limited resources, policy-makers and funders therefore are hard-pressed to commit funds to psychotherapy in situations of large-scale refugee flows. Additional constraints include deep-seated stigma and prejudice, even within health services, against the mental health enterprise in general, an attitude that extends to skepticism about the effectiveness of psychotherapy as an intervention. The sheer size and location of refugee groups make the equitable provision of even brief psychotherapies a daunting challenge. For the present and foreseeable future, the reality is that most refugees experiencing common mental disorders will never receive any mental health intervention, let alone psychotherapy or counseling.

From a public health perspective, therefore, the selection of those in greatest need requires priority attention in relation to future research. A fruitful area of exploration would be to define more clearly those refugees with mental health symptoms who are unlikely to recover spontaneously but are potentially responsive to brief psychotherapies. At the less severe end of the spectrum, effective psychosocial programs should assist most refugees to recover naturally, whereas at the extreme end, those with the most chronic and disabling conditions may require more comprehensive, multimodal approaches to rehabilitation. Broader systemic factors that are known to undermine recovery, such as risk of future conflict and persecution, extreme poverty, insecure residency, and violence against women and children, should receive a stronger advocacy focus from mental health professionals and helping agencies. In that sense, there is a need to reconcile the use of brief, structured forms of psychotherapy that are the subject of most scientific trials in the field and the realities of contemporary practice, where a diversity of psychiatric and psychosocial needs is encountered.

References

Acarturk, C., Konuk, E., Cetinkaya, M., Senay, I., Sijbrandij, M., Cuijpers, P., & Aker, T. (2015). EMDR for Syrian refugees with posttraumatic stress disorder symptoms: Results of a pilot randomized controlled trial. *European Journal of Psychotraumatology*. *6*, 27414. https://doi.org/10.3402/ejpt.v6.27414.

American Psychiatric Association (1980). *Diagnostic and statistical manual of mental disorders* (3rd ed.). Retrieved from Washington, DC.

American Psychiatric Association (1994). *Diagnostic and statistical manual of mental disorders* (4th ed.). Retrieved from Washington, DC.

Bass, J. K., Annan, J., McIvor Murray, S., Kaysen, D., Griffiths, S., Cetinoglu, T., … Bolton, P. A. (2013). Controlled trial of psychotherapy for Congolese survivors of sexual violence. *New England Journal of Medicine*, *368*(23), 2182–2191. https://doi.org/10.1056/NEJMoa1211853.

Beiser, M., Turner, R. J., & Ganesan, S. (1989). Catastrophic stress and factors affecting its consequences among Southeast Asian refugees. *Social Science and Medicine*, *28*(3), 183–195.

Beiser, M., & Wickrama, K. A. S. (2004). Trauma, time and mental health: A study of temporal reintegration and depressive disorder among southeast Asian refugees. *Psychological Medicine*, *34*(5), 899–910.

Beltran, R. O., Silove, D., & Llewellyn, G. M. (2009). Comparison of ICD-10 diagnostic guidelines and research criteria for enduring personality change after catastrophic experience. *Psychopathology*, *42*(2), 113–118 https://doi.org/000204761.

Betancourt, T. S. (2005). Stressors, supports and the social ecology of displacement: Psychosocial dimensions of an emergency education program for Chechen adolescents displaced in Ingushetia, Russia. *Culture, Medicine and Psychiatry*, *29*(3), 309–340.

Bichescu, D., Neuner, F., Schauer, M., & Elbert, T. (2007). Narrative exposure therapy for political imprisonment-related chronic posttraumatic stress disorder and depression. *Behaviour Research and Therapy*, *45*(9), 2212–2220.

Boehnlein, J. K. (1987). Clinical relevance of grief and mourning among Cambodian refugees. *Social Science and Medicine*, *25*(7), 765–772.

Bolton, P., Bass, J., Neugebauer, R., Verdeli, H., Clougherty, K. F., Wickramaratne, P., ... Weissman, M. (2003). Group interpersonal psychotherapy for depression in rural Uganda: A randomized controlled trial. *Journal of the American Medical Association*, *289*(23), 3117–3124.

Bolton, P., Lee, C., Haroz, E. E., Murray, L., Dorsey, S., Robinson, C., ... Bass, J. (2014). A transdiagnostic community-based mental health treatment for comorbid disorders: Development and outcomes of a randomized controlled trial among Burmese refugees in Thailand. *PLoS Medicine*. *11*(11), e1001757. https://doi.org/10.1371/journal.pmed.1001757.

Bryant, R. A., Schafer, A., Dawson, K. S., Anjuri, D., Mulili, C., Ndogoni, L., ... van Ommeren, M. (2017). Effectiveness of a brief behavioural intervention on psychological distress among women with a history of gender-based violence in urban Kenya: A randomised clinical trial. *PLoS Medicine*. *14*(8), e1002371https://doi.org/10.1371/journal.pmed.1002371.

Buhmann, C. B., Nordentoft, M., Ekstroem, M., Carlsson, J., & Mortensen, E. L. (2016). The effect of flexible cognitive-behavioural therapy and medical treatment, including antidepressants on post-traumatic stress disorder and depression in traumatised refugees: Pragmatic randomised controlled clinical trial. *British Journal of Psychiatry*, *208*(3), 252–259. https://doi.org/10.1192/bjp.bp.114.150961.

Carlsson, J. M., Mortensen, E. L., & Kastrup, M. (2005). A follow-up study of mental health and health-related quality of life in tortured refugees in multidisciplinary treatment. *Journal of Nervous and Mental Disease*, *193*(10), 651–657.

Carlsson, J. M., Olsen, D. R., Kastrup, M., & Mortensen, E. L. (2010). Late mental health changes in tortured refugees in multidisciplinary treatment. *Journal of Nervous and Mental Disease*, *198*(11), 824–828. https://doi.org/10.1097/NMD.0b013e3181f97be3.

Charlson, F. J., Flaxman, A., Ferrari, A. J., Vos, T., Steel, Z., & Whiteford, H. A. (2016). Post-traumatic stress disorder and major depression in conflict-affected populations: An epidemiological model and predictor analysis. *Global Mental Health (Cambridge)*. *3*, e4, https://doi.org/10.1017/gmh.2015.26.

Chodoff, P. (1968). Late effects of the concentration camp syndrome. *Archives of General Psychiatry*, *8*, 323–333.

Cienfuegos, A. J., & Monelli, C. (1983). The testimony of political repression as a therapeutic instrument. *American Journal of Orthopsychiatry*, *53*(1), 43–51.

Cloitre, M., Courtois, C. A., Charuvastra, A., Carapezza, R., Stolbach, B. C., & Green, B. L. (2011). Treatment of complex PTSD: Results of the ISTSS expert clinician survey on best practices. *Journal of Traumatic Stress*, *24*(6), 615–627. https://doi.org/10.1002/jts.20697.

Creamer, M., Burgess, P., & McFarlane, A. C. (2001). Post-traumatic stress disorder: Findings from the Australian National Survey of mental health and well-being. *Psychological Medicine*, *31*(7), 1237–1247.

Crumlish, N., & O'Rourke, K. (2010). A systematic review of treatments for post-traumatic stress disorder among refugees and asylum-seekers. *Journal of Nervous and Mental Disease*, *198*(4), 237–251.

Dawson, K. S., Bryant, R. A., Harper, M., Kuowei Tay, A., Rahman, A., Schafer, A., & van Ommeren, M. (2015). Problem management plus (PM+): A WHO transdiagnostic psychological intervention for common mental health problems. *World Psychiatry*, *14*(3), 354–357.

Dawson, K. S., Schafer, A., Anjuri, D., Ndogoni, L., Musyoki, C., Sijbrandij, M., ... Bryant, R. A. (2016). Feasibility trial of a scalable psychological intervention for women affected by urban adversity and gender-based violence in Nairobi. *BMC Psychiatry*, *16*(1), 410. https://doi.org/10.1186/s12888-016-1117-x.

Drozdek, B. (1997). Follow-up study of concentration camp survivors from Bosnia-Herzegovina: Three years later. *Journal of Nervous and Mental Disease*, *185*(11), 690–694.

Drozdek, B., Kamperman, A. M., Tol, W. A., Knipscheer, J. W., & Kleber, R. J. (2014). Seven-year follow-up study of symptoms in asylum seekers and refugees with PTSD treated with trauma-focused groups. *Journal of Clinical Psychology*, *70*(4), 376–387. https://doi.org/10.1002/jclp.22035.

Dzubur-Kulenović, A., Weine, S. M., & Pavković, I. (2001). Psychotherapeutic testimony be refugees from Bosnia-Herzegovina: A pilot study. *Medicinski Arhiv*, *55*(1 Suppl. 1), 47–51.

Ehntholt, K. A., & Yule, W. (2006). Practitioner review: Assessment and treatment of refugee children and adolescents who have experienced war-related trauma. *Journal of Child Psychology and Psychiatry and Allied Disciplines*, *47*(12), 1197–1210. https://doi.org/10.1111/j.1469-7610.2006.01638.x.

Eitinger, L. (1980). The concentration camp syndrome and its late sequelae. In J. E. Dimsdale (Ed.), *Survivors, victims, and perpetrators: Essays on the Nazi holocaust* (pp. 127–162). New York: Hemisphere Publishing Corporation.

Ezard, N., Oppenheimer, E., Burton, A., Schilperoord, M., Macdonald, D., Adelekan, M., ... van Ommeren, M. (2011). Six rapid assessments of alcohol and other substance use in populations displaced by conflict. *Conflict and Health*, *5*(1), 1. https://doi.org/10.1186/1752-1505-5-1.

Foa, E. B., Steketee, G., & Rothbaum, B. O. (1989). Behavioral/cognitive conceptualizations of post-traumatic stress disorder. *Behavior Therapy*, *20*(2), 155–176.

Gwozdziewycz, N., & Mehl-Madrona, L. (2013). Meta-analysis of the use of narrative exposure therapy for the effects of trauma among refugee populations. *The Permanente Journal*, *17* (1), 70–76. https://doi.org/10.7812/tpp/12-058.

Hall, G. C., Ibaraki, A. Y., Huang, E. R., Marti, C. N., & Stice, E. (2016). A meta-analysis of cultural adaptations of psychological interventions. *Behavior Therapy*, *47*(6), 993–1014. https://doi.org/10.1016/j.beth.2016.09.005.

Herman, J. L. (1992). Complex PTSD: A syndrome in survivors of prolonged and repeated trauma. *Journal of Traumatic Stress*, *5*(3), 377–391.

Hewage, K., Zachary, S., Mohamed, M., Tay, A. K., De Oliveira, J. C., Da Piedade, M., ... Silove, D. (2017). A wait-list control study of a trauma-focused cognitive behavioural treatment for intermittent explosive disorder (IED) in Timor-Leste. *American Journal of Orthopsychiatry*, *88*(3), 282–294.

Hinton, D. E., & Patel, A. (2017). Cultural adaptations of cognitive behavioral therapy. *Psychiatric Clinics of North America*, *40*(4), 701–714. https://doi.org/10.1016/j.psc.2017.08.006.

Hobfoll, S. E., Watson, P., Bell, C. C., Bryant, R. A., Brymer, M. J., Friedman, M. J., … Ursano, R. J. (2007). Five essential elements of immediate and mid-term mass trauma intervention: Empirical evidence. *Psychiatry*, *70*(4), 283–315. discussion 316-269. https://doi.org/10.1521/psyc.2007.70.4.283.

Jordans, M. J., Komproe, I. H., Tol, W. A., Kohrt, B. A., Luitel, N. P., Macy, R. D., & de Jong, J. T. (2010). Evaluation of a classroom-based psychosocial intervention in conflict-affected Nepal: A cluster randomized controlled trial. *Journal of Child Psychology and Psychiatry and Allied Disciplines*, *51*(7), 818–826. https://doi.org/10.1111/j.1469-7610.2010.02209.x.

Karam, E. G., Friedman, M. J., Hill, E. D., Kessler, R. C., McLaughlin, K. A., Petukhova, M., … Koenen, K. C. (2014). Cumulative traumas and risk thresholds: 12-month ptsd in the world mental health (WMH) surveys. *Depression and Anxiety*, *31*(2), 130–142. https://doi.org/10.1002/da.22169.

Kessler, R. C., Sonnega, A., Bromet, E., Hughes, M., & Nelson, C. B. (1995). Posttraumatic stress disorder in the national comorbidity survey. *Archives of General Psychiatry*, *52* (12), 1048–1060. https://doi.org/10.1001/archpsyc.1995.03950240066012.

Kohrt, B. A., Jordans, M. J., Tol, W. A., Perera, E., Karki, R., Koirala, S., & Upadhaya, N. (2010). Social ecology of child soldiers: Child, family, and community determinants of mental health, psychosocial well-being, and reintegration in Nepal. *Transcultural Psychiatry*, *47*(5), 727–753. https://doi.org/10.1177/1363461510381290.

Lin, E. H., Carter, W. B., & Kleinman, A. M. (1985). An exploration of somatization among Asian refugees and immigrants in primary care. *American Journal of Public Health*, *75* (9), 1080–1084.

Liu, H., Petukhova, M. V., Sampson, N. A., Aguilar-Gaxiola, S., Alonso, J., Andrade, L. H., … Kessler, R. C. (2017). Association of DSM-IV posttraumatic stress disorder with traumatic experience type and history in the World Health Organization world mental health surveys. *JAMA Psychiatry*, *74*(3), 270–281. https://doi.org/10.1001/jamapsychiatry.2016.3783.

Maercker, A., Brewin, C. R., Bryant, R. A., Cloitre, M., Ommeren, M., & Jones, L. M. (2013). Diagnosis and classification of disorders specifically associated with stress: Proposals for ICD-11. *World Psychiatry*. *12*, https://doi.org/10.1002/wps.20057.

Meffert, S. M., Osman Abdo, A., Ahmed Abd Alla, O., Omer Mustafa Elmakki, Y., Abdelrahim Omer, A., Yousif, S., … Marmar, C. (2011). A pilot randomized controlled trial of interpersonal psychotherapy for Sudanese refugees in Cairo, Egypt. *Psychological Trauma: Theory, Research, Practice, and Policy*, *6*(3), 240–249.

Miller, K. E., & Rasmussen, A. (2010). War exposure, daily stressors, and mental health in conflict and post-conflict settings: Bridging the divide between trauma-focused and psychosocial frameworks. *Social Science and Medicine*, *70*(1), 7–16.

Mollica, R. F. (2001). The trauma story: A phenomenological approach to the traumatic life experiences of refugee survivors. *Psychiatry*, *64*(1), 60–63.

Mollica, R. F. (2011). Medical best practices for the treatment of torture survivors. *Torture*, *21* (1), 8–17.

Mollica, R. F., Sarajlic, N., Chernoff, M., Lavelle, J., Vukovic, I. S., & Massagli, M. P. (2001). Longitudinal study of psychiatric symptoms, disability, mortality, and emigration among Bosnian refugees. *JAMA*, *286*(5), 546–554.

Mollica, R. F., Wyshak, G., & Lavelle, J. (1987). The psychosocial impact of war trauma and torture on Southeast Asian refugees. *American Journal of Psychiatry*, *144*(12), 1567–1572.

Mollica, R. F., Wyshak, G., Lavelle, J., Truong, T., Tor, S., & Yang, T. (1990). Assessing symptom change in Southeast Asian refugee survivors of mass violence and torture. *American Journal of Psychiatry*, *147*(1), 83–88.

Momartin, S., Silove, D., Manicavasagar, V., & Steel, Z. (2004). Complicated grief in Bosnian refugees: Associations with posttraumatic stress disorder and depression. *Comprehensive Psychiatry*, *45*(6), 475–482.

Morina, N., Malek, M., Nickerson, A., & Bryant, R. A. (2017a). Meta-analysis of interventions for posttraumatic stress disorder and depression in adult survivors of mass violence in low- and middle-income countries. *Depression and Anxiety*, *34*(8), 679–691. https://doi.org/10.1002/da.22618.

Morina, N., Malek, M., Nickerson, A., & Bryant, R. A. (2017b). Psychological interventions for post-traumatic stress disorder and depression in young survivors of mass violence in low- and middle-income countries: Meta-analysis. *British Journal of Psychiatry*, *210*(4), 247–254. https://doi.org/10.1192/bjp.bp.115.180265.

Murray, L. K., Dorsey, S., Bolton, P., Jordans, M. J., Rahman, A., Bass, J., & Verdeli, H. (2011). Building capacity in mental health interventions in low resource countries: An apprenticeship model for training local providers. *Int J Ment Health Syst*, *5*(1), 30. https://doi.org/10.1186/1752-4458-5-30.

Murray, L. K., Dorsey, S., Haroz, E., Lee, C., Alsiary, M. M., Haydary, A., … Bolton, P. (2014). A common elements treatment approach for adult mental health problems in low- and middle-income countries. *Cognitive and Behavioral Practice*, *21*(2), 111–123. https://doi.org/10.1016/j.cbpra.2013.06.005.

Neuner, F., Kurreck, S., Ruf, M., Odenwald, M., Elbert, T., & Schauer, M. (2010). Can asylum-seekers with posttraumatic stress disorder be successfully treated? A randomized controlled pilot study. *Cognitive Behaviour Therapy*, *39*(2), 81–91. https://doi.org/10.1080/16506070903121042.

Neuner, F., Schauer, M., Klaschik, C., Karunakara, U., & Elbert, T. (2004). A comparison of narrative exposure therapy, supportive counseling, and psychoeducation for treating posttraumatic stress disorder in an African refugee settlement. *Journal of Consulting and Clinical Psychology*, *72*(4), 579–587.

Nicholl, C., & Thompson, A. (2004). The psychological treatment of post traumatic stress disorder (PTSD) in adult refugees: A review of the current state of psychological therapies. *Journal of Mental Health*, *13*(4), 351–362.

Nickerson, A., Bryant, R., Silove, D., & Steel, Z. (2011). A critical review of psychological treatments of posttraumatic stress disorder in refugees. *Clinical Psychology Review*, *31* (3), 399–417. https://doi.org/10.1016/j.cpr.2010.10.004.

Nickerson, A., Bryant, R. A., Brooks, R., Steel, Z., Silove, D., & Chen, J. (2011). The familial influence of loss and trauma on refugee mental health: A multilevel path analysis. *Journal of Traumatic Stress*, *24*(1), 25–33. https://doi.org/10.1002/jts.20608.

Nickerson, A., Cloitre, M., Bryant, R. A., Schnyder, U., Morina, N., & Schick, M. (2016). The factor structure of complex posttraumatic stress disorder in traumatized refugees. *European Journal of Psychotraumatology*. *7*, 33253https://doi.org/10.3402/ejpt.v7.33253.

Oruc, L., Kapetanovic, A., Pojskic, N., Miley, K., Forstbauer, S., Mollica f, R., & Henderson, D. C. (2008). Screening for PTSD and depression in Bosnia and Herzegovina: Validating the Harvard trauma questionnaire and the Hopkins symptom checklist. *International Journal of Culture and Mental Health*, *1*(2), 105–116. https://doi.org/10.1093/jrs/feq053.

Palic, S., & Elklit, A. (2011). Psychosocial treatment of posttraumatic stress disorder in adult refugees: A systematic review of prospective treatment outcome studies and a critique. *Journal of Affective Disorders*, *131*(1–3), 8–23. https://doi.org/10.1016/j.jad.2010.07.005.

Patel, V., Maj, M., Flisher, A. J., De Silva, M. J., Koschorke, M., & Prince, M. (2010). Reducing the treatment gap for mental disorders: A WPA survey. *World Psychiatry*, *9*(3), 169–176.

Purgato, M., Gross, A. L., Betancourt, T., Bolton, P., Bonetto, C., Gastaldon, C., … Barbui, C. (2018). Focused psychosocial interventions for children in low-resource humanitarian settings: A systematic review and individual participant data meta-analysis. *The Lancet Global Health*, *6*(4), e390–e400. https://doi.org/10.1016/s2214-109x(18)30046-9.

Rahman, A., Riaz, N., Dawson, K. S., Usman Hamdani, S., Chiumento, A., Sijbrandij, M., … Farooq, S. (2016). Problem management plus (PM+): Pilot trial of a WHO transdiagnostic psychological intervention in conflict-affected Pakistan. *World Psychiatry*, *15*(2), 182–183. https://doi.org/10.1002/wps.20312.

Rasmussen, O. V., Dam, A. M., & Nielsen, I. L. (1977). Torture: A study of Chilean and Greek victims. In *Evidence of torture, Studies by Amnesty International Danish Medical Group* (pp. 9–19). London: Amnesty International.

Rees, S., & Silove, D. (2011). Sakit Hati: A state of chronic mental distress related to resentment and anger amongst West Papuan refugees exposed to persecution. *Social Science and Medicine*, *73*(1), 103–110. https://doi.org/10.1016/j.socscimed.2011.05.004.

Rees, S., Silove, D., Verdial, T., Tam, N., Savio, E., Fonseca, Z., … Steel, Z. (2013). Intermittent explosive disorder amongst women in conflict affected Timor-Leste: Associations with human rights trauma, ongoing violence, poverty, and injustice. *PLoS ONE*. *8*(8) e69207. https://doi.org/10.1371/journal.pone.0069207.

Rees, S., Thorpe, R., Tol, W., Fonseca, M., & Silove, D. (2015). Testing a cycle of family violence model in conflict-affected, low-income countries: A qualitative study from Timor-Leste. *Social Science and Medicine*, *130*, 284–291. https://doi.org/10.1016/j.socscimed.2015.02.013.

Schaal, S., Elbert, T., & Neuner, F. (2009). Narrative exposure therapy versus interpersonal psychotherapy. A pilot randomized controlled trial with Rwandan genocide orphans. *Psychotherapy and Psychosomatics*, *78*(5), 298–306. https://doi.org/10.1159/000229768.

Scholte, W. F., Verduin, F., Kamperman, A. M., Rutayisire, T., Zwinderman, A. H., & Stronks, K. (2011). The effect on mental health of a large scale psychosocial intervention for survivors of mass violence: A quasi-experimental study in Rwanda. *PLoS ONE*. *6*(8) e21819. https://doi.org/10.1371/journal.pone.0021819.

Silove, D. (2013). The ADAPT model: A conceptual framework for mental health and psychosocial programming in post conflict settings. *Intervention*, *11*.

Silove, D., Momartin, S., Marnane, C., Steel, Z., & Manicavasagar, V. (2010). Adult separation anxiety disorder among war-affected Bosnian refugees: Comorbidity with PTSD and associations with dimensions of trauma. *Journal of Traumatic Stress*, *23*(1), 169–172.

Silove, D., Steel, Z., & Psychol, M. (2006). Understanding community psychosocial needs after disasters: Implications for mental health services. *Journal of Postgraduate Medicine*, *52* (2), 121–125.

Silove, D., Tarn, R., Bowles, R., & Reid, J. (1991). Psychosocial needs of torture survivors. *Australian and New Zealand Journal of Psychiatry*, *25*(4), 481–490.

Silove, D., Tay, A. K., Kareth, M., & Rees, S. (2017). The relationship of complex post-traumatic stress disorder and post-traumatic stress disorder in a culturally distinct, conflict-affected population: A study among west Papuan refugees displaced to Papua New Guinea. *Frontiers in Psychiatry*. *8*, 73, https://doi.org/10.3389/fpsyt.2017.00073.

Silove, D., Ventevogel, P., & Rees, S. (2017). The contemporary refugee crisis: An overview of mental health challenges. *World Psychiatry*, *16*(2), 130–139. https://doi.org/10.1002/wps.20438.

Silove, D. M., Tay, A. K., Steel, Z., Tam, N., Soares, Z., Soares, C., … Rees, S. (2017). Symptoms of post-traumatic stress disorder, severe psychological distress, explosive anger and grief amongst partners of survivors of high levels of trauma in post-conflict Timor-Leste. *Psychological Medicine*, *47*(1), 149–159. https://doi.org/10.1017/s0033291716002233.

Somnier, F. E., & Genefke, I. K. (1986). Psychotherapy for victims of torture. *British Journal of Psychiatry*, *149*, 323–329.

Steel, Z., Bateman Steel, C. R., & Silove, D. (2009). Human rights and the trauma model: Genuine partners or uneasy allies? *Journal of Traumatic Stress*, *22*(5), 358–365.

Steel, Z., Chey, T., Silove, D., Marnane, C., Bryant, R. A., & Van Ommeren, M. (2009). Association of torture and other potentially traumatic events with mental health outcomes among populations exposed to mass conflict and displacement: A systematic review and meta-analysis. *Journal of the American Medical Association*, *302*(5), 537–549.

Steel, Z., Momartin, S., Silove, D., Coello, M., Aroche, J., & Tay, K. W. (2011). Two year psychosocial and mental health outcomes for refugees subjected to restrictive or supportive immigration policies. *Social Science and Medicine*, *72*(7), 1149–1156. https://doi.org/10.1016/j.socscimed.2011.02.007.

Steel, Z., Silove, D., Brooks, R., Momartin, S., Alzuhairi, B., & Susljik, I. (2006). Impact of immigration detention and temporary protection on the mental health of refugees. *British Journal of Psychiatry*, *188*, 58–64.

Steel, Z., Silove, D., Chey, T., Bauman, A., & Phan, T. (2005). Mental disorders, disability and health service use amongst Vietnamese refugees and the host Australian population. *Acta Psychiatrica Scandinavica*, *111*(4), 300–309.

Steel, Z., Silove, D., Phan, T., & Bauman, A. (2002). Long-term effect of psychological trauma on the mental health of Vietnamese refugees resettled in Australia: A population-based study. *Lancet*, *360*(9339), 1056–1062.

Tay, A. K., Rees, S., Chen, J., Kareth, M., & Silove, D. (2015a). The coherence and correlates of intermittent explosive disorder amongst West Papuan refugees displaced to Papua New Guinea. *Journal of Affective Disorders*, *177*, 86–94. https://doi.org/10.1016/j.jad.2015.02.009.

Tay, A. K., Rees, S., Chen, J., Kareth, M., & Silove, D. (2015b). Factorial structure of complicated grief: Associations with loss-related traumatic events and psychosocial impacts of mass conflict amongst West Papuan refugees. *Social Psychiatry and Psychiatric Epidemiology*. https://doi.org/10.1007/s00127-015-1099-x.

Tay, A. K., Rees, S., Chen, J., Kareth, M., & Silove, D. (2015c). Pathways from conflict-related trauma and ongoing adversity to posttraumatic stress disorder symptoms amongst west Papuan refugees: The mediating role of anxiety and panic-like symptoms. *Comprehensive Psychiatry*, *63*, 36–45. https://doi.org/10.1016/j.comppsych.2015.08.005.

Tay, A. K., Rees, S., Chen, J., Kareth, M., & Silove, D. (2015d). The structure of post-traumatic stress disorder and complex post-traumatic stress disorder amongst west Papuan refugees. *BMC Psychiatry*. *15*, 111, https://doi.org/10.1186/s12888-015-0480-3.

Tay, A. K., Rees, S., Kareth, M., & Silove, D. (2016). Associations of adult separation anxiety disorder with conflict-related trauma, ongoing adversity, and the psychosocial disruptions of mass conflict among west Papuan refugees. *American Journal of Orthopsychiatry*. https://doi.org/10.1037/ort0000126.

Tay, A. K., Rees, S., Liddell, B., Tam, N., Nickerson, A., Steel, C., & Silove, D. (2016). The role of grief symptoms and a sense of injustice in the pathways to post-traumatic stress symptoms in post-conflict Timor-Leste. *Epidemiology and Psychiatric Sciences*, *26*(2), 1–4.

Tay, A. K., Rees, S., Tam, N., Savio, E., Da Costa, E., & Silove, D. (2017). The role of trauma-related injustice in pathways to post-traumatic stress symptoms amongst conjugal couples; a multilevel, dyadic analysis in post-conflict Timor-Leste. *SageOpen*, 1–10.

Tay, A. K., & Silove, D. (2016). *The ADAPT model: Bridging the gap between psychosocial and individual responses to mass violence and refugee trauma*: (pp. 1–4). Epidemiology and Psychiatric Sciences.

Ter Heide, F. J., Mooren, T. M., Kleijn, W., de Jongh, A., & Kleber, R. J. (2011). EMDR versus stabilisation in traumatised asylum seekers and refugees: Results of a pilot study. *European Journal of Psychotraumatology*. *2*, https://doi.org/10.3402/ejpt.v2i0.5881.

Ter Heide, F. J., Mooren, T. M., van de Schoot, R., de Jongh, A., & Kleber, R. J. (2016). Eye movement desensitisation and reprocessing therapy v. stabilisation as usual for refugees: Randomised controlled trial. *British Journal of Psychiatry*, *209*(4), 311–318. https://doi.org/10.1192/bjp.bp.115.167775.

The ICD-10 Classification of Mental and Behavioural Disorders: Diagnostic Criteria for Research (1992). *The ICD-10 classification of mental and behavioural disorders*.

Tol, W. A., Komproe, I. H., Susanty, D., Jordans, M. J., Macy, R. D., & De Jong, J. T. (2008). School-based mental health intervention for children affected by political violence in Indonesia: A cluster randomized trial. *JAMA*, *300*(6), 655–662. https://doi.org/10.1001/jama.300.6.655.

UNHCR (2018). *UNHCR projected global resettlement needs*. Retrieved from Geneva. http://www.unhcr.org/en-au/protection/resettlement/593a88f27/unhcr-projected-global-resettlement-needs-2018.html.

United Nations Convention Against, T (2006). *Convention against torture and other cruel, inhuman or degrading treatment or punishment*.

Van Der Kolk, B. A., Roth, S., Pelcovitz, D., Sunday, S., & Spinazzola, J. (2005). Disorders of extreme stress: The empirical foundation of a complex adaptation to trauma. *Journal of Traumatic Stress*, *18*(5), 389–399.

Van Ee, E., Mooren, T., & Kleber, R. (2014). Helping children cope with trauma, individual, family and community perspectives. In R. Pat-Horenzcyk, D. Brom, & J. M. Vogel (Eds.), *Helping children cope with trauma, individual, family and community perspectives* (pp. 146–162). New York: Routledge.

Van Ommeren, M., Sharma, B., Sharma, G. K., Komproe, I., Cardeña, E., & De Jong, J. T. V. M. (2002). The relationship between somatic and PTSD symptoms among Bhutanese refugee torture survivors: Examination of comorbidity with anxiety and depression. *Journal of Traumatic Stress*, *15*(5), 415–421.

van Wyk, S., & Schweitzer, R. D. (2014). A systematic review of naturalistic interventions in refugee populations. *Journal of Immigrant and Minority Health*, *16*(5), 968–977. https://doi.org/10.1007/s10903-013-9835-3.

Verduin, F., Smid, G. E., Wind, T. R., & Scholte, W. F. (2014). In search of links between social capital, mental health and sociotherapy: A longitudinal study in Rwanda. *Social Science and Medicine*, *121*, 1–9. https://doi.org/10.1016/j.socscimed.2014.09.054.

Wagenaar, W. A., & Groeneweg, J. (1990). The memory of concentration camp survivors. *Applied Cognitive Psychology*, *4*(2), 77–87.

Weine, S., Kulauzovic, Y., Klebic, A., Besic, S., Mujagic, A., Muzurovic, J., … Rolland, J. (2008). Evaluating a multiple-family group access intervention for refugees with PTSD. *Journal of Marital and Family Therapy*, *34*(2), 149–164. https://doi.org/10.1111/j.1752-0606.2008.00061.x.

Weine, S. M., Kulenovic, A. D., Pavkovic, I., & Gibbons, R. (1998). Testimony psychotherapy in Bosnian refugees: A pilot study. *American Journal of Psychiatry*, *155*(12), 1720–1726.

Weiss, W. M., Murray, L. K., Zangana, G. A., Mahmooth, Z., Kaysen, D., Dorsey, S., … Bolton, P. (2015). Community-based mental health treatments for survivors of torture and militant attacks in southern Iraq: A randomized control trial. *BMC Psychiatry. 15*, 249. https://doi.org/10.1186/s12888-015-0622-7.

Westermeyer, J., Bouafuely, M., Neider, J., & Callies, A. (1989). Somatization among refugees: An epidemiologic study. *Psychosomatics, 30*(1), 34–43.

Westermeyer, J., & Janca, A. (1997). Language, culture and psychopathology: Conceptual and methodological issues. *Transcultural Psychiatry, 34*(3), 291–311.

Wickrama, K. A. S., Beiser, M., & Kaspar, V. (2002). Assessing the longitudinal course of depression and economic integration of south-east Asian refugees: An application of latent growth curve analysis. *International Journal of Methods in Psychiatric Research, 11*(4), 154–168.

Index

Note: Page numbers followed by *f* indicate figures, *t* indicate tables, and *b* indicate boxes.

F

G

H

I

Q

R

S

Kolibri 360 GmbH
Ferdinand-Jühlke-Straße 7
99095 Erfurt, Deutschland
produktsicherheit@kolibri360.de